T0213739

# Lecture Notes in Artificial Intelligence    10285

Subseries of Lecture Notes in Computer Science

More information about this series at http://www.springer.com/series/1244

Dylan D. Schmorrow · Cali M. Fidopiastis (Eds.)

# Augmented Cognition

## Enhancing Cognition and Behavior in Complex Human Environments

11th International Conference, AC 2017
Held as Part of HCI International 2017
Vancouver, BC, Canada, July 9–14, 2017
Proceedings, Part II

 Springer

*Editors*
Dylan D. Schmorrow
SoarTech
Orlando, FL
USA

Cali M. Fidopiastis
Design Interactive, Inc.
Orlando, FL
USA

ISSN 0302-9743          ISSN 1611-3349   (electronic)
Lecture Notes in Artificial Intelligence
ISBN 978-3-319-58624-3       ISBN 978-3-319-58625-0   (eBook)
DOI 10.1007/978-3-319-58625-0

Library of Congress Control Number: 2017940250

LNCS Sublibrary: SL7 – Artificial Intelligence

Printed on acid-free paper

This Springer imprint is published by Springer Nature
The registered company is Springer International Publishing AG
The registered company address is: Gewerbestrasse 11, 6330 Cham, Switzerland

# Foreword

The 19th International Conference on Human–Computer Interaction, HCI International 2017, was held in Vancouver, Canada, during July 9–14, 2017. The event incorporated the 15 conferences/thematic areas listed on the following page.

A total of 4,340 individuals from academia, research institutes, industry, and governmental agencies from 70 countries submitted contributions, and 1,228 papers have been included in the proceedings. These papers address the latest research and development efforts and highlight the human aspects of design and use of computing systems. The papers thoroughly cover the entire field of human–computer interaction, addressing major advances in knowledge and effective use of computers in a variety of application areas. The volumes constituting the full set of the conference proceedings are listed on the following pages.

I would like to thank the program board chairs and the members of the program boards of all thematic areas and affiliated conferences for their contribution to the highest scientific quality and the overall success of the HCI International 2017 conference.

This conference would not have been possible without the continuous and unwavering support and advice of the founder, Conference General Chair Emeritus and Conference Scientific Advisor Prof. Gavriel Salvendy. For his outstanding efforts, I would like to express my appreciation to the communications chair and editor of *HCI International News*, Dr. Abbas Moallem.

April 2017                                                      Constantine Stephanidis

# HCI International 2017 Thematic Areas
# and Affiliated Conferences

Thematic areas:

- Human–Computer Interaction (HCI 2017)
- Human Interface and the Management of Information (HIMI 2017)

Affiliated conferences:

- 17th International Conference on Engineering Psychology and Cognitive Ergonomics (EPCE 2017)
- 11th International Conference on Universal Access in Human–Computer Interaction (UAHCI 2017)
- 9th International Conference on Virtual, Augmented and Mixed Reality (VAMR 2017)
- 9th International Conference on Cross-Cultural Design (CCD 2017)
- 9th International Conference on Social Computing and Social Media (SCSM 2017)
- 11th International Conference on Augmented Cognition (AC 2017)
- 8th International Conference on Digital Human Modeling and Applications in Health, Safety, Ergonomics and Risk Management (DHM 2017)
- 6th International Conference on Design, User Experience and Usability (DUXU 2017)
- 5th International Conference on Distributed, Ambient and Pervasive Interactions (DAPI 2017)
- 5th International Conference on Human Aspects of Information Security, Privacy and Trust (HAS 2017)
- 4th International Conference on HCI in Business, Government and Organizations (HCIBGO 2017)
- 4th International Conference on Learning and Collaboration Technologies (LCT 2017)
- Third International Conference on Human Aspects of IT for the Aged Population (ITAP 2017)

# Conference Proceedings Volumes Full List

1. LNCS 10271, Human–Computer Interaction: User Interface Design, Development and Multimodality (Part I), edited by Masaaki Kurosu
2. LNCS 10272 Human–Computer Interaction: Interaction Contexts (Part II), edited by Masaaki Kurosu
3. LNCS 10273, Human Interface and the Management of Information: Information, Knowledge and Interaction Design (Part I), edited by Sakae Yamamoto
4. LNCS 10274, Human Interface and the Management of Information: Supporting Learning, Decision-Making and Collaboration (Part II), edited by Sakae Yamamoto
5. LNAI 10275, Engineering Psychology and Cognitive Ergonomics: Performance, Emotion and Situation Awareness (Part I), edited by Don Harris
6. LNAI 10276, Engineering Psychology and Cognitive Ergonomics: Cognition and Design (Part II), edited by Don Harris
7. LNCS 10277, Universal Access in Human–Computer Interaction: Design and Development Approaches and Methods (Part I), edited by Margherita Antona and Constantine Stephanidis
8. LNCS 10278, Universal Access in Human–Computer Interaction: Designing Novel Interactions (Part II), edited by Margherita Antona and Constantine Stephanidis
9. LNCS 10279, Universal Access in Human–Computer Interaction: Human and Technological Environments (Part III), edited by Margherita Antona and Constantine Stephanidis
10. LNCS 10280, Virtual, Augmented and Mixed Reality, edited by Stephanie Lackey and Jessie Y.C. Chen
11. LNCS 10281, Cross-Cultural Design, edited by Pei-Luen Patrick Rau
12. LNCS 10282, Social Computing and Social Media: Human Behavior (Part I), edited by Gabriele Meiselwitz
13. LNCS 10283, Social Computing and Social Media: Applications and Analytics (Part II), edited by Gabriele Meiselwitz
14. LNAI 10284, Augmented Cognition: Neurocognition and Machine Learning (Part I), edited by Dylan D. Schmorrow and Cali M. Fidopiastis
15. LNAI 10285, Augmented Cognition: Enhancing Cognition and Behavior in Complex Human Environments (Part II), edited by Dylan D. Schmorrow and Cali M. Fidopiastis
16. LNCS 10286, Digital Human Modeling and Applications in Health, Safety, Ergonomics and Risk Management: Ergonomics and Design (Part I), edited by Vincent G. Duffy
17. LNCS 10287, Digital Human Modeling and Applications in Health, Safety, Ergonomics and Risk Management: Health and Safety (Part II), edited by Vincent G. Duffy
18. LNCS 10288, Design, User Experience, and Usability: Theory, Methodology and Management (Part I), edited by Aaron Marcus and Wentao Wang

19. LNCS 10289, Design, User Experience, and Usability: Designing Pleasurable Experiences (Part II), edited by Aaron Marcus and Wentao Wang
20. LNCS 10290, Design, User Experience, and Usability: Understanding Users and Contexts (Part III), edited by Aaron Marcus and Wentao Wang
21. LNCS 10291, Distributed, Ambient and Pervasive Interactions, edited by Norbert Streitz and Panos Markopoulos
22. LNCS 10292, Human Aspects of Information Security, Privacy and Trust, edited by Theo Tryfonas
23. LNCS 10293, HCI in Business, Government and Organizations: Interacting with Information Systems (Part I), edited by Fiona Fui-Hoon Nah and Chuan-Hoo Tan
24. LNCS 10294, HCI in Business, Government and Organizations: Supporting Business (Part II), edited by Fiona Fui-Hoon Nah and Chuan-Hoo Tan
25. LNCS 10295, Learning and Collaboration Technologies: Novel Learning Ecosystems (Part I), edited by Panayiotis Zaphiris and Andri Ioannou
26. LNCS 10296, Learning and Collaboration Technologies: Technology in Education (Part II), edited by Panayiotis Zaphiris and Andri Ioannou
27. LNCS 10297, Human Aspects of IT for the Aged Population: Aging, Design and User Experience (Part I), edited by Jia Zhou and Gavriel Salvendy
28. LNCS 10298, Human Aspects of IT for the Aged Population: Applications, Services and Contexts (Part II), edited by Jia Zhou and Gavriel Salvendy
29. CCIS 713, HCI International 2017 Posters Proceedings (Part I), edited by Constantine Stephanidis
30. CCIS 714, HCI International 2017 Posters Proceedings (Part II), edited by Constantine Stephanidis

# Augmented Cognition

Program Board Chair(s): **Dylan D. Schmorrow and Cali M. Fidopiastis, USA**

- Débora N.F. Barbosa, Brazil
- Murat Perit Çakir, Turkey
- Martha E. Crosby, USA
- Rodolphe Gentili, USA
- Michael W. Hail, USA
- Monte Hancock, USA
- Øyvind Jøsok, Norway
- Ion Juvina, USA
- Benjamin J. Knox, Norway
- Chloe Chun-Wing Lo, Hong Kong, SAR China
- David Martinez, USA
- Santosh Mathan, USA
- Chang S. Nam, USA

- Banu Onaral, USA
- Robinson Pino, USA
- Mannes Poel, The Netherlands
- Stefan Sütterlin, Norway
- Anna Skinner, USA
- Robert A. Sottilare, USA
- Midori Sugaya, Japan
- Ayoung Suh, Hong Kong, SAR China
- Christian Wagner, Hong Kong, SAR China
- Peter Walker, USA
- Martin Westhoven, Germany
- John K. Zao, Taiwan

The full list with the Program Board Chairs and the members of the Program Boards of all thematic areas and affiliated conferences is available online at:

**http://www.hci.international/board-members-2017.php**

# HCI International 2018

The 20th International Conference on Human–Computer Interaction, HCI International 2018, will be held jointly with the affiliated conferences in Las Vegas, NV, USA, at Caesars Palace, July 15–20, 2018. It will cover a broad spectrum of themes related to human–computer interaction, including theoretical issues, methods, tools, processes, and case studies in HCI design, as well as novel interaction techniques, interfaces, and applications. The proceedings will be published by Springer. More information is available on the conference website: http://2018.hci.international/.

General Chair
Prof. Constantine Stephanidis
University of Crete and ICS-FORTH
Heraklion, Crete, Greece
E-mail: general_chair@hcii2018.org

**http://2018.hci.international/**

# Contents – Part II

## Brain-Computer Interfaces

## Human Cognition and Behavior in Complex Tasks and Environments

# Contents – Part I

## Eye Tracking in Augmented Cognition

## Physiological Measuring and Bio-sensing

## Machine Learning in Augmented Cognition

# Cognitive Load and Performance

# Comparing Capacity Coefficient and Dual Task Assessment of Visual Multitasking Workload

Leslie M. Blaha[✉]

Pacific Northwest National Laboratory, Richland, WA, USA
leslie.blaha@pnnl.gov

**Abstract.** Capacity coefficient analysis offers a theoretically grounded alternative approach to subjective measures and dual task interference assessment of mental workload. Workload efficiency is a human information processing modeling construct defined as the efficacy with which the system responds to increases in the number of cognitive processes. In this paper, I explore the relationship between capacity coefficient analysis of workload efficiency and dual task interference response time measures. I examine how the relatively simple assumptions underlying capacity coefficient analysis parallel those made in dual task interference workload assessment. For the study of visual multitasking, capacity coefficient analysis enables a comparison of visual information throughput as the number of tasks increases from one to two to any number of simultaneous tasks. By using baseline models derived from transformations of response time distribution, capacity coefficient analysis enables theoretically grounded interpretations of workload. I illustrate the use of capacity coefficients for visual multitasking, compared to dual task interference analysis, on sample data from dynamic multitasking in the modified Multi-attribute Task Battery.

**Keywords:** Capacity coefficient · Workload · Dual-task · MAT-B · Multitasking

## 1 Introduction

Visual multitasking is the simultaneous execution of at least two distinct visual tasks. In visual multitasking, each task is comprised of separate, potentially unique, visual stimuli, independent events and timing characteristics, and separate decisions and responses. For example, texting while driving requires visual attention to the environmental cues external the car to maintain lane position, as well as attention to the screen and buttons of the mobile phone to input responses to the incoming messages. When multiple simultaneous tasks require the same perceptual processing resources, degradations in performance are often observed as the number of tasks increases.

The goal of the present work is to explore the applicability of workload efficiency analysis to the study of performance in multitasking situations. Workload efficiency, or processing capacity, is the information processing modeling

© Springer International Publishing AG 2017
D.D. Schmorrow and C.M. Fidopiastis (Eds.): AC 2017, Part II, LNAI 10285, pp. 3–19, 2017.
DOI: 10.1007/978-3-319-58625-0_1

construct that characterizes the response of cognitive information processing mechanism to changing tasks demands [28,29]. That is, as the number of decisions (processing stages or subtasks) increase, how do information processing rates respond? There exists a set of theoretically grounded, model-based measures for workload capacity, derived from the distributions of task response times, that may offer useful insights about multitasking, both about the mechanisms involved and about the mental workload demands for a given situation. In the following, I will explore the use of the capacity coefficient, in particular, as a potential metric for multitasking workload efficiency. I compare it to the very similar notion of dual task interference effects, which are often utilized as an objective metric for mental workload when clear, repeated behavioral measures can be collected empirically.

## 1.1   Characteristics of Multitasking

Salvucci and colleagues have defined several dimensions along which multitasking scenarios can be characterized. First, the multitasking continuum defines the timescales at which activity occurs before a person switches between tasks [24,27]. At one end of the continuum are tasks that require seconds to complete, like driving and talking. The other end of the multitasking continuum is tasks requiring hours to complete before switching, such as cooking and reading a book. Another facet of multitasking is the degree to which tasks are concurrent or sequential in execution [25,26]. True sequential tasks are performed with discrete yet well-defined boundaries between tasks, such as switching between writing an email and making a phone call. One task is completed before the next is initiated. Concurrent tasks are executed simultaneously with overlapping temporal events, such as simultaneously baking a cake and holding a conversation with someone else in the kitchen. The concurrent-sequential nature of the tasks has implications for the organization of the mental resources, including perceptual, memory, decision making, and motor resources, needed to support effective performance. Note that these dimensions (concurrency and time scale) of multitasking can be defined separately for any given combination of tasks. However, concurrent tasks typically require frequent attention switching on the order of seconds, and so they often align with the shorter time scale end of the multitasking continuum. Likewise, sequential tasks often occur on longer time scales at the upper end of the multitasking continuum [26].

Multitasking tasks can further be placed on an application continuum based on the real-world nature of the tasks under observation. The application continuum ranges from abstract laboratory tasks (e.g., visual or memory search for simple targets) to real-world multitasking (e.g., management of attention while driving busy city streets involving other cars, signals, and pedestrians). Finally, the abstraction continuum is used to characterize the nature of theories developed to characterize multitasking as well as the related methodologies developed to study multitasking through those theoretical lenses. The abstraction continuum is akin to Newell's bands of cognition, defining the timescales at which behavior can be decomposed and appropriately measured and modeled [2,20].

The information processing mechanisms of interest in the present work fall into the cognitive band, on the order of seconds for the completion of individual mental operations or single task units.

## 1.2 Dual Task Assessment of Workload

In many ways, the assessment of performance during multitasking falls into the general problem of measuring operator mental workload, from both the objective behavioral impacts and the subjective experience of changing processing demands. Generally, mental workload is conceptualized as the demands placed on information processing resources, which are recognized to be limited [36]. The assessment of mental workload, however, is difficult as the workload experience is a latent factor and can only be assessed indirectly. The goal of workload assessment measurements is to translate the subjective experience of workload together with the impacts of varying workload into something quantifiable, like a numerical scale [18]. Approaches include subjective assessments of workload, such as the popular subjective workload assessment technique (SWAT [22]), or the NASA task-load index (NASA-TLX [11]). While popular and easy to administer, subjective techniques have faced extensive criticism for being only indirect measures of resource allocation and information processing capacity. Objectively, the impacts of multitasking on behavioral performance are often addressed with a measure of dual task interference, derived from total task accuracy or mean response times. To perform a dual task interference assessment, the difference between a task performed in isolation and the task performed in multitasking conditions is computed to assess the degree of impact of the multiple competing task demands. Drops in performance or increases in subjective workload can successfully describe some aspects of the impact of multitasking.

The popular terminology for the components of dual task assessment is primary and secondary task measures. Primary task measures are defined as some aspect of performance on a task of interest, which has generally been predetermined by the experimenter. Secondary tasks are then used to load more cognitive demands onto available processing resources, to impact the primary task measures in some way. There are two ways in which a secondary task can be used empirically. First, in a task loading paradigm, participants are asked to maintain high performance on the secondary task, at the expense of the primary task. The second approach uses the secondary task in a subsidiary role, in which the participant is asked to maintain high performance on the primary task. In this latter case, the secondary task serves to degrade the primary task by distraction or utilizing needed resources. A balance of both approaches could be engaged in laboratory settings to assess bi-directionality of interference effects, though there are often practical limitations to this being accomplished.

There is a set of critical assumptions that must be met for effective assessment of workload using dual task interference approaches [5]. The first is that baseline measures can be taken from both the primary and secondary task, separately and independently of the dual task scenario. This would mean being able collect data from at least three total experimental conditions: (1) primary task alone,

(2) secondary task alone, and (3) dual task combination. The second assumption is that both the primary and secondary task tap into common resource requirements, which is considered critical for the tasks to interfere or compete for the limited resources. This reflects the notion that performance in multi-task situations can be limited in different ways, and that it is possible for two concurrently performed tasks to draw from different pools of cognitive resources [21].

The next assumptions are that the secondary task places continuous demands on the user and that the participant has had sufficient practice on the secondary task to achieve stable performance. Both are necessary for the secondary task to offer competing resource demands on the user but not to distract the participant from the primary task onto training of the secondary task. Because practice and task learning can improve performance, it is possible that a secondary task performed without initial practice can result in enough learning that the secondary task becomes trivial and no longer places enough demands on the user to compete with the primary task for resources. Additionally, multiple levels of difficulty can be used in the secondary task to vary the level of effort needed (e.g., [35]). This, in turn, influences the degree of interference the secondary task places on the primary task, which can affect both the dual task interference effects and perhaps the subjective experience of workload.

## 2   Workload versus Workload Efficiency

In their efforts to assess mental workload, researchers have consistently found that mental workload may be a multi-faceted or multidimensional construct. This is because the subjective experience of higher workload may result from cognitive moderators, like stress, that influence physiological responses, in addition to the information processing and motor response demands of the tasks themselves [9,19,37]. Certainly one of the key dimensions that should be considered in the assessment of workload is the degree to which cognitive information processing mechanisms are able to effectively perform the work demanded of them.

Workload efficiency is a human information processing modeling construct defined as the amount of information that can be processed by the cognitive system given a specified of amount of time. The range of time is defined by the range of response times required for the task under consideration. Here, I emphasize visual tasks, so the information processing mechanisms entail visual perception and decision making. In the visual domain, workload efficiency measures are typically applied to redundant targets task designs, such as the identification or discrimination of multiple features within a single visual object (e.g., eyes, nose, and mouth within a face [34]) or the visual search in a redundant targets array (e.g., [17]). The workload capacity of a system describes the way in which changes in information processing demands influence the rate of processing. If increases in demands slow processing, then the system's efficiency is termed limited capacity. If increases in demands do not change the processing rates, then the system's efficiency is termed unlimited capacity. If increases in demands increase the speed of processing, which seems counterintuitive but has been observed (e.g., Gestalt processing [14]), then the system's efficiency is termed super capacity. In this framework, three broad classes of workload efficiency are defined in terms of task completion rates, which can be measured with completion or response times.

Workload capacity analysis makes a set of basic assumptions similar to those required by effective dual task interference analysis. First, the multiple tasks used should require comparable demands on the participant as each other. That is, they should both be similarly discrete or continuous over the course of task performance, and be at a similar level of complexity (i.e., both are single perceptual or choice decisions, or both are at the same level of realism on the application continuum). It is also assumed that all tasks have been practiced to a similar degree of stable performance such that learning and practice effects are accounted for in all tasks. Workload capacity analysis assumes that performance can be assessed for the component tasks alone as well as for the tasks combined, identical to the assumption in the dual task approach. However, the component tasks need not necessarily tap into the same cognitive or perceptual resources for capacity analysis to work. With this approach, available information processing models offer some degree of characterization of the system regardless if the component tasks utilize all, none, or partially overlapping resources. As discussed in the next section, capacity characteristics reflect situations in which tasks can interfere with each other, not interfere at all, and even cases when they facilitate each other. In terms of processing resources, these cases, respectively, may reflect situations wherein the two tasks compete for resources, may not need common resources, or mutually augment the resources available to a single task alone.

Identical to dual task interference analysis, workload efficiency requires that separate measurements be taken from the component tasks as well as performance on the combination of tasks together. For two-task cases, this means collecting data from the same three experimental conditions: (1) primary task alone, (2) secondary task alone, and (3) dual task combination. This requirement is necessary to formulate model-based predictions for multitasking performance. And similar to the recommendation for dual task interference analysis, the difficulty level of the tasks can be varied. However, because of the use of model-based predictions as workload efficiency baseline estimates, it is important that if the difficulty levels are varied, then data must be collected in both the single-task and multi-task conditions at the same difficulty levels. This ensures that the capacity interpretation reflects the workload manipulations without potential confounds of task difficulty.

## 3   The Capacity Coefficient

Capacity coefficient analysis enables inferences about information processing efficiency by comparing the amount of cognitive work completed while multiple tasks are performed together to a prediction about cognitive work made by a baseline model. Cognitive work is measured with the integrated hazard and reverse hazard functions of response times. The hazard function is defined as $h(t) = \frac{f(t)}{S(t)}$, where $f(t)$ is the probability density function and $S(t) = 1 - \int f(t)$ is the survivor function. Hazard functions can be interpreted as the amount of instantaneous effort or energy in a system at any point in time, $t$ [29]. Consequently, the integrated hazard, $H(t) = \int_0^t h(\tau)d\tau = -log(S(t))$, can be interpreted as the total amount of work completed from the start of a task to time $t$. Similarly, the reverse integrated hazard function, defined as $K(t) = \int_0^t \frac{f(\tau)}{F(\tau)}d\tau = log(F(t))$ is interpreted as the amount of work left to be completed by the system after $t$ time has passed. Note that when applied to a cognitive task, $t$ is measured as the response time on each trial, or the time between some stimulus or alert and the observer's response.

The baseline performance model engaged in capacity coefficient analysis is an independent, parallel, unlimited capacity (UCIP) model system. In a UCIP system, the number of tasks can be increased without changing the speed at which any individual task is completed. For multitasking, this means that a person can complete a combination of multiple simultaneous tasks at the same speed as when completing the tasks individually. The system exhibits unlimited processing capacity. An implication of this is that the amount of mental effort should remain consistent under increasing demands. Against the UCIP baseline, if additional tasks slow processing, the capacity coefficient analysis will show limited capacity. If additional tasks should benefit the person and speed up performance, the capacity coefficient analysis will indicate super capacity.

The choice of hazard or reverse hazard function and the specific definition of the UCIP model depend on the nature of the task under study, particularly the nature of the stopping rule governing the termination of processing to make a response. For dynamic visual multitasking, I consider the case in which each task engages a single cognitive decision in response to a single alert event, separate and independent of the decisions made in the other tasks. Using information processing modeling terminology, this is a single-target self-terminating (ST-ST) stopping rule. This means that for each task at a given time there is a single target event that triggers a response, and that the response can be made after that target event has been observed by the participant. Cognitive work for ST-ST processing is typically measured with the integrated reverse hazard function. For ST-ST processing, the amount of work predicted by a UCIP baseline system for each individual task during multitasking is identical to the amount of work completed on each task performed individually. That is, for given task $A$ among a set of tasks $M$, the UCIP baseline prediction is defined as $K_A(t)$, estimated from the participant performing task $A$ alone. Then the observed performance of $A$ during multitasking is defined as $K_{A,M}(t)$. The capacity coefficient for ST-ST processing is defined as

$$C_{\text{ST}}(t) = K_A(t) - K_{A,M}(t). \tag{1}$$

If the processing efficiency for task $A$ during multitasking is unlimited, then $C_{\text{ST}}(t) = 0$. Limited capacity is inferred if $C_{\text{ST}}(t) < 0$, and super capacity is inferred if $C_{\text{ST}}(t) > 0$.

Note that these inference reference values are similar to those used in dual task interference effects at the mean level, when applied to response times. If there is no decrement in performance under dual task conditions, then the difference in mean response time for the primary task between the single and dual task conditions will be zero. Interference caused by an increase in workload under dual task conditions will produce a negative impact on response time in that $\overline{RT}_{Single} - \overline{RT}_{Dual} < 0$. Though not common in the workload literature, should moving from a single task to dual task condition improve performance, then a dual task facilitation could be inferred, when $\overline{RT}_{Single} - \overline{RT}_{Dual} > 0$.

The key difference in these approaches is that $C_{ST}(t)$ provides a functional measure of the influence of multitasking on workload efficiency. That is, we get a value over the entire range of response times. This allows for a more nuanced interpretation of the impact of moving from a single task to dual task situation. With the capacity coefficient, it is possible to observe $C_{ST}(t)$ values that vary between levels of efficiency over time. For example, fast detection responses may be super capacity in nature, $C_{ST}(t) > 0$. But if the observer did not immediately detect a stimulus and performed a more effortful target search, then the responses may reflect limited capacity processing, $C_{ST}(t) < 0$. In this way, we can get a more detailed but still objective description of the impact of increasing cognitive load on task performance.

## 4   Application to Dynamic Visual Multitasking

I demonstrate the dual task response time analysis and capacity coefficient analysis on sample data from two-task combinations from multitasking software that supports up to four simultaneous tasks. Consistent with the traditional applications of the capacity coefficient, tasks were selected because they all entail reactionary responses to alerting events. The alerting events can be considered the stimulus onset event, and the reactionary response times can be recorded. In this way, a distribution of response times can be collected that is similar to the response time distributions collected in single visual decision tasks in which capacity analysis has been previously utilized.

A key difference between discrete trial experiments and dynamic visual multitasking is that dynamic visual multitasking does not include well-defined intertrial intervals. But such intervals are not a critical assumption of capacity coefficient analysis. A potentially larger challenge in dynamic multitasking is that the time of an alerting event may not be the identical to the time at which the participant observes the alerting event. This is because the alerts may not occur while the participant is foveating on the alert, as is expected in discrete trial experiments with centrally presented stimuli. However, I leave treatment of this detail to future efforts. For the present, I make the reasonable assumption that response time can measured from the timestamp of an alert to the timestamp of keyboard or mouse response.

The tasks herein can be characterized using the various continua discussed above. On the multitasking continuum, these tasks are continuous and concurrent in nature. Participants must monitor all activity in the tasks for alerting events. The alerting events occur on the order of seconds, with response times also on the order of seconds or even milliseconds. Along the application continuum, these tasks represent a laboratory abstraction of pilot-like multitasking. The nature of the task is a realistic reflection of some demands occurring in real-world pilot multitasking. However, the display and details are greatly simplified. Thus, these tasks reside more toward the first third-to-half of the application continuum.

## 4.1  Task Environment

Sample data from one well-practiced team member were captured in both single and dual visual decision making tasks within a JavaScript implementation of a modified multi-attribute task battery (mMATB-JS; [8,10]).[1] This lightweight, web-based version of the MAT-B contains up to four simultaneous visual tasks: continuous object tracking, alert monitoring, communication (channel cuing), and resource management. Any individual task within the mMATB-JS can be used as a single visual decision making task; any combination can be leveraged for visual multitasking. The specific combinations of tasks used herein are shown in Fig. 1. Note that the resource management task is a strategic task requiring participants to manage simulated fuel levels. It is not used in the current demonstration, so is not depicted in Fig. 1.

The monitoring task (upper left quadrant, Fig. 1), consists of a set of sliders and two color indicator blocks. The participant's task is to provide the appropriate button press (F1–F6, labeled on each indicator/slider) if a parameter is out of its normal state. For the sliders, this means moving above or below ±1 notch from the center. Participants must respond with the appropriate button press before the slider moves back into the central range; if the slider returns to the central range before a response, then an event miss is recorded. For the indicators, the normally green block might turn black, or the normally black block might turn red. The participant must respond before the event timeout, when the color reverts to the normal value.

The continuous tracking task (upper right quadrant, Fig. 1 top and middle) requires the participate to continuously track a moving circular target with the mouse. At any time, one of the circles can turn red, indicating it is the target to be acquired and tracked. When this occurs, the participant clicks to acquire the target (which turns green) and then tries to keep the mouse cursor centered on the target as it moves along an ellipsoid track. A target will remain in an alert (red) state until either acquired by the user or the next alerting event occurs, which is recorded as an event miss.

The communications task (lower left quadrant, Fig. 1 middle and bottom) requires the participant to adjust channel frequencies when cued. The display includes four channels, labeled INT1, INT2, OPS1, OPS2, together with the current channel values; the topmost line gives a target channel and value. If a red cued target appears in the top box, the participant uses the up/down

---

[1] Available online at http://sai.mindmodeling.org/mmatb/index.html.

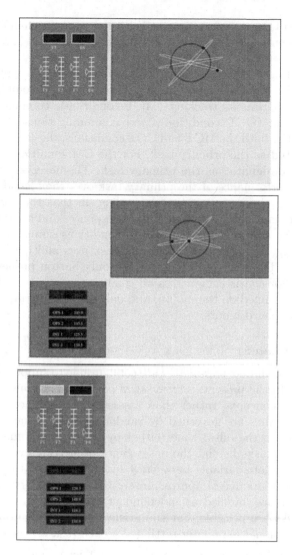

**Fig. 1.** Screen shots of the three dual tasks combinations used in the present demonstration. The top shows the monitoring-plus-continuous tracking condition (MCT) with the F5 color out of state (black) and the tracking task in a cue alert (red) state. The middle shows the communications-plus-continuous tracking condition (CCT) with the communications cuing a new channel value for INT2 and the tracking in a target acquired (green) state. The bottom shows the communications-plus-monitoring condition (CM) with the slider F4 out of range and a new channel value cued for OPS1. The frame indicates edges of the monitor, and the layout and sizing of the tasks are preserved from the full four-task mMATB-JS environment. (Color figure online)

arrow keys to select the cued channel and the right/left arrow keys to adjust the channel value to the new cued value. The enter key submits the corrected channel, which changes the topmost cue box to white until the next channel cue appears. The cued target remains red until either the correct channel adjustment is input with the enter key or the operation times out, which is recorded as an event miss.

As illustrated in Fig. 1, three dual task conditions were created to capture different task/response characteristics. These dual task combinations were: monitoring–plus–continuous tracking (MCT condition), communication–plus–continuous tracking (CCT condition), and communications–plus–monitoring (CM condition). For both the MCT and CCT conditions, the continuous tracking task was designated as the primary task. For the CM condition, the communications task was designated as the primary task. The observer was instructed to prioritize the performance of the primary task over the secondary task. The MCT condition required two-handed responding, in that the monitoring task uses the non-dominant hand for single-button responses and the dominant hand for mouse clicking and tracking. The CCT conditions similarly required two handed responding, but the communications task uses multiple button pushes for each response. The CM condition required only button pushes by the non-dominant hand. For consistency across all conditions, during the CM task, the dominant hand remained on the mouse, and only the non-dominant hand could be used for all keyboard inputs.

### 4.2   Task Parameters

In the mMATB-JS, all task parameters are configurable to support varying levels of task difficulty. In the present, a fixed set of parameters were selected to illustrate the analysis concepts, rather than assessing performance under variable conditions. Alert times are governed by random variables that add a random inter-trial interval to the offset time (either by response or timeout) following each event. For all tasks herein, the onset times of alerting events were drawn from a uniform random variable between 8 and 14 s. For a 20 min session, this results in an expected value of approximately 109 events per task. The timings within each event are handled as independent event sequences. Simultaneous events across tasks are possible, but simultaneous alerts within a task are not possible. The additional parameter settings for each task are as follows:

**Communication.** Frequency ranges were 110–160, with random starting values chosen; maximum frequency differential per alert was 6.
**Monitoring.** The slider speeds were 2 s/tic, 1.4 s/tic, 1 s/tic, and 1.6 s/tic for F1 through F4, respectively. Timeout rate for F5 and F6 was 8 s.
**Tracking.** For all paths, path interval set to 30; satellite radius was 13 pixels. The movement refresh was 100.

Capacity analyses were completed in R using the *capacity.stst()* function in the sft package [13].

### 4.3   Results

Table 1 shows the traditional dual task interference effects for the two-task scenarios in all three conditions. Interference effects were computed by taking

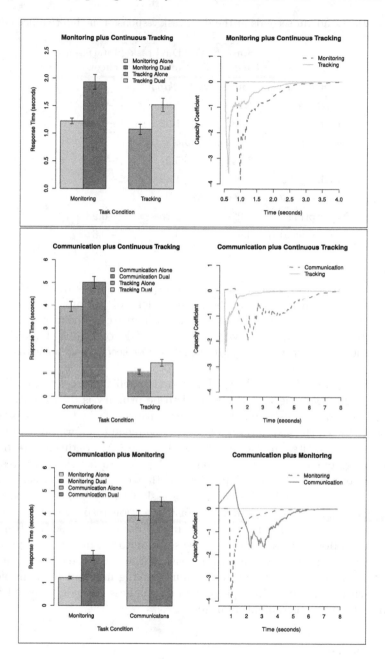

**Fig. 2.** Plots of the mean response times (left column) for the single and dual task conditions; corresponding capacity coefficient functions (right column). From top to bottom, the figure contains the MCT, CCT, and CM conditions. Error bars show ±1 standard error of the mean.

**Table 1.** Magnitude in seconds of the dual task response time interference effects

|  | Single task mean RT | Dual task mean RT | Interference effect |
|---|---|---|---|
| *Monitoring plus continuous tracking* | | | |
| Monitoring | 1.22 | 1.93 | −0.71 |
| Tracking | 1.08 | 1.52 | −0.44 |
| *Communication plus continuous tracking* | | | |
| Communication | 3.94 | 5.01 | −1.06 |
| Tracking | 1.08 | 1.49 | −0.42 |
| *Communication plus monitoring* | | | |
| Monitoring | 1.22 | 2.20 | −0.98 |
| Communication | 3.94 | 4.55 | −0.61 |

$\overline{RT}_{Single} - \overline{RT}_{Dual}$ for each task. The corresponding plots of the single and dual task mean response times are shown in the left column of Fig. 2. Consistent with dual task expectations, all tasks show an increase in mean response time under dual task conditions, relative to the single task conditions. This is regardless of whether the task was designated primary or secondary; both tasks show performance interference.

The right column of Fig. 2 shows the capacity coefficient results for all tasks. Note that in all plots, the task designated to be primary is drawn with a solid line, and the secondary task capacity is drawn with the dashed line. As expected, and consistent with the interference effects at the mean level, we observe limited capacity during multitasking for all tasks. For the CM condition, we observe some surprising evidence of super capacity $C_{ST}(t) > 0$ for the early response times in the communication task. This means that the additional task demands placed on the participant by the monitoring task actually boosted performance on events when the participant made a fast detection response. It is not clear from this analysis alone if that boost resulted from an increase in attentional resources to support the task, or an increase in motor resources to support the need to use one hand for two concurrent tasks. Either way, the capacity analysis suggests that workload efficiency during multitasking may not be a simple unidirectional effect on processing speed. Similar nuances are not reflected in the traditional dual task decrement analyses.

## 5   Discussion

Capacity coefficient analysis and traditional mean response time dual task interference analysis for mental workload rely on similar assumptions and techniques for assessing the impact increasing task demands have on performance. Both require the use of single and multiple task conditions, and leverage response time as the dependent measure of task performance. Both attempt to assay the degree to which tasks require common resources and impact cognitive effort through measurable interference (or lack thereof). As I have illustrated herein, when applied to two-task visual multitasking, with tasks that tap into common visual perception and motor response mechanisms requiring concurrent performance on the order of seconds, both measures lead to consistent interpretations about limitation in workload capacity. The presence of workload capacity limitations means that the information processing mechanisms must work harder to achieve the same amount of information throughput in any given amount of time. That is, capacity limitations imply a higher mental workload.

So why bother with a more complicated analysis that seems to give us the same basic interpretation? Capacity coefficient analysis, because of its theoretical grounding in information processing modeling and the use of a baseline model, immediately provides hypotheses about the mechanisms producing the observed workload efficiency. When observed performance is not equivalent to the UCIP model, we have three candidate mechanisms to investigate. First, performance could be non-UCIP if the assumption of parallel processing architecture is not correct. In the visual multitasking herein, the tasks are concurrent in nature. However, the organization of the mental information processing channels could be parallel (cues from each task processed simultaneously) or serial (cues from each task process sequentially). The latter implies fast mental switching between tasks is required, which is possible if attention is regularly switched between the task quadrants and independent alerting cues. If a person engages a standard serial processing architecture, then the resulting comparison to the UCIP baseline will produce limited capacity performance. Additional tests of processing architecture are available (see, e.g., [13,31]).

The second mechanism that can be tested is the degree to which the information processing mechanisms are operating independently. Process independence refers to stochastic dependencies between the information processing channels. Non-independence can arise from correlated inputs or cross-talk between the channels over the course of task execution [32]. This is not the same as concept of independence as resource independence, in which two or more tasks require the use of separate mental resources, such as visual and auditory perceptual mechanisms [36]. Inhibitory stochastic dependencies between the tasks will produce limited capacity performance relative to the UCIP baseline.

The third mechanism producing non-UCIP performance is the employment of a stopping rule or decision mechanism different from the one assumed by the $C_{ST}(t)$ implementation. In the present effort, a single-target self-terminating stopping rule was assumed based on the nature of the concurrent visual alert response tasks. However, other decision rules are possible, such as an exhaustive cue processing strategy in which all cues within a task are examined before a decision-response is made. Use of a strategy requiring more decisions to be made than the ST-ST assumption will result in limited capacity performance relative to the baseline UCIP model defined for the assumed stopping rule (see [16] for an example of people engaging a stopping rule other than the one specified by the task).

There are additional sources of capacity limitations that may play into mental workload that are not captured by the capacity coefficient analysis. Working memory capacity, for example, represents a different set of mental resources that are known to be limited in nature but that are not assessed by a measure of information throughput. Recent work has attempted to determine the ways in which working memory capacity and workload efficiency capacity may reflect any common resources or may be measured conjointly [12,38]. However, evidence suggests the two are uncorrelated, consistent with multiple resource theory of mental workload [36].

Capacity coefficient analysis can scale to multitasking that includes more than two tasks, which is more difficult for dual task interference measures. While mean response times can be collected for any number of tasks, the generalization of the dual task comparison approach would be similar to an analysis of variance with pairwise comparisons between subsets of tasks. This approach based on purely empirical comparisons offers little theoretical foundation for predicting and interpreting the underlying mechanisms behind the empirical observations. Capacity coefficient analysis, together with other variations on the component hazard functions, naturally generalize to $n \geq 2$ tasks by straightforward extension of the baseline UCIP model [4]. The interpretation of the mechanisms of workload efficiency remain consistent because the fundamental baseline model remains consistent [30,32].

Objective, functional assessment of cognitive workload efficiency with the capacity coefficient offers a novel tool to support the goal of real-time cognitive state assessment [6,23]. Real-time state assessment is the process of inferring some aspect of a person's state, such as fatigue [3] or workload, online during task execution. Development of such a capability is considered critical for developing effective automation or adaptive machine aiding to mitigate the negative effects of cognitive moderators (e.g., task overload). Subjective measures of workload are considered too disruptive to be used frequently for online assessment; psychophysiological data streams can be measured continuously but they offer only indirect correlates of the cognitive states of interest. If a task offers a behavior for which response time can be measured with some regularity, then the task has the potential to leverage capacity analysis for objective assessment and mechanistic interpretation of cognitive states. There is much work left to be done in order to determine minimal task and data requirements to support robust inference, as well as to hone techniques for estimating the capacity models continuously. But the consistency of the interpretation of workload between standard dual task approaches and capacity analysis suggest this is a fruitful workload assessment technique to continue developing.

For multitasking scenarios in particular, real-time state assessment of workload will support adaptive machine determining when to interrupt tasks or to switch between tasks. Evidence consistently supports that task switching is most effective at points of low mental workload [1,7,33]. Iqbal and Bailey [15] demonstrated efficacy of this principle by using task models to predict points of low workload for best switching opportunities. Such task models, however, are not dynamically adaptive to changing environment, task, or human operator state demands. Model-based approaches to workload assessment, like the capacity coefficient, could supply critical input data for adaptive computational models that might be embedded into human-machine systems engaging adaptive machine intelligence to provide external support for effective multitasking or that attempt to mitigate cognitive overload.

**Acknowledgments.** The research described in this document was sponsored the U.S. Department of Energy (DOE) through the Analysis in Motion Initiative at Pacific Northwest National Laboratory. The views and conclusions contained in this document are those of the author and should not be interpreted as representing the official policies, either expressed or implied, of the U.S. Government.

# References

1. Altmann, E.M., Trafton, J.G.: Timecourse of recovery from task interruption: data and a model. Psychon. Bull. Rev. **14**(6), 1079–1084 (2007)
2. Anderson, J.R.: Spanning seven orders of magnitude: a challenge for cognitive modeling. Cogn. Sci. **26**(1), 85–112 (2002)
3. Blaha, L.M., Fisher, C.R., Walsh, M.M., Veksler, B.Z., Gunzelmann, G.: Real-time fatigue monitoring with computational cognitive models. In: Schmorrow, D.D.D., Fidopiastis, C.M.M. (eds.) AC 2016. LNCS, vol. 9743, pp. 299–310. Springer, Cham (2016). doi:10.1007/978-3-319-39955-3_28
4. Blaha, L.M., Houpt, J.W.: An extension of workload capacity space for systems with more than two channels. J. Math. Psychol. **66**, 1–5 (2015)
5. Boff, K.R., Lincoln, J.E.: Engineering data compendium. Human perception and performance, vol. 3. Technical report, DTIC Document (1988)
6. Borghetti, B.J., Rusnock, C.F.: Introduction to real-time state assessment. In: Schmorrow, D.D.D., Fidopiastis, C.M.M. (eds.) AC 2016. LNCS, vol. 9743, pp. 311–321. Springer, Cham (2016). doi:10.1007/978-3-319-39955-3_29
7. Borst, J.P., Taatgen, N.A., van Rijn, H.: What makes interruptions disruptive? A process-model account of the effects of the problem state bottleneck on task interruption and resumption. In: Proceedings of the 33rd Annual ACM Conference on Human Factors in Computing Systems, pp. 2971–2980. ACM (2015)
8. Cline, J., Arendt, D., Geiselman, E., Blaha, L.M.: Web-based implementation of the modified multi-attribute task battery. In: Fourth Annual Midwestern Cognitive Science Conference, Dayton, OH (2015)
9. Derrick, W.L.: Dimensions of operator workload. Hum. Factors **30**(1), 95–110 (1988)
10. Halverson, T., Reynolds, B., Blaha, L.M.: SIMCog-JS: simplified interfacing for modeling cognition-javascript. In: Proceedings of the International Conference on Cognitive Modeling, Groningen, The Netherlands, pp. 39–44 (2015)
11. Hart, S.G., Staveland, L.E.: Human Mental Workload. Elsevier Science, Amsterdam (1988)
12. Heathcote, A., Coleman, J.R., Eidels, A., Watson, J.M., Houpt, J., Strayer, D.L.: Working memory's workload capacity. Mem. Cogn. **43**(7), 973–989 (2015)
13. Houpt, J.W., Blaha, L.M., McIntire, J.P., Havig, P.R., Townsend, J.T.: Systems factorial technology with R. Behav. Res. Methods **46**(2), 307–330 (2014)

14. Houpt, J.W., Townsend, J.T., Donkin, C.: A new perspective on visual word processing efficiency. Acta Psychol. **145**, 118–127 (2014)
15. Iqbal, S.T., Bailey, B.P.: Investigating the effectiveness of mental workload as a predictor of opportune moments for interruption. In: CHI 2005 Extended Abstracts on Human Factors in Computing Systems, pp. 1489–1492. ACM (2005)
16. Johnson, S.A., Blaha, L.M., Houpt, J.W., Townsend, J.T.: Systems factorial technology provides new insights on global-local information processing in autism spectrum disorders. J. Math. Psychol. **54**(1), 53–72 (2010)
17. Little, D.R., Eidels, A., Fific, M., Wang, T.: Understanding the influence of distractors on workload capacity. J. Math. Psychol. **68**, 25–36 (2015)
18. Matthews, G., Reinerman-Jones, E., Barber, D.J., Abich, J.I.: The psychometrics of mental workload: multiple measures are sensitive but divergent. Hum. Factors **57**, 125–143 (2015)
19. Matthews, G., Reinerman-Jones, L., Wohleber, R., Lin, J., Mercado, J., Abich, J.: Workload is multidimensional, not unitary: what now? In: Schmorrow, D.D., Fidopiastis, C.M. (eds.) AC 2015. LNCS, vol. 9183, pp. 44–55. Springer, Cham (2015). doi:10.1007/978-3-319-20816-9_5
20. Newell, A.: Unified Theories of Cognition. Harvard University Press, Cambridge (1994)
21. Norman, D.A., Bobrow, D.G.: On data-limited and resource-limited processes. Cogn. Psychol. **7**(1), 44–64 (1975)
22. Reid, G.B., Nygren, T.E.: The subjective workload assessment technique: a scaling procedure for measuring mental workload. Adv. Psychol. **52**, 185–218 (1988)
23. Rusnock, C., Borghetti, B., McQuaid, I.: Objective-analytical measures of workload – the third pillar of workload triangulation? In: Schmorrow, D.D., Fidopiastis, C.M. (eds.) AC 2015. LNCS, vol. 9183, pp. 124–135. Springer, Cham (2015). doi:10.1007/978-3-319-20816-9_13
24. Salvucci, D.D.: Multitasking. In: Lee, J.D., Kirlik, A. (eds.) The Oxford Handbook of Cognitive Engineering, pp. 57–67. The Oxford Library of Psychology, Oxford University Press, New York (2013)
25. Salvucci, D.D., Taatgen, N.A.: Threaded cognition: an integrated theory of concurrent multitasking. Psychol. Rev. **115**(1), 101 (2008)
26. Salvucci, D.D., Taatgen, N.A.: The Multitasking Mind. Oxford University Press, Oxford (2010)
27. Salvucci, D.D., Taatgen, N.A., Borst, J.P.: Toward a unified theory of the multitasking continuum: from concurrent performance to task switching, interruption, and resumption. In: Proceedings of the SIGCHI Conference on Human Factors in Computing Systems, pp. 1819–1828. ACM (2009)
28. Townsend, J.T.: Issues and models concerning the processing of a finite number of inputs. In: Kantowitz, B.H. (ed.) Human Information Processing: Tutorials in Performance and Cognition, pp. 133–168. Lawrence Erlbaum Associates, Hillsdale (1974)
29. Townsend, J.T., Ashby, F.G.: Methods of modeling capacity in simple processing systems. In: Castellan, J., Restle, F. (eds.) Cognitive Theory, vol. 3, pp. 200–239. Lawrences Erlbaum Associates, Hillsdale (1978)
30. Townsend, J.T., Ashby, F.G.: Stochastic Modeling of Elementary Psychological Processes. Cambridge University Press, Cambridge (1983)
31. Townsend, J.T., Nozawa, G.: Spatio-temporal properties of elementary perception: an investigation of parallel, serial, and coactive theories. J. Math. Psychol. **39**(4), 321–359 (1995)

32. Townsend, J.T., Wenger, M.J.: A theory of interactive parallel processing: new capacity measures and predictions for a response time inequality series. Psychol. Rev. **111**(4), 1003 (2004)
33. Trafton, J.G., Altmann, E.M., Brock, D.P., Mintz, F.E.: Preparing to resume an interrupted task: effects of prospective goal encoding and retrospective rehearsal. Int. J. Hum. Comput. Stud. **58**(5), 583–603 (2003)
34. Wenger, M.J., Townsend, J.T.: Basic response time tools for studying general processing capacity in attention, perception, and cognition. J. Gen. Psychol. **127**(1), 67–99 (2000)
35. Whitaker, L.A.: Dual-task interference as a function of cognitive processing load. Acta Psychol. **43**(1), 71–84 (1979)
36. Wickens, C.D.: Multiple resources and mental workload. Hum. Factors: J. Hum. Factors Ergon. Soc. **50**(3), 449–455 (2008)
37. Yeh, Y.Y., Wickens, C.D.: Dissociation of performance and subjective measures of workload. Hum. Factors **30**(1), 111–120 (1988)
38. Yu, J.C., Chang, T.Y., Yang, C.T.: Individual differences in working memory capacity and workload capacity. Front. Psychol. **5**, 1465 (2014)

# Moving Vigilance Out of the Laboratory: Dynamic Scenarios for UAS Operator Vigilance Training

Tarah Daly[1]([✉]), Jennifer Murphy[1], Katlin Anglin[1], James Szalma[2],
Max Acree[3], Carla Landsberg[4], and Laticia Bowens[4]

[1] Quantum Improvements Consulting, Orlando, FL, USA
{tdaly, jmurphy, kanglin}@quantumimprovements.net
[2] University of Central Florida, Orlando, FL, USA
james.szalma@ucf.edu
[3] GameSim, Orlando, FL, USA
max.acree@gamesim.com
[4] Naval Air Warfare Center Training Systems Division, Orlando, USA
{carla.landsberg, laticia.bowens}@navy.mil

**Abstract.** Our technology laden world continues to push the limits of human cognitive performance. Human performers are increasingly expected to assume roles of passive monitors rather than active engagers of technology systems [1]. Active and physical tasks have shifted to more sedentary tasks requiring significant cognitive workload at a rapid pace. Consequently, researchers and academics alike struggle to find a balance between effective user interface, usability, and ergonomic designs that will allow the performer to successfully complete their tasks while sustaining attention in these complex environments. It is no surprise that human error is at the root of tragic mishaps relating to vigilance across a wide range of applications and operational environments [2–4].

Researching vigilance is not new [5–7]. In fact, vigilance has been studied in laboratory settings for nearly seventy years across many conditions and tasks [8]. Traditional laboratory tasks involve static displays with simple image targets presented to individuals over prolonged periods of time. Participants are required to detect rare and temporally spaced targets among abundant "noise" images while sustaining their attention. The results using these vigilance tasks have found evidence of vigilance decrements, increased stress [7], and high cognitive demand [9]. The issue of training the skill to sustain attention has also been addressed [10, 11]. Findings from traditional research show that the most effective way of improving vigilance performance is through providing feedback in the form of knowledge of results [12].

Although the contrived, laboratory-based vigilance tasks can produce and mitigate the vigilance decrement, tasks that directly relate to complex operational environments are severely underrepresented in research. There have only been few researchers that utilize dynamic environments in vigilance research. For example, Szalma et al. [13] developed a video game-based training platform with the goal to extend the traditional vigilance training paradigm to complex, dynamic, and virtual environments that are more representative of visual detection tasks in the real world. Our current research is focused on extending

© Springer International Publishing AG 2017
D.D. Schmorrow and C.M. Fidopiastis (Eds.): AC 2017, Part II, LNAI 10285, pp. 20–35, 2017.
DOI: 10.1007/978-3-319-58625-0_2

the vigilance training paradigm to operationally relevant areas with the development of a game-based system for training operator attention within unmanned aerial systems (UAS).

UAS are an integral part of mission operations within many branches of our military. New developments and improved technology allow extended mission operations of UAS up to, and exceeding 12 h. However, many UAS mishaps are the result of mechanical failures, and an alarming rate – 60.2% – of mishaps have been attributed to operator error [2]. This finding is not surprising, as UAS operations are highly cognitively demanding. Prolonged shiftwork and surveillance missions require sustained attention toward tracking or identifying rare targets, often in visually degraded conditions. This paper discusses current efforts to take the vigilance training paradigm out of the laboratory setting and into operational environments, including our current work in creating game-based training of vigilance for UAS operators. We describe the challenges associated with defining and standardizing targets, developing scenarios, and assessing performance.

**Keywords:** Vigilance · Game-based training · Sustaining attention · Vigilance decrement · Operational environment · UAS training · Game attributes

# 1 Introduction

Technological innovations, those which purport to improve human performance, allow operators to extend work hours significantly, and keep operators safe in hostile or extreme environments are increasingly pushing humans to assume roles of passive monitors within technology systems [1]. This shift, while certainly allowing the extension of human capabilities in some regards, has left the operator in a state of required sustained attention, under alerted conditions, to perform vigilance tasks. Vigilance refers to the ability to sustain attention for rare, temporally spaced signals among noise over prolonged periods of time. As time on task progresses, performance tends to decline as difficult task requirements decrease engagement and increase distress [7]. It is no surprise that human error is at the root of tragic mishaps relating to vigilance across a wide range of applications and operational environments [2–4].

Many occupational and operational settings require operators to perform vigilance tasks. Air traffic controllers, Transportation Security Administration (TSA) agents, and nuclear power plant controllers are more obvious occupations requiring continuous monitoring of information. However, other operational environments require extreme vigilance including unmanned aerial systems operations. Improved technology allows extended mission operations of UAS up to, and exceeding, 12 h. While many UAS mishaps are the result of mechanical failures, an alarming rate – 60.2% – of mishaps have been attributed to operator error [2]. Real-world data suggest that the vigilance paradigm observed in the laboratory is a phenomenon occurring in operational settings as well, and poses a significant threat to the safety and wellbeing of individuals in the real-world.

## 1.1    Training for Vigilance

Vigilance has been studied in laboratory settings for nearly seventy years [8] across many conditions and tasks. A consistent finding in this research is the *vigilance decrement,* in which performance on tasks that require vigilance declines over time. Traditionally, laboratory vigilance tasks involve a response to a relatively rare target over a lengthy period of time. The vigilance decrement usually occurs within the first 15 min of task performance, however, if the task is sufficiently cognitively demanding, it can take as little as five minutes for performance to decline [9]. While this effect has been historically interpreted as a decline in arousal, research investigating perceived workload and task induced stress show that vigilance tasks are in fact very stressful to the participant [7]. Thus, the vigilance decrement can be attributed to the high cognitive demands of the task. Under an Army effort investigating vigilance in route clearance missions, it was found that Warfighters are aware of these strains and attempt to mitigate them with energy drinks, cigarette smoking, and other stimulants [14].

Research shows that vigilance depends upon a combination of participant characteristics, environmental conditions, and task characteristics and performance varies widely from person to person [15]. In a previous Army Research Institute (ARI) study, performance on a vigilance task predicted peer ratings of Soldiers' intelligence, decision-making ability, attentiveness, and resilience [16]. Vigilance also depends upon the physiological state of the participant; arousal may be influenced by stimulant use, fatigue, time of day, and numerous other factors. Importantly, the extent to which a participant exhibits relatively high levels of vigilance has been found to predict performance in game platform-based training for Warfighter tasks [16]. Environmental conditions could include stimulant usage, sleep, or time of day which have been shown to affect vigilance performance [17, 18]. Additionally, task characteristics refer to vigilance task parameters and these range from static, laboratory-based tasks, dynamic stimuli within videogame-based environments, or even feedback presented to the trainee during or after a vigil.

There have been substantial research efforts to identify effective training methods for vigilance. Research indicates that the most effective way of improving sustained attention is through performance feedback in the form of knowledge of results (KR) (for early reviews see [12, 19]). KR has been shown to improve operators' perceptual sensitivity (the ability to discriminate signal from nonsignal; [20]). Early research demonstrated that providing feedback regarding performance outcomes (i.e., detections, false alarms, missed targets, or response time) improved performance during both a training session where feedback on these outcomes is provided as well as in a test or transfer session in which the feedback is withdrawn. The transfer of training to a test vigil is commonly used to establish that skill retention (i.e., learning) is a result of training intervention (in this case, feedback in the form of KR) rather than due to the immediate performance support afforded by the intervention itself during the training session [21].

Several studies have shown that KR training can improve vigilance, but there has been some debate regarding whether KR effectiveness is due primarily to operator motivation or to learning mechanisms. There is evidence to support both perspectives. Mackworth [22] demonstrated that performance improvement can be achieved using false feedback, i.e., feedback provided on a random schedule that provides no accurate information regarding performance, pointing to KR's motivational influences (see [23, 24]). Later studies established that performance can be improved by the use of partial KR schedules (KR only provided some of the time), goal setting interventions, or providing monetary awards in addition to KR [25–29]. These findings support a motivational explanation.

There is also evidence to support a non-motivational role for KR. Much of this evidence derives from evaluation of the transfer of training from one task to another. The nature of the vigilance task itself has been found to moderate differences in performance. Vigilance tasks may be categorized into those requiring successive discriminations and those requiring simultaneous discrimination. In successive discrimination tasks the observer must compare a stimulus event against a standard in memory (absolute judgment), and in simultaneous discrimination tasks the observer must compare a stimulus element to another element present in the display (comparative judgment). If KR effectiveness were due only to increasing motivation, then task type should not affect transfer. However, research has shown that training on a task requiring simultaneous or a successive discrimination transfers to a criterion task within the same task type but not across types [10, 11]. These findings suggest a strong learning component to vigilance training using this paradigm. The task specificity of vigilance training has important implications for training the vigilance component of any task. To maximize the effectiveness of SkySpotter, it is important to replicate the sorts of tasks end users will be performing in the operational setting.

## 1.2   Vigilance Training in Simulated Environments

The research summarized above describes training for vigilance as it has been traditionally examined in a laboratory setting. In these experiments, participants view static displays that feature simple targets in order to maximize experimental control. While these paradigms have been effective in inducing a vigilance decrement, they do not capture the complexity of the operational environment. As sustaining attention becomes more difficult as cognitive demands increase, a true understanding of how vigilance works in the real world is required. Further, because previous research shows successful training transfer depends upon the extent to which a training task mirrors the transfer task, it is imperative to accurately represent operator tasks.

Under an ARI funded effort, Szalma and colleagues [13] developed vigilance training in a videogame-based platform. The goal of this research was to extend the traditional vigilance paradigm to a dynamic, complex virtual environment that more accurately represents the visual detection tasks required of route clearance personnel engaged in improvised explosive device (IED) detection. The primary challenge the team faced was developing scenarios that were sufficiently boring and monotonous to induce a vigilance decrement despite the engaging and motivating aspects characteristic of game-based training platforms. An additional challenge was to design scenarios in such a way to define consistent, equivalent "trials," which is required in order to examine the degradation of performance over time. To accomplish this goal, scenarios were designed in which participants engaged in a virtual dismounted route clearance mission. Movement was limited to guided navigation at a steady pace, effectively putting the participant "on rails." The participant's goal was to identify suspicious targets known to be indicators of IEDs (e.g. fuel cans, command wire, pressure plates) that appeared sporadically throughout the scenario. The participant received KR feedback about the accuracy of their response: "Correct" for a correct detection, "Miss" for a missed target, and "False Alarm" for a response when no target was present. Figure 1 depicts screenshots of a correct identification and sample feedback.

**Fig. 1.** Screenshots from Vigilance Training Module in VBS2 [13]

After participants completed the training phase in which feedback was presented, transfer was assessed by completing a similar scenario with no feedback. Interestingly, these participants did not exhibit a vigilance decrement, either during training or transfer. However, scores on measures of perceived workload and stress indicated task engagement declined over the course of the training, while distress and avoidant coping increased, a finding consistent with previous vigilance research [8]. Importantly, participants who received feedback in terms of KR outperformed those who did not, identifying more targets and responding more quickly. These findings hold promise for the development of videogame-based training for UAS operators.

### 1.3 Videogame-Based Training

The use of videogame-based simulation by the military has steadily increased as these technologies have improved in popularity, fidelity, and accessibility. Videogame-based platforms are typically used for training purposes within a military context and provide an inexpensive, flexible means of introducing Soldiers to a variety of domains. The effectiveness of videogame-based platforms for training has been demonstrated for a variety of cognitive skills and abilities [30]. Skills acquired have been shown to transfer to external tasks, particularly if the skills and abilities required to succeed in the game and the transfer task are consistent [31].

There is an important distinction between training using a videogame-based platform and training using "serious games." Typical military applications of game-based training platforms, such as VBS2 and *America's Army*, provide a moderate level of fidelity in a low-cost desktop simulation. These applications are not truly "games" as they lack many of the attributes of games that provide an engaging, motivating experience. In his review of game-based training, Hays [32] defines a game as "an artificially constructed, competitive activity with a specific goal, a set of rules, and constraints that is located in a specific context." Wilson et al. [33] provide an extensive review of these game attributes, and consider the most important to be fantasy, representation, sensory stimuli, challenge, mystery, assessment, and control. These attributes determine the extent to which a game is, among other things, fun.

Our goal with SkySpotter is to develop a true game. A hallmark of vigilance tasks is the extent to which they induce stress, high cognitive workload, and decreased motivation. Consequently, these tend to be tasks that individuals avoid. For vigilance training to be maximally effective, trainees must continue to practice in order to maintain their skill level. Our aim is to develop a program that is challenging enough to be effective but also engaging enough that trainees will continue to put effort into developing their vigilance skills despite the stress or other negative emotions they may feel.

## 1.4   Adaptive Training Technology

Adaptive training has been defined as the personalization of training content during the course of instruction to the individual student, based on an assessment of that student's knowledge, abilities, experiences, and/or skills [34]. The Navy, as well as the other services, is increasingly interested in implementing adaptive training technologies as a means of providing effective learning experiences while reducing costs. To date, most adaptive training interventions have focused on improving the learner's understanding of a particular knowledge domain, such as math (e.g., [35]), conceptual science (e.g., [36]), or vocabulary (e.g., [37]). Adaptive training tends to be more effective for well-defined domains in which there is a "right" answer to a problem. In these cases, adaptive techniques tend to involve manipulating the challenge or complexity of information based on a real-time assessment of student understanding. Such techniques include scaffolding [38, 39], fading of worked examples [40–42], and comprehension gauging [39, 43–45], among others.

Unlike knowledge-based domains, sustained attention is a cognitive skill. Adaptive algorithms have been successfully used in training programs for cognitive and perceptual skills. In these paradigms, the difficulty of a discrimination or similar task is manipulated based on an ongoing assessment of the trainee's performance. While these programs have shown improvement in trainee performance, the extent to which the adaptation itself provides a benefit is unclear [46–48]. This is likely because the costs associated with developing adaptive and non-adaptive versions of the same training simply for research purposes are prohibitive [49]. Further, there is little opportunity to evaluate long-term benefits of these programs and generalize the empirical evidence of adaptive training to complex environments [50].

In addition to real-time adaptations, macro-level adaptive strategies can be employed in order to determine placement within a training program, adjust content format, or appropriate level of control. These adaptations are often based on learner characteristics related to performance, such as aptitude, personality, and learning style. Because individual differences are suggested to influence the effectiveness of training instruction, content, feedback, and difficulty, these variables may be critical in determining how and when to adapt training [50]. In the context of vigilance, age, physiological state (e.g. fatigue and stress), learning difficulties (e.g. ADHD), and other characteristics influence an individual's ability to sustain attention.

Elements of adaptive training will be applied to SkySpotter to support individualized approaches to ongoing assessment of performance with the use of the system. Macro-level adaptions will be leveraged to place trainees, pre-task, based on predictor variables such as participant characteristics (individual differences) and environmental factors. Adaptive placement will provide opportunities for trainees to experience task challenges and appropriate levels of effort and stress while not feeling overwhelmed and disengaged. The goal is to achieve maximal motivation so trainees feel compelled to return to training for challenges, personal achievement, and improved performance.

## 2   Current Research

Presently, work is being conducted for the design and development of a videogame-based adaptive attentional training platform for UAS operators under an effort supported by the Naval Air Warfare Center Training Systems Division (NAWCTSD). SkySpotter is the current effort researching the effectiveness of vigilance training within a videogame-based platform. While previous research has leveraged dismounted, ground-based environments [13] this domain is novel. However, the innate characteristics of vigilance tasks remain consistent within this instantiation of dynamic, operationally relevant work.

UAS long-duration mission operations are the primary point of concern, given the expanded capabilities of more technologically sound unmanned aircraft. Current and new UAS will allow for prolonged mission duration up to, and even exceeding, 12 h. This extended operational environment causes UAS operators to work in extreme, alerted conditions, while expected to perform at optimal levels. To maintain training gains, it is imperative that trainees maintain continued practiced and while improvements in vigilance can be found after just one session, sustained attention is a perishable skill. Therefore, it is imperative that a sound, scientifically-based, effective training system be available to UAS operators at all times, to improve their ability to sustain attention.

SkySpotter is a web-based training program composed of four core functionalities: a pre-training assessment, vigilance training scenarios, a test scenario, and a profile. The pre-training assessment is designed to capture state, trait, and demographic characteristics, predictor variables that could have an effect on vigilance performance. The vigilance training scenario and test scenarios simulate a UAS performing a sweep of an area, a geo-typical middle eastern terrain. The scenarios follow a very precise prescription for target and environmental elements so that vigilance performance may be evaluated with the same laboratory scrutiny. Finally, a user profile tracks performance progression through training. Not only will data be collated here to provide trainees feedback and after action review (AAR), data will drive adaptive training elements as well.

## 2.1 Predictor Variables

Vigilance depends upon a combination of participant characteristics, environmental conditions, and task characteristics. Vigilance also depends upon the physiological state of the participant; arousal may be influenced by stimulant use, fatigue, time of day, and numerous other factors. Importantly, the extent to which a participant exhibits relatively high levels of vigilance has been found to predict performance in game platform-based training for Warfighter tasks [16]. As such, research suggests that it is possible to predict vigilance (e.g., [36, 51–54].

Traits, characteristic behaviors and attitudes that are long-term and consistent, that predict vigilance include personality (extroversion, conscientiousness, and neuroticism/ trait anxiety; [51]), cognitive skills (working memory and spatial ability; [51, 52]), and fatigue proneness (propensity for sleepiness and boredom; [54]).

States, temporary behaviors or attitudes that depend on a person's situation at a specific time, have also been identified to predict vigilance. State variables of interest include stress/coping and sleepiness (different from fatigue proneness). Subjective state and coping dimension questionnaires are typically used to identify elements that reduce task engagement, leading to vigilance decrements. Sleepiness has been found to impair vigilance. Usually occurring during night shifts, sleepiness is more prevalent at the end of the night [55], as there are significant correlations between errors and subjective sleepiness [18]. Sleep restriction may also contribute to sleepiness and vigilance decrements, greatly impacting response time and alertness.

Environmental influences are variables such as stimulant consumption, time of day, and sleep the previous night. To maintain vigilance, stimulants are often used to enhance performance and attention. A 32-mg dose of caffeine, which is equivalent to the amount of caffeine in a typical cola drink and less than that of a cup of coffee, improved auditory vigilance hit rates and visual reaction time [17]. Caffeine given in the early morning also improved overall vigilance performance during late morning [56].

Additional items for consideration include demographics information such as age, academic achievement, videogame experience, etc. While age is found to influence vigilance, performance was more variable among older adults as stimulus degradation increased and the vigil progressed [57]. Furthermore, vigilance is associated with video game experience. Research has found that videogame players (VGPs) outperform non-video game players (NVGPs) in attention and visual search that are most commonly used during vigilance tasks [58–60].

## 2.2 Scenario Elements (Training and Test Vigils)

Researching vigilance in a dynamic, videogame-based environment is relatively novel. Only a few have performed this work in the past [13, 16]. In order to scientifically evaluate vigilance performance within a novel platform, one must validate that the vigilance paradigm is being replicated in that environment. Distinct paradigm parameters include rare and temporally spaced targets separated by "noise" or distractor elements (context and environment specific), sufficient task length (vigilance decrements have been seen in a little as five minutes [9]), and the phenomenon known as the vigilance decrement, when performance declines as time on task or task difficulty increases [61].

A review of literature and publicly available doctrine and handbooks was conducted as well as interviews with a subject matter expert. This requirement collection procedure informed content and environment creation for the vigils (both training and test scenarios). Most notably, SME input informed targets of interest to include that would be both operationally relevant and effective for vigilance training within the UAS context. In addition to targets, environmental conditions (e.g., smoke, fog, rain), distractors (e.g., civilians), and other contextually relevant information were included in scenario development. The scene in which trainees will view content consists of a bird's eye view through a clear scope (natural eye view) whereby the rural geo-typical middle eastern terrain will pass by. Buildings, vehicles, people, animals, foliage, and terrain features will also be included.

Following laboratory based vigilance tasks, training scenarios typically employ KR while test vigils remove this feedback to gauge transfer of training [19]. Following this approach, training scenarios within SkySpotter display KR, real-time feedback of trainee performance, while the test vigils do not provide KR. Scenario length must be sufficiently long enough to capture performance decrements while also providing time to collect performance data across time on task. Additionally, target appearance should be relatively random throughout the scenarios and follow parameters previously set by Szalma and colleagues [13]. The duration of the scenario should consist of distinct epochs of time in which targets are randomly selected to appear within the scene. Speed through the scene should accommodate target appearance interval time to allow the target to remain onscreen from moment of visibility (through line of sight) for a short variable duration. Only one target will be presented on screen at a time, such that as soon as the current target flows off screen, the next target shall appear in the allotted epoch of time. Targets should be a mixture of all variable types (those selected for inclusion in the scenario). These parameters cause trainees to remain alerted to scenario elements while looking for targets on screen (there are no repeated elements and trainees cannot anticipate what will come on screen).

Game elements are an additional feature included in the scenarios that are not typical to laboratory-based vigilance tasks. For this effort, game features were an important part in developing a true vigilance training game. Since vigilance tasks tend to induce stress, high cognitive workload, and decreased motivation, trainees are likely to abandon or avoid the training system. However, with the inclusion of game elements, the goal was to develop a program that is challenging enough to be effective but also engaging enough that trainees will continue to use the system in order to develop their vigilance skills despite stress they may feel. Gameplay aspects including a storyline and mission, leveling, engaging characters, performance goals, mystery, and consistent style will be utilized to maximize immersion and presence.

## 2.3   Performance Tracking

In order to instantiate adaptive training within SkySpotter, the system will collect various demographic and performance metrics across training sessions to utilize in providing a tailored training experience. First time users will be presented with an introduction and tutorial to system functionality and game play. However, subsequent game play will be based on quick state assessments captured at the beginning of a training session. The predictor variables collected will inform the system of which training level a trainee will encounter. Levels vary in difficulty (e.g., target type, target rate, signal-to-noise ratio, speed of presentation, etc.). The system will recommend a level to trainees based on current state and past performance (percent correct, positive predictive power, etc.). Once in a level, real-time feedback will be presented across training vigils (i.e., hits, misses, and false alarms) and users will be shown a summary screen of their performance at the end of a completed session (e.g., KR, percent correct score, and feedback). Various performance metrics across time can be accessed through the user profile at any time (e.g., last session, last session score, current level, current score, improvement over time, etc.).

## 2.4  Research Questions

There are challenges associated with providing a novel platform to train vigilance tasks. For one, the dynamic environment must be created to afford the replication of the vigilance performance decrement and other salient vigilance paradigm parameters. Additionally, unique challenges also occur with performance metrics themselves. How would one evaluate a simultaneous false alarm and miss? Static vigilance tasks would not allow this type of behavior to occur. Not only do our research questions focus on the design and validation of a videogame-based adaptive training platform for vigilance, we also consider the effectiveness of the training delivery system once developed. There are five major steps for experimentation in support of the development of SkySpotter. Following a prescription of experimental scenario development, we can hope to address some of the more unique challenges associated with the use of dynamic environments.

### 2.4.1  Identify a Target Set

First, we must identify a set of potential targets. Although the final number of targets for inclusion in the scenario may between 5–7, more should be identified in this step in case some selected targets do not have the desired psychophysical properties (too small and can't be seen, too salient and always seen, etc.). Work toward this step has already been accomplished. Based on SME interviews we have identified a list of several targets that can also be modified for additional permutations of the base target.

Identification of non-target objects with features that are similar to those of targets must be performed. Non-target objects can potentially be used as "distractors" and will provide greater flexibility in manipulating task difficulty (civilians, animals, buildings, miscellaneous everyday objects, etc.). Distractor objects will be used to fill the environment within the scenario with sufficient "noise". Additionally, distractor objects will give the scenario a more realistic and operationally relevant context.

Environmental features must also be identified for scenario development, specifically target placement within the scenario. Targets that come on screen should not just appear. They should slowly come into view as they would in a real-world context.

Large objects or structures that can occlude targets and non-targets will be placed strategically so that target/non-target objects may emerge from behind them.

### 2.4.2    Create Testing Clips

Parameters surrounding the game environment, specifically for UAS operations include altitude and speed. A selection of 3–5 levels of altitude should be considered as well as 3–5 levels of speed. Testing can be accomplished with the creation of brief clips of movement through the environment. The set of clips should represent the range of environments under consideration for use in the scenarios. A sufficiently large set of clips would allow a selection of a random sample to control for environmental variations. This step would also strengthen any inferences we make regarding the psychophysical characteristics of the target and non-target stimuli.

An equal number of clips should be created for each combination of altitude and speed and each should contain sufficient clutter to prevent easy target identification. Impoverished environments would make it difficult to control task difficulty. Target placement would need to remain identical throughout each clip. When feasible, a third version of each clip can be created in which a non-target is placed at the same location. This step allows researchers to evaluate target control specifications. After a set of targets has been identified, a set of locations throughout the scenario (with occlusion and non-target influences to keep in mind) should then be selected. These locations, however, should be held constant across varying altitudes and speed clips. The number of target placement locations should be sufficiently large so that a randomly sampled selection can be treated as a random effects variable. In past instantiations of videogame-based vigilance tasks, computer software selected targets (from a pool of available targets) at a given location across an epoch of time. It is likely that will be executed here as well.

### 2.4.3    Establish Psychophysical Parameters of the Task

It is necessary to establish the psychophysical parameters of the task to avoid either floor or ceiling effects during the target detection task. To do so, a two-alternative forced choice (2AFC) procedure will be conducted to establish how variations in target type, presence of distractors, altitude, and speed of movement affect detectability of targets under alerted conditions. In this procedure, a trial consists of two versions of stimuli that are presented sequentially. On each trial, one stimulus always includes a target to be detected and the other stimulus is the identical environment but without the target present. The observer's task is to decide whether the target was presented first or second. The 2AFC procedure permits evaluation of the discriminability under alerted conditions because the participant knows that a target is presented on each trial and decides when in the sequence that target was presented. The iterative approach to stimulus development provides stronger empirical evidence for the validity of the stimulus parameters used in developing the vigilance task.

### 2.4.4    Develop and Validate the Vigilance Task

Once psychophysical parameters have been established, task and stimuli identified should be adopted to create a full vigilance task of 15–30 min. A sufficient duration will induce monotony. The changing environment should not appear novel. Without the monotony element, it may be difficult to establish this as a vigilance task.

To validate the vigilance task, an evaluation on performance decrements and trainee stress and workload need to be conducted. If the performance decrement was induced and trainee stress and workload are high, this provides a strong argument that the task is a vigilance task as it contains paradigm features seen in laboratory vigilance tasks and research. If indicators emerge that indicate performance is not declining as time on task increases there are several ways to manipulate the task. These manipulations include altering and editing stimuli and target/non-target parameters to better accommodate the performance decrement.

Lastly, gamification needs to the tested for motivational effects. Game elements can be tested by adding them in systematically or simultaneously and evaluating performance, workload, and stress associated with the task. Developing game elements will need to consider the vigilance requirement that always needs to remain present (i.e., continuous demand to monitor the environment for targets over prolonged watch periods). Other items for consideration include manipulating motivational variables to determine their effects on the outcome measures. This includes instructional manipulations and game rules and structure that facilitate autonomous motivation and an experience of competence in game-play, as well as instructions and a game environment that convey the importance of the task. If a person has a good rationale for why a task is important they tend to experience stronger autonomous motivation for it even if the task is boring. KR effects should also be tested. This could be done in tandem with gamification, or as a separate step prior to gamification. The latter approach would determine whether the vigilance task we develop shows typical training effects when using KR. The latter approach would test the effects of KR in the context of the gamified version. Testing KR effects would involve manipulating the provision of feedback during a training phase, and then testing all participants in a transfer phase consisting of the same task without feedback.

# 3 Closing Remarks

Vigilance is both a laboratory phenomenon and a serious real-world issue. After approaching vigilance questions in the laboratory for over 60 years, the meticulously contrived static tasks became irrelevant in today's fast paced, technologically advanced environment. The vigilance paradigm needed an upgrade to accommodate the study and evaluation of its effects within contextually relevant settings. Operators do not perform their tasks in isolation. They are, more often, typically observing incredible amounts of data within highly complex systems, a task that humans are not particularly good at doing. This necessitates an equally effective adaptive training solution to prepare operators for the task, provide opportunities for remediation of skill degradation, and encourage optimal performance through maintained gains.

Leveraging state-of-science contributions in the novel exploration of vigilance using videogame-based platforms, SkySpotter aims to provide engaging and effective adaptive vigilance training to UAS operators. Following a careful prescription of target element and scenario parameters, SkySpotter can be used to perform effectiveness evaluations on the vigilance paradigm itself (performance decrements, stress, and workload), gamification, and vigilance gains with use of the system compared to those who are not receiving adaptive vigilance training. This gamified vigilance platform provides a way to answer many research questions regarding vigilance in the real-world while offering solutions to current and emerging critical issues in the operational landscape today.

# References

1. Hancock, P.A.: Mind, Machine, and Morality: Toward a Philosophy of Human-Technology Symbiosis. Ashgate Publishing, Burlington (2009)
2. Tvaryanas, A.P., Thompson, B.T., Constable, S.H.: U.S. military unmanned aerial vehicle mishaps: assessment of the role of human factors using HFACS. Technical report, Brooks City-Base, TX, USAF Human Performance Directorate (2005)
3. Reinach, S., Gertler, J.: An examination of railroad yard worker safety. Technical report. U.S. Department of Transportation (2001). https://www.fra.dot.gov/Elib/Document/2938
4. Reinerman-Jones, L., Matthews, G., Mercado, J.E.: Detection tasks in nuclear power plant operation: vigilance decrement and physiological workload monitoring. Saf. Sci. **88**, 97–107 (2016)
5. Parasuraman, R., Davies, D.R.: A taxonomic analysis of vigilance performance. In: Mackie, R.R. (ed.) Vigilance: Theory, Operational Performance, and Physiological Correlates. Plenum Press, New York (1977)
6. See, J.E., Howe, S.R., Warm, J.S., Dember, W.N.: Meta-analysis of the sensitivity decrement in vigilance. Psychol. Bull. **117**(2), 230–249 (1995)
7. Warm, J.S., Parasuraman, R., Matthews, G.: Vigilance requires hard mental work and is stressful. Hum. Factors **50**(3), 433–441 (2008)
8. Mackworth, N.H.: The breakdown of vigilance during prolonged visual search. Q. J. Exp. Psychol. **1**, 6–21 (1948)
9. Helton, W.S., Dember, W.N., Wann, J.S., Matthews, G.: Optimism, pessimism, and false failure feedback: Effects on vigilance performance. Curr. Psychol. **18**, 311–325 (2000)
10. Becker, A.B., Warm, J.S., Dember, W.N.: Specific and nonspecific transfer effects in training for vigilance. In: Mouloua, M., Parasuraman, R. (eds.) Human Performance in Automated Systems: Current Trends, pp. 294–299. Erlbaum, Hillsdale (1994)
11. Szalma, J.L., Miller, L.C., Hitchcock, E.M., Warm, J.S., Dember, W.N.: Intraclass and interclass transfer of training for vigilance. In: Scerbo, M.W., Mouloua, M. (eds.) Automation Technology and Human Performance, pp. 183–187. Erlbaum, Mahwah (1999)
12. Mackworth, J.F.: Vigilance and Attention: A Signal Detection Approach. Penguin, Middlesex (1970)
13. Szalma, J.L., Schmidt, T.N., Teo, G.W., Hancock, P.A.: Vigilance on the move: video game-based measurement of sustained attention. Ergonomics **57**(9), 1315–1336 (2014)
14. Schweitzer, K.M., CuQlock-Knopp, V.G., Klinger, D.K., Martinsen, G.L., Rodgers, R.S., Murphy, J.S., Stanard, T.W., Warren, R.: Preliminary research to develop methodologies for identifying experts in the detection of Improvised Explosive Devices (IEDs): Phase I. Technical report, Aberdeen Proving Ground, MD. Accession number: ADB337683 (2008)
15. Ballard, J.C.: Computerized assessment of sustained attention: a review of factors affecting vigilance performance. J. Clin. Exp. Neuropsychol. **18**, 843–863 (1996)

16. Murphy, J.S.: Identifying experts in the detection of improvised explosive devices: IED2 Technical report, TR 1269, Arlington, VA (2010)
17. Lierberman, H.R., Wurtman, R.J., Emde, G.G., Roberts, C., Coviella, I.L.: The effects of low doses of caffeine on human performance and mood. Psychopharmacology **92**(3), 308–312 (1987)
18. Manly, T., Huetink, J., Evans, K., Woldt, K., Robertson, I.: Rehabilitation of executive function: facilitation of effective goal management on complex tasks using periodic auditory alerts. Neuropsychologica **40**, 271–281 (2002)
19. Davies, D.R., Tune, G.S.: Human Vigilance Performance. American Elsevier, Oxford (1969)
20. Szalma, J.L., Hancock, P.A., Warm, J.S., Dember, W.N., Parsons, K.S.: Training for vigilance: using predictive power to evaluate feedback effectiveness. Hum. Factors **48**(4), 682–692 (2006)
21. Salmoni, A.W., Schmidt, R.A., Walter, C.B.: Knowledge of results and motor learning: a review and critical reappraisal. Psychol. Bull. **95**, 355–386 (1984)
22. Mackworth, J.F.: The effect of true and false knowledge of results on the detectability of signals in a vigilance task. Can. J. Psychol. **18**, 106–117 (1964)
23. Antonelli, D.C., Karas, G.G.: Performance on a vigilance task under conditions of true and false knowledge of results. Percept. Mot. Skills **25**(1), 129–138 (1967)
24. Weidenfeller, E.W., Baker, R.A., Ware, J.R.: Effects of knowledge of results (true and false) on vigilance performance. Percept. Mot. Skills **14**, 211–215 (1962)
25. Montague, W.E., Webber, C.E.: Effects of knowledge of results and differential monetary reward on six uninterrupted hours of monitoring. Hum. Factors **7**(2), 173–180 (1965)
26. Sipowicz, R.R., Ware, J.R., Baker, R.A.: The effects of reward and knowledge of results on the performance of a simple vigilance task. J. Exp. Psychol. **64**(1), 58–61 (1962)
27. Warm, J.S., Hagner, G.L., Meyer, D.: The partial reinforcement effect in a vigilance task. Percept. Mot. Skills **23**(3), 987–993 (1971)
28. Warm, J.S., Kanfer, F.H., Kuwada, S., Clark, J.L.: Motivation in vigilance: effects of self-evaluation and experimenter-controlled feedback. J. Exp. Psychol. **92**(1), 123–127 (1972)
29. Warm, J.S., Riechmann, S.W., Grasha, A.F., Seibel, B.: Motivation in vigilance: a test of the goal-setting hypothesis of the effectiveness of knowledge of results. Bull. Psychon. Soc. **1** (5–A), 291–292 (1973)
30. Wong, J., Nguyen, A., Ogren, L.: Serious game and virtual world training: instrumentation and assessment. Naval Undersea Warfare Center Division, Newport, RI. Accession number: ADA582003 (2012)
31. Tobias, S., Fletcher, J.D., Dai, D.Y., Wind, A.P.: Review of research on computer games. In: Tobias, S., Fletcher, J.D. (eds.) Computer Games and Instruction, pp. 127–222. Information Age, Charlotte (2011)
32. Hays, R.T.: The effectiveness of instructional games: a literature review and discussion Technical report. 2005–004. Naval Air Warfare Center, Orlando, FL (2005)
33. Wilson, K., Bedwell, W., Lazzara, E., Salas, E., Burke, C., Estock, J., Orvas, K., Conkey, C.: Relationships between game attributes and learning outcomes. Simul. Gaming **40**(2), 217–266 (2009)
34. Spain, R.D., Priest, H.A., Murphy, J.S.: Current trends in adaptive training with military applications: an introduction. Mil. Psychol. **24**(2), 87–95 (2012)
35. Chien, T.C., Yunus, A.S., Ali, W.C.W., Bakar, R.: The effect of an intelligent tutoring system (ITS) on student achievement in algebraic expression. Int. J. Instr. **1**, 25–38 (2008)
36. Rosé, C.P., Jordan, P.W., Ringenberg, M., Siler, S., VanLehn, K., Weinstein, A.: Interactive conceptual tutoring in Atlas-Andes. In: Moore, J.D., Redfield, C., Johnson, W.L. (eds.) Artificial Intelligence in Education: Ai-ED in the Wired and Wireless Future, pp. 256–266. IOS, Washington, DC (2001)

37. Metzler-Baddeley, C., Baddeley, R.J.: Does adaptive training work? Appl. Cogn. Psychol. **23**, 254–266 (2009)
38. VanLehn, K.: The relative effectiveness of human tutoring, intelligent tutoring systems, and other tutoring systems. Educ. Psychol. **46**(4), 197–221 (2011)
39. Chi, M.T.H., Siler, S., Jeong, H., Yamauchi, T., Hausmann, R.G.: Learning from human tutoring. Cogn. Sci. **25**, 471–533 (2001)
40. Renkl, A., Atkinson, R.K., Maier, U.H., Staley, R.: From example study to problem solving: Smooth transitions help learning. J. Exp. Educ. **70**(4), 293–315 (2002)
41. Salden, R., Aleven, V., Schwonke, R., Renkl, A.: The expertise reversal effect and worked examples in tutored problem solving. Instr. Sci. **38**, 289–307 (2010)
42. Salden, R.J.C.M., Aleven, V.A., Renkl, A., Schwonke, R.: Worked examples and tutored problem solving: redundant or synergistic forms of support? Top. Cogn. Sci. **1**(1), 203–213 (2009)
43. Chi, M.T.H.: Active-Constructive-Interactive: a conceptual framework for differentiating learning activities. Top. Cogn. Sci. **1**, 73–105 (2009)
44. Graesser, A.C., Person, N., Magliano, J.: Collaborative dialog patterns in naturalistic one-on-one tutoring. Appl. Cogn. Psychol. **9**, 359–387 (1995)
45. Graesser, A.C., Person, N.K.: Question asking during tutoring. Am. Educ. Res. J. **31**(1), 104–137 (1994)
46. Montani, V., De Filippo De Grazia, M., Zorzi, M.: A new adaptive videogame for training attention and executive functions: design principles and initial validation. Frontiers in Psychology **13**(5), 409 (2014). doi:10.3389/fpsyg.2014.00409
47. Lintern, G., Gopher, D.: Adaptive training of perceptual-motor skills; issues, results, and future directions. Int. J. Man Mach. Stud. **10**, 521–551 (1978)
48. Peng, P., Miller, A.C.: Does attention training work? A selective meta-analysis to explore the effects of attention training and moderators. Learn. Individ. Differ. **45**, 77–87 (2016)
49. Durlach, P.J., Ray, J.M.: Designing adaptive instructional environments: insights form empirical evidence. Technical report no. 1297. U.S. Army Research Institute for the Behavioral and Social Sciences, Arlington, VA (2011)
50. Landsberg, C.R., Astwood Jr., R.S., Van Buskirk, W.L., Townsend, L.N., Steinhauser, N.B.: Review of adaptive training system techniques. Mil. Psychol. **24**, 96–113 (2012)
51. Finomore, V., Matthews, G., Shaw, T., Warm, J.: Predicting vigilance: a fresh look at an old problem. Ergonomics **52**, 791–808 (2009). doi:10.1080/00140130802641627
52. Matthews, G., Warm, J., Shaw, T., Finomore, V.: Predicting battlefield vigilance: a multivariate approach to assessment of attentional resources. Ergonomics **57**(6), 1–19 (2014)
53. Shaw, T., Matthews, G., Warm, J., Finomore, V., Silverman, L., Costa Jr., P.: Individual differences in vigilance: personality ability and states of stress. J. Res. Pers. **44**, 297–308 (2010)
54. Teo, G.W.L., Szalma, J.L., Schmidt, T.N., Hancock, G.M., Hancock, P.A.: Evaluating vigilance in a dynamic environment: methodological issues and proposals. Poster presented at the 56th Annual Meeting of the Human Factors and Ergonomics Society, Boston, MA, October 2012
55. Boivin, D.B., Boudreau, P.: Impacts of shift work on sleep and circadian rhythms. Pathol. Biol. (Paris) **62**(5), 292–301 (2014)
56. Smith, A.P., Kendrick, A.M., Maben, A.L.: Effects of breakfast and caffeine on performance and mood in the late morning and after lunch. Neuropsychobiology **26**(4), 198–204 (1992)
57. Bunce, D.: Age differences in vigilance as a function of health-related physical fitness and task demands. Neuropsychologia **39**(8), 787–797 (2001)
58. Green, C.S., Bavelier, D.: Action video game modifies visual selective attention. Nature **423**, 534–537 (2003)

59. Pavlas, D., Rosen, M.A., Fiore, S.M., Salas, E.: Using visual attention video games and traditional interventions to improve baggage screening. In: Proceedings of the Human Factors and Ergonomics Society, vol. 52 (2008)

60. Schmidt, TN., Teo, G.W.L., Szalma, J.L., Hancock, G.M., Hancock, P.A.: The effect of video game play on performance in a vigilance task. Poster presented at the 56th Annual Meeting of the Human Factors and Ergonomics Society, Boston, MA, October 2012

61. Tiwari, T., Singh, A.L., Singh, I.L.: Task demand and workload: Effects on vigilance performance and stress. J. Indian Acad. Appl. Psychol. 35(2), 265–275 (2009)

# Cognitive Augmentation Metrics Using Representational Information Theory

Ron Fulbright(✉)

University of South Carolina Upstate, Spartanburg, SC, USA
rfulbright@uscupstate.edu

**Abstract.** In the coming era of *cognitive augmentation*, humans will work in natural, collegial, and peer-to-peer partnerships with systems able to perform expert-level cognition. However, we lack theoretically grounded fundamental metrics describing and characterizing this kind of human cognitive augmentation. The pursuit of such metrics leads us to some of the most fundamental questions about the nature of information and cognition. We define a cognitive process as the transformation of data, information, knowledge, or wisdom. We then employ representational information theory to calculate the effect a cognitive process has on the information. We then use that metric as the basis for deriving several other metrics such as cognitive gain, work, power, density, and efficiency to analyze a cognitively augmented human. We also propose a metric called the augmentation factor to indicate the level to which a human is augmented by working with one or more cognitive systems.

**Keywords:** Information theory · Representational information · Cognitive work · Cognitive power · Cognitive augmentation · Cognitive systems · Cognitive computing

## 1 Introduction

Until now, humans have had to do all of the thinking however, we are at the beginning of a new era in human history—the cognitive augmentation era. Cognitive systems are being developed in every domain in which a human can be an expert. We are about to be inundated with a host of intelligent applications, devices, products, and services fueled by a confluence of deep learning, big data, the Internet of things, and natural language interfaces. These systems will communicate with us in spoken natural language but also know things about us from our emails, tweets, and daily activities. In much the same way we work with our family members, loved ones, and co-workers, humans and cognitive systems will work together in natural, collegial, peer-to-peer partnerships. The age of the augmented human is upon us.

In 2011, a cognitive computing system called Watson, built by IBM, defeated two of the most successful human Jeopardy champions of all time [1]. Watson communicated in natural language and deeply reasoned about its answers using several different techniques from artificial intelligence research. In 2016, GoogleMind's AlphaGo computer defeated the reigning world champion in Go using a deep neural network and advanced Monte Carlo tree search [2]. Although not the first time computers have

© Springer International Publishing AG 2017
D.D. Schmorrow and C.M. Fidopiastis (Eds.): AC 2017, Part II, LNAI 10285, pp. 36–55, 2017.
DOI: 10.1007/978-3-319-58625-0_3

beaten human champions (checkers, chess, and various card games for example), Watson and AlphaGo are different. Watson and AlphaGo learned how to play their respective games using a variety of deep learning techniques [3, 4]. Watson and AlphaGo learned and practiced to ultimately achieve expert-level performance within their respective domains.

These systems were not built just to play games. Watson and AlphaGo represent a new kind of computer system built as a platform for a new kind of application [5, 6]. This new type of system is intended to act as partners with and alongside humans. John Kelly, Senior Vice President and Director of Research at IBM describes the coming revolution in cognitive augmentation as follows [6]:

> The goal isn't to... replace human thinking with machine thinking. Rather...humans and machines will collaborate to produce better results – each bringing their own superior skills to the partnership. The machines will be more rational and analytic – and, of course, possess encyclopedic memories and tremendous computational abilities. People will provide judgment, intuition, empathy, a moral compass and human creativity.

Since 2011, IBM has been actively commercializing Watson technology to serve (and in many ways create) the emerging multi-billion dollar cognitive computing market. The Cognitive Business Solutions group consults with companies to create cogs. The Watson Health group's focus is to commercialize Watson technology for the health sector [7–10]. In her keynote address at the 2016 Consumer Electronics Show, Chairwoman, President, and CEO of IBM Ginni Rometty announced more than 500 partnerships with companies and organizations across 17 industries each building new applications and services utilizing cognitive computing technology based on Watson [11, 12]. Many of these systems currently under development are intended for use by the average person.

IBM is not alone. Most major technology companies are actively researching and developing new artificial intelligence-based products and services. Voice-activated personal assistants will be one of the first battlegrounds. Apple's Siri, Microsoft's Cortana, Google Now, Facebook's M, and Amazon Echo's Alexa each accept natural-language requests from users, reply in natural language, and perform services on behalf of the user [13–17]. But currently, these tools simply retrieve information, and perform minor clerical tasks such as creating appointment calendar items. Each of these are steadily increasing in the complexity and variety of tasks they can perform. The voice-controlled assistant represents the primary user interface connecting hundreds of millions to their technology, so the major technology companies are understandably competing for control in this area.

As cogs become able to perform higher-order cognitive processing, human-cog partnerships of the future will go far beyond what is possible today. Cogs will be able to consume vast quantities of unstructured data and information and deeply reason to arrive at novel conclusions and revelations, as well as, or better than, any human expert. Cogs will then become colleagues, co-workers, and confidants instead of tools. Because cogs will interact with us in natural language and be able to converse with us at human levels, humans will form relationships with cogs much like we do with friends, fellow workers, and family members. These systems may very well lead to the democratization of expertise [49].

In the early 1960s, Engelbart was among the first to describe human-computer partnerships and famously developed a framework modeling a human being as being part of an integrated system consisting of: the human, language (concepts, symbols, representations), artifacts (physical objects), methodologies (procedures, know-how), and training or H-LAM/T [18]. As shown in Fig. 1, Engelbart's framework envisions a human interacting with an artificial entity (or entities) working together on a cognitive task. To perform the task, the system as a whole executes a series of cognitive processes with the human performing (called *explicit-human* processes) and the artificial entities performing some (called *explicit-artif*act processes). Other processes are performed by a combination of human and machine (called *composite* processes). In Engelbart's framework, the cognitive ability of the human can be augmented by making improvements to any component (human, artifact, language, methodologies, or training). When the paper was written artifacts were seen as making it easier for the human to perform the cognitive task. Engelbart's artifacts perform a relatively small amount of cognitive work. Instead, they make the human able to perform their cognitive work more efficiently. However, in the cog era, cogs will be artifacts capable of performing cognitive work of their own at a level rivaling or surpassing humans. This represents a fundamental shift in what we mean when we say "cognitive augmentation."

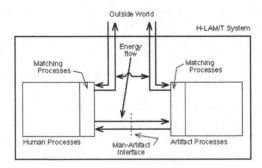

**Fig. 1.** Englebart's H-LAM/T Framework.

The entire discussion of augmented cognition becomes a matter of how cognitive processes are distributed across the human and cog infrastructure. However, we currently lack the metrics and general theory to describe cognitive processes or the distribution. Currently, we are not able to measure how much the human is augmented. To develop such metrics, we must first define the very nature of a cognitive process. At the very core of this effort are basic questions like: "What is information?" "What is cognition?" and "What does it mean to be cognitively augmented?".

## 2   Literature

This work lies at the intersection of three different fields: knowledge management, information theory, and cognitive computing.

## 2.1    Knowledge Management and Information Science

From the knowledge management and information science fields, we adopt a widely accepted view of data, information, knowledge, and wisdom (DIKW) [19]. The DIKW hierarchy represents information as processed data, knowledge as processed information, and wisdom as processed knowledge. Each level is of a higher value than the level below it because of the processing and therefore represents a higher level of understanding. However, lacking are metrics allowing us to measure data, information, knowledge, and wisdom and measure the effect of processing as we climb the levels. The metrics we present here can be used in this manner.

## 2.2    Physics and Thermodynamics

There is a long history of entropic measures of information. In physics, particularly statistical mechanics and thermodynamics, such metrics are associated with the concept of order and disorder. In the mid-1800s, Clausius coined the term *entropy* to describe the amount of heat energy dissipated across the system boundary ultimately leading to the Second Law of Thermodynamics. In the late 1800s, Boltzmann related thermodynamic entropy of a system, S, to the number of equally likely arrangements (states) $W$, where $k$ is Boltzman's constant [20].

$$S = k \ln W. \tag{1}$$

Boltzmann's entropy is a measure of the amount of disorder in a system. In 1929, Szilard was one of the first to examine the connection between thermodynamic entropy and information by analyzing the decrease in entropy in a thought experiment called Maxwell's Demon [21]. Szilard reasoned the reduction of entropy is compensated by a gain of information:

$$S = k \sum_i p_i \ln p_i, \tag{2}$$

where $p_i$ is the probability of the $i^{th}$ event, outcome, or state in the system. In 1944, Schrodinger wondered how biological systems (highly ordered systems) can become so structured, in apparent violation of the Second Law of Thermodynamics and realized the organism increases its order by decreasing the order of the environment [22]:

$$S = k \ln D \tag{3a}$$

$$-S = k \ln(1/D) \tag{3b}$$

Schrodinger calls $-S$, the negative entropy (or negentropy), a measure of order in a system. Brillouin refined the idea and described living systems as importing and storing negentropy [23]. The ideas of Schrodinger, Szilard, and Brillouin involve a flow of information from one entity to another and use entropy to measure the flow.

## 2.3  Information Theory

In the field of *information theory*, Hartley was one of the first to define the information content, H, of a message of N symbols chosen from an alphabet of S symbols as [24]

$$H = \log S^N = N \log S \tag{4}$$

Since $S^N$ messages are possible, one can view the number of messages as the number of possible arrangements or states and therefore see the connection to thermodynamic entropy equations. Hartley's equation represents a measure of disorder in probability distribution across the possible messages, Hartley simply defines this measure of disorder to be equivalent to the information content of a message. In 1948, Shannon developed the basis for what has become known as information theory [25–27]. Shannon's equation for entropy, H, is

$$H = -K \sum_{i=1}^{v} p(i) \log_2 p(i), \tag{5}$$

where p(i) is the probability of the $i^{th}$ symbol in a set of $v$ symbols and K, is an arbitrary constant enabling the equation to yield any desired units. Shannon, as did Hartley, equates order/disorder and information content. Shannon's equation gives the average information content per symbol. The information content, I, of a message consisting of $m$ symbols is

$$I = mH = -mK \sum_{i=1}^{m} p(i) \log_2 p(i) \tag{6}$$

Shannon's information theory is the most widely used measure of information but yields anomalous results for our purposes. In the 1960's, Chaitin and others developed the concept of algorithmic information content as a measure of information [28–31]. The algorithmic information content, I, of a string of symbols, w, is defined as the size of the minimal program, s, running on the universal Turing machine that generates the string

$$I(w) = |s|, \tag{7}$$

where the vertical bars indicate the length, or size, of the program s. This definition of information concerns the compressibility of a string of symbols. A string with regular patterns can be "compressed" to a much shorter representation whereas the shortest description of a string of random symbols is a verbatim listing, the string itself. This description also equates order/disorder to information content, although in a different manner. In 1990, Stonier suggested an exponential relationship between entropy, S, and information, I [32–34]:

$$I = I_0\, e^{-S/K}$$

$$\text{where } S = -k \sum_i p_i \ln p_i \tag{8}$$

where $k$ is Boltzmann's constant, and $I_0$ is the amount of information in the system at zero entropy. The measure of entropy, $S$, is the thermodynamic form of Shannon's equation which is mathematically equivalent to Szilard's and Boltzmann's earlier general entropic equations. Stonier's equation is interesting because it is similar mathematically to the one we will use, as described below, but differs theoretically.

We employ a relatively new form of information theory, called representational information theory (RIT) [35, 36]. Unlike entropy-based traditional information theory metrics, such as those discussed above, the fundamental unit in RIT is the *concept*. The value of a piece of information in RIT is relative to the concept to which the information refers and how well the information represents the concept. This brings meaning and understanding to information calculus for the first time. We will discuss RIT in detail in a later section.

## 2.4    Cognition, Cognitive Systems, Artificial Intelligence

There is no widely accepted general theory of cognition although the topic has been studied for decades by researchers in several different disciplines. At the outset of this research, it seemed reasonable to look to the cognitive science field for metrics of information value, content, and measures of cognition. However, all findings in this area are unsatisfactory because any metrics developed apply only to a specific implementation, the cognitive architecture, for which it was developed. A number of cognitive architectures and models have been developed. Computational cognitive architectures such as Soar [37–39], ACT and ACT-R [40], CLARION [41, 42], and EPIC [43] are ultimately based on the idea of reducing human cognition to symbol manipulation—Newell and Simon's famous physical symbol system hypothesis [44]. In these architectures, reasoning is achieved by the matching, selection, and execution of if-then statements called production rules representing procedural, declarative, and episodic knowledge. However, we seek metrics applicable to all forms of inference and cognitive processing fully recognizing not all cognitive systems are production systems.

Connectionist models and architectures are based on mental or behavioral phenomena being the emergent result of interconnected networks of simple units such as artificial neural networks (ANNs) and include: Holographic Associative Memory [45], Hierarchical Temporal Memory [46], Society of Mind [47], and more recently, Google DeepMind [48]. However, we find these unsatisfactory for our purposes because any metrics from this field is too heavily invested in the neural network architecture and do not apply generically. We seek a more general description of cognition and one independent of implementation details.

Vigo's RIT, described in detail in the next section, is such an effort to define the general principles of human conceptual behavior. At the core is the concept and the effort associated with learning the concept given one or more representations of the concept. We feel this is a superior model of cognition for our purposes because we can use it to define a cognitive process, define the value of information, and, when combined with the DIKW view of information, construct cognitive performance metrics applicable to any biological or artificial system performing cognitive processing.

## 3 Representational Information Theory

There are two problems with using entropic information measures for the cognitive augmentation metrics we seek here. The first problem is entropic measures do not take into account *meaning*. Intuitively, we known information has different value based on the context of the production, consumption, and processing of the information. Therefore, a measure of information must be relative to context in some manner. In this section, we describe how representational information theory measures information relative to a concept. The second problem is entropic measures ascribe the highest amount of information content to totally random ensembles. This contradicts intuition. Imagine a completely random collection of letters compared to a novel. Regardless of who reads it, the random letters will never convey a large amount of information. However, even though not random, the novel conveys a tremendous amount of information to a reader. It is true, the amount of information actually conveyed varies depending on the reader's own ability, knowledge, and comprehension. However, this just further illustrates the need for a *relative* measure of information.

We employ a relatively new form of information theory, called representational information theory (RIT) [35, 36]. Unlike entropic-based information theory treatments the fundamental component in RIT is the concept. The value of a piece of information in RIT is always relative to the concept to which the information refers. Incorporating the concept into the measure of information is different than any other version of information theory. This brings meaning and understanding to information calculus for the first time.

In RIT, a *concept* is a mental construct in the mind be it biological or artificial. One should think of concepts as existing in abstract concept space. The only way to experience a concept in the real world is via some kind of *representation*. A representation can be a description, model, or a collection of example objects belonging to or describing the concept. Thus, one should think of a representation as an instance of a concept. Some representations convey the concept better than other representations. The more ambiguous the representation is, the more difficult (or complex) it is to discern the concept it refers to. RIT measures the strength of a representation by a metric called *structural complexity* where the complexity refers to how difficult it is to discern the concept from the representation. Representations with a low level of structural complexity convey the concept easier. Representations with a high level of structural complexity convey the concept with more difficulty. The goal, of course, are representations with minimal structural complexity.

In RIT, structural complexity is proportional to the size of the representation and inversely proportional to a quality of the representation called *invariance*. Invariance relates how robust a representation is in the face of change. For example, consider the concept *sports car* and a representation of this concept consisting of instances of red, white, blue, and yellow sports cars. If we change the color of one of the cars, say change the blue one to an orange sports car, one could still easily discern the concept. However, if we change one of the cars to a truck, ambiguity and uncertainty is introduced. More interpretations of the representation are possible thus discerning the concept *sports car* is more complex. This representation is invariant with respect to *color* but not to *type* of car with respect to the *sports car* concept. Stated alternatively, the representation is *variant* with respect to *type* but not variant with respect to *color*. In general, stable, robust, highly invariant representations convey concepts easier (with less complexity in understanding). In RIT, the structural complexity of a representation is given by

$$\Psi(\widehat{F}) = \frac{p}{f(\Phi(F))} \tag{9}$$

where $F$ is the representation of a concept, $p$ is the size of the representation, $\phi$ is the invariance of the representation, and $f$ is a monotonic function. Of course, this begs the question of the nature of $f$. Researchers in the field of human cognitive behavior have shown empirically discerning the concept becomes exponentially more difficult as the ambiguity of a representation increases [35, 36]. This allows us to assign the exponential function to $f$ above yielding

$$\psi(\widehat{F}) = pe^{-\Phi(F)} = pe^{-\left[\sum_{i=1}^{D}\left[\left\|\frac{\partial F(x_1,\cdots,x_D)}{\partial x_i}\right\|\right]^2\right]^{1/2}} \tag{10}$$

where the partial differential represents the sensitivity of each item in the representation to change. The similarity of Eq. 10 to Stonier's equation, Eq. 8, is striking and reassuring since Stonier deduced the exponential relationship in an entirely different way than RIT. To illustrate the calculation of structural complexity consider the following representation, $S$:

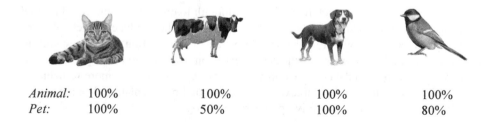

| | | | |
|---|---|---|---|
| *Animal:* 100% | 100% | 100% | 100% |
| *Pet:* 100% | 50% | 100% | 80% |

This representation can represent a number of different concepts but here we consider just two concepts: *animal* and *pet*. We have assigned a "fitness" value between 0% and 100% indicating the robustness of each of the items in representing the concepts *animal* and *pet*. (These fitness values are just for illustration only and are not the result of any rigorous study.) The fitness values capture the fact that while all are unambiguously animals, birds and cows are not usually viewed as pets but birds are considered pets more so than cows. Substituting these values into Eq. 10 gives us

$$\psi(s) = |s|e^{-\sqrt{v_1^2 + v_2^2 + \dots + v_n^2}} \tag{11}$$

where $p = |S| = 4$ and $v_i$ is the fitness value of the $i^{th}$ item in the presentation. We can now calculate the structural complexity of this representation relative to each concept:

$$\psi(s \mid animal) = 4e^{-\sqrt{1^2 + 1^2 + 1^2 + 1^2}} \quad \psi(s \mid pet) = 4e^{-\sqrt{1^2 + .5^2 + 1^2 + .8^2}}$$
$$\psi(s \mid animal) = 4e^{-2} \quad\quad\quad\quad \psi(s \mid pet) = 4e^{-1.7}$$
$$\psi(s \mid animal) = 0.5413 \quad\quad\quad \psi(s \mid pet) = 0.7307$$

These calculations indicate it is easier to learn the concept animal than it is to learn the concept pet given this particular representation. As another illustration of structural complexity, consider the case in which we change one of the animals in the above $S$:

Animal:    100%              100%              100%              0%

Now, the representation contains three excellent examples of the concept *animal* but one example not representing the concept at all. The structural complexity of this representation with respect to the concept *animal* is:

$$\psi(s \mid animal) = 4e^{-\sqrt{1^2 + 1^2 + 1^2 + 0^2}}$$
$$\psi(s \mid animal) = 4e^{-1.732}$$
$$\psi(s \mid animal) = 0.7077$$

indicating, as one might expect, that it is more difficult to discern the concept of *animal* from this new representation because of the presence of the airplane. Structural complexity gives us a new way to calculate the value of information and a new way to calculate information content with dependence on the concept in question. For example, with respect to the concept *animal*, the first representation is more valuable by virtue of its lower structural complexity than the second representation. We next show how this is used to define cognitive processes and cognition.

## 4    Definition of a Cognitive Process

We adopt the view of data, information, knowledge, and wisdom known as the DIKW [19]. The DIKW hierarchy represents information as processed data, knowledge as processed information, and wisdom as processed knowledge. Each level is of a higher value than the lower level because of the processing. Data is considered to be of the lowest value and the closest to the physical world (and therefore the least abstract of the levels). Data is generated when physical phenomena are sensed. For example, the measure of the surge of electrical current from an optical sensor on a piece of rotating machinery is data. If multiple surges are sensed and counted over a measured period of time, then revolutions per minute (RPM) can be determined. RPM is information not able to be sensed directly from the environment. It must be synthesized as a result of some amount of processing in which two pieces of data, electrical current surges and time, are compared. This is an illustration of how data is transformed into information by the effort of the processing involved. Likewise, information can be processed and transformed into knowledge. In our example, if we combine the information RPM with other information, say humidity and temperature, dependencies are revealed explaining the behavior of the RPM. Ultimately, knowledge is transformed into wisdom.

We maintain transformation of data, information, knowledge, and wisdom is the essential aspect of a cognitive action we call a *cognitive process*. Instead of repeating the four words over and over, we refer generically to any data, information, knowledge, and wisdom as *information stock*. We can then visualize a cognitive process as the transformation of information stock as shown in Fig. 2 where $S_{in}$ is the information stock in its original form and $S_{out}$ is the information stock after the transformation.

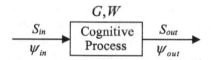

**Fig. 2.** A cognitive process as a transformation of information stock.

The structural complexity of the information stock prior to and after execution of the cognitive process, $\psi_{in}$ and $\psi_{out}$ respectively is calculated using Eq. 11. The difference in structural complexity represents a certain amount of *cognitive gain* denoted by $G$ and explained in more detail in the next section. Cognitive gain is achieved by the expenditure of a certain amount of *cognitive work* denoted by $W$ and explained in more detail in the next section. This affords us a precise definition of a cognitive process:

**Definition 1.** A *cognitive process* is defined as the transformation of information stock from an input form to an output form achieving a certain amount of cognitive gain requiring the expenditure of a quantity of cognitive work.

## 5   Cognitive Gain

If we use Eq. 11 from representational information theory (RIT) to calculate the structural complexity of the information stock before and after the cognitive process is executed we can then calculate the amount of change effected by the cognitive process's transformation, $\psi_{out} - \psi_{in}$. RIT represents the change in structural complexity as a percentage using

$$G = \frac{\psi_{out} - \psi_{in}}{\psi_{in}} \tag{12}$$

and calls this *representational information*. We call this the *cognitive gain* of a cognitive process. Note that a cognitive process can either increase or decrease the structural complexity of the information stock it transforms (or leave it the same), so $G$ can be negative, positive, or zero. Recalling structural complexity measures the ambiguity of a representation relative to a concept, a negative cognitive gain represents a transformation resulting in a more robust representation of a concept while a positive cognitive gain represents a transformation resulting in a less robust representation. Stated another way, if a cognitive process achieves a reduction in structural complexity it moves the information stock closer to the concept at hand. If a cognitive process achieves an increase in structural complexity, it has moved the information stock further away from the concept at hand. Using RIT, we are now able to express and calculate cognitive processing in terms relative to a specific concept.

## 6  Cognitive Work

Cognitive gain is certainly a useful measure of a cognitive process but is not sufficient. It is possible for a cognitive process to produce, after some amount of transformation, an output with exactly the same structural complexity as the input resulting in zero cognitive gain. While it is true zero cognitive gain was achieved in this case it is also true that *something* happened and this escapes measurement by the cognitive gain formula alone. For this reason, we developed the concept of cognitive work.

Cognitive work is a measure of all transformation of information stock regardless of the cognitive gain achieved. If we look at only the input and output, we miss everything that might have went on *inside* and *during* the cognitive process. Any information stock transformation achieved during the execution of the cognitive process but not represented in the output is not visible to the outside world. We call such internal transformations *lost* as is represented in Fig. 3.

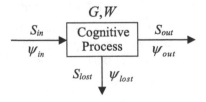

**Fig. 3.** A cognitive process with full accounting of information stock transformations.

Cognitive work, then, is an accounting of all information stock transformations achieved by a cognitive process as given by

$$W = |\Psi(S_{out}) - \Psi(S_{in})| + \Psi_{lost} \tag{13}$$

We use the absolute value form of the cognitive gain because we are concerned only with positive values since a negative amount of cognitive work is meaningless. Cognitive work is a measure of the total effort expended in the execution of a cognitive process. It is important to note it requires both cognitive gain and cognitive work to characterize a cognitive process. A cognitive process could perform an enormous amount of transformation and yet achieve very little, if any, real cognitive gain. In such a case, cognitive gain would be near zero but cognitive work would be large. A cognitive process could also achieve an enormous amount of cognitive gain yet do so with very little transformation. In this case, cognitive work would be small but cognitive gain large. Cognitive gain provides a magnitude and direction of the result while cognitive work provides the amount of effort.

With these metrics, we can compare and analyze all cognitive processes regardless of how the entity performs the cognitive process. The most efficient cognitive processes are those which achieve a large cognitive gain while expending little cognitive work. It is important to not forget the connection of cognitive gain and cognitive work to the *concept*. Since structural complexity is relative to the concept described by the information stock, cognitive gain and cognitive work is also relative to the concept at hand. A cognitive process achieves different amounts of cognitive gain and cognitive work depending on the concept being considered. As an example, consider a cognitive process that sums a list of numbers. Relative to the concept *sorted* numbers, this process achieves nothing but expends an amount of cognitive work. However, relative to the concept of *average value*, this process moves decidedly closer toward that goal so achieves a substantial cognitive gain by expending an amount of cognitive work. The dependency on the relationship of information to concept is unique in RIT and a powerful notion to our cognitive work theory.

## 7 Cognitive Gain and Cognitive Work of Bubble Sort

To illustrate the calculation of cognitive work and cognitive gain, we consider the bubble sort algorithm. An algorithm is a sequence of steps to perform a task and therefore is simply a step-by-step description of a cognitive process. By Definition 1 then, bubble sort achieves a cognitive gain and expends an amount of cognitive work.

Bubble sort is a well-known algorithm to sort any collection of items for which a "less than" relationship can be determined between the items. Here, unless otherwise stated, we assume "sorted" refers to items sorted in ascending order and "inversely sorted" refers to items in descending order. We can visualize bubble sort as a cognitive process accepting as input an unsorted collection of items and outputting the collection of items in a sorted order as shown in Fig. 4.

For this sample calculation, the items to be sorted are the letters C, B, D, A, E. The "fit" of each letter is based on its position relative to the position it should be in when sorted. If any letter is in the correct sorted position, we assign a fit of 100% (1). If a letter is not in the correct position, we assign a fit based on the number of positions away from the correct position at 20% (.2) per position. For example, if the letter B is in

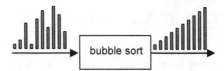

**Fig. 4.** Bubble sort as a cognitive process.

the 1st or 3rd position, its fitness is 80% (.8) because it is one position, or 20%, away from the correct position. Therefore, the input sequence C, B, D, A, E has fitness values of 0.6, 1.0, 0.8, 0.4, 1.0 respectively allowing the structural complexity of the unsorted letters to be calculated as follows using Eq. 11:

$$\psi(C,B,D,A,E) = 5e^{-\sqrt{.6^2 + 1^2 + .8^2 + .4^2 + 1^2}}$$
$$\psi(C,B,D,A,E) = 5e^{-\sqrt{.36 + 1 + .64 + .16 + 1}}$$
$$\psi(C,B,D,A,E) = 5e^{-\sqrt{3.16}}$$
$$\psi(C,B,D,A,E) = 5e^{-1.7776}$$
$$\psi(C,B,D,A,E) = 5(0.1690)$$
$$\psi(C,B,D,A,E) = 0.8452$$

The bubble sort cognitive process produces the sorted letters A, B, C, D, and E as output. Since, when sorted, each letter is in the correct position, we can assign a fitness of 100% ($p = 1$) to each allowing us to calculate the structural complexity of the five sorted letters:

$$\psi(A,B,C,D,E) = 5e^{-\sqrt{1^2 + 1^2 + 1^2 + 1^2 + 1^2}}$$
$$\psi(A,B,C,D,E) = 5e^{-2.2361}$$
$$\psi(A,B,C,D,E) = 5(0.1069)$$
$$\psi(A,B,C,D,E) = 0.5344$$

The cognitive gain achieved by the bubble sort algorithm in this case is:

$$G = \frac{\psi_{out} - \psi_{in}}{\psi_{in}}$$
$$G = \frac{0.5344 - 0.8452}{0.8452}$$
$$G = -0.3677$$
$$G = -36.77\%$$

Recall the concept to which the above is calculated relative is the *sorted* concept. The unsorted input does not represent the *sorted* concept as well as the sorted output so as expected, the structural complexity of the input (unsorted letters) is higher than the output (sorted letters). The bubble sort cognitive process reduces the structural complexity in this instance by 36.77%.

Bubble sort swaps letters when it finds an unsorted adjacent pair of letters. Each time the algorithm swaps letters it creates an intermediate sequence of letters each resulting in a change in structural complexity of the information stock being transformed. To calculate the cognitive work of the above instance of bubble sort, we must consider all of the intermediate configurations the algorithm creates before it arrives at the final output. The following shows the five versions of the letters (including the three intermediate versions) and the structural complexity of each.

|         |       | $\psi$ | $\Delta\psi$ |
|---------|-------|--------|--------------|
| Input:  | CBDAE | 0.8452 |              |
| #1:     | BCDAE | 0.8645 | 0.0193       |
| #2:     | BCADE | 0.7420 | 0.1225       |
| #3:     | BACDE | 0.6317 | 0.1103       |
| Output: | ABCDE | 0.5344 | 0.0973       |

Allowing the calculation of cognitive work as follows:

$$W = |\psi_{out} - \psi_{in}| + \psi_{lost}$$
$$W = |0.5344 - 0.8452| + (0.0193 + 0.1225 + 0.1103 + 0.0973)$$
$$W = 0.6602$$

## 8 Cognitive Augmentation Metrics

The ability to calculate cognitive gain and cognitive work, as demonstrated above, gives us a new and powerful capability. In this section, we use these metrics to derive several other metrics to describe a human augmented by one or more artificial systems (cogs).

### 8.1 Cognitive Work and Gain of the Ensemble

Figure 1 shows Englebart's original vision of human/computer symbiosis in which a human is augmented by one or more artificial systems. In Fig. 5, we update this vision to the cognitive systems era in which one or more humans work in partnership with one or more cogs to execute a cognitive task.

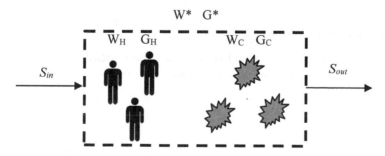

**Fig. 5.** Humans and cogs participating in a cognitively augmented ensemble.

The ensemble, inside the dashed border, receives information stock as input and transforms it to produce transformed information stock as output. In the execution of the cognitive task, the humans achieve a certain cognitive gain and expend a certain amount of cognitive work, $G_H$ and $W_H$ collectively. Likewise, cogs achieve a cognitive gain and expend a certain amount of cognitive work, $G_C$ and $W_C$ collectively, where:

$$W_H = \sum_i W_H^i \quad G_H = \sum_j G_H^j$$
$$W_C = \sum_i W_C^i \quad G_C = \sum_j G_C^j \tag{14}$$

The total amount of cognitive gain, and cognitive work by the ensemble is

$$W^* = W_H + W_C \quad G^* = G_H + G_C \tag{15}$$

We have good reason to believe $W^*$ is actually *greater than* the sum of the human and cog cognitive work but this will be the subject of a future paper.

## 8.2   Augmentation Factor

Given that we can calculate the individual cognitive contributions of the humans and the cogs, it is natural to compare their efforts. In fact, doing so yields the *augmentation factor, $A^+$*. Note we can use either the cognitive gain or the cognitive work, or both, to calculate the augmentation factor.

$$A_W^+ = \frac{W_C}{W_H} \quad A_G^+ = \frac{G_C}{G_H} \tag{16}$$

Note humans working alone without the aid of artificial systems ($W_C = G_C = 0$) are not augmented at all and have an $A^+ = 0$. As long as the humans are performing more cognitive work or cognitive gain than the cogs, $A^+ < 1$. This is the world in which we have been living so far. However, when cogs start performing more cognitive work or cognitive gain than humans, $A^+ > 1$ with no upward bound. We believe the cognitive systems era will see $A^+$ continually increase. In fact, we propose $A^+$ as a global metric for cognitive augmentation to be tracked over the coming years.

## 8.3   Cognitive Efficiency

The goal of any cognitive effort is to have the most effect (measured as cognitive gain) but expend the least amount of effort (measured by cognitive work). Therefore we define *cognitive efficiency* as

$$\xi = \frac{G}{W} \tag{17}$$

Note, the above equation is written in a generic form. One can calculate cognitive efficiency of just the human component $(G_H/W_H)$, just the cog component $(G_C/W_C)$, or for the entire ensemble $(G*/W*)$.

## 8.4   Cognitive Power

A common way to analyze performance is in the time domain. If we relate how much time it takes to achieve an amount of cognitive gain and expend an amount of cognitive work we have the metric we call *cognitive power*.

$$P_G = \frac{G}{t} \quad P_W = \frac{W}{t} \tag{18}$$

Again, note the above equation is written in a generic form. One can calculate cognitive power of just the human component $(G_H/t)$ or $(W_H/t)$, just the cog component $(G_C/t)$ or $(W_C/t)$, or for the entire ensemble $(G*/t)$ or $(W*/t)$.

In terms of cognitive power, artificial systems have a distinct advantage over humans. Computers are able to perform trillions of operations per second, so the time it takes for them to achieve the same thing a human does is many orders of magnitude greater.

## 8.5   Cognitive Density

Another useful way to analyze performance is the energy domain. Relating how much energy it takes to achieve an amount of cognitive gain or expend an amount of cognitive work yields a metric we call *cognitive density*.

$$D_G = \frac{G}{E} \quad D_W = \frac{W}{E} \tag{19}$$

The cognitive density of just the human component is $(G_H/E)$ or $(W_H/E)$, just the cog component is $(G_C/E)$ or $(W_C/E)$, or for the entire ensemble $(G*/E)$ or $(W*/E)$. Currently, electronic circuits in a computer require milliwatts of electrical power on par with neurons in the human brain, but large computers, where cognitive systems are implemented, consume many times that to operate. As cognitive systems improve and begin to be implementable on portable, handheld electronic devices, the cognitive density with respect to energy will change dramatically.

## 8.6   Discussion: Watson vs. Humans

An interesting illustration of the cognitive augmentation metrics introduced here is to consider what occurred in 2011 when IBM Watson played human champions in *Jeopardy!* Both Watson and the human players received the same clue and both were able to correctly state the answer (in a form of a question of course). In terms of a cognitive process, the information stock input and output was exactly the same for Watson and the humans. Since their outputs were the same, each achieved exactly the same cognitive gain, $G_{Human} = G_{Watson}$.

However, to answer each clue, Watson performed billions of operations and analyzed potentially millions of pieces of information as it reasoned its way to the answer. Most observers would agree Watson performed a much greater amount of cognitive work than the humans simply because it performed millions of transformations. If we use cognitive gain as the basis, Watson and human exhibited the same cognitive power. If we use cognitive work as the basis, Watson exhibited a much greater cognitive power (simply by virtue of transforming so much information stock in so little amount of time as compared to humans), $P_{Watson} \gg P_{Human}$.

On the other hand, if we agree Watson performed more cognitive work, then the humans achieved a much greater cognitive efficiency because they expended far less cognitive work than Watson yet achieved the same cognitive gain. The 2011 version of Watson consumed on the order of 20 kW of electrical power while the human brain consumes about 20 W of power. In terms of cognitive gain, humans achieved a cognitive density 1000 times greater than Watson. However, in terms of cognitive work, even though Watson consumed 1000 times more energy, most would agree it performed millions of times more cognitive work so therefore achieved a greater cognitive density.

In terms of cognitive power, the rules of *Jeopardy!* assured both human and computer had to answer in about the same amount of time. Since each achieved the same cognitive gain, one would reason they exhibited the same cognitive power. However, in terms of cognitive work, Watson achieved a significantly greater cognitive power.

## 9  Conclusion and Future Work

We have employed a new kind of information theory, called representational information theory, to form the basis of a set of metrics we can use to characterize and analyze the coming revolution in the cognitive systems era. In the near future, we will all be interacting with cogs capable of performing human-level cognition. All of us will become augmented humans where our cognitive ability is enhanced by working in partnership with cogs. The metrics presented here, cognitive work, cognitive gain, cognitive power, cognitive efficiency, cognitive density, and augmentation factor can be used to study this new era of human/computer interaction.

We have offered a new, generic definition of cognition in defining a cognitive process as the transformation of information stock resulting in a cognitive gain at the expenditure of an amount of cognitive work. We think these metrics could be adopted and used in the field of cognitive systems architectures as an implementation-independent way to compare architectures.

Similarly, we feel neuroscientists, psychologists, behaviorists, and computer scientists studying human cognitive performance can adopt our notion of cognition, cognitive work, and cognitive gain, and other metrics, as an implementation-independent way to compare and contrasts research findings. For example, we urge researchers in computational complexity to use cognitive gain and cognitive work to analyze complexity classes such "NP-complete" and "NP-hard." Currently these can be analyzed statistically, but the notions of cognitive gain and cognitive work give the possibility of measuring specific instances of algorithms.

Finally, we certainly hope the cognitive systems and cognitive augmentation community will adopt, further explore, and extend the cognitive augmentation metrics presented here. We urge researchers to include in their analyses of cognitive systems discussion and calculations using the metrics introduced here.

# References

1. Jackson, J.: IBM Watson Vanquishes Human Jeopardy Foes. PC World (2011). Internet page http://www.pcworld.com/article/219893/ibm_watson_vanquishes_human_jeopardy_foes.html. Accessed May 2015
2. Science Staff: From AI to protein folding: our breakthrough runners-up. Science, 22 December 2016. Internet page located at: http://www.sciencemag.org/news/2016/12/ai-protein-folding-our-breakthrough-runners. Accessed Jan 2017
3. Ferrucci, D.A.: Introduction to "this is watson". IBM J. Res. Dev. 56(3/4), 1 (2012)
4. Ferrucci, D., Brown, E., Chu-Carroll, J., Fan, J., Gondek, D., Kalyanpur, A., Lally, A., Murdock, J.W., Nyberg, E., Prager, J., Schlaefer, N., Welty, C.: Building watson: an overview of the DeepQA project. AI Mag. 31(3), 59–79 (2010)
5. Wladawsky-Berger, I.: The era of augmented cognition. Wall Street J.: CIO Rep. (2013). Internet page located at: http://blogs.wsj.com/cio/2013/06/28/the-era-of-augmented-cognition/. Accessed May 2015
6. Isaacson, W.: The Innovators: How a Group of Hackers, Geniuses, and Geeks Created the Digital Revolution. Simon & Schuster, New York (2014)
7. IBM: IBM Forms New Watson Group to Meet Growing Demand for Cognitive Innovations (2014). IBM Internet page located at: https://www03.ibm.com/press/us/en/pressrelease/42867.wss. Accessed May 2015
8. IBM: IBM Launches Industry's First Consulting Practice Dedicated to Cognitive Business (2015a). IBM Internet page: https://www-03.ibm.com/press/us/en/pressrelease/47785.wss. Accessed Nov 2015
9. IBM: Watson Health (2015b). IBM Internet page located at: http://www.ibm.com/smarterplanet/us/en/ibmwatson/health/. Accessed Nov 2015
10. Sweeney, C.: Tech leader brings Wellville initiative to Lake County. North Bay Bus. J. (2015). Internet page located at: http://www.northbaybusinessjournal.com/northbay/lakecounty/4293852-181/tech-leader-brings-wellville-initiative#page=0#kXTgUCrErV81oRDk.97. Accessed Nov 2015
11. Gugliocciello, G., Doda, G.: IBM Watson Ecosystem Opens for Business in India (2016). IBM News Release https://www-03.ibm.com/press/us/en/pressrelease/48949.wss. Accessed Mar 2016
12. Rometty, G.: CES 2016 Keynote Address (2016). YouTube Video https://www.youtube.com/watch?v=VEq-W-4iLYU
13. Apple: Siri (2015). Apple Internet page located at: http://www.apple.com/ios/siri/. Accessed Nov 2015
14. Microsoft: What is Cortana? (2015). Microsoft Internet page: http://windows.microsoft.com/en-us/windows-10/getstarted-what-is-cortana. Accessed Nov 2015

15. Google: Google Now: What is It? (2015). Google Internet page located at: https://www.google.com/landing/now/#whatisit. Accessed Nov 2015
16. Hempel, J.: Facebook Launches M, Its Bold Answer to Siri and Cortana. Wired (2015). Internet page: http://www.wired.com/2015/08/facebook-launches-m-new-kind-virtual-assistant/. Accessed Nov 2015
17. Colon, A., Greenwald, M.: Amazon echo. PC Mag. (2015). Internet page located at: http://www.pcmag.com/article2/0,2817,2476678,00.asp. Accessed Nov 2015
18. Engelbart, D.C.: Augmenting human intellect: a conceptual framework. Summary Report AFOSR-3233, Stanford Research Institute, Menlo Park, CA, October 1962
19. Ackoff, R.: From data to wisdom. J. Appl. Syst. Anal. **16**, 3–9 (1989)
20. Jaynes, E.T.: Gibbs vs Boltzmann entropies. Am. J. Phys. **33**, 391–398 (1965)
21. Szilard, L.: On the decrease of entropy in a thermodynamic system by the intervention of intelligent beings. Behav. Sci. **9**, 301–310 (1964)
22. Schrodinger, E.: What is Life?. Cambridge University Press, Cambridge (1944)
23. Brillouin, L.: Physical entropy and information. J. Appl. Phys. **22**, 338–343 (1951)
24. Hartley, R.V.L.: Transmission of information. Bell Syst. Tech. J. **7**, 535–563 (1928)
25. Weaver, W., Shannon, C.E.: The Mathematical Theory of Communication. University of Illinois Press, Urbana (1949)
26. Pierce, J.R.: An Introduction to Information Theory, revised 2 edn. Dover Publications, New York (1980)
27. Goldman, S.: Information Theory. Dover Publications, New York (1953)
28. Chaitin, G.J.: On the length of programs for computing finite binary sequences. J. Assoc. Comput. Mach. **13**, 547–569 (1966)
29. Chaitin, G.J.: Algorithmic information theory. IBM J. Res. Dev. **21**, 350–359, 496 (1977)
30. Kolmogorov, A.N.: Three approaches to the quantitative definition of information. Probl. Inf. Transm. **1**, 1–17 (1965)
31. Solomonoff, R.J.: A formal theory of inductive inference. Inf. Control **7**(1–22), 224–254 (1964)
32. Stonier, T.: Information and the Internal Structure of Universe. Springer, London (1990)
33. Stonier, T.: Beyond Information: The Natural History of Intelligence. Springer, London (1992)
34. Stonier, T.: Information and Meaning: An Evolutionary Perspective. Springer, Berlin (1997)
35. Vigo, R.: Complexity over uncertainty in generalized representational information theory (GRIT). Information **4**, 1–30 (2013)
36. Vigo, R.: Mathematical Principles of Human Conceptual Behavior. Psychology Press, New York (2015). ISBN 978-0-415-71436-5
37. Laird, J.E.: The Soar Cognitive Architecture. MIT Press, Cambridge (2012)
38. Laird, R., Newell, A.: Soar: an architecture for general intelligence. Artif. Intell. **33**, 1–64 (1987)
39. Newell, A.: Unified Theories of Cognition. Harvard University Press, Cambridge (1990)
40. Anderson, J.R.: The Architecture of Cognition. Psychology Press, Philadelphia (2013)
41. Sun, R.: Duality of the Mind: A Bottom-up Approach Toward Cognition. Lawrence Erlbaum Associates, Mahwah (2002)
42. Sun, R., Merrill, E., Peterson, T.: From implicit skills to explicit knowledge: a bottom-up model of skill learning. Cogn. Sci. **25**, 203–244 (2001)
43. Kieras, D.E., Meyer, D.E.: An overview of the EPIC architecture for cognition and performance with application to human-computer interaction. Hum.-Comput. Interact. **12**, 391–438 (1997). Lawrence Erlbaum Associates, Inc.
44. Newell, A., Simon, H.: Computer science as empirical inquiry: symbols and search. Commun. ACM **19**, 3 (1976)

45. Sutherland, J.: Holographic models of memory, learning and expression. Int. J. Neural Syst. **1**, 3 (1990)

46. Hawkins, J., George, D.: Hierarchical Temporal Memory - Concepts, Theory, and Terminology (2006). PDF: http://numenta.com/learn/hierarchical-temporal-memory-white-paper.html. Accessed Feb 2016

47. Minsky, M.: The Society of Mind. Simon & Schuster, New York (1986)

48. Silver, D., et al.: Mastering the game of Go with deep neural networks and tree search. Nature **529**, 484–489 (2016)

49. Fulbright, R.: How personal cognitive augmentation will lead to the democratization of expertise. In: 4th Annual Conference on Advances in Cognitive Systems, June 2016, Evanston, IL (2016). http://www.cogsys.org/posters/2016. Accessed Jan 2017

# Neurophysiological Impact of Software Design Processes on Software Developers

Randall K. Minas[1(✉)], Rick Kazman[1], and Ewan Tempero[2]

[1] Shidler College of Business, University of Hawaii at Manoa,
2404 Maile Way, Honolulu, HI 96822, USA
{rminas,kazman}@hawaii.edu
[2] Department of Computer Science, The University of Auckland,
303/38 Princes St, Auckland 1010, New Zealand
e.tempero@auckland.ac.nz

**Abstract.** Software development often leads to failed implementations resulting from several factors related to individual reactions to software design. Some design metrics give software developers guidelines and heuristics for use in software design. Furthermore, many metrics have been created to measure outcomes in terms of "code quality." However, these guidelines and metrics have been shown only to have a weak relationship and are poorly implemented. This study takes a new approach using tools from cognitive neuroscience to examine the cognitive load and arousal level placed on software engineers while working with different software designs. Specifically, we use electroencephalography (EEG) and skin conductance (SCR) to examine cognitive and emotional reactions to software structure. We propose to examine whether modular design affects levels of cognitive load and arousal. Our findings open the door for future research that combines software engineering and cognitive neuroscience. The potential implications of this study extend beyond optimal ways to structure software to leading the software engineering field to study individual cognition and arousal as a central component in successful software development. This opens a wide array of potential studies in the software engineering field.

**Keywords:** Cognitive load and performance · Emotion · Electroencephalography · Augmented cognition · Arousal · Software engineering

## 1 Introduction

Developing software systems is difficult and often leads to failed implementations, resulting from non-completion, reduced confidence, or budgetary overruns [1, 2]. Central to software development is design and development of the code that drives the system. Software engineering is focused on the development of software using a systematic, structured, repeatable approach. These systematic approaches to software development leave an engineer with many decisions on how to organize their software. Researchers in the software engineering field have explored the consequences of different design decisions, such as the choice of identifiers [3], code branching operations [4], and modular structure [5]. The problem, however, is that the evidence of the

© Springer International Publishing AG 2017
D.D. Schmorrow and C.M. Fidopiastis (Eds.): AC 2017, Part II, LNAI 10285, pp. 56–64, 2017.
DOI: 10.1007/978-3-319-58625-0_4

effectiveness of many of these guidelines and heuristics is, at best, weak. Furthermore, there is plenty of evidence that software developers routinely ignore this advice, even when they are aware of it and know the claimed benefits [6–8]. Much research has focused on the outputs of the development process, or aspects of a software engineer's decision making process. But little research has focused on the affective and cognitive responses software engineers have to the structure—the design—of their software. Taken together, the rate of software development failures and our relative immaturity at dealing with their root causes call for a new approach to understanding the benefits and problems associated with the design of software.

Many disciplines, from marketing to information systems, have begun to apply the tools of cognitive neuroscience to open the "black-box" of the brain, examining areas such as cognitive load, arousal, decision-making, and others [9, 10]. Cognitive neuroscience uses methods such as electroencephalography (EEG), function magnetic resonance imaging (fMRI), and psychophysiological responses (e.g., skin conductance and facial electromyography) to understand how individuals process information, stress levels, cognitive load, and emotion. Some cognitive neuroscience studies have also examined software engineering problems, such as [11] where the author used fMRI to understand program comprehension. However, this study did not elucidate how different types of designs may affect a programmer's cognitive load and arousal. The use of tools from cognitive neuroscience can generate new insights into how software engineers develop software from shedding light on optimal software structure to uncovering the best practices, from a cognitive standpoint, that will lead to better system development and fewer software implementation failures.

The purpose of this study is two-fold. First, it seeks to determine the differences in cognitive load and arousal related to different software designs, identifying from a cognitive and arousal standpoint, which designs lead to lower cognitive load and arousal for the software engineer. Second, and perhaps more importantly, this study seeks to establish a framework from which future software engineering studies can employ the use of cognitive neuroscience methods to gain further insight into the effects individual cognition and emotion have on software engineering efficiency and effectiveness. Our findings should have implications for future software engineering studies and could open a door to a new research agenda within software engineering.

## 2 Theoretical Background

### 2.1 Software Engineering and Development Metrics

Much research exists in software engineering that examines different metrics to understand code and design quality. This has been an active research area in software engineering for over four decades (see, for example [12–14]). There are a plethora of metrics that have been proposed to measure the quality of code in Object Oriented (OO) programming, such as CK Metrics [15], LK Metrics [16], and MOOD Metrics [17]. All of these metrics take a different approach to measuring code quality. For example, the MOOD Metrics contains six metrics that examine data encapsulation (e.g., the ability of a program to hide implementation through separate compilation of modules), information hiding (e.g., visibility of methods and/or attributes to other code), inheritance (e.g., when an object or class is based on another object), and coupling (e.g., the degree of interdependence between modules) [17, 18].

The aforementioned metrics examine the output artifact—the code that has been written—and do not examine the arousal or cognitive load it takes for a software engineer to understand, debug, or update this code. Since there are many ways to structure coding from full object-orientation, to naïve object-orientation, to a relatively unstructured "God Class" [19], the metrics are only providing a relative comparison of the output artifacts. As they give no insight into the cognitive load or arousal level placed on the software engineer, the usefulness of these metrics is limited.

## 2.2   Cognitive Load and Arousal and Software Engineering

Cognitive load theory is a major theory in the cognitive science literature that provides a framework for investigating cognitive processes, simultaneously considering the structure of information and cognitive architecture that allows learners to process information efficiently [20]. Cognitive load refers to the amount of cognitive resources that are needed to process a given task. Low cognitive load tasks require fewer cognitive resources, while high cognitive load tasks require higher cognitive resources [20]. One of the key cognitive resources that underlies cognition is working memory [21]. It encapsulates both what many consider "short-term memory" and attention. Therefore, working memory is pivotal for both information processing and specific tasks (i.e., software engineering), responsible for encoding information from the environment and retrieving information from long-term memory in order to make sense of it [21–23]. A useful computer analogy for understanding working memory is that it represents the brain's RAM, storing of information currently undergoing processing but limited in its capacity [24].

Working memory is most heavily associated with the frontal areas of cortex, namely Dorsolateral Prefrontal Cortex (DLPFC) [25]. However, it is important to note that neural networks distribute working memory to multiple areas of cortex. Changes in activity in the DLPFC indicate changes in working memory load and attention [26]. In EEG, attenuation of the alpha rhythm over DLPFC indicates increases in working memory load [27]. Cognitive load in working memory (in the frontal and temporal regions of the brain) is reduced when irrelevant information is presented, as less information needs to be maintained for subsequent recall [28]. Skin conductance, a measure of autonomic nervous system arousal, is also closely tied to cognitive load [29]. As cognitive load increases, autonomic system arousal increases [30].

In software engineering, there have been some studies on cognitive load. One study applied design techniques from other disciplines that have found to be low in cognitive load and applied them to software engineering, finding that current visual implementations for software engineers need improvement to lower cognitive load on software engineers [31]. Another study has applied cognitive models to the novice software analyst, finding that novices often have trouble in scoping the problem and poor formation of the conceptual model of the problem domain [32]. However, despite these studies and others, no studies have instituted the tools of cognitive neuroscience to directly measure cognitive load and arousal during software updating tasks. Our study examines the link between cognitive load, arousal and structured and unstructured software engineering tasks. In cases where the code is highly structured, we believe the individual's cognitive load and arousal will be lower. Moreover, in cases where the code is unstructured, we believe there will be a greater cognitive load and arousal. Therefore, we hypothesize:

> H1: An individual's cognitive load and arousal will be higher when there is less structure in the code (e.g., God Class) than in a fully object-oriented design.

## 3  Method

Our goal in this study is to understand how individual software engineers respond cognitively and emotionally to different software structures. Therefore, the unit of analysis will be the individual. The study participant will be given a software update task to perform in Java using the Eclipse IDE environment.

### 3.1  Participants

Participants will be undergraduate students from a state university who will receive $75 compensation for their time. The participants were drawn from upper-level computer science courses and had experience with both Java and the Eclipse environment. We aim to collect data on 50 subjects in a repeated measures design.

### 3.2  Task

We will use an implementation of the game Kalah in the Eclipse environment. Participants will be asked to make a changes to the code to implement different functionality for the game. One task will ask the participant to change the number of initial seeds in the houses from two to three. This is a trivial change. The second task will ask the subject to institute an AI player for the game. This is a more involved change in the code. We will examine cortical changes and skin conductance during each task. The participants will also have practice task to gain familiarity with the game in the Eclipse environment. We use a repeated measures design in this study, so each participant will be exposed to both tasks.

### 3.3  Treatments

There will be two treatments. One treatment will be the God Class for a program of the game Kalah—a single class that implements all of the game's functions. The second treatment will be a fully object-oriented modular design of the game Kalah. This will be a repeated measures design with participants being exposed to both treatments.

**Independent Variable**

The independent variable in this study is the task the participant is making changes in the code. There are two levels of difficulty in the task, trivial and non-trivial. We will examine these along with the two treatment levels: God Class and full object-orientation.

**Dependent Variables**

Our dependent variables are cortical alpha wave activity, autonomic arousal, and emotional valence. These are operationalized using neurological and psychophysio-logical measures. EEG measures will be collected using a 14-channel headset (Emotiv Systems, San Francisco, CA, USA) with electrodes dispersed over the scalp along the 10–20 system [33] (see Fig. 1). The electrodes will make connection with the scalp surface via felt pads saturated in saline solution. The reference electrodes will be located at P3 and P4 over the inferior, posterior parietal lobule [33]. All other channels will be measured in relation to the electrical activity present at these locations, sampled at 128 Hz. Impedances will be verified and data collected using Emotiv TestBench Software Version 1.5.0.3, which will export it into comma-delimited format for subsequent analysis.

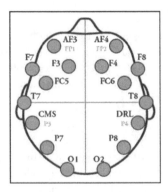

**Fig. 1.** Position of the electrodes on the EEG headset with labels along the 10–20 system.

Autonomic arousal will be operationalized as skin conductance level measured with disposable electrodes filled with electrically neutral gel and adhered planar surface of the foot. A Biopac MP150 system will be used to collect the skin conductance data at 1000 Hz. Emotional valence will be operationalized as the relative activation of the corrugator supercilli muscle group (facial EMG). Corrugator EMG will be measured using a pair of mini (4 mm) reusable AG/AGCL electrodes filled with electrolyte gel placed above the subject's left eye after dead skin cells has been removed by a skin prep pad containing rubbing alcohol and pumice. The bipolar corrugator measures will be collected using the Biopac MP150 system with high pass filters set at 8 Hz. The full wave signal will be rectified and then contour integrated online at a time constant of 100 ms, and then sampled at 1000 Hz by the Biopac MP150 system.

## 3.4   Procedures

Participants will complete the experimental procedure individually after providing informed consent approved by the university's Institutional Review Board. The experiment will take place in an individual lab room. The entire research session will take about 120 min.

Participants will be seated in a high back chair to minimize movement. They will be provided a standard keyboard and a mouse. The experimenter will then explain the procedure for attaching the physiological electrodes and fitting the EEG cap, answering any questions posed by the participant. After obtaining adequate impedance readings for the EDA, EMG and EEG measures, the protocol will continue with another brief handedness questionnaire.

Next the participant will watch two videos, one familiarizing them with the rules of the game Kalah and one familiarizing them with the Eclipse environment. They will then be instructed to attempt the practice task, which is changing the capture rule to the empty house capture rule. Upon successful completion of the practice tasks they will receive the next four tasks in a fully counterbalanced format (2 tasks in 2 treatments).

After the tasks are completed, the experimenter will remove the EEG cap and physiological sensors. The participant will then complete the post-experiment questionnaire. Finally, the participant will be debriefed, compensated for their time, and released.

## 3.5   Data Cleaning and Preparation

EEG data will be cleaned and analyzed using EEGLab [34]. One limitation of EEG is that cortical bioelectrical activity is extremely small in magnitude when compared to muscle movements across the head. Therefore, participant movement introduces artifacts of high-frequency and magnitude into the EEG data. These will be removed using two methods: EEGlab probability calculations and visual inspection. The EEGLab artifact rejection algorithm uses deviations in microvolts greater than three standard deviations from the mean to reject specific trials. However, additional artifacts are also apparent to the trained eye, so visual inspection of trials is essential in artifact removal [34].

In addition to trial-by-trial removal of artifacts, occasionally specific EEG channels must be rejected in an individual subject's data due to unacceptable impedance levels. This can be done in the current study using an automatic impedance detection feature of EEGLab.

Electrodermal and facial EMG data will be aggregated to mean values per second using Biopac's Acqknowledge software. Change scores will be calculated by subtracting the physiological level at the onset of each target statement during the online discussion from each subsequent second across a 6-second window.

## 3.6   ICA Analysis of EEG Data

The first step of the EEG analysis will be an Independent Components Analysis (ICA) at the individual level. A common problem in neurophysiology research results from the collection of large amounts of data which, based upon the Central Limit Theorem, become normally distributed. However, the brain is comprised of discrete patches of cortex that are very active at some points in time and relatively non-active at others (i.e. – activity is not normally distributed across the scalp) [35]. ICA overcomes this problem by taking this Gaussian data and rotating it until it becomes non-Gaussian, thereby isolating independent components of activation. The ICAs are distributed patterns of activation across the 14-electrodes in the EEG system.

Initially, an EEGLab ICA performs a Principal Components Analysis (PCA). At each electrode site the program assesses which of the other electrode sites account for the most variance in the signal. Taking these weighted values it then relaxes the orthogonality constraint of PCA to isolate individual components of activation [35]. Each ICA component then represents a pattern of activation over the entire brain, not solely the activity present at a specific electrode. The number of independent components (ICs) depends on the number of electrodes in the dataset, as the algorithm is working in an $N$-dimensional space (where N is the number of electrodes). Most participants in the current study are expected to generate 14 distinct ICs, since our recording device has 14 electrodes.

Finally, using the $K$-means component of EEGlab the independent components at the individual level will be grouped into clusters containing similar components using procedures recommended by [36]. This procedure clusters similar ICs based upon their latency, frequency, amplitude, and scalp distribution [36]. Relevant clusters will be identified and a time-frequency decomposition will be performed to examine changes in event-related desyncronization of the alpha rhythm.

## 4  Potential Implications

This study seeks to better understand the effects of software design strategies on cognitive load and arousal. The findings will have two strong implications for future research. First, the study will elucidate which design structures create the greatest level of cognitive load and arousal on software engineers, which has significant practical implications for software development. Second, and perhaps more importantly, this study will employ tools from cognitive neuroscience to examine how software engineers react to software design. This introduces what we term Neuro Software Engineering or NeuroSE into the software engineering field. Further research can examine other types of code and design structures and strategies in a similar way as this study to determine optimal design structures and strategies, from a cognitive and emotional standpoint.

Furthermore, the software engineering field can apply these tools to other research and practice areas such as language design and software engineering education. By understanding the cognitive load that various language artifacts and software structures impose on (experienced and novice) developers, we can better design these artifacts and structures, so that the experience of software development and the way that we teach it is better attuned to human cognitive capabilities and limitations.

# References

1. Chow, T., Cao, D.-B.: A survey study of critical success factors in agile software projects. J. Syst. Softw. **81**(6), 961–971 (2008)
2. DeMarco, T., Lister, T.: Waltzing with Bears: Managing Risk on Software Projects. Addison-Wesley, Boston (2013)
3. Lawrie, D., Morrell, C., Feild, H., Binkley, D.: What's in a Name? a study of identifiers. In: 14th IEEE International Conference on Program Comprehension (ICPC 2006), pp. 3–12 (2006)
4. Dijkstra, E.W.: Cooperating sequential processes. In: Hansen, P.B. (ed.) The Origin of Concurrent Programming: From Semaphores to Remote Procedure Calls, pp. 65–138. Springer, New York (2002)
5. Parnas, D.L.: On the criteria to be used in decomposing systems into modules. Commun. ACM **15**, 1053–1058 (1972)
6. Tempero, E.: An empirical study of unused design decisions in open source java software. In: 2008 15th Asia-Pacific Software Engineering Conference, pp. 33–40 (2008)
7. Gorschek, T., Tempero, E., Angelis, L.: A large-scale empirical study of practitioners' use of object-oriented concepts. In: 2010 ACM/IEEE 32nd International Conference on Software Engineering, pp. 115–124 (2010)
8. Kazman, R., Cai, Y., Mo, R., Feng, Q., Xiao, L., Haziyev, S., Fedak, V., Shapochka, A.: A case study in locating the architectural roots of technical debt. Presented at the Proceedings of the 37th International Conference on Software Engineering, Vol. 2, Florence (2015)
9. Dimoka, A.: What does the brain tell us about trust and distrust? evidence from a functional neuroimaging study. MIS Q. **34**, 373–396 (2010)
10. Minas, R.K., Potter, R.F., Dennis, A.R., Bartelt, V., Bae, S.: Putting on the thinking cap: using neurois to understand information processing biases in virtual teams. J. Manag. Inf. Syst. **30**, 49–82 (2014)
11. Siegmund, J.: Measuring Program Comprehension with Fmri
12. McCabe, T.J.: A complexity measure. IEEE Trans. Softw. Eng. **2**, 308–320 (1976)
13. Halstead, M.H.: Elements of Software Science **7**. Elsevier, New York (1977)
14. Mo, R., Cai, Y., Kazman, R., Xiao, L.: Hotspot patterns: the formal definition and automatic detection of architecture smells. In: 2015 12th Working IEEE/IFIP Conference on Software Architecture, pp. 51–60 (2015)
15. Chidamber, S.R., Kemerer, C.F.: A metrics suite for object oriented design. IEEE Trans. Softw. Eng. **20**, 476–493 (1994)
16. Lorenz, M., Kidd, J.: Object-Oriented Software Metrics: A Practical Guide. Prentice-Hall Inc, Upper Saddle River (1994)
17. e Abreu, F.B.: The mood metrics set. In: Proceedings of ECOOP, p. 267 (1995)
18. Harrison, R., Counsell, S.J., Nithi, R.V.: An evaluation of the mood set of object-oriented software metrics. IEEE Trans. Softw. Eng. **24**, 491–496 (1998)
19. Lang, J.E., Bogovich, B.R., Barry, S.C., Durkin, B.G., Katchmar, M.R., Kelly, J.H., McCollum, J.M., Potts, M.: Object-oriented programming and design patterns. ACM SIGCSE Bull. **33**, 68–70 (2001)
20. Paas, F., Renkl, A., Sweller, J.: Cognitive load theory and instructional design: recent developments. Educ. Psychol. **38**, 1–4 (2003)
21. Baddeley, A.: Working memory. Science **255**, 556–559 (1992)
22. Conway, A.R.A., Engle, R.W.: Working memory and retrieval: a resource-dependent inhibition model. J. Exp. Psychol. Gen. **123**, 354–373 (1994)

23. Welsh, M.C., Satterlee-Cartmell, T., Stine, M.: Towers of hanoi and london: contribution of working memory and inhibition to performance. Brain Cogn. **41**, 231–242 (1999)
24. D'Esposito, M.: From cognitive to neural models of working memory. Philos. Trans. Royal Soc. B Biol. Sci. **362**, 761–772 (2007)
25. D'Esposito, M., Detre, J.A., Alsop, D.C., Shin, R.K., Atlas, S., Grossman, M.: The neural basis of the central executive system of working memory. Nature **378**, 279–281 (1995)
26. Wager, T.D., Jonides, J., Reading, S.: Neuroimaging studies of shifting attention: a meta-analysis. NeuroImage **22**, 1679–1693 (2004)
27. Gevins, A., Smith, M.E., McEvoy, L., Yu, D.: High-resolution EEG mapping of cortical activation related to working memory: effects of task difficulty, type of processing, and practice. Cereb. Cortex **7**, 374–385 (1997)
28. Lavie, N.: Distracted and confused? selective attention under load. Trends Cogn. Sci. **9**, 75–82 (2005)
29. Shi, Y., Ruiz, N., Taib, R., Choi, E., Chen, F.: Galvanic skin response (Gsr) as an index of cognitive load. Presented at the CHI 2007 Extended Abstracts on Human Factors in Computing Systems. San Jose (2007)
30. Mehler, B., Reimer, B., Coughlin, J., Dusek, J.: Impact of incremental increases in cognitive workload on physiological arousal and performance in young adult drivers. Transp. Res. Rec. J. Transp. Res. Board **2138**, 6–12 (2009)
31. Moody, D.: The "Physics" of notations: toward a scientific basis for constructing visual notations in software engineering. IEEE Trans. Softw. Eng. **35**, 756–779 (2009)
32. Sutcliffe, A.G., Maiden, N.A.M.: Analysing the novice analyst: cognitive models in software engineering. Int. J. Man-Mach. Stud. **36**, 719–740 (1992)
33. Herwig, U., Satrapi, P., Schönfeldt-Lecuona, C.: Using the international 10–20 EEG system for positioning of transcranial magnetic stimulation. Brain Topogr. **16**, 95–99 (2003)
34. Delorme, A., Makeig, S.: EEGLAB: an open source toolbox for analysis of single-trial EEG dynamics including independent component analysis. J. Neurosci. Methods **134**, 9–21 (2004)
35. Onton, J., Makeig, S.: Information-based modeling of event-related brain dynamics. In: Christa, N., Wolfgang, K. (Eds.) Progress in Brain Research, vol. 159, pp. 99–120. Elsevier, Amsterdam (2006)
36. Delorme, A., Makeig, S.: EEGLAB Wikitutorial, 12 May. http://sccn.ucsd.edu/wiki/PDF: EEGLAB_Wiki_Tutorial

# Text Simplification and Pupillometry:
# An Exploratory Study

Mina Shojaeizadeh[1], Soussan Djamasbi[1(✉)], Ping Chen[2],
and John Rochford[3]

[1] User Experience & Decision Making Research Laboratory,
Worcester Polytechnic Institute, Worcester, MA, USA
{minashojaei,djamasbi}@wpi.edu
[2] University of Massachusetts, Boston, MA, USA
ping.chen@umb.edu
[3] University of Massachusetts Medical School, Worcester, MA, USA
john.rochford@umassmed.edu

**Abstract.** Cognitive load is a major factor affecting user performance. Hence, a better understanding of cognitive load can help design better information systems. To achieve this goal, in this study we looked at the relationship between cognitive load and pupillary responses for a task that required people to either read a text passage from an actual website or read the simplified version of the same text passage. The simplified text passage was constructed in a way to assure reduced cognitive load, that is, to facilitate communication of textual information in a way that it can be read and understood easily and quickly. In our previous study, we showed that by applying a set of plain language standards (PLS) to online passages we can simplify the passages in a way that they induce less cognitive demand and hence can improve performance. In this study, we extended our research by investigating time series analysis of eye-movement (pupil dilation) as a proxy for measuring cognitive load during reading these passages. To this end, we conducted an exploratory analysis in order to understand how text simplification, which was used to reduce cognitive load during reading, affected pupil dilation over time. Our results show that text simplification had a significant impact on pupil dilation and that it affected pupil dilation differently at different reading intervals. Additionally, our results show that examining pupil dilation during fixations and saccades separately can provide new insights for understating cognitive load.

**Keywords:** Eye tracking · Cognitive load · Information processing · Pupillometry · Time series analysis

## 1 Introduction

In this study we focus on the relationship between the pupillary responses and cognitive load. Pupil dilation can be measured continuously during processing of a task, therefore; it could be used as a robust measure for cognitive load [1, 2].

In our previous study [3] we showed that by applying a set of plain language standards (PLS) to online passages adopted from internet we can simplify the passages [4]

© Springer International Publishing AG 2017
D.D. Schmorrow and C.M. Fidopiastis (Eds.): AC 2017, Part II, LNAI 10285, pp. 65–77, 2017.
DOI: 10.1007/978-3-319-58625-0_5

so that there is less cognitive demand on the readers and hence the user's performance in answering questions related to passages improved significantly. Additionally, we showed that readers who read the simplified version of the passage had shorter average fixations and exhibited a more efficient visual search behavior as compared to those who read the original version of the passage. In this study, we extended our previous work by investigating time series analysis of pupil dilation as a proxy for measuring cognitive effort. To this end, we conducted an exploratory analysis in order to understand how text simplification affected pupil dilation over time and whether or not this effect was consistent over different time intervals during reading. In a recent study, pupillary data during fixation were separated from pupillary data during saccade [5]. It was shown that there was a significant difference between PD during these two types of eye-movements. Grounded in this pervious results, we separated PD data during fixation (PD-fixation) from PD data during saccade (PD-saccade) and investigated the effect of text simplification on these two variables separately over time. Time series analysis was conducted on the same eye tracking data set reported in our previous study that showed text simplification was effective in reducing cognitive load (i.e., it improved performance significantly) [3]. In the following sections, we provide a brief review of related Pupillometry literature, explain the experimental set up used to collect the eye movement data, and discuss the time series analysis that was conducted to examine whether and how pupil dilation during reading was affected by cognitive load manipulated through text simplification.

## 2 Theoretical Background

Pupillary response is an involuntary reflex and the pupil size can range in diameter from 1.5 mm to more than 8 mm [6]. For more than twenty years psychologists have argued that changes in pupil dilation accompany cognitive processing. Many studies have validated this argument using a variety of tasks, such as sentence comprehension [7], mental arithmetic [8], as well as letter matching [9]. Zehui Zhan et al. [10] used pupil dilation to assess the reading ability of online learners.

A number of studies have shown that users' pupils dilate when the difficulty of the task increases. For example Siyuan Chen et al. [11] manipulated the level of task difficulty in recalling number of player positions (defender and attacker) in a basketball game which was played in a computer based training application and showed that in some cases pupil size was larger in the more difficult task. Klinger et al. [12] measured pupil dilation during a mental multiplication and found a task difficulty effect on dilation magnitude. They showed that easy manipulation problems caused the smallest pupil dilations and hard problems caused the largest. Other studies also suggest that pupil dilation is a reliable proxy of cognitive load [13–15].

A recent study argues that because fixations and saccades reflect different types of processing, it is useful to examine pupil dilation during these events separately [5]. Fixations are relatively stable gazes that allow us to focus on objects that we like to inspect. Hence, fixations have been identified as reliable indicators of attention. Saccades are rapid movements of the eye when moving from one fixation to another. During saccades we are not able to process visual information [16, 17].

# 3   Methodology

This section provides a brief review of the laboratory experiment that was conducted to collect eye movement data used in this study. It also explains how the pupil data was prepared for time series analysis.

## 3.1   Eye-Tracking Experiment

A comprehensive set of plain language standards [3] were used to convert an actual online text passage about sports (18th grade reading level) to a simpler version (10th grade reading level). Each participant was randomly assigned to one of the two versions of the text passage, which was displayed on a computer screen. Participants were recruited from a pool of college students. Out of the 54 collected datasets, 26 were from participants assigned to read the original version of the text and the rest were from those who were assigned to read the simplified version of the same passage.

We used a commercially available eye tracking device, Tobii x300, to collect eye movement data. This remote eye tracking device can capture eye movements unobtrusively at the rate of 300 samples per second. The eye tracker was calibrated for each participant before starting the task. This process requires participants to observe a moving dot on the eye-tracking screen. Tobii software version 3.2.3, and I-VT filter with 30 °/sec saccadic velocity threshold was used to process raw gaze data into fixations and saccades.

## 3.2   Time Series Analysis of Pupil Dilation

Eye-movement data were individually saved in .csv format for further processing. Because the task was not time limited, the duration of reading was different among participants, which resulted in different number of data points for each participant. To facilitate the comparison of time series analysis, studies often equalize the number of data points by designing the task in a way to have pre-specified time windows [18–20]. While this approach is useful and relevant for many experiments, we were interested in examining reading behavior in a setting that allowed users take as much time they needed to read and understand the text. To compensate for the unequal number of data points in such a setting, we used cubic spline interpolation method [21] to construct equal size arrays of PD data for all participants. Interpolation is the estimation of intermediate values between precise data points [22]. This process allowed us to have an equal number of pupil data points for each of the participants in each of the two experimental groups (original and simplified conditions). To look at the changes in pupil dilation over time, average PD values for all participants were calculated for each data point.

As mentioned earlier, the results of a previous research [5] shows that pupil dilation during fixation is different from pupil dilation during saccade. Thus, in this study we examined both overall pupil dilation as well as pupil dilation during fixations and saccades. We also looked at changes in PD over three distinct reading periods, beginning, middle, and end. To do so interpolated data points were divided into three equal intervals.

## 4   Results

The comparison between PD when reading original and simplified passages was indicated in Fig. 1. PD-saccade and PD-fixation were not yet separated in this plot. Figure 1 displays the trend of overall PD over time. As shown in Fig. 1 the overtime PD trend is similar between reading the original and simplified version of the text except for the beginning and the end part of the graph. We used a t-test to see whether the overall averages for these two trends were different. The results of the two-sample t-test for the means of the overall PD during reading the original or simplified passages showed that there were no significant differences between the two trends (t-stat = 0.93, p = 0.35). In other words, no significant differences were detected in pupil dilation during reading original vs. simplified versions of the same text.

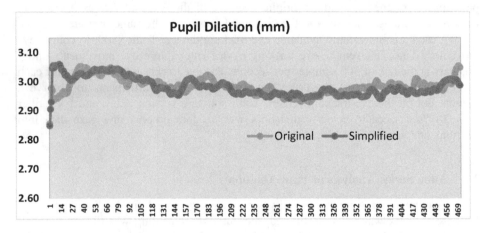

**Fig. 1.** Time series trend of pupil dilation, red: simplified, blue: original passage (Color figure online)

Next, we refined the above analysis by investigating differences in the means of PD during three different time intervals (beginning, middle and end). A two-way factorial ANOVA was conducted to compare the effects of two independent variables (1) text simplification, and (2) time interval. Text simplification included 2 levels (1. Original and 2. Simplified) and time interval included 3 levels (1. Beginning, 2. Middle and 3. End). The results, shown in Table 2, indicated that text simplification did not have a main effect on pupil dilation (F (1,938) = 0.88, p = 0.35). The results, however, show that time interval did have a main effect on PD (F (2,938) = 17.44, p = 0.00). The interaction effect was almost significant (F (2,944) = 2.44, p = 0.09). By comparing the pairwise interactions between time intervals and text simplification, as shown in Table 3 and Fig. 2, we can see that there is a significant difference in PD between simplified and original versions in the last time interval. There are no significant differences between simplified and original versions in the beginning and the middle reading intervals (p-beginning = 0.32, p-middle = 0.63).

**Table 1.** Descriptive statistics and t-test for PD during reading original and simplified passages

|  | Mean | SD | t-Stat | df | p-value |
|---|---|---|---|---|---|
| Original | 2.982 | 0.0298 | 0.926 | 905 | 0.354 |
| Simplified | 2.978 | 0.036 |  |  |  |

**Table 2.** ANOVA results comparing the means of PD during different intervals and among original and simplified passages

|  | F | P-value |
|---|---|---|
| Orig-Simp | 0.88 | 0.35 |
| Intervals | **17.44** | **0.00** |
| (Orig_Simp)*Intervals | 2.44 | 0.09 |

**Table 3.** Pairwise comparison between different time intervals for overall PD

| Time intervals | Mean ± SD (PD-original) | Mean ± SD (PD-simplified) | P-value |
|---|---|---|---|
| Beginning | 2.99 ± 09 | 3.00 ± 0.11 | 0.32 |
| Middle | 2.97 ± 02 | 2.97 ± 0.01 | 0.63 |
| End | 2.98 + 01 | 2.97 + 0.01 | **0.03** |

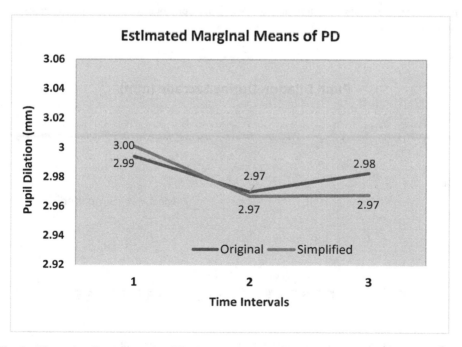

**Fig. 2.** The main effect of text simplification and time intervals and their interaction effect on the dependent variable PD

Next, we ran the same analysis but this time we examine PD during fixation and saccades separately. Figures 3, and 4 show the time series trend of PD-Fixation and PD-Saccade when reading original versus simplified passages. These graphs show more nuanced differences between PD trends in the original simplified conditions.

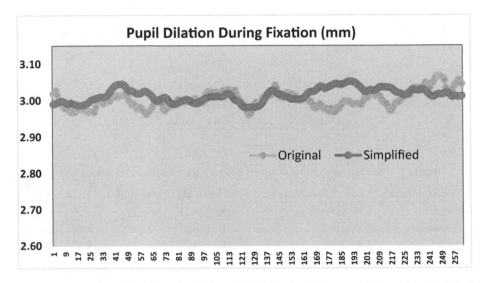

**Fig. 3.** Time series plot of pupil dilation during fixation (blue = original, red = simplified) (Color figure online)

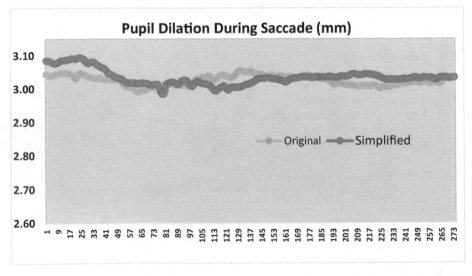

**Fig. 4.** Time series plot of pupil dilation during saccade (blue = original, red = simplified) (Color figure online)

A two-way ANOVA was performed to investigate the effects of (1) text simplification and (2) fixation/saccade separation on PD. The results of ANOVA in Table 4 show that PD is significantly affected by text simplification regardless whether it is measured during fixations or saccades (F (1, 1068) = 68.71, p = 0.00) and that PD values are significantly different during saccades and fixations regardless of text condition (original vs. simplified) (F (1, 1068) = 331.64, p = 0.00). There is no significant interaction effect between text simplification and fixation/saccade separation as indicated in Table 4 (F (1, 1072) = 1.63, p = 0.20). The graphical representation of this analysis is displayed in Fig. 5, which shows that no matter what type of passage the participant was reading (original or simplified) the average PD during fixation (blue line) was smaller than average PD during saccade (red line), and this difference remains almost the same either when reading the original passage or the simplified passage. Both PD-Fixations and PD-Saccades had larger average values in the simplified text condition. These results show that separating PD-Fixation and PD-Saccade provides additional information that is useful when performing time-series analysis of pupil dilation (Table 1).

**Table 4.** ANOVA results comparing the means of PD between fixation and saccade during original and simplified passages

|  | F | P-value |
|---|---|---|
| Original-Simplified | 68.71 | 0.00 |
| Fixation_Saccade | 331.64 | 0.00 |
| (Original_Simp)*(Fixation_Saccade) | 1.63 | 0.20 |

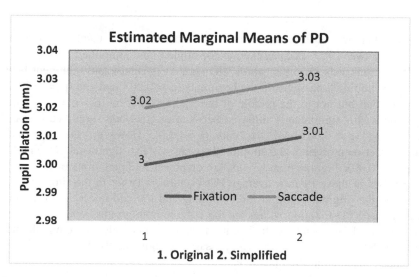

**Fig. 5.** The main effect of text simplification and fixation/saccade separation and their interaction effect on the dependent variable PD (Color figure online)

Having separated PD-Fixation from PD-Saccade, next we investigated this data using the three reading time intervals. The two-way ANOVA test was used for PD-Fixation and PD-Saccade to compare the overall effects of two independent variables (1) text simplification, and (2) time interval separation.

Table 5 displays the overall results of the ANOVA tests. The results show that PD values are significantly different both during fixations and saccades when people read original vs. simplified text passages ($F(1,518) = 54.23$, $p = 0.00$ for PD-fixation and $F(1, 542) = 35.885$, $p = 0.00$ for PD-saccade). The results show that PD values during fixations are also significantly different over the three time intervals ($F(1,518) = 65.17$, $p = 0.00$ for PD-fixation). Additionally, the differences in PD-fixations between the original and simplified conditions are significantly different in the three time intervals ($F (2,524) = 10.13$ and $p = 0.00$). The same is true for PD values during saccades ($F(1,542) = 17.05$, $p = 0.00$). The results show significant interaction effect between text simplification conditions and time intervals ($F (2,548) = 75.59$, $p = 0.00$).

**Table 5.** ANOVA results comparing the means of PD-Fixation and PD-Saccade within different time intervals

| PD-Fixation | F | P-value |
|---|---|---|
| Orig-Simp | 54.23 | p = 0.00 |
| Intervals | 65.17 | p = 0.00 |
| (Original_Simplified)*Intervals | 10.13 | p = 0.00 |
| PD-Saccade | F | P-value |
| Orig-Simp | 35.88 | p = 0.00 |
| Intervals | 17.05 | p = 0.00 |
| (Original_Simplified)*Intervals | 75.59 | p = 0.00 |

These differences are further shown in Table 6, which displays the pairwise comparison between PD saccade/fixation for original and simplified passages among different time intervals. In other words, PD-fixation is significantly different between original and simplified passages in the beginning ($p = 0.00$), and end ($p = 0.00$) of the reading duration but not in the middle of the reading duration ($p = 0.53$). Identically, PD-saccade is also significantly different between original and simplified passages in the beginning ($p = 0.00$) and the end ($p = 0.00$). However, the difference in PD-saccade between original and simplified passages is also significant in the middle of reading ($p = 0.00$). Figures 6 and 7 display graphical interpretations of these results. As we can see in these figures, average PD-Fixation is larger in the simplified group compared to the original group at the beginning and the end intervals. In the middle interval Average PD-Fixation values are the same in both groups. While we observe a similar trend for PD-Saccade in the beginning and end intervals, in the middle interval average PD-Saccade for the original passage is significantly larger than average PD-Saccade for the simplified passage.

**Table 6.** Pairwise comparison between different time intervals for PD-Fixation and PD-Saccade

| PD-Fixation | | | |
| --- | --- | --- | --- |
| Time intervals | Mean ± SD (original) | Mean ± SD (simplified) | P-value |
| Beginning | 2.99 ± 0.01 | 3.01 ± 0.02 | p = 0.00 |
| Middle | 3.00 ± 0.02 | 3.00 ± 0.01 | p = 0.53 |
| End | 3.01 ± 0.02 | 3.03 ± 0.01 | p = 0.00 |
| *PD-Saccade* | | | |
| Time intervals | Mean ± SD (original) | Mean ± SD (simplified) | P-value |
| Beginning | 3.02 ± 0.2 | 3.05 ± 0.03 | p = 0.00 |
| Middle | 3.04 ± 0.01 | 3.02 ± 0.01 | p = 0.00 |
| End | 3.02 ± 0.01 | 3.04 ± 0.00 | p = 0.00 |

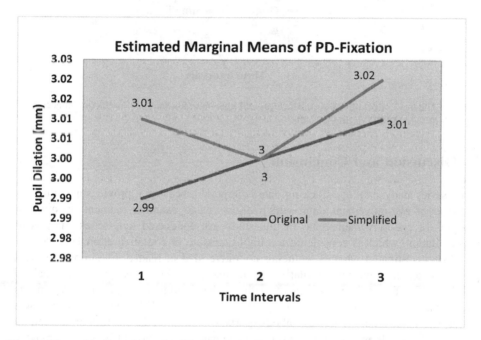

**Fig. 6.** The main effect of text simplification and time intervals and their interaction effect on the dependent variable PD during fixation

These findings are consistent with previous literature [11–15] that identify pupil dilation as a reliable measure of cognitive load in cognitive tasks. In addition; these results indicate that separating pupil dilation during fixation and saccades can provide more nuanced information that is not available when considering only the overall PD. Furthermore, these results open new research questions in the field of pupillometry related to HCI research, which will be discussed in the next section of this paper.

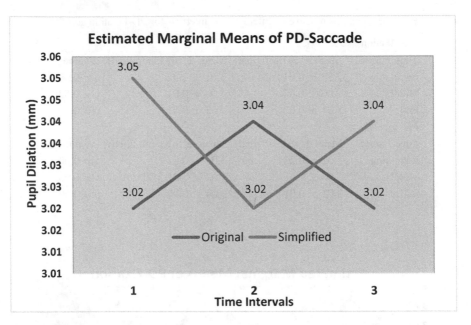

**Fig. 7.** The main effect of text simplification and time intervals and their interaction effect on the dependent variable PD during saccade

## 5   Discussion and Conclusion

Time series analysis of eye-tracking data is important because it provides a continuous measure of eye-movement data, which allows us to examine moment by moment analysis of eye-movement data. In this study, we conducted time-series analysis of pupil dilation, which is considered a reliable measure of cognitive effort [11–15].

We investigated whether reducing cognitive load of readers by simplifying text passages can affect their pupil dilation during reading and whether this effect remained steady over different time intervals of reading. The simplified text passage used in this study was developed using a set of plain language rules [3]. The original passage, which was an actual news passage about sports, was simplified from 18th grade reading level to 10th grade reading level through systematic application of the plain language rules described in [3].

The time series PD analysis in our study was based on eye movement data of 54 participants, 26 reading the simplified version of the passage and 28 reading the original passage. Gaze data was recorded using Tobii X-300 eye-tracker with sampling rate of 300 Hz. Eye-movement data were then obtained from eye-tracking software (Tobii studio V3.2.3). Cubic splines interpolation method [21] was used to interpolate the data points and to make arrays of equal sizes of pupil data among participants in different conditions. For each cell in the array averages among all participants were calculated and used to compare the trend of PD over time between simplified and original passages.

The results of t-test comparing overall PD values between the original and simplified groups showed that text simplification did not significantly affect pupil dilation over time. However, when dividing the data points into three equally size intervals, the results showed that PD values were significantly different between the original and simplified groups in the last part of reading. Because pupil dilation is generally associated with increased cognitive load [20, 23], the results displayed in Fig. 2 suggest that participants were experiencing more cognitive load at the beginning of the task (compared to the two other time intervals) when they were familiarizing themselves with the text. The results also show that cognitive load was similar for the two text conditions (original vs. simplified) at the beginning and middle time intervals but it was significantly lower for people in the simplified text condition at the end interval. These results provide evidence that examining PD in various time intervals can provide additional information for understanding cognitive load.

Next, we examined PD for fixations and saccades separately. Our analysis, showing that the impact of text simplification on PD was significant when separating PD-Fixation from PD-Saccade, supported the study that argues examining PD during fixations and saccades separately is useful in refining the explanatory power of pupillemotry. Our results are consistent with the argument that the observed differences are due to differences in the nature of fixation and saccadic eye-movements [5]. Our results show that pupil dilation was slightly larger during saccades compared to pupil dilation during fixations (Fig. 5). The results also show that PD regardless whether it was measured during fixations or saccades was larger in simplified version of the text. Note that PD during fixations refers to visual information processing. Because during saccades we cannot process visual information (our eyes move too fast to be able to take foveal snapshots), PD during saccades may indicate cognitive processing beyond what is typically associated with attention measured as foveal processing of visual information. Given this interpretation, the results in Fig. 5, suggests higher cognitive activity during saccades compared to fixations regardless whether participants were reading the original or the simplified versions of the text. It also suggests higher cognitive activity in the group that were reading simplified text. Given that the performance for the same set of data indicated that people provided significantly more accurate answers to questions about the text in the simplified group [4], higher cognitive activity in the simplified group in this case may indicate higher level of engagement with the task.

Next, we examined PD during fixations and saccades over the three reading intervals: beginning, middle, and end. The results, displayed in Fig. 6 and Fig. 7, reveals different effects. During fixations, PD increases consistently over the three time periods when people read the original version of the text. However, when people read the simplified version, PD in the middle of the reading is significantly smaller than the two other intervals. During the saccades, PD values in the middle interval are higher than the two other intervals for the original version of the text while they are lower than the two other intervals for the simplified version of the text. These results indicate the presence of different types of activities in the middle of reading as represented by PD during saccades and fixations. While future experiments are needed to fully explain these differences, these results provide evidence for the usefulness of examining PD during fixations and saccades separately during various intervals.

Overall our findings are consistent with previous literature that have employed pupil dilation as a reliable measure of cognitive load. Additionally, our results indicate that investigating pupil dilation in different time intervals is useful in providing a better understanding of cognitive load and that separating the analysis of pupil dilation during fixations and saccades can provide additional useful information about cognitive load. These results provide a rationale for new research questions in the field of pupillometry related to HCI research. For example, why PD-Fixation and PD-Saccade show similar behavior at the beginning and end of the reading when comparing reaction to original and simplified passages, but show different behavior in the middle of reading? Is this a consistent behavior even when we test different passages or with a different population of readers?

## 6   Limitations and Future Research

As in any other research our study has some limitations, which provides opportunity for directing future research efforts. For example, future studies, including some of our own planned experiments, are needed to test passages with different content other than sports to see whether similar results are obtained. Expanding population to include older users or those with limitations in reading proficiency can also help to improve our understanding of the relationship between cognitive load and pupillometery.

## 7   Contributions

In this exploratory study, we set out to examine the impact of cognitive load (manipulated via text simplification) on pupillometry. In particular, we examined (1) how pupil dilation was affected when people read simplified vs. original versions of a passage, (2) whether this impact was different if we separate pupil dilation during fixations and saccades, and (3) whether pupillary responses were different during various time intervals. Our results provide evidence that all these types of exploratory investigations can provide useful information for refining our understanding of the relationship between cognitive load and pupillometry.

## References

1. Beatty, J.: Task-evoked pupillary responses, processing load, and the structure of processing resources. Psychol. Bull. **91**, 276–292 (1982)
2. Iqbal, S.T., Zheng, X.S., Bailey, B.P.: Task-evoked pupillary response to mental workload in human-computer interaction. In: CHI, 1477–1480 (2004)
3. Djamasbi, S., Rochford, J., DaBoll-Lavoie, A., Greff, T., Lally, J., McAvoy, K.: Text simplification and user experience. In: Schmorrow, D.D.D., Fidopiastis, C.M.M. (eds.) AC 2016. LNCS (LNAI), vol. 9744, pp. 285–295. Springer, Cham (2016). doi:10.1007/978-3-319-39952-2_28

4. Djamasbi, S., Shojaeizadeh, M., Chen, P., Rochford, J.: Text simplification and generation Y: an eye tracking study. In: SIGHCI 2016 Proceedings, Paper 12 (2016). http://aisel.aisnet.org/sighci2016/12
5. Shojaeizadeh, M., Djamasbi, S., Trapp, A.C.: Does pupillary data differ during fixations and saccades? does it carry information about task demand? In: Proceedings of the Thirteenth Annual Workshop on HCI Research in MIS, Fort Worth, Texas, USA, 13 December 2015
6. Zagermann, J., Pfeil, U., Reiterer, H.: Measuring cognitive load using eye tracking technology in visual computing. In: Sedlmair, M., Isenberg, P., Isenberg, T., Mahyar, N., Lam, H. (eds.) Proceedings of the Sixth Workshop on Beyond Time and Errors on Novel Evaluation Methods for Visualization (BELIV 2016), New York, USA, pp. 78–85. ACM (2016)
7. Just, M.A., Carpenter, P.A.: The intensity dimension of thought: pupillometric indices of sentence processing. Can. J. Exp. Psychol. **47**, 310–339 (1993)
8. Hess, E.H.: Attitude and pupil size. Sci. Am. **212**, 46–54 (1965)
9. Beatty, J., Wagoner, B.L.: Pupillometric signs of brain activation vary with level of cognitive processing. Science **199**, 1216–1218 (1978)
10. Zhan, Z., Zhang, L., Mei, H., Fong, P.S.W.: Online learners' reading ability detection based on eye-tracking sensors. Sensors **16**, 1457 (2016)
11. Chen, S., Epps, J., Ruiz, N., Chen, F.: Eye activity as a measure of human mental effort in HCI. In: Proceedings of the 16th International Conference on Intelligent User Interfaces (IUI 2011), New York, USA, pp. 315–318. ACM (2011)
12. Klingner, J., Tversky, B., Hanrahan, P.: Effects of visual and verbal presentation on cognitive load in vigilance, memory, and arithmetic tasks. Psychophysiology **48**(3), 323–332 (2011)
13. Pomplun, M., Sunkara, S.: Pupil dilation as an indicator of cognitive workload in human-computer interaction. In: Proceedings of the International Conference on HCI, pp. 542–546 (2003)
14. Klingner, J., Kumar, R., Hanrahan, P.: Measuring the task-evoked pupillary response with a remote eye tracker. In: Proceedings of the 2008 Symposium on Eye tracking Research & Applications, pp. 69–72. ACM (2008)
15. Pfleging, B., Fekety, D.K., Schmidt, A., Kun, A.L.: A model relating pupil diameter to mental workload and lighting conditions. In: Proceedings of the 2016 CHI Conference on Human Factors in Computing Systems (CHI 2016), New York, USA, pp. 5776–5788. ACM (2016)
16. Poole, A., Ball, L.J.: Eye tracking in HCI and usability research. Encycl. Hum. Comput. Interact. **1**, 211–219 (2006)
17. Djamasbi, S.: Eye tracking and web experience. AIS Trans. Hum.-Comput. Inter. **6**(2), 37–54 (2014)
18. Simpson, H.M., Hale, S.M.: Pupillary changes during a decision-making task. Percept. Mot. Skills **29**, 495–498 (1969)
19. Beatty, J., Wagoner, B.L.: Pupillometric signs of brain activation vary with level of cognitive processing. Science **199**, 1216–1218 (1978)
20. Einhäuser, W., Stout, J., Koch, C., Carter, O.: Pupil dilation reflects perceptual selection and predicts subsequent stability in perceptual rivalry. PNAS **105**(5), 1704–1709 (2008). Published ahead of print 4 February 2008
21. McKinley, S., Levine, M.: Cubic spline interpolation. vol. 45, no. 1, pp. 1049–1060, College of the Redwoods, January 1998
22. Reinsch, C.H.: Numer. Math. **10**, 177 (1967). doi:10.1007/BF02162161
23. Wang, J.T-y., Spezio, M., Camerer, C.F.: Pinocchio's pupil: using eyetracking and pupil dilation to understand truth telling and deception in sender-receiver games. Am. Econ. Rev. **100**(3), 984–1007 (2010)

# Attentional Trade-Offs Under Resource Scarcity

Jiaying Zhao[1,2]($\boxtimes$) and Brandon M. Tomm[1]

[1] Department of Psychology, University of British Columbia,
Vancouver, BC V6T 1Z4, Canada
jiayingz@psych.ubc.ca
[2] Institute for Resources, Environment and Sustainability,
University of British Columbia, Vancouver, BC V6T 1Z4, Canada

**Abstract.** Resource scarcity poses challenging demands on the cognitive system. Budgeting with limited resources induces an attentional focus on the problem at hand, but it also comes with a cost. Specifically, scarcity causes a failure to notice beneficial information in the environment, or remember to execute actions in the future, that help alleviate the condition of scarcity. This neglect may arise as a result of attentional narrowing. Attentional trade-offs under scarcity can further determine memory encoding. In five experiments, we demonstrated that participants under scarcity prioritized price information but neglected a useful discount when ordering food from a menu (Experiment 1); they showed better recall for information relevant to the focal task at a subsequent surprise memory test (Experiments 2 and 3); they performed more efficiently on the focal task but neglect a useful cue in the environment that could save them resources (Experiment 4); and they failed to remember the previous instructions to execute future actions that could save them resources (Experiment 5). These results collectively demonstrate that scarcity fundamentally shapes the way people process information in the environment, by directing attention to the most urgent task, while inducing a neglect of other information that can be beneficial. The attentional neglect and memory failures may lead to suboptimal decisions and behaviors that further aggravate the condition of scarcity. The results provide new insights on the behaviors of the poor, and also important implications for public policy and the design of welfare services and programs for low-income individuals.

**Keywords:** Poverty · Visual attention · Memory · Encoding · Decision making

## 1 Introduction

Scarcity is an urgent and pervasive problem in the world: Roughly 1.2 billion people live in extreme poverty with less than \$1.25 a day, 1.3 billion people live without electricity, and more than 780 million lack access to clean water. Scarcity is the condition of having insufficient resources to cope with the demands, and presents significant challenges to the cognitive system. For example, having limited financial

© Springer International Publishing AG 2017
D.D. Schmorrow and C.M. Fidopiastis (Eds.): AC 2017, Part II, LNAI 10285, pp. 78–97, 2017.
DOI: 10.1007/978-3-319-58625-0_6

resources requires the meticulous calculation of any expenses. Similarly, having limited time requires stringent management of schedules.

The cognitive consequences of scarcity are recently revealed by a number of studies [14]. For example, scarcity causes myopic behavior which results in the neglect of future events [18]. Specifically, people under scarcity tend to prioritize the task at hand and over-borrow resources from the future. Financial scarcity directly impairs cognitive function, reducing fluid intelligence and the ability to exert cognitive control [12]. These cognitive and behavioral consequences are particularly problematic because these impairments can lead to suboptimal decision making and behaviors (e.g., poor time management or financial planning skills) that further perpetuate the condition of scarcity.

Currently, it is still unclear what cognitive mechanisms underlie the impairments caused by scarcity. A possible explanation is that scarcity presents urgent demands that hijack attentional resources, causing a strong focus on the task at hand. Such focus can induce a neglect of other potentially important information.

Support for this explanation comes from the previous theoretical and empirical work on the limits of the cognitive system. Specifically, the cognitive system has a finite capacity, and people can only receive and process a limited amount of information at a time [1, 11, 13, 15]. Given this limited capacity, engaging in one process consumes cognitive resources needed for another, thus causing interference. For example, studies on inattentional blindness [20] show that performing a demanding task (e.g., counting how often the basketball is passed around) results in an inability to notice a salient event (e.g., a man dressed as a gorilla passing by). Basic visual features of unattended stimuli may not even be perceived [17]. In addition to perception, this interference can cause serious behavioral consequences such as impaired driving [21]. The limited cognitive resources given competing demands can thus result in attentional trade-offs between focus and neglect.

Here, we propose that scarcity forces attentional trade-offs. Specifically, people operating under scarcity may prioritize urgent tasks at hand, leaving other information unattended. This process can be counter-productive because the attentional neglect can cause the failure to notice useful and beneficial information in the environment that alleviates the condition of scarcity. To investigate the attentional trade-offs under scarcity and the resulting cognitive consequences of such trade-offs, we conducted five experiments in the current study.

## 2   Experiment 1

The goal of this experiment was to examine the effects of scarcity on visual attention. We predict that scarcity draws attention to the information relevant to the task at hand, but at the same time, also causes the neglect of other useful information in the environment.

## 2.1    Participants

One hundred and ninety undergraduate students (152 female, 35 male, 3 unspecified; mean age = 20.39 years, $SD$ = 3.92) were recruited from the Human Subject Pool at the Department of Psychology at the University of British Columbia (UBC), and participated in the experiment for course credit. Participants in all experiments reported normal or corrected-to-normal vision and provided informed consent. All experiments reported here were approved by the UBC Behavioral Research Ethics Board.

## 2.2    Stimuli and Procedure

Participants were presented with a restaurant menu which contained 24 food items. For each item, the price and the calories were listed in two columns on the menu (Fig. 1). The menu subtended 12.4° of visual angle in width and 16.2° in height. A discount clause was shown on the bottom of the menu ("You may ask for an 18% student discount.").

Participants were randomly assigned with either a small budget ($20; the poor condition) or a large budget ($100; the rich condition). Thus, the experiment used a between-subjects design. Participants were asked to view the items on the menu and think about what they would like to order, as if they were ordering a meal from a restaurant. They were given unlimited time to place the order, and were told not to exceed the assigned budget, but they were not required to spend the entire budget.

The eye gaze of each participant was monitored throughout the experiment using SMI RED-250 Mobile Eyetracking System (60 Hz). To examine which part of the menu was attended to, the menu was divided into four areas of interest: food items (left column), price information (middle column), calorie information (right column), and discount clause (on the bottom).

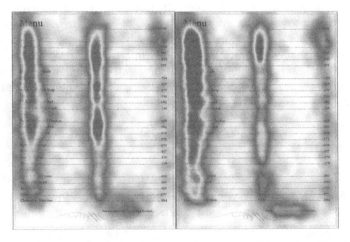

**Fig. 1.** Left: A heat map of the menu showing the distribution of the average dwell time for the participants in the poor condition (who ordered a meal with $20). Right: A heat map showing the distribution of the average dwell time for the participants in the rich condition (who ordered a meal with $100). Warmer colors represent longer average dwell time. (Color figure online)

## 2.3    Results and Discussion

To measure visual attention, we calculated the dwell time and the number of fixations in each area of interest. The heat maps of the average duration of dwell time between the poor and the rich conditions were shown in Fig. 1.

Since there was no time limit in the experiment, participants could spend as much time as they needed to make the order. We found that participants in the rich condition took more time to order ($M = 89$ s) than the participants in the poor condition ($M = 76$ s) [$t(188) = 2.24$, $p = .03$, $d = .33$]. Thus, we used the proportional dwell time (the dwell time spent in each area divided by the total dwell time on the menu) and the proportional fixations (the number of fixations in each area divided by the total number of fixations on the menu) as two measures of visual attention. In addition, participants with more than 3 standard deviations away from the mean in each measure were excluded (between 1 and 4 participants in total, depending on the measure).

For the food items (Fig. 2), participants in the poor condition spent less dwell time ($M = 35.11\%$) than those in the rich condition ($M = 51.98\%$) [$t(185) = 3.91, p < .001$, $d = .57$]. The poor also made few fixations ($M = 36.66\%$) on the food items than the rich ($M = 48.50\%$) [$t(187) = 3.08$, $p = .002$, $d = .45$]. This suggests that the poor participants spent less time considering which food items they would like to order than the rich participants did.

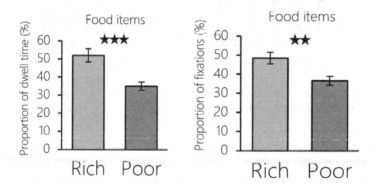

**Fig. 2.** The proportional dwell time and fixations on food items between participants in the poor and the rich conditions (error bars reflect $\pm 1$ SEM; $**p < .01$, $***p < .001$).

For price information (Fig. 3), participants in the poor condition dwelled longer at prices ($M = 21.08\%$) than those in the rich condition ($M = 15.23\%$) [$t(185) = 2.16$, $p = .03, d = .32$]. Participants in the poor condition also made more fixations on prices ($M = 23.07\%$) than those in the rich condition ($M = 15.81\%$) [$t(185) = 2.91, p < .01$, $d = .43$]. This suggests that the poor attended more to prices than the rich participants.

This result could be driven by the possibility that scarcity enhanced attention to all numerical information. Thus, we examined attention to the calorie information (Fig. 4). Participants in the poor condition dwelled less on calories ($M = 2.92\%$) than those in the

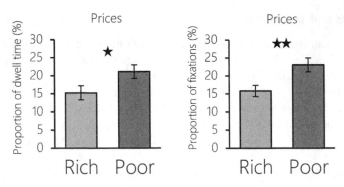

**Fig. 3.** The proportional dwell time and fixations on prices between participants in the poor and the rich conditions (error bars reflect ±1 SEM; *$p$ < .05, **$p$ < .01).

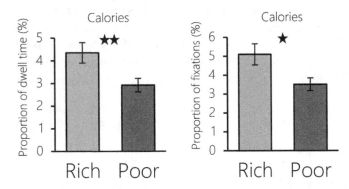

**Fig. 4.** The proportional dwell time and fixations on calories between participants in the poor and the rich conditions (error bars reflect ±1 SEM; *$p$ < .05, **$p$ < .01).

rich condition ($M$ = 4.35%) [$t(185)$ = 2.65, $p$ < .01, $d$ = .39]. The poor ($M$ = 3.51%) also made fewer fixations on calories than the rich did ($M$ = 5.09%) [$t(184)$ = 2.39, $p$ = .02, $d$ = .35]. This indicates that financial scarcity draws attention more to prices and induces a neglect of calories.

Importantly, for the discount clause (Fig. 5), participants in the poor condition spent less dwell time ($M$ = 0.83%) than those in the rich condition ($M$ = 1.83%) [$t(184)$ = 3.51, $p$ < .001, $d$ = .52]. The poor also made fewer fixations on the discount clause ($M$ = 0.85%) than the rich ($M$ = 1.82%) [$t(184)$ = 3.51, $p$ < .001, $d$ = .52]. This suggests that the poor neglected the discount, compared to the rich participants.

As another measure of attention to the discount, after placing the order the participants were asked if they had noticed other information on the menu besides the price and calorie information. While measures of visual attention showed that the poor looked less at the discount than the rich did, there was no reliable difference between the number of poor ($N$ = 36) and rich ($N$ = 33) participants who explicitly reported noticing the discount [$X^2(1,190)$ = .09, $p$ = .76].

An alternative explanation for the finding that the poor attended less to the discount was that scarcity might result in more efficient processing of task-relevant information. This would suggest that the poor did not need to look at the discount as much as the rich, because they were faster in seeing the discount. Since both the prices and the discount were task-relevant, this explanation would predict that the poor would be efficient in processing both price information and the discount. However, we found that the poor looked more at the prices but less at the discount than the rich did, which could not be explained by the efficiency account.

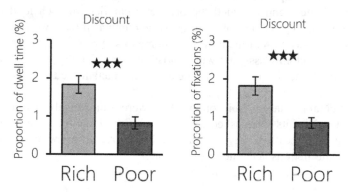

**Fig. 5.** The proportional dwell time and fixations on the discount clause between participants in the poor and the rich conditions (error bars reflect ±1 SEM; ***$p < .001$).

The discount on the menu could in theory help the poor participants save money and stay within their budget. Despite this usefulness, the poor participants still neglected the discount and focused more on the prices of the food items. This finding is ironic and could help explain why the low-income individuals engage in neglectful behaviors that are counter-productive.

## 3   Experiment 2

Experiment 1 demonstrated that financial scarcity prioritizes the processing of price information, at the cost of other useful information. Given the attentional prioritization of prices, we predict that memory encoding of prices will also be enhanced. This prediction is supported by the recent work that suggests that visual working memory can be construed as visual attention preserved internally over time [2, 3]. Feature-based theories of attention also predict selective facilitation in visual processing for task-relevant features [8, 9]. Thus, in Experiment 2 we examined the effects of scarcity on memory encoding, as a result of attentional prioritization. We predict that financial scarcity facilitates memory encoding specifically for price information, and not for other types of information.

## 3.1    Participants

A new group of 60 undergraduate students (43 female, 17 male; mean age = 19.95 years, *SD* = 2.30) from UBC participated in the experiment for course credit.

## 3.2    Stimuli and Procedure

To increase the demand for memory encoding, we increased the number of items on the menu. Participants were presented with a menu which now contained 50 food items. As in Experiment 1, the menu included the price and calories for each food item. Participants were asked to place a meal order from the menu as if they were ordering from a restaurant. There was no set time limit for participants to place their order. As before, participants were randomly assigned with a small budget ($20; the poor condition) or a large budget ($100; the rich condition). The experiment again used a between-subjects design.

After participants placed their order, they were immediately given a surprise memory test. Participants were asked to recall as many items from the menu as possible. For each item recalled, they were also asked to recall the price and the calorie information of the item as accurately as possible.

## 3.3    Results and Discussion

To measure memory encoding, we calculated the average absolute error between the recalled prices (and calories) and the objective prices (and calories) for each participant (Fig. 6). Participants in the poor condition (*Mean error* = $1.32) were reliably more accurate in the price recall than those in the rich condition (*Mean error* = $2.19) [*t*(58) = 2.42, *p* = .02, *d* = .63]. However, there was no reliable difference in the calorie recall between the poor and the rich participants [*t*(58) = .81, *p* = .42, *d* = .21].

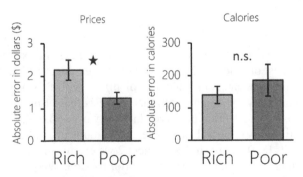

**Fig. 6.** The absolute error in the price recall and the calorie recall between participants in the price poor and the price rich conditions (error bars reflect ±1 SEM; *p < .01).

This enhanced performance in price recall in the poor cannot be explained by the fact that the poor participants ordered fewer items ($M = 2.13$) than the rich ($M = 3.70$) [$t(58) = 3.85, p < .001, d = .99$]. First, there was no reliable difference in the number of recalled times between the poor and the rich [$t(58) = 1.38, p = .17, d = .36$]. Second, there was no difference in the time taken to place the order between the poor and the rich participants [$t(58) = 1.58, p = .12, d = .41$]. Third, even if ordering fewer items might improve memory recall, this benefit would be seen in both price and calorie recall, but we found that the poor were more accurate only in price recall, not in calorie recall. Thus, these findings suggest that financial scarcity improves memory encoding for task-relevant information (i.e., prices), but not for task-irrelevant information (i.e., calories). Scarcity selectively facilitates memory encoding.

# 4   Experiment 3

To generalize the findings in Experiment 2 to a different domain, we examined how calorie scarcity affects memory encoding. We predict that calorie scarcity facilitates memory encoding specifically for calorie information, and not for price information.

## 4.1   Participants

A new group of 60 undergraduate students (49 female, 11 male; mean age = 20.03 years, $SD = 2.11$) from UBC participated in the experiment for course credit.

## 4.2   Stimuli and Procedure

The stimuli and the procedure were identical to those in Experiment 2, except for a critical difference. Participants were randomly assigned with a small calorie budget (500 calories; the poor condition) or a large calorie budget (2000 calories; the rich condition). As before, participants were then asked to place a meal order from the menu as if they were ordering from a restaurant. After the order, participants were given a surprise memory test, where they recalled items from the menu with the price and calorie information.

## 4.3   Results and Discussion

To measure memory encoding, we calculated the average absolute error between the recalled calories (and prices) and the objective calories (and prices) for each participant (Fig. 7). Participants in the poor condition (*Mean error* = 48.05) were reliably more accurate in the calorie recall than those in the rich condition (*Mean error* = 71.61) [$t(58) = 2.27, p = .03, d = .58$]. This suggests that the calorie poor showed better memory encoding of calorie information than the calorie rich.

A critical test of our prediction was whether this memory facilitation is specific to task-relevant information (i.e., calories). We found that there was no reliable difference in the price recall between the two conditions [$t(58) = 0.19$, $p = .85$, $d = .04$]. Thus, memory encoding was selectively enhanced for the calorie information in the calorie poor participants. Interestingly, we did not observe worse memory encoding for the task-irrelevant information. That is, the calorie recall was the same for the price poor and the price rich in Experiment 2, and the price recall was the same for the calorie poor and the calorie rich in Experiment 3. The lack of difference between the rich and poor in memory encoding of task-irrelevant information could be driven by the possibility that neither the rich nor the poor needed to pay attention to this information in these experiments.

**Fig. 7.** The absolute error in the calorie recall and the price recall between participants in the calorie poor and the calorie rich conditions (error bars reflect ±1 SEM; *$p < .01$).

## 5    Experiment 4a

In this experiment we investigated how time scarcity affects the online detection of information. Past work shows that people only start to increase their efforts to accomplish their goals when a deadline becomes salient [4]. Further, time pressure causes fewer attributes to be considered when choosing between alternatives [22]. The goal of this experiment was to investigate how time scarcity affects the online detection of information in the environment. We hypothesize that time scarcity draws attention to the focal task, while inducing neglect of other useful information in the environment.

### 5.1    Participants

Undergraduate students ($N = 90$) were recruited from the UBC Human Subject Pool, and participated in the experiment in exchange for course credit.

### 5.2    Stimuli and Procedure

Each participant was asked to solve a series of puzzles on the computer screen. The puzzles were 50 trials of the Raven's Progressive Matrices [16]. Each matrix appeared at the centre of the screen, and contained a pattern of objects. The bottom right corner of the matrix was missing, and participants had to find the right piece that fits with the general pattern in the matrix. The participant was asked to correctly solve as many matrices as possible in exchange for points. In each trial, participants were presented with one Raven's matrix, with the numbered pieces appearing below. The response keys appeared in a vertical list on the left side of the screen. In the top-left corner of the screen, the questions number and time remaining were displayed (see Fig. 8). To solve a given matrix, participants had to press a number key that corresponds to the piece that fits into the missing corner of the matrix.

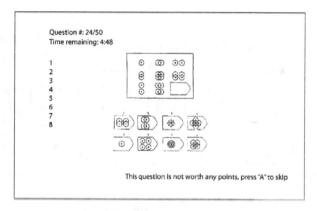

**Fig. 8.** Trial screen for Experiment 4a.

To manipulate time scarcity, participants were randomly assigned with either a rich time budget (they had 40 min in total to solve the matrices; the time-rich condition, $N = 45$), or a poor time budget (they only had 10 min in total to solve the matrices; the time-poor condition, $N = 45$). Without explicit instruction or prompting, a time-saving cue appeared in the lower right part of the screen during the experiment. Specifically, on even-numbered trials starting from trial #24, the cue appeared on the screen stating: "This question is not worth any points. Press 'A' to skip." (see Fig. 8) Thus, 14 of the 50 trials were allowed to be skipped without any loss of points. The cue appeared at the same time as the matrix for those trials, and remained on the screen for 2000 ms, and then disappeared. These trials presented an opportunity to skip the question in order to save time. Participants were not told anything about the cue. We wanted to see if they were able to detect this message during the experiment and skipped the even-numbered questions from trial #24.

## 5.3   Results and Discussion

Participants in the time-poor condition almost unanimously used their entire time budget while participants in the time-rich condition used less than half of their time budget. Given this constraint, the time-poor participants spent less time on the task overall compared to time-rich participants [$t(88) = 6.51, p < .001, d = 1.37$] (Fig. 9a).

The time-poor participants completed fewer trials than the time-rich participants [$t(88) = 4.71$, $p < .001$, $d = .99$] (Fig. 9b).

Notably, there was marginal difference in accuracy on the Raven's Progressive Matrices between the time-poor and the time-rich participants [$t(88) = 1.69$, $p = .09$, $d = .36$] (Fig. 9c). When accounting for the total amount of time spent on the task, the time-poor participants scored higher accuracy per minute than time-rich participants [$t(88) = 8.09$, $p < .001$, $d = 1.71$]. This result suggests that time scarcity can cause a greater focus on the task at hand, enhancing task performance within the time limit.

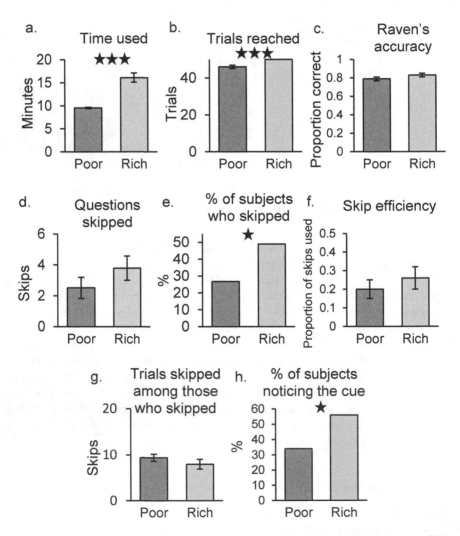

**Fig. 9.** Results for Experiment 4a (Error bars represent ±1 SEM. *$p < .05$, ***$p < .001$).

Examining the number of questions skipped, we found that there was no difference in the average number of questions skipped between the time-poor and the time-rich participants [$t(88) = 1.23$, $p = .22$, $d = .26$] (Fig. 9d). However, only 26.7% of the participants in the time-poor condition skipped at least once, and there were more time-rich participants (48.9%) who skipped at least once [$X^2(1,90) = 4.72$, $p = .03$] (Fig. 9e). This result suggests that time scarcity caused a failure to use the time-saving cue appearing on the bottom of the screen.

To control for the total number of trials completed, we calculated skip efficiency as the number of questions skipped divided by the number of possible questions that could be skipped. There was no difference in skip efficiency between the time-poor and the time-rich participants [$t(88) - .91$, $p - .36$, $d = .19$] (Fig. 9f).

Among those who skipped at least once, there was no difference in the number of questions skipped between the time-poor and the time-rich participants [$t(31) = .89$, $p = .38$, $d = .34$] (Fig. 9g). This means that if the participant noticed the cue at least once, they were able to skip the same number of questions, regardless of scarcity.

To measure retrospective recall of the time-saving cues, we asked participants after completing the task during debriefing to report whether they saw any messages appearing on the screen during the task. We found that the time-poor participants were less likely to report seeing the cues than the time-rich participants [$X^2(1,84) = 3.81$, $p = .05$] (Fig. 9h).

These results showed that fewer participants under time scarcity skipped the questions at least once, and reported seeing the cues, compared to time-rich participants. This suggests that time scarcity may narrow attention to the central task, while inducing a neglect of peripheral, even beneficial information in the environment. An alternative explanation is inattentional blindness, suggesting that the time-poor participants were less able to attend to salient but task-irrelevant information, than the time-rich participants. To tease these two accounts apart, we conducted the next experiment, probing whether scarcity alters the spatial scope of attention, or the ability to notice salient stimulus. Specifically, we manipulated the location of the time-saving cue, and examined the likelihood of skipping questions as a function of the spatial location of the cue under scarcity.

# 6  Experiment 4b

In this experiment, we reduced the spatial distance between the time-saving cue and the matrix (i.e., the focal task) by moving the cue closer to the center of the screen, and investigated how the spatial proximity of the time-saving cue to the focal task impacted its detection.

## 6.1  Participants, Stimuli, and Procedure

Participants ($N = 87$) were recruited from the Human Subject Pool at UBC, and participated in the experiment in exchange for course credit. The stimuli and the procedure were exactly the same as those in Experiment 4a, except one important change: the time-saving cue (i.e., the message to skip even-numbered questions after trial #24) now appeared directly underneath the Raven's Matrix after trial #24 for even-numbered questions (Fig. 10).

If the neglect of the time-saving cue in Experiment 4a was due to the spatial narrowing of attention under scarcity, we would predict that the time-poor participants would be more likely to notice the cue if it were moved closer to the central task. On the other hand, if the neglect of the time-saving cue was due to inattentional blindness, moving the cue closer to the central task would not affect performance.

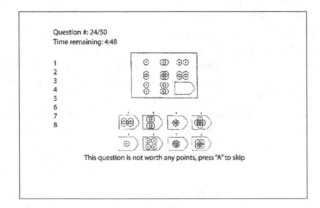

**Fig. 10.** Trial screen for Experiment 4b, where the time-saving cue appeared right below the matrix.

## 6.2   Results and Discussion

Since in Experiment 4a, time scarcity influenced the number of participants who skipped at least once, we examined the same measure here again. We found that now there was no statistical difference in the percent of participants who skipped at least once [$X^2(1,87) = .56$, $p = .46$]. Comparing Figs. 11a to 9e, the time-rich participants were not influenced by the change in the position of the cue, but the poor seemed to benefit from the closer proximity of the cue to the central task. This suggests that if the cue falls within the spatial scope of attention, the time-poor participants could still take advantage of the cue.

During debriefing, the time-poor participants were marginally less likely to report seeing any messages during the task compared to the time-rich participants [$X^2(1,85) = 3.583$, $p = .06$] (Fig. 11b). Compared to the time-poor participants in Experiment 4a (34% reported noticing the cue), the closer proximity seemed to provide a large benefit to the time-poor participants in Experiment 4b (49% reported noticing the cue). These results support the account that scarcity narrows spatial attention to the focal task.

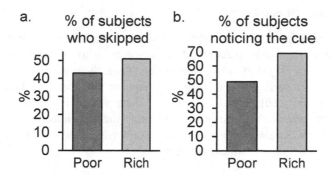

**Fig. 11.** Results for Experiment 4b.

# 7 Experiment 4c

To further explore the boundary condition of the spatial narrowing effect of scarcity, in this experiment we moved the time-saving cue farther away from the focal task, and examined how likely participants were to notice the cue.

## 7.1 Participants, Stimuli, and Procedure

Participants ($N = 86$) were recruited from the Human Subject Pool at UBC, and participated in the experiment in exchange for course credit. The stimuli and the procedure were identical to those of Experiment 4a, but this time the time-saving cue appeared in the bottom right corner of the screen (Fig. 12), which was even farther away from the focal task than in Experiment 4a.

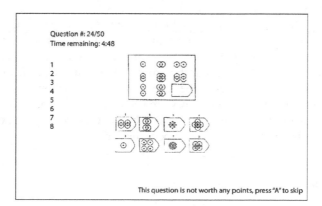

**Fig. 12.** Trial screen for Experiment 4c, where the time-saving cue appeared far from the matrix, on the bottom right corner of the screen.

## 7.2    Results and Discussion

We found that participants in both conditions failed to take advantage of the cue. There was no difference in the percent of participants who skipped at least once [$X^2(1,86) = .93$, $p = .33$] (Fig. 13a). During debriefing, there was no difference in the likelihood to report seeing any messages during the task between both conditions [$X^2(1,83) = 2.00$, $p = .16$] (Fig. 13b). In fact, there was a floor effect in both the time-poor and the time-rich participants in skipping the questions or noticing the cue. This suggests that when the cue was spatially far away from the focal task, participants could not notice the cue, regardless of scarcity.

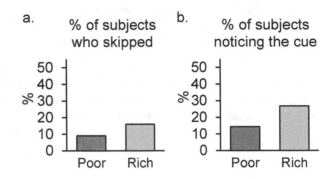

**Fig. 13.**    Results for Experiment 4c.

# 8    Experiment 5

Experiments 4a-c showed that time scarcity narrowed attention on the focal task, resulting in the neglect of a time-saving cue which appeared in the peripheral during the experiment. However, in daily life, we do not always have cues in the external environment as reminders for certain actions. Instead, we need to rely on internal cues from memory that need to be activated at the right time to direct actions. For example, in order to pick up groceries on the way home from work, we must remember to turn at the right intersection in order to go to the grocery store. This depends on prospective memory, which is the ability to remember to executive future actions based on previous instructions. Cues for prospective memory are internal, and must be present in mind in order to cue behavior at the right time [6, 10]. In this experiment, we examined how time scarcity affects prospective memory performance.

## 8.1    Participants

Participants ($N = 90$) were recruited from the Human Subject Pool at UBC and completed the study in exchange for course credit.

## 8.2   Stimuli and Procedure

Participants were asked to solve the same set of 50 Raven's Progressive Matrices used in Experiments 4a–c. As before, participants were randomly assigned either a small time budget (5 min; the time-poor condition), or a large time budget (20 min; the time-rich condition). A critical difference in this experiment was that the time-saving cue never appeared in the experiment. Rather, all participants were explicitly instructed at the start of the experiment the following: "Even-numbered questions from number twenty-four on are not worth any points. You can skip these questions without losing any points." This instruction was presented on paper to participants to read, and the experimenter also read through these instructions with each participant to maximize the comprehension of the instruction. As before, the question number and remaining time appeared in the top-left corner of the screen, and the keys available for the participants to press were listed on the left side of the screen. Note that now the "A (skip)" key is listed among the available keys and was listed for every single question (Fig. 14). There were no visual cues during the experiment to remind participants which questions they were allowed to skip. Thus, participants needed to remember to use the opportunity to skip when the applicable questions were reached.

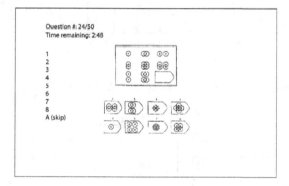

**Fig. 14.** Trial screen for Experiment 5.

## 8.3   Results and Discussion

Participants in the time-poor condition almost unanimously exhausted their time budgets, while participants in the time-rich condition usually completed the experiment with some time to spare (Fig. 15a). The time-poor participants spent less time solving the Raven's Matrices than the time-rich participants [$t(88) = 13.33$, $p < .001$, $d = 2.81$]. They also completed significantly fewer trials than the time-rich participants [$t(88) = 10.14$, $p < .001$, $d = 2.14$] (Fig. 15b), and were significantly less accurate [$t(88) = 2.29$, $p = .02$, $d = .48$] (Fig. 15c). When accounting for the total amount of time spent on the task, the time-poor participants scored higher accuracy per minute than time-rich participants [$t(88) = 9.53$, $p < .001$, $d = 2.01$], suggesting that time scarcity enhancing performance on the focal task.

The time-poor participants on average skipped fewer questions than the time-rich participants [$t(88) = 2.52$, $p = .01$, $d = .53$] (Fig. 15d). However, this result is likely driven, at least in part, by the considerably smaller number of questions completed by the time-poor participants. Similarly, we found that fewer time-poor participants skipped at least once compared to the time-rich participants [$X^2(1,90) = 10.08$, $p < .01$] (Fig. 15e), but this could be due to the smaller number of possible skips experienced by the time-poor participants. Thus, we examined the skip efficiency defined as the number of questions skipped divided by the number of possible questions that could be skipped experienced by the participant. We found that the time-poor participants were less likely to skip than time-rich participants (two time-poor participants were excluded from this analysis due to failing to reach trial number twenty-four) [$t(86) = 2.01$,

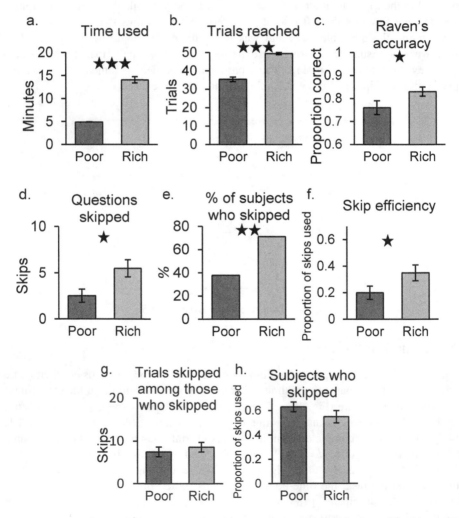

**Fig. 15.** Results for Experiment 5 (Error bars represent ±1 SEM. *$p < .05$, **$p < .01$, ***$p < .001$).

$p = .05$, $d = .43$] (Fig. 15f). This finding suggests that time scarcity impairs prospective memory performance. We should note that among participants who skipped at least once, there was no difference in the number of questions skipped between the time-poor and the time-rich participants [$t(40) = .59$, $p = .56$, $d = .19$] (Fig. 15g), or in skip efficiency [$t(40) = .76$, $p = .45$, $d = .26$] (Fig. 15h).

## 9  General Discussion

The goal of the current study was to examine how scarcity forces attentional trade-offs and influences memory encoding driven by such trade-offs. When operating under a limited financial budget, the poor focused more on the price information, compared to the rich (Experiment 1). This focus came with the neglect of other information in the environment, even if the information could be useful or beneficial to the poor (e.g., the discount). The attentional prioritization of prices also resulted in enhanced memory encoding of price information among the poor participants (Experiment 2). Likewise, the attentional prioritization of calories led to better memory encoding of calorie information among the calorie poor (Experiment 3). We also found that people under time scarcity were less likely to take advantage of a time-saving cue that appeared peripheral to the focal task (Experiment 4a), but nonetheless performed well on the focal task under the time constraint. This suggests that people under time scarcity are ironically less likely to notice opportunities to save time. This effect could be explained by a narrowing of spatial attention to the focal task (Experiments 4b & 4c). In the absence of an external cue, participants under time scarcity were less likely to remember to skip questions in the future (Experiment 5), suggesting that they failed to retrieve a cue from memory to execute actions at the right time.

These findings were particularly problematic for people under scarcity because the attentional neglect of resource-saving opportunities or the failure to remember to save resources could be detrimental, perpetuating the condition of scarcity and creating a vicious cycle of poverty. These cognitive impairments could explain a range of counter-productive behaviors observed in the low-income individuals, such as forgetting to follow instructions, or not signing up for public benefit programs. In addition, prospective memory errors can be seen by others as an indication of incompetence of the poor [5]. The present findings instead attribute the memory failures not to the poor individuals themselves but to the condition of scarcity. The current study provides useful implications for designing policies and programs to mitigate the impact of scarcity, such as the use of reminders, automatic enrolment, or setting the right default, to reduce the attentional and memory burdens in the poor.

The current findings provide a new perspective on how scarcity shapes the way people perceive and experience the external environment. While the perceptual experiences can be largely characterized by information overload, scarcity selectively orients people's attention to specific aspects of the environment. When operating with financial constraints, people automatically prioritize price-relevant information. Such prioritization facilitates memory encoding of these information, but crucially it comes with a cost, which is the neglect of other information in the environment.

The current study also reveals a painful irony of scarcity. People with limited resources were too focused on prices, such that they neglected the beneficial discount that could save money and alleviate the financial burden. This irony can help explain why low-income individuals sometimes engage in neglectful behaviors that are counter-productive (e.g., missing an appointment for a health checkup, or failure to sign up for benefit programs).

It is worth noting that the current experiments involved an artificial simulation of scarcity in the lab. In fact, just by randomly assigning people to receive a hypothetical small or large budget, we observed a strong effect of scarcity on attention and memory. Moreover, the participants in our experiments were not provided with real money, were not rewarded for frugality, and knowingly were not to receive any food from the menu. In the absence of possible consequences of their decisions, the poor participants still focused on task-relevant information and neglected a help to alleviate the condition of scarcity. This raises the possibility that, outside the lab when people operate with scarce resources and can face real consequences of their actions, the effects of scarcity on attention and cognition observed in this study may be amplified.

The current findings can help inform public policy and services targeting low-income populations. Among the OECD countries, enrollment in social assistance and public benefit programs is estimated to range between 40% and 80% [7]. Our current study provides a new explanation for the low participation rate. That is, the poor who are eligible for these programs fail to participate because of the attentional trade-offs under scarcity. Low-income individuals may need to focus on their financial challenges and deadlines under scarcity, and either are not aware of these benefit programs and services, or neglect the enrollment procedures. This attentional account is not the only factor that can explain the low participation rate, as there are many other social barriers and stigmas related to enrollment in assistance programs.

Given the attentional constraints under scarcity, we propose that social assistance and public benefit programs should be designed to avoid the attentional neglect in the poor under scarcity. It may be helpful to streamline assistance applications and services to make them more salient, more accessible, and easier to process for the poor. The amount of effort and attention required from the poor should be minimized to increase or maintain participation. Benefit programs and social services can also be made more salient by using prompts and reminders. This could be done through any messaging medium such as text-message or email, and could be effective in catching the attention of those living under scarcity. Based on our current findings, future research can design behavioral interventions to avoid attentional neglect in the poor. Future studies can also test the hypothesis that certain mindfulness training programs (e.g., EEG-enhanced biofeedback) would reduce the cost of scarcity-induced attentional bias, through a reduction of reactivity to scarcity-related thoughts and emotions.

**Acknowledgements.** We thank the research assistants at the Zhao Lab for assistance with data collection. We also thank Anuj Shah, Darko Odic, Alan Kingstone, Rebecca Todd, and the members in the Zhao Lab for helpful comments. This work was supported by NSERC Discovery Grant (RGPIN-2014-05617 to JZ), Sloan Foundation Grant (2014-6-16), Russell Sage Foundation Grant (98-15-01), the Canada Research Chairs program (to JZ), and the Leaders Opportunity Fund from the Canadian Foundation for Innovation (F14-05370 to JZ).

# References

1. Baddeley, A.D., Hitch, G.J.: Working memory. Psychol. Learn. Motiv. **8**, 47–89 (1974)
2. Chun, M.M.: Visual working memory as visual attention sustained internally over time. Neuropsychologia **49**, 1407–1409 (2011)
3. Chun, M.M., Golomb, J.D., Turk-Browne, N.B.: A taxonomy of external and internal attention. Annu. Rev. Psychol. **62**, 73–101 (2011)
4. Gersick, C.J.: Time and transition in work teams: toward a new model of group development. Acad. Manag. J. **31**(1), 9–41 (1988)
5. Graf, P.: Prospective memory: faulty brain, flaky person. Can. Psychol. **53**(1), 7 (2012)
6. Graf, P., Uttl, B., Dixon, R.: Prospective and retrospective memory in adulthood. In: Lifespan Development of Human Memory, pp. 257–282 (2002)
7. Hernanz, V., Malherbet, F., Pellizzari, M.: Take-up of welfare benefits in OECD countries: a review of the evidence. In: OECD Social, Employment and Migration Working Papers, no. 17. OECD Publishing, Paris (2004)
8. Hayden, B.Y., Gallant, J.L.: Combined effects of spatial and feature-based attention on responses of V4 neurons. Vis. Res. **49**, 1182–1187 (2009)
9. Jehee, J.F., Brady, D.K., Tong, F.: Attention improves encoding of task-relevant features in the human visual cortex. J. Neurosci. **31**, 8210–8219 (2011)
10. Loftus, E.F.: Memory for intentions: the effect of presence of a cue and interpolated activity. Psychon. Sci. **23**(4), 315–316 (1971)
11. Luck, S.J., Vogel, E.K.: The capacity of visual working memory for features and conjunctions. Nature **390**, 279–281 (1997)
12. Mani, A., Mullainathan, S., Shafir, E., Zhao, J.: Poverty impedes cognitive function. Science **341**, 976–980 (2013)
13. Miller, G.A.: The magical number seven, plus or minus two: some limits on our capacity for processing information. Psychol. Rev. **63**(2), 81 (1956)
14. Mullainathan, S., Shafir, E.: Scarcity: Why Having Too Little Means So Much. Henry Holt and Company, New York (2013)
15. Pashler, H., Johnston, J.C., Ruthruff, E.: Attention and performance. Annu. Rev. Psychol. **52**, 629–651 (2001)
16. Raven, J.: The Raven's progressive matrices: change and stability over culture and time. Cogn. Psychol. **41**(1), 1–48 (2000)
17. Rock, I., Gutman, D.: The effect of inattention on form perception. J. Exp. Psychol. Hum. Percept. Perform. **7**, 275 (1981)
18. Shah, A.K., Mullainathan, S., Shafir, E.: Some consequences of having too little. Science **338**, 682–685 (2012)
19. Shah, A.K., Shafir, E., Mullainathan, S.: Scarcity frames value. Psychol. Sci. **26**(4), 402–412 (2015)
20. Simons, D.J., Chabris, C.F.: Gorillas in our midst: sustained inattentional blindness for dynamic events. Perception **28**, 1059–1074 (1999)
21. Strayer, D.L., Drews, F.A., Johnston, W.A.: Cell phone-induced failures of visual attention during simulated driving. J. Exp. Psychol. Appl. **9**, 23–32 (2003)
22. Wright, P.: The harassed decision maker: time pressures, distractions, and the use of evidence. J. Appl. Psychol. **59**(5), 555–561 (1974)

# Adaptive Learning Systems

# Towards a Dynamic Selection
# and Configuration of Adaptation Strategies
# in Augmented Cognition

Sven Fuchs[(✉)] and Jessica Schwarz

Department of Human-Systems Engineering,
Fraunhofer Institute for Communication,
Information Processing and Ergonomics,
Fraunhoferstraße 20, 53343 Wachtberg, Germany
{sven.fuchs,jessica.schwarz}@fkie.fraunhofer.de

**Abstract.** Most Augmented Cognition systems use physiological measures to detect critical cognitive states and trigger adaptation strategies to address the problem state and restore or augment performance. Without accounting for context, however, it is likely that adaptations are triggered or withdrawn at inopportune moments, potentially disrupting or confusing the user. We have developed an approach to dynamic adaptation management that processes task and operator state indicators to dynamically select and configure context-sensitive adaptation strategies in real time. This dynamic approach is expected to avoid much of the potential cognitive cost associated with adaptations. We provide an overview of our conceptual approach, describe a proof-of-concept implementation, and summarize user feedback and initial lessons-learned from a small survey.

**Keywords:** Adaptive systems · Augmented Cognition · Cognitive state assessment · Dynamic adaptation management

## 1 Introduction

Interaction is a dynamic adaptation of behavior and actions between actors. It requires effective communication, cooperation, and coordination to adequately interpret the other's goals, expectations, and reactions. Humans possess such abilities and naturally apply these in social interaction, machines do not. But in its attempt to revolutionize the interaction between humans and machines, the field of Augmented Cognition (Aug-Cog) has long recognized the need for technology to adapt to the state of the operator.

Most AugCog systems use physiological measures to detect critical cognitive states and trigger adaptation strategies to address the problem state and restore or augment performance. However, mere detection of a critical state may indicate a need for adaptation – for example to address excessive workload – but reveals little about the type of adaptation that would be appropriate with respect to the given situation [1]. Also, adaptation strategies in demonstrated AugCog systems are often hard-coded, i.e., whenever a critical operator state X is detected, the machine triggers a predetermined strategy $A_X$ to address the problem. But without accounting for context, it is likely that adaptations are triggered or withdrawn at inopportune moments, potentially disrupting

D.D. Schmorrow and C.M. Fidopiastis (Eds.): AC 2017, Part II, LNAI 10285, pp. 101–115, 2017.
DOI: 10.1007/978-3-319-58625-0_7

or confusing the user. The associated cognitive costs may include task switching issues, situation awareness problems, and workload increases. In these cases, adaptations may even have a negative impact on performance, outweighing the benefit of adaptation altogether. This inconsiderate application of adaptation strategies has been labeled 'brute force mitigation' [2]. As a first step to addressing this problem, we have identified various aspects of where and how context sensitivity is essential for effective adaptation in AugCog systems:

1. When assessing operator state, it is important to realize that there are various states that have been found to be interdependent [3]. Adaptation based on a single problem state may lead to oversimplification by addressing the symptom rather than the cause. For example, attention may be modulated by workload, fatigue, and even the emotional state, but depending on the modulating state, attention may be impacted in very different ways. For an adaptation strategy to be effective, context is necessary to understand the relationship between the detected problem state and related states.
2. Cognitive states are hypothetical constructs (cf. [4]) that cannot be manipulated directly. To be able to impact cognitive state X, adaptation strategy $A_X$ requires an appropriate environmental variable for manipulation. For example, a plausible way to mitigate high workload could be to reduce the number of simultaneous tasks. However, this strategy will only work if the number of tasks is sufficiently high. If task load is low and workload is up for other reasons (e.g. lack of experience), this strategy will not be effective. Thus, context information is essential for determining the adequacy of an adaptation strategy.
3. The adaptation should be capable of adapting itself to the situation and the user [5]. As situation and context evolve, a once adequate adaptation strategy may become inadequate. For example, brute force adaptation may automate a task the user has already started to perform or attempt to restore global situation awareness by shifting the user's focus away from a new high-priority task.

## 2    Advanced Dynamic Adaptation Management (ADAM)

To overcome challenges with brute force adaptation, we have developed an "Advanced Dynamic Adaptation Management" component (ADAM). Instead of triggering a static adaptation $A_X$ to respond to a critical cognitive state X, the goal of ADAM is to select, configure, and trigger adequate adaptation when and where needed.

Dynamic adaptation management requires extensive amounts of task and user context. Therefore, we also developed a diagnostic engine – our Realtime ASsessment of Multidimensional User State (RASMUS) – that implements a multidimensional approach to user state assessment. RASMUS diagnoses up to six cognitive and emotional problem states, of which three cognitive states – workload, attention, and fatigue – were recently validated. RASMUS evaluates a multitude of individual and task-related indicators known to impact these cognitive states, as well as physiological and behavioral reactions. Based on this information, it returns user states assumed to be critical and reports which indicators have likely contributed to this state on a second-by-second basis. RASMUS diagnostics enable technology to detect not only when the human operator's performance declines and what cognitive states are insufficient, but also indicates contextual factors (system state, task state, user state as indicated by physiological and behavioral metrics) that may have contributed to the situation. More detail on RASMUS is provided in another article within this volume [6].

ADAM assumes that declines in performance are symptoms caused by underlying cognitive problem states. For example, task omission may be caused by excessive workload, a lack of attention, or even motivational issues. Accordingly, ADAM assumes that task performance can be restored by addressing that cognitive problem state through adaptation. According to Breton and Bossé [7], humans should receive support when their "cognitive capabilities are not sufficient to adequately perform the task" (pp. 1–4). Thus, ADAM assumes a need for adaptation when a performance decrement occurs in conjunction with at least one critical cognitive state. The condition of a performance decrement was included to allow operators to self-adapt to the problem state, considering that "having an adaptive system working together with an adaptive operator will likely be unsuccessful. An adaptive system is more likely to work successfully when it starts reallocating tasks as soon as the operator is no longer able to adapt properly to changing task demands" ([8], p. 10). Also, intervening too early may favor complacency ("based on an unjustified assumption of satisfactory system state," [9], p. 23) and hinder development of resilience and coping strategies.

For adaptation to be triggered, ADAM also requires that the pool of adaptation strategies includes a strategy that is (a) capable of addressing the cognitive problem state and (b) suitable in the given context. For example, it is only possible to automate tasks if enough tasks are present). ADAM then draws from a pool of candidate strategies and configures them based on RASMUS diagnostic output. This dynamic approach is expected to avoid much of the potential cognitive cost associated with brute force adaptations. Once a need for adaptation is detected, dynamic adaptation management involves five steps (Fig. 1) that are explained in detail below.

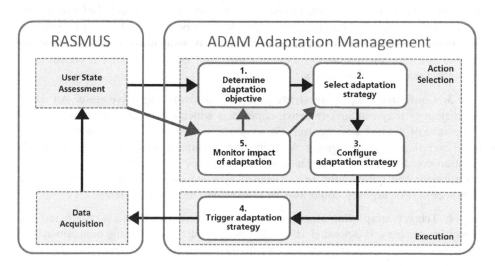

**Fig. 1.** Five steps of dynamic adaptation management

**Step 1: Determine an adaptation objective.** Adaptation objectives are rather abstract descriptions of cognitive manipulations that describe how a certain cognitive problem state could be manipulated in a way that it is no longer critical. ADAM will select an adequate adaptation objective based on the diagnosed problem state. For example, when a performance problem occurred along with a state of high workload, ADAM's objective may be to decrease task load to address the problem. In contrast, if the performance problem coincided with fatigue, a further decrease in task load would be counterproductive and ADAM may instead attempt to increase operator activation and arousal. There may be different strategies available for achieving each objective.

**Step 2: Select adaptation strategy.** From a pool of available adaptations, ADAM selects a strategy that is designed to address the adaptation objective and that is suitable under current conditions.

Each strategy is associated with at least one adaptation objective. All adaptations able to achieve the adaptation objective determined in Step 1 become candidate strategies. Known prerequisites for all candidate strategies are then evaluated to determine the best strategy under current circumstances. Given that adaptation cannot directly affect cognitive states, one prerequisite is the availability of a manipulable variable that is related to the cognitive state to be addressed. Moreover, it is possible that other conditions must be met in order for a strategy to work. If prerequisites are not fulfilled, the strategy is deemed unsuitable in the given context and further strategies from the pool will be evaluated for their suitability.

As an example for strategy-specific prerequisites, consider that RASMUS diagnostics report a decline in performance in conjunction with critical workload. RASMUS also indicates that a high number of simultaneous tasks contributed to the critical workload condition. A rather intuitive adaptation objective in this case is to decrease workload by reducing the number of simultaneous tasks. Available candidate adaptation strategies to address this objective are automation and task sequencing. Both require multiple tasks to be simultaneously active (which is the case here). Adaptive automation would take over certain tasks until performance is restored but would only be useful if a certain minimum number of tasks must be processed at that time and at least one of these can be automated. In contrast, task sequencing would schedule the tasks to distribute them more evenly over time, but is only appropriate if certain tasks have a lower priority than others.

**Step 3: Configure adaptation strategy to suit task and cognitive state.** An adaptation strategy may contain contextual parameters which can be used to tailor it further to the state of the task and the user. For example, a task sequencing strategy could be based on task priority or urgency. A cueing strategy aimed at refocusing the operator's attention could consider his current focus to determine cue location or select the best modality for cue presentation (e.g. visual if eyes are on-screen, auditive if eyes are off-screen). Task urgency could also be used to determine cue salience.

**Step 4: Trigger adaptation strategy.** Once dynamically selected and configured, the adaptation strategy is activated in the information display, altering human-machine interaction in a way that impacts the cognitive problem state and serves the adaptation objective.

**Step 5: Monitor the impact of the adaptation.** Monitoring the effects of adaptation with respect to task performance and cognitive state changes will determine whether and how adaptation should be continued. If the adaptation objective was accomplished and the underlying problem states are no longer present, it is important to withdraw adaptation, as inappropriate continuation could have negative effects on the operator and task performance. For example, an inadequate adaptation may occupy cognitive resources, interrupt a high priority task, or refocus the operator's attention away from it. There are four possible monitoring results with different implications for adaptation management (Table 1).

**Table 1.** Implications of monitoring the impact of an adaptation

|  | Performance restored | Performance remains critical |
|---|---|---|
| Targeted cognitive state not critical | **Withdraw adaptation** <br><br> The adaptation was successful and there is no longer a need for adaptation | **Change adaptation strategy** <br><br> Although the adaptation successfully altered the targeted cognitive state, it did not affect performance. In this case, consider using a different adaptation strategy (cf. Step 2) |
| Targeted cognitive state remains critical | **Withdraw adaptation** <br><br> Although the adaptation strategy has not been able to impact the critical cognitive state, there is no longer a need for adaptation, as long as performance remains adequate. This result may indicate successful self-adaptation of the user | **Change adaptation objective** <br><br> The adaptation did not have the desired effect on cognitive state and performance. This may indicate that another cognitive state was the underlying reason for the performance drop. If other cognitive states were diagnosed as critical, adaptation should target a different cognitive state, which may have a better effect on performance |

## 3   Proof-of-Concept Implementation

### 3.1   Task Environment

For an initial demonstration of ADAM's capabilities, an adaptation manager was implemented for a naval anti-air-warfare simulation (Fig. 2). The simulation includes four tasks that were simplified for learnability but designed to maintain the essential cognitive demands of the real-world task.

During the simulation the operator is to perform all occurring tasks with a focus on keeping the Identification Safety Range (ISR) around the ownship clear of threats. Tasks with different priorities (detailed in Table 2) occur at scripted times throughout the scenario. In the case of multiple simultaneous tasks, users were instructed to perform higher priority tasks first. RASMUS diagnostics report an instance of critical performance whenever a task is not completed within the time limits indicated in Table 2.

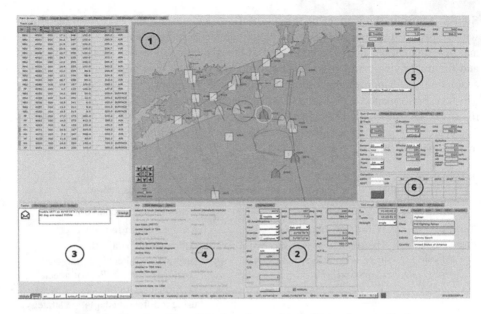

**Fig. 2.** User interface of the experimental task (Color figure online)

**Table 2.** Task descriptions and properties (numbers in parentheses refer to display areas marked in Fig. 2)

| Task | Description | Priority | Time limit |
|------|-------------|----------|------------|
| Identify | Any unidentified contacts in the tactical display area (TDA; 1) must be identified as friendly, neutral, or hostile based on certain criteria presented in the Track Attribute Control (TAC) panel (2). If identified tracks change their behavior in a way that changes the criteria, they must be reassessed and identification reassigned if necessary | 100 (outside ISR), 300 (within ISR) | 60 s |
| Create NRTT | From time to time, envelopes will appear in a message panel (3), announcing non-real-time tracks (NRTT) that must be added to the TDA by selecting "new track" in (4), placing it in the TDA and entering the corresponding track data into the respective text boxes in the TAC panel (2) | 200 | 90 s |
| Warn | Contacts identified as hostile must be warned using the communications panel (5) as soon as they enter the Identification Safety Range (ISR; large blue circle around ownship) | 400 | 30 s |
| Engage | Contacts identified as hostile that have been warned must be engaged using the gun control panel (6) as soon as they enter Weapon Range (WR; small red circle around ownship) | 500 | 10 s |

In addition to performance, three cognitive states are monitored in the proof-of-concept system:

1. (high) workload
2. (incorrect) attentional focus
3. passive task-related (TR) fatigue (cf. [10])

These cognitive states, further detailed in [6], were chosen because of their relevance to the task and because RASMUS diagnostics were successfully validated for these states in a recent experiment [11]. Along with every critical cognitive state, RASMUS reports the status of contextual indicators that contributed to the state diagnosis. Table 3 shows the contextual indicators considered for cognitive state detection.

**Table 3.** Contextual indicators associated with cognitive problem states

| High workload | Incorrect attentional focus | Passive TR fatigue |
|---|---|---|
| Number of tasks high | Number of tasks > 1 | Number of tasks low |
| Click frequency high | Highest priority contact not selected | Click frequency low |
| Heart rate variability low | | Heart rate variability high |
| Pupil size high | | Pupil size low |
| Respiration rate high | | Respiration rate low |

Using this diagnostic setup, the dynamic adaptation management must distinguish between the five critical state combinations depicted in Fig. 3 to adapt human-machine interaction in a context-adequate manner. High workload and passive TR fatigue are mutually exclusive; however, attentional problems can certainly occur in conjunction with the two other states.

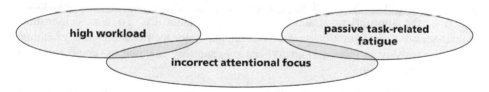

**Fig. 3.** Five critical state combinations to be considered by dynamic adaptation management

### 3.2  Adaptations

In our proof-of-concept system, the adaptation objective to be pursued is determined based on cognitive problem states reported at the time of critical performance. To demonstrate dynamic selection of an adaptation based on diagnosed cognitive state problems, an adequate adaptation objective was formulated for each cognitive problem state (Fig. 4).

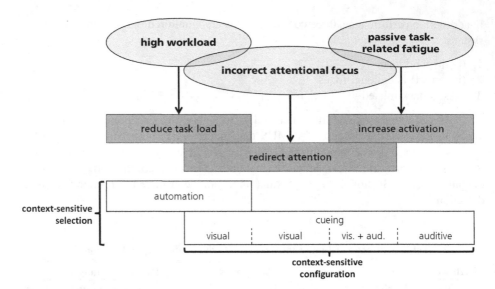

**Fig. 4.** Context-sensitive selection and configuration of adaptation strategies in the prototype system

- The adaptation objective for high workload is reduction of task load. This can be achieved, for example, by temporarily reducing the number of tasks to be processed.
- The adaptation objective for incorrect attentional focus is to redirect the user's attention to the highest priority task.
- The adaptation objective for passive TR fatigue is activation of the operator to combat his passivity. The activation of the user can be accomplished by increasing arousal.

When performance decrements occur, the system dynamically selects from two implemented strategies – automation and cueing. Depending on the adaptation objective, the appropriate strategy is invoked dynamically. To also demonstrate context-sensitive configuration, task context and operator metrics are used to configure the cueing strategy in three variants: visual cue, auditory cue, and the combination of visual and auditory cue.

**Automation.** Automation changes the extent of human involvement in the task by taking over tasks previously performed by a human operator. Automation is particularly helpful when operator workload is high. Under low workload conditions, however, it may have undesirable effects such as boredom and fatigue [12]. Therefore, automation can be used to address the adaptation objective for the high workload (i.e. reduce task load) but is unsuitable strategy to address the other adaptation objectives.

For our proof-of-concept system we chose to implement simple dual mode automation: Under normal circumstances, the operator is responsible for all tasks. Only when high workload is diagnosed along with critical performance, all low priority tasks (identification of contacts outside the ISR) are automated. This frees up cognitive resources that can be used to perform higher-priority tasks. It has also been recommended that safety-critical tasks remain with the human to maintain situation awareness [13]. To prevent automation errors and avoid complacency effects (e.g., [14]), all automated identifications are marked with a badge (Fig. 5) and must be manually verified by the user for the badge to disappear. In high workload situations, the user can thus focus on the most important tasks; when less taxed, he can verify the automatically assigned identities, distributing task load more evenly. Future iterations of the automation strategy could be enabled to dynamically select the task to be automated and choose between different levels of automation.

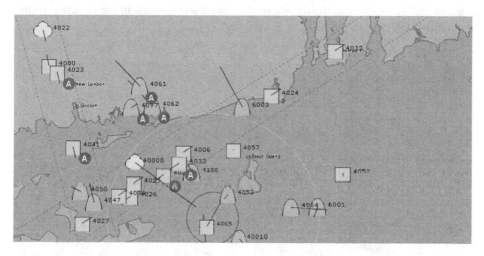

**Fig. 5.** Automated identification; contacts with automatically assigned identities are marked with red badges (Color figure online)

**Cueing.** This strategy manipulates the user's attention by enhancing the information presentation. Often, attention is shifted by increasing the saliency of relevant information objects. Cues are not limited to the visual modality, but can also be implemented as auditive, tactile, or multimodal cues, as well as in different levels of intrusiveness to enable context-sensitive configuration. However, cueing should also be used with caution, as cued attention may be narrowed to such an extent that other high-priority information may not be perceived [15]. Also, task interruption, as initiated by refocused attention, has unfavorable effects on stress and performance, in particular with regard to complex or cognitively demanding tasks [16, 17].

To demonstrate context-sensitive configuration of an adaptation strategy two cueing variants – visual and auditive cueing – were implemented and are activated depending on the adaptation objective.

Passive TR fatigue, often caused by prolonged monotonous tasks, can lead to performance problems if the operator drifts off or becomes distracted. In this case, the adaptation objective is to address the passivity by activating the user. A visual cue may not be effective here as it may not even be perceived. Thus, if a performance problem occurs along with passive TR fatigue, an auditory cue in the form of an intrusive alarm tone is triggered to indicate the presence of an unnoticed task and increase the operator's arousal.

In contrast, the occurrence of a performance problem along with an incorrect attentional focus indicates that the operator is attentive, albeit not focused on the most important task. Thus, the adaptation objective is to refocus the operator's attention to the highest-priority task. In this case, use of a visual cue is appropriate because it can be assumed that the user's attention is directed at the task environment and all tasks in the simulation concern visual information objects. The visual cue indicates the presence and location of a task more important than the one currently attended to. It consists of an arrow that is attached to the mouse pointer and always points in the direction of the information object with the highest priority task (Fig. 6).

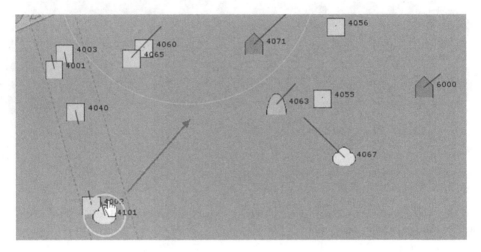

**Fig. 6.** Cueing (visual configuration); the arrow points to the highest-priority contact (4071) (Color figure online)

### 3.3    Monitoring of Adaptation Effects

After an adaptation was triggered, performance and cognitive state criteria are continuously monitored to examine whether a strategy was successful in achieving the associated adaptation objective. In the proof-of-concept implementation, monitoring results determine the withdrawal of adaptation strategies.

In the case of automation, new contacts are no longer automatically identified when the tasks that caused the performance problem no longer exist or when workload is no longer critically high. However, the identity of automatically identified tracks and their badges are preserved in order to avoid inconsistencies in the information presentation. Reversing automatically assigned identities to "unknown" would cause a sudden increase in task load which could lead to undesired oscillation effects in the adaptation management [18].

The visual cue has achieved its objective of shifting the operator's attention when the contact with the highest priority task is selected. It is then deactivated. The objective of the auditory cue (i.e. activate the operator and alert him to the presence of a task) is achieved when the user resumes task processing. Consequently, the audible alarm is turned off as soon as the user selects a relevant information object.

## 4   User Feedback

To obtain initial feedback and user insights regarding the effectiveness and adequacy of the dynamic adaptation, we asked three subjects (m36, m34, f31) that had already participated in our validation experiment to perform the task and then complete a survey.

Participants were not informed about the functionality of the adaptive features. It was only mentioned that under certain circumstances the system will automatically identify contacts and participants were asked to manually confirm automatic identifications as soon as workload permits. After performing the task, participants completed a questionnaire to assess their subjective impression of effectiveness and adequacy of adaptations. Further questions asked for potential improvements and other qualitative feedback. Due to the small number of participants, the results were only evaluated qualitatively.

### 4.1   Occurrence and Perception of Adaptations

Only two subjects triggered all implemented adaptations. One subject did not experience an auditory cue because no performance problems occurred along with diagnosed fatigue. Although subjects were not informed about the adaptive features, they recognized all adaptations. However, two subjects overestimated, and one subject underestimated how often adaptations were triggered (Table 4).

**Table 4.** Number of adaptations triggered (subject estimates in parenthesis)

| Subject | Total | Auto ID | Cue (visual) | Cue (auditive) |
|---------|-------|---------|--------------|----------------|
| 1 | 10 (14) | 2 (6) | 6 (6) | 2 (2) |
| 2 | 9 (25) | 5 (15) | 4 (10) | 0 (0) |
| 3 | 10 (7) | 2 (1) | 5 (8) | 1 (1) |

### 4.2   Perceived Effects on Performance

Subjects perceived the effects of adaptation differently: One subject felt that adaptations generally had a positive effect on performance and the presence of the adaptations for the overall task was helpful. One subject perceived some aspects enhanced and others impaired performance. One respondent indicated that the adaptations in his opinion had no effect on performance.

Feedback can be further differentiated when considering the individual strategies (Table 5). None of the participants found the automation strategy disturbing, two people rated it helpful. The visual cue was perceived as very helpful by two subjects, while one perceived it as "somewhat disturbing". One person perceived the alarm sound as "somewhat disturbing" but pointed out that this impression was linked to the specific signal tone (similar to an alarm clock buzzer). Also, in this case the auditory cue was triggered when an unidentified contact was overlooked in a noncritical location. The respondent criticized the high intrusiveness despite the low priority of the task, and suggested that tone and volume should be tailored to the priority of the task.

**Table 5.** Ratings of perceived effects on performance

|  | Very helpful | Somewhat helpful | Neither helpful nor disturbing | Somewhat disturbing | Very disturbing |
|---|---|---|---|---|---|
| Auto ID | ● | ■ | ◆ |  |  |
| Cue (visual) | ■● |  |  | ◆ |  |
| Cue (auditive) |  |  | ◆ | ■ |  |

■ Subject 1 ● Subject 2 ◆ Subject 3

### 4.3 Appropriateness of Adaptation Timing

Due to the cognitive costs associated with inadequate adaptation, an important aspect of adaptation management is adequate timing. Adaptations are only useful in situations when the benefits outweigh these costs. The participants' overall impression was that the timing was appropriate (Table 6). With regard to individual strategies, the vast majority of ratings indicated appropriate timing. The "very inappropriate" rating for the auditory cue followed a programming bug that made it impossible to engage a hostile contact. Although the subject had performed the task correctly, the system diagnosed a performance problem and triggered the auditory cue. The same subject rated the timing of the automatic identification "somewhat inappropriate", commenting that he was not aware of the adaptation and was surprised when he noticed the changes. Considering that automation is only invoked under high workload conditions, it is likely that workload-induced attentional tunneling [19] inhibited the perception of automated changes in peripheral contacts.

**Table 6.** Ratings of perceived appropriateness of adaptation timing

|  | Very appropriate | Somewhat appropriate | Somewhat inappropriate | Very inappropriate |
|---|---|---|---|---|
| Overall impression | ● | ■◆ |  |  |
| Auto ID | ● | ■ | ◆ |  |
| Cue (visual) | ● | ■◆ |  |  |
| Cue (auditive) |  | ■ |  | ◆* |

■ Subject 1 ● Subject 2 ◆ Subject 3
* Cue was triggered unnecessarily due to a programming bug.

## 4.4  Appropriateness of Adaptation Withdrawal

Another question addressed the withdrawal of the adaptation. Since the automated identification of contacts was not reversed for consistency reasons, withdrawal could not be assessed for this strategy. For the remaining strategies, two participants found the duration of adaptation to be appropriate (Table 7). One person indicated a positive overall impression but rated the withdrawal of the cues as somewhat inappropriate. In the case of the visual cue, the subject felt that the arrow disappeared too quickly.

**Table 7.**  Ratings of perceived appropriateness of adaptation withdrawal

|  | Very appropriate | Somewhat appropriate | Somewhat inappropriate | Very inappropriate |
|---|---|---|---|---|
| Overall impression | ● | ■◆ |  |  |
| Auto ID | n/a |  |  |  |
| Cue (visual) | ● | ■ | ◆ |  |
| Cue (auditive) |  | ■ | ◆* |  |

■ Subject 1 ● Subject 2 ◆ Subject 3
\* Cue was triggered unnecessarily due to a programming bug.

## 5  Conclusions

With our prototype implementation of context-sensitive adaptation, we were able to demonstrate the concept and feasibility of near real-time selection and configuration of adaptation strategies and have thus made important steps towards a truly dynamic adaptation management. Our proof-of-concept implementation was limited in that only one adaptation objective was assigned to each critical cognitive state, and only one adaptation strategy was implemented for each adaptation objective, but conceptually ADAM supports multiple adaptation objectives per problem state and multiple strategies per adaptation objective. Future work will expand the prototype system to include more adaptation objectives and strategies, consider additional diagnostic results in the selection of adaptations, and enable truly dynamic configuration of strategies in real-time. Once these enhancements are implemented, we plan to conduct empirical evaluations to validate the effectiveness of dynamic adaptation management and quantify the effects on the performance of operators.

Dynamically invoked adaptations were generally triggered as expected and predominantly well received by survey participants. Some characteristics perceived as disruptive must be attributed to a technical problem; others can be addressed by slight changes to the strategies or trigger rules. Despite the small number of survey participants, initial lessons learned can be drawn from the results and the qualitative feedback we received: Although participants mostly felt that adaptations were triggered at appropriate times, two subjects noted that their occurrence was sometimes perceived as random. It was not intuitively clear to them why and under what circumstances certain adaptations appeared. This demonstrates a need for providing users of adaptive systems with sufficient understanding of the system's behavior. Another lesson learned is that perception and appraisal of adaptations is very individual: an adaptation praised as particularly helpful by one subject may be perceived as disturbing by another. If the system was provided with such personal preferences, this information could be used just like other contextual information to further individualize adaptation.

The combination of multidimensional user state diagnostics and dynamic adaptation management offers potential far beyond what was described in this paper. Both components were developed as generalizable concepts that we seek to apply to different application areas. We expect particular benefits for the operation of highly automated task environments and safety-critical systems where performance decrements and critical cognitive states may have serious consequences. The approach could also be used for adaptive training applications to individualize training on the fly based on real-time context information about the task, trainee state, and performance.

# References

1. Fuchs, S., Hale, K.S., Stanney, K.M., Berka, C., Levendowski, D., Juhnke, J.: Physiological sensors cannot effectively drive system mitigation alone. In: Schmorrow, D.D., Stanney, K.M., Reeves, L.M. (eds.) Foundations of Augmented Cognition, 2nd edn, pp. 193–200. Strategic Analysis Inc, Arlington (2006)
2. Stanney, K., Reeves, L.: Mitigation strategies and performance effects. White Paper Outbrief from a Working Session at Improving Warfighter Information Intake Under Stress, AugCog PI Meeting, 2–4 March 2005, Chantilly, VA (2005)
3. Schwarz, J., Fuchs, S., Flemisch, F.: Towards a more holistic view on user state assessment in adaptive human-computer interaction. In: Proceedings of the IEEE International Conference on Systems, Man, and Cybernetics, pp. 1247–1253. IEEE Press, New York (2014)
4. MacCorquadale, K., Meehl, P.E.: On a distinction between hypothetical constructs and intervening variables. Psychol. Rev. **55**, 95–107 (1948)
5. Fuchs, S., Schwarz, J., Flemisch, F.O.: Two steps back for one step forward: revisiting augmented cognition principles from a perspective of (social) system theory. In: Schmorrow, D.D., Fidopiastis, C.M. (eds.) AC 2014. LNCS (LNAI), vol. 8534, pp. 114–124. Springer, Cham (2014). doi:10.1007/978-3-319-07527-3_11
6. Schwarz, J., Fuchs, S.: Multidimensional real-time assessment of user state and performance to trigger dynamic system adaptation. In: Schmorrow, D.D., Fidopiastis, C.M. (eds.) AC 2017. LNCS (LNAI), vol. 10285, pp. 383–398. Springer, Cham (2017)
7. Breton, R., Bossé, É.: The cognitive costs and benefits of automation. In: The Role of Humans in Intelligent and Automated Systems. Proceedings of the RTO Human Factors and Medicine Panel (HFM) Symposium (RTO-MP-088). NATO RTO, Neuilly-sur-Seine, France (2003). doi:10.14339/RTO-MP-088
8. Veltman, H.J.A., Jansen, C.: The adaptive operator. In: Vincenzi, D.A., Mouloua, M., Hancock, P. (eds.) Human Performance, Situation Awareness, and Automation: Current Research and Trends. Lawrence Erlbaum Associates, vol. 2, pp. 7–10. Mahwah, London (2004)
9. Billings, C.E., Lauber, J.K., Funkhouser, H., Lyman, G., Huff, E.M.: NASA Aviation Safety Reporting System (Technical report TM-X-3445), NASA Ames Research Center Moffett Field, CA (1976)

10. May, J.F., Baldwin, C.L.: Driver fatigue: the importance of identifying causal factors of fatigue when considering detection and countermeasure technologies. Transp. Res. Part F: Psychol. Behav. **12**(3), 218–224 (2009)
11. Fuchs, S., Schwarz, J., Werger, A.: Adaptive Mensch-Maschine-Interaktion: Ganzheitliche Onlinediagnose und Systemadaptierung. Final project report (grant no. E/E4BX/EA192/CF215. Fraunhofer FKIE, Wachtberg, Germany (2016)
12. Kaber, D.B., Riley, J.M., Tan, K.W., Endsley, M.R.: On the design of adaptive automation for complex systems. Int. J. Cogn. Ergon. **5**(1), 37–57 (2001)
13. Arciszewski, H.F.R., de Greef, T.E., van Delft, J.H.: Adaptive automation in a naval combat management system. IEEE Trans. Syst. Man and Cybern. - Part A: Syst. Hum. **39**(6), 1188–1199 (2009). doi:10.1109/TSMCA.2009.2026428
14. Parasuraman, R., Molloy, R., Singh, I.L.: Performance consequences of automation-induced complacency. Int. J. Aviat. Psychol. **3**(1), 1–23 (1993). doi:10.1207/s15327108ijap0301_1
15. Wickens, C.D., Conejo, R., Gempler, K.: Unreliable automated attention cueing for air-ground targeting and traffic maneuvering. In: Proceedings of the Human Factors and Ergonomics Society 43rd Annual Meeting, pp. 21–25. HFES, Santa Monica (1999)
16. Gopher, D., Armony, L., Greenspan, Y.: Switching tasks and attention policies. J. Exp. Psychol. Gen. **129**, 229–308 (2000)
17. McFarlane, D.C.: Comparison of four primary methods for coordinating the interruption of people in human-computer interaction. Hum.-Comput. Interact. **17**(1), 63–139 (2002)
18. Stanney, K.M., Schmorrow, D.D., Johnston, M., Fuchs, S., Jones, D., Hale, K.S., Ahmad, A., Young, P.: Augmented cognition: an overview. In: Durso, F.T. (ed.) Reviews of Human Factors and Ergonomics, vol. 5, pp. 195–224. HFES, Santa Monica (2009). doi:10.1518/155723409X448062
19. Wickens, C.D.: Attentional tunneling and task management. Technical report AHFD-05-01/NASA-05-10. NASA Ames Reseach Center, Moffett Field, CA (2005)

# Adaptive Training Across Simulations in Support of a Crawl-Walk-Run Model of Interaction

Benjamin Goldberg[1(✉)], Fleet Davis[2], Jennifer M. Riley[3], and Michael W. Boyce[1]

[1] U.S. Army Research Laboratory, Orlando, FL, USA
{benjamin.s.goldberg.civ,
michael.w.boycell.civ}@mail.mil
[2] Humanproof, Washington, D.C., USA
fleet.davis@humanproof.com
[3] Design Interactive, Orlando, FL, USA
jennifer.riley@designiteractive.net

**Abstract.** In this paper we present a model of training interaction based on tenets of intelligent tutoring systems and skill development and acquisition. We present a Crawl-Walk-Run approach to training management that associates with the utility of complimentary simulation environments to build a set of skills across multiple exercises and scenarios. In addition, we highlight the role adaptive training technologies can play in this model of interaction, along with technologies being developed to support the authoring and configuration of these experiences. The work presented within is based on the Generalized Intelligent Framework for Tutoring (GIFT) and discusses the development of tools and methods to author and deliver adaptive training content grounded in skill development.

**Keywords:** Authoring · Gift Wrap · Adaptive training · Assessment

## 1 Introduction

The concept of adaptive training involves the use of Artificial Intelligence (AI) tools and methods to augment a learning experience based on the needs of a given individual, or in future instances, a set of individuals (i.e., team). This entails tracking what an individual knows and doesn't know within a domain and using that information to guide the training experience. These automated techniques are intended to provide personalized training in the absence of live instruction through modeling approaches that balance challenge levels and recognize errors and misconceptions during a practice scenario. These models are also used to invoke feedback and guidance strategies designed to aid a learner in overcoming an impasse. Using a simple analogy, adaptive training systems apply AI methods to mimic the interactions conducted by an effective human tutor engaging with single learner.

Adaptive training programs are commonly referred to as Intelligent Tutoring Systems (ITS), with ITS examples dating back to the 1970s [1]. There are notable

© Springer International Publishing AG 2017
D.D. Schmorrow and C.M. Fidopiastis (Eds.): AC 2017, Part II, LNAI 10285, pp. 116–130, 2017.
DOI: 10.1007/978-3-319-58625-0_8

success stories looking at the effect ITSs have when compared against more traditional classroom methods [1, 2]. However, many of these success stories associate with well-defined domains (e.g., physics, algebra, computer programming) and are mostly confined to stove-piped training environments. A current goal of the U.S. Army Research Laboratory (ARL) is investigating how to extend these technologies into military relevant domains through the development of the Generalized Intelligent Framework for Tutoring (GIFT) [3]. As such, it is important to conceptualize how ITS methods fit within the context of a unified Army training model that manages skill acquisition through identifying approaches to leverage multiple systems and simulations. This requires approaches that leverage ITS methods to track progress and manage interaction at the individual level. In this paper, we present current work surrounding the development of GIFT, a generalized ITS environment in support of a skill acquisition model of training. We present the foundations associated with ITS implementation in a military context and provide a breakdown of technologies required to create this type of training spectrum.

## 1.1   Training Foundations

A common research question is: How can ITS tools and methods be applied in a training continuum that incorporates multiple training platforms and events to progress an individual from novice to expert in a single domain? Before a solution can be devised, it is important to discuss the theory and foundations of military based training. In the context of this paper, we present training foundations as they pertain to simulation-based exercises devised in support of skill development and application. The majority of training practices adhere to commonly known theories of skill acquisition that associate with phases of application (e.g., cognitive phase, associative phase, and autonomous phase) [4, 5]. In each phase, varying instructional approaches and training exercises are organized to assist an individual in developing an understanding of not only what to do, but also an understanding of how to do it. Anderson's ACT-R* [6] distinguishes these processes as either containing declarative information associated with the domain, or procedural information that associates with performing a task as they adhere to the declarative constraints of the task environment.

The goal of an effective training program is to the balance the interplay of declarative and procedural knowledge training, so as to accelerate an individual's sequence through the phases of skill acquisition. This interplay is based on a Crawl-Walk-Run (CWR) model of interaction [7, 8], where training programs are designed to: (1) establish the rules and requirements associated with task performance (Crawl), (2) provide opportunities for skill development through scenario exercises with performance monitoring and real-time coaching (Walk), and (3) provide opportunities for trainees to execute tasks based on their ability with little instructor intervention (Run) [8]. Taking it a step further, we propose an additional layer of abstraction to the CWR model by including the sequencing of training exercises across complimentary simulation platforms (see Fig. 1). In these instances, you apply CWR pedagogical practices within each event, while using those individualized events to prepare that trainee for subsequent training interactions that build on one another.

**Fig. 1.** The CWR model of adaptive interaction applied across multiple simulation platforms

To reduce the cost and manpower associated with military training, simulation-based methods have been developed to compliment the training process, especially as they associate to the crawl and walk phases of skill development. Resulting simulation platforms provide cost-effective, safe environments that allow individuals to practice procedures and tasks. These simulation exercises support a drill-and-repeat task approach with little time and post-acquisition cost constraints, with the notion that repetitive scenario interactions will prepare an individual for live task execution when the time comes. The limitation of simulation-based training is often linked to an instructor-in-the-loop requirement for the purpose of monitoring training interactions to make sure errors are corrected and training principles are reinforced. As such, many of these platforms require coordination at the trainee/trainer level to make sure the simulations are used in a way that promotes efficient skill transfer.

With advancements in adaptive training research and the Army Research Lab's investment in the Generalized Intelligent Framework for Tutoring (GIFT) [3], utilizing ITS tools and methods to automate the CWR model of training is achievable. The goal is to manage an interplay of simulation exercises that enforce different training principles, along with configuring ITS functions in each simulation for the purpose of monitoring performance and providing guidance and adaptation at the individual level. In the following sections, we discuss the utility of ITS technologies to support the CWR model of adaptive interaction in a self-regulated training context. This will include a use case centered on land navigation to guide the discussion.

## 2   Creating a Network of Simulations in Support of Self-regulated Training

To fully implement ITS services in an adaptive CWR context, an architecture is required that enables interoperability across multiple sets of simulation platforms. Each platform can vary in the types of tasks and interactions it supports, so the architecture must account for exercises that train similar concepts at varying phases of the skill acquisition process. In addition, each platform can also incorporate varying data formats and messaging protocols that are unique to that specific application. Therefore, assessing performance in each environment requires specific modeling approaches that account for the data made available by the training environment as it pertains to a set of established concepts and training objectives [9]. Despite these complexities, a CWR instantiation of ITS methods is possible. It requires a network of simulations that build on one another in support of skill development, and a generalized framework to manage the interactions across each experience. For the purposes of this discussion and the defined use case, we are focused on existing stand-alone platforms and applications that are used for training land navigation oriented concepts and skills. These applications are available, and in some instances used in training programs by instructors in controlled settings with human-in-the-loop monitoring.

To take full advantage of available training simulation tools, we advocate the use of ITS technologies to manage training delivery across simulations based on a self-regulated learning construct. To support adaptive functions in all phases of training, the ITS architecture must be able to integrate with all platforms for the purpose of retrieving necessary data sources for managing assessment and driving pedagogical decisions. This includes being able to collect information in real-time produced from the training environment itself and from relevant sensing technologies linked to physiological and behavioral markers. In support of this approach, we are leveraging GIFT's modular architecture to demonstrate the utility of using ITSs to automatically manage multiple training events across disparate simulations.

## 2.1   Generalized Intelligent Framework for Tutoring (GIFT)

GIFT is a domain-independent framework and serves as a set of best-practices for constructing, delivering, and evaluating ITS technologies [9]. GIFT provides an ontological schema for linking observable interactions occurring in a training environment with concepts and competencies linked to that interaction. Through this mapping, GIFT can monitor what a trainee is doing within an environment, and use that information to assess performance based on established models configured around data-informed thresholds. These thresholds associate with three common modeling techniques: (1) expert models used to identify interaction and behavior that deviates from a desired path, (2) buggy models that map interactions to specific common error types and misconceptions, and (3) event-based models used for triggering situational relevant training interventions [10]. With established models and threshold values linked to domain concepts, instructional interventions can now be enacted based on what a trainee does during their training event.

GIFT is unique in that its generalizability provides a means for leveraging multiple systems to train common domain concepts and skill sets. The framework supports interoperability across multiple training environments, with persistent modeling components in place to track a set of skills across multiple training instantiations. GIFT also supports a mastery learning approach, where lessons can be structured and delivered in a way that adheres to common learning theory. In this fashion, subsequent lessons are dependnent on the materials and skills trained prior to, with criteria defined to warrant an individual to progress to the next lesson/skill set. The architecture is comprised of the modular components necessary to develop adaptive training functions across a seamlessly endless number of domains, with schemas in place to support cognitive, affective, and psychomotor training spaces [11].

## 3   A Real-World Use Case: Land Navigation

The goal of this use case is to establish a set of procedures and interactions that will dictate the training experience an individual will receive during a CWR adaptive training event, utilizing GIFT tools. To frame the discussion, we are using the domain of land navigation. Land navigation is a great example to work from, as it incorporates a mix of cognitive and psychomotor task components that are critical to effectively performing the skills required to orienteer unknown terrain. In establishing the criteria for driving an adaptive training approach, we are leveraging currently available training platforms that are used to train varying aspects of the land navigation domain. From an adaptive training standpoint, each platform facilitates a specific aspect of the training experience that adheres to the CWR model of interaction.

The notion is to utilize a set of independent training programs to facilitate the CWR phases of skill acquisition (see Fig. 2). Secondly, through the incorporation of GIFT, each of these independent programs can be configured to support adaptive training at the individual level. As such, we will frame the sub-sections as follows. We start by identifying the tasks prescribed in each phase of the training model, followed by a description of their role in the training process. Next, we will highlight specific concepts each phase will target and the types of assessments required for determining proficiency and competency across each. To round out each sub-section, we will present conceptual adaptive training functions that can be configured in each phase based on GIFT capabilities.

Land Nav 101 -- Lesson 01 -- Terrain Association and Route Planning -- CRAWL    Land Nav 101 -- Lesson 02 -- Simulation-Based Training in VBS -- WALK    Land Nav 101 -- Lesson 03 -- Live Training - - RUN

**Fig. 2.** GIFT lesson structure for land navigation training with CWR sequencing

### 3.1   CRAWL: Terrain Association Exercises

**Task Description.** In this phase, the training focus will be on the fundamentals of land navigation according to FM3-25.26 [12]. Initial instruction will be on three primary components: (1) map reading, (2) terrain association, and (3) route planning. Each of these areas has specific training objectives that can be taught via simulation. Exercises and interactions are designated in this portion of the training to instill the required cognitive components required to perform land navigation procedures. As the primary components of the identified objectives are cognitive in nature, this crawl portion of training will heavily center on all elements related to the planning portion of a navigation exercise.

**Training Environment.** The environment used in the crawl session of this use case is ARL's Augmented REality Sandtable (ARES) [12]. ARES is a research testbed which aims to provide a common operating picture at the point of need for military planning. ARES uses low-cost commercially available technologies (Microsoft Kinect®, a projector, a large screen television monitor, a laptop, and a sand table) to project map data and visualizations onto the sand surface. ARES allows customized presentations of terrain for training purposes. This includes features such as: the use of contours as well as being able to place military standard units. Once a particular terrain is configured, a scenario file can be saved for later use. ARES is currently integrated with GIFT through a gateway configuration that allows the delivery and assessment of ARES configured scenarios, with GIFT driving training prompts and assessments.

**How GIFT can Personalize this Interaction.** Through the integration of GIFT with ARES [14], a training event can be created that prompts a user to interact with ARES scenarios that target land navigation type concepts. An example would be displaying a map on ARES, with GIFT asking the trainee to plot a way point based on specific GPS coordinates. Scenarios can be defined that progress in complexity, with pedagogical practices in place to devise a CWR approach to interaction within this specific environment. The culminating 'Run' type event would include an individual devising a planned route to be executed in the 'Walk' training environment, which is described next.

During all ARES events, GIFT can correct trainees when they perform erroneous actions based on configured assessment criteria. GIFT can also use information pro vided from ARES-based assessments to support personalized remediation through responses to GIFT driven questions. With learner models in place, GIFT can progress a trainee through content and scenarios based on performance outcomes, and can personalize feedback and interactions based on individual differences. As the crawl portion is primarily problem-based, GIFT can sequence a set of ARES scenarios for preparing that trainee for the subsequent 'Walk' portion of training. When all concepts have been deemed mastered through GIFT assessments, this phase of training can be completed and the trainee progressed on to a new training environment for further application of land navigation skill sets.

## 3.2   WALK: Game-Based Interactive Exercises

**Task Description.** The next phase of events in the proposed training interaction model associate with procedural applications using the knowledge learned in the ARES crawl session. The goal is to immerse an individual in a set of interactive exercises that elicit the application of knowledge associated with land navigation, while introducing additional concepts that associate with the psychomotor components of task execution. To facilitate this walk phase of training, utilizing a game-based land navigation scenario provides the environment necessary to replicate the decisions and movements associated with performing the domain tasks without subjecting the trainee to the live environment and all the associated constraints that come with that. This allows a trainee to go through the procedural steps of performing land navigation tasks, while having the ability to make critical mistakes without consequence and the ability to replay events to get multiple trials of skill application.

The tasks in this phase of training are inherently designed to mimic a live training event, with the exception of physically walking the course itself. This includes rehearsing cognitive and psychomotor task components that would be performed in the real-world. The cognitive aspects include: plotting a set of waypoints, devising a route based on known location and terrain features, measuring distance between route points for referencing, and calculating azimuths that will guide navigation practices. Each of these factors coincides with the psychomotor aspect of the domain, where the route is executed based on upfront planning. With a plan in place, the psychomotor task components include: shooting an azimuth vector with a compass, walking along that vector while maintaining pace count to judge distance, and identifying land features to maintain orientation.

**Training Environment.** For the purpose of the walk phase of training, we are leveraging Bohemia Interactive's Virtual Battle Space 3 (VBS3) to drive the use case development. VBS3 is an excellent platform for this phase of training as it mimics real-world tasks through first-person shooter gaming methods. GIFT is integrated with VBS3 through a configured gateway module that can receive and route Distributed Interactive Simulation (DIS) protocol data units. These data units provide real-time game-state information across a number of environment related variables. This integration is important, as it provides the GIFT framework with valuable interaction data that can be used for assessment purposes. The DIS data types of most interest to this use case associate with entity information (i.e., location, movement, collision) and known scenario objects that impact task interactions (i.e., way points, buildings and structures, terrain features).

**How GIFT can Personalize this Interaction.** GIFT is designed to integrate with game-based applications for the purpose of monitoring player actions and assessing performance against a set of specified objectives [9]. In the context of land navigation in VBS3, GIFT supports concept assessments as they relate to available DIS information produced during run-time. These DIS data units are applied as inputs to inform condition classes designed to assess the concepts identified above. These condition classes are established to produce measurable metrics from available interaction data (e.g., measuring the distance of an entity to an object). In addition, GIFT provides mechanisms in each condition class to establish configured thresholds that designate performance states based on associated data types. For example, a condition class might be used to determine how much a player is staying on a path (i.e., vector). Through a condition class, you can update a performance state for the concept 'stay on path' when a player is measured greater than 10 feet off path based on current location and their starting point. With a set of established training concepts, and defined condition classes informing their real-time performance, GIFT can monitor interaction and trigger feedback and scenario adaptations based on changes in performance states.

## 3.3 Live Training Exercises (RUN)

**Task Description.** In this phase of training, individuals will be tasked with completing a land navigation course in a live training environment. Trainees will be asked to conduct all required tasks to navigate across a set of waypoints using a map, a compass, and known GPS coordinates. This will require individuals to apply all components of the crawl and walk phases of training, thus providing a metric of training transfer as it relates to going from simulation to live exercise. The main addition to this level of interaction is the full incorporation of psychomotor task components. This includes walking the course based on designated routes, monitoring distance traveled through pace counts, and maintaining appropriate orientation through registered land marks (e.g., roads and rivers) and observable points (e.g., large hilltops, unique rock formations).

A benefit to the CWR adaptive interaction model is that more complex concepts are integrated as trainees progress through the designated training environments. An assumption is that individuals should have gained all basic and procedural knowledge to more effectively exploit the training benefits of live events when the 'Run' exercise is initiated. That is, they are no longer struggling with lower level concepts and skills which could hinder higher level integration and transfer of knowledge in very active training. This results in better skill integration as well as better cost/time effectiveness with live environments which can be expensive and where we don't want people struggling on basic elements.

**Training Environment.** The training environment for the 'Run' phase of this use case is a live land navigation course. The course will consist of designated waypoints a trainee will be asked to navigate. The trainee will also be outfitted with a map, a protractor, a pencil, and a compass. Depending on the location, individuals will need to navigate the optimal route based on land features and vegetation. The environment itself is rugged in nature and will require physical endurance to complete the course in a timely fashion.

**How GIFT can Personalize this Interaction.** A dependency of personalized training interactions is that there are assessments in place that can drive performance determinations and guide pedagogical strategy selections. In GIFT, this requires data sources that can be used to designate what a trainee is doing in relation to a set of defined concepts and objectives. In this phase of training, we are now implementing GIFT modeling techniques in a 'in-the-wild' type environment, where simulation data is not conveniently made available. As such, future GIFT-based research is focused on the integration of cellular device data feeds to capture behavioral information as it relates to a known environment. In this instance, GIFT will need to receive real-time location data as informed through GPS and cell network tracking technologies. With real-time location data, we can recreate the assessment conditions performed within the VBS3 land navigation scenario. This requires the ability to author similar assessments performed in VBS3, with the main difference being the incorporation of new map data sources and linking those to location data for tracking trainee interactions.

The benefit with this integration is the ability to apply crawl and walk type training interventions in a 'Run' type training environment. We now have the capacity to enact 'crawl' based pedagogical interventions in the live environment with the ability fade support as a trainee progresses through the run designated exercise. This allows GIFT to create an interplay between training and transfer, with the latter focusing on performance with the removal of training supports and scaffolds.

## 4   Authoring Adaptive Functions Across Disparate Systems

Integrating all land navigation oriented training environments with GIFT provides the ability to create a unified adaptive training experience that guides individuals through phases of training based on the delivery of customized lessons. These lessons are authored using the GIFT Authoring Tool (GAT; see Fig. 3). At its foundation, GIFT lessons are created by configuring GAT course objects that drive learner interaction [15]. For the purpose of this paper, we are focusing on the Adaptive Course Flow object and its associated practice delivery component. This course object manages the delivery of instructional content and guides practice events with available external training applications [16]. An authoring burden is building GIFT logic for managing assessment and pedagogy for all external training environments used for practice exercises. To put it simple, without assessment, these systems cannot support ITS instructional practices. In the following sub-sections, we present a relevant problem statement and research targeting the development of authoring tools to support an intuitive approach to authoring assessment logic for training environment applications integrated in GIFT.

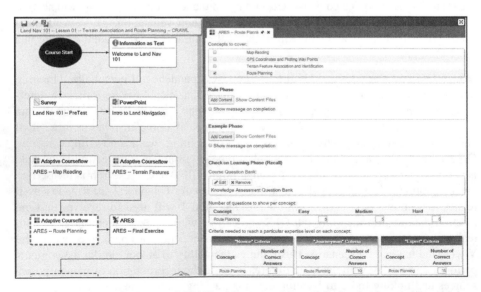

**Fig. 3.** The GIFT Authoring Tool (GAT) with course objects linked to land navigation training in ARES.

## 4.1    Assessment Authoring Considerations

The GAT primarily addresses the authoring processes associated with creating and organizing course objects that define the sequence of events an individual will experience (e.g., surveys, tests, lesson materials, etc.). However, GIFT interactions go well beyond these more conventional training formats. GIFT provides developers with authoring capabilities for creating an adaptive training experience across interactive external training environments that associate with actual skill application and practice opportunities. This will involve the incorporation of both virtual and augmented reality technologies.

Authoring Adaptive Course Flow objects for these external training applications poses a number of authoring challenges. Continuing with the VBS3 land navigation example, let's say a developer has created a land navigation course and would like to assess the learner's ability to navigate across various waypoints within the environment. In addition to authoring and configuring the condition classes associated with this assessment (e.g., how much a player is staying on a path (i.e., vector)), the developer may also need to make edits to the VBS3 scenario itself (e.g., add a waypoint to reference for assessment purposes). Or perhaps even create the VBS3 land navigation scenario in the first place. This disconnect between the GIFT authoring environment and the VBS3 scenario editor requires users to constantly switch between each tool and can be very cumbersome, often leading to increases in development time and potential user error and frustration from the authoring standpoint.

Beyond the challenges associated with toggling between authoring environments, there are also authoring challenges associated with creating adaptive assessment logic for a variety of disparate training applications. GIFT uses a Domain Knowledge File (DKF), to configure the adaptive training experience for any training application by associating generalized schemas that map concept ontologies to condition classes used for assessment, and linking the outcomes of those assessments with available pedagogical interventions. The DKF Authoring Tool (DAT) is designed to allow developers to create adaptive training across any GIFT integrated training application (i.e., training environment with an established gateway). However, due to the wide variety of training applications developers could employ, as well as the unique types of assessments one may potentially use within, the DAT was designed to be an extremely flexible tool; however, this flexibility required that users possess the technical skills necessary to use such a tool. While this flexibility extended the reach of GIFT to many training applications, it limited the accessibility of the tool for users without particular technical expertise.

## 4.2    GIFT Wrap

ARL is currently investigating new methods to address the authoring challenges described above. This includes the development of GIFT Wrap, a fully-integrated, user-friendly tool for authoring adaptive assessment logic and instruction within external training applications.

First, GIFT Wrap seeks to overcome the disconnect between the GIFT authoring environment, in this case the DAT, and a training application's scenario editor through the use of an overlay interface. When configuring a condition class within a DKF, the GIFT Wrap provides the ability to manipulate objects in a training applications scenario editor, with relevant information automatically populating within the DKF's xml schema. For example, if the user wanted to designate a specific set of waypoints to associate within a scenario, GIFT Wrap would enable a user to establish waypoints in the scenario editor, with those coordinates being referenced in the DKF for assessment configuration. While being somewhat linear in nature, this user-friendly interface allows for the flexibility to make changes within either tool at any time.

Second, GIFT Wrap addresses the technical skills gap by providing an intuitive user interface for configuring the adaptive training experience. For example, rather than editing a specific condition class and it's corresponding assessment parameters within an XML editor, users access the same functionality via the GIFT Wrap user interface. No specific technical skills are required to use the tool. By adopting a user-centered approach, GIFT Wrap will greatly increase access for those seeking to develop and deploy adaptive training.

In general, GIFT Wrap allows instructional designers to designate triggers for when an intervention or tutoring event will take place within a training application. When the trigger is invoked the tutoring event is initiated. Triggers available depend upon the training application (ARES, VBS3, Live environment, etc.) in use, and the available assessment techniques supported within (i.e., existing condition classes based on available data inputs). GIFT Wrap is designed to provide a training developer with the information to understand what type of assessments can be supported within a training application through descriptions of assessment types once they designate what application will be used for a lesson/exercise. The first development iteration of GIFT Wrap is focused on ARES training events, with VBS3 and live training next in the queue.

**GIFT Wrap in ARES.** In ARES, GIFT Wrap includes features to develop specific tests of knowledge and skill. Two existing assessments have been conceptualized to guide initial development efforts, including a check on learning and a terrain layout task (see Fig. 4 for notional terrain layout task configurations). With the check on learning, GIFT Wrap facilitates the development of queries assessing land navigation knowledge for which a trainee provides answers by selecting icons through the ARES interface. Interaction with these queries may be embedded within a larger ARES tactical scenario. For example, a GIFT Wrap instructional designer may use GIFT Wrap and the ARES interface to create a map scene in which trainees must evaluate the scenario to identify relevant landmarks. The instructional designer could then create a set of queries, through a GIFT survey item, requesting the trainee to identify specific landmarks.

With an ARES gateway module in place, GIFT would utilize the established conditions for the check on learning to evaluate in real-time the correctness of the answer. Correct answers might result in adaptation of the training through GIFT to include another test or review of a different map scene. Wrong answers might result in feedback through GIFT, highlighting the correct answer; or it may include instructional

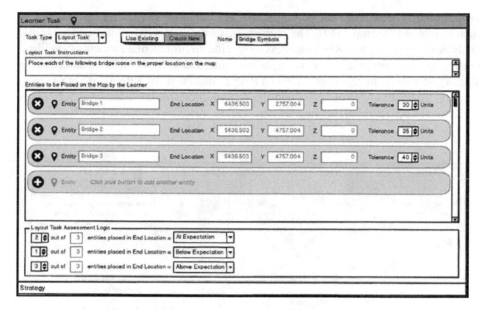

**Fig. 4.** GIFT wrap layout task configuration interface.

material that guides the user through remedial content focused on the underlying concepts assessed within that ARES scenario.

For a terrain layout tasks, GIFT WRAP facilitates the development of assessments that evaluate the degree to which users place icons in the correct location on an ARES presented map. Here the GIFT WRAP author selects an ARES scenario, designs a query regarding positioning elements on the ARES map, and designates the correct positions of elements via the interface. Trainees using ARES and experiencing the test would position icons, the positions of which would be compared to the correct positions for determining skill level. As with check on learning events, feedback or scenario adaptations can be initiated based on performance outcomes. Assessment capabilities will be further extended to support more sophisticated measures required for route planning type exercises.

**GIFT Wrap in VBS3.** In VBS3, GIFT Wrap is being conceptualized to support a variety of real-time assessments driven by the data that can be directly received from the game environment. Multiple trigger types, tutoring events, and performance tests are supported. For example, taking an event-based approach GIFT Wrap can be used to author tutoring events triggered by entity states (avatar health) or environmental events (weapons fired). In a land navigation example, tutoring events may easily be triggered based on user/entity locations within the VBS3 environment as they relate to identified way points and scenario objects. Say a trainee reaches a GIFT Wrap–specified location. The system may prompt the user to complete a task or it may automatically begin to assess behaviors. Past research has demonstrated the capability for using triggers (time, location, entity state, etc.) for automatically and intelligently presenting interventions such as real-time prompts [17]. The prompts may guide users in building metacognitive skills or they may assess user awareness of specific environmental elements (See Fig. 5 illustrating the presentation of prompts to trainees during a VBS3 land-navigation training scenario). In any case, GIFT WRAP is designed for authors to configure all triggers, associated tests or tasks, and the condition classes used for assessing trainee performance across those varying events.

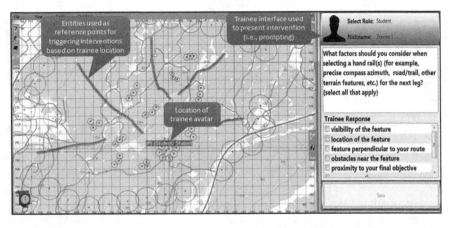

**Fig. 5.** VBS3 assessment configurations and notional GIFT training intervention prompt based on a configured trigger.

**GIFT Wrap in Live Training.** Conceptually, GIFT Wrap would perform similarly in a live training environment. Authored triggers however would be based on data pulled from the live interaction (e.g., trainee location as tracked via GPS-capable technology). Real time assessment may include automated assessment of physical behaviors (e.g., how long a trainee stayed in a specific location, how many time a trainee "backtracked" to a specific location). Intelligent tutoring could take the form of prompts or coaching messages, as described within the VBS3 example. In this case, the trainee interface would be presented via smart-phone or tablet technologies, which would present user tasks and collect data from assessments that require user response to cognitive tasks while they complete physical tasks during a land navigation training event. To support this approach to adaptive training, two functions need to be addressed: (1) the ability to configure assessment data based on real-world terrain data, as represented across multiple map data resources (e.g., google maps interface), and (2) a GIFT mobile app that manages the transmission of GPS data to a centralized server for assessment purposes and for the delivery of prompts triggered during training based on GIFT Wrap oriented assessments.

# 5 Conclusions

Developing training to support a CWR adaptive model of interaction in a self-regulated environment requires technology to facilitate the assessment and coaching required to guide a trainee through the varying phases of skill acquisition. GIFT provides the tools and methods to build intelligent tutoring functions across an array of instructional domains, but there are no mechanisms to assist a training developer in building a set of lessons that build upon each other and incorporate a sequence of complimentary training events and simulations. In this paper, we present a use case showing GIFT's utility in training a set of knowledge and skills across multiple environments that incorporate scenarios intended to progress a trainee from novice to expert. In addition, we show how GIFT can support personalized instruction during each training interaction. Lastly, we present current research surrounding the development of a new generalized tool, GIFT Wrap, to assist training developers in building the assessment logic required to drive these adaptive experiences.

# References

1. Kulik, J.A., Fletcher, J.: Effectiveness of intelligent tutoring systems: a meta-analytic review. Rev. Educ. Res. **86**(1), 42–78 (2016)
2. VanLehn, K.: The relative effectiveness of human tutoring, intelligent tutoring systems, and other tutoring systems. Educ. Psychol. **46**(4), 197–221 (2011)
3. Sottilare, R.: Challenges in moving adaptive training & education from state-of-art to state-of-practice. In: Developing a Generalized Intelligent Framework for Tutoring (GIFT) Workshop at the 17th International Conference on Artificial Intelligence in Education (AIED), Madrid, Spain (2015)
4. Nicholls, D., Sweet, L., Muller, A., Hyett, J.: Teaching psychomotor skills in the twenty-first century: revisiting and reviewing instructional approaches through the lens of contemporary literature. Med. Teach. **38**(10), 1056–1063 (2016)
5. Fitts, P., Posner, M.: Human Performance. Brooks/Cole, Oxford (1969)
6. Anderson, J.R., Schunn, C.: Implications of the ACT-R learning theory: no magic bullets. In: Advances in Instructional Psychology, Educational Design and Cognitive Science, pp. 1–33 (2000)
7. Mueller-Hanson, R.A., Wisecarver, M.M., Dorsey, D.W., Ferro, G.A., Mendini, K.: Developing adaptive training in the classroom: DTIC Document (2009)
8. Kinney, M.: What the Army Taught Me About Teaching. Inside Higher Ed (2008)
9. Goldberg, B., Brawner, K.W., Holden, H., Sottilare, R.: Adaptive game-based tutoring: mechanisms for real-time feedback and adaptation. In: Defense and Homeland Security Simulation (DHSS) Workshop, Vienna, Austria (2012)
10. Woolf, B.P.: Building Intelligent Interactive Tutors: Student-Centered Strategies for Revolutionizing E-Learning. Morgan Kaufmann, Burlington (2009)
11. Krathwohl, D.R.: A revision of Bloom's taxonomy: an overview. Theory Pract. **41**(4), 212–218 (2002)
12. U.S. Army: Map Reading and Land Navigation. Washington, DC, FM, 3–25.26 (2007)
13. Amburn, C.R., Vey, N.L., Boyce, M.W., Mize, J.R.: The augmented reality sandtable (ARES) (No. ARL-SR-0340). Army Research Laboratory (2015)

14. Boyce, M.W., Reyes, R.J., Cruz, D.E., Amburn, C.R., Goldberg, B., Moss, J.D., Sottilare, R.A.: Effect of Topography on Learning Military Tactics - Integration of Generalized Intelligent Framework for Tutoring (GIFT) and Augmented REality Sandtable (ARES) (ARL-7792). Army Research Laboratory (2016)
15. Ososky, S., Brawner, K., Goldberg, B., Sottilare, R.: GIFT cloud improving usability of adaptive tutor authoring tools within a web-based application. In: Human Factors and Ergonomics Society Annual Meeting Proceedings (2016)
16. Goldberg, B., Hoffman, M., Tarr, R.: Authoring instructional management logic in GIFT using the engine for management of adaptive pedagogy (EMAP). In: Sottilare, R., Graesser, A., Hu, X., Brawner, K. (eds.) Design Recommendations for Intelligent Tutoring Systems: Authoring Tools, vol. 3. U.S. Army Research Laboratory (2015)
17. Davis, F., Priest, H. W., Riley, J. M., Scielzo, S.: Developing effective adaptive training systems to enhance military instruction. In: Interservice/Industry Training, Simulation, and Education Conference (I/ITSEC), Orlando, FL (2014)

# Modeling Training Efficiency in GIFT

Gregory A. Goodwin[1]($\boxtimes$), James Niehaus[2], and Jong W. Kim[1]

[1] U.S. Army Research Laboratory, Orlando, FL, USA
gregory.a.goodwin6.civ@mail.mil
[2] Charles River Analytics Inc., Cambridge, MA, USA

**Abstract.** The US Army Learning Model (ALM) emphasizes the importance of deployable, individualized, adaptive training technologies to help Soldiers better learn and improve critical skills in dynamic and challenging environments. The Army is developing one such technology known as the Generalized Intelligent Framework for Tutoring (GIFT). GIFT is an open-source, domain-independent intelligent tutoring framework that facilitates reuse of components in an effort to reduce the expense of developing and delivering adaptive training. Adaptive training offers the promise of higher levels of proficiency, but another important benefit is that it is more efficient than one-size-fits-all training. Put another way, intelligent, adaptive training should require less time to train a population of learners to a given level of proficiency than non-adaptive training. The gains in efficiency should be a function of several factors including learner characteristics (e.g., aptitude, reading ability, prior knowledge), learning methods employed by the adaptive training system, course content (e.g., difficulty and length, adaptability), and test characteristics (e.g., difficulty, number of items). Optimizing training efficiency requires one to tune the instructional design and course content to the characteristics of the learners. GIFT currently lacks the ability to model or predict the efficiency with which training can be delivered based on these factors. This paper presents a process, and proposed architecture to enable GIFT to make estimates of training efficiency. How this architecture supports authoring and how machine learning can be used to improve the predictive model are also discussed.

**Keywords:** Adaptive training · Probabilistic programming · Return on investment · Training duration

## 1 Introduction

The Generalized Intelligent Framework for Tutoring (GIFT) is an open-source, modular architecture developed to reduce the cost and skill required for authoring adaptive training and educational systems, to automate instructional delivery and management, and to develop and standardize tools for the evaluation of adaptive training and educational technologies (Sottilare et al. 2012a, b). By separating the components of ITSs, GIFT seeks to reduce development costs by facilitating component reuse.

Meta-analyses and reviews support the claim that intelligent tutoring systems (ITS's) improve learning over typical classroom teaching, reading texts, and/or other traditional learning methods. (Dynarsky et al. 2007; Dodds and Fletcher 2004; Fletcher 2003;

© Springer International Publishing AG 2017
D.D. Schmorrow and C.M. Fidopiastis (Eds.): AC 2017, Part II, LNAI 10285, pp. 131–147, 2017.
DOI: 10.1007/978-3-319-58625-0_9

Graesser et al. 2012; Steenbergen-Hu and Cooper 2013, 2014; VanLehn 2011). In fact, ITS's have been shown to improve learning to levels comparable to Human tutors (VanLehn et al. 2007; VanLehn 2011; Olney et al. 2012).

While improved training effectiveness is certainly a benefit of ITS technology, another important benefit is improved training efficiency over one-size-fits-all training. The goal of an ITS is to identify the gaps in knowledge specific to each learner so that training can focus on filling just those gaps. One of the problems of one-size-fits-all training is that to insure all trainees can comprehend the instruction, it must be developed for trainees with the least experience, knowledge, and aptitude. Though less costly to develop, the material is presented a pace that is slow and that includes content not needed for more experienced, higher aptitude trainees. An ITS would be expected to reduce the time needed to deliver training to such trainees.

The reduction in time to train (i.e., improved acquisition rate) is an important metric because reductions in training time represent cost savings. This is especially true for military trainees who are paid a salary. Reductions in the time needed to train those trainees saves salary costs for both trainees and instructors. For large-volume courses, those savings can be substantial.

All of this highlights the need for a means to model and predict training efficiency gains by ITSs generally and GIFT specifically. Having the ability to model time saved by the use of adaptive, intelligent training, as compared to existing or non-adaptive training would have benefits throughout the lifecycle of a course. During the design of new training, the training developer could more easily make decisions about the relative costs and benefits of adding adaptive features. For example, adding extensive remedial training for easy-to-understand concepts may benefit such a small percent of the population of learners, that the net reduction in training time would be too small to make those features worth the cost of development.

During training delivery, actual trainee data could be used to verify and/or improve the model. For example, suppose the model assumed that learners with an aptitude above criteria A would have a 95% probability of understanding concept B without needing any remediation. Learner data could then be used to validate or adjust that probability. This improved model could then be used to better determine the true time-savings of the course when delivered by GIFT.

During training evaluation and refinement, the disparity between predicted and observed training outcomes could be used to refine the training. For example, if a segment of training proves to be more difficult than anticipated for a group of learners, it is possible that the training segment should be refined or redeveloped.

An example of such a model was developed by McDonnell Douglas (1977). This model incorporated predictor variables in four broad categories: course content (e.g., difficulty, length of content), instructional design (e.g., instructional strategies/ techniques), test characteristics (e.g., difficulty, number of items), and trainee characteristics (e.g., aptitude, motivation). The model predicted about 39% of the variability in trainee's first-attempt lesson time for self-paced computer-based instruction.

To understand how GIFT might begin to model and predict training time for learners, it is necessary to understand how training is adapted by this system. GIFT is a framework that modularizes the common components of intelligent tutoring systems. These components include a learner module, an instructional or tutor module, a domain module, and a user interface. One of the main motivations for creating this framework was to lower the cost and labor needed to create intelligent tutoring systems by facilitating re-use of components and by simplifying the authoring process (Sottilare et al. 2012a).

GIFT adapts training using the learning effects model depicted in Fig. 1 below. At the first point of this model, learner data informs learner state in the learner module. The learner module receives assessments from both sensors and the domain module. The learner state is used to determine the appropriate instructional strategy by the tutor module. The instructional strategy is then interpreted by the domain module and used to determine the domain specific learning activities needed to instruct the learner in that domain. The responses of the learner to that activity then update the learner module which starts the cycle over again.

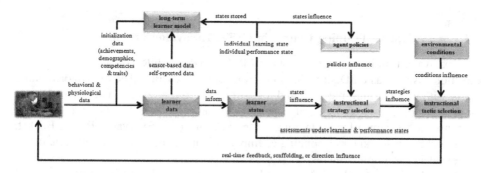

**Fig. 1.** The learning effects model

As can be seen, developing a predictive model in GIFT is not a straightforward process given the ways that training is adapted to each individual. We should note that our goal is not to predict the single path that a trainee would be expected to take through a specific course, but rather the probability associated with all possible paths through the training for a given learner. From that we can determine the range and distribution of times that would be expected for that learner to complete the training. Taking this one step further, we could apply this to a population of learners and predict the range and distribution of the time for that population to complete that training.

The development and integration of a probabilistic model for predicting time to train into the GIFT architecture is currently in the first phase of a three phase plan. In this paper, we describe work being done in the first phase. In this phase we are developing the structure of the Bayesian probabilistic model, identifying factors that are expected to impact training time, and mapping those to a specific course delivered by GIFT. In the second phase, we will integrate this model into the GIFT framework and develop the user interface to allow for authoring of new predictive models for other GIFT courses. In the third phase of the work, we will empirically validate the predictive model in GIFT and make adjustments to try to improve it.

## 2   Methods

This section describes our method for modeling adaptive training content and predicting distributions of completion times for both individuals and groups using the GIFT excavator trainer. This course is available with public version of GIFT. The training content includes text, images, video demonstrations, and practice opportunities in a virtual simulator.

First we describe an example adaptive training course in GIFT, the excavator training. Second, we describe the approach to modeling this content of adaptive training using the Methodology for Annotated Skill Trees (MAST). And finally, we describe our approach to developing probabilistic models of trainees executing the task, including static variables (e.g., prior knowledge and expertise in the domain) and dynamic variables (e.g., fatigue and boredom) which may be observed or latent.

### 2.1   An Adaptive Training Course in GIFT: Excavator Training

The excavator training course consists of MS PowerPoint slides that have text and text questions as well as a 3D simulation environment for practice. The excavator training starts with a welcoming message and a set of survey questions that extract the learner characteristics of motivation, grit, and self-regulatory ability. The GIFT tutor, then, presents the concepts of rules to control the excavator (i.e., Excavator, Boom, Bucket, Arm, and Swing), and corresponding examples. Figure 2 shows the overall structure of the excavator training contents.

GIFT has been developed to strengthen the capability of adaptive courses. One of recent advances is an implementation of "Adaptive Course Flow" in GIFT (e.g., Sottilare 2014; Goldberg and Hoffman 2015). This was formerly known as the Engine for Management of Adaptive Pedagogy (EMAP) which supports adaptive capabilities for training based on the Component Display Theory (CDT, Merrill 1983). The CDT supports a general framework of skill training that progresses through two types of learning activities, each with two categories: expository (rules and examples) and inquisitory (recall and practice). According to Merrill, learners should progress through these four quadrants in order starting with rules (presentation of general principles), then to examples (presentation of a specific instance), then to recall (declarative knowledge test of the trainee's comprehension), and finally to practice (opportunity for the trainee to perform the skill). By sorting learning activities into these four quadrants, adaptive training systems like GIFT can apply the CDT to any domain as long as content for that domain is so labeled.

The Adaptive Courseflow (AC) object also considers learner traits and states when determining the most appropriate content to present to the learner in each quadrant. For example, content can be tailored to the motivation, experience, arousal, etc. of the trainee. For example, when initiating the course, students self-identify as either: novice, journeyman, or expert. The learner progresses through the expository quadrants and then is evaluated in the inquisitory quadrants. So, if the learner fails to demonstrate an understanding of the rules or examples in the recall or practice quadrants, the AC object

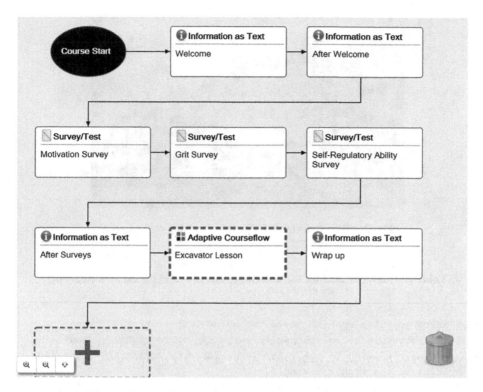

**Fig. 2.** The overall structure of the excavator training in GIFT.

attempts to remediate and reevaluate the trainee before progressing him or her to the next quadrant or lesson. Performance is assessed at either below, at, above expectation.

In the excavator training, rules to control the excavator for each concept (i.e., Boom, Bucket, Arm, Swing) are presented to the learner in the Rule phase, and corresponding examples are presented in the Example phase. In the Recall phase, a batch of assessment questions, shown in Table 1, is presented to the learner in an attempt to identify the learner's knowledge of each concept. The adaptive behavior of the GIFT tutoring system is dependent on the number of correct answers for each concept as defined by the course author. Within the allowed number of attempts, the learner receives adaptive instructions based on his or her performance. For example, a novice would receive the Rule or Example remediation content, and a journeyman would receive the Example remediation content. The adaptive behavior of the concept remediation occurs up to the total number of three attempts—if the learner fails to reach the anticipated level within the total number of three attempts, the learner is advised to see an instructor. In the practice phase, the learner can practice the acquired knowledge and skills through a practice training application that can be information as text, information from file, or information from web. The excavator training uses the Dynamic Environment Testbed program shown in Fig. 3.

**Fig. 3.** The excavator 3D simulation training environment.

**Table 1.** Questions used for the knowledge assessment in the excavator training.

Q1 Which joystick control moves the swing left or right? (Swing)
Q5 What controls would you use to swing the cabin right? (Swing)
Q7 Moving the swing to the right is perfomed by moving the right-side joystick to the right? (Swing)
Q9 What functionality allows you to move the cabin right and left? (Swing)
Q12 Which control is labeled 'C' on the Excavator? (Swing)

Q2 What action is performed when you move the right joystick to the left (towards the driver)? (Bucket)
Q3 What action is perfomed when you move the right joystick to the right (away from the driver)? (Bucket)
Q6 You can perform a loading function by moving the left-side joystick forward? (Bucket)
Q13 Which control is labeled 'D' on the Excavator? (Bucket)'

Q4 How do you move the boom up? (Boom)
Q11 Which control is labeled 'B' on the Excavator? (Boom)

Q8 Which joystick controls move the arm down? (Arm)
Q10 Which control is labeled 'A' on the Excavator? (Arm)
Q14 The Arm function is performed using the Right Joystick. (Arm)

## 2.2    Modeling the Content of Adaptive Training

To model the content of adaptive training, we use MAST skill trees. Figure 4 shows a visual representation of a MAST skill tree. The "skeleton" of the skill tree is a procedure model that breaks down entire procedures into constituent steps, tasks, and subtasks. Annotations (shown as colored boxes in the tree and in greater detail on the right) are added to the procedure model; these annotations make MAST unique. For example, consider completing a set of questions in the excavator tutor that features hints and feedback. This step includes tasks for reading the introduction to the problems, each problem, reading hints, and reviewing feedback. Critical for adaptive training, the MAST procedure model represents not only the base procedure of answering each question correctly without hints, but also the optional hints and feedback steps, variations, and multiple potential paths among questions as chosen by GIFT.

Annotations within the MAST skill tree include the following additional information for each step, task, and subtask (that is, for each *skill tree node*).

- *Information Elements:* Information or knowledge needed by the trainee to perform the actions required by the skill tree node. These requirements are commonly called the "knowledge map" in ITS literature. In the example of completing a set of GIFT questions, this is the knowledge used to answer the question correctly.
- *Instructional Resources:* Resources to teach the skills needed to perform the actions required by the node. In the question example, these are pointers to additional training content.

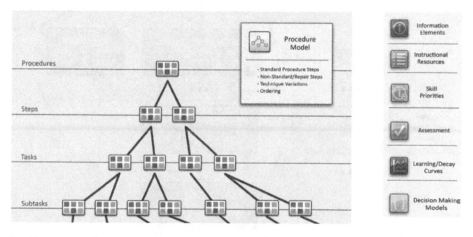

**Fig. 4.** PAST Time uses MAST skill trees to represent adaptive training content (Color figure online)

- *Skill Priorities:* Ratings of the difficulty and criticality of the skills needed to perform the actions required by the node. These ratings enable training systems to prioritize skills for training and optimize ROI. In the question example, ratings express the criticality of answering the questions correctly to the overall learning goals.

- *Assessments*: Methods of assessing the skills required by the node. These methods enable training systems to determine trainee ability. In the question example, assessment methods include secondary measures of trainee cognitive workload, motivation, or affect that may influence completion time.
- *Decision Making Models*: Computational models of how the procedure steps, tasks, and subtasks are chosen and ordered. These models enable some of the adaptation logic to be represented in the skill tree. In the question example, these models encode the rules for providing hints, providing feedback, and selecting the next question.

For this effort, we have extended this set of annotations to include a *Completion Time* Data annotation that describes a distribution of completion time based on past data or an estimate of completion time based on type. This data will be used to train the prediction algorithms. Figure 5 shows a portion of a MAST skill tree for the excavator training GIFT course. This skill tree focuses on the information elements that most heavily influence completion time. On the left, the overall course on Excavator is the root of the tree structure. Its children are the different topics covered by the course, including the Boom Movement topic. This topic features a number of slides with Pictures, Audio, and Text components. Individual trainees may vary in the amount of

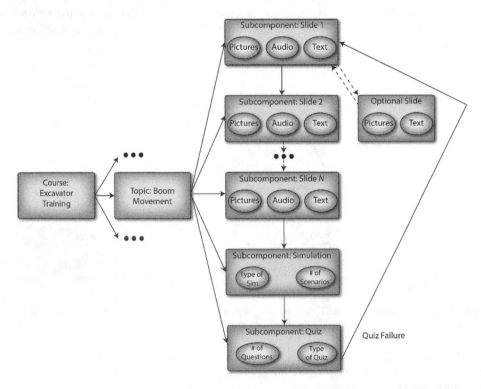

**Fig. 5.** High-level design of a MAST skill tree of a GIFT module with representations of individual instructional elements, branching content, and variables that influence completion times

time they spend examining the Pictures, whether or not they listen completely to the Audio, and the amount of time taken to read the Text. Trainees may also choose to view optional Slides explaining concepts that they may not be familiar with, adding more time. If trainees fail to demonstrate sufficient knowledge in the quiz or fail to complete the simulation tasks appropriately, they are sent back to the beginning of the Boom Movement topic on Slide 1, adding significant time to completion of the course. This model may be expanded to represent a maximum number of failures before the trainee either moves to a different topic or ends the course.

After reviewing the Slides, the trainees are asked to practice their skills in Simulation. The MAST model of the simulation can be either a complex procedure describing the steps needed to complete the scenario and optional steps that may or may not contribute to the overall goal. The MAST simulation model may also be simple, as shown in Fig. 5 representing just the type of simulation and the number of scenarios. To save modeling time and effort, these MAST models are constructed with only the level of detail needed to sufficiently accurately predict completion time.

## 2.3   Modeling the Adaptive Training Execution

We use a probabilistic model to represent the different factors and instructional strategies that impact the completion time of a MAST module, as well as probabilistic inference techniques to determine a distribution of course completion time. Not only must our model represent relationships between variables and paths in the MAST skill tree, but it must also recognize and model the impact of time as well; many variables can change as the trainee is completing a training module. Building this model consists of two basic steps: developing a model that estimates completion time for nodes in the MAST skill tree, and temporally linking these models together to enable inference of the entire module completion time.

Figure 6 shows part of an example model for estimating the completion time of a node. This example shows some contributing factors that could be used by PAST Time

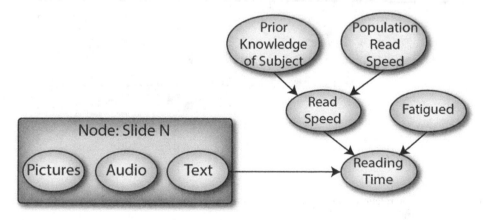

**Fig. 6.** Example model for estimating the time to read text on a slide node

to estimate the time it takes for a trainee to read the text on the slide. There are also variables that estimate the time to process the pictures and audio on the slide, but that these have been omitted from this example for brevity. The model includes a Reading Time variable, which represents the time it takes for the user to read the text. The value of this variable is a function of the amount of text on the slide, the speed at which the trainee can read the text (Read Speed), and the current alertness of the trainee (Fatigued). These relationships are probabilistic. For example, if a trainee normally reads at 100 words per minute, there are 100 words in the text, and the trainee is tired, the reading time of the trainee could be distribution uniformly from 1 to 2 min. The reading speed of the trainee is also a non-deterministic variable that depends on how much prior knowledge the trainee possesses about the subject, and statistics about how fast the general population of trainees read.

One of the benefits of building a probabilistic model to represent completion time is that not all of the information in the model is needed to estimate the completion time. For example, if we know how much prior knowledge the user has about the subject (for example, from a pre-instruction questionnaire), we can post that knowledge as *evidence* to the model that would be taken into account when estimating the completion time. If we do not possess that information, we can treat the variable as *latent* and use a prior distribution to represent the state of the variable. For example, we can estimate that only 20% of trainees taking the course have prior knowledge of the subject. These prior distributions can be estimated from the literature review or expert knowledge, and then *learned* over time based on the outcomes of actual testing.

Once we determine the probabilistic relationships between the variables in each node, we will develop a *dynamic relational model* that models the actual temporal process of instruction and the uncertain paths that a trainee may take through the MAST skill tree. Figure 7 shows an example dynamic relational model.

This dynamic relational model is intended to capture two critical elements of predicting completion time: the dynamic process of learning (e.g., becoming fatigued)

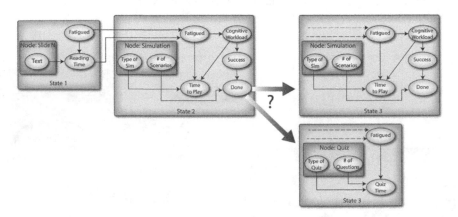

**Fig. 7.** Dynamic relational probabilistic model that includes variable relationships over time and traversal uncertainty

and the uncertainty inherent in traversing the MAST skill tree. The example shown in the figure shows three states of the learning process. The first state models the completion time to read the text on slide N of a module (this is the same node in Fig. 6, but other variables have been removed for clarity). Once the trainee completes the instruction on the slide, they progress to the simulation node of the module. Here, we model the completion time of the node as the amount of time it takes to complete a scenario in the simulation. The time to play a scenario depends on whether the trainee is fatigued which affects their current cognitive workload. One important aspect of this model is that we create temporal relationships between the variables to model the explicit process of a trainee taking this course. For example, at State 2 in this figure, the probability that a trainee is fatigued increases if the trainee was already fatigued or they spent a significant amount of time completing the previous node.

State 3 in Fig. 7 explicitly shows the relational uncertainty that can impact completion time. In this example, a trainee is required to successfully pass a minimum number of individual training scenarios. We explicitly model the number of passes and failures of a trainee, since each time a trainee engages in a scenario, the completion time is impacted. Therefore, we have a variable that represents whether the trainee succeeded in the scenario, and a variable that represents whether the user is done with the node. If the trainee has not successfully completed the required number of scenarios, then State 3 again models the trainee engaging in a simulation scenario; otherwise, State 3 models the completion time of the next node in the MAST tree (a quiz). This modeling of the relational nature between nodes in the MAST tree is critical for accurate completion time prediction.

Once these probabilistic models are defined, they can be used to compute a distribution over the course completion time. To generate this distribution, a modeler first provides knowledge about a trainee, group of trainees, or a module as evidence to the model. This could be statistical information obtained from the trainees from a pre-course questionnaire, or data obtained from prior training. Then, given the posted evidence, the user can apply standard probabilistic inference techniques (e.g., variable elimination, importance sampling, Metropolis-Hastings, support computation, most probable explanation (MPE), and particle filtering) to generate a distribution over the completion time of the module. These specific methods are included in the Figaro libraries. Statistical moments of this distribution (e.g., mean and variance) can be easily computed and presented to a module designer.

A significant advantage of combining this probabilistic modeling with the MAST skill tree representation is the capability to ascribe time to individual models, and perform "what if" analysis by adding or removing components. For example, a node for a module requiring detailed arithmetic may take little time in and of itself, but it may be fatiguing, causing significant downstream effects in terms of overall training completion time.

# 3 Results

## 3.1 Implementing the Adaptive Training Models

The probabilistic model is being implemented using Charles River Analytics' open source probabilistic programming language, Figaro™ (Pfeffer 2012), to construct and learn probabilistic models of the relationships between these factors. The use of Figaro will greatly simplify the authoring of these models which can be complex and require a high degree of experience by users who may not be experts in probabilistic reasoning.

Creating probabilistic models for specific analytical applications, such as this training completion time prediction problem, presents both representation and reasoning challenges. Figaro enables the easy creation and manipulation of these probabilistic models. Figaro is extremely expressive and can represent a wide variety of models, including:

- Directed and undirected models with latent relationships, such as trainee motivation
- Dynamic models with temporal factors, such as trainees completing several nodes of a module
- Models in which conditions and constraints are expressed by arbitrary functions to represent a wide variety of relationships among the trainee model and adaptive training content
- Open universe models in which we do not know what or how many objects exist, such as the number of times that a trainee will exercise a particular simulation scenario
- Models in which the elements themselves are rich data structures, such MAST skill trees

Figaro provides a rich library of constructs to build these models, and provides ways to extend this library to create new model elements. Figaro's library of reasoning algorithms is also extensible. Current built-in algorithms include exact inference using variable elimination, importance sampling, Metropolis-Hastings with an expressive language to define proposal distributions, support computation, most probable explanation (MPE) using variable elimination, and particle filtering for dynamic models. Figaro also contains built-in learning algorithms based on Expectation-Maximization so that prior distributions can be updated over time. To ease user adoption, PAST Time will leverage Charles River's previous efforts to provide an easy-to-use graphical interface to build these models that compiles into Figaro programs.

Figure 8 shows an example Figaro program that creates the completion time model for the node slide shown previously in Fig. 6. Note that the probabilities and values in this program are notional.

First, we define the amount of text in the node as 1000 characters. Then, we define two latent variables, one representing the prior knowledge of the trainee and the other representing typical reading speeds. In this case, we specify that a trainee has prior knowledge with 0.2 probability, and the trainee's reading speed is normally distributed around 100 characters a second. Next, we define the actual reading speed of this trainee. In this example, if the trainee has prior knowledge of this subject, we increase their reading speed by a value normally distributed around 50 characters a second.

```
val text = Constant(1000.0)
val priorKnowledge = Flip(0.2)
val populationReadSpeed = Normal(100.0, 50.0)
val readSpeed = If(priorKnowledge,
  populationReadSpeed ++ Normal(50.0, 25.0), populationReadSpeed)
val fatigued = Flip(0.4)
val readingTime = If(fatigued,
  text / (readSpeed * Constant(0.5)), text / readSpeed)

val algorithm = Importance(10000, readingTime)
algorithm.start
println(algorithm.distribution(readingTime))
```

**Fig. 8.** Figaro program that models reading time of a slide node

We next represent the fatigued state of the trainee (0.4 probability that the trainee is fatigued). Finally, we define the reading time of this node as the amount of text divided by the reading speed of the trainee; if the trainee is fatigued, however, we assume they can only read at 50% capacity. To use this model to estimate the completion time of the module, we use Figaro's built-in importance sampling algorithm to sample the model and print the distribution over the reading time variable. Observe that invoking an inference algorithm to estimate the completion time is a single line of code, and any other Figaro inference algorithm can be substituted into this program with no other changes.

Figaro probabilistic programming is useful in this context for a number of reasons: We can automatically build a model given a specification of the MAST skill tree, the trainee model, and a set of known relationships. Prediction based on the model is already coded in Figaro's inference algorithm, so additional effort is not required to use the model. Figaro supports the creation of dynamic Bayesian networks that model the temporal processes of variables, simulating fatigue and practice effects. We can continuously learn using these models; the probabilistic programs are flexible enough to update relationships between variables based on historical or dynamic data. Figaro's encapsulation mechanism enables easy creation of reusable components. Trainee models and MAST skill trees can be reused for future prediction models. It is embedded in a general purpose language, Scala, which allows the creation of front end graphical interfaces that can edit and invoke the models created in Figaro. Figaro is free and open source, enabling the Sponsor and others to edit, create, and share source code for models.

Figure 9 shows the results of running this Figaro model. The distribution of reading times has three modes. At about 7 s, individuals that have prior knowledge and are not fatigued read the slide quickly. At 10–11 s are individual that have no prior knowledge and are not fatigued. At 20–21 s are individuals without prior knowledge and who are fatigued, reading slowly to absorb more information. An instructor may use a model like this one to examine how individual slide contents may be processed by a class of students, and make small changes to the presentation to increase learning efficiency.

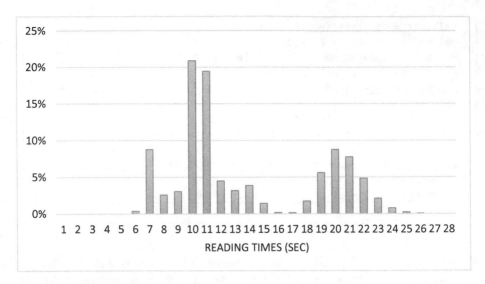

**Fig. 9.** Probability density of reading times for one slide

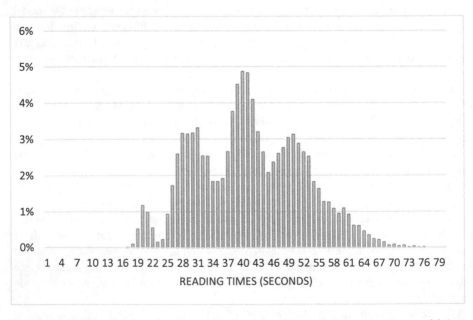

**Fig. 10.** Probability density of reading times for three slides with increasing chance of fatigue

Figure 10 shows the probability density of reading times over three slides with the student having increased chance of fatigue (40%, 45%, and 50%) on each successive slide. In this simulation, only a small portion of the students are in the fastest group, completing three slides in about 20 s. The bulk of the students range from 25–55 s for these three slides, with three modes in this range covering the combinatorics of prior knowledge and different possible fatigue states on each slide. Also, a significant portion of the students take longer than 55 s, with a possibility of up to 76 s to complete. An instructor can use this model to examine the differential effects of fatigue, prior knowledge, and reading speeds of a heterogeneous group of students, and adjust learning content or course expectations accordingly.

This modeling can reveal underlying properties of adaptive learning content that may be counter-intuitive at first glance. For example, the most likely reading speed of a single slide (according to the first model) is about 10 s. For three slides, one might assume 10 * 3 = 30 s, but the distribution in Fig. 10 shows the mean of the predicted time about 41 s with significant standard deviation. Allotting only 10 s on average per slide in a course would prevent about two-thirds of students from completing all of the course content.

Adaptive training content with significant remedial steps has a much wider variance of completion times. We hypothesize that retraces through previous material (e.g., reviewing the boom operation slides) will be performed much faster than the initial trace. Trainees may also be able to optimize their reading and comprehension strategies if they know how they will be tested and what the consequences for failing are. Therefore, later sections in an adaptive training course (e.g., excavator bucket handling after boom handling) may have significantly different variable interactions than earlier sections, as trainees learn the training structure.

Fatigue, boredom, and other dynamic variables that represent aspects of trainee state may be heavily influenced by elements outside of the tutor, such as the time of day the training is taken, the amount of sleep the trainees received, or the amount of prior instruction (e.g., after a long day of lectures or first learning activity of the day). This may cause a seemingly high degree of variance within the completion times that may be accounted for by measuring these external variables, estimating them from data, or controlling them such that they do not vary among trainees and training instances.

Short training content, such as a course that can be completed in 30 min to an hour, has a significantly different models than extended and repeated training content, such as a course that lasts for multiple hours or content that is experienced over many sessions. Using tools such as the approaches described here can help training staff make intelligent tradeoffs between alternate course structures (e.g., a single 3–4 h session once a week or 3 sessions of approximately an hour per week).

## 4  Discussion

We believe that including a capability to predict training time for trainees in GIFT has several significant advantages. First, it facilitates return on investment calculations by enabling the author to determine training time reductions resulting from the addition of adaptive features. Second, it provides a means for GIFT to monitor student progress against an expected timeline. Students who take much longer to complete training than expected may not be fully engaged in the training or may be having difficulty with the material. These are conditions that might prompt a response by GIFT. Finally, it can play a role in quality control of GIFT courses. For example, if segments of a course take much longer than expected across multiple trainees, GIFT could flag those sections for review by the course author to insure that the material is presented clearly.

There are several challenges we may face as we move into the second and third phases of this effort. First, the initial MAST skill trees may not contain sufficient variables to predict adaptive training completion times. Our initial literature review and analysis has identified a potential set of most influential variables, but these variables may not be reflective of completion time upon closer inspection. We will mitigate this risk by widening the scope of task models to incorporate more predictive variables if necessary.

Second, while the model predictions may be highly accurate, there is a risk that the system will be too difficult or time consuming to use for some or all of the target populations of instructional designers, course managers, and instructional staff. We mitigate this risk by conducting a requirements analysis early in the effort to closely examine the needs of these user groups and design our system and interfaces to best meet those needs. We will apply human factors and user-centered design and understand the challenges of and methods for developing highly useful and usable decision-aiding tools for practitioners.

Third, while this approach combines state of the art probabilistic approaches and identifies key variables from the literature and past experience, there is a potential that the initial predictions will not sufficiently account for the variability of trainee completion times. We plan to mitigate this risk by incorporating historical data early and adjusting the analysis techniques to capture the maximum amount of variability from data that can be reasonably collected in the field.

When complete, this will be the first system to predict the completion times of GIFT modules from module and trainee data and the first to enable effective assessments of the ROI of key design and implementation decisions for adaptive training systems. It includes an innovative application of procedural skill modeling using demonstrated MAST skill trees to flexibly represent adaptive training content for analysis. It is the first application of Figaro probabilistic programming to predict completion times for adaptive training technologies, including both unobserved latent variables and temporal factors, such as trainee fatigue, boredom, or flow.

The ability to predict the completion time of adaptive training content directly supports the ARL mission and the Army Learning Model (ALM). This approach, if successful, enables instructional designers, course managers, and instructors to make intelligent decisions about adaptive training development, implementation, and use within Army training by providing critical metrics of time to complete training. These metrics significantly impact the ROI of adaptive training and can differentiate between feasible and infeasible training approaches. Optimizing this metric can yield significant cost savings for large Army training courses, where the total cost of trainee time is very high. Tools such as the models described in this paper enable the Army to better understand and streamline adaptive training, as well as invest intelligently in new training technologies by providing accurate estimates of these technologies' impact on cost and force readiness.

# References

Dodds, P., Fletcher, J.D.: Opportunities for new "smart" learning environments enabled by next generation web capabilities. J. Educ. Multimedia Hypermedia **13**, 391–404 (2004)

Dynarsky, M., Agodini, R., Heaviside, S., Novak, T., Carey, N., Camuzano, L., Sussex, W.: Effectiveness of reading and mathematics software products: findings from the first student cohort, March Report to Congress 2007. http://ies.ed.gov/ncee/pdf/20074005.pdf. Accessed 15 May 2015

Fletcher, J.D.: Evidence for learning from technology-assisted instruction. In: O'Neil, H.F., Perez, R. (eds.) Technology Applications in Education: A Learning View, pp. 79–99. Erlbaum, Mahwah (2003)

Goldberg, B., Hoffman, M.: Adaptive course flow and sequencing through the engine for management of adaptive pedagogy (EMAP). In: Proceedings of the AIED Workshop on Developing a Generalized Intelligent Framework for Tutoring (GIFT): Informing Design through a Community of Practice, pp. 46–53. Madrid, Spain (2015)

Graesser, A.C., Conley, M., Olney, A.: Intelligent tutoring systems. In: Harris, K.R., Graham, S., Urdan, T. (eds.) APA Educational Psychology Handbook, vol. 3, pp. 451–473. American Psychological Association, Washington, D.C. (2012). Applications to Learning and Teaching

McDonnell Douglas Corporation. A survey and analysis of military computer-based training systems: (A two part study). Vol II: A descriptive and predictive model for evaluating instructional systems. Defense Advanced Research Projects Agency (1977). http://www.dtic.mil/dtic/tr/fulltext/u2/a043358.pdf. Accessed October 2015

Merrill, M.D.: Component display theory. In: Reigeluth, C.M. (Ed.) Instructional-Design Theories and Models: An Overview of their Current Status, pp. 282–333. NJ: Lawrence Erlbaum Associates, Hillsdale (1983)

Olney, A.M., Person, N.K., Graesser, A.C.: Guru: designing a conversational expert intelligent tutoring system. In: Boonthum-Denecke, C., McCarthy, P., Lamkin, T. (eds.) Cross Disciplinary Advances in Applied Natural Language Processing: Issues And Approaches, pp. 156–171. Information Science Publishing, Hershey (2012)

Pfeffer, A.: Creating and manipulating probabilistic programs with Figaro. Workshop on Statistical Relational Artificial Intelligence (StarAI) (2012)

Sottilare, R., Brawner, K.W., Goldberg, B.S., Holden, H.K.: The generalized intelligent framework for tutoring (GIFT). Army Research Laboratory (US), Human Research and Engineering Directorate (HRED), Orlando (2012a). https://gifttutoring.org/attachments/152/GIFTdescription_0.pdf. Accessed May 2015

Sottilare, R., Goldberg, B.S., Brawner, K.W., Holden, H.K.: A modular framework to support the authoring and assessment of adaptive computer-based tutoring systems (CBTS). In: Proceedings of the Interservice/Industry Training Simulation and Education Conference, 3–6 December 2012, Orlando, FL. National Defense Industrial Association, Arlington (2012b)

Sottilare, R.A.: Using learner data to influence performance during adaptive tutoring experiences. In: Schmorrow, D.D., Fidopiastis, C.M. (Eds.) AC 2014. LNAI, vol. 8534, 265–275. Springer, Cham (2014). doi:10.1007/978-3-319-07527-3_25

Steenbergen-Hu, S., Cooper, H.: A meta-analysis of the effectiveness of intelligent tutoring systems on K-12 students' mathematical learning. J. Educ. Psychol. **105**(4), 970–987 (2013)

Steenbergen-Hu, S., Cooper, H.: A meta-analysis of the effectiveness of intelligent tutoring systems on college students' academic learning. J. Educ. Psychol. **106**, 331–347 (2014)

VanLehn, K., Graesser, A.C., Jackson, G.T., Jordan, P., Olney, A., Rosé, C.P.: When are tutorial dialogues more effective than reading? Cogn. Sci. **31**(1), 3–62 (2007)

VanLehn, K.: The relative effectiveness of human tutoring, intelligent tutoring systems, and other tutoring systems. Educ. Psychol. **46**(4), 197–221 (2011)

# Personalizing Training to Acquire and Sustain Competence Through Use of a Cognitive Model

Tiffany S. Jastrzembski[1]([✉]), Matthew Walsh[2], Michael Krusmark[3],
Suzan Kardong-Edgren[4], Marilyn Oermann[5], Karey Dufour[6],
Teresa Millwater[7], Kevin A. Gluck[1], Glenn Gunzelmann[1],
Jack Harris[8], and Dimitrios Stefanidis[9]

[1] Air Force Research Laboratory, Wright-Patterson Air Force Base,
Dayton, OH, USA
{tiffany.jastrzembski,kevin.gluck,
glenn.gunzelmann}@us.af.mil
[2] Tier1 Performance Solutions, Pittsburgh, PA, USA
m.walsh@tier1performance.com
[3] L-3 Communications, Dayton, OH, USA
michael.krusmark.ctr@us.af.mil
[4] Robert Morris University, Pittsburgh, PA, USA
kardongedgren@rmu.edu
[5] Duke University, Durham, NC, USA
marilyn.oermann@duke.edu
[6] Defense Health Headquarters, Falls Church, VA, USA
karey.dufour@us.af.mil
[7] The SALUS Group Incorporated, Dayton, OH, USA
teresa.millwater.ctr@us.af.mil
[8] Infinite Tactics, Wright-Patterson Air Force Base, Dayton, OH, USA
jack@infinitetactics.com
[9] Dimitrios Stefanidis, Bloomington, IN, USA
dimstefa@iu.edu

**Abstract.** One-size-fits-all fixed calendar date approaches to training have proven to be inadequate across an array of domains and contexts, and in the medical field specifically, many studies document that skills deteriorate as early as two months after training (e.g., Madden 2006; Woollard et al. 2006). Given the individual differences learners inherently possess, we posit that it would be much more prudent to personalize training around individual learner needs, so that competency could be both attained and sustained in a tailored and streamlined fashion. We hypothesize that through the application of an innovative new cognitive technology, known as the Predictive Performance Optimizer (PPO), individual trainees may reduce unnecessary time in training while increasing performance effectiveness compared to learners given similar training opportunities at fixed times. PPO functions by capitalizing on the fidelity of objective performance data captured through simulation to prescribe training events/refreshers that help individuals both acquire and sustain competency in specific skills, including CPR, trauma assessment, laparoscopic surgery, and intracranial pressure monitoring. We have amassed increased levels of evidence

© Springer International Publishing AG 2017
D.D. Schmorrow and C.M. Fidopiastis (Eds.): AC 2017, Part II, LNAI 10285, pp. 148–161, 2017.
DOI: 10.1007/978-3-319-58625-0_10

revealing the ability of PPO to personalize training and prescribe tailored, customized regimens designed to help trainees both acquire and sustain competencies both efficiently and effectively.

**Keywords:** Cognitive model · Learning · Retention · Personalized training · Competency · Acquisition · Sustainment

# 1  Introduction

Simulation-based learning for the acquisition and maintenance of skills plays an increasingly integral role in most medical training curricula. Reasons for this shift in teaching and assessment include changes in health care delivery resulting in academic environments where patient-based teaching is limited, a desire to reduce the likelihood of medical errors and enhance patient safety, and a paradigm shift to competence-based demonstrations of performance, for which simulation technology enables objective performance measurement (Scalese et al. 2007).

Fortunately, momentum has gained in recent years to establish proficiency-based criteria for specific medical tasks. This is a good first step towards quantifying the return on investment of simulation use for training acquisition purposes and ensures each individual is competent to pass the program when specific criteria are met. Unfortunately, little guidance exists regarding the duration of acquired skills or the appropriate dosing of simulation experiences – meaning how much simulation is optimal, what type of simulation would best achieve goals, and when should those training experiences optimally be delivered. It is our argument that sustainment should also be proficiency-driven, meaning that individual training schedules should be determined on the basis of when individuals skills are predicted to decay below acceptable criteria. This paper seeks to present several case studies demonstrating the ability to personalize and tailor medical simulation training around individual learning needs.

Within the Air Force, medical sustainment requirements are arguably even more acute. A primary emphasis of the Air Force Medical Service (AFMS) is to maintain the readiness of personnel to perform wartime healthcare. Over the past decade, the AFMS has been successful in achieving these goals because clinicians routinely care for combat casualties in a wartime environment. Of considerable concern is the impact that the recent decreased military operations in Iraq and Afghanistan will have on sustaining readiness skills. Further, because skill retention across an array of medical tasks tends to decay between three and six months if not practiced (Stefanidis et al. 2006; Oermann et al. 2011; Tuttle et al. 2007), it is likely the case that Air Force nurses attempting to demonstrate competency every 24 months will find that their skills not only have decayed below reasonable levels, but will need to be reacquired.

## 1.1  The Simulation Environment

Use of effective simulation is key towards helping nurses both acquire and sustain performance effectiveness when real-world exposures and opportunities are lacking. For these reasons, a number of simulators have been validated as training tools and simulation centers have been established in many educational and training institutions and environments (Fried et al. 2004; Korndorffer et al. 2006). Simulation provides participants with the opportunity to practice clinical judgment and apply problem solving skills in a risk-free, replicable clinical environment (Jha et al. 2001; Rosen 2008; Ziv et al. 2000; Prion 2008). Further, medical simulation technology provides a platform for trainees to practice and acquire relevant clinical skills that will later translate to clinical outcomes on patient care (Dunn et al. 2004; Tekian et al. 1999).

In the specific case of laparoscopic surgery, evidence for benefits of using simulation technology is even more compelling. Laparoscopic surgery imposes specific hindrances such as the loss of 3-dimensional visualization, loss of tactile feedback, and counterintuitive instrument movement (Ahlberg 2007). Given these challenges, a conventional apprenticeship model of skill development does not fit well. Further, during the period before technical proficiency has been reached, the risk for complications is greatly increased (Moore et al. 1995; Deziel et al. 1993; Joice et al. 1998). Thus, it is critically important to objectively assess the performance levels of trainees as they acquire laparoscopic surgical skills, to mitigate risk and maximize patient safety.

Despite advances in objective performance measurement, simulation technology, proficiency-based curricula, it is unfortunately the case that few guidelines exist for how simulation may be used most effectively, what type of simulation platform would be most beneficial for specific individuals, whether specific skills trained will transfer to the clinical environment, and the longevity of specific skills trained using simulation (Stefanidis et al. 2005). Further, no evidence exists regarding how to use proficiency-based data to predict the future performance effectiveness of a learner or determine when refresher training show optimally occur to mitigate skill decay. Consequently, medical simulation curricula could benefit greatly from such affordances. Providing instructors with a principled approach towards tracking individual performance and prescribing tailored training schedules around individual needs could transform the current state-of-the-art and effectively and efficiently ensure that trainees would acquire or maintain proficiency at specific points in time. The current research assesses the extent to which the application of a cognitive model could provide accurate predictions of future performance at the individual learner level of analysis.

## 1.2    Cognitive Model of Learning and Decay

Briefly stated, a cognitive model's purpose is to scientifically and formally translate a conceptual theoretical framework of a basic cognitive process (i.e., learning, perceiving, remembering, problem solving, decision making) by reformulating those assumptions into a more rigorous mathematical or computer language (Busemeyer and Diederich 2009). They are derived from basic principles of cognition (Anderson and Lebiere 1998) and produce precise, quantitative predictions of performance that may be empirically tested. The cognitive model we will now describe lays its roots in this type of mathematical foundation.

Over a hundred years of research in the field of learning and forgetting has robustly demonstrated that the temporal spacing of training has a dramatic effect on the individual's ability to retain the knowledge or skill (Ebbinghaus 1885). If training is scheduled in such a way that knowledge and skills are more susceptive to decay, then additional training resources and time must be put forth to ensure that the individual reacquires the knowledge and skills. This results in higher training costs, more training hours, and may ultimately risk patient safety.

Conversely, maintaining knowledge and skills efficiently leads to the graduation of short-term memory to long-term memory, which is much less susceptible to decay. When the knowledge and skills are committed to long-term memory, the learner does not need sustainment training as frequently. Therefore, prescribing deliberate and individualized training may result in greater knowledge and skill retention (less decay), faster knowledge and skill accessibility, and reduced chance of error.

**Predictive Performance Equation.** Recently, several researchers on this proposal who work within the Cognitive Models and Agents Branch of the Air Force Research Laboratory have developed a cognitive computational model to explain how the spacing of practice and other factors affect knowledge and skill acquisition and retention. The model is an extension of the general performance equation (Anderson and Schunn 2000) called the predictive performance equation, or PPE (c.f. Jastrzembski et al. 2009).

In PPE, three factors impact the acquisition and retention of knowledge: (1) amount of practice (*frequency effect*); (2) elapsed time since practice occurred (*recency effect*); and (3) the temporal distribution of practice over time (otherwise known as the *spacing effect*).

The spacing effect is a robust phenomenon of human memory revealing that separating practice repetitions by a delay slows learning but enhances retention (for review, see Benjamin and Tullis 2010; Cepeda et al. 2006; Delaney et al. 2010). The spacing effect is extremely general. It occurs in tasks that involve declarative knowledge (Hintzman and Rogers 1973; Janiszewski et al. 2003), procedural skills (Lee and Genovese 1988; Moulton et al. 2006), and academic competencies (Rohrer and Taylor 2006; Seabrook et al. 2005). The spacing effect has been replicated in laboratory studies (Cepeda et al. 2006), and in ecologically-valid educational settings (Carpenter et al. 2012). Children and adults show spacing effects, as do different animal species (Delaney et al. 2010).

PPE captures the spacing effect by using a multiplicative effect of practice and elapsed time, meaning that more recent training experiences are weighted more heavily than early ones, and weights associated with training experiences decrease exponentially with time. These mechanistic details allow PPE to capture learning trends across a depth and breadth of empirical data sets where spacing effects are present.

In PPE, as in other cognitive models, the psychological parameters that control cognitive processes vary across individuals. We have developed techniques to estimate these parameters at the level of the individual in order to quantify latent characteristics of the learner (i.e. decay rate, susceptibility to spacing, and retrieval variability). To the extent that these parameters and the psychological processes they represent are engaged in different and unique tasks and contexts, they provide a novel way to predict generalization and future performance. In the research presented here, we examine the predictive validity of PPE to longitudinal, repeated measures assessments of performance across laparoscopic surgery, CPR, and trauma assessment domains.

The model accounts for numerous empirical phenomena in the memory literature, demonstrating its sufficiency as a theoretical account of the spacing effect (Walsh et al. submitted). It has been validated using data from more than a dozen experiments that involve the acquisition of factual knowledge and procedural skill across timescales ranging from minutes to years. For these reasons, we are assessing PPE's validity in more applied and complex training domains.

## 2    Case Examples

PPE is currently being tested in a nationwide, multi-site field study with the American Heart Association and Laerdal to assess the validity of personalizing cardiopulmonary resuscitation skills training for medical care providers. PPE is also being used to prescribe refresher training for nurses performing trauma assessment on higher fidelity mannequin training platforms, and has been used to track and predict performance in virtual reality laparoscopic surgery domains. Plans to assess PPE using virtual and virtual reality training environments for trauma assessment, and intracranial pressure monitoring skill decay of critical care nurses (a collaboration with the United States Air Force School of Aerospace Medicine) are funded and underway as well.

### 2.1    Cardiopulmonary Resuscitation Skills Acquisition and Retention

**Purpose.** The current standard for hospital employees to maintain certification for cardiopulmonary resuscitation (CPR) skills is taking the American Heart Association course every 2 years. Literature reveals that most medical skills, including CPR, have decayed below proficient levels somewhere between 3 and 6 months post-acquisition, however. As such, the American Heart Association is using that evidence to make a potential policy shift, mandating that hospital employees increase their training 8-fold, and complete CPR training every 3 months, rather than every 2 years. This policy shift also changes the nature of training from a curriculum that is subjectively assessed, to one that is objectively measured using more intelligent manikin training systems. The problem is that the potential policy shifts seeks to fix the problem with undertraining trainees, by potentially overtraining individuals who do not need the additional training. For this reason, researchers at AFRL are collaborating with the American Heart Association and Laerdal to determine whether CPR skills could be personalized around individual learning needs, saving both time in training and reducing patient risk through proficiency-based training scheduling.

**Participants.** We recruited nursing students from a total of 9 nursing schools around the United States of America, and have enrolled approximately 400 students in a 2 year, repeated measures field study thus far.

**Materials.** CPR was assessed using the ResusciAnne Simulator designed by Laerdal. This system provides real-time, dynamic, visual feedback to trainees regarding compression depth, compression rate, compression hand placement, compression hand release, ventilation volume, and ventilation rate. The simulation system produces a score ranging from 0–100% regarding the quality of both compressions and ventilations. These scores are used in the American Heart Association's Resuscitation Quality Index (RQI) program. Proficiency was set at 75% in concordance with the RQI program. All data were recorded using Laerdal's learning management system (LMS), so that individuals could easily log in, examine their performance profile and history, and receive real-time training prescriptions immediately following the current training session for those enrolled in the PPE-prescribed condition (as described in the Design section below).

**Design.** The empirical design consisted of a 24 month, repeated measures training and assessment schedule. We employed a pre-test (no feedback), training with real-time, dynamic feedback, post-test (no feedback) design across sessions. Compressions and ventilations were each performed for approximately 1 min for each assessment (e.g., pre-test, training with feedback, and post-test). We included a pre-test/post-test design in order to provide the cognitive model with as much information as possible to adequately estimate its parameters in a very short amount of time. In this way, we could quantify the efficacy of the training itself and how much trainees learned within a session (between the pre and post-test), and estimate the degree of decay that occurred between unique sessions.

We included multiple conditions in this large-scale research design. Firstly, we manipulated the training calibration schedule, meaning we had participants come in for initial acquisition training for 4 sessions spread either daily, weekly, monthly, or quarterly (every 3 months). The purpose of having a difference in our initial acquisition sessions was to assess the validity of PPE model prescriptions as a function of how quickly those individual learning and decay parameters were estimated.

Next, we compared performance of trainee groups across 2 fixed retention intervals of either 3 or 6 months, to groups of individuals assigned to a PPE-prescribed training schedule. For those in the fixed interval condition, they completed 2 reassessments. For those in the PPE-prescribed training condition, they could complete up to a maximum of 10 training sessions or up to 2 years of training time total. In the PPE-prescribed training condition, a subsequent training session was scheduled according to either when that individual's performance was predicted to decay below 75%, or to help them acquire 75% proficiency in the first place.

Results from the full field study are not yet available as the study is set to complete about 9 months from now. As such, we seek to present pilot results demonstrating how the model functions and results from the smaller pilot group.

**Model Application.** Data from the pre and post-tests from the first 4 training sessions were used to estimate unique learning and decay parameters for individual trainees. The model produces empirical predictions of human performance for subsequent training sessions using a one-step-look-ahead procedure, and iteratively update unique learning and decay parameter estimates as new data become available.

Figure 1, below, reveals empirical data from a portion of our pilot sample, examining performance differences as a function of either daily or weekly initial acquisition of skill, and returning for reassessment 3 months post-acquisition. We will focus our analyses on compressions only at this time.

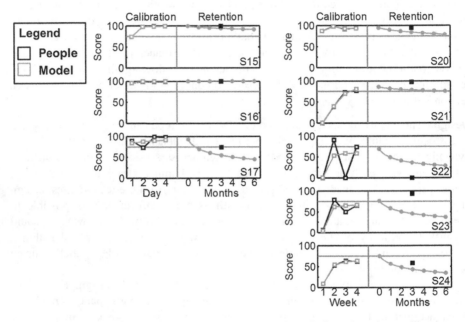

**Fig. 1.** Empirical data for 8 participants with PPE model predictions, based on calibration to initial 4 sessions. Right panel of each graph reveals projected decay curve for each participant.

Pilot study results reveal key findings. (1) Acquisition is faster when participants train ore quickly, in line with effects of recency, and (2) PPE may be used to successfully track and predict trauma assessment skills performance at the individual learner level. Extrapolations of decay curves indicate that PPE correctly classified 7/8 participants correctly when it came to who would and who would not be proficient at the 3 month retention assessment. In the larger field study, we are doing more than simply classifying who needs training at fixed intervals. We are prescribing precisely when individuals need to return for retraining to either (1) acquire skills initially (as would be the case for S24 in Fig. 1, above), or (2) utilize the decay curves to determine precisely when a participant should return for training to sustain skills before they are predicted to dip below the 75% criterion (e.g., S17 in Fig. 1, above, would be required to return approximately 3.5 weeks post-training acquisition, as that is the point in the decay curve that dips below proficiency). Interestingly, in this very small sample we did not see a trend toward enhanced retention as a function of more distributed training upfront. It will be interesting to see whether true effects of spacing are present in the larger field study.

At a finer level of detail, Fig. 2, below, reveals how the model functions at the individual learner level of analysis. This figure takes pilot data from S24 and extrapolates forward in time to reveal how this individual would likely perform under the current standard of training cycle, which is every 2 years. In this scenario, this participant wouldn't achieve proficiency until nearly 12 years into their career, meaning they would be performing "at risk" approximately 43% of their career.

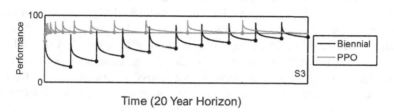

Time (20 Year Horizon)

**Fig. 2.** PPE model predictions of performance for S24 over a 20 year horizon, based on calibration to initial 4 sessions, compared to PPE model predictions of performance based on a PPE-prescribed training schedule over the same timeframe.

By contrast, Fig. 2 also reveals a PPE-prescribed training regimen, demonstrating that more training would be required upfront to help this individual first attain proficiency. After proficiency is attained, then training refreshers are principally spaced farther and farther apart temporally, as knowledge and skills become more and more stable. This simple comparison revealed a 45% decrease in training time, and a 99% reduction in risk over the same 20 year horizon.

## 2.2 Trauma Assessment Skills Acquisition and Retention

**Purpose.** Air Force nurses must acquire and sustain a high level of trauma assessment skills to manage patient wounds from current and future conflicts and to be prepared for mass casualty events. Due to drawdowns from Iraq and Afghanistan, decreased deployments have resulted in reduced exposure to trauma management and care, and Air Force nurses do not have frequent enough opportunities to care for trauma patients stateside to maintain currency. This case study sought to determine whether:

(1) Trauma assessment skills may be objectively assessed using simulation
(2) A trauma assessment curriculum could be established to help nurses establish and sustain proficiency
(3) The application of PPE may capture and predict learning and decay so that principled prescriptions may be assessed in an a priori fashion in a follow-on study.

There is also a vacuum in trauma assessment training, as performance is subjectively measured, self-assessed, and trained only once every four years in the Trauma Nurse Core Course (TNCC).

**Participants.** Active duty United States Air Force nurses stationed at Wright-Patterson Air Force Base were targeted for inclusion in this 12 month, repeated measures pilot study. Any type of nurse (i.e., medical-surgical, critical care, emergency department) was deemed acceptable to participate, as all types have the core requirement to perform trauma assessment. A total of 5 active duty nurses were successfully recruited and due to deployments, 3 were able to successfully complete the project.

**Materials.** Trauma assessment performance was assessed using a moderate to high-fidelity Advance Life Support Patient Simulator designed by Laerdal, and individual-level objective performance metrics were developed and validated by Lt Col Dufour and Jastrzembski (2015), using an adaptation of a previously validated trauma assessment tool for teams (Holcomb et al. 2002). This measurement tool allowed for a detailed quantitative examination of performance across specific portions of the trauma assessment task. Proficiency was set at 70% in concordance with the Trauma Nurse Core Course criterion.

**Design.** The empirical design consisted of a 12 month, repeated measures training and assessment schedule. We employed a pre-test ($\sim 20$ min), didactic training (45 min at initial training, 15 min for subsequent refreshers), post-test design ($\sim 20$ min + 40 min debriefing) across sessions. Rationale for including both a pre-test and post-test within a session mirrored that of the CPR study – namely, we wished to determine how effective training was within a session, and we wished to assess how rapidly skills decayed between sessions by establishing a baseline. Participants came in for a total of 5 sessions, occurring at onset of the study, 1 month, 3 months, 6 months, and 12 months. At the 12 month session, only an assessment occurred (no didactics or post-test was administered).

**Model Application.** The first 3 training points (pre and post tests at baseline, and reassessment at 1 month) were used to estimate unique learning and decay parameters. The model produced empirical predictions of human performance for subsequent training sessions using a one-step-look-ahead procedure, and iteratively updated unique learning and decay parameter estimates as new data became available. Not surprisingly, use of additional data for model calibration purposes produces better predictions for future events, as shown in Table 1 below, though calibrating with more than 3 training points produced diminishing returns, suggesting that for this skill set, at this cadence of training, PPE makes valid predictions out to 12 months based on only 1 month of data to calibrate with.

**Table 1.** Correlation and mean-squared error values between model and empirical data based on the number of data points calibrated with.

|          | Number of data points | | | |
|----------|-------|-------|-------|-------|
| Measure  | 2     | 3     | 5     | 8     |
| $R^2$    | 0.18  | 0.89  | 0.94  | 0.99  |
| *MSE*    | 0.200 | 0.002 | 0.001 | 0.001 |

The model was able to track performance extremely well when compared against empirical data, as shown in Fig. 3, below.

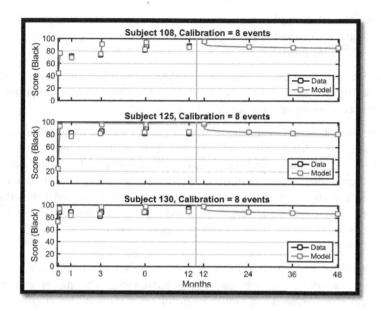

**Fig. 3.** Empirical data for 3 participants with PPE model predictions, based on calibration to initial 3 data points. Right panel of each graph reveals projected decay curve for each participant.

Based on this small sample, we demonstrated that PPE may be used to successfully track and predict trauma assessment skills performance at the individual learner level. Based on our extrapolations of projected sustainment, we also argue that restructuring the way trauma assessment is taught could produce a 75% reduction in training time with the added benefit of more prolonged skills sustainment. A follow-on study testing the model prescriptions with a larger sample is currently underway.

## 2.3   Laparoscopic Surgery Skills Acquisition and Retention

**Purpose.** Training laparoscopic surgical techniques is not a skill that is amenable to the typical apprenticeship training model, as specific hindrances including loss of 3-dimensional visualization, loss of tactile feedback, and counterintuitive instrument movement are the nature of the beast (Ahlberg et al. 2005). Additionally, during the period before proficiency has been attained, the risk for complications is dramatically higher (Moore and Bennet 1995; Deziel et al. 1993; Joice et al. 1998). Thus, great care has been placed into developing proficiency-based simulation training environments, so that students may practice and hone their craft without risking patient safety. Though this represents a huge shift in the right direction, the question still remains how long skills trained in simulation will last. As such, researchers at the Carolinas Simulation

Center collaborated with AFRL to assess whether PPE could be applied to the laparoscopic surgery domain. We used archival data as a starting point, to assess how well PPE could track and predict performance in a 12 month longitudinal study.

**Participants.** Our data analysis examined performance of seventeen second-year medical students, who were trained to proficiency in a laparoscopic suturing task (see Stefanidis et al. 2005, for details).

**Materials.** Students trained using the Fundamentals of Laparoscopic Surgery (FLS) training model, and performance was assessed using an objective performance measurement scale based on time and accuracy.

**Design.** The empirical design consisted of a 6 month, repeated measures training and assessment schedule. All students were initially trained to proficiency at session 1 (mean of 54 ± 22 repetitions and 5.6 ± 1.4 h). Students were then split into 2 conditions – either a proficiency control or proficiency + maintenance-based training group. Reassessments occurred at 2 weeks, 1 month, 3 months, and 6 months. The ongoing proficiency-based training group received additional training at the 1 and 3 month sessions in order to maintain criterion performance. At 6 months, a single reassessment was performed.

**Model Application.** Data up to and including the 2-week reassessment data were used to calibrate the model's learning and decay parameters. The model extrapolated learning trajectories for each individual to generate predictions for suturing performance at the 1, 3, and 6 month follow-up sessions.

The model was able to track performance extremely well when compared against empirical data, as shown in Fig. 4, below.

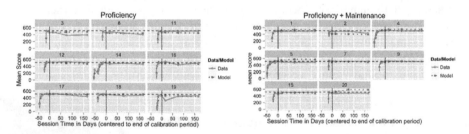

**Fig. 4.** Empirical data for 17 participants with PPE model predictions, based on calibration to initial 2 weeks of data.

These results provide a proof-of-concept that PPE may be used to successfully track and predict laparoscopic suturing skills performance at the individual learner level. In the next phase of studies, we seek to use PPE to drive principled training prescriptions around individual learning needs to determine when students should return for simulation training to sustain competencies.

# 3  Summary

It is evident that calendar-based, subjectively rated training schedules and programs are antiquated training methodologies that possess huge costs in terms of training time, training dollars, and increased performance risk. We argue that incorporating our state-of-the-art cognitive modeling approach, personalization of training is not only possible, it is affordable, feasible, and can dramatically reduce risk. It is necessary that appropriate care be given to lay a foundation of objective performance measurement systems so that $21^{st}$ century approaches to personalized learning may be validly applied. We are enthusiastic about the momentum we have gained thus far and are encouraged by government, academic, and industry investments being made to fundamentally help change the training status quo.

# References

Ahlberg, G., Kruuna, O., Leijonmarck, C.E., et al.: Is the learning curve for laparoscopic fundoplication determined by the teacher or the pupil? Am. J. Surg. **189**, 184–189 (2005)

Ahlberg, G., Enochsson, L., Gallagher, A.G., Hedman, L., Hogman, C., McClusky Iii, D.A., et al.: Proficiency-based virtual reality training significantly reduces the error rate for residents during their first 10 laparoscopic cholecystectomies. Am. J. Surg. **193**(6), 797–804 (2007)

Anderson, J.A., Lebiere, C.: The Atomic Components of Thought. Lawrence Erbaum Associates, Mahwah (1998)

Anderson, J.R., Schunn, C.D.: Implications of the ACT-R learning theory: no magic bullets. In: Glaser, R. (ed.) Advances in Instructional Psychology: Educational Design and Cognitive Science, vol. 5. Erlbaum, Mahwah (2000)

Benjamin, A.S., Tullis, J.: What makes distributed practice effective? Cogn. Psychol. **61**, 228–247 (2010)

Busemeyer, J., Diederich, A.: Cognitive Modeling. Sage Publications, Thousand Oaks (2009)

Carpenter, S., Cepeda, N., Rohrer, D., Kang, S.K., Pashler, H.: Using spacing to enhance diverse forms of learning: review of recent research and implications for instruction. Educ. Psychol. Rev. **24**, 369–378 (2012)

Cepeda, N.J., Pashler, H., Vul, E., Wixted, J.T., Rohrer, D.: Distributed practice in verbal recall tasks: a review and quantitative synthesis. Psychol. Bull. **132**, 354–380 (2006)

Deering, S., Johnston, L.C., Colacchio, K.: Multidisciplinary teamwork and communication training. Semin. Perinatol. **35**(2), 89–96 (2011)

Delaney, P.F., Verkoeijen, P.P., Spirgel, A.: Spacing and testing effects: a deeply critical, lengthy, and at times discursive review of the literature. Psychol. Learn. Motiv. **53**, 63–147 (2010)

Deziel, D.J., Millikan, K.W., Economou, S.G., et al.: Complications of laparoscopic cholecystectomy: a national study of 4,292 hospital and analysis of 77,605 cases. Am. J. Surg. **165**, 9–14 (1993)

Dufour, K.M., Jastrzembski, T.S.: The Use of a Hybrid Educational Method for Trauma Training Among US Air Force Nurses. Aerospace Medical Association annual meeting, Lake Buena Vista (2015)

Dunn, W.F. (ed.): Simulators in Critical Care Education and Beyond. Society of Critical Care Medicine, Des Plaines (2004)

Ebbinghaus, H.: Memory: A Contribution to Experimental Psychology. Columbia University Press, New York (1885). Trans. H.A. Ruger and C.E. Bussenius

Fried, G.M., Feldman, L.S., Vassiliou, M.C., et al.: Proving the value of simulation in laparoscopic surgery. Ann. Surg. **240**, 518–525 (2004)

Hintzman, D.L., Rogers, M.K.: Spacing effects in picture memory. Mem. Cogn. **1**, 430–434 (1973)

Holcomb, J.B., Dumire, R.D., Crommett, J.W., Stamateris, C.E., Fagert, M.A., Cleveland, J.A., Mattox, K.L.: Evaluation of trauma team performance using an advanced human patient simulator for resuscitation training. J. Trauma **56**(6), 1078–1086 (2002)

Janiszewski, C., Noel, H., Sawyer, A.G.: A meta-analysis of the spacing effect in verbal learning: Implications for research on advertising repetition and consumer memory. J. Consum. Res. **30**, 138–149 (2003)

Jastrzembski, T.S., Gluck, K.A., Rodgers, S.: Improving military readiness: a state-of-the-art cognitive tool to predict performance and optimize training effectiveness. In: I/ITSEC Annual Meetings, Orlando (2009)

Jha, A.K., Duncan, B.W., Bates, D.W.: Chapter 45: simulator-based training and patient safety (2001). http://www.ahrq.gov/legacy/clinic/ptsafety/chap45.htm

Joice, P., Hanna, G.B., Cuschieri, A.: Errors enacted during endoscopic surger – a human reliability analysis. Appl. Ergon. **29**, 409–414 (1998)

Korndorffer Jr., J.R., Stefanidis, D., Scott, D.J.: Laparoscopic skills laboratories: current assessment and a call for resident training standards. Am. J. Surg. **191**, 17–22 (2006)

Lee, T.D., Genovese, E.D.: Distribution of practice in motor skill acquisition: learning and performance effects reconsidered. Res. Q. Exerc. Sport **59**, 277–287 (1988)

Madden, C.: Undergraduate nursing students' acquisition and retention of CPR knowledge and skills. Nurse Educ. Today **26**(3), 18–27 (2006)

Moore, M.J., Bennet, C.L.: The learning curve for laparoscopic cholecystectomy. Am. J. Surg. **170**, 55–59 (1995)

Moulton, C.A.E., Dubrowski, A., Macrae, H., Graham, B., Grober, E., Reznick, R.: Teaching surgical skills: what kind of practice makes perfect? A randomized, controlled trial. Ann. Surg. **244**, 400–409 (2006)

Oermann, M.H., et al.: Effects of monthly practice on nursing students' CPR psychomotor skill performance. Resuscitation **82**(4), 47–53 (2011)

Prion, S.K.: A practical framework for evaluating the impact of clinical simulation experiences in prelicensure nursing education. Clin. Simul. Nurs. **4**, e69–e78 (2008)

Rohrer, D., Taylor, K.: The effects of overlearning and distributed practice on the retention of mathematics knowledge. Appl. Cogn. Psychol. **20**, 1209–1224 (2006)

Rosen, K.R.: The history of medical simulation. J. Crit. Care **23**(2), 157–166 (2008). doi:10.1016/j.jcrc.2007.12.004

Scalese, R.J., Obeso, V.T., Issenberg, B.: Simulation technology for skills training and competency assessment in medical education. J. Gen. Intern. Med. **23**(1), 46–49 (2007)

Seabrook, R., Brown, G.D.A., Solity, J.E.: Distributed and massed practice: from laboratory to classroom. Appl. Cogn. Psychol. **19**, 107–122 (2005)

Stefanidis, D., Korndorffer Jr., J.R., Markley, S., Sierra, R., Scott, D.J.: Skill retention following proficiency-based laparoscopic simulator training. Surgery **138**, 165–170 (2005)

Stefanidis, D., Korndorffer, J.R., Markley, S., Sierra, R., Scott, D.: Proficiency maintenance: Impact of ongoing simulator training on laparoscopic skill retention. J. Am. Coll. Surg. **202**(4), 599–603 (2006)

Tekian, A., McGuire, C.H., McGaghie, W.C. (eds.): Innovative Simulations for Assessing Professional Competence. Department of Medical Education, University of Illinois College of Medicine, Chicago (1999)

Tuttle, R.P., Cohen, M.H., Augustine, A.J., Novotny, D.F., Delgado, E., Dongilli, T.A., DeVita, M.A.: Utilizing simulation technology for competency skills assessment and a comparison of traditional methods of training to simulation-based training. Respir. Care **52**(3), 263–270 (2007)

Walsh, M., Gluck, K.A., Gunzelmann, G., Jastrzembski, T.S., Krusmark, M.: Evaluating the theoretical adequacy and applied potential of computational models of the spacing effect (submitted)

Woollard, M., et al.: Optimal refresher training intervals for AED and CPR skills: a randomised controlled trial. Resuscitation **71**(2), 37–47 (2006)

Ziv, A., Small, S.D., Wolpe, P.R.: Patient safety and simulation-based medical education. Med. Teach. **22**(5), 489–495 (2000)

# A Cognitive Modeling Approach - Does Tactical Breathing in a Psychomotor Task Influence Skill Development during Adaptive Instruction?

Jong W. Kim[1]([✉]), Christopher Dancy[2], Benjamin Goldberg[1],
and Robert Sottilare[1]

[1] US Army Research Laboratory, Orlando, FL, USA
jong.w.kim20.ctr@mail.mil
[2] Bucknell University, Lewisburg, PA, USA

**Abstract.** This paper reports the relationship between cognitive (e.g., attentional resources) and physiological (e.g., breathing) factors in executing a psychomotor task (i.e., golf putting). We explore performance from a series of computational models in the ACT-R and ACT-R/Φ architecture in an attempt to improve adaptive instruction and feedback using a predictive model. We particularly investigate the effect of tactical breathing during a psychomotor task of golf putting. In general, learners are instructed to perform proper breathing while executing actions. However, it is not well understood that how the corresponding mechanisms of attentional control interact with the physiological factors as the learner progresses to the learning stage. In addition the instruction and feedback policy in a training system need to deal with the changing attentional capacity in the learning stage. One of the advantages using an adaptive training system (e.g., Generalized Intelligent Framework for Training: GIFT) is to provide tailored feedback to the leaner. It is, thus, necessary to understand what influences skill development, and how physiological and cognitive processes work together to reinforce correct behaviors. Our study starts to answer such questions for psychomotor instruction within intelligent tutoring systems.

**Keywords:** Attention · Breathing · Psychomotor tasks · Intelligent Tutoring Systems (ITSs) · Generalized Intelligent Framework for Tutoring (GIFT) · High Level Behavior Representation Language (HERBAL) · ACT-R/Φ

## 1 Introduction

Intelligent Tutoring Systems (ITSs) provide adaptive instruction to learners in a variety of cognitive domains (e.g., mathematics, physics, software programming). A new trend is to begin examining how ITSs might provide instruction in psychomotor domains (e.g., sports tasks, marksmanship, medical procedures) and measure learner behaviors directly to assess skill development [1, 2]. To support the adaptive instruction of psychomotor tasks, the US Army Research Laboratory is developing the Generalized

© Springer International Publishing AG 2017
D.D. Schmorrow and C.M. Fidopiastis (Eds.): AC 2017, Part II, LNAI 10285, pp. 162–174, 2017.
DOI: 10.1007/978-3-319-58625-0_11

Intelligent Framework for Tutoring (GIFT) with the goal of providing tools and methods to enable easy authoring, delivery, and evaluation of adaptive instruction in a wider variety of domains (e.g., cognitive, affective, psychomotor, and social/collaborative). This paper focuses on the challenges of providing adaptive instruction for psychomotor tasks and specifically addresses the question: Does tactical breathing in a psychomotor task influence skill development during adaptive instruction?

Tactical breathing is a specific breath-control technique used by individuals to perform a precision required psychomotor task under a stressful situation [3, 4]. Tactical breathing has been introduced to soldiers to control physiological responses and to stay in a zone where their performance is anticipated to be successful [5, p. 39].

In this paper, we provide a new methodology to examine the functional relationship of cognitive and physiological factors. We use a cognitive modeling approach in an attempt to predict performance and to improve assessment methods, which can be applied to an adaptive instructional system. Our target task is golf-putting that requires precision. Particularly, we explore the functional relationship of tactical breathing and cognitive factors (i.e., attentional control) in terms of the learning stage. We believe that our effort combining a computational cognitive and physiological model will lead to better predictions of human performance, and can help us to make our assumptions explicit and to expose the veracity/fallacy of such assumptions. Finally, we describe how a model prediction can be used in GIFT in an attempt to generalize psychomotor tasks training, which can be useful to implement an adaptive and instructional training system.

## 2  The ABC of Psychomotor Tasks Training

In this section, we describe some background about the ABC (attention, breathing, and choking) of psychomotor tasks training. Supposed that you are hitting a golf ball. This action induces an effect that we may call the *movement effect* [6, p. 137]. The movement effect includes several sub-actions: the motion of your club, the trajectory of the golf ball you hit, the landing point of the golf ball, etc. It is argued that an optimal attentional focus exists, and it helps to develop the expertise skill by facilitating the process of learning [7]. In general, the beginner golfer should focus on the movement of the golf club that is outside of the golfer's body. You might also recognize that many golfers focus on their body movements (hands, hips, legs, etc.).

How about breathing? Focusing on breathing can affect one's attentional resources during the performance. Tactical breathing can be a useful tool for the precision-required task, but it might influence one's attentional capacity. Then, what theories should we rely on in an attempt to instruct effectively? Are these useless for the beginner to focus on? Probably not. Then, when and what should the golfer (a novice or an expert) focus on?

### 2.1  Attention and Psychomotor Performance

Attentional control relates to learning and performance in psychomotor tasks. Wulf and her colleagues mention that the focus of attention not only affects performance but also facilitates learning/retention of psychomotor skills [6]. The focus of attention indicates that the learners direct attention either to body movements or the effects of movement. In general, the former is called *internal focus* and the latter is called *external focus*. A study reveals the benefits of learning by directing attention to other cues including task-relevant or task-irrelevant cues [8].

For example, in the task of learning to balance on a stabilometer, participants grouped into three conditions: (a) directing attention to the effects of the learners' movement effects (external cues, task-relevant), (b) directing attention to the learners' movements themselves (internal cues, task-relevant), and (c) directing attention to the attention-demanding secondary task (shadowing a story-telling: external cues, task-irrelevant). This study suggests that the learners are benefited from the attentional control instruction of directing attention to external cues that are the effects of the movement (task-relevant external cues). The underlying hypothesis is that adopting an external focus reduces conscious interference in the process that controls our movements and a consequence result. In this context, some scientists argue that it is effective for an expert golfer would perform better with less explicit knowledge about the task; not thinking about the movements (i.e., putting strokes) while executing the actions [9].

To address successful skill learning and performance, it is necessary to consider what mechanisms are responsible for the aforementioned phenomena in terms of the stages of learning (from a novice through to an expert). At the very beginning of the learning stage, the learners need to adopt internal focus to direct attention to coordination of various submovements that constitute the movement of a task skill. In the early stages, more attentional resources are required to execute the skill (i.e., step-by-step execution of the skill). On the other hand, in the later stage (i.e., the third stage), the task skill can be executed without excessive effort as related to attentional resources that is known as the autonomous stage in a theory (that is represented as the procedural stage in ACT-R).

We may also observe that a professional athlete performs much more poorly than expected when faced with an outcome-defining action, which is termed *choking under pressure*. For example, under highly stressful situations, a golfer, who is endeavoring to make the cut for the PGA tour, would perform more poorly than his/her skill level and capability. Performance degrades and performance gaps exist! Is it because attentional focus is shifted to task-irrelevant cues [10, 11]? Is it because there is increase in attention that is being paid to step-by-step execution of the task skill set rather than the proceduralized skill set in the later stage of learning [12, 13]? Can we, then, minimize the influence of stressors on performance by strategic practice of tactical breathing?

It has been reported that there is a functional relationship between attentional control and psychomotor performance [14]. Particularly, skill levels (from a novice to an expert) are related to attentional resources (i.e., step-by-step execution of skill components and proceduralized performance). In addition, it is reported that a physiological change (e.g., breathing, heart rate) is related to psychomotor performance under stressful situations [5]. It can be, therefore, argued that physiological and cognitive factors are interrelated with psychomotor performance, and, thus, an advanced understanding of such factors is highly necessary to improve instruction and feedback.

There are two competing theories. The different stages of learning would require different attentional resources. That is, in the earlier stage, if the task skill execution depends on retrieval of memory items in declarative memory, a stress factor would create the potential distraction to shift attentional focus to task-irrelevant cues such as worries, a process known as distraction theories [11]. Another relevant theory applies to explicit monitoring of task skill execution. In the middle and later stages, task skills are proceduralized, indicating execution of task skill is largely unattended without the service of working memory, like the skilled typist. In this explicit monitoring theory, a stress factor raises anxiety about performing correctly, which causes the reversion of attentional focus to step-by-step control of skill processes [12, 13]. Thus, this theory can explain performance failure in the later stage.

Beilock and Carr [15] pointed out that the aforementioned theories have been seemingly considered to be mutually exclusive but should, in fact, be considered to be complimentary. This complimentary understanding is possible when we consider the three stages of learning and retention [16]. That is, under the distraction theory, task skills reside in the early stage and rely on declarative memory item retrieval, and under explicit monitoring theory, task skills reside in the later stages and rely on production rules. The aforementioned distraction and explicit monitoring theories can partly account for the phenomenon, how are physiological factors interrelated with attention resources in terms of skill learning stages.

## 2.2  Physiological Factors and Psychomotor Performance

Neumann and Thomas [3, 4] investigated measures of cardiac and respiratory activities when individuals at different levels of skill development during the golf putting task. Compared to a novice golfer, the expert golfers showed a pronounced phasic deceleration in heart rate immediately prior to the putt, and greater heart rate variability in the very low frequency band, and a greater tendency to show a respiratory pattern of exhaling immediately prior to the putt [3]. And, in a follow up investigation of Neumann and Thomas, participants performed the putting task to measure both cardiac and respiratory activity under with or without attentional focus instructions [4]. The results show that the experienced and elite golfers showed better performance and reduced heart rate (HR), greater heart rate variability (HRV), pronounced HR deceleration prior to the putt, and a greater tendency to exhale prior to the putt, compared to novice golfers. This study shows a relationship between psychomotor performance, physiological factors, and the skill level.

It is reported that a range of heart rates is related to psychomotor skill performance— i.e., around 115 beats per minute (bpm), fine motor skills are beginning to deteriorate, and complex psychomotor skills are degraded around 145 bpm, and gross motor skills (e.g., running) start to break down above 175 bpm [5, p. 31]. As a training regimen, a tactical breathing method is used to address psychomotor performance under pressure [5], and, it also has been reported that a breathing technique can lower blood pressure [17]. Furthermore, there is a report that psychological performance training including tactical breathing help to manage stress; i.e., tactical breathing and mental imagery can mitigate negative effects of stress for police officers [18], and stress management training with tactical breathing is effective in reducing stress in soldiers [19]. As a technique to delink memory from a physiological arousal, soldiers are trained to do tactical breathing to lower their heart rates.

One of the major causes of choking is self-focused attention [6]. It is very curious what the individuals focus on under time stress; do they control their movements (i.e., internal focus)? If so, instead of internal focus, it might be desirable to direct attention to external cues so that it can prevent (or reduce) choking. If we view tactical breathing as a task-irrelevant internal cue, a novice would suffer from performance degradation by tactical breathing that would demand additional attention, but, in the meantime, it could help the expert to better deal with choking. It is still necessary to further investigate the functional relationship between the cognitive factor (attentional control) and the physiological factors (breathing and heart rate variability) in terms of the skill level. Tactical breathing can be considered as a means to control attentional focus. Thus, if you use tactical breathing, you may have better performance by controlling your attention (breathing as an attentional focus training method).

# 3 The Cognitive Model

We seek to implement a series of computational models that can summarize the relationship between cognitive and physiological aspects for psychomotor tasks. We chose to use ACT-R [20] to implement a cognitive model since it is one of the widely used cognitive architectures. Also, we use a high-level behavior representation language (Herbal) [21] to organize the task knowledge of a golf-putting task.

The task knowledge used in this study adopts the instruction developed in the previous study by Beilock and her colleagues [14]. Knowledge components for a typical golf putting can be separated into (a) assessment, and (b) execution steps. For the assessment step, a golfer gathers information to judge the line of the ball, the grain of the turf, and distance/angle to the hole. Then, a golfer sequentially executes a series of mechanical actions: (a) position the ball between the center of the feet, (b) align shoulders, hips, knees, and feet, (c) check postures of grip, standing, arms, hands, and head, (d) check weight distribution, (e) stroke, (f) keep appropriate postures after stroke. As you see, the putting task requires cognitive resources during the action.

## 3.1 High Level Behavior Representation Language: Herbal

Herbal supports ontological representation of the task knowledge based on the Problem Space Computational Model [PSCM, 22]. A computational model can be created by editing Herbal's classes with an Eclipse plug-in or directly in XML. Developers can directly modify the Herbal XML code, and Herbal compiles the XML representation into low-level rule-based representations that can be run in several architectures such as Soar, Jess, and ACT-R. A recent addition to Herbal provides a capability to efficiently support ontological representation of task knowledge and to automatically generate a series of ACT-R models [23]. Table 1 shows the XML structure of the declarative memory elements.

**Table 1.** The XML structure of the declarative memory element of "Assessment".

```
<declarativememory name='Assessment'>
   <rationale>
      <what></what>
      <how></how>
      <why></why>
   </rationale>
   <parent name='Putting'/>
   <firstchild name='JudgeLineOfBall'/>
   <nextsibling name='Execution'/>
   <action name='none'/>
   <perceptualmotor name='none'/>
   <chunktype name='none'/>
   <key name='none' isString='false'/>
   <nextperceptualmotor name='none'/>
   <prerequest name='none'/>
</declarativememory>
```

In our study, Herbal helps to clarify the task knowledge structure of the golf-putting task as shown in Fig. 1. In Herbal, the topmost entity, the agent, operates within a problem space which contains a global goal. Each problem space is a collection of several subproblem spaces with a local goal that serves for the topmost problem space.

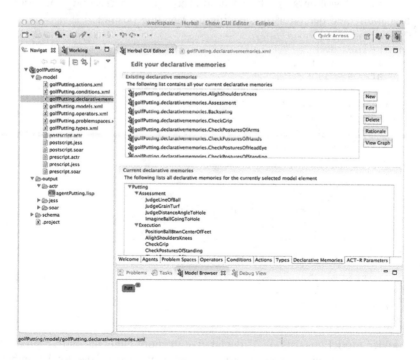

**Fig. 1.** The structure of the golf-putting task in the Herbal GUI environment.

For the golf-putting task, we created the agent named `golfPutting` with a problem space of `Putt`.

## 3.2    The ACT-R Model of Putting

We created a series of ACT-R models that represent the golf-putting performance—the time to complete a putting task in terms of the varying skill levels (e.g., a novice, a journeyman, and an expert). The ACT-R theory assumes distinctive memory systems of declarative and procedural memory. Declarative knowledge is factual or experiential. One of the declarative memory item is "Judge Line of the Ball", as shown below. It is associated with assessment to gather information before the stroke—it has a parent of `GatherInfo` in the ontological hierarchy. Also, it has a next sibling subtask, `JudgeGrainTurf`.

```
(JudgeLineOfBall ISA task-DMs Element_Name JudgeLineOfBall
Parent_Name GatherInfo Next_Sibling_Name JudgeGrainTurf
isString false Action_Name none Post JudgeGrainTurf)
```

Procedural knowledge in the model is goal-directed. The following two productions show how goals are satisfied in the condition statement. The first production is to start the putting task by checking the goal buffer if the slot values are doing a putt and ready to retrieve the next sibling subtask that is to check grip. The second production also shows a goal-directed behavior of checking the standing posture.

```
(P Start
 =goal> isa  dm
      Start  Putting
      state  nil
 ==>
 =goal> state  Putting
 +retrieval>  isa  task-dms
      element_name CheckGrip
      !output! (none)
)

(P CheckPosturesOfStanding
 =goal> isa  dm
      state  CheckPosturesOfStanding
 =retrieval>  isa  task-dms
      element_name CheckPosturesOfStanding
      post =post
 ==>
 =goal> state  CheckPosturesOfArms
 +retrieval>  isa  task-dms
      element_name =post
      !output! (none)
)
```

The novice model consists of 22 declarative memory elements and 25 production rules to produce behavior. Accordingly, for the journeyman, the total number of declarative memory items is 22 and the total number of production rules is 22. The expert model uses the same number of declarative memory that the journeyman and the novice model use, but uses 20 production rules to produce behavior; that is, it takes less explicit, goal-directed, steps for experts to complete the putt problem-space. In this manner, we can present levels of expertise.

Based on the task knowledge structure, the ACT-R model predicts learning performance—the time to complete the task in terms of the three stages of learning. In the first stage, the model learns task knowledge from instructions. It is an initial encoding of facts about task knowledge. Then, in the second stage (declarative + procedural), the acquired task knowledge is interpreted to produce behavior. Through a mechanism called knowledge compilation (or production compilation), the acquired task knowledge is converted to a procedural form with practice. After knowledge compilation, further tuning of task knowledge occurs in the third stage, producing a speedup of the knowledge application process. This is referred to as the procedural stage.

Figure 2 shows the time decreasing both by the skill level and by practice trials. The ACT-R model's learning is dependent on the activation mechanism that controls the probability and time to retrieve knowledge from declarative memory and the production compilation mechanism that is in charge of a production rule learning.

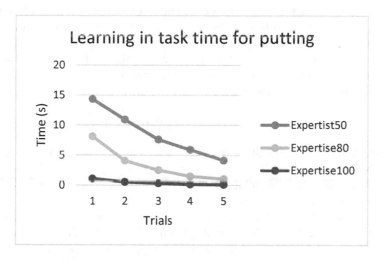

**Fig. 2.** Learning curves by the different skill level.

### 3.3 Computational Explorations of Breathing Using ACT-R/Φ

The ACT-R/Φ architecture extends the ACT-R cognitive architecture with the Hum-Mod physiological model and simulation system [24–26]. Physiological variables within the HumMod system modulate certain cognitive parameters so that changes in physiology subsymbolically affect memory—e.g., stress variables such as epinephrine modulate the ability for a model to successfully retrieve the correct declarative memory. Even though ties between stress-related variables and cognitive parameters have been previously explored [25, 26], modulations of physiological and cognitive processes due to tactical breathing have not previously been studied using cognitive architectures.

Given that tactical breathing modulates physiological systems that affect stress systems, these mechanisms are somewhat already present within the ACT-R/Φ architecture. Indeed, respiratory-related sensory mechanisms (e.g., those related to tidal volume and pulmonary stretch reflexes) have been shown to modulate sympathetic and parasympathetic nervous systems activity [27, 28]. Deep slow breathing (i.e., similar to the breathing exhibited during tactical breathing) enhances parasympathetic activation and tends to inhibit sympathetic activity [28].

Tactical breathing produces a calming effect that can, in a stressful situation, allow one to better focus on current goals and reduce stress (e.g., see [e.g., 19, for a study on related techniques used to reduce stress during a battle simulation]). Following the respiratory effects on peripheral release of catecholamines [29], one can trace potential effects on cognitive abilities; the aforementioned catecholamines modulate behavioral arousal (including through indirect mechanisms via afferents that modulate the locus coeruleus (LC)-noradrenergic system). Previous work on LC-noradrenergic (arousal) modulation of behavior [30] provides some clarity on a way to connect known respiratory effects on autonomic activity to cognitive processes and behavioral effects.

Figure 3 gives a high-level picture of the effects of arousal on memory systems in ACT-R/Φ. With this representation, low arousal (e.g., being tired) results in an overall lowering of all subsymbolic properties of memory elements. The properties all increase non-linearly as the arousal representation increases. In ACT-R/Φ, arousal is determined using cortisol, epinephrine, corticotrophin releasing hormone (CRH). Equation 1 reflects the involvement of these variables in arousal.

$$Arousal = f(cort) * [\alpha * g(crh) + \beta * h(epi)] \tag{1}$$

The equation reflects evidence that cortisol seems to serve more of a multiplicative than additive role in memory-based arousal due to the LC system [31, 32]. In Eq. 1, $\alpha$ and $\beta$ are parameters that determine the slope of the linear relation between deviation from the normal physiological state; $f(cort)$, $g(crh)$, and $h(epi)$ are a function of the change in cortisol, CRH, and epinephrine (respectively) from the baseline state. It is important to note that the non-linearity displayed in Fig. 3 (within the "arousal vs x" graphs) is accomplished intrinsically within the physiology system: physiological variables involved in the stress system change non-linearly via interactions with other variables over-time.

To accomplish tactical breathing within ACT-R/Φ, the physiology system (i.e., HumMod) is made to breath with certain parameters (e.g., tidal volume). The Integrative HumMod provides built-in mechanisms to change and track breathing over simulated time. This direct change in the physiological system, coupled with the existing arousal representation, allows the use of an Herbal compiled ACT-R model in the ACT-R/Φ architecture. Only a few parameters must be added to the model to allow it to use the physiological representations.

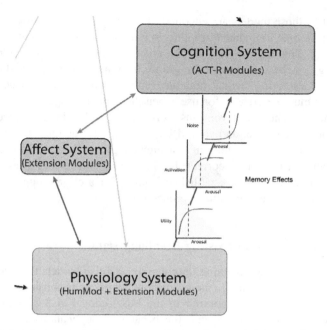

**Fig. 3.** A high-level picture of the memory effects of arousal between the physiology and cognition systems in ACT-R/Φ.

## 4    Discussion and Conclusions

In this paper, we presented the importance of tactical breathing in psychomotor tasks, and the methodology of integrating a cognitive model with physiological modulations. We suggested a convincing solution to implement the ACT-R model that can be efficiently generated by Herbal in an attempt to represent a real world sports task, a golf-putting. The major advantage of such a cognitive model provides cognitive process of learning and skill development, which is useful to improve an intelligent tutoring system. Our attempts in this paper can persuade researchers to incorporate computational model predictions to improve skill assessment strategies in the development of adaptive instruction and feedback. The following paragraphs describe future directions illuminated by the current study.

### 4.1    Toward an Adaptive Feedback and Instruction in GIFT

Establishing a predictive model of tactical breathing in GIFT requires some architectural considerations. With GIFT being a domain-independent framework, a concept must be established in a domain's ontological representation of the things to be assessed, as configured through a domain knowledge file (DKF). The DKF is used to associate a concept, such as tactical breathing, with a designated Java condition class designed to inform state assessments. The condition class is used to configure the model parameters and thresholds that will be used at training runtime.

The output of those models are encoded in a domain module message, and sent to GIFT's learner module to update the trainee's state as it associates with the event they are experiencing. This trainee state is then communicated to the pedagogical module for determining how best to manage the trainee from a pedagogical standpoint. With a model in place monitoring tactical breathing application, specific instructional strategies and tactics must be created for use when the model designates an individual as needing assistance. These interventions must be grounded in the concept they are intended to correct/reinforce, and should be based on instructional design and expert opinion. If someone is not breathing in a fashion congruent to tactical application, what intervention can be triggered to correct that individual's behavior? These elements of pedagogy and content must be established upfront for a closed-loop trainer that can focus application on tactical breathing procedures.

## 4.2    Lessons Learned from Existing Breathing Data

An analysis on the existing breathing data was to establish models for incorporation in a closed-loop ITS. The breathing data corresponds with an established fundamental of marksmanship procedures, as captured in the U.S. Army FM 3-22.9 [33]. The first analysis approach was associated with the behavioral application of breathing while executing a marksmanship grouping exercise. The goal was to investigate the utility of a generalized model of breathing based on expert application.

Data was collected across eight experts. With a large corpus of behavioral measures, we constructed models through the following procedure: (a) we computed the derivative for all associated values captured in the raw breathing wave form, (b) we established a time-window around the shot event to parse out data values (i.e., looking at breathing 1.5 s before the shot to 0.5 s following), (c) we calculated the Area Under the Curve (AUC) for that configured time-window, and (d) we performed a cross-fold validation procedure on expert data through an $n-1$ approach [34]. Outcomes of this analysis demonstrated a generalizable model of breathing application during the marksmanship task. The resulting AUC descriptive models were integrated in GIFT for assessment criteria during a training event. Then, the system can identify erroneous breathing application based on a comparison of trainee data with expert model values, with an associated 2-standard deviation threshold being defined for classifying improper breathing technique. These models can then be used to provide feedback contents and to instruct proper breathing techniques.

Based on this previous investigation on marksmanship, the cognitive modeling approach presented in this paper can provide much more generalized behavior regularity with predictions for other psychomotor tasks domains (e.g. sports, medical practices, and other military related tasks), which can be used for skill assessment and adaptive instructions. Also, a greater advantage can be expected to provide a stress resistant training by a computational understanding of cognitive and physiological characteristics (e.g., ACT-R/$\Phi$). The use of stress management training including tactical breathing is a promising method to effectively reduce stress to improve psychomotor performance. Furthermore, this attempt provides a step toward an intelligent psychomotor tasks tutoring beyond the desktop environment.

# References

1. Sottilare, R.A., LaViola, J.: Extending intelligent tutoring beyond the desktop to the psychomotor domain. In: Interservice/Industry Training, Simulation, and Education Conference (I/ITSEC) 2015, Orlando (2015)
2. Sottilare, R., et al.: Adaptive instruction for medical training in the psychomotor domain. J. Defense Model. Simul. Appl. Method. Technol. (2016). doi:10.1177/1548512916668680
3. Neumann, D.L., Thomas, P.R.: The relationship between skill level and patterns in cardiac and respiratory activity during golf putting. Int. J. Psychophysiol. **72**(3), 276–282 (2009)
4. Neumann, D.L., Thomas, P.R.: Cardiac and respiratory activity and golf putting performance under attentional focus instructions. Psychol. Sport Exerc. **12**(4), 451–459 (2011)
5. Grossman, D., Christensen, L.W.: On combat: the psychology and physiology of deadly conflict in war and in peace, 3rd edn. Warrior Science Publications (2008)
6. Wulf, G.: Attention and motor skill learning. Human Kinetics, Champaign (2007)
7. Wulf, G., Prinz, W.: Directing attention to movement effects enhances learning: A review. Psychon. Bull. Rev. **8**(4), 648–660 (2001)
8. Wulf, G., McNevin, N.: Simply distracting learners is not enough: more evidence for the learning benefits of an external focus of attention. Eur. J. Sport Sci. **3**(5), 1–13 (2003)
9. Masters, R.S.W.: Knowledge, knerves and know-how: the role of explicit versus implicit knowledge in the breakdown of a complex motor skill under pressure. Brit. J. Psychol. **83**, 343–358 (1992)
10. Easterbrook, J.A.: The effect of emotion on cue utilization and the organization of behavior. Psychol. Rev. **66**(3), 183–201 (1959)
11. Wine, J.: Test anxiety and direction of attention. Psychol. Bull. **76**(2), 92–104 (1971)
12. Baumeister, R.F.: Choking under pressure: self-consciousness and paradoxical effects of incentives on skillful performance. J. Pers. Soc. Psychol. **46**(3), 610–620 (1984)
13. Lewis, B.P., Linder, D.E.: Thinking about choking? attentional process and paradoxical performance. Pers. Soc. Psychol. Bull. **23**, 937–944 (1997)
14. Beilock, S.L., et al.: Haste does not always make waste: expertise, direction of attention, and speed versus accuracy in performing sensorimotor skills. Psychon. Bull. Rev. **11**(2), 373–379 (2004)
15. Beilock, S.L., Carr, T.H.: On the fragility of skilled performance: What governs choking under pressure? J. Exp. Psychol. Gen. **130**(4), 701–725 (2001)
16. Kim, J.W., Ritter, F.E.: Learning, forgetting, and relearning for keystroke and mouse driven tasks: Relearning is important. Hum.-Comput. Inter. **30**(1), 1–33 (2015)
17. Grossman, E., et al.: Breathing-control lowers blood pressure. J. Hum. Hypertens. **15**(4), 263–269 (2001)
18. Page, J.W., et al.: Brief mental skills training improves memory and performance in high stress police cadet training. J. Police Crim. Psychol. **31**, 122–126 (2015)
19. Bouchard, S., et al.: Using biofeedback while immersed in a stressful videogame increases the effectiveness of stress management skills in soldiers. PLoS ONE **7**(4), e36169 (2012)
20. Anderson, J.R.: How can the human mind occur in the physical universe? In: Ritter, F. (ed.) Oxford Series on Cognitive Models and Architectures. Oxford University Press, New York (2007)
21. Cohen, M.A., Ritter, F.E., Haynes, S.R.: Herbal: a high-level language and development environment for developing cognitive models in Soar. In: 2005 Conference on Behavior Representation in Modeling and Simulation (BRIMS), Universal City (2005)
22. Newell, A.: Unified Theories of Cognition. Harvard University, Cambridge (1990)

23. Paik, J., et al.: Predicting user performance and learning in human-computer interaction with the herbal compiler. ACM Trans. Comput.-Hum. Interact. **22**(5), 1–26 (2015)
24. Dancy, C.L.: ACT-RΦ: a cognitive architecture with physiology and affect. Biol. Inspired Cogn. Architect. **6**, 40–45 (2013)
25. Dancy, C.L., et al.: Using a cognitive architecture with a physiological substrate to represent effects of a psychological stressor on cognition. Comput. Math. Organ. Theory **21**(1), 90–114 (2015)
26. Dancy, C.L., Ritter, F.E., Gunzelmann, G.: Two ways to model the effects of sleep fatigue on cognition. In: Proceedings of the 13th International Conference on Cognitive Modeling, Groningen (2015)
27. Seals, D.R., Suwarno, N.O., Dempsey, J.A.: Influence of lung volume on sympathetic nerve discharge in normal humans. Circ. Res. **67**(1), 130–141 (1990)
28. Jerath, R., et al.: Physiology of long pranayamic breathing: neural respiratory elements may provide a mechanism that explains how slow deep breathing shifts the autonomic nervous system. Med. Hypotheses **67**(3), 566–571 (2006)
29. Berntson, G.G., Cacioppo, J.T., Quigley, K.S.: Respiratory sinus arrhythmia: autonomic origins, physiological mechanisms, and psychophysiological implications. Psychophysiology **30**(2), 183–196 (1993)
30. Aston-Jones, G., Cohen, J.D.: An integrative theory of locus coeruleus-norepinephrine function: adaptive gain and optimal performance. Annu. Rev. Neurosci. **28**, 403–450 (2005)
31. Roozendaal, B., et al.: Glucocorticoid enhancement of memory requires arousal-induced noradrenergic activation in the basolateral amygdala. Proc. Natl. Acad. Sci. **103**(17), 6741–6746 (2006)
32. Roozendaal, B., McGaugh, J.L.: Memory modulation. Behav. Neurosci. **125**(6), 797–824 (2011)
33. US Army, Rifle Marksmanship M16-/M4-Series Weapons (FM 3-22.9). Fort Benning, GA (2011)
34. Amburn, C., et al.: Effects of equipment on model development for adaptive marksmanship trainers. In: Proceedings of Interservice/Industry Training, Simulation, and Education Conference (I/ITSEC), Orlando (2016)

# Assessing Motivation to Individualize Reinforcement and Reinforcers for an Intelligent Tutor

Elizabeth Lameier[1(✉)], Lauren Reinerman-Jones[1],
Michael W. Boyce[2], and Elizabeth Biddle[3]

[1] Institute for Simulation and Training, University of Central Florida,
Orlando, USA
{elameier, lreinerm}@ist.ucf.edu
[2] Advanced Training and Simulation Division, Army Research Laboratory,
Human Research and Development Command, Orlando, FL, USA
michael.w.boycell.civ@mail.mil
[3] The Boeing Company, Orlando, FL, USA
elizabeth.m.biddle@boeing.com

**Abstract.** Personalized learning with technology is in full demand across all context. Learning occurs through motivation therefore, personalizing motivation is key to enhancing learning rate and retention for the learner. Supplying the intelligent tutors with key information not will advance the familiarity of individual's motivational factors and interest for individualizing motivation. Building this relationship stems from a streamlined Motivational Assessment Tool (MAT), aimed at assessing several motivation factors. The Motivation Assessment Tool is based on the interconnectedness of motivational factors with personality. The creation of the assessment allows the intelligent tutor to implement reinforcers that influence motivational level based off individual variances such as personality.

**Keywords:** Motivational factors · Intelligent tutor · Individualized motivation · Personality · Motivation Assessment Tool

## 1 Introduction

Personality traits and motivation impact learning strategies and outcomes [1]. They are titled as separate entities, yet interconnected by similar influential factors. Personality traits set the tone (positive or negative) that influence motivation by pre-disposing the individuals to be more or less comfortable in different types of situations and activities. Motivation increases or decreases as a person involved in an activity that is compatible or incompatible, respectively, with their unique make-up of personality traits. With respect to learning, the compatibility of the learner's personality traits and learning environment impacts the learner's motivation. Consequently, learners benefit from instruction that is tailored to their personality traits and motivation levels.

Motivation and personality are both complex because they are influenced by various factors. Personality traits are generally stable and unchanging, although outward

© Springer International Publishing AG 2017
D.D. Schmorrow and C.M. Fidopiastis (Eds.): AC 2017, Part II, LNAI 10285, pp. 175–184, 2017.
DOI: 10.1007/978-3-319-58625-0_12

display can vary across short timespans depending on the environmental context [2]. Motivation also changes based on a person's value [3], relevance of the activity [4], interest in the subject matter [5], ability to persist [6], and level of support needed on a task [7]. The use of a motivational strategy that recommends reinforcers that leverage the learner's personality traits and level of intrinsic motivation can support and increase the learner's motivation. The Motivational Assessment Tool (MAT) will perform an upfront assessment of the learner's personality and motivation. The results can then be used to determine what type of reinforcers to provide and a schedule for providing reinforcement. For this specific effort, the MAT will feed into the Generalized Intelligent Framework for Tutoring (GIFT) long term learner model [8] to recommend a personalized motivation strategy. The goal is to provide an extended representation of motivation pursuing personalized motivation though an assessment.

## 2 Personality Interaction with Motivational Factors

Research has investigated correlations presented in motivation, interest, and personality. The interrelationship of personality, motivational variables, and interest are recognized, but not fully established. Personality traits describe relatively fixed attributes that shape how an individual perceives and interacts with their environment. Consequently, an individual's set of personality traits often influence the types of activities they pursue [9]. One of the most commonly used set of personality traits is the Big Five [10–12]: Extraversion (preference for active/social environments), Agreeableness (preference for cooperation vs. competition), Conscientiousness (preference to attend to details, self-focused), Neuroticism (predisposed to viewing the environment as negative or threatening) and Openness (preference to try new things, creative). Motivation refers to an individual's desire and drive to succeed, or in this case, to learn, and has been categorized into two types: intrinsic and extrinsic. Intrinsic motivation refers to an internal desire to achieve, while extrinsic motivation refers to the situation in which the individual requires an external source that compels them to achieve [13–15]. Examples of the interaction between personality traits and motivation include individuals high in Conscientiousness tending to be intrinsically-motivated, while individuals high in Agreeableness (and low in Conscientiousness) tend to be extrinsically motivated. In addition to the interaction between personality traits and motivation, other attributes compound to further influence a learner's motivation. In order to develop a method for assessing motivation and determining an appropriate reinforcement strategy, the linkages between motivation and personality traits were further decomposed and defined by values, reinforcement sensitivity, vocational interest, and learning styles.

Values refer to what a person finds important [3]. Values are a part of personality and associated with motivation. Something an individual values also serves to motivate. For example, individuals with high Extraversion value social interaction [16] and are motivated when in social environment. Values and motivation are formed partially from their environment [17, 18] or from genetic factors [19]. Research has also supported that vocational interest are pieces of a person's personality [20, 21]. Table 1 identifies the linkages found between each of the Big Five personality traits and values, using the Schwartz Value Theory to define value.

A person's vocational interests reflect their personality. For example, individuals low in Extraversion prefer solitary activities, and therefore, their interests tend towards activities with low social interaction [9]. Self-efficacy [22] and interest also remain connected [23] and therefore, personality is connected to self-efficacy [24, 25]. The relation to self- efficacy is possibly through relations to the variables of personality or possibly an extension of one's personality. [24, 25]. Vocational interest is included in the Motivation Factors Interdependencies shown in Table 1 given that training with an intelligent tutoring with respect to GIFT is vocationally focused. Also, a learner's vocational interest provides insight into types of reinforcers for that individual.

Reinforcement Sensitivity Theory (RST) [26–28], which proposes that motivation is changed by a person's sensitivity to rewards (SR) and punishments (SP), explains a person's personality behaviorally and physiologically with respect to the provision of reinforcements in learning. For example, individuals with high Conscientiousness are highly sensitive to punishment, which would be viewed as a criticism of the perfection they strive to achieve, whereas they have little sensitivity to rewards since they are pushing themselves to achieve internally. Table 1 further describes the relationship between RST and the Big Five personality traits.

Deep level learning versus surface level learning has also been connected to personality types [29]. Understanding an individual's proclivity towards surface or deep learning is important when considering an intelligent tutor environment to ensure the information is being conveyed in a manner that is compatible with the learner's style. Further, ensuring that the format of the instructional content is provided in either a deep versus surface level format is important to keeping the student motivated with the learning task. Consequently, the relationship between deep versus surface level learning, referred to as learning style, is included in Table 1.

All of this research seem to point in the direction that personality is interconnected with facets of motivation. When combined, these interdependencies add more pieces to the puzzle when determining a person's motivation. However, providing a big picture, by stringing all the pieces together for a complete representation of a person's motivation by personality has yet to be determined. Table 1 shows some of the different interdependencies between the Big Five personality and motivational variables at a high level and how placing the research together begins connecting the pieces towards a more complete view of an individual's motivation.

**Table 1.** Interdependencies of motivation factors to personality.

| Motivation | | | | | |
|---|---|---|---|---|---|
| Openness | Conscientiousness | Extraversion | Agreeableness | Neuroticism | [10–12] |
| Stimulation, self-direction, hedonism, universalism and benevolence. negatively with conformity, tradition, and security | Conformity, security, achievement, and to a lesser degree tradition. negative to hedonism and stimulation | Stimulation, self-direction, hedonism, power, and achievement. negative to conservation, tradition, and conformity | Strong link for benevolence and universalism. Negative link to power and achievement | No links | Schwartz value theory [3, 30, 31] |

(*continued*)

**Table 1.** (*continued*)

| | | | | | |
|---|---|---|---|---|---|
| Sensitivity to punishment is negatively associated | Sensitivity to punishment is positively associated. negatively associated to sensitivity to reward | Positive correlation to sensitivity to reward and negative to sensitivity to punishment | Associated positively to sensitivity to punishment and negatively to sensitivity to reward | Sensitivity to punishment and reward is positively associated | Reinforcement sensitivity theory [26–28 47–49] |
| Investigative, social interest, and artistic | Conventional interest, and stability | Enterprising and social interest | Low relation to social interest | No links found | Vocational interest Holland (RIASEC) [20, 21, 32, 33] |
| Positively relates to all 6 self-efficacy types | Related to social, enterprising, and conventional self-efficacy | Related to artistic, social, and enterprising self-efficacy | Related to social self-efficacy | Negatively related to investigative and enterprising self-efficacy. Lower self-efficacy for 5 out of 6 RIASEC types | Self-Efficacy and interest Holland (RIASEC) [21, 22, 24, 25, 34, 46] |
| Prefers a deep learning | Strategic and deep approach to learning | Deep and strategic | Results are not consistent | Prefers surface level learning | Learning Style [1, 35] |
| Connected with intelligence and GPA. [36] Like more open assessments that not analytic, concise, or multiple-choice [37] | Associated with Grit [38] and negatively to procrastination [39, 40, 45]. Prefer continuous assessment [37] | Grade dependent on the type of assessment. Oral exams, short-multiple choice, and group work. [37] | Relation to oral exams and group work [37] | Has ties to procrastination. [39, 40] tendency towards being negative [41] Prefer assessment to not be continuous low Neuroticism associated with essay or oral exams. [37] | Other |

Each of these factors identified in Table 1 have a separate assessment. Some of the assessments look at one factor value, such as procrastination while others combine a few factors. While the interconnectedness is not completely understood, acknowledgement of their connection is agreed upon [1, 29–33, 35, 45–49].

## 3   Creation of the Multifactor Motivation Assessment

As shown above, research has provided overtones from personality with motivation factors. This interrelationship between the factors of motivation and personality provides similarities on all their assessments. This connected relationship is key for developing an assessment that covers the multidimensional approach for assessing motivation. The relationship is key for developing the new assessment because it allows it to be pared down and streamlined while still capturing the variables presented in the interconnected factors for an intelligent tutoring system.

## 3.1    Specific Development of the Motivational Assessment Tool

To begin the process, foundational work needed to be established from prior assessments, reinforcers, and taxonomies. This was prepared by creating a list for each of the sections and used to guide in the formation of the Motivational Tool Assessment (MAT). During the creation of the tool, a layout of the assessment was established. The assessment layout consisted of a list of factors in the assessment, which included demographics and interest. The foundation of the tool identified analogous structures between the assessments. The discovery of the related structures was accomplished by color-coding by motivational variable type (e.g. intrinsic, student autonomy) and listing items from each assessment, about 500 question/statements in all. Then the assessment questions/statements were clustered together by similarities. The clustering yielded the questions that were connected. During this process, we also discarded any motivational question/statement that did not apply to an intelligent tutor or teaming situation. Teaming was eliminated because of the current capabilities of the intelligent tutor of interest. Similar questions were rewritten into one or two questions. The motivational type categorizations were merged in some cases because of different connections in other areas. However, categorizations that appeared distinctly different remained separated. These motivation factors are related but still separate entities. Some of the questions that only applied to one motivation factor remained if applicable. A new, comprehensive assessment was generated from this qualitative factor analysis process.

The resulting MAT areas that did not capture a person's full motivation because it left out the link to their interest. Consequently, a list of reinforcers was assembled from different context and interest inventories, such as the Dunn-Rankin Reward Preference Inventory. [42]. Both non-tangible (e.g. on-line scorecard) and tangible (e.g. paper based scorecard) were included. An intelligent tutor can integrate and present many of the non-tangible reinforcers such as digital tokens, recognition, or brain breaks. However, tangibles require an onsite human teacher to provide the reinforcer in a timely manner. Therefore, the use of tangibles will be added by the instructor's availability of the items to bridge the barrier for supplying these types of reinforcers that are given very selectively. It will remain available for situations that are capable of blended learning approaches. Otherwise, it will remain off when a trainer is not available. It was noted that some pieces of information were required for the intelligent tutor to tailor and reinforce motivation. Therefore, we added sections to the MAT that is addressed in the gap areas, which will further guide the intelligent tutor towards maintaining a desired motivation level.

## 3.2    Gap Areas in the Motivation Assessment Tool

While aligning the assessment categories, there were some categories that had many fewer statements than others. To help improve the reliability of the MAT, additional items were recommended for these smaller categories- specifically in the goals/task and reward orientation sections. Another gap was the lack of specificity in the assessment items to develop actionable reinforcement strategies. The questions were then geared towards personal learning styles, choices, and strategies learners require to achieve maximum learning and retention to aid in determining the best means of providing reinforcement to the learner. Some of the sections were included to specifically gain insight on the learner's strategies for retention. This enables the intelligent tutor to provide support to a person's motivation and preference to be challenged, while also helping him or her to be a successful learner.

The task section was included to help, providing personalization to the task to influence motivation. Examples of this type of personalization are: (a) providing the learner with an option to pick the level of complexity they need to reach the goal: (b) displaying questions prior to the task, or just after the task, to help maintain focus during the learning session or after learning; (c) proving an outline to help them or preference to take their own notes, and (d) increasing the type of learning such as video, text, or listening. Some examples of the statements learners were asked to rate themselves on are:

1. In order to understand the content, I need information from different sources.
2. I am able to focus better when the text is provided to me in smaller amounts.
3. I am able to learn information faster by watching a video.

These types of questions are geared towards self-regulation and organizing preferences that have an impact on motivation. Knowing the way a student learns and the type of strategies that help learners to retain information and work hard is key in this section. Assessments of learning style exist, but were not specific enough to reinforce with an intelligent tutor, so questions were developed to help tailor motivation on a smaller scale.

The other gap in the available assessment dealt with rewards. In particular, a reward orientation section is included in the MAT. The aim for this section was to provide insight into an individual's competition perspective, types of recognition preferred (anonymous, informal, ranking, and recognition by peers), leaders, points, reinforcers, and frequency of praise or feedback needed. Tendencies towards ascetics, progress bars, type of guidance needed, grades, and unexpected rewards etc. This allows the computer to select from the taxonomy the type of rewards of interest and other functions that would enhance learning.

## 3.3   Linking the Motivational Assessment Tool and the Implication

After the MAT questions were solidified, each assessment item was liked to one or more of the five personality traits. By determining the association with an assessment item and a personality trait, the number of potential reinforcement's strategies suitable for the individual can be reduced. The goal of this is to make judgments prior to the data analysis after data is collected. The Intelligent tutor then has a wealth of knowledge on the person and their thought process for motivation. To prep for linkage, an organizer was created based on the Five Factor Personality model [10–12]. Then, judgments on the connectedness to personality for each motivation assessment statement were made. There were a few statements applicable to all personality traits. Personality can also be linked to many of the reinforcers. As previously discussed, a preference for reinforcement through the use of social recognition is linked to individuals high in Extraversion [9]. Another example pertains to a brain break reinforcer that is administered to help regain focus for individuals that are impulsive or easily stressed as seen with high Neuroticism or low Conscientious personality types. Personalities that are high in Openness are linked with artistic interest and low Extraversion prefer independent activities. There are some additional small links towards physical activity, musical preference etc. with personality [43, 44]. However, the research is very limited in linking specific reinforcers to personality. That limitation is one challenge that will be addressed by the development of the MAT. Other individual differences will also be considered for motivational links. These differences will be asked during the demographics sections. Factors that may influence a person's motivation other than personality is their social economic status, GPA, or type of community the individual lives in (rural, suburban, or urban). As with the qualitative factor analysis completed for personality and motivation, the same type of process can be applied here. These other considerations will direct us to motivate more specifically and begin to drill down on individual differences and personalizing reinforcers towards them by a more robust picture of a person.

Once the assessment is distributed to analyze the data, a taxonomy that stands across context will be hunted. Current taxonomies are divided by peer approval, tangibles, non-tangibles, etc. [42] However, without linkage to personality trait, this does not allow for personalization that may occur across the taxonomies. For example, the learner may be motivated by tangibles and peer approval equally. The data provided from the assessment will guide the creation of a taxonomy that will allow more personalization of reinforcers. Once the MAT taxonomy is created, it will be implemented into specific task experiments to test its validity and into the GIFT platform. Physiological measures will be collected to obtain data for measuring states of motivation during the task and effect of different reinforcers.

# 4 Next Steps

The next step is to incorporate the use of real-time physiological measures to evaluate student engagement and activity levels to provide additional inputs to the intelligent tutor to further refine the reinforcement strategy selection. This physiologically-based assessment of engagement will alert the tutor to different states, such as high stress, frustration, or boredom. Identification of real-time engagement between the different states will allow the intelligent tutor to determine the optimal strategy for supporting the student's motivation – such as providing motivational reinforcement or initiating an intervention. It may be possible in the future to link dopamine release with another physiological device that is cheaper and more accessible such as the FNIR, skin conductance, heart rate, or eye blinking.

With respect to rewards and reinforcement, a future effort is to determine the value of each reinforcer based on personality. This project will validate a select few reinforcers although there are a multitude of reinforcers available. Knowing the effect size for each personality will give the intelligent tutor input on what reinforcer will boost the learner to an optimal learning state. If the physiological measure detects only a slight decrease from the pendulum then the effect size needed is small as well. If the tutor does not provide anything, the motivational gap will increase and effectiveness of the motivational reinforcer will need to be larger.

The last step to be expanded is perfecting the intelligent tutor's capability with in the zone of proximal development. The intelligent tutor cannot just provide the student the right answer when they are wrong. There needs to be a balancing system that challenges the learner. This also could be linked with physiological measures. For example, if the brain is not showing maximum effort then the intelligent tutor will redirect the learner to try again versus another person might need more assistance. The high level of stress would tell the intelligent tutor that this learner need more guided support or to back up to the previous concept. This requires incorporating real-time assessments that distinguishes different engagement states and provides a deeper level of understanding for motivation and learning strategies needed for the learner.

## 5   Conclusion

The demand for personalized learning is in full force across context. Motivation allows for learning and success to occur. It too, is an individualized process. Finding a proper fit that is relevant to the learner is key. This process begins by creating an assessment tool that streamlines important relationship factors that an intelligent tutor cannot form without being provided the information. This enables the development of a taxonomy of reinforcers that personalizes methods for the intelligent tutor, which can boost an individual to optimal motivation. This assessment, links to individualization, and prior research provides a vision of a framework for personalizing motivation by personality. This framework provides guidance on effective reinforcement schedules and applies the reinforcer immediately. It directs learners in a path towards increasing the learning rate and retention. Ultimately, accomplishing this effort will result in learning that is accessible to all and deployed from the Long Term Learner Model within GIFT tutoring system.

## References

1. Busato, V., Prins, F.J., Elshout, J.J., Hamaker, C.: The relation between learning styles, the Big Five personality traits and achievement motivation in higher education. Pers. Individ. Differ. **26**(1), 129–140 (1998)
2. Fleeson, W.: Toward a structure and process-integrated view of personality: traits as density distributions of states. J. Pers. Soc. Psychol. **80**, 1011–1027 (2001)
3. Schwartz, S.H.: Universals in the content and structure of values: theory and empirical test in 20 countries. Adv. Exp. Soc. Psychol. **25**, 1–65 (1992)
4. Keller, J.M.: IMMS: instructional materials motivation survey. Florida State University (1987)

5. Harackiewicz, J.M., Tibbetts, Y., Canning E., Hyde, J.S.: Harnessing values to promote motivation in education. In: Motivational Interventions, pp. 71–105. Emerald Group Publishing Limited (2014)

6. Driskell, J.E., Willis, R.P., Cooper, C.: Effect of overlearning on retention. J. Appl. Psychol. **77**, 615–622 (1002)

7. Kember, D., Wong, A., Leung, D.: Reconsidering the dimensions of approaches to learning. Br. J. Educ. Psychol. **60**, 323–343 (1999)

8. Sottilare, R.A., Brawner, K.W., Goldberg, B.S., Holden, H.K.: The generalized intelligent framework for tutoring (GIFT). In: Concept Paper Released as Part of GIFT Software Documentation. Army Research Laboratory, Orlando (2012)

9. Matthews, G.: Personality and skill: a cognitive-adaptive framework. In: Learning and Individual Differences Process, Trait and Content Determinants, pp. 251–270. American Psychological Association, Washington D.C. (1999)

10. Costa, P.T., McCrae, R.R.: NEO-PI-R professional manual. Psychological Assessment Resources, Odessa (1992)

11. Goldberg, L.R.: The development of markers for the Big Five factor structure. Psychol. Assess. **4**(1), 26–42 (1992)

12. Dingman, J.M.: Personality structure: emergence of the five factor model. Annu. Rev. Psychol. **41**(1), 417–440 (1990)

13. Kember, D., Wong, A., Leung, D.: Reconsidering the dimensions of approaches to learning. Br. J. Educ. Psychol. **69**, 323–343 (1999)

14. del Soldato, T., du Boulay, B.: Implementation of motivational tactics in tutoring systems. J. Artif. Intell. Educ. **6**(4), 337–378 (1995)

15. Noels, K., Clement, R., Pelletier, L.: Perception of teachers' communicative style and students' intrinsic and extrinsic motivation. Mod. Lang. J. **83**(1), 23–34 (1999)

16. Odum, M., Pourjalai, H.: Effects of personality and expert system instruction on knowledge development in managerial accounting. Percept. Mot. Skills **36**, 267–272 (1994)

17. McCrae, R.R., Cosata Jr., P.T., Ostendorf, F., Angleitner, A., Hrebickova, M., Avia, M.D., Saunders, P.R.: Nature over nurture: temperament, personality, and life span development. J. Pers. Soc. Psychol. **78**(1), 173 (2000)

18. McCrae, R.R., Costa, P.T.: A five-factor theory of personality. In: Pervin, L.A., John, O.P. (eds.) Handbook of Personality: Theory and Research, vol. 2, pp. 139–153 (1999)

19. Schermer, J.A., Vernon, P.A., Maio, G.R., Jang, K.L.: A behavior genetic study of the connection between social values and personality. Twin Res. Hum. Genet. **14**, 233–239 (2011)

20. Larson, L.M., Rottinghaus, P.J., Borgen, F.H.: Meta-analyses of Big Six interest and Big Five personality variables. J. Vocat. Behav. **61**(2), 217–239 (2002)

21. Holland, J.L.: Making Vocational Choices: A Theory of Vocational Personalities and Work Environments, 3rd edn. Psychological Assessment Resources, Odessa (1997)

22. Bandura, A.: Self-efficacy: toward a unifiying theory of behavioral change. Psychol. Rev. **82**(2), 191 (1977)

23. Donnay, D.C., Borgen, F.H.: The incremental validity of vocational self-efficacy: an examination of interest, self-efficacy, and occupation. J. Couns. Psychol. **46**(4), 432–447 (1999)

24. Rottinghaus, P.J., Lindley, L.D., Green, M.A., Borgen, F.H.: Educational aspriations: the contribution of personality, self-efficacy, and interests. J. Vocat. Behav. **61**, 1–19 (2002)

25. Nauta, M.M.: Self-efficacy as a mediator of the relationships between personality factors and career interest. J. Career Assess. **12**(4), 381–394 (2004)

26. Gray, J.A.: The psychophysiological basis of introversion-extroversion. Behav. Res. Ther. **8**(3), 249–266 (1970)

27. Gray, J.A.: The Neuropsychology of Anxiety: An Enquiry into the Functions of the Septo-hippocampal System. Oxford University Press, Oxford (1982)

28. Gray, J.A., McNaughton, N.J.: The Neuropsychology of Anxiety, 2nd edn. Oxford Medical Publications, Oxford (2000)

29. Graesser, A., Chipman, P., Leeming, F., Biedenbach, S.: Deep learning and emotion in serious games. In: Serious Games: Mechanisms and Effects, pp. 81–100 (2009)

30. Parks-Leduc, L., Feldman, G., Anat, B.: Personality traits and personal values: a meta-analysis. Pers. Soc. Psychol. Rev. **19**(1), 3–19 (2015)

31. Fischer, R., Boer, D.: Motivational basis of personality traits: a meta-analysis of value-personality correlations. Personality **83**(5), 491–510 (2015)

32. Mount, M.K., Barrick, M.R., Scullen, S.M., Rounds, J.: Higher-order dimensions of the Big Five personality traits and the Big Six vocational interest types. Pers. Psychol. **58**(2), 447–478 (2005)

33. Barrick, M., Mount, M., Gupta, R.: Meta-analysis of the relationship between the five-factor model of personality and Holland's occupational types. Pers. Psychol. **56**, 45–74 (2003)

34. Hartman, R., Betz, N.E.: The five-factor model and career self-efficacy: general and domain-specific relationships. J. Career Assess. **15**(2), 145–161 (2007)

35. Swanberg, A.B., Martinsen, O.L.: Personality, approaches to learning and achievement. Educ. Psychol. **30**(1), 75–88 (2010)

36. Connelly, B.S., Ones, S., Chernyshenko, O.S.: Introducing the special section on openness to experience review of openness taxonomies, measurement, and nomological net. J. Pers. Assess. **96**(1), 1–16 (2013)

37. Chamorro-Premuzic, T., Furnham, A., Dissou, G., Heaven, P.: Personality and preference for academic assessment: a study with Australian university students. Learn. Individ. Differ. **15**(4), 247–256 (2005)

38. Duckworth, A.L., Peterson, C., Matthews, M.D., Kelly, D.R.: Grit: perseverance and passion for long-term goals. J. Pers. Soc. Psychol. **92**(6), 1087 (2007)

39. Watson, D.: Procrastination and the five-factor model: a facet level analysis. Pers. Individ. Differ. **30**, 149–158 (2001)

40. Steel, P., Brothen, T., Wambach, C.: Procratination and personality, performance, and mood. Pers. Individ. Differ. **30**, 95–106 (2001)

41. Matthews, G., Zeidner: Traits, states, and the trilogy of mind: an adaptive perspective on intellectual functioning. In: Motivation, Emotion, and Cognition: Integrative Perspectives on Intellectual Functioning and Development, pp. 143–174 (2004)

42. Landschulz, M.: A validity test of the Dunn-Rankin reward preference inventory. Doctoral dissertation, Ohio State University (1978)

43. Rentfrow, P.J., Gosling, S.D.: The Do Re Mi's of everyday life: the structure and personality correlates of music preferences. J. Pers. Soc. Psychol. **84**(6), 1236–1256 (2003)

44. Hoyt, A.L., Rhodes, R.E., Hausenblas, H.A., Giacobbi, P.R.: Integrating five-factor model facet-level traits with the theory of planned behavior and excercise. Psychol. Sports Exerc. **10**(5), 565–572 (2009)

45. Johnson, J.L., Bloom, M.A.: An analysis of contribution of the factors of personality to variance in academic procrastination. Pers. Individ. Differ. **18**(1), 127–133 (1995)

46. Rottinghaus, P.J., Lindley, L.D., Green, M.A., Borgen, F.H.: Educational aspirations: the contribution of personality, self-efficacy, and interest. J. Vocat. Behav. **61**(1), 1–19 (2002)

47. Corr, P.J.: Reinforcement sensitivity theory and personality. Neurosci. Biobehav. Rev. **28**(3), 317–332 (2004)

48. Mitchell, J.T., Kimbrel, N.A., Hundt, N.E., Cobb, A.R., Nelson-Gray, R.O., Lootens, C.M.: An analysis of reinforcement sensitivity theory and the five-factor model. Eur. J. Pers. **21**(7), 869–887 (2007)

49. Smits, D.J., Boeck, P.D.: From BIS/BAS to the Big Five. Eur. J. Pers. **20**, 255–270 (2006)

# Flow Experience in AR Application: Perceived Reality and Perceived Naturalness

Hansol Lee and Sangmi Chai[(⊠)]

School of Business, Ewha Womans' University, Seoul, Republic of Korea
1989luna@ewhain.net, smchai@ewha.ac.kr

**Abstract.** As the emergence of augmented reality (AR), game industry has promptly adopted AR to their products for better user experiences. Due to fact that the AR could deliver more realistic experience to users, AR based applications received a lot of attentions from various industries. Recent researches revealed that AR game can enhances users' flow experience more than ordinary game applications leading to better educational performance. This study pays attention to the phenomenon that AR based application can lead users' flow more than simple online applications and explored antecedent factors users' flow experiences.

By utilizing text mining method and structured interview with AR Application users, this study discovered two influential factors on users flow experience; perceived reality and perceived naturalness. We also found that perceived naturalness is a more influential factor than perceived reality on users' flow in AR context. In addition, this research discovered privacy concerns as a main cause of decreasing flow.

**Keywords:** Augmented reality · Perceived reality · Perceived naturalness · Privacy concern · Flow experience · Experiment · Text mining

## 1 Introduction

Since augmented reality (AR) was developed in 1990s, it has been commercialized in various fields such as medical, broadcasting, architecture and game industry. Because AR provides more realistic experience to user by mixing real world and virtual information compared to ordinary online environment, game industry enthusiastically adopted AR on their applications. According to SuperData's research, there are 55.8 million users in virtual and augmented reality game [31]. Investment in virtual and augmented reality game would be 3 billion dollar in 2017 and 4 billion dollar by 2018 [31].

Recently, education field also start to aware the value of AR application for educational purpose. In education perspectives, learners' state of flow is one of most important factors increasing learning outcomes. According to research of Noh et al. AR applications enhance users' interest, enjoyment, flow compared with simple applications in game context [21]. Even though there is growing popularity of AR applications for various field, there is little research empirically investigating AR app's utilities in terms of users' flow experiences. This study, as a preliminary study, explored factors affecting users flow experience in AR applications. Flow, which is mental state,

© Springer International Publishing AG 2017
D.D. Schmorrow and C.M. Fidopiastis (Eds.): AC 2017, Part II, LNAI 10285, pp. 185–198, 2017.
DOI: 10.1007/978-3-319-58625-0_13

concentration on what people are doing with feeling of full involvement and enjoyment about their activity, is one of main factors accelerating learners' proficiency in learning process [32]. This study focused on characteristics of AR application enhancing users' flow state. The main characteristics of AR application differentiate with ordinary application is users' enhanced reality perception through combining real spatial information with informational layer. Two factors, reality and naturalness, are discussed as important influencers increasing users flow using AR applications. This study also tried to discover other factors which have a potential to influence on flow experience and then discovered privacy concerns. The results of this study could provide useful insights to AR application developers by suggesting factors which they must consider.

In Sect. 2, we explain theoretical background with literature review. We also suggest a research model and hypotheses in Sect. 3. Methodology, result and conclusion are discussed in the flowing sections.

# 2 Literature Review

## 2.1 Augmented Reality

Augmented reality (AR), as a one form of virtual reality (VR) technology, allows application can mix real world and virtual information. In 1960s, a device called head mounted display (HDM) was first invented could overlap virtual information and real environment [28]. However, no specific term was used for a technology which combines real world and the virtual information until 1990s. Tom Caudell of the Boeing Company first used a term "augmented reality" to refer the technology combining real spatial world with information [3]. The first functional AR system 'Virtual Fixtures' was developed to train surgeons in early 1990s at the U.S. Air Force's Armstrong Labs [22]. And Azuma suggested the definition of AR as a system with specific characteristics [2]; AR combines real and virtual and AR Is interactive in real time. From early 1990s, AR has been widely used in military, motor and aerospace industries. In 2000s, AR technology began to be used in various industries such as game, mining, and tourism [11, 16, 30]. Especially, game industry is a first mover in adopting AR technology on their services. AR provides higher presence to game players and flow is one of main predictor of game service satisfaction [9].

## 2.2 Augmented Reality in Learning

A few studies in education field have been conducted to find out an impact of using AR contents in learning process. Ibanez et al. (2014) and Bressler et al. (2013) found out that students' flow on the class increased when they use augmented reality applications [34, 35]. Mostly, studies on AR contents in education suggested that students' level of understanding on complicated concepts can be increased by realistic experience with AR contents through virtual objects in 3D environment [4, 15, 24, 25]. Learning based on AR contents is also effective in enhancing students' interest on the class compared to traditional textbook based learning [21].

Past studies on AR in education area assented to positive effect of AR contents in learning process for increasing flow. However, there is no research uncovers what factors affecting to flow state in AR based learning so that further research is needed.

### 2.3 Purpose of This Study

Realistic experience in AR applications allows better employee training, service, and way of working, with these reasons, organizations consider implementation of AR applications [46]. To achieve expected results of AR applications, organizations need to know characteristics of AR applications leading users' flow. Based on situated learning theory and flow theory, this study explores main characteristics of AR applications fostering users flow. Findings of this study can provide important insights for AR industries when they develop AR applications.

## 3 Theoretical Background

### 3.1 Flow Theory

According to Csíkszentmihályi, when people concentrated on what they are doing, they could feel full involvement and enjoyment about their activity [7]. To fulfill flow state, there should be a balance between challenge of activity and people's skill [8]. Flow theory has been widely adopted in various contexts such as sport, gaming and education [5, 14, 18]. In business context, flow state corresponds to optimal state in work [38]. Flow state stimulates employees' motivation of achievement in their work [36] so that they can show high performance in their complicated knowledge works [37]. Flow state of employees at work also affects to increase their intension of using information technology [44] resulting in enhancement of employees' performance [45] Recently organizations implement AR applications in employee training for workers to provide real workplace experience [39]. Based on flow theory, it is better for employees archive flow state to maximize training outcome.

### 3.2 Situated Learning Theory

Situated learning theory derived from Constructivism [1] assuming that there is a positive relationship between human experience and learning. The theory insists that there is difference between school learning environment and real world so that knowledge acquired in school cannot be properly applied in real world situations [6]. To solve this problem, researchers suggested that it is important for teachers to make learning environment similar to the real world [17]. In business context, organizations implement learning by experience training due to increase training results by reducing gaps between learning environment and work place [47]. From this situational context, AR applications are widely used in the training to provide more realistic experience for employees [40]. Based on situated learning theory, this study figured out perceived reality and naturalness are the most important factors increasing users' realistic experiences through AR applications. Sensory realism is a prerequisite in making realistic environment with virtual 3D environment [41]. Perceived reality is related to visual reality in real world representation [23] and perceived naturalness is related to feeling correspondence between environment and manipulation so that it contribute to experiencing presence in AR environment [20].

### 3.3 Perceived Reality

Perceived reality was first suggested in television media studies. Hawkins suggested the term "perceived reality" to explain how people judge the reality of television media in the first time [13]. A common definition of perceived reality is the degree of correspondence between the media texts and the real-world [18]. Malliet introduced concept of perceived reality to the video game context [19]. Malliet asserted that users' perceived reality of game be critical to increase players' concentration in the game [19]. Shafer et al. used the extended definition of perceived reality examining perceived reality of various media such as animations, dramas and video games [23]. They focused on "perceptual fidelity" which is visual reality. Based on their research results, we can conclude that visual reality is also very important in AR application since most of AR applications provide visual information through combination of real space with visual information.

### 3.4 Perceived Naturalness

Natural mapping is suggested as a related factor of perceived naturalness. Natural mapping means "a system's ability to map its controls to correspond to changes within a mediated environment, doing so in a manner that is natural and predictable (p. 104) [27]." Natural mapping help their players to make accurate and quick decision on game situation so that player could align the real-world and virtual world behavior closer [29]. Skalski explained that natural mapping increases the degree of perceived naturalness [26], which means the degree of congruent feeling between the virtual world and their manipulation in the game through controller [20]. However, perceived naturalness was never explored in AR application context.

## 4 Research Model and Hypotheses

When students use AR application in study, AR technology adds virtual objects on the real environment. They can observe and experience phenomena with AR application. This allows them to develop better conceptual understanding about what they learn,

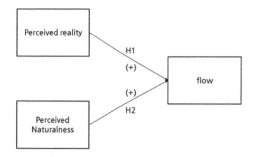

**Fig. 1.** Conceptual research model of this study

leading to have interest about it. By adopting AR application, students easily concentrate on the class and feel enjoyment [25].

Previous research proved that the similarity between the representation of world in game and real world has a positive relationship with players' flow experience [29]. Likewise, if virtual objects in AR environment are similar to the real objects, students could have more realistic experience like applying their real world skill [33]. Therefore, interest on the class would be increased. Interest on the study subject makes students concentrate on the class so that they could have a higher probability of experiencing flow state. Therefore we posit this hypothesis 1 (Figure 1).

**H1: Perceived reality in AR application and flow has a positive relationship.**

Students could manipulate virtual objects in real environment with educational AR application. They experience phenomena by navigating AR environment, feel enjoyment and interest about the class [21]. If the objects in AR game were controlled in a lifelike manner, students don't have to care about game control and could fully concentrate on the game [10]. Higher perceived naturalness contributes to the students' concentration so that it performs a key role in achieving flow experience with AR game. Therefore, we suggest following hypothesis.

**H2: Perceived naturalness in AR application and flow has a positive relationship.**

## 5   Research Methodology

### 5.1   Study 1: Text Mining

To select smart phone AR applications to fit our study purpose which provide differences in perceived reality and perceived naturalness, this study applied text mining method. We selected 2 AR smart phone astronomy applications that have same operation system and functions. To find out differences in perceived reality and perceived naturalness of 2 applications, we collected the review of last 18 months (June 1, 2015–December 31, 2016) from Google play store. Application A received 258

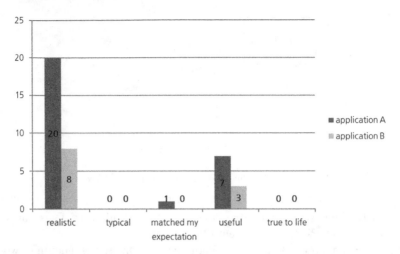

**Fig. 2.** The frequency of keyword/key phrase in perceived reality

reviews from players and Application B received 220 reviews from players during the time (Fig. 2). Because reviews contain free expression of customer opinion, it is useful to know true reactions of customers on products or services [42]. We deployed text mining technique called word frequency analysis on the reviews. Customer review text mining is often used in a customer satisfaction research, and word frequency analysis is widely used to find out how many reviews give positive/negative opinions on products or services [43] (Table 1).

**Table 1.** Frequency of top 10 word in the reviews

| A | Frequency | B | Frequency |
|---|---|---|---|
| Constellation | 46 | Constellation | 34 |
| Best | 40 | Best | 25 |
| Location | 14 | Planet | 18 |
| Thank | 11 | Amazing | 16 |
| Extraction | 10 | Study | 13 |
| Camera | 10 | Name of B | 10 |
| Science | 8 | This | 8 |
| Cool | 8 | Accurate | 8 |
| Subscription | 8 | Universe | 7 |
| Screen | 8 | Location | 7 |

To conduct key term extraction, we collected keywords and key phrases from measures of perceived reality [23] and perceived naturalness [20]. We counted the frequency of keywords and key phrases with R 3.3.2 ver. The analysis result shows that application A has higher frequency of perceived reality keywords and application. (Figure 3) B has higher frequency of perceived naturalness keywords (Fig. 4). Based on this result, we conclude that app A has higher perceived reality and app B has higher perceived naturalness.

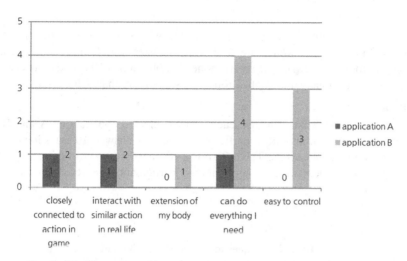

**Fig. 3.** The frequency of keywords/key phrases in perceived naturalness

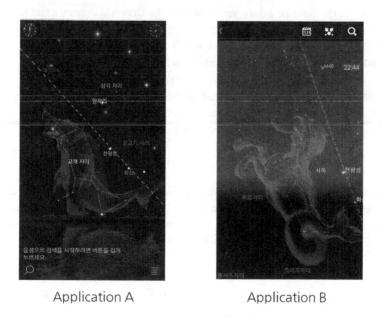

Application A                    Application B

**Fig. 4.** Representation of same constellation in 2 applications

## 5.2    Study 2: An Experiment

Users evaluated that A was better than B in perceived reality. Likewise, users evaluated that B was better that in perceived naturalness. To find out the impact of perceived reality and perceived naturalness on flow state, we conducted an experiment and carried out structured in-depth interviews.

### Subject
The participants for this study were 10 Koreans who have never experienced AR application. 2 interviewees were male, and 8 interviewees were female. All of 10 interviewees spent more than 2 h on the smartphone manipulation per day and 8 interviewees were regular smartphone game application users spent more than 1 h per day.

### Procedure
Study participants were asked to use each of two selected applications A and B. By using two AR applications each, participants need to answer 10 questions during 30 min for each of applications. Table 2 shows 10 questions used in this study. After each 30 min experience for two applications, participants answered 50 min longs in-depth interview.

**Table 2.**  10 questions to answer in 30 min

| | |
|---|---|
| 1. | Please find out satellites of the Jupiter(write down at least 4 satellites) |
| 2. | The moon is _____ km in diameter. |
| 3. | What is the name of galaxy surrounded by the Corvus, Centaurus, and Libra? |
| 4. | Please write down 3 signs of zodiac which can be seen in the northerly sky. |
| 5. | Please write down 2 planets which can be seen in the westerly sky. |
| 6. | What are the nickname of Cetus alpha and its origin? |
| 7. | What are the names of stars located on Orion's belt? |
| 8. | What is the name of galaxy located on the head of Andromeda? |
| 9. | Please find out satellites of the Saturn (write down 3 satellites). |
| 10. | Please write down 3 constellations which can be seen in the southerly sky. |

### The Interview Question
We developed interview questions based on perceived reality measure of Shafer et al. [36] and perceived naturalness measure of McGloin et al. [20], and flow measure of Jackson et al. [14]. The measurement questions are modified to fit AR application environment and they went through a pilot study to ensure reliability of measurements. The interview questions are as follows;

(1) Perceived reality

- Please choose one application whose feature of night sky was more realistic and explain your own reason to make a choice.

(2) Perceived naturalness

- Please choose one application that actions you performed with smartphone were closely connected to the actions happening in the AR environment and explain your own reasons to make a choice.
- Please choose one application that can be control naturally and explain your own reasons to make a choice.

(3) Flow experience

- While you find out the answers for the questions with 2 applications, were the challenge and your ability at an equally high level? Please describe your thought and feeling.
- While you find out the answers for the questions with 2 applications, which application was easy to concentrate on? Please describe why and how that application was helpful for you.
- Did realistic feature of night sky help you to concentrate on the challenge?
- Did natural control help you to be concentrate on the challenge?

(4) Additional factors which could affect to flow state

- If there were additional factors that enhance you to fully concentrate on the task, please describe which factor is it and why.
- If there were additional factors that disturb you to fully concentrate on the task, please describe which factor is it and why.

# 6    Result

## 6.1    Perceived Reality and Flow Experience

Among interviewees, 6 interviewees explained that application A was better than application B in perceived reality. 2 interviewees were male, and 4 interviewees were female. They suggested that "A's virtual environment is similar to the real environment (2 times).", "the color of night sky was realistic (2 times)."

Among 10 interviewees, 7 interviewees stated that higher perceived reality affected to the higher flow experience. They suggested that "As the night sky of the application seemed more real, it helps me to feel more curiosity and interest on it (2 times).", "More realistic graphic helps me to concentrate (4 times).", "Realistic graphic is attractive to me (1 time)."

Interviewee 10: Compare to application B, It feels like I was watching the star at the countryside (when I use application A). So I could deeply concentrate on it.
Interviewee 7: I could see the stars with application A that I cannot see on the earth. So I could concentrate on it more.

## 6.2 Perceived Naturalness and Flow Experience

Among 10 interviewees, 6 interviewees explained that application B was better than application A in perceived naturalness. 2 interviewees were male and 4 interviewees were female. "Application B reflects my control more effectively (2 times).", "Application B moves faster than application A (1 time)." Among 10 interviewees, 9 interviewees explained that higher perceived naturalness affected to the higher flow experience. They suggested 'When it has a lot of lag, I feel so frustrated (1 times).' 'Easy control helps me to freely explore the galaxy with application.'(3 times), and 'definitely yes (1 times).'

Interviewee 2: When it has a lot of lag, I feel so frustrated. So I chose application B, which has no lag in control and could concentrate on it more.
Interviewee 3&4: Easier control helps me to freely explore the galaxy with applications. I feel very comfortable and concentrated on.
Interviewee 5: When easier control is available, it was feel like I am really watching stars. I feel more immersion with application B.

## 6.3 Perceived Reality vs Perceived Naturalness

6 Interviewees stated that application B was more immersive than application A. 2 interviewees said that application A was more immersive that B. 1 interviewees stated there was no difference between 2 applications (Fig. 4).

6 interviewees choosing application B explained that impact of perceived naturalness on the flow experience was stronger than impact of perceived reality on flow state. Interviewees stated; "When I have trouble in controlling the applications, I couldn't care about graphic at all (2 times)." and "The graphic is good enough. I think easy control or naturalness is more important in playing (1 time)." (Fig. 5).

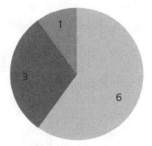

application A    application B    There were no difference between 2 applications

**Fig. 5.** Answer about the question "which application was easy to concentrate on?"

**Interviewee 1**: I am totally satisfied with graphic. There is no need to upgrade it. However, naturalness needs to be upgraded. I have much experience in manipulating smart phone, so I didn't have any difficulty in manipulation. But I think that people who don't have much experience in manipulating smart phone would feel uncomfortable due to insufficient naturalness.

**Interviewee 6**: I was hard to control the application. I could not care about anything except manipulation. So, I think that easy control is a very important factor. I think if I used bigger device, it would be easy to control applications.

### 6.4 Additional Factor Affecting to Flow Experience

2 of Interviewees stated that they feel privacy concerns due to Global Positioning System (GPS). They feel uncomfortable when they turn on GPS function in smart phone. Interviewee 1 and 3 stated about their privacy concerns.

**Interviewee 1**: I could concentrate on using applications with GPS function. However, if I have a chance to use the game with risky device, I don't want to play game.

**Interviewee 3**: I care about my privacy a lot. If there is a big privacy invasion risk caused by using GPS function, it will make me hard to concentrate on. I hope games have strong security measure to protect it.

## 7  Discussion and Implication

In this exploratory research, we suggested a model of flow in the context of AR application. After carrying out a text mining and an experiment with 10 participants, we discovered that perceived reality and perceived naturalness have positive relationships with users' flow state. This means that users achieve higher flow state when they use the application with higher perceived reality and perceived naturalness. Therefore, it is important to enhance perceived reality and perceived naturalness when companies develop new AR applications.

We also found out that perceived naturalness have stronger impact on flow experience compared to perceived reality. Study participant stated that they think perceived naturalness was more important than perceived reality. AR application provides information with actual spatial image through camera so users may feel high level of perceived reality in application usage. Due to this reason, users may focus on easy manipulation and naturalness more than reality itself.

Participants point out that when they have privacy concerns related to AR applications, they would experience lower flow experience and their intention to play AR application would decrease. Recently, many AR applications provide realistic experience based on GPS or camera functions in the smart device. Adopting GPS or camera can enhance players' realistic experiences so that players could achieve higher flow state. However when those AR applications don't have enough information security measures to protect users' privacy, users could be disrupted to reach flow even with two major characters; perceived reality and naturalness, are ensured in an application.

# 8 Conclusion

This research adds new dimensions on literature body in an AR application by focusing on users flow. Especially, this study examined users' perceived reality and perceived naturalness which have not been explored in prior research. Based on our study results, this research confirmed that positive impact of perceived reality and perceived naturalness on users flow state in an application context.

However, the study results indicate that perceived naturalness has more influence on users flow state compared with perceived reality. Our research findings are differentiated from prior studies in a way that the role of reality on flow is weaker in AR environment. Beside of two main factors, this research discovered a negative impact of privacy concerns on users' flow experience.

This research has a practical contribution to the industries by suggesting useful insights for application developers. Study results suggest that it be important to provide privacy protection measure in AR applications for flow experience. In addition to the privacy protection measure, it is important for developers to enhance perceived reality and perceived naturalness. By enhancing realistic AR environment with higher perceived reality and naturalness, users' flow experience could be maximized.

This exploratory research has several limitations. First, only few factors were tested to develop the model of AR application flow. Likewise, study participant were 10 people which is hard to generalize our results. To overcome these limitations, we plan to conduct future studies discover more predicting factors of AR application flow experience. By executing survey with large study participants, we expect to find out a powerful explanatory model to users flow state in AR environment.

# References

1. Anderson, J.R., Reder, L.M., Simon, H.A.: Situated learning and education. Educ. Res. 25(4), 5–11 (1996)
2. Azuma, R.T.: A survey of augmented reality. Presence: Teleoperators Virtual Environ. 6(4), 355–385 (1997)
3. Caudell, T.P., Mizell, D.W.: Augmented reality: an application of heads-up display technology to manual manufacturing processes. In: Proceedings of the Twenty-Fifth Hawaii International Conference on System Sciences, vol. 2, pp. 659–669. IEEE, January 1992
4. Cheng, K.H., Tsai, C.C.: Affordances of augmented reality in science learning: Suggestions for future research. J. Sci. Educ. Technol. 22(4), 449–462 (2013)
5. Chou, T.J., Ting, C.C.: The role of flow experience in cyber-game addiction. CyberPsychology Behav. 6(6), 663–675 (2003)
6. Cobb, P., Bowers, J.: Cognitive and situated learning perspectives in theory and practice. Educ. Res. 28(2), 4–15 (1999)
7. Csikszentmihalyi, M., Larson, R., Prescott, S.: The ecology of adolescent activity and experience. J. Youth Adolesc. 6(3), 281–294 (1977)
8. Csikszentmihályi, M., Abuhamdeh, S., Nakamura, J.: "Flow", in Elliot, A., Handbook of Competence and Motivation, New York: The Guilford Press, pp. 598–698 (2005)

9. Felnhofer, A., Kothgassner, O.D., Hauk, N., Beutl, L., Hlavacs, H., Kryspin-Exner, I.: Physical and social presence in collaborative virtual environments: exploring age and gender differences with respect to empathy. Comput. Hum. Behav. **31**, 272–279 (2014)

10. Fontaine, G.: The experience of a sense of presence in intercultural and international encounters. Presence: Teleoperators Virtual Environ. **1**(4), 482–490 (1992)

11. Guttentag, D.A.: Virtual reality: applications and implications for tourism. Tourism Manag. **31**(5), 637–651 (2010)

12. Hall, A.: Reading realism: audiences' evaluations of the reality of media texts. J. Commun. **53**, 624–641 (2003)

13. Hawkins, R.P.: The dimensional structure of children's perceptions of television reality. Commun. Res. **4**, 299 (1977)

14. Jackson, S.A., Ford, S.K., Kimiecik, J.C., Marsh, H.W.: Psychological correlates of flow in sport. J. Sport Exerc. Psychol. **20**(4), 358–378 (1998)

15. Kaufmann, H., Schmalstieg, D.: Mathematics and geometry education with collaborative augmented reality. Compt. Graph. **27**, 339–345 (2003)

16. Kizil, M.S.: Virtual reality applications in Australian minerals industry. In: APCOM 2003, vol. 31, pp. 569–574. The South African Institute of Mining and Metallurgy (2003)

17. Lave, J., Wenger, E.: Situated Learning: Legitimate Peripheral Participation. Cambridge University Press, Cambridge (1991)

18. Liao, L.F.: A flow theory perspective on learner motivation and behavior in distance education. Distance Educ. **27**(1), 45–62 (2006)

19. Malliet, S.: An exploration of adolescents' perceptions of videogame realism. Learn. Media Technol. **31**(4), 377–394 (2006)

20. McGloin, R., Farrar, K.M., Krcmar, M.: The impact of controller naturalness on spatial presence, gamer enjoyment, and perceived realism in a tennis simulation video game. Presence: Teleoperators Virtual Environ. **20**(4), 309–324 (2011)

21. Noh, K., Jee, H., Lim, S.: Effect of augmented reality contents based instruction on academic achievement. Interest Flow Learn. J. Korea Contents Assoc. **10**(2), 1–13 (2010)

22. Rosenberg, L.B.: The Use of Virtual Fixtures as Perceptual Overlays to Enhance Operator Performance in Remote Environments. Stanford Univ Ca Center for Design Research (1992)

23. Shafer, D.M., Carbonara, C.P., Popova, L.: Spatial presence and perceived reality as predictors of motion-based video game enjoyment. Presence: Teleoperators Virtual Environ. **20**(6), 591–619 (2011)

24. Shelton, E., Hedley, N.: Using augmented reality for teaching earth-sun relationships to undergraduate geography students. In: Proceeding of First IEEE International Augmented Reality Toolkit Workshop, Darmstadt, Germany (2002)

25. Shelton, B., Stevens, R.: Using coordination classes to interpret conceptual change in astronomical thinking. In: Kafai, Y., Sandoval, W., Enyedy, N., Nixon, A., Herrera, F. (eds.) Proceedings of the 6th International Conference for the Learning Sciences. Lawrence Erlbaum & Associates, Mahweh (2004)

26. Skalski, P., Tamborini, R., Shelton, A., Buncher, M., Lindmark, P.: Mapping the road to fun: natural video game controllers, presence, and game enjoyment. New Media Soc. **13**(2), 224–242 (2011)

27. Steuer, J.: Defining virtual reality: dimensions determining telepresence. J. Commun. **42**(4), 73–93 (1992)

28. Sutherland, I.E.: A head-mounted three dimensional display. In: Proceedings of the Fall Joint Computer Conference, Part I, 9–11 December 1968, pp. 757–764. ACM, December 1968

29. Tamborini, R., Skalski, P.: The role of presence in the experience of electronic games. In: Vorderer, P., Bryant, J. (eds.) Playing video games: Motives, responses, and consequences, pp. 225–240. Erlbaum, Mahwah (2006)

30. Zyda, M.: From visual simulation to virtual reality to games. Computer **38**(9), 25–32 (2005)
31. Gaudiosi, J.: Virtual Reality Video Game Industry to Generate $5.1 Billion in 2016. Fortune, 05 January 2016. http://fortune.com/2016/01/05/virtual-reality-game-industry-to-generate-billions/
32. Ahlberg, G., Enochsson, L., Gallagher, A.G., Hedman, L., Hogman, C., McClusky, D.A., Ramel, S., Smith, C.D., Arvidsson, D.: Proficiency-based virtual reality training significantly reduces the error rate for residents during their first 10 laparoscopic cholecystectomies. Am. J. Surg. **193**(6), 797–804 (2007)
33. Kiili, K.: Digital game-based learning: towards an experiential gaming model. Internet Higher Educ. **8**(1), 13–24 (2005)
34. Ibáñez, M.B., Di Serio, A., Villarán, D., Kloos, C.D.: Experimenting with electromagnetism using augmented reality: impact on flow student experience and educational effectiveness. Comput. Educ. **71**, 1–13 (2014)
35. Bressler, D.M., Bodzin, A.M.: A mixed methods assessment of students' flow experiences during a mobile augmented reality science game. J. Comput. Assist. Learn. **29**(6), 505–517 (2013)
36. Eisenberger, R., Jones, J.R., Stinglhamber, F., Shanock, L., Randall, A.T.: Flow experiences at work: for high need achievers alone? J. Organ. Behav. **26**, 755–775 (2005)
37. Quinn, R.W.: Flow in knowledge work: high performance experience in the design of national security technology. Adm. Sci. Q. **50**(4), 610–641 (2005)
38. Fullagar, C.J., Kelloway, E.K.: Flow at work: an experience sampling approach. J. occup. organ. Psychol. **82**(3), 595–615 (2009)
39. Lopez, M.: Augmented and Virtual Reality Fuel the Future Workplace, Forbes, 11 November 2016. http://www.forbes.com/sites/maribellopez/2016/11/11/augmented-and-virtual-reality-fuel-the-future-workplace/#2acad902198e
40. Sanjiv, K.R.: Wipro. How VR and AR will be training tomorrow's workforce. Venturebeat, 21 February 2016. http://venturebeat.com/2016/02/21/how-vr-and-ar-will-be-training-tomorrows-workforce/
41. Dalgarno, B., Lee, M.J.: What are the learning affordances of 3-D virtual environments? Br. J. Educ. Technol. **41**(1), 10–32 (2010)
42. Gamon, M., Aue, A., Corston-Oliver, S., Ringger, E.: Pulse: mining customer opinions from free text. In: Famili, A.Fazel, Kok, Joost N., Peña, José M., Siebes, A., Feelders, A. (eds.) IDA 2005. LNCS, vol. 3646, pp. 121–132. Springer, Heidelberg (2005). doi:10.1007/11552253_12
43. Hu, M., Liu, B.: Mining and summarizing customer reviews. In: Proceedings of the Tenth ACM SIGKDD International Conference on Knowledge Discovery and Data Mining, pp. 168–177. ACM, August 2004
44. Heo, M., Cheon, M.: An empirical study on the relationship of antecedents of flow, organizational commitment, knowledge sharing and job satisfaction. The. J. Inf. Syst. **16**(4), 1–31 (2007)
45. Lucas, H.C., Spitler, V.K.: Technology use and performance: a field study of broker workstations. Decis. Sci. **30**(2), 291–311 (1999)
46. Nick Heath, "Five ways augmented reality will transform your business", ZDnet, 1 February 2016. http://www.zdnet.com/article/five-ways-augmented-reality-will-transform-your-business/
47. Billet, S.: Situated learning—a workplace experience. Aust. J. Adult Community Educ. **34**(2), 112–130 (1994)

# Using Mobile Technology to Generate Learning Content for an Intelligent Tutoring System

Rodney A. Long[1]([⊠]), Jennifer M. Riley[2], and Christina K. Padron[2]

[1] Army Research Laboratory, Orlando, FL, USA
Rodney.A.Long3.Civ@mail.mil
[2] Design Interactive, Inc., Orlando, FL, USA
{Jennifer.Riley,Christina.Padron}@designinteractive.net

**Abstract.** With the release of the "Army Learning Concept for 2015," the Army signaled a need to change the way it trained. One goal was to reduce the amount of lecture-based classes, and move towards "...more engaging technology-delivered instruction that will be used as part of a blended learning approach, distributed to the workforce for job-related sustainment learning, and as performance support applications." As a result, a repository of learning modules will be needed to support career progression, assignment-oriented learning, operational lessons, and performance support. In addition, intelligent tutors, generated with the Generalized Intelligent Framework for Tutoring (GIFT), will tailor the learning experience to the individual learner.

Our research examined effective ways for guiding users, e.g. subject matter experts, instructional systems designers, etc. in the development of reusable learning objects (RLOs) to support adaptive learning. RLOs are small "chunks" of instructional content which are associated with learning objectives. The research included studying the common structure of RLOs and defining approaches for creating RLOs via easy-to-use, guided user interactions. In addition, a prototype authoring system was developed to provide a robust set of capabilities for quick and easy development of effective RLOs, leveraging the capability of mobile devices to create rich, multi-media assets. The resulting Android-based mobile app: (1) guides users through the development of instructionally sound RLOs and lessons that are created from sequencing multiple RLOs; (2) provides support for including multimedia assets such as video, audio, still imagery, and text to convey knowledge, (3) supports the development of embedded assessments within RLOs, and (4) saves/packages the instructional content in a sharable format (as a sharable content object). This paper discusses the user needs analysis, requirements definition, authoring tool prototype, exemplar training content development, and results from preliminary usability and instructional system design evaluations.

**Keywords:** Intelligent tutoring systems · Learning content generation · Mobile

© Springer International Publishing AG 2017
D.D. Schmorrow and C.M. Fidopiastis (Eds.): AC 2017, Part II, LNAI 10285, pp. 199–209, 2017.
DOI: 10.1007/978-3-319-58625-0_14

# 1 Introduction

Advances in technology have led to increased opportunities for computer-based training (CBT) that can be accessed anytime and anyplace for self-guided learning. Effective computer-based instruction can provide extremely flexible training that is less costly, labor- intensive and time-consuming than classroom training. It can also provide a complement to traditional learning environments that can increase the rate of knowledge acquisition along the spectrum from basic to higher-order cognitive skills.

The challenge in the development of CBT is the rapid and cost effective creation of robust and meaningful training content that can be used across multiple contexts, truly advances learning, and promotes retention over the long term. The military and other organizations have explored the benefit of RLOs, which "chunk" small learning components together that can be used over and over for promoting operational skill development (Beck and Baggio 2007). While emerging as a viable content reusability concept, RLOs are only effective if they are high in quality.

As such, content developers need support in authoring RLOs that are effective, situation-appropriate and meet the educational needs of a multitude of trainees. This is critical as training that fails to adequately address the key knowledge, skills, abilities, and other attributes (KSAOs) pertinent to a context will fail to convey what, in some cases, may be a complicated set of instructional elements that underlie core competencies of the domain.

The aim of our research was to study effective and appropriate methods to provide guided instructional design support to subject matter experts (SMEs), instructional designers, and inexperienced training developers for rapidly generating RLOs. An emphasis was placed on defining methods for integrating best practices and proven instructional design principles within the authoring component to aid the end user in building good instructional strategies within RLOs. This research resulted in the development of an easy-to-use authoring tool, implemented for a mobile platform that effectively guides users in the rapid development of instructional content that promotes learning. The mobile app was developed to advance the Army's goals for rapidly addressing emerging training needs by helping users organize their knowledge into effective learning objects and by supporting ongoing training research initiatives, such as the Army Research Laboratory's Adaptive Training Research program which is exploring rapid, reusable content development for intelligent tutoring systems.

# 2 Adaptive Training

With the release of the "Army Learning Concept for 2015," (TRADOC 2011) the Army signaled a need to change the way it trained. One goal was to reduce the amount of lecture-based classes, and move towards "…more engaging technology-delivered instruction that will be used as part of a blended learning approach, distributed to the workforce for job-related sustainment learning, and as performance support applications." As a result, a repository of learning modules will be needed "…to support career progression, assignment-oriented learning, operational lessons, and performance support aids and applications." In addition, intelligent tutors will be able to tailor the learning experience to the individual learner.

To support this vision, the Army Research Laboratory began its Adaptive Training research program. The focal point of the program is the Generalized Intelligent Framework for Tutoring (GIFT), an open source software package to build intelligent tutoring systems. The cloud version of the GIFT authoring tools provides an easy to use flow chart for developing the tutors and allows incorporation of multimedia objects, quizzes/surveys, etc. (Fig. 1). GIFT also has a pedagogy module that supports adaptation based on learner characteristic and performance (Sottilare et al. 2012).

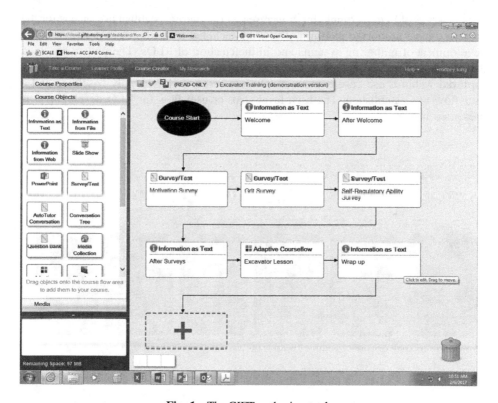

**Fig. 1.** The GIFT authoring tool

## 3  Prototype Development

Our research studied effective ways for guiding users in the development of RLOs. The work included the development of a functional authoring system prototype that provides a robust set of capabilities for rapid authoring of instructional content for a mobile computing environment. Specifically, the rapid authoring platform (RAP) is an Android-based mobile platform that:

- steps users through the development of RLOs, Lessons, and short performance assessments associated with RLOs and lessons
- provides means to integrate multi-media assets such as video, text, audio, and still imagery within RLOs
- provides guidance that ensures the inclusion of various instructional system design (ISD) elements within RLOs and Lessons
- supports the saving of RLOs in a sharable content format

## 3.1    User Needs Analysis

This task was aimed at completing user research in order to establish user needs for the proposed rapid authoring platform. The work included reviewing best practices in the development of authoring systems and in the creation of RLOs. The review provided the initial basis of use cases for the application. Formal use cases were created and captured within a use case document. The use cases were internally baselined and a user flow was established. The high level steps or user flow for RLO development is presented in Fig. 2.

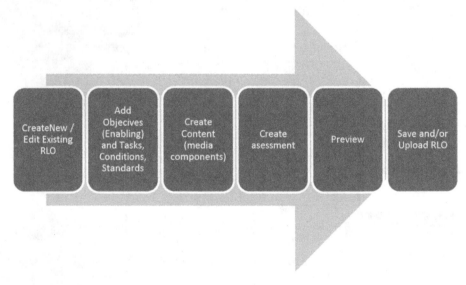

**Fig. 2.** Steps for RLO development supported by RAP

Based on our user need analysis, a guided authoring approach was conceptualized to "walk" the user through numbered steps for the creation or editing of RLOs and/or lessons of grouped RLOs. The instructional content development starts with the establishment of enabling learning objectives and capturing relevant actions (tasks), conditions, and standards which are familiar to military users. The next step involves adding or creating media content for the RLO. Multiple media components may be utilized within a single

RLO. The media content may be a video, an audio file, text, a graphic or image, or some combination of these elements. For easy authoring, the user selects an instructional template. The templates ensure some standardization in the development of multimedia components. As media is added to RLO, it can be sequenced to meet learning objectives. Once an RLO is created, the system takes the user to the next step, the creation of an assessment for the RLO. The RLO assessment may be one or more questions to test knowledge acquisition. The last two steps that the users are guided through involve previewing the RLO and completing the creation by saving and/or uploading the RLO.

In a similar manner to what has been described for RLO creation, the RAP was conceptualized to guide a user through the authoring of lessons. Lessons are RLOs that are sequenced together to create a "larger" or more complex instructional object. Multiple RLOs are utilized to make a lesson. The RLOs can be sequenced as needed to meet terminal learning objectives. Lessons include assessments that are associated with the included RLOs and may include additional assessments to evaluate knowledge acquisition for the learning objectives. The high level steps or user flow for lesson development with RAP is presented in Fig. 3.

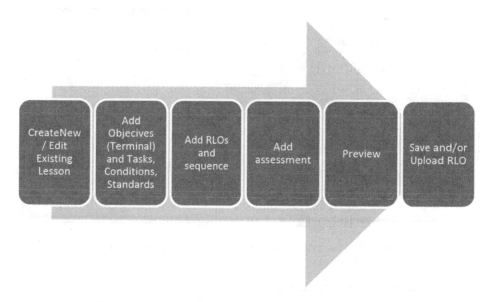

**Fig. 3.** Steps for lesson development supported by the RAP

## 3.2 System Design Requirements

The user experience (UX) process begins with understanding user needs. This key component is accomplished through UX methods such as contextual inquiries, interviews, task analyses and persona creation. While there was limited access to subject matter experts within specific domain of interest (e.g., military maintenance), the research team and instructional system design personnel worked to develop exemplar personas for identifying user needs. An in-house military domain expert answered a series of questions regarding use of a computer-based tool for creating quick "hip pocket" lessons for short impromptu training opportunities. The information gathered was utilized to create work flows, as well as use cases for the RAP. This information informed the initial design of the user's experience and user interface (UI).

Wireframing was used as an iterative process that combined the information architecture, navigation and UI component placement for the application. The wireframes were internally baselined and utilized in the development of initial system design requirements. Dynamic wireframes were completed to support walkthroughs and early evaluation of the design concepts. The multidisciplinary team worked together to evaluate the user flow, and projected functional components of the system. As the design solidified, user interface design and interaction design were completed as part of the system design. The final UI design and interaction design guided the refinement of the design specification which guided the prototype development. Figure 4 shows the progression from rough sketch wireframes of the RAP to high fidelity interactive wireframe of the user interface.

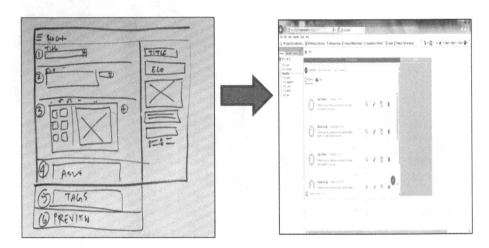

**Fig. 4.** Wireframing iterations of the RAP user interface

### 3.3 Building the Prototype Authoring Tool

An agile software development process, including full regression quality assurance (QA) testing at each software release, was implemented in the development of the RAP. The agile development process relies on solid code being generated and functionality being completed in two-week sprint cycles. User interface designs consisting of high-fidelity mockups, along with associated use cases, were reviewed at least one sprint in advance by the engineering team. QA testing was performed one sprint after the sprint in which development work was completed. The independent team of QA personnel verified the functionality of each deliverable software feature. The code was deemed completed when it passed internal unit testing written by the developer, external integration testing with the overall build, and QA testing for the overall product. Evaluations of functions and features at each sprint were also completed by the human factors personnel on the team. At the later stages of development, the sponsor was able to review the working software product for functionality and suitability for meeting operational utility.

## 3.4    Creating Exemplar RLOs

During the RAP development, instructional system design (ISD) personnel supported the RLO team with instructional design, user experience and usability testing. In order to create reusable learning objects on the app, solid content was needed. The team searched for appropriate media for illustrating military-relevant content within the RAP. A video was selected – "Disassembly, Assembly and Cleaning of the M16 A2." The video is adequate for novice warfighters/learners who are unfamiliar with the disassembly, assembly, and cleaning of a weapon. The ISD team constructed a list that explained each step in the three sections of the video. The video was downloaded and edited using Giphy Capture [https://giphy.com/apps/giphycapture] to create a series of animations in the Graphics Interchange Format (GIF). All of the GIF files were labeled and organized in a Google Drive folder.

In the creation of lessons and RLOs with the RAP, the ISD team began by establishing the learning goals or objectives, which drove the requirements for the associated RLOs. For the RAP example content, the goal and outcome of one lesson was defined – to support a single learner in gaining the ability to identify parts of the M16 A2 rifle and the steps needed to effectively disassemble the rifle. Enabling and terminal learning objectives were established. The learning objectives were conceptualized in three commonly identified components: actions, conditions, and standards. For setting the condition, the ISD team reviewed the video to identify supplies required to complete the task. For the standard, the team included criteria that should be met by the learner, for example, disassemble the M16 A2 rifle within 60 s. The system is designed to guide users in setting up enabling and terminal learning objects, thereby embedding important instructional system design components to boost quality of learning content. For an RLO, a single action (i.e., what the trainee should be able to do) is captured for the objectives, though multiple conditions under which the actions must be completed may be set. Similarly, a single standard (i.e., the required level/quality of performance) is put in place. Standards may include reference to number of errors or time to complete an action. The system guides the user, but allows for flexibility with establishing the learning objectives.

Following the establishment of the objectives of the RLO, the ISD team created instructional content utilizing the embedded templates as part of the RAP tool. The templates were designed by the UI/UX and ISD team to guide users in the integration of multimedia with instructional material and content. Templates provide a standardization among RLOs that increases their overall quality and utility. A screen capture of available RAP templates for integrating images, text, video, and audio is presented in Fig. 5. Multiple options exist for each media type.

## 4    Prototype Evaluation

An informal subjective assessment of the software was conducted during RAP development. Five (5) target users completed a walkthrough of the tool with a researcher and utilized the tool to create an example RLO. Feedback was collected from the users on potential pain-points, usability concerns, and areas of improvement with regard to features and functions. In addition, a preliminary evaluation of the RAP prototype was conducted using internal ISD reviews as described below.

### 4.1    Method

Three people with experience in developing training content were asked to provide feedback on the content creation portion of the RAP. The researchers specifically wanted people who varied in level of experience in creating training content, level of comfort with technology, domain of training content. Level of experience in creating content varied from 5–10 years across participants (average of 6.67 years), level of comfort ranged from 3–4 (average of 3.67), with 5 being the highest level of comfort, and the domain of training content varied widely (e.g., project management and sales content vs. employee relations and communication content vs. industrial machinery and medical content).

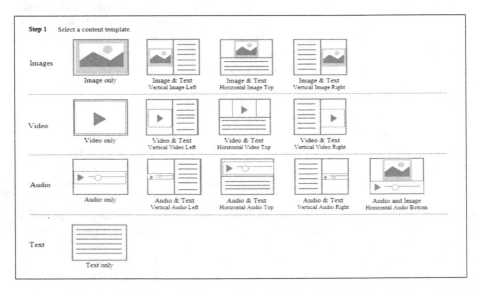

**Fig. 5.** Templates available to guide standardized RLO development

Each person was first given a quick, high-level demonstration of the RAP. They then completed a cognitive walkthrough procedure in which they performed a series of tasks within the RAP and were asked to simultaneously speak aloud what they were trying to do and any thoughts they had about things they liked, things they didn't understand or what they expected to happen, and things that could be improved. Tasks included aspects of creating a new RLO, editing the title and objective, adding new content, adding assessments, and previewing the RLO), editing a current RLO (e.g., adding content and assessments), copying RLOs, and deleting RLOs. In addition to the insights gained during the cognitive walkthrough, they were asked for any additional thoughts after completing the tasks. They then completed a System Usability Scale (SUS) questionnaire (Brooke 1996), which provides a composite usability score.

## 4.2    Results and Discussion

Feedback on the RLO system was generally positive, and most tasks could be completed quickly with very minimal support from the facilitator. The system was found to be overall well-designed for the intended purpose, and all three people said that they would like to use the system for the creation of content. However, there were some themes of improvements that would be helpful to the RAP system that came out of the usability testing in addition to some smaller detailed improvements. Some of the major themes will be discussed in the following sections, along with the SUS results.

## 4.3    Tutorial

Though each person was mostly able to get through the tasks without help, there were a few instances where they could not locate a particular aspect of the interface when it was not immediately obvious (e.g. the arrow that brings out the RLO preview bar). It became clear quite quickly that the addition of a simple user interface tutorial to walk the user through some of the common interface elements would go a long way in terms of preventing situations where the user took a long time or was not able to locate an aspect of the system. In most cases, when the aspect of the system was pointed out to them once, there was no future need to help them find it.

## 4.4    Overall Organization

The RAP system has a hierarchy made up of a variety of levels, including lessons made up of RLOs and RLOs made up of pieces of content (e.g. text, pictures, videos) and assessments (e.g. true/false and multiple choice questions). The current design of the RAP system interface does not easily distinguish (besides with labels) which level you are in when you are adding something new. The feedback was that the consistency of the interaction with the system is great, but the users would sometimes get disoriented in terms of where they were in the hierarchy. Two recommendations came out of this issue. One is to incorporate some type of design element into the interface to clearly distinguish which level the user is currently adding to, such as a different background color per level. The other recommendation was to add a bar on the left that provides an outline of the lesson or RLO currently being edited as a reference point for the user. It would also increase efficiency of use if there were hyperlinks within the outline that allowed the user to quickly move between levels.

## 4.5    Button Design and Placement

Although the buttons in the RAP interface were generally self-explanatory, there were a few exceptions that caused some confusion for the users. One was the plus sign button that is used throughout the system as a type of an enter button whenever a new item is being added (e.g., new title). The users repeatedly commented that it was a bit confusing because a plus sign generally indicates that you are about to add something new, not that you are entering information. This symbol can easily be changed to an arrow or another symbol that indicates entering information. Another example of a button that can use improvement is the arrow that brings out the preview panel when selected. This button seemed to be easy to miss, and even when it was detected, it was not clear what it did. Though the tutorial would help to let users know what it is there for, a redesign including possibly increasing the size and or color of the button would help it to stand out more as well.

## 4.6    SUS Results

The results of the SUS were mostly promising. The three scores were 67.5, 65, and 30 out of 100. A couple of the categories where the RAP system received high marks from all three users included the consistency of the system and the expectations that not much technical support would be needed to use the system. The two users with the higher scores also thought the system was not too complex and that not a lot of learning was needed to start using the system. The results of the SUS are certainly promising, given that this is the first version of the RAP system. It is expected that with a few revisions to the design and the addition of a tutorial, the usability of the system would increase a good amount.

## 5    Conclusion

The RAP prototype was developed to provide a robust set of capabilities for quick and easy development of effective RLOs, leveraging the capability of mobile devices to create rich, multimedia assets. The resulting Android-based mobile app: (1) guides users through the development of instructionally sound RLOs and lessons that are created from sequencing multiple RLOs; (2) provides support for including multimedia assets such as video, audio, still imagery, and text to convey knowledge, (3) supports the development of embedded assessments within RLOs, and (4) saves/packages the instructional content in a sharable format (as a sharable content object). In the near future, the resulting RLOs will be able to be imported into the GIFT authoring tools to create an individualized, adaptive learning experience.

**Acknowledgments.** The research described herein has been sponsored by the U.S. Army Research Laboratory. The statements and opinions expressed in this article do not necessarily reflect the position or the policy of the United States Government, and no official endorsement should be inferred.

# References

Beck J., Baggio, B.: Meeting Training and Learning Challenges with Reusable Learning Objects. Learning Solutions Magazine, 6 August 2007

Brooke, J.: SUS: a quick and dirty usability scale. In: Jordan, P.W., Thomas, B.A.W., McClelland, I.L. (eds.) Usability Evaluation in Industry, pp. 189–194 (1996)

Sottilare, R.A., Brawner, K.W., Goldberg, B.S., Holden, H.K.: The Generalized Intelligent Framework for Tutoring (GIFT). U.S. Army Research Laboratory – Human Research & Engineering Directorate, Orlando (2012)

U.S. Army Training and Doctrine Command. The United States Army Learning Concept for 2015 (TRADOC PAM 525-8-2). Department of the Army, Training and Doctrine Command, Monroe (2011)

# A Conceptual Assessment Model (CAM) for Operationalizing Constructs in Technology-Augmented Assessments

Mark E. Riecken[1], Clayton W. Burford[2(✉)], Grace Teo[3],
Joseph McDonnell[4], Lauren Reinerman-Jones[3], and Kara Orvis[5]

[1] Trideum, Orlando, FL, USA
mriecken@trideum.com
[2] Army Research Laboratory, Orlando, FL, USA
clayton.w.burford.civ@mail.mil
[3] Institute for Simulation and Training,
University of Central Florida, Orlando, FL, USA
{gteo,lreinerm}@ist.ucf.edu
[4] Dynamic Animation Systems, Fairfax, VA, USA
joe.mcdonnell@d-a-s.com
[5] Aptima, San Diego, CA, USA
korvis@aptima.com

**Abstract.** The concept of the "construct" is essential and ubiquitous in the social and psychological sciences, but is often glossed over as being well understood by members of a single community of interest (COI) and not necessarily used uniformly across communities. With the explosive increase in digital augmentation technologies, there is an opportunity, even a necessity, to quantify and possibly standardize what is meant by particular constructs. The opportunity is especially apparent as constructs are "operationalized," or made measurable through the specification of data elements. We use techniques borrowed from computer science, specifically the Unified Modeling Language (UML), to build a conceptual assessment model (CAM) that can aid in specifying a systematized process of operationalizing constructs. We examine several use cases that can benefit from this approach. We also discuss how we anticipate using the CAM in our program of research into human-machine teaming (HMT) assessments called UMMPIREE.

**Keywords:** Assessment · Conceptual model · Construct · Unified Modeling Language · Human machine teaming · Operationalization

## 1 Introduction

The work described in this paper is a result of the efforts of the Unified Multi-modal Measurement for Performance Indication Research, Evaluation, and Effectiveness (UMMPIREE) project. The UMMPIREE project is sponsored by the U.S. Army Research, Development, and Engineering Command (RDECOM), Army Research Laboratory (ARL), Human Research and Engineering Directorate (HRED), Advanced

© Springer International Publishing AG 2017
D.D. Schmorrow and C.M. Fidopiastis (Eds.): AC 2017, Part II, LNAI 10285, pp. 210–222, 2017.
DOI: 10.1007/978-3-319-58625-0_15

Training & Simulation Division (ATSD), Advanced Modeling & Simulation Branch (AMSB). The UMMPIREE research team has a diverse background including experience in cognitive assessment, software engineering, and modeling and simulation.

## 2   Research Background and Motivation

ARL conducts both pure and applied research of importance to the U.S. Army. As such, ARL has an interest not only in pure science [1, 2], but in how that science can be uniformly applied in real-world applications [3]. The U.S. Army is looking at ways to better understand, characterize, and improve human performance both individually and in teams [4]. Given this research focus and the resulting real-world applications, it is prudent for the Army to also develop ways and means in which to more accurately and consistently assess human performance in all relevant contexts. This is important to assure that the research results are founded in a shared and thorough scientific approach and those results can be transferred validly and effectively to the engineering domain where they can support the warfighters' needs.

In addition to the challenges of characterizing and improving human performance, the availability of technology relevant to human performance, especially augmentation capabilities, is rapidly increasing. This can be seen in all sectors of society and is already so ubiquitous as to not be noticed. Some simple examples of human performance augmentation include smart phones, internet search engines, and prosthetic limbs and organs. It is expected that this trend will continue and furthermore will be characterized by an increasing presence of machine intelligence and autonomy of the augmentations [5]. This can be seen in the field of robotics and autonomous vehicles [6] to cite an obvious example. It is expected that the increasing demands on human performance [7], coupled with more robust machine intelligence, will strain the ability of prevailing methods and concepts in assessment to keep pace. Assessment is important for at least the following two reasons: (1) the ability to accurately portray performance in engineering and development efforts so the best acquisition decisions can be made; and (2) the ability to adequately train the soldier to perform using the augmentation capabilities in order to meet the objectives of a given mission.

Some of the key concepts that underpin research in human performance and teaming (and the assessment thereof) are well known and have been part of the literature in psychology and related fields for many years [8]. It is the observation of this research team, however, that in order to advance the state of the practice to meet the challenges just discussed that the discipline of assessment will benefit from an increased level of rigor. It is also our observation that one of these key concepts is that of the psychological "construct," and concepts closely associated with constructs, including operationalization, and construct validity. This field of psychological and social research is too vast and the state of human knowledge too meagre to universalize these concepts for all communities, but we believe that it is possible, even essential, to make progress in standardization across specific communities of interest (COI), especially within the U.S. Army. The UMMPIREE project is addressing how it can support the maturation of these ideas in the context of the Human Machine Teaming

(HMT) domain in particular. Part of this effort is the proposed Conceptual Assessment Model (CAM) discussed in this paper.

## 3   Key Terminology Used in Our Research with Discussion

Before describing the CAM, we present a short survey of selected key terms with definitions that are of use within our research effort. We use commonly available sources from the internet for definitions.

### 3.1   Key Terminology

**Construct.** "Construct, also called hypothetical construct or psychological construct, in psychology, a tool used to facilitate understanding of human behaviour [*sic*]. All sciences are built on systems of constructs and their interrelations. The natural sciences use constructs such as gravity, temperature, phylogenetic dominance, tectonic pressure, and global warming. Likewise, the behavioral sciences use constructs such as conscientiousness, intelligence, political power, self-esteem, and group culture. [...] In a sense, a psychological construct is a label for a cluster or domain of covarying behaviours [*sic*]. For example, if a student sees another sitting in a classroom before an examination biting her nails, fidgeting, lightly perspiring, and looking somewhat alarmed, the interpretation might be that she is experiencing test anxiety" [9].

**Operationalization.** "Operationalization is [...] the process of defining a fuzzy concept so as to make it clearly distinguishable, measurable, and understandable in terms of empirical observations" [10].

**Construct Validity.** "Construct validity refers to the degree to which inferences can legitimately be made from the operationalizations in your study to the theoretical constructs on which those operationalizations were based" [11]. A further clarification: "Construct validity refers to the extent to which a test, device, or instrument measures what it purports to measure. This impacts the degree to which inferences be legitimately made from the operationalizations in a study to the theoretical constructs on which those operationalizations were based." The reader is also referred to the seminal paper on this subject by Cronbach and Meehl [12].

**Unified Modeling Language (UML).** "The Unified Modeling Language (UML) is a general-purpose, developmental, modeling language in the field of software engineering, that is intended to provide a standard way to visualize the design of a system. [...] In 1997 UML was adopted as a standard by the Object Management Group (OMG), and has been managed by this organization ever since. In 2005 UML was also published by the International Organization for Standardization (ISO) as an approved ISO standard" [13].

**Conceptual Model (Per Wikipedia).** "A conceptual model is a representation of a system, made of the composition of concepts which are used to help people know, understand, or simulate a subject the model represents. Some models are physical objects; for example, a toy model which may be assembled, and may be made to work like the object it represents" [14].

**Conceptual Model (Authors' Addition to the Wikipedia Definition).** A conceptual model makes explicit and unambiguous the specific concepts which are being examined or represented – and therefore the observables from which data will be collected. It also serves to codify the researchers' presuppositions about the problem space. Anything not explicitly represented in the conceptual model cannot be fully and correctly reasoned about or analyzed since it will lack objective evidence.

**Measurement.** "Measurement is the assignment of scores to individuals so that the scores represent some characteristic of the individuals." [15] Measurement can also be defined as the assignment of a number or score on a scale to a characteristic of an individual, object, or event to enable comparison to other individual, objects, and events.

**Assessment (Educational).** "A tool or method of obtaining information from tests or other sources about the achievement or abilities of individuals. Often used interchangeably with test" [16].

**Assessment (Psychological).** "Psychological assessment is a process of testing that uses a combination of techniques to help arrive at some hypotheses about a person and their behavior, personality and capabilities."

**Operationalized Construct (Authors' Definition).** A construct that has been defined, at least partially, in terms of a finite and discrete set of measurable quantities.

## 3.2   Discussion

The focus of this paper is on developing a tool, the CAM, that can increase clarity in research involving constructs. It is noted, however, that terms closely associated with constructs, especially measurement and assessment, seem to have multiple meanings and their usage is sometimes conflated one with the other. For purposes of this research we refer to assessment as the broad, overall process that may involve quantitative data from measurements, qualitative data from observations or other sources, and expert (or not so expert) judgment. It is also observed that the usage of terms like assessment vary by context (e.g., psychology or education).

Figure 1 depicts the purpose of a conceptual model in the UMMPIREE project. A conceptual model articulates the finite observables that are used in an assessment thereby both limiting the scope of the assessment and enabling a clear understanding of all the factors in the assessment.

The real world has many features and attributes that may be of interest to a given assessment, so many that the number may approach infinity. The purpose of the conceptual model is to identify and make discrete a finite set of those features and attributes in a way that allows that finite set to be measured. The resulting quantitative data then forms a significant portion of the overall assessment. We recognize that

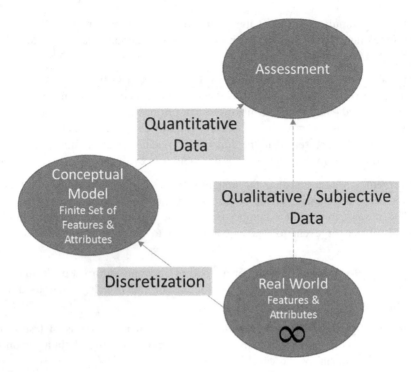

**Fig. 1.** Purpose of the conceptual model in UMMPIREE

quantitative data alone is not necessarily sufficient for a good assessment and that qualitative and subjective data form key contributions to assessment as well.

## 4   Conceptual Assessment Model (CAM)

In this section we discuss UML diagrams of the CAM. We use UML merely as a convenient way of articulating a model structure in a conventionally accepted way. In other words, UML is a commonly used modeling technique. We use only two concepts from UML: classes and compositions. The classes are represented as boxes. Classes associated with other classes are indicated by the diamond shape.

Figure 2 illustrates the CAM using a UML representation. The CAM is composed of one Subject Model, one to many Operationalized Constructs, and is associated with one Mission or Assessment Context. This Mission or Assessment context may also influence the Operationalized Construct that is part of the CAM.

The assumption is that "what is being assessed" is the Operationalized Construct of which there is at least one, but could be several. The purpose of the CAM is not to prescribe any particular method of executing assessment (or experiment), but to increase the level of uniformity across similar assessments by framing the assessment in a common, yet flexible, structure.

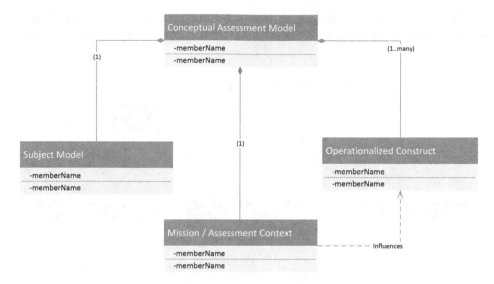

**Fig. 2.** The Conceptual Assessment Model (CAM)

Figure 3 illustrates the Subject Model class of the CAM. In this example, the Subject Model is specific to the HMT problem space.

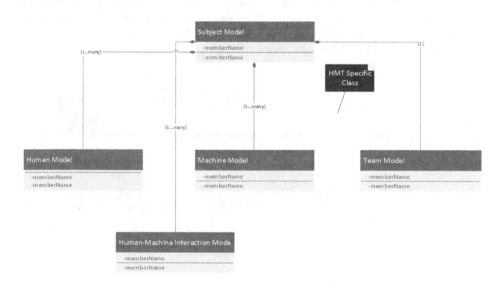

**Fig. 3.** The CAM subject model

The Subject Model for the HMT problem space is composed of one to many Human Models, one to many machine models, and one Team Model. In addition, there are one to many Human-Machine Interaction modes.

Figure 4 illustrates the Mission or Assessment Context that is an essential element of the CAM and may influence the Operationalized Constructs that compose the CAM.

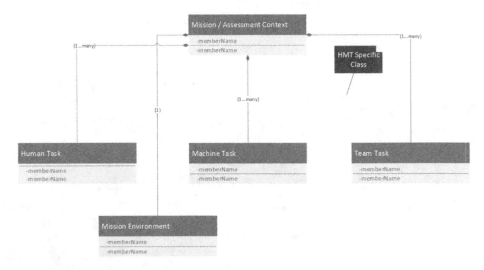

**Fig. 4.** The CAM mission/assessment context

This Mission or Assessment Context model is also specific to the HMT problem domain. It is composed of one to many Human Tasks, one to many Machine Tasks, one to many Team Tasks, and a unique (one) Mission (or Assessment) environment.

We define the Operationalized Construct class as shown in Fig. 5.

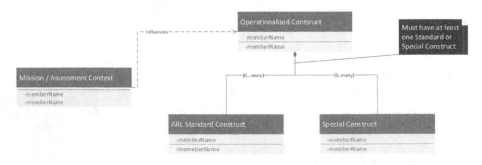

**Fig. 5.** The CAM operationalized construct

The Operationalized Construct is composed of at least one ARL Standard Construct or Special Construct, but there could be multiples of each of these standard and special models. The Operationalized Construct is influenced by the Mission or Assessment Context model.

We define the Construct model itself as shown in Fig. 6. Not surprisingly, the Construct model can be complex. It can be composed of multiple theories, although none are required. The only requirement is that an Evidence model is defined.

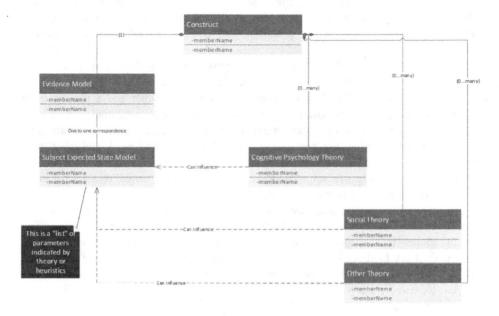

**Fig. 6.** The CAM construct model

In summary, the assessment process can benefit from the use of the CAM through the following steps:

1. Identify and detail (provide specificity) the components of the CAM that will be used for a particular assessment.
2. Develop a data collection and measurement plan for each element of the CAM that is identified as useful for the assessment.
3. Articulate how the components and elements relate to one another (e.g., how do the tasks relate to the constructs? What data elements will be used for calculating what assessment measures?) from an analysis perspective.
4. Articulate how these data will be analyzed using Measures of Performance (MOPs) and Measures of Effectiveness (MOEs) and other high level measures.

## 5    Applying the CAM to a "Trust" Construct

The construct of "trust" and related constructs such as "transparency" occur many times in the literature; the references found in this paper cite only a few [17–22]. These constructs are widely used yet in some papers no definition is offered[1]. It is possible

---

[1] See (Lee & See, 2004) for a good summary of trust definitions in the literature.

that the reader is expected to have a shared, cultural definition in mind, or that the construct itself is too difficult to define, or that only concepts or measures somehow ancillary to the construct itself can be articulated or operationalized. We presume, however, that in some cases, it will benefit the research to operationalize these well-used constructs as much as possible, even if it means greatly simplifying the situation by putting aside many potential, but difficult to articulate or measure, possibilities.

To explore how the CAM might help develop an explicit definition of trust in a specific context, we imagine a simple, fictional assessment use case. The situation is that we wish to assess "trust" in the context of a single soldier and a robotic mule device that is designed to follow the soldier while carrying a given load.

If this were an actual assessment (or experiment), we would want to determine how we were going to conduct the assessment, what data we would need, and what measures or analysis would need to be observed and calculated. In this hypothetical example, we simply identify some obvious, and presumably "easy," measures – those measures are highlighted in the tables below.

The tables below represent instantiations of the UML classes described above. Table 1 includes the particular CAM Name (Trust in Soldier-Robot Teams). The Subject Model is the Soldier-Robot. The Mission-Assessment Context Name is "Transport heavy load/field environment." We identify two operationalized constructs: "Trust – Will Follow" and "Transparency – Soldier Knows State of Robot."

**Table 1.** Example trust CAM

|  | Name |
| --- | --- |
| CAM name | Trust in soldier-robot teams |
| Subject model name | Soldier-robot |
| Mission/assessment context name | Transport heavy load/field environment |
| Operationalized construct name - 1 | Trust - will follow |
| Operationalized construct name - 2 | Transparency - soldier knows state of robot |

In Table 2 our hypothetical example is further developed by describing the "Trust in Soldier-Robot Teams" Subject Model. For this table and subsequent tables, several columns are added. These can be thought of as "attributes" of the model. If there are

**Table 2.** Example subject model

|  | Name | Variables/values | Measure | Constraints & characterizations |
| --- | --- | --- | --- | --- |
| Subject model | Soldier-robot | None | None | None |
| Human model | Soldier | None | None | None |
| Machine model | Robot | None | None | None |
| Team model | Soldier-robot | None | None | None |
| Human-machine interaction mode - 1 | Wireless controller | Connectivity | % Time connected | None |
| Human-machine interaction mode -2 | Visual | Line of Sight | % LOS in place | None |

measurable quantities associated with a particular class, those are identified along with suitable measures. For example, the Human-Machine Interaction Mode – 1 is a Wireless Controller. The Variable is Connectivity and is measured by % time connected. The final column includes other constraints or characterizations that should be associated with a given class.

Table 3 describes the example Mission-Assessment Environment. It is comprised of two human tasks, two machine tasks, and one team task. The mission-assessment environment is an open field – in this case a parking lot. (LOS = Line of Sight)

**Table 3.** Example mission-assessment environment

|  | Name | Variables/values | Measure | Constraints & characterizations |
|---|---|---|---|---|
| Mission-assessment model | Go to waypoint in open field | None | None | None |
| Human task - 1 | Go from waypoint A to B | None | None | None |
| Human task - 2 | Monitor robot |  |  |  |
| Machine task - 1 | Follow and maintain pace with soldier | None | None | None |
| Machine task - 2 | Carry load with no damage |  |  |  |
| Team task | Collaboratively move from waypoint A to B | None | None | None |
| Mission environment | Open field | None | None | Parking lot |

Table 4 describes the top level of the hypothetical Operationalized Trust Construct.

**Table 4.** Example operationalized trust construct (top level)

|  | Name | Variables/values | Measure | Constraints & characterizations |
|---|---|---|---|---|
| Mission-assessment model | Go to waypoint in open field | None | None | None |
| ARL standard construct | ARL Basic Two-Party Trust | None | None | None |
| Special construct | ARL HMT Trust | None | None | None |

Table 5 describes the hypothetical ARL Basic Two-Party Trust Construct. In this example, the single feature of the Evidence Model is a Reliance Agreement between the two parties. In this case, the reliance agreement is simply a functioning communications device.

**Table 5.** Example ARL basic two-party trust construct

| | Name | Variables/values | Measure | Constraints & characterizations |
|---|---|---|---|---|
| Mission-assessment model | ARL basic two-party trust | None | None | None |
| Evidence model | Reliance | Reliance agreement in place | None | Functioning wireless communications link |
| Subject expected state model | None | None | None | None |
| Cognitive psychology theory | None | None | None | None |
| Social theory | None | None | None | None |
| Other theory | None | None | None | None |

The Transparency construct can be similarly described, but we do not do so in this paper.

## 6   Extensions to a Network Approach

Starting at least as far back as Cronbach [12] the relationship between constructs and networks or graphs has been recognized. Recently multiple researchers [23–25] have introduced concepts from network theory [26] to this problem space as well and in so doing, greatly enriching the potential for further research. The authors see the potential for data mining of current research, especially if a structure similar to the CAM is used to "normalize" different research approaches and methods. The CAM could then be used in conjunction with network approaches to further discover commonality (and variability) across research and thereby support systemization of constructs and the assessments in which they are used.

## 7   Further Research

The CAM is a concept that is intended to explore how activities like human or human-machine team assessments may be improved through a more systematic and standardizes approach to defining constructs within a given research or assessment context. Using the UML formalism to define a conceptual model leads to many questions about how constructs are defined and relationships between concepts within such a model. Using a UML class approach is only a beginning at describing some of the static relationships between concepts. UML (or other modeling approaches for that matter) also provide for ways to further delineate static aspects but also dynamic aspects. This could be particularly relevant for a construct such as trust since trust can be expected to vary over time.

The most important future research is an attempt to use the CAM in a real assessment or experimental setting. The "real world" or "in the wild" settings can be expected to introduce many challenges that could easily overwhelm a CAM implementation that is too literal. This in itself is a challenge to any research intended to further systematize the field of human performance assessment, especially in complex, cognition-intensive, and machine intelligence augmented situations. It is the authors' belief that to continue to make progress in this increasingly complex operational environment, progress must be made in systemization and standardization.

Finally, the authors intend to further explore the potential connections between the CAM and network approaches to constructs, measures, and assessments.

## 8  Summary and Conclusions

We have presented a Conceptual Assessment Model (CAM) using the UML methodology. The CAM provides a potential tool that could be used in a structured method of assessment. The CAM, or other similar concepts, could be particularly useful across an enterprise in serving to standardize the way constructs are defined and what measures are used to describe them.

**Acknowledgements.** The authors would like to thank Professor Peter Hancock of the University of Central Florida for his review of this material.

## References

1. Army Research Laboratory: Army Research Laboratory S&T Campaign Plans 2015–2035. U.S. Army RDECOM, Adelphi (2014)
2. Army Research Laboratory: Army Research Laboratory Technical Strategy 2015–2035. U.S. Army RDECOM, Adelphi (2014)
3. Army Research Laboratory: ARL Technical Implementation Plan
4. Wharton, J.F.: Army Soldier & Squad Performance Optimization Strategy. Aberdeen Proving Ground. (2015)
5. Bostrom, N.: Superintelligence Paths, Dangers, and Strategies. Oxford University Press, Oxford (2014)
6. U.S. Army: The U.S. Army Robotic and Autonomous Systems Strategy. U.S. Training and Doctrine Command, Maneuver, Aviation, and Soldier Division Army Capabilities Integration Center, Fort Eustis (2016)
7. Tamilio, D.: Modern Warrior 2050 Soldier and Team Performance Baseline Proposed Army Capability Enabler (ACE) (n.d.)
8. Stevens, S.S.: The operational definition of psychological concepts. Psychol. Rev. **42**, 517–527 (1935)
9. Binning, J.F.: Construct. Encyclopedia Britannica. https://www.britannica.com/science/construct
10. Wikipedia: Operationalization. https://en.wikipedia.org/wiki/Operationalization
11. Web Center for Social Research Methods. Construct Validity. (Cornell Office for Research on Evaluation). http://www.socialresearchmethods.net/kb/constval.php

12. Cronbach, L.J., Meehl, P.E.: Construct validity in psychological tests. Psychol. Bull. **52**, 281–302 (1955)
13. Wikipedia: Unified Modeling Language. https://en.wikipedia.org/wiki/Unified_Modeling_Language
14. Wikipedia: Conceptual Model. https://en.wikipedia.org/wiki/Conceptual_model
15. Univ of Minnesota: Understanding Psychological Measurement. Univ of Minnesota, Research Methods in Psychology. University of Minnesota Libraries Publishing. http://open.lib.umn.edu/psychologyresearchmethods/chapter/5-1-understanding-psychological-measurement/
16. National Council on Measurement in Education: Glossary of Important Assessment and Measurement Terms. http://www.ncme.org/ncme/NCME/Resource_Center/Glossary/NCME/Resource_Center/Glossary1.aspx?
17. Chen, J.Y., Procci, K., Boyce, M., Wright, J., Garcia, A., Barnes, M.: Situation Awareness-Based Agent Transparency. Army Research Laboratory. U.S. Army Research Laboratory. http://www.arl.army.mil/arlreports/2014/ARL-TR-6905.pdf (2014)
18. Lee, J.D., See, K.A.: Trust in automation: designing for appropriate reliance. Hum. Factors, **46**, 50–80 (2004). http://user.engineering.uiowa.edu/~csl/publications/pdf/leesee04.pdf
19. Hancock, P.A., Billings, D.A., Schaefer, K.E., Chen, J.Y., de Visser, E.J., Parasuraman, R.: A meta-analysis of factors affecting trust in human-robot interaction. Hum. Factors: J. Hum. Factors Ergon. Soc. (2011). http://hfs.sagepub.com/content/53/5/517
20. Lyons, J.B.: Being transparent about transparency: a model for human-robot interaction. In: Trust and Autonomous Systems: Papers from the 2014 AAAI Spring Symposium (2013)
21. Hieb, M.R.: Developing and communicating intent for distributed staff. In: 20th ICCRTS - C2, Cyber, and Trust
22. Hieb, M.R.: Command and control in multiteam systems: measuring and building trust between people and groups. In: 20th ICCRTS - C2, Cyber, and Trust
23. Borrsboom, D., Cramer, A.O., Schmittmann, V.D., Epskamp, S., Waldrop, L.J.: The small world of psychopathology. PLOS **6**(11), 27407 (2011)
24. Schmittmann, V.D., Cramer, A.O., Waldorp, L.J., Epskamp, S., Kievit, R.A., Borsboom, D.: Deconstructing the construct: a network perspective on psychological phenomena. New Ideas Psychol. **31**, 43–53 (2013)
25. Watts, D.J., Steven, H.S.: Collective dynamics of "small-world" networks. Nature **393**, 440–442 (1998)
26. Boccaletti, S., Latora, V., Moreno, Y., Chavez, M., Hwang, D.-U.: Complex networks: structure and dynamics. Phys. Rep. **424**, 175–308 (2006)

# Recommendations for Use of Adaptive Tutoring Systems in the Classroom and in Educational Research

Anne M. Sinatra[1]([⊠]), Scott Ososky[1,2], Robert Sottilare[1], and Jason Moss[1]

[1] U.S. Army Research Laboratory, Orlando, FL, USA
[2] Oak Ridge Associated Universities, Orlando, FL, USA
{anne.m.sinatra.civ, scott.j.ososky.ctr,
robert.a.sottilare.civ, jason.d.moss11.civ}@mail.mil

**Abstract.** The current paper and presentation provide background on the different uses of intelligent tutoring systems (ITSs) in context of course instruction, discusses specific instructor considerations that are associated with their use, and ways to use ITSs for educational research. Instructor considerations include the time necessary to plan prior to constructing an ITS, the process of constructing ITS lessons for use by students, the method in which students will interact with the ITS, approaches to incorporating ITS use into classes, and the information that instructors would find useful to be output from the ITS. Specifically, the Generalized Intelligent Framework for Tutoring (GIFT), an open-source, domain independent ITS framework will be discussed as an approach to creating adaptive tutoring content for classroom use. GIFT includes straightforward authoring tools for instructors and Subject Matter Experts (SMEs). These authoring tools are powerful, do not require a background in computer science to use, and result in fully adaptive computer-based lessons. Additionally, GIFT provides the flexibility for instructors to bring their pre-generated and already existing instructional material to the system and use it to create ITS lessons. The authoring tools allow the instructor to determine the path of their lesson and the components that their students will experience (i.e. surveys, quizzes, lesson materials, videos). The paper includes details about the development of an instructor dashboard in GIFT, ways for an instructor to use GIFT for educational research, and a discussion of general output information from ITSs that would be relevant to instructors.

**Keywords:** Intelligent tutoring systems · Classroom · Generalized Intelligent Framework for Tutoring · Educational research · Adaptive tutoring

## 1 Introduction

Intelligent Tutoring Systems (ITSs) provide an opportunity for instructors to create adaptive content that their students can engage with as a supplement to their courses. In the current education landscape, even lecture based courses often times have a website associated with them that allows students to download course material, engage

© Springer International Publishing AG 2017
D.D. Schmorrow and C.M. Fidopiastis (Eds.): AC 2017, Part II, LNAI 10285, pp. 223–236, 2017.
DOI: 10.1007/978-3-319-58625-0_16

in discussions and receive grades. Providing student access to web-based ITSs through these websites is a natural next step. ITSs offer benefits such as personalized adaptive learning, and have been shown to be as effective as a human tutor [1]. One of the major benefits of ITSs, is that unlike a human tutor they can be easily accessed at all hours of the day, and do not get tired or frustrated. ITSs can adapt based on prior knowledge of the individual student, individual differences, or within-tutor performance. This method of instruction provides a tailored, personalized version of lesson materials that can include remediation and clarification of topics. Instructors who author ITSs can make the determination on what type of adaptations they want to occur, and which student individual differences/actions they want to use to determine the adaptations of the system. ITSs can have different benefits and uses based on the type of course that is being taught: online, mixed mode, or lecture [2]. In the case of online courses they may be a vital component of the class that provides important material, whereas, in a lecture course they may serve as an independent supplement to the material that is taught in class. Further, some instructors may want students to engage with ITSs on their own, while others may want them to be used in a computer lab environment with the instructor present for clarification or to assist in classroom management [2].

## 2   Intelligent Tutoring Systems in the Classroom

Research has shown that ITSs can have positive impacts on learning in a number of different educational domains [1, 3, 4]. Additionally, ITSs can be used either as an added supplement to teaching, or as a component of the classroom. The advantages of ITSs include that they can be used on the student's own time, allow for remediation as needed, and can be engaging as well as motivational. However, the time spent creating materials and remediation for an ITS, is likely to impact the overall adaptivity and outcomes of the ITS. A more adaptive ITS will require more time spent on authoring alternative methods of teaching the required concepts. For instance, if there are 10 different remediation options available to the system based on one concept it will be more adaptive than if there were only 3 pieces of material available. However, authoring this material and considering the situations in which it will be presented does add to the instructor's workload.

While ITSs are a computer-based medium, they can be utilized in both traditional in-person lecture courses, as well as online courses. They can even be beneficial in reduced-seat mixed mode courses. In lecture-based classes, ITSs may be used to provide review and remediation of material that was previously taught, potentially as a review prior to a test. In online classes, ITSs may be one of the primary ways of presenting materials to the students. Mixed-mode classes could potentially integrate ITSs by providing ITS experiences related to the specific material prior to in-class lectures, in order to provide a foundation and context for the material to be learned. ITSs can be useful for not only providing information to students, but also it could be advantageous for students to learn how to create their own ITSs. By planning and creating ITSs about specific concepts students can reflect upon the material, as well as learn about the functions of these adaptive systems [2]. The utilization of an ITS in these different environments can also provide meaningful output to instructors that can be compiled in the form of a dashboard and be leveraged so that they can adapt their teaching methods as needed. Additionally, ITSs and generalized ITS frameworks can provide a means to perform educational research and examine the impact of different adaptations and interventions within the ITS.

## 3   Intelligent Tutoring Systems in Educational Research

The use of ITSs as a tool in the classroom has continued to increase throughout the years in U.S. schools. For example, Cognitive Tutor by Carnegie Learning was used in over 2,600 U.S. schools as of 2010 [3]. ITSs have been used for a variety of different age levels spanning from kindergarten to college students. Further, there have been many different ITSs developed in domains as wide-ranging as algebra, physics, medical physiology, law, language learning, and meta-cognitive skills [4]. Comprehensive research examining the effectiveness of ITSs can be found in recent meta-analyses. These meta-analyses examined the effectiveness of ITSs as compared to the effectiveness of typical classroom instruction (i.e., large group and small group human instruction), individual human instruction (i.e., one on one human tutoring), individual computer based instruction (i.e., non-adaptive/intelligent tutoring lacking student/learner modeling), and when the student interacted with an individual textbook [4].

As a tool used in the classroom, ITSs track students' domain knowledge of a subject, learning skills, learning strategies, emotions, or motivation through learner modeling. Further, Steenbergen-Hu and Cooper [3] identified the actions of an ITS as the delivery of learning content to students, tracking and assessing of students' learning progress and adapting to said progress (or lack thereof), and the delivery of appropriate feedback to students. ITSs in the classroom are considered to be superior to traditional computer-based training (CBT) and computer-assisted instruction (CAI) in that ITSs afford unlimited interactions between the ITS and the learner [5].

Steenbergen-Hu and Cooper [3] conducted one of the first meta-analyses examining the effectiveness of math ITSs among K-12 students. The meta-analysis included samples from 1997 to 2010 which had information regarding achievement level, learning outcomes, and an independent comparison group. Overall, their findings suggested that ITS had no negative impact on learning, but only a small positive effect on K-12 mathematical learning was revealed as compared to regular classroom instruction [3]. However, effectiveness of ITSs was greater when compared with homework or human tutoring (i.e., effect sizes of ITS ranged from .20 to .60) [3].

Although small effects were revealed for the effectiveness of ITS on mathematical learning for K-12 grade students, the meta-analysis revealed robust findings to support the use and development of ITSs. Two interesting findings of the meta-analysis were that shorter uses of the ITS were found to be more effective than long term uses, and that low achievers did not benefit as much from an ITS as other students [3]. These results suggest that individual differences and the length of the exposure to the ITS may have an impact on learning outcomes.

An additional meta-analysis by Ma et al. [4] compared effect sizes from ITS studies that included students of different grade levels, different ITS topic areas, and the way that the ITS was incorporated into the learning environment. In general, ITSs were found to be more effective than standard computer based learning and large lecture classes. The ITSs were effective regardless of how they were incorporated into class (i.e. as a primary means of instruction, as a supplement to material, or an aid). However, ITSs still were not as effective as human one-to one tutoring. These results are insightful, as they show that ITSs may important components of a classroom environment, but the approaches taken with their integration into the classroom should be carefully thought out to ensure that their use is optimized. It was revealed by Ma et al. [4] that the domains of humanities and social sciences are the greatest beneficiaries of ITS use with an effect size of .63. In their meta-analysis, chemistry was the only domain that did not reveal a significant nor moderate effect size.

Although ITSs continue to demonstrate positive achievement outcomes over traditional instruction across a variety of subject domains and education levels, research questions still remain in the use of ITSs and how ITSs can address educational research questions. Also, there are recommendations that ITS researchers can follow in reporting and documenting their results to improve the overall ability for ITS researchers to draw more consistent and reliable conclusions from reported research. Steenbergen-Hu and Cooper [3] found ITSs to have a greater impact on moderate achieving students than low achievers. There is a need to examine how ITSs can better impact the learning outcomes of the students that need it the most. How can ITSs be leveraged to affect students of different and lower achieving levels? Further, research using ITSs should examine and develop a better understanding of why higher achieving students benefit more from the use of ITSs. It is not unlikely to hypothesize that lower achieving students may have less motivation than higher achieving students. Therefore, how ITSs better leverage intrinsic and extrinsic motivational factors is an example of a research question worth further pursuing.

As pointed out by Ma et al. [4], although ITSs have demonstrated effectiveness, it is still difficult to definitively come to a consensus on explanations for the effectiveness of ITSs. Further research is necessary to address and offer explanations for why ITSs are effective in order to improve the development of ITSs. Also, this research should provide further insight on how to improve the efficacy of instructors in the classroom.

Lastly, there are some recommendations researchers can adhere to when reporting and documenting the results of their research in order for others to draw more reliable and consistent conclusions from the reported research. Researchers should adhere to the standards of reporting basic statistics such as means and standard deviations, and Ma et al. [4] recommend development of a taxonomy of ITS design. Developing a taxonomy of ITS design would enhance the standardization of ITS research reporting, ideally resulting in quicker ITS research advancements and a common framework for researchers and practitioners to draw reliable and valid conclusions for the use of ITSs in education.

## 4 The Generalized Intelligent Framework for Tutoring (GIFT) and Educational Research

In order to study the effectiveness of ITSs, an ITS not only has to be created, but researchers must put together carefully constructed experiments to determine the real world application and benefits of ITS use. Different approaches can be taken to conducting educational research with ITSs. Comparisons can be made between grades from students who were in a previous ITS-less versions of the course as opposed to an ITS-enhanced version. Pre and post test can be given before and after ITS use. In an online class, the pre and post performance of students that engaged with an ITS can be compared to those who just received non-adaptive computer-based material. One of the inherent difficulties with designing a study that actively uses students and provides different means of providing material to them is that the instructor does not want to offer more of an advantage to one student over another by providing them with better instructional materials. Therefore, it is important to carefully design the materials to make sure that they are equivalent in content. The time the student spends with the material can also be a metric to examine, as those with the ITS may more efficiently peruse the material as opposed to receiving a regular all inclusive version.

While meta-analyses were able to compare overall effect sizes for ITSs, they do not allow for direct comparisons between ITSs of different subject types in controlled experimental fashion. If ITSs in different subject areas were constructed using the same framework and with consistency, then perhaps their learning outcomes can be more directly compared to each other. For instance, are there more learning gains when ITSs are used for algebra as opposed to when they are used for learning a language? Further, an area that has not received as much attention is the components of the learner model that are tracked during interaction with the ITS or that result in adaptations [6]. Research could further investigate these questions by engaging in experiments that vary the individual differences or characteristics that adaptation occurs based on. For instance, is there an improved outcome to adapting based on prior knowledge and motivation level in an algebra tutor, or is it more advantageous to adapt just based on prior knowledge? Generalized frameworks for ITSs can help offer an opportunity to research these types of questions.

Most ITSs are tightly coupled with the material that they are teaching, and are not reusable. However, the Generalized Intelligent Framework for Tutoring (GIFT), is a domain-independent ITS framework. The tools that exist within GIFT can be used to create adaptive tutoring in any subject or topic. Due to this, it allows for reusability of material and adaptability of the ITS without needing to start from scratch or develop an entirely new framework. GIFT is made up of different modules and components: the learner module, pedagogical module, domain module, sensor module, gateway module, and the tutor-user interface [7]. The only module that is tied to the domain content is the domain module. The flexibility that exists within GIFT also allows for changes to be made to the types of information that is being tracked in the learner module, the types of adaptations that are recommended by the pedagogical module, as well as the material in the domain module. Therefore, GIFT provides an opportunity to examine the impact of changing the selected characteristics and representations within these modules without needing to dramatically change or reprogram an already established ITS. This functionality opens up opportunities for further expanding educational research using ITSs. These types of research questions allow for educators to research what the optimal individual differences to adapt to are, as well as if there are advantages to one type of adaptation over another type. The information gathered from this can then be applied in educational environments whether they are online or in in-person classes. Additionally, the flexibility of GIFT allows for instructors to utilize the elements of it in the classroom to add to and enhance the way that they interact with their students.

## 5  Applying GIFT in the Classroom

While much of the research conducted to enable GIFT as an adaptive training tool has been focused on standalone (no human-in-the-loop) one-to-one tutoring capabilities, the goal has always been to have GIFT used in a classroom environment as an aid to human instructors too. This section discusses the information needs of human instructors which would enable them to evaluate and manage concurrent computer-based tutoring sessions of their students. We examine what information the instructor might need to optimize decisions about when and where they allocate their time to intercede with students who need help beyond what a computer-based tutor is able to provide. We begin by discussing what information about the student is already available to GIFT-based tutors and later extend this model to support the classroom paradigm.

The learner model in GIFT-based tutors includes information from various sources. As noted in the various updates of the Learning Effect Model (LEM) [8–10], this information originates from five primary sources: (1) real-time student interaction with the tutor and the training environment (e.g., responses to requests for information); (2) real-time sensor data and physiological states based on sensor data; (3) historical data from record stores which include demographics, domain experiences, knowledge, achievements and the results of validated assessments (e.g., grit surveys, personality and other trait appraisal instruments); (4) real-time assessment of performance based on learner progress toward learning goals and other behavioral states based on sensor data; and (5) external environments (e.g., entity level data from a simulation integrated with a GIFT-based tutor through a standardized GIFT gateway).

GIFT uses this information to select strategies and implement instructional tactics with the goal of accelerating and optimizing learning, performance, retention, and the transfer of skills developed during training to the work or operational environment. A consideration in developing a dashboard (information resource) for application in a classroom is the migration of each student from one quadrant (i.e., rules, examples, recall, and practice) to the next as described by Merrill's [11] Component Display Theory and implemented in GIFT. In the classroom use case, GIFT should be able to provide a comprehensive picture of the student population at a glance so the instructor can decide where to allocate their time in support of student learning objectives. This could mean alerting the instructor when students struggle with domain concepts and content or when they fall below expectations based on past performance.

Bull and Nghiem [12] and Guerra et al. [13] recommend an open learner modeling approach which is designed to help learners to better understand their learning processes with a model which is accessible to the student, the instructor, and their peers. Bull and Ngheim [12] also note the following benefits of the open learner modeling approach: (1) improves the accuracy of the learner model by allowing students to contribute information to it; (2) promotes reflection; and (3) helps the tutor plan and monitor learning based upon the foundation of information available in the learner model. The information available in an open learner model ranges from performance statistics (e.g., quiz grades) to progress toward goals (e.g., completed 58% of assigned work). Guerra et al. [13] suggest a graphic visualization of the learner's activities (e.g., quizzes, examples) and domain topics in their mastery grids system which uses various shades of green to indicate student performance, shades of blue to represent reference group performance, and a combination of green and blue to indicate how an individual student is performing with respect to the reference group. This system allows a student, instructor or peers to quickly assess their performance in a variety of activities and topical areas.

Considering the open learner model and various states and traits available within the GIFT architecture, we recommend a hybrid system to allow instructors to address not only performance concerns, but also the affective state, domain competency, and learning readiness of their students. A simple dashboard (Fig. 1) might show a classroom of 20 student icons color coded to show the instructor the overall state of the student. Students with green status (e.g., Students A, C and D) are on track in the pursuit of their learning goals and are not currently experiencing any negative affective

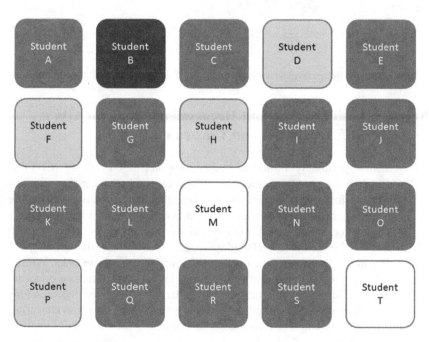

**Fig. 1.** Top level view of notional GIFT Dashboard (Color figure online)

states. Students with yellow status (e.g., Students D, F and H) may be performing slightly below expectation based on their domain competency and/or experiencing negative affective states relative to learning readiness. Students with red status (e.g., Student B) may be significantly underperforming or experiencing negative affective states that significantly curtail learning. Finally, white squares represent neutral status which may mean that the student has not yet begun the set of tasks in the domain under instruction.

Details about any of the students represented in this dashboard may be viewed by clicking on the appropriate student icon. Figure 2 shows an example of the status of an individual student. There is a breakdown of status based on concept, affective state, and quadrant based on Component Display Theory. The same color scheme as the top level dashboard view is used.

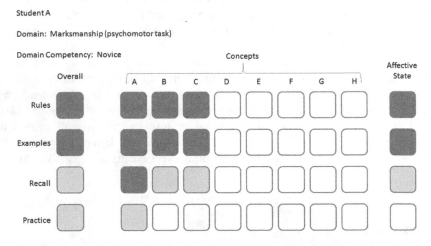

**Fig. 2.** Student detail level view of notional GIFT Dashboard (Color figure online)

## 6   Future Considerations and Recommendations for GIFT to Assist in Educational and Classroom Use

ITSs may seem superficially similar to linear, computer-based training (CBT). However, ITSs adapt to the profile of a learner, which can include their current and prior experiences and performance, learning preferences, affective states, and so on. Thus the resources, authoring, and pre-production required in order to build an effective tutor are greater than that of computer based training. GIFT, as an intelligent tutoring platform, intends to provide the means to create, deploy, and manage adaptive training content while lowering the skill and resource barriers to accomplishing those tasks. While great progress has been made in service of those core principles, there remain opportunities for improvement. Here, we will describe considerations and recommendations for future research, design, and development in GIFT supporting classroom education and educational research, along the dimensions of *authoring, instructional support, and research management.*

## 6.1    Considerations and Recommendations for Classroom Education: Authoring

The concept of creating a tutor is a relatively new content creation paradigm. Therefore, one of the greatest challenges to tutor authoring is how to best cultivate mental models of ITSs in novice end-users, and cultivating an authoring user experience for users that encourages the creation of truly adaptive tutors (as opposed to producing linear CBT). GIFT currently provides a series of authoring tools, intended to reduce the time and skill required to produce tutors. Our current approach in developing a user experience for tutor authoring is based upon tenants of mental model theory: when confronted with a new system, individuals will rely upon mental models of systems perceived to be familiar to the new system [14]; and that mental models help make sense of the form, function, and purpose of a system [15].

With that in mind, GIFT's current authoring tools use interfaces and interaction paradigms that are intended to look and feel familiar to other productivity tasks such as building a flow chart, filling out a form, or creating a web-page. The idea is that familiar interface elements from other productivity applications will help to form the foundation of a mental model for tutor authoring. Much of this effort has been targeted at the core elements of the authoring experience (e.g., sequencing elements, adding media, developing survey material) as well as quality-of-life improvements (e.g., auto-save, copy/paste, minimizing clicks and pop-ups) [16].

With a system that is reasonably learnable and usable, we are discovering new considerations for education with an expanded user base. Particularly, many authors bring their existing content to GIFT (or any ITS), however this content is largely not in a format suitable for adaptation. That content is generally intended to be viewed in its entirety by all of the learners, constituting CBT. While GIFT is not a media creation tool, future GIFT development should support the semi-automated process of content generation and/or formatting for adaptation based on learner characteristics. For example, that might involve assisting the author in sub-diving an existing slide show or print material into core, remedial, and advanced content and then placing that content in the appropriate course elements within a GIFT course. Or, authoring support may take the form of intelligently interfacing with external content repositories to help locate and suggest additional content to the author to include in their tutor.

Future GIFT-related research should consider novel ways to provide adaptations beyond content selection. GIFT, for instance, presents tutors within its own custom tutor-user interface (TUI). Improvements to the TUI could be made, configurable via the authoring tools, which would provide certain overlays and interface elements that would change and/or appear based on the learner's profile. For example, a learner that is highly competitive may be presented with the option to view a leaderboard in an effort to build motivation, but such a TUI element would not be shown if the system believes it would only demoralize that learner. The actual learning content remains unchanged. Leaderboards, specifically, come from a larger class of TUI elements inspired by gamification [17], however, there are other ways in which existing media content can be enhanced or modified through the TUI, such as options for background music, context personalization [18], or the ability to customize the tutor avatar with which a learner interacts.

## 6.2  Considerations and Recommendations for Classroom Education: Instructional Support

As described in Sect. 5, ITSs have the potential to produce large amounts of data, including those about the learner (e.g., profile, sensors, preferences), the learner's interaction within the ITS (and linked, external practice environments), actions taken by the ITS based on the learner model, as well as the learning content and assessments presented to each individual learner. Data sources may also include information external to GIFT, such as a learner record store [19]. With respect to instructional support, the primary consideration for GIFT is to provide a *dashboard* that enables instructors to quickly perform data exploration and high level analyses in order to ascertain the health of the class, and make decisions regarding interventions for high or low performing students.

Given the nature of a flexible, adaptive system like GIFT, there may not be a single best solution for a dashboard. Each row of student data within the same course may contain different columns of information, depending on the adaptive paths encountered within the tutor. Since GIFT is a domain-independent platform, the types of data that are generated across courses will vary wildly. Further, different instructors in different courses may need to answer different types of questions regarding their courses, suggesting that there may not be a single user experience that best fits all these cases. To that end, GIFT should consider the perspective that adaptive tutoring systems will require adaptive instructional dashboards.

The high-level notional concepts presented in Figs. 1 and 2 (above) help to answer questions regarding *how* the students in the class are performing, and those views may remain fairly consistent across GIFT modules. As an instructor drills down into the data however, customizable views will be required to help answer questions about *why* the students are exhibiting certain levels of performance [20]. Again, the data available to answer these questions depends upon the unique composition of the tutor. Therefore, a user-centered design strategy should be followed in pursuit of a GIFT instructor dashboard. Operationally, a modular dashboard should be built around instructors' work goals, and the associated tasks required in order to meet those goals (Fig. 3). Specifically, GIFT would provide semi-automated support to the instructor in constructing figures and charts, and the instructor should be able to organize those reports into a customizable view, similar to the interface of an analytics dashboard for website usage.

Consider a use case illustrated in Fig. 3. Using the dashboard, an instructor notes that one student is performing poorly in a course, relative to the performance of the other students. Note that Fig. 1 is one of the views that the instructor has added to their custom dashboard. On the surface, the student appears to be engaging with the tutor, and the course materials contained within, but the instructor wants to investigate the low-performing student's actions within the system in greater detail. Using a modular instructor dashboard in GIFT, the instructor decides to begin examining the extent to which students of different performance levels interact with various types of instructional media contained within that lesson. From a list automatically-populated of available charts, figures, and tables, the instructor adds the relevant module to their dashboard view, and selects three students for comparison. The instructor notes that the

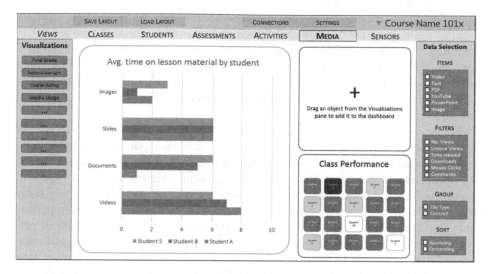

**Fig. 3.** Conceptual mock-up of a modular, semi-automated instructor dashboard for GIFT

low-performing student appears to have spent the same amount of time viewing the lesson material with the exception of some of the image content. The instructor can now investigate whether the low performing student missed important information contained within some of the images in the lesson. Data exploration can continue in this way to corroborate this potential linkage between the student's performance and the time spent with a particular type of lesson material.

Functional considerations should also be made to improve the usability of the dashboard tools. Layouts and configured visualizations should be able to be saved as views, for use in future courses, or to share with other instructors. Dashboard elements should be interactive: Hovering the cursor over individual data points should provide pop-ups with additional details. Clicking on a relevant data point, such as "Student A" in the Class Performance visualization in Fig. 3, should produce the view found in Fig. 2, by "zooming into" that view as an underlying element. Elements should be movable, resizable, and support common productivity functions such as cut, copy, and paste. Similar to the authoring tools UX, overall quality-of-life improvements will help to make the tools more efficient and allow the instructor to spend less time setting up the dashboard, and more time exploring the data [21].

### 6.3  Considerations and Recommendations for Education Research: Management

GIFT has been used for research purposes since its inception, and it is upon research that GIFT's pedagogical engine and other features are based [22]. GIFT has only recently, however, been updated with features directly supporting tasks associated with preparing, administering, and managing research. Currently, core functionality is in place that allows an existing GIFT module to be spawned into a "research version" of that module [16]. Doing that creates a non-editable version of the module, with the intent of maintaining the consistency of the trials across participants. A unique URL is generated that allows participants to directly access the course without a GIFT Account, with the intent of protecting the anonymity of their data. Access to the study can be paused and resumed in accordance with data collection timelines and regulatory bodies. GIFT's research tools also provide interfaces for downloading customized data files and reports when desired.

Future considerations for GIFT in support of educational research could include explicit features for creating and managing treatments/manipulations within *experimental* versions of the material to be learned, as well as the distribution of participants into those sets of materials. Consider a use case in which a researcher wants to implement three versions of a educational material covering a concept that only differ by a specific element. The researcher also wants to semi-randomly distribute participants into the three versions of the material, but ensure that each cell has equal participants with similar distributions of high/low motivated learners. GIFT might handle this use case in one of two ways, either internally or externally to the course. One implementation would use the same overall GIFT course with a special course element containing all three versions and logic for specifying the distribution into the permutations. Alternatively, three separate versions of the material could be somehow "linked" together in a way that version control is maintained across them with the exception of the elements intended to be manipulated. Randomization and assignment of participants would then be handled through the top-level Research UI of the GIFT interface. Determining the "best" design implementation for this functionality may come down to preference, as the design of adaptive tutors themselves is still evolving.

Finally, more robust reporting tools are needed for educational research using adaptive tutors. GIFT is intended to be a flexible, domain independent platform, therefore the types of tutors that can be created will vary wildly. GIFT also adapts on a number of learner characteristics using both discrete-time, outer-loop logic as well as real-time (or near real-time), inner-loop logic. Sources of learner data may also come from various sources (described earlier in this work). It logically follows that the data outputs from educational research will require different reporting formats as well beyond the current capabilities of the reporting tool currently provided by the GIFT web-application. Instructor dashboards, described in the prior section, may assist the researcher as well in conducting exploratory analyses with partial or complete data sets.

## 7 Conclusions and Recommendations

ITSs can be extremely useful to instructors of courses, regardless of the modality. They have the ability to engage students with material that may have been missed, or that was not completely understood. Additionally, they are adaptive to the individual such that the prior knowledge and performance of the student will impact the material that they are provided. ITSs have been demonstrated to be useful in both the laboratory environment as well as in classroom environments [23–25].

There are many educational research questions that can still be examined in ITSs, such as what the ideal components of the learner model are, a comparison in effectiveness of ITSs between domains, and the impact ITSs have when implemented in an in-person vs. an online course. A domain-independent ITS framework such as GIFT provides opportunities to construct ITSs to contribute to the answers to these questions, and to enhance the classroom experience. It is recommended that GIFT be used to pursue these and similar research questions that are not practical or able to be asked in traditional ITSs. As GIFT and other ITSs continue to be developed for both practical use and educational research, it is recommended that instructor dashboards are designed to be customizable and provide a way to harness the rich data that is available from ITSs about student performance, states, and progress. ITSs can be extremely useful to instructors, and can be incorporated into classes in a number of different meaningful ways including as a means to: provide information, remediate information, monitor student performance/state, and to conduct educational research.

**Acknowledgements.** The research described herein has been sponsored by the U.S. Army Research Laboratory. The statements and opinions expressed in this article do not necessarily reflect the position or the policy of the United States Government, and no official endorsement should be inferred.

# References

1. VanLehn, K.: The relative effectiveness of human tutoring, intelligent tutoring systems, and other tutoring systems. Educ. Psychol. **46**(4), 197–221 (2011)
2. Sinatra, A.M., Ososky, S., Sottilare, R.: Assessment in intelligent tutoring systems in traditional, mixed mode and online courses. In: Design Recommendations for Intelligent Tutoring Systems, Volume 5: Assessment (in press)
3. Steenbergen-Hu, S., Cooper, H.: A meta-analysis of the effectiveness of intelligent tutoring systems on K-12 students' mathematical learning. J. Educ. Psychol. **105**(4), 970–987 (2013)
4. Ma, W., Adesope, O.O., Nesbit, J.C., Liu, Q.: Intelligent tutoring systems and learning outcomes: a meta-analysis. J. Educ. Psychol. **106**(4), 901–918 (2014)
5. Graesser, A.C., Conley, M., Olney, A.: Intelligent tutoring systems. In: Harris, K.R., Graham, S., Urban, T. (eds.) APA Educational Psychology Handbook. Applications to Learning and Teaching, vol. 3, pp. 451–473. American Psychological Association, Washington, D.C. (2011)
6. Holden, H. K., Sinatra, A. M.: The need for empirical evaluation of learner model elements. In: Design Recommendations for Intelligent Tutoring Systems, Volume 1: Learner Modeling, p. 87 (2013)
7. Sottilare, R.A., Goldberg, B.S., Brawner, K.W., Holden, H.K.: A modular framework to support the authoring and assessment of adaptive computer-based tutoring systems (CBTS). In: Proceedings of the Interservice/Industry Training, Simulation, and Education Conference, pp. 1–13 (2012)
8. Sottilare, R.: Considerations in the development of an ontology for a generalized intelligent framework for tutoring. In: International Defense and Homeland Security Simulation Workshop in Proceedings of the I3M Conference, Vienna, Austria, September 2012

9. Sottilare, R., Ragusa, C., Hoffman, M., Goldberg, B.: Characterizing an adaptive tutoring learning effect chain for individual and team tutoring. In: Proceedings of the Interservice/Industry Training Simulation and Education Conference, Orlando, Florida, December 2013

10. Sottilare, R.: Elements of a learning effect model to support an adaptive instructional framework. In: Sottilare, R., Ososky, S. (eds.) 4th Annual GIFT Users Symposium (GIFTSym4) Army Research Laboratory, Orlando, Florida (2016). ISBN: 978-0-9977257-0-4

11. Merrill, M.D.: Component display theory. Instr.-Des. Theor. Models: Overview Their Curr. Status **1**, 282–333 (1983)

12. Bull, S., Nghiem, T.: Helping learners to understand themselves with a learner model open to students, peers and instructors. In: Proceedings of Workshop on Individual and Group Modelling Methods that Help Learners Understand Themselves, International Conference on Intelligent Tutoring Systems, pp. 5–13 (2002)

13. Guerra, J., Hosseini, R., Somyurek, S., Brusilovsky, P.: An intelligent interface for learning content: combining an open learner model and social comparison to support self-regulated learning and engagement. In: Proceedings of the 21st International Conference on Intelligent User Interfaces, pp. 152–163. ACM, March 2016

14. Craik, K.: The Nature of Explanation. Cambridge University Press, Cambridge (1943)

15. Rouse, W.B., Morris, N.M.: On looking into the black box: prospects and limits in the search for mental models. Psychol. Bull. **100**(3), 349–363 (1986). doi:10.1037/0033-2909.100.3.349

16. Ososky, S.: Designing the user experience of the GIFT Cloud authoring tools. In: Sottilare, R., Ososky, S. (eds.) Proceedings of the 4th Annual GIFT Users Symposium, vol. 4, pp. 145–156. Army Research Laboratory, Orlando (2016)

17. Ososky, S.: Opportunities and risks for game-inspired design of adaptive instructional systems. In: Schmorrow, D.D., Fidopiastis, C.M. (eds.) AC 2015. LNCS (LNAI), vol. 9183, pp. 640–651. Springer, Cham (2015). doi:10.1007/978-3-319-20816-9_61

18. Sinatra, A.M.: A review of self-reference and context personalization in different computer-based educational domains. In: Design Recommendations for Intelligent Tutoring Systems: Volume 4-Domain Modeling, p. 107 (2016)

19. Sabin, M.: Student-pull instead of instructor-push: in preparation for a student learning dashboard. J. Comput. Sci. Coll. **27**(6), 70–72 (2012)

20. Siemens, G., Gasevic, D., Haythornthwaite, C., Dawson, S., Shum, S.B., Ferguson, R., Duval, E., Verbert, K., Baker, R.S.J.D.: Open learning analytics: an integrated & modularized platform. Open University Press Doctoral dissertation (2011)

21. Lightbown, D.: Designing the User Experience of Game Development Tools. CRC Press, Boca Raton (2015)

22. Wang-Costello, J., Goldberg, B., Tarr, R.W., Cintron, L.M., Jiang, H.: Creating an advanced pedagogical model to improve intelligent tutoring technologies. In: The Interservice/Industry Training, Simulation and Education Conference (I/ITSEC) (2013)

23. Corbett, A.T., Koedinger, K.R., Hadley, W.H.: Cognitive tutors: from the research classroom to all classrooms. In: Technology Enhanced Learning: Opportunities for Change, pp. 235–263 (2001)

24. Koedinger, K.R., Aleven, V., Roll, I., Baker, R.: In vivo experiments on whether supporting metacognition in intelligent tutoring systems yields robust learning. In: Handbook of Metacognition in Education, pp. 897–964 (2009)

25. Yacef, K.: The Logic-ITA in the classroom: a medium scale experiment. Int. J. Artif. Intell. Educ. **15**(1), 41–62 (2005)

# Defining Complexity in the Authoring Process for Adaptive Instruction

Robert Sottilare[1(✉)] and Scott Ososky[1,2]

[1] U.S. Army Research Laboratory, Orlando, FL, USA
{robert.a.sottilare.civ,scott.j.ososky.ctr}@mail.mil
[2] Oak Ridge Associated Universities, Orlando, FL, USA

**Abstract.** Adaptive instruction is computer-based training or education that is tailored to match the difficulty of the content to the states and traits of the learner. Since the individual differences of learners vary widely and contribute greatly to the adaptation decisions by the tutor, adaptive instructional systems (e.g., Intelligent Tutoring Systems – ITSs) need much more content and make many more instructional decisions than non-adaptive instructional systems that instruct all learners only based on their performance level (e.g., low, moderate, high) using identical instructional strategies. Since the authoring of adaptive instruction varies with the complexity of its content and instructional decisions, it is difficult to compare the efficiency of the adaptive instructional authoring tools and methods, and the effort and skill required to use them in the construction of ITSs. This paper puts forth a methodology to assess ITS complexity and operationalize it in an index to enable adaptive instructional scientists to compare authoring tools and methods. The baseline for this initial comparative index is the Generalized Intelligent Framework for Tutoring (GIFT) authoring tools.

**Keywords:** Adaptive instruction · Intelligent Tutoring Systems · Generalized Intelligent Framework for Tutoring (GIFT) · Authoring tools

## 1 Introduction

Adaptive tutors, also known as Intelligent Tutoring Systems (ITSs), deliver instructional (training or educational) content to individual learners or teams of learners that is tailored to match the capabilities, states, and traits of each learner [1]. Adaptive instruction guides the learner(s) based on their individual differences with the goal of optimizing learning, performance, retention, and transfer of skills from instruction to work/operational environments [2]. Since the individual differences of learners vary widely and contribute greatly to the adaptation decisions by the tutor, adaptive instructional systems (e.g., Intelligent Tutoring Systems – ITSs) need much more content and make many more instructional decisions than non-adaptive instructional systems (e.g., computer-based training systems) that instruct all learners and only adapt content and flow based on their performance level (e.g., low, moderate, high).

Since the authoring of adaptive instruction varies with the complexity of its content and instructional decisions, it is difficult to compare the efficiency of the adaptive

© Springer International Publishing AG 2017
D.D. Schmorrow and C.M. Fidopiastis (Eds.): AC 2017, Part II, LNAI 10285, pp. 237–249, 2017.
DOI: 10.1007/978-3-319-58625-0_17

instructional authoring tools and methods, and the effort and skill required to use them in the construction of ITSs. This paper puts forth a methodology to assess ITS complexity and codify it in an index to enable adaptive instructional scientists to compare authoring tools and methods. The baseline for this initial comparative index is the Generalized Intelligent Framework for Tutoring (GIFT) authoring tools [3].

Often, ITS authoring is cited as taking X number of hours to produce one hour of adaptive instruction. The differences in domain complexity, authoring tool usability and author competency make it difficult to compare the efficiency of one ITS toolset versus another. Currently, we have no method to compare the efficiency of processes for ITSs developed with the same authoring toolset.

For example, a three-bedroom house and a skyscraper are both buildings, but the amount of material, skill, and effort to construct them is significantly different. If we wanted to understand and compare the skills and efficiency of two builders, one that built the house and the other the skyscraper, it would be difficult without some measure or index (e.g., building rate). In order to compare the complexity of authoring tasks for building one ITS to another, we need to define what contributes to authoring complexity and establish an index of authoring. In this way, we can compare one authoring task to another, and the performance of one set of authoring tools fairly and objectively to another.

We chose to examine both the performance and skill of the author as well as the complexity of any ITS examined by our index. This was done to be able to compare the effectiveness of authoring tools for low, moderate, and highly skilled authors. As basic measures of ITS authoring performance, we considered efficiency, the time or rate of progress, and effectiveness which involves assessment of the quality of the resulting ITS in terms of the ratio of increases in learning to time on task. For example, a tutor that averages increases in knowledge and skill of 50% and 20% respectively is twice as effective as one that averages increases of 25% and 10% for learners spending the same amount of time in training.

To understand the complexity of any ITS that might be authored, we examined three contributing factors: (1) task complexity, (2) tutor authoring tool usability, and (3) author competency and interaction. We examined these factors in relationship to the Generalized Intelligent Framework for Tutoring (GIFT) authoring process to provide context, but these principles could be applied to any ITS authoring system. Factors that contribute to increased task complexity include: the number of concepts or learning objectives; the amount and diversity of content (including media and surveys) required/curated/created/used in the instruction; and the number of assessments, decisions or adaptations required during the instruction.

Factors which decrease complexity include: automation and ease of use. What parts of the authoring process can be handled by an artificially intelligent method? Is it clear to the author what the authoring process is and should be done next? The competency of the learner is inversely related to their time on task or contact time with the ITS, and therefore influences the perception of the ITSs effectiveness. Other learner behaviors have variable influence on the effectiveness of the ITS. For example, off-task behaviors (e.g., doing other than what they should be doing, sleeping, or daydreaming) negatively impact ITS effectiveness while learner familiarity and confidence with the instructional environment have positive effects. An examination of the GIFT authoring tools and processes reveals how task complexity, tutor usability, and learner competency and interaction might be used to define ITS authoring complexity. This paper puts forward a concept for assessing ITS complexity as a method to compare the effectiveness of ITS authoring systems.

## 2 Examining Task Complexity in the ITS Authoring Process

As part of our quest to define complexity in the ITS authoring process, we begin by examining elements of task complexity. Our goal is to provide a practical method for defining ITS complexity within GIFT and this begins with concepts or learning objectives. GIFT represents concepts to be learned as either a list (i.e., no hierarchical relationship) or a hierarchy as shown in Fig. 1.

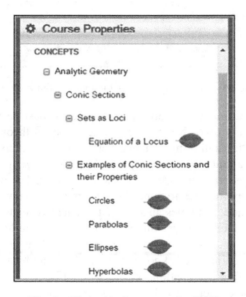

**Fig. 1.** Hierarchical concepts in GIFT

In GIFT, the lowest level in the hierarchy of concepts (shown in Fig. 1 as leaves) require an assessment to determine if the learner has mastered that concept. Leaves may be defined as any concept without a child. Concepts at the leaf level may be rolled up to determine proficiency in higher level concepts. For example, the assessments for concepts noted as circles, parabolas, ellipses, and hyperbolas may be used to assess the parent concept "Examples of Conic Sections and their properties." This means that each leaf in the hierarchy or item on a list that is assessed contributes to authoring complexity as it requires the development of an assessment (e.g., knowledge, skill test, or real-time assessment coupled with an external environment).

In addition to concept-specific content, there may be amplifying content/media that is presented to the learner to provide context or background as shown in Fig. 2. The complexity of the authoring task varies based on the amount of content that must authored/found/retrieved/implemented in GIFT.

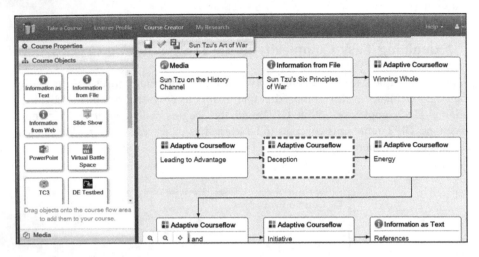

**Fig. 2.** Adaptive course flow and course objects for a GIFT course on Sun Tzu's Art of War

In GIFT's *adaptive courseflow* object, each concept must be tied to content presented to the learner as part of Merrill's component display theory (CDT) [4] implemented within the GIFT authoring schema. For a set of concepts, this CDT content includes information about *rules* (facts, principles), *examples* (models of successful behavior), recall (an assessment also known as a check on learning or a knowledge test), and *practice* (opportunities to apply knowledge and develop skill).

Within the rules and examples phases of the adaptive courseflow object GIFT delivers content (e.g., media, presentations, audio, text) to the learner to support the acquisition of knowledge. For the recall quadrant, GIFT assesses domain knowledge and for the practice quadrant, both knowledge and skill may be assessed as part of an interactive experience (e.g., simulation, serious game). Figure 3 provides details for the recall phase or check on learning. For the concept called *deception*, the learner's knowledge of information presented in the rules and examples phases is assessed through random selection of questions from a question bank of 25 questions in which 2 each (easy, medium, and hard) are presented to the learner. GIFT may also have a fixed survey/test in which the author only generates the number and difficulty level of the questions needed. Either way, the complexity of authoring is tied to the number of assessment questions generated.

In the practice quadrant, GIFT is capable of using either an existing environment, one already integrated though the GIFT gateway or the author will need to develop a new gateway interop to support the exchange of information between GIFT and the application. Reuse of the already integrated applications reduces the authoring burden, but is limited to about 6 publicly available practice environments at the time of this publication.

| Check on Learning Phase (Recall) | | | |
|---|---|---|---|
| Course Question Bank: | | | |

✏ Edit   ✖ Remove
Knowledge Assessment Question Bank

Number of questions to show per concept:

| Concept | Easy | Medium | Hard |
|---|---|---|---|
| Deception | 2 | 2 | 0 |

Criteria needed to reach a particular expertise level on each concept:

| "Novice" Criteria | | "Journeyman" Criteria | | "Expert" Criteria | |
|---|---|---|---|---|---|
| Concept | Number of Correct Answers | Concept | Number of Correct Answers | Concept | Number of Correct Answers |
| Deception | 0 | Deception | 2 | Deception | 4 |

**Fig. 3.** Details of adaptive courseflow object as part of GIFT authoring process

Each practice environment will require a real-time assessment which includes four steps to be completed by the author to define: (1) scenario properties, (2) tasks and concepts (Fig. 4), (3) instructional strategies (Fig. 5), and (4) state transitions (Fig. 6) as shown below for a virtual excavator trainer.

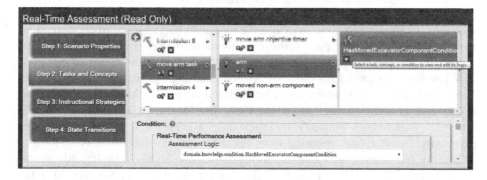

**Fig. 4.** Defining tasks and concepts for real-time assessment in external environments

Real-Time Assessment (Read Only)

Step 1: Scenario Properties

Step 2: Tasks and Concepts

Step 3: Instructional Strategies

Step 4: State Transitions

arm instructions    Valid    ✖

Strategy Logic:
This strategy should...
  ● Give feedback to the learner (e.g. messages, audio cues, etc.)
  ○ Adapt the scenario in some way (e.g. changing the learning environment)
  ○ Request an assessment of the learner's performance in a specific task or concept
  ○ Do nothing

Instructional Feedback:
  Feedback to present:    ⊕

**Fig. 5.** Defining instructional strategies in response to real-time assessment in external environments

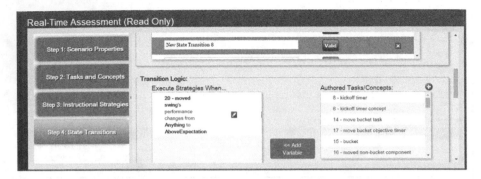

**Fig. 6.** Defining state transitions during real-time assessment in external environments

## 3   Examining ITS Authoring Complexity

Authoring complexity is largely a function of the type of tutor that needs to be produced, with respect to dimensions like those described in the previous sections. Authoring tools, then, are productivity applications that aid a developer (or team of developers) in the creation of tutors. If all authoring tools were created equally, more complex tutors will require more time and effort to create than less complex tutors. Therefore, authoring tools seek to reduce the time and effort required to develop tutors, through functions that provide various levels of automated support in organizing content, setting conditions for assessments, configuring adaptations, and so on.

While the core models/modules of adaptive training systems [5] are well established, the functions with which tutors are built and the modes through which they can be delivered is still evolving. Authoring tools, therefore, are also evolving with ITS platforms. That creates difficulty in establishing a generalized model of authoring complexity, as individual authoring tools can differ widely from one another [6–9].

Murray has written that that authoring tools "are highly complex educational software applications used to produce highly complex software applications" [10]. His work described challenges in developing tutor authoring tools with respect to design tradeoffs between *usability*, *depth*, and *flexibility* [11, 12]. In summary, increasing the power of the authoring tools (i.e., depth), the applicability of the tools to different domains and problem spaces (i.e., flexibility), or the usability of the tools themselves (i.e., learnability, productivity), comes at a cost to one or both of the other two [13]. Those characteristics provide a suitable reference for examining authoring complexity through the lens of the authoring tools, using GIFT as our reference baseline.

### 3.1   Authoring Tool Usability

The GIFT authoring tools have evolved the task of authoring a tutor from the direct manipulation of extensible markup language (XML) code to an object oriented visual interface similar to those associated with developing discrete event simulation models. Redesigning GIFT's authoring tools were motivated, in part, by the desire to allow users to create tutors without requiring specific knowledge of instructional design or computer programming. Further, mental model theory served as one of the core principles of newer user-centered interface designs in two important ways: 1. Prior versions of GIFT authoring tools were structured very closely to the system conceptual model, creating a burden on the author to configure system variables that were tangential to the task of creating a tutor [14]; and 2. There simply isn't another productivity or content creation task that is a suitable and/or complete analogy for tutor authoring, however current designs leveraged familiar interaction patterns and thoughtful interface representations from various productivity applications in order to assist the user in developing accurate mental models of the authoring process [15].

The usability of authoring tools differently benefits users of various skill levels and experience. The usability authoring tool characteristic might be further divided into *learnability* and *efficiency*. For novice users, authoring tools must be learnable, GIFT has an opportunity to improve upon learnability by making it easier for new authors to figure out what to do first/or next. Likewise, authoring tools must not be intimidating or frustrating to the point where a user gives up (a point at which subjective authoring complexity supersedes objective complexity). The GIFT authoring tools support that notion by displaying only the most common and straightforward functions by default, a technique referred to as *progressive disclosure* [16]. Authors only see what they need to see, and can explore further into the interface as they become more comfortable, or require advanced functionality.

Progressive disclosure is also related to authoring efficiency, which is beneficial for author of all skill levels. Spending less time scanning an interface for a specific option allocates more effort toward the actual authoring task. Lightbown [16] also noted that a balance must be found between progressive disclosure and *excise*, which is the physical effort involved in using the interface (e.g., mouse movement, clicks, visually scanning the UI). As an example, the latest update to GIFT's authoring interface includes an improved survey editing experience, which reduces the amount of physical effort required to quickly create questions.

Finally, authoring tool usability feeds into the larger notion of an authoring user experience (UX), which seeks to support the author from concept to deployment. In this area we consider elements external to the authoring tools including publications and documentation, course management/organization, and community building through forums and face-to-face meetings [17, 18].

Depth and flexibility are the other two aspects of the authoring tool design tradeoff space. Those might collectively be referred to as *authoring tool complexity*. It is the position of one of the authors of this paper that separation can be placed between authoring tool complexity and usability [17]. Further, complex authoring tools can be usable, given a thoughtful focus on usability in a way that does not provide a detriment to depth and flexibility. For what good is depth and flexibility if no one can (or wants to) use the authoring tools?

## 3.2   Authoring Tool Depth

Depth in authoring tools refers to the "structural or casual depth of any of the ITS modules" [11]. Depth varies within the authoring tools for each of the various modules of GIFT. Within the learner module, GIFT can track a variety of affective (e.g., anxiety, arousal) and performance based variables. These are configurable through the authoring tool user interface, but GIFT provides default configurations for those variables, as well as the logic with which to interpret them within the pedagogical module. The variables tracked within the learner module, as well as the logic contained with the pedagogical module, was determined by research and literature review. The author does not have to edit these modules, unless they wish to do so.

The domain module offers, perhaps, the greatest depth within the GIFT authoring tools. GIFT currently uses two primary mechanisms for adaptation. The first is through the adaptive courseflow object (Fig. 3, above), a discrete-time adaptation capability based on a learner's proficiency within the object. The depth of this experience can quickly expand, given even a modest number of concepts to assess, and learning the content required to sufficiently populate the adaptations for this object. The second core mechanism for adaptation within GIFT is the real-time assessment engine most commonly associated with external training applications or sensors. This aspect of GIFT is highly configurable for a variety of external applications, subject to the data that is able to be exchanged between GIFT and the application, as well as the variables that the author wishes to assess (see Figs. 4, 5 and 6, above).

Finally, GIFT provides variable depth within the authoring tools for the tutor user interface (TUI) module (Fig. 7). GIFT supports a variety of different learning content types including web-based and local resources (e.g., PDF, PowerPoint shows). The author can also construct different types of interactions using virtual avatars, and branching conversations. The overall look and feel of the TUI (to the learner) is not currently directly configurable; however, authors can use built-in rich-text editing tools or write custom HTML to add styling to individual elements within a course.

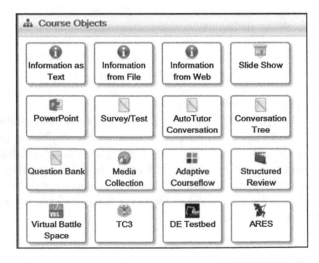

**Fig. 7.** Part of GIFT's growing list of course objects. Each is highly configurable, providing depth to how content can be displayed to the learner through the tutor-user interface.

## 3.3  Authoring Tool Flexibility

Flexibility refers to the ability to "author a diversity of types of" tutors [11]. This characteristic of tutor authoring tools may be the most difficult to quantify, especially in the case of GIFT. GIFT was built to be domain independent, meaning that the same authoring tools could be used to generate tutors for cognitive tasks, psychomotor tasks and so on. The GIFT authoring tools provide a number of intelligent defaults; however, it is possible to create new features in support of creating new types of tutors. Some of these manual options are natively available within the current authoring tool interfaces (e.g., altering learner or pedagogical models), while others may require some external development (e.g., interfacing with a new physiological sensor).

GIFT is an open-source platform, meaning that developers can extend the functionality of GIFT to accommodate new training applications, deliver tutors through different platforms (e.g., virtual and augmented reality), or build new pedagogy based on a preferred learning theory. From that perspective, GIFT is highly flexible. The caveat, however, is that a developer would also need to create authoring tool interfaces (as opposed to hard-coded solutions) to support those enhancements.

Given the rapid pace at which tutors, in general, continue to evolve, flexibility may be most at odds with usability. It takes time, resources, and testing to develop new tutor functionality. Often, the actual authoring tool supporting the use of the new functionality is one of the last pieces to fall in place, because the tool cannot be truly finished until all of the configurable parameters are known. From a usability perspective, support material and error-prevention measures cannot be established until the limits of the new functionality is well understood. That being said, GIFT continues to expand to meet new challenges across the ITS waterfront. Once a new function is developed and integrated into the baseline, that functionality becomes available to all users. The most direct example of this is GIFT's interoperability with external applications. Some back-end development is required in order to establish a communication gateway between the two systems. However, because GIFT is modular, additional development in other modules would not be necessary. GIFT Components like these are also re-usable once this is done, thus expanding the overall flexibility of the authoring tools for all GIFT users.

## 4  Examining Author Competency

As part of our examination of complexity in the authoring process, we discuss the impact of author competency on the ITS authoring process in GIFT. While the author's familiarity and expertise influence the time needed to develop a tutor using GIFT or other authoring tools, the author's competency does not affect the complexity of the tutor. We acknowledge that some factor may be needed to accurately compare the authoring process for a novice, journeyman, and expert developing the same tutoring content with the same authoring tools, our understanding of what this factor might be has no empirical basis yet.

# 5  Applying a Comparative Index to the GIFT Authoring Tools

Specifically, within the GIFT authoring, we have identified several variables contributing to the complexity of building ITSs. We make the assumption that content curation is an integrated part of the authoring process. In other words, we don't break out the effort to find, retrieve, and organize content. We assume this must be done with all content. So, if you need content, you must curate it, but you might not build it from scratch. Some content (e.g., presentation material, surveys, quizzes, multimedia, or simulation scenarios) can be reused. The need for content is primarily driven by the total number of concepts (or learning objectives) designated "TC" and associated leaf nodes designated "LN". Leaf nodes within a hierarchical or non-hierarchical set of concepts (learning objectives) are nodes without children.

Assuming each major concept requires an adaptive courseflow object, the author is responsible to curate content for use in all phases of learning (rules, examples, recall, and practice). This might be done manually or with the use of curation tools. As we review the application of our model of complexity with respect to GIFT authoring, we will refer to examples provided previously in figures above. In Fig. 1, we show a hierarchical set of concepts for analytic geometry in GIFT. A tutor built around these concepts would have TC = 9 and LN = 5. While each concept requires content, not all concepts require assessments. Typically, the lowest levels of concept, LNs are where assessments are authored (e.g., surveys, real-time assessments).

We chose to simplify the modeling of content development complexity because the complexity of content development processes varies so widely. For example, building a slide for a presentation is a much different task from building a three-dimensional, interactive, immersive virtual simulation. To simplify our model, we chose to use interactive multimedia instruction (IMI) levels [19] already defined in GIFT as a meta-data element of our ITS authoring complexity model. The IMI schema in GIFT is described by four levels as shown below in Table 1.

**Table 1.**  Interactive Multimedia Instruction (IMI) levels.

| |
|---|
| Level 1 – Low interaction and low user control: primarily passive with minimal action required by the learner |
| Level 2 – Limited interaction, low user control: some recall required |
| Level 3 – Significant interaction and moderate user control: primarily requires learner to make decisions, solve problems or interpret results |
| Level 4 – Full interaction and user control: real-time interaction and responses to complex cues; learner required to demonstrate specific skills with measurable results |

The following factors were identified through our review process as required to define ITS complexity in GIFT:

- TC = total number of concepts defined by the author
- LN = Leaf Nodes = total number of concepts without children which require assessments

- CDT = Component Display Theory Phases = usually four (rules, examples, recall and practice)
- W, X, Y, Z = number of separate pieces of content for each CDT phase respectively under a given concept
- IMI = IMI Level of Content

Based on these factors, we determined that ITS complexity is the sum of the complexity for each of the concepts (Eq. 1), and the complexity for each concept is dependent on the number of pieces of content available to the learner for each CDT phase and the IMI level of each piece of content. For the recall phase, the number of pieces of content developed is equal to the number of questions in the question bank, survey, or check-on-learning. This led us to formulate the following equations:

$$\text{ITS Complexity} = \sum_{a=1}^{a=TC} \text{Complexity Concept}_i \tag{1}$$

$$\left.\begin{aligned}\text{ITS Complexity} = \sum_{a=1}^{a=TC} \Big( \sum_{b=1}^{b=W} (\text{IMI for Rules}_{ab}) + \sum_{c=1}^{c=X} (\text{IMI for Examples}_{ac}) \\ + \sum_{d=1}^{d=Y} (\text{IMI for Recall}_{ad}) + \sum_{e=1}^{e=Z} (\text{IMI for Practice}_{ae})\Big) + \text{LN}\end{aligned}\right\} \tag{2}$$

$$\text{where}\begin{cases} \text{Rules}_{ab} = \text{content \#b for Concept}_a \text{ in the Rules Phase} \\ \text{Examples}_{ac} = \text{content \#c for Concept}_a \text{ in the Examples Phase} \\ \text{Recall}_{ad} = \text{content \#d for Concept}_a \text{ in the Recall Phase} \\ \text{Practice}_{ae} = \text{content \#e for Concept}_a \text{ in the Practice Phase} \end{cases}$$

## 6  Next Steps

In this paper we have highlighted three primary components that influence the authoring process: the tutor itself, the authoring tools used to build the tutor, and the competency of the author. We have discussed, mostly qualitatively, what factors into each of those areas, and have started to identify how each of these aspects affects one another. However, continued work is needed to formalize this logic into a quantifiable comparison metric, and to refine such a metric through research and case studies.

Regarding authoring tools specifically, more work is needed in service of quantifying their value. We used the characteristics of usability, depth, and flexibility to differentiate authoring tools from one another, but it is likely that those three areas can be further subdivided to offer greater detail to our metrics. Usability, for instance, includes learnability and efficiency. Depth and flexibility might be further categorized at the ITS model level. Determining how to segment authoring tool properties, and determining the relative importance of each could yield a useful taxonomy. Such a taxonomy could be used to compare authoring tools directly to one another, or even serve as a blueprint for identifying opportunities for future authoring tool development.

Regarding, complexity across the entire authoring process, future work should continue to refine the models for relationships between pairs of components, along a theoretical X-Y axis. For example, there may be points at which an author's competency is high enough that a more usable set of authoring tools offer little additional benefit. Likewise, different sets of authoring tools may seem relatively comparable with simple tutors, but those same platforms may actually be vastly different in efficiency with more complex tutors. Identifying the critical features of these relationships may help to determine where the best effort can be put forth in future research into the complexity of ITS development.

# References

1. Sottilare, R.: Fundamentals of adaptive intelligent tutoring systems for self-regulated learning. In: Proceedings of the Interservice/Industry Training Simulation & Education Conference, Orlando, Florida, December 2014 (2014)
2. Sottilare, R.: Elements of a learning effect model to support an adaptive instructional framework. In: Sottilare, R., Ososky, S. (eds.) 4th Annual GIFT Users Symposium (GIFTSym4). Army Research Laboratory, Orlando (2016). ISBN 978-0-9977257-0-4
3. Sottilare, R.A., Brawner, K.W., Goldberg, B.S., Holden, H.K.: The Generalized Intelligent Framework for Tutoring (GIFT). U.S. Army Research Laboratory – Human Research & Engineering Directorate (ARL-HRED), Orlando (2012)
4. Merrill, M.D.: The descriptive component display theory. Educational Technology Publications, Englewood Cliffs (1994)
5. Woolf, B.P.: Building Intelligent Interactive Tutors: Student-Centered Strategies for Revolutionizing e-Learning. Morgan Kaufmann, Burlington (2009)
6. Olsen, J.K., Belenky, D.M., Aleven, V., Rummel, N.: Intelligent tutoring systems for collaborative learning: enhancements to authoring tools. In: Lane, H.C., Yacef, K., Mostow, J., Pavlik, P. (eds.) AIED 2013. LNCS (LNAI), vol. 7926, pp. 900–903. Springer, Heidelberg (2013). doi:10.1007/978-3-642-39112-5_141
7. Aleven, V., Sewall, J.: Hands-on introduction to creating intelligent tutoring systems without programming using the cognitive tutor authoring tools (CTAT). In: Proceedings of the 9th International Conference of the Learning Sciences, vol. 2, pp. 511–512. International Society of the Learning Sciences (2010)
8. Suraweera, P., Mitrovic, A., Martin, B.: Widening the knowledge acquisition bottleneck for constraint-based tutors. Int. J. Artif. Intell. Educ. (IJAIED) 20, 137–173 (2010)
9. Mitrovic, A., Martin, B., Suraweera, P., Zakharov, K., Milik, N., Holland, J., McGuigan, N.: ASPIRE: an authoring system and deployment environment for constraint-based tutors. Int. J. Artificial Intell. Educ. 19, 155–188 (2009)
10. Murray, T.: Coordinating the complexity of tools, tasks, and users: on theory-based approaches to authoring tool usability. Int. J. Artif. Intell. Educ. 26, 1–35 (2015)
11. Murray, T.: Theory-based authoring tool design: considering the complexity of tasks and mental models. In: Sottilare, R.A., Graesser, A.C., Hu, X., Brawner, K. (eds.) Design Recommendations for Intelligent Tutoring Systems. Authoring Tools and Expert Modeling Techniques, vol. 3, pp. 9–29. U.S. Army Research Laboratory, Orlando (2014)
12. Murray, T.: Having it all, maybe: design tradeoffs in ITS authoring tools. In: Frasson, C., Gauthier, G., Lesgold, A. (eds.) ITS 1996. LNCS, vol. 1086, pp. 93–101. Springer, Heidelberg (1996). doi:10.1007/3-540-61327-7_105

13. Murray, T.: Design tradeoffs in usability and power for advanced educational software authoring tools. Educ. Technol. **44**, 10–16 (2004)
14. Ososky, S., Sottilare, R.A.: Heuristic evaluation of GIFT authoring tools. US Army Research Laboratory, Orlando (2016)
15. Ososky, S., Brawner, K., Goldberg, B., Sottilare, R.: GIFT cloud improving usability of adaptive tutor authoring tools within a web-based application. In: Proceedings of the Human Factors and Ergonomics Society Annual Meeting, pp. 1389–1393. SAGE Publications (2016)
16. Lightbown, D.: Designing the User Experience of Game Development Tools. CRC Press, Boca Raton (2015)
17. Ososky, S.: Practical requirements for ITS authoring tools from a user experience perspective. In: Schmorrow, D.D.D., Fidopiastis, C.M.M. (eds.) AC 2016. LNCS (LNAI), vol. 9744, pp. 55–66. Springer, Cham (2016). doi:10.1007/978-3-319-39952-2_6
18. Ososky, S.: Designing the user experience of the GIFT cloud authoring tools. In: Sottilare, R., Ososky, S. (eds.) Proceedings of the 4th Annual GIFT Users Symposium, vol. 4, pp. 145–156. U.S. Army Research Laboratory, Orlando (2016)
19. Schwier, R., Misanchuk, E.R.: Interactive multimedia instruction. Educational Technology (1993)

# Brain-Computer Interfaces

# Validation of a Brain-Computer Interface (BCI) System Designed for Patients with Disorders of Consciousness (DOC): Regular and Sham Testing with Healthy Participants

Brendan Z. Allison[1](✉), Woosang Cho[2], Rupert Ortner[1,2],
Alexander Heilinger[1], Guenter Edlinger[1,2], and Christoph Guger[1,2](✉)

[1] Guger Technologies OG, Herbersteinstrasse 60, 8020 Graz, Austria
allison@gtec.at
[2] g.tec medical engineering GmbH,
Sierningstrasse 14, 4521 Schiedlberg, Austria
guger@gtec.at

**Abstract.** Brain-computer interface (BCI) technology is increasingly used to research new methods to provide assessment and communication for patients diagnosed with a disorder of consciousness (DOC). As this technology advances, it could lead to tools that could support clinical diagnoses, provide communication to some persons who cannot otherwise communicate, and further impact families, friends, and carers. Hence, validation studies are needed to ensure that BCI systems that are intended for these patients operate as expected. This study aimed to validate different components of a hardware and software platform that is being used for research with patients with DOC called mind-BEAGLE. This real-time EEG system uses four different paradigms for assessment and communication. We assessed regular and sham conditions with healthy participants and report on the resulting EEG data and BCI performance results.

**Keywords:** Communication · Assessment · DOC · BCI · EP · Motor imagery

## 1 Introduction

Figure 1 presents some conditions that can impair cognitive and/or motor function. The bottom half of this figure includes locked-in syndrome (LIS) and complete locked-in syndrome (CLIS). In these syndromes, patients have little or no remaining motor control. Thus, they may not even be able to communicate with assistive technologies or alternative and augmentive communication systems that are designed for disabled persons with some remaining movement. For these patients, a brain-computer interface (BCI), which can provide communication without movement, could be the only means of communication possible for them. A BCI is a real-time system that measures activity from the brain, automatically analyzes the data, and provides some output that influences user interaction. Classic BCI review articles have focused on BCIs as

© Springer International Publishing AG 2017
D.D. Schmorrow and C.M. Fidopiastis (Eds.): AC 2017, Part II, LNAI 10285, pp. 253–265, 2017.
DOI: 10.1007/978-3-319-58625-0_18

communication systems for persons with LIS and CLIS, such as patients with late-stage Amyotrophic Lateral Sclerosis (ALS; [1, 2]). Over the past several years, BCI research has also begun to address new BCI approaches that can help broader groups of patients [3–6]. One prominent new approach uses BCIs to assess conscious awareness and provide communication for persons diagnosed with a disorder of consciousness (DOC). Figure 1 includes three different categories of DOC. In coma, patients do not appear to have any cognitive or motor functions. In the unresponsive wakefulness state (UWS), patients may indicate arousal but do not seem to have any awareness. Minimal consciousness (MCS) patients also do not have reliable voluntary motor control, and have substantial cognitive impairment, although their awareness and cognitive function may fluctuate.

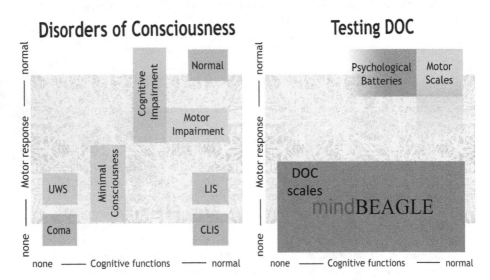

**Fig. 1.** The left panel shows the types of DOC as well as other conditions, categorized by remaining cognitive and motor functions. The right panel shows that typical psychological and testing batteries are not designed for DOC patients or some other persons with disabilities. DOC assessment such as the CRS-R and GCS scales are designed for DOC patients, but provide behavioral measures only. The mindBEAGLE system has an EEG-based assessment battery and communication tools for patients with DOC, as well as locked-in syndrome (LIS) and complete locked-in syndrome (CLIS).

Different factors have indicated a growing interest in BCIs for DOC patients. Numerous peer-reviewed articles on this topic have been published from several groups (e.g. [7–14]), including recent review articles [15–17]. Several major international conferences in 2016 alone held workshops, special sessions, symposia, or related events focused on this research direction. Examples include the Sixth International Brain Computer Interface Meeting (Pacific Grove, CA), 18th International Conference on Human Computer Interaction (Toronto, ON), 46th Annual Society for Neuroscience meeting (San Diego, CA), 38th Annual International Conference of the IEEE Engineering in Medicine and Biology Society (Orlando, FL), and the 9th International Joint Conference on Biomedical Engineering Systems and Technologies (Rome, IT). These and other conferences have also featured talks, posters, papers, and other work presenting new research with BCIs for DOC. The Annual Brain-Computer Interface Research Award has had a growing number of submitted projects, and more projects nominated for awards, that relate to BCIs for DOC [6]. Most importantly, ongoing advances in relevant technologies and validation efforts with patients provide growing hope that BCI technology can help patients and their families.

These articles, conference activities, and award submissions have presented different BCI platforms from different groups that use a variety of analysis methods, hardware, and software. One of the platforms that several groups have used across different studies is the mindBEAGLE platform [17]. This system provides BCIs based on motor imagery (MI) and different evoked potential (EP) paradigms, and has been used with over 100 persons with DOC to date. Given the growing usage of mindBEAGLE and related systems with a vulnerable patient group, and the potentially life-changing impact of a system error, there is an increasingly pressing need for basic validation studies with healthy people to confirm that the BCI system works as expected. Such studies may provide limited new scientific knowledge, but are crucial precursors to wider adoption.

The main goal of the present study was to validate different components of the mindBEAGLE system with healthy users. We evaluated assessment tools that used motor imagery and three types of EP paradigms that relied on auditory or vibrotactile stimuli. We tested the hypothesis that healthy persons would exhibit indicators of conscious awareness, and be able to communicate, using the mindBEAGLE system. Obviously, results indicating that any healthy person did not exhibit conscious awareness would raise serious concerns about the system. We evaluated the assessment tools with regular system operation and "sham" testing. We also evaluated the BCI-based communication components with the MI approach and one of the vibrotactile EP paradigms.

## 2    Methods

### 2.1    Equipment

All of the hardware and software used for data recording, stimulus presentation, and data analysis were implemented through the mindBEAGLE platform. The mindBEAGLE platform has a laptop, a g.USBamp signal amplifier, one g.STIMbox, one EEG cap, three vibrotactile stimulators, two earbuds, and all cables required to connect system components to each other. The g.USBamp provided 24 bit ADC resolution, and the cap contained 16 g.LADYbird active electrodes positioned at sites FC3, Fz, FC4, C1, C2, C3, Cz, C4, C5, C6, CP1, CP3, CPz, CP2, CP4 and Pz. Figure 2 shows the mindBEAGLE system used in this study.

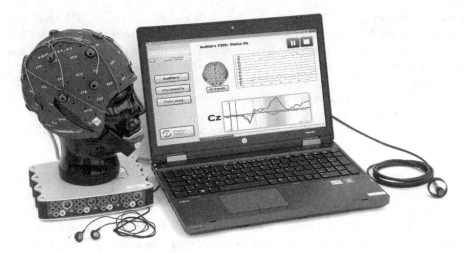

**Fig. 2.** This image shows mindBEAGLE system components. The left side shows the amplifier, electrode cap, and earbuds. The middle part of the image shows a laptop with mindBEAGLE software running, and the right side shows one of the vibrotactile stimulators. The image on the laptop shows some of the real-time feedback during the AEP paradigm. This includes an electrode signal quality check, raw EEG from different channels, and EPs from target and nontarget stimuli (with differences between them shaded in green). The green progress bar on the bottom of the monitor shows the time remaining before a break. Operators can also pause or stop the system using the icons in the top right. (Color figure online)

## 2.2    Participants

The participants were three healthy persons (2 male, age 38–43, SD = 2.6). All participants reported that they had never been diagnosed with any DOC, neurological damage, or psychiatric conditions. The participants signed a consent form, and the procedure was approved by the local ethics committee. All participants' native language was German. Hence, the mindBEAGLE system was set to provide all instructions in German.

## 2.3    Experimental Procedure

The participants were seated during the study. Participants were positioned so they could not see the mindBEAGLE laptop monitor, since the monitor activity might have distracted participants and disrupted the sham condition. Each recording session began with mounting the electrode cap, earbuds, and vibrotactile stimulators. One stimulator was placed on each hand, and a third was placed on the middle of the back. The experimenter explained the procedure for each run and played examples of each stimulus to the subject. For example, the experimenter played the words "left" and "right" in the motor imagery paradigm, and showed the subject what each of the three vibrotactile stimuli felt like.

The mindBEAGLE system has software modules that can manage four types of paradigms. These paradigms are: Auditory evoked potential (AEP); Vibro-tactile stimulation with 2 tactors (VT2); Vibro-tactile stimulation with 3 tactors (VT3); and Motor imagery (MI). The first three of these paradigms rely on EPs, while the MI paradigm relies on event-related (de) synchronization (ERD/S) around roughly 10–12 Hz [3]. All four paradigms can be used for assessment, while the VT3 and MI paradigms can also be used for communication. All instructions, stimuli, and feedback were presented to the participants via the earbuds, and the VT2 and VT3 paradigms also utilized the vibrotactile stimulators. The software presented information to the system operator through the laptop monitor as well (see Fig. 2).

Each participant performed two regular runs and one sham run across each of the AEP, VT2, VT3, and MI assessment paradigms. Next, each participant performed two regular runs with each of the VT3 and MI communication paradigms. Therefore, there were twelve assessment and then four communication runs. Aside from the constraint that all assessment runs occurred before any communication run, the order of the runs was decided pseudo-randomly. The communication runs each entailed five or ten yes/no questions. Subjects took a brief break between each run.

### 2.3.1 Assessment Runs

The AEP paradigm utilized two stimuli: high and low pitch tones (1000 and 500 Hz) presented at a ratio of 1:7. Each tone lasted 100 ms, and the delay between tone onset was 900 ms. Participants were instructed to silently count the less frequent high tones and ignore the low tones, thus creating a classic "oddball" paradigm [18]. Each run had four trial groups. Each trial group had 30 trials that each contained one high tone and seven low tones, in pseudorandom order. Thus, each run presented 480 tones in total. There was no pause between trial groups.

The two stimuli in the VT2 paradigm were vibrotactile stimulators on the left and right wrists. Like the AEP paradigm, each run contained 4 trial groups with 30 trials each. At the beginning of each trial group, each participant was instructed via earbuds to silently count each pulse to the target wrist and ignore pulses to the nontarget wrist. Each trial presented one vibrotactile pulse to the target wrist and seven pulses to the nontarget wrist. Each pulse lasted 100 ms with a 300 ms delay between pulse onset. The software automatically decided which wrist to designate as the target wrist (left or right) at a 1:1 ratio, and provided instructions and stimuli accordingly.

The VT3 paradigm was identical to VT2, except as follows. First, a third vibro-tactile stimulator was placed on the back. Second, each trial presented three types of stimuli – one to the left wrist, one to the right wrist, and six to the back, determined pseudorandomly. Like VT2, the instructions prior to each trial group instructed the participants to silently count pulses to either the left or right wrist at a 1:1 ratio. The back was never designated as a target, and was thus intended as a "distracter" stimulus within the oddball paradigm [18].

Since each trial presented one target stimulus and seven other stimuli (non-target or distracter), chance accuracy was 12.5%. The mindBEAGLE software treated all eight stimuli within each trial equally in terms of classification; that is, non-target stimuli were not grouped together and the classifier was blind to the target stimulus.

In the MI paradigm, each participant heard the word "left" or "right" at the beginning of the trial, followed by a tone 2 s later. These two cues instructed the participant to imagine moving the left or right hand (1:1 ratio, determined randomly) for four seconds when the tone begins. Next, another tone cued the participant to relax. Next, a random interval of 0.5–2 s provided a brief break before the next trial. Each MI run had 60 trials (30 for each hand) and lasted about 9 min.

### 2.3.2    Communication Runs

The VT3 and MI communication runs were identical to the corresponding assessment runs, with several differences. Prior to each trial group, the system provided a pause during which the experimenter asked the participant a YES/NO question. In this study, we only asked questions in copy-spelling mode, meaning that the answers were known beforehand.

In the VT3 paradigm, subjects were told to count pulses to the left wrist to answer YES or right wrist to answer NO. Each VT3 communication run consisted of one trial group with 15 trials (120 total stimuli), and lasted about 38 s. At the end of each run, a circle near the bottom of the monitor moved to YES or NO if the classifier chose the left or right wrist, or remained in the center if the distracter was selected, reflecting an indeterminate response.

In the MI paradigm, each participant was asked to imagine left hand movement to answer YES and right hand movement to answer NO. Each MI run consisted of one trial lasting about eight seconds, and thus could potentially provide faster communication. At the end of the run, the circle moved to YES or NO; indeterminate responses were not possible. The time estimates for VT3 and MI communication runs do not include the time required to ask a question, convey the answer, or pause before the next run if desired.

### 2.3.3    Regular vs. Sham Runs

During the regular runs, the mindBEAGLE system performed normally. During the sham runs for the assessment paradigms, the subjects still wore the cap and followed a similar procedure, but did not receive critical stimuli from the mindBEAGLE system. The vibrotactile stimulators were unplugged during the VT2 sham runs. Thus, while subjects still heard instructions during the VT2 sham runs, they never received tactile stimuli required to elicit EPs. During the AEP, VT3, and MI sham runs, the system was muted. Thus, the participants did not hear the auditory cues that elicit EPs (AEP) or the system's instructions cueing them to the left or right and information about trial timing (VT3 and MI).

### 2.4    Signal Processing and Classification

The mindBEAGLE software installed on the laptop in Fig. 2 managed all data recording and processing in real-time to allow real-time feedback. Data were sampled at 256 Hz and bandpass filtered from .1-30 Hz. In the AEP, VT2 and VT3 paradigms, data from eight sites (Fz, C3, Cz, C4, CP1, CPz, CP2, and Pz) were used. First, epochs were created with the data from -100 ms before to 600 ms after each auditory or vibrotactile stimulus began. Automated tools then performed baseline correction based on the 100 ms preceding stimulus onset and rejected all trials in which EEG amplitude exceeded $\pm 100$ $\mu$V. Next, a linear discriminant analysis (LDA) classifier attempts to identify which of the eight stimuli presented in each run is the target stimulus. The LDA classifier then checks to see which stimulus was the target and calculates a classification accuracy that ranges from 0% to 100%. This process is repeated as more trials are presented within each trial group, and classifier accuracy can be plotted against the number of events required to attain that level of classifier performance. The software also presents the EPs on the laptop, updated as new epochs are created. A significance test is performed that presents areas with significant differences between targets and non-targets as green-shaded areas in the EPs ($p < 0.05$). Trials where the amplitude of the EEG signal exceeds a threshold are rejected from the EP and classifier calculation.

In the MI paradigm, a common spatial patterns (CSP) classifier is trained on data from 3–5 s after the cue to begin an imagined movement (left or right). This training creates weights for each electrode that reflect the relative contributions of different electrode sites to correct classification. The system then estimates the variance of a 1.5 s window and trains an LDA classifier to calibrate the system for the participant. Like the EP paradigms, the LDA classifier then outputs a classification accuracy that can range from 0% to 100%. The mindBEAGLE manual recommends a threshold of 64% for MI assessment paradigm, which is calculated with a binomial test (alpha $< 0.05$). We used a threshold of 60% for EP assessment paradigms based on our experience with patients.

The four paradigms were trained as follows. Within each paradigm, data from the first assessment run was used to train the classifier that was used for real-time analysis during the second assessment run. The resulting classifier settings were then used for real-time analysis in the communication runs for the VT3 and MI paradigms. Also, when mindBEAGLE presents classifier results at the end of each run and in saved files, these results are based on a classifier that was updated based on that same run. For example, the results displayed on the monitor at the end of the first VT2 assessment run reflect a classifier that was trained on the first VT2 assessment run. Otherwise, accuracy would have to be based on generic data templates, which would be less accurate. All accuracy plots employed a cross-validation strategy to counteract overfitting.

# 3   Results

Table 1 summarizes results from the regular and sham runs. The table includes classification accuracies during assessment runs and communication. Next, Fig. 3 shows results from all three of the participants.

**Table 1.** This presents results from the three participants (S1–S3), including the BCI classification accuracies from assessment and communication runs. This table also shows number of questions answered correctly and the number of questions asked (e.g. 5 questions are answered correctly out of 5).

| Subject | | S1 | | S2 | | S3 | | Total | |
|---|---|---|---|---|---|---|---|---|---|
| | Exp. | Ass. Acc. [%] | Comm. [%]; [correct/total] | Ass. Acc. [%] | Comm. [%]; correct/total] | Ass. Acc. [%] | Comm. [%]; correct/total] | Mean Ass. Acc. [%] | Mean Comm. Acc. [%] |
| AEP | Run 1 | 100 | | 100 | | 100 | | 100 | |
| | Run 2 | 100 | | 100 | | 100 | | 100 | |
| | Sham | 15 | | 0 | | 0 | | 5 | |
| VT2 | Run 1 | 100 | | 100 | | 65 | | 88 | |
| | Run 2 | 100 | | 100 | | 100 | | 100 | |
| | Sham | 0 | | 25 | | 10 | | 12 | |
| VT3 | Run 1 | 90 | 100, [5/5] | 60 | 20, [1/5] | 100 | 100, [5/5] | 83 | 73,3 |
| | Run 2 | 100 | 80, [4/5] | 100 | 100, [5/5] | 80 | 80, [4/5] | 93 | 86,7 |
| | Sham | 0 | | 10 | | 10 | | 6,6 | |
| MI | Run 1 | 70 | 80, [4/5] | 71 | 60, [3/5] | 78 | 80, [4/5] | 73 | 73,3 |
| | Run 2 | 90 | 80, [4/5] | 67 | 80, [4/5] | 62 | 90, [9/10] | 73 | 83,3 |
| | Sham | 55 | | 50 | | 59 | | 57 | |

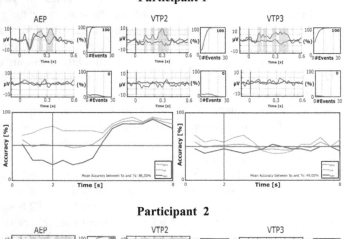

**Participant 1**

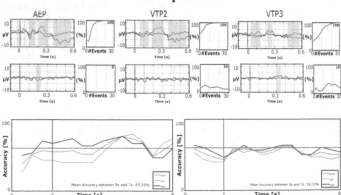

**Participant 2**

**Participant 3**

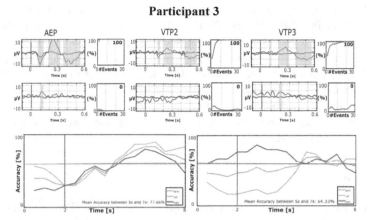

**Fig. 3.** These images show results from assessment runs from all three participants. Each group of images for each participant contains three rows of images. The top row presents EPs from site Cz, and BCI accuracy, for one of the two regular runs in the AEP, VT2 and VT3 paradigms. We selected a representative image from each of the two regular assessment runs for each of these paradigms. In the EP plots, the vertical red line shows the onset of the stimulus (tone or vibrotactile pulse), EPs elicited by target stimuli are shown in green, and EPs from non-target stimuli are shown in blue. The areas that are shaded light green reflect time periods with significant targets vs. non-target differences (Kruskal-Wallis test). The BCI accuracy, shown to the right of each of the EP plots, shows classification accuracy on the y-axis plotted against the number of trials that the classifier averaged together in the x-axis. The median accuracy is shown at the top right of each accuracy plot. Chance performance in all three EP paradigms is 12.5%. Middle: These images have the same format as the top images, but show results from the sham run with all three participants. Bottom: These images show changes in BCI classification accuracy during trial execution. Presentation of the cue indicating which hand movement to imagine occurred 2 s in to each trial, shown by the vertical red line. The horizontal red line reflects the chance performance accuracy of 50% for the MI paradigm. Each image shows the results averaged across all trials from left hand imagination, right hand imagination and imagination of both hands. The left image shows results from regular runs, and the right image shows sham results. (Color figure online)

## 3.1    Regular Runs

Across the four paradigms, assessment accuracy ranged from 60% to 100%. These results are above the thresholds we recommend, which are 60% for the EP paradigms and 61% for the motor imagery paradigm. The assessment accuracy was not always 100% and did vary between runs. Fluctuations in accuracy have been widely reported in the BCI literature [3], and the fluctuations did not push the results from any regular assessment run below the threshold. Nonetheless, these results underscore the importance of multiple recording sessions to properly assess patients, discussed below. For the communication runs, results generally showed that the BCI could answer YES/NO questions. S2's performance fluctuated from 20% to 100%, while the two other participants each achieved 80% to 100% accuracy.

The EPs from the regular runs in Fig. 3 show common EP components such as the N1 (most distinct in AEP), P2, and P3 [19]. The N1 does not differ substantially for target vs. nontarget trials, as expected for such an early EP component. The green shaded areas show that the P2 and P3 exhibit significant target vs. nontarget differences. BCI classification accuracy reaches 100% after about five events and remains at 100% as more events are averaged together. The MI accuracy plots in Fig. 3 indicate that S1's average performance (green line) increased from about 50% (chance accuracy) early in the trial to over 80% about two seconds after cue onset, as typical of MI BCI paradigms [3, 20].

## 3.2   Sham Runs

For the three EP paradigms, accuracy ranged from 0% to 25%. This is well below the EP threshold of 60%, and is closer to the chance accuracy of 12.5%. Assessment results from the MI paradigm ranged from 50% to 59%. This is also below the threshold of 64%, and near the chance accuracy of 50%. Hence, results from sham assessments across all four paradigms did not cross the threshold.

The results shown in Fig. 3 further indicate that the system did not detect activity that reflects stimulus and task following during any of the sham run. The EPs do not reflect any activity associated with selective attention to stimuli, the target and nontarget lines look similar to each other (without noteworthy significant differences shaded green), and classification accuracy is very low regardless of how many trials are averaged together. The MI classification accuracy remains near chance level throughout the trial with a low median accuracy. All of these MI results, like the EP results, are consistent with expectations for regular and sham operation.

## 4   Discussion

Results from all four paradigms (AEP, VT2, VT3, and MI) were appropriate for healthy persons. That is, these four paradigms indicated that the three healthy participants did exhibit conscious awareness, and could communicate using the BCI tools, in regular and (for assessment) not sham paradigms. These results indicate that the system is working as expected. However, one participant did not perform well in the first VT3 communication run, which may be due to training effects (learning the relatively difficult VT3 paradigm), distraction, or other causes. Patients may exhibit greater fluctuations. Thus, when working with patients whose conscious awareness may fluctuate, repeated assessments are strongly recommended. We also recommend attempting BCI communication as soon as possible after an assessment indicates this is possible in many cases. If patients may present only a limited window of awareness when communication is possible, then opportunities for them to communicate be rare.

This ties in to a related question. What does the assessment assess? The most direct answer is that the assessment protocol assesses the user's ability to generate distinct EEG signals, by performing simple tasks that do not require movement, which a specific signal processing platform can discriminate. The results may be used to infer the potential for communication through a BCI. More broadly, proof that a patient can perform the required mental activities could influence the views of family, friends, and physicians relating to the patient's state and treatment.

BCIs for this latter type of assessment may develop into clinical decision support tools. This prospect raises many issues relating to new standards and norms. Prior work has suggested standardized scales for clinical DOC diagnosis that include the EEG. Recording and utilizing EEG activity using auditory BCI methods during the CRS-R scale could also provide supplemental information [14]. Other standards could address the number and types of assessments needed, training requirements and recommended methods, ethical guidelines, and certifications for equipment and staff expertise. The hierarchical approach to assessing conscious function that has been proposed [21, 22] could lead to standardized scales and testing methods that conduct specific tests in sequence to provide a much richer picture of remaining cognitive function.

The hierarchical approach entails passive vs. active paradigms. In passive para-digms, the user is not instructed to perform any task. Passive paradigms can thus assess relatively basic brain function. For example, the mismatch negativity (MMN) is a signal that may be elicited by an oddball stimulus even without any instructions. The P300 and other signals can also be elicited through passive paradigms. Indeed, the AEP and VT2 paradigms presented here could be adapted to passive paradigms by removing the instruction to count the oddball stimulus. These modified paradigms could sup-plement existing and new paradigms to evaluate different levels of cognitive function. Other simple modifications to existing paradigms could involve removing distractor and even non-target stimuli to assess both active and passive P300s and related EPs [18, 23]. Auditory tests could present more complex information, such as different words, which could add established paradigms for DOC assessment such as the sub-ject's own name (SON) paradigm [7] or N400 priming [9].

We do note some limitations of this study. We did not explore a communication sham condition. The AEP and VT2 sham runs did not present any stimuli. Thus, EEG activity or noise that could have been caused by stimuli would not occur in the sham condition. The reason is that presenting stimuli could have led to passive P300s. Also, both the experimenter and the subject were aware of which runs were regular or sham. Blinding the experimenter and especially the subject would have required changing the paradigm in some way, which we did not want to do. Furthermore, the differences between regular and sham performance are quite pronounced, both in BCI performance and EPs, and these minor confounds are probably irrelevant. Also, we could study performance across many recording sessions in future work. Additional sessions with healthy users might have indicated training effects and provided more information about system consistency.

In future work, the YES/NO communication tools could become faster, such as by training persons with the MI approach or reducing the number of events before the classifier reaches a decision. New devices such as belts, necklaces, bracelets, or other wearable devices with a variety of stimulators could provide broader communication options, as could more varied auditory stimuli. These new communication approaches must account for many unique design issues for interacting with target users, including non-visual stimuli [24–27]. Future systems might further leverage the "hybrid BCI" approach in mindBEAGLE with a broader variety of BCI communication tools [28]. The inclusion of MI and other approaches in mindBEAGLE provides some flexibility for end users. MI BCIs may require more training and may not work for some users, but could provide faster communication, at least with the settings used here.

Many other future directions merit further research. In addition to advanced communication, patients might be provided with sensory, cognitive, and/or motor rehabilitation tools. New methods could aim to predict recovery or periods of conscious awareness. Improved hardware might provide more EEG channels, higher signal quality and smaller and more comfortable electrodes (perhaps allowing long recording periods that could detect conscious awareness and inform staff). Improved software could incorporate new protocols for assessment and communication, perhaps within a hierarchy or scale, as well as better signal processing that might use ECG, EOG, EMG, and/or other signals. This approach could provide a hybrid BCI for communication for persons with LIS and CLIS who cannot use visual stimuli [3]. Perhaps most importantly, additional research with target patients in real-world settings is essential for validating systems and approaches and providing new data.

In summary, the present results indicate that the mindBEAGLE assessment tools work when expected, providing correct results that indicate conscious awareness during regular operation and indicating otherwise during sham operation. The communication components of mindBEAGLE were also successful, although (like the assessment components), the MI approach should be supplemented with other tools. Overall, these results could support and encourage wider system use.

# References

1. Kübler, A., Kotchoubey, B., Kaiser, J., et al.: Brain–computer communication: unlocking the locked in. Psychol. Bull. **127**, 358 (2001)
2. Wolpaw, J.R., Birbaumer, N., McFarland, D.J., et al.: Brain–computer interfaces for communication and control. Clin. Neurophysiol. **113**, 767–791 (2002). doi:10.1016/S1388-2457(02)00057-3
3. Wolpaw, J.R., Wolpaw, E.W.: Brain-Computer Interfaces: Principles and Practice, 1st edn. Oxford University Press, Oxford (2012)
4. Allison, B.Z., Dunne, S., Leeb, R., et al.: Recent and upcoming BCI progress: overview, analysis, and recommendations. In: Allison, B.Z., et al. (eds.) Towards Practical Brain-Computer Interfaces, pp. 1–13. Springer, Heidelberg (2012)
5. Brunner, C., Birbaumer, N., Blankertz, B., et al.: BNCI Horizon 2020: towards a roadmap for the BCI community. Brain-Comput. Interfaces **2**, 1–10 (2015). doi:10.1080/2326263X.2015.1008956
6. Guger, C., Allison, B.Z., Ushiba, J.: The BCI Award 2015: A State-of-the-Art Summary 5. Springer, Heidelberg (2017)
7. Risetti, M., Formisano, R., Toppi, J., Quitadamo, L.R., Bianchi, L., Astolfi, L., Cincotti, F., Mattia, D.: On ERPs detection in disorders of consciousness rehabilitation. Front. Hum. Neurosci. 7, 775 (2013). doi:10.3389/fnhum.2013.00775
8. Cruse, D., Chennu, S., Chatelle, C., et al.: Bedside detection of awareness in the vegetative state: a cohort study. Lancet **378**, 2088–2094 (2012)
9. Cruse, D., Beukema, S., Chennu, S., et al.: The reliability of the N400 in single subjects: implications for patients with disorders of consciousness. NeuroImage: Clin. **4**, 788–799 (2014)

10. Monti, M.M., Vanhaudenhuyse, A., Coleman, M.R., et al.: Willful modulation of brain activity in disorders of consciousness. N. Engl. J. Med. **362**, 579–589 (2010). doi:10.1136/bmj.313.7048.13
11. Lugo, Z.R., Rodriguez, J., Lechner, A., et al.: A vibrotactile P300-based BCI for consciousness detection and communication. Clin. EEG Neurosci. (2014). doi:10.1177/1550059413505533
12. Ahn, S., Kim, K., Jun, S.C.: Steady-state somatosensory evoked potential for brain-computer interface—present and future. Front. Hum. Neurosci. 9, 716 (2016). doi:10.3389/fnhum.2015.00716
13. Gibson, R.M., Chennu, S., Fernández-Espejo, D., et al.: Somatosensory attention identifies both overt and covert awareness in disorders of consciousness. Ann. Neurol. **80**, 412–423 (2016)
14. Xiao, J., Xie, Q., He, Y., Yu, T., Lu, S., Huang, N., Yu, R., Li, Y.: An auditory BCI system for assisting CRS-R behavioral assessment in patients with disorders of consciousness. Sci. Rep. 6, 32917 (2016). doi:10.1038/srep32917
15. Guger, C., Sorger, B., Noirhomme, Q., Naci, L., Monti, M.M., Real, R., Pokorny, C., Veser, S., Lugo, Z., Quitadamo, L., Lesenfants, D.: Emerging Theory and Practice in Neuroprosthetics. In IGI Global (2014)
16. Lesenfants, D., Chatelle, C., Saab, J., Laureys, S., Noirhomme, Q.: Neurotechnological communication with patients with disorders of consciousness. In: Neurotechnology and Direct Brain Communication: New Insights and Responsibilities Concerning Speechless but Communicative Subjects, p. 85 (2016)
17. Ortner, R., Allison, B.Z., Heilinger, A., Sabathiel, N., and Guger, C.: Assessment of and communication for persons with disorders of consciousness. J. Vis. Exp. (in press)
18. Gonsalvez, C.J., Polich, J.: P300 amplitude is determined by target-to-target interval. Psychophysiology **39**, 388–396 (2002)
19. Kutas, M., Dale, A.: Electrical and magnetic readings of mental functions. Cogn. Neurosci. 197–242 (1997)
20. Guger, C., Edlinger, G., Harkam, W., et al.: How many people are able to operate an EEG-based brain-computer interface (BCI)? IEEE Trans. Neural Syst. Rehabil. Eng. **11**, 145–147 (2003). doi:10.1109/tnsre.2003.814481
21. Laureys, S., Giacino, J.T., Schiff, N.D., et al.: How should functional imaging of patients with disorders of consciousness contribute to their clinical rehabilitation needs? Curr. Opin. Neurol. **19**, 520 (2006)
22. Gerrard, P., Zafonte, R., Giacino, J.T.: Coma recovery scale–revised: evidentiary support for hierarchical grading of level of consciousness. Arch. Phys. Med. Rehabil. **95**, 2335–2341 (2014)
23. Allison, B.Z., Polich, J.: Single stimulus activity across workload levels during computer game play. Biol. Psychol. **77**(3), 277–283 (2008)
24. Allison, B.: The I of BCIs: next generation interfaces for brain–computer interface systems that adapt to individual users. In: Jacko, J.A. (ed.) HCI 2009. LNCS, vol. 5611, pp. 558–568. Springer, Heidelberg (2009). doi:10.1007/978-3-642-02577-8_61
25. Fazel-Rezai, R., Allison, B.Z., Guger, C., et al.: P300 brain computer interface: current challenges and emerging trends. Front. Neuroeng. **5**, 14 (2012)
26. Scherer, R., Faller, J., Balderas, D., et al.: Brain–computer interfacing: more than the sum of its parts. Soft. Comput. **17**, 317–331 (2013)
27. McCullagh, P., Brennan, C., Lightbody, G., Galway, L., Thompson, E., Martin, S.: An SSVEP and eye tracking hybrid BNCI: potential beyond communication and control. In: Schmorrow, D., Fidopiastis, C. (eds.) AC 2016. LNCS, vol. 9743, pp. 69–78. Springer, Cham (2016). doi:10.1007/978-3-319-39955-3_7
28. Pfurtscheller, G., Allison, B.Z., Bauernfeind, G., et al.: The hybrid BCI. Front. Neurosci. **4**, 3 (2010)

# Wheels Within Wheels: Brain-Computer Interfaces as Tools for Artistic Practice as Research

Andrés Aparicio[1,2(✉)] and Rodrigo F. Cádiz[1]

[1] Centro de Investigación en Tecnologías de Audio, Instituto de Música,
Pontificia Universidad Católica,
Avenida Jaime Guzmán Errázuriz 3300, Santiago, Chile
{aaparicio,rcadiz}@uc.cl
[2] Centro de Desarrollo de Tecnologías de Inclusión (CEDETi UC),
Pontificia Universidad Católica, Avenida Vicuña Mackenna 4860, Santiago, Chile
http://cita.uc.cl/,
http://www.cedeti.cl/

**Abstract.** Practice as research (PaR) is concerned with practice both as a method for inquiry and as evidence of the research process, producing embodied knowledge. It has been proposed that it is the foundational strategy in *performative research*, a kind of research apart from quantitative and qualitative research, characterized by being expressed using forms of symbolic data different from quantities or words in discursive texts. In this context, practice requires constant reflection upon itself to yield insights that can be used in a never-ending loop of creation. As practice is performed by the body and produces embodied knowledge, tools that allow querying the body during the artistic process may provide information that supports this creation/reflection loop. Previous artistic BCI applications have shown that they are suited to work as introspection tools (affective states, correlation between performed actions and area activations), as the source of raw material to be used in the creative process (raw signal, patterns of activation, band power), and as controllers for artistic instruments. We believe that previous research has laid the groundwork for the use of BCIs as tools in PaR. In this paper, we propose a framework for this and review three examples of previous artistic work using BCIs that illustrate different aspects of said framework.

**Keywords:** Brain-computer interfaces · Practice as research · Embodied knowledge

This research was partially funded by Fondecyt grant 1161328; Dirección de Artes y Cultura, Vicerrectoría de Investigación, Pontificia Universidad Católica de Chile; and "Proyecto basal de centros de investigación interdisciplinaria", Vicerrectoría de Investigación, Pontificia Universidad Católica de Chile.

D.D. Schmorrow and C.M. Fidopiastis (Eds.): AC 2017, Part II, LNAI 10285, pp. 266–281, 2017.
DOI: 10.1007/978-3-319-58625-0_19

# 1    Introduction

There is a long tradition of using brain signals in artistic practice. Since Lucier's *Music for Solo Performer* [12], there have been further explorations of these signals in music, visual arts and performance. In parallel, in the last forty years, *practice as research* (PaR) has become an accepted methodology for research in the arts. A key characteristic of PaR is that it deals with *embodied knowledge*, knowledge that is located in the body and cannot be reduced to a set of quantities or a discursive text. Nevertheless, there is a need for descriptions about practice both for critical reflection and to evidence the research inquiry [16]. During our work with an artist with Locked-In Syndrome, we have identified a possible enhancement upon the kinds of available descriptions. Following Nelson [17], we think that these descriptions should be multi-modal and, as embodied knowledge is central to PaR, we propose that the methodology may benefit from tools that provide information about the body. This paper presents a framework for using BCI in PaR and it is organized as follows: Sect. 2 is a short explanation of PaR and its process, Sect. 3 describes our work, the documentation possibilities we have identified and presents the concept of *body queries* as a way to obtain and interpret data from the body, Sect. 4 explains the framework for using BCI in practice as research projects, Sect. 5 provides a review of three examples of BCI in artistic or art-related to illustrate the framework, and Sect. 6 presents the discussion.

# 2    Practice as Research

In his 2006 manifesto, Haseman [7] made the case for the formalization of a new paradigm of research, different from quantitative and qualitative, that he called *performative research*. In this paradigm, practice is central to the research process and its findings are presented as symbolic data in the particular forms of the practice. He argued that, while methods from the other paradigms might be adapted and used, practitioner-researchers[1] can also invent their own methods to inquire upon their practices. This was exemplified by the method of *artistic audit*, where the focus is placed on attending the symbolic forms of the artwork in performance while placing them in the context of the practice and the research inquiry. An artistic audit of a painting, for example, implies going beyond the mere act of gazing by placing the information gathered by the gaze in the traditions and conventions that contextualize the piece. Later, Nelson [17] encoded information from past experiences using the paradigm and proposed a multi-mode epistemological model to support *practice as research* (PaR), which he defined as involving projects

> in which practice is a key method of inquiry and where, in respect of the arts, a practice (creative writing, dance, musical score/performance, theatre/performance, visual exhibition, film or other cultural practice) is submitted as substantial evidence of a research inquiry.

---

[1] A *practitioner-researcher* is an artist involved in a PaR process.

Nelson's model (Fig. 1) articulates three modes of knowledge in a loop, modes that resonate between them and across *arts praxis*, or "theory imbricated with practice". These modes of knowledge are: (i) *know-how*, located in the body, experiential and tacit; (ii) *know-what*, the result of critical reflection aiming to make the tacit explicit; and (iii) *know-that*, explicit, shared, articulated socially, and propositional.

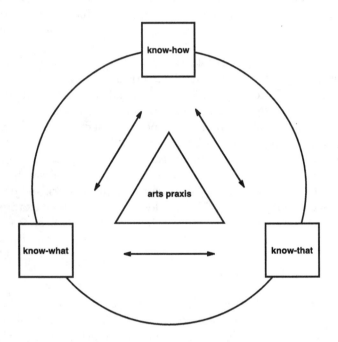

**Fig. 1.** Simplified version of Nelson's multi-mode epistemological model. Each mode of knowing resonates with the others in order to "articulate the tacit" inherent in practice. The original is found in [16].

The model codifies the idea that knowledge exists on a spectrum that goes from tacit (embodied, performative, semi-conscious or unconscious) to explicit (objective or maximally intersubjective, susceptible of representation by numbers or words), and that practitioner-researchers should strive to find processes that articulate the tacit even if cannot be made thoroughly explicit. To that end, Nelson [15] recommends that "if practitioner-researchers wish their embodied cognitions to be better recognised, means of identifying and disseminating them must be sought".

Complementary documentation and writing are the means to make the tacit explicit. Their goal is to draw attention to the doing-thinking of the practitioner-researcher during the process. They are *thick descriptions*, that is, descriptions that explain the activity and the broader context which makes it meaningful in order to provide a better understanding of it. By working on these documents, practitioner-researchers engage in critical reflection about their practice, moving from *know-how* to *know-what* and finding resonances to *know-that*. As a result, their practice is enhanced and the loop begins anew.

## 3   Body Queries

We have been working with an actor and playwright with Locked-In Syndrome[2] since 2009. We developed a custom-built communication system based on an eye-tracking device to support him both in daily life and in his artistic practice. He has written a play, a book and has participated in several research teams. He is working on a new play and collaborating with our team in the design and implementation of a brain-computer music interface, in the context of finding ways to implement BCI-based systems for the performing arts [1].

During our work, and due to his condition, we have faced an increasing need for information about the body state of the artist during practice. As documentation of process in PaR is a multi-modal affair, its sources can be words, diagrams, drawings, sketches, video and sound recordings of rehearsals, material objects produced during practice, or printed material related to the activity [18]. However, these sources are once or twice removed from the body that performs the activity. By this we mean that they gather information about the body from the results of the activity, or by the recording of those results. The closest to directly asking the body comes when expert practitioner-researchers are able to recognize changes in their bodies as they perform and reflect upon them afterwards.

Documentation is mostly created and analyzed by the practitioner-researchers themselves. In our case, this is not possible with the usual methods. While there are methods to guide the design of BCI tools for users with motor impairments (see [9, 11] for examples), they are focused on the design of the BCI system itself and not in its role in a PaR process.

Keeping in mind that the goal is to make the tacit explicit, we think there is a documentation gap between first-person experience and currently used methods. This gap could be filled by technological tools that query the body directly and provide information about its state and its changes during practice. This information, in turn, can be interpreted according to the requirements of the practice and the *know-that* that supports the tool being used. We propose the term *body query* to name this process of obtaining information about the body using technology and interpreting that information according to previously agreed-upon criteria (Fig. 2).

### 3.1   Bodily Sources

Any signal produced by the body that can be gathered with a technological device is a potential source for body queries. These signals must have, at least,

---

[2] This is a neurological condition characterized by preserved cognition, quadriplegia, aphonia, and, in some cases, some kind of preserved voluntary ocular movement [10].

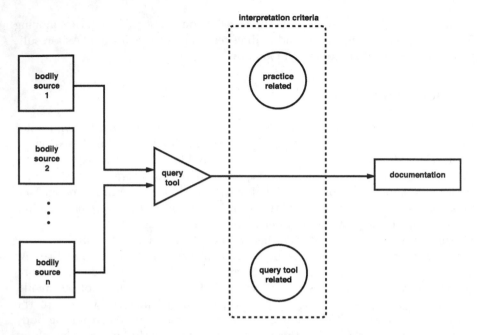

**Fig. 2.** The *body query* process. Bodily source information is gathered by the query tool, this information is interpreted according to criteria related to practice and the specific query tool, and this interpretation is compiled as documentation.

a previously agreed-upon interpretation related to the query tool being used. That is, there should be a consensus about what kind of information the signal obtained with the device provides about the body and its state. Thus, there must be a context upon which the information from the signal can be interpreted. We place this constraint upon the source to guarantee the contextualization of the documentation in the *know-that*. It also works as a safeguard against reductionist interpretations by forcing reflection upon the kinds of claims a practitioner-researcher can make about the information gathered from the signal.

For example, writing about the trend of linking neuroscience and performance studies, May [13] proposes that practitioner-researchers should be aware that they can make four kinds of claim about the relationship between brain and practice:

1. Activation in brain area(s) X is correlated with Y.
2. Activation in brain area(s) X is necessary for Y to occur.
3. Activation in brain area(s) X is necessary and sufficient for Y to occur.
4. Y is actually, or is reducible to, activation in brain area(s) X.[3]

In order to make one of these claims in a body query, a practitioner-researcher must be aware of the burden of proof their choice entails. As they are listed in increasing order of difficulty to prove, reducing one aspect of a practice to

---

[3] These claims are taken verbatim from [13].

activation in one area of the brain is more difficult to support than saying that the aspect and the activation are correlated. In general, while executing body queries care must be exercised in what kind of interpretative claims are made and whether they are supported by existing evidence.

The signals may also be interpreted according to criteria based on the practice, whether extracted from previous uses in other projects or built during the course of practice. In this case, interpretation is more open in the sense that, while the criteria may change during the process, those changes should be adequately contextualized in the broader context of the research inquiry. This constraint should enforce the requirement of critical reflection upon the process while keeping interpretation flexible enough to adapt to the dynamics of the practice.

## 3.2   Query Tools

Any technological device that can gather signals from the body is a query tool. This implies that devices originally created for purposes other than artistic expression can be used as tools in a body query. Thus, those used in medicine, marketing, sports, or gaming, for example, are susceptible to be repurposed while their original uses serve as *know-that* context for interpretation. Such devices include, but are not limited to: electroencephalographs, electrocardiographs, electromyographs, thermometers, skin conductance meters, pupillometers, inertial measurement units, and eye trackers.

Devices may also be grouped to provide more complex descriptions of body states. Cruz-Garza et al. [5] present a protocol that combines electroencephalography, inertial measurement units, video recordings and behavioral analysis to study the development of neural networks in freely-behaving human infants. *Body area networks* [4] are another example of devices grouped to gather information from different bodily sources and produce a coherent description of body state.

## 3.3   Documentation

The goal of a body query is to produce documentation about the process, that is, a set of interpretations of signals obtained at a given moment during practice. As explained before, these interpretations must be made according to criteria contextualized by the practice and by the *know-that* that supports the query tools. To illustrate, we offer an example cribbed from the dramaturgical practice of the playwright in our team while using his eye-tracker enabled communication system.

The eye-tracking device translates user's gaze to positions on a screen coordinate system. Changes in the position are in turn translated to navigation and selection commands upon a fixed menu according to predetermined rules; this means that the signal is interpreted according to the characteristics of the device. We add a new piece of interpretation related to practice by combining information about the sequence of commands with the selected characters during the writing process. By doing this, we fulfill the body query and produce documentation that can be used to reflect upon both the practice and the usability of the communicator system. Figure 3 shows a word annotated with the following interpretation of eye movements: the number of dots represents the ratio between the amount of choices made to select the letter and the minimum choices required to select that letter (one dot represents flawless use, more dots represents more choice errors).

**Fig. 3.** Example documentation stemming from a body query based on eye movements.

This illustrates the possibility to reflect upon the practice: an increasing number of dots as the writing progresses may be interpreted as fatigue from the user or a bug in the system. Such interpretations can then guide adjustments before the next practice session while further body queries can be used to analyze what effect those changes have in the practice. This kind of documentation may also be delivered as part of the thick description of the practice, helping build a shared pool of knowledge.

## 4   BCI in PaR

While a variety of signal types can be used, we are particularly interested in body queries using the brain as bodily source. Wadeson et al. [20] offer an overview of artistic BCI where they identify four types of systems: (i) *passive*, those that respond to signals but do not require interaction of intention from the user; (ii) *selective*, those that allow the user to interact but do not allow direct control of the output; (iii) *direct*, those that enable users to choose specific outputs; and (iv) *collaborative*, those that allow multiple user interaction through subsystems that fall under the previous types.

Each of these types can be seen as incomplete body queries that must be completed by practice-related interpretations specific to a project. As practice requires constant reflection upon itself, the results of those body queries can be used by a practitioner-researcher as raw material, introspection information, or control commands for artistic tools that affect the next stage in the doing-thinking process. Thus, we have three interlocked loops: practice, body queries, and the BCI system itself (as defined in [21]). Figure 4 shows these loops and how they interact.

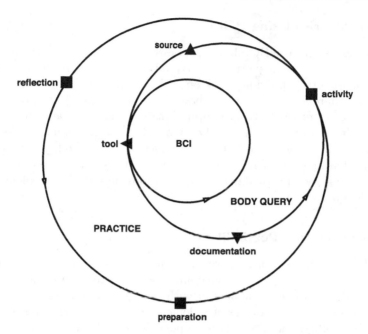

**Fig. 4.** The interlocked loops model of BCI in PaR. Each loop contains an inner loop that is repeated when the outer loop reaches a certain stage. In turn, each inner loop yields information that is used in the following stages of the outer loop.

The PRACTICE outer loop begins with the *preparation* of the activity: contextualization from literature-practice review, reflections from previous iterations, planning of the practice session, etc. Afterwards, the practitioner-researcher undertakes the creative *activity* and, while performing, one or more concurrent or sequential body queries can be executed. Each BODY QUERY is an inner loop started during the *activity* and gathers information from a *bodily source* through the use of a *tool* (in this case BCI) while adding automatic interpretations, if possible, to produce live documentation that may be used as real-time feedback. After the *activity* ends, further interpretations can be assigned to the results of body queries and the resulting documentation is used in the *critical reflection* stage. All the loops repeat as needed.

It is important to note that body queries are central to this model and that their definition is flexible enough to allow for using BCI either as an integral part of the practice or as a process documentation tool. In the first case, BCI is used as a tool for artistic practice during a research inquiry in a PaR process. In the second case, the use of BCI is akin to the use of video recordings, journal annotations, etc. One case does not exclude the other, however. If used as part of the practice, BCI can also be used as documentation tool; if used as documentation tool, the dynamic nature of the process may suggest using it as part of the practice.

## 4.1  Body Queries Using BCI

In PaR processes that use BCI, body queries should be designed around existing tool-related interpretation paradigms. By this we mean that the practitioner-researcher must review previous work on BCI to identify the kind of information gathered by different techniques and how it can be mapped to the practice and documentation of process. To accomplish that, it may be useful to frame the design of body queries according to the set of possible commands afforded by the query tool [2]. In this way the practitioner-researcher may codify previous work in a format that enables them to reflect upon the possibilities open for practice while decoupling each particular body query from the technical implementation details of its query tool.

## 4.2  Documentation Possibilities

As stated before, documentation resulting from body queries may be used in real-time during the creative activity, afterwards during the critical reflection stage, or as descriptions to be shared with the community. Which kind of use the practitioner-researcher makes of it depends on the aim of the practice, implementation feasibility, and interpretation possibilities. The first item refers to the fact that documentation should contribute to the thick description of the practice in the context of the research inquiry. The second, implementation feasibility, deals with more technical aspects of the body query and whether they can be ethically, safely and timely implemented for use during the creative activity. Finally, the possibilities of interpretation refer to which interpretations may be automatically assigned to information coming from the query tool, either in real-time or during a post-process step; which interpretations should be assigned manually by the practitioner-researcher; and the methods to do so.

Beyond the possible ways in which documentation may be realized, it is useful also to think about it in terms of its purpose. Given a set of body queries, each with its own set of interpretations, those interpretations may be codified in order to achieve one of these goals:

**Transcription:** Codification occurs sequentially in time to produce transcriptions of the activity. This process may occur in real-time and the resulting transcripts dynamically presented as feedback for the practitioner-researcher. Example of this kind of documentation are Miranda's *Activating Memory* [14], a piece for a string quartet and a BCMI quartet, and Cádiz and de la Cuadra's *Kara I* [3], a piece for flute, violoncello, BCI, computer music and visuals. In both cases, the signal from the performers is codified as a musical score in real-time.

**Annotation:** The codification is incorporated into the piece created during the activity. In this way the piece is annotated with the results of the body queries and the documentation is embedded on the objects produced by the practice. The documentation described in Subsect. 3.3 and Fig. 3 is an example of this.

**Insight Identification:** Codification is oriented to identify inflection points in the practice; moments when one or more conditions about the practice are met. These conditions are defined during the preparation stage according to known characteristics of the query tool and the practice. The research with jugglers by Schiavone et al. [19] suggest a way to differentiate between expert and non-expert jugglers according to the spectral power in certain frequency bands. In this case, a practitioner-researcher might be notified when the spectral power profile changed from non-expert to expert. This example will be further explored in Sect. 5.

**Multiple Performer Relationships:** If there is more than one person involved in the activity, codifications may be extended to include information about participants (either practitioners or audience members) with the goal to describe their interactions as the practice progresses. Any of the previous examples could be extended to include information about each performer.

## 5    Examples

To illustrate aspects of the framework described in the previous sections, we will review previous uses of BCI in research projects involving artistic practice. For each one, we will show how some aspects of the model are exemplified by each project and suggest possible documentations approaches based on the available information.

### 5.1    Eaton et al. *The Space Between Us*

This example is based on the report of a live performance of the musical piece *The Space Between Us* used in the research of affective states of performers and audience members [6]. The main goal of the BCMI system described was to "move the affective states of two users closer together, creating a shared emotional experience through the music that is based on the emotional measures extracted from the EEG".

To accomplish their goal, the authors used existing literature to create a coordinate system of possible affective states and then defined a mapping between alpha and beta band power from an EEG signal to the coordinate system. Each affective state is mapped to a set of pre-composed musical sequences. During the live performance of the piece, EEG data is obtained for a performer and an audience member, their affective states measured and, using some of those states, trajectories upon the coordinate system towards a target affective state are built. These trajectories are used to select musical sequences that are performed.

To summarize, the authors describe:

(1) A device for capturing EEG signals from the brain.
(2) A set of electrodes placed across the prefrontal cortex.
(3) A mapping from EEG signal to affective state coordinate system.
(4) A mapping from affective states to pre-composed musical sequences.
(5) A display system for the selected pre-composed musical sequence.

Each item in the previous list can be contextualized as part of a body query: (1) is the query tool, (2) is one bodily source, (3) is the query tool related interpretation criteria, (4) is the practice related interpretation criteria, and (5) may be seen as an instance of real-time documentation fulfilling a transcription goal.

From the information available in the paper, we suggest another type of documentation that may fulfill the transcription and multiple performer relationship goals. As the aim of the research is moving the affective states of the users along trajectories to reach a target state, these trajectories may be visualized upon the affective state coordinate system. Figure 5 shows a possible diagram evidencing affective state dynamics during a live performance.

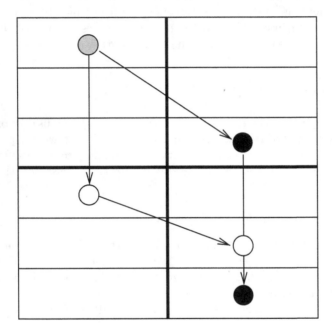

**Fig. 5.** An example of trajectories over an affective state coordinate system. The horizontal axis is *valence* (negative and positive) and the vertical axis is *arousal* (from low to high), each cell represents a possible affective state resulting from their combination. The gray dot is the initial state, the white dots show the proposed trajectory, and the black dots are the real trajectory. We have purposefully left out dimension labels to emphasize the visual aspect of the documentation.

## 5.2 Zioga et al. *Ehneduanna: A Manifesto of Falling*

The second example builds upon *Ehneduanna: A Manifesto of Falling*, a real-time audio-visual and mixed-media performance that uses of multiple BCI systems [22]. According to the authors, the performance is an artistic research project, which aims to investigate in practice the challenges of the design and implementation of multi-brain BCIs in mixed-media performances (...) and develop accordingly a combination of creative and research solutions.

Although there are more participants, we will focus on those fitted with EEG devices: an actress and two audience members. Raw data is processed to obtain frequency band information for each participant, the frequencies selected are supposed to be meaningful in the context of the performance: beta and lower gamma associated with intense mental activity and tension, alpha to a relaxed and awake state, and theta to both deep relaxation and emotional stress. This information is then mapped to RGB color values: beta and lower gamma to the red value, alpha to the green value, and theta to the blue value.

The work is structured in two parts divided in five scenes total. An actress performs on stage with the exception of scene 4, when she leaves the stage and returns at the beginning of stage 5. Fragments of texts and videos are projected on a screen and the video stream is filtered with a color determined by the signals from the participants: scenes 1, 2 and 3 use information from the actress; scene 4 use information from two audience members; and scene 5 uses information from the actress and one audience member. In scenes where there is information from two participants, each color filter is applied to one half of the projected image. In scene 5, the colors gradually merge towards an average color. The color dynamics during the performance "not only correspond to a unique real-time combination of the three selected brain activity frequencies of multiple participants, but also serve as visualisation of their predominant cognitive states, both independently as well as jointly".

As we did in the previous example, we can summarize the process:

(1) A device for capturing EEG signals from the brain.
(2) One electrode placed in the prefrontal lobe.
(3) A mapping from EEG signal to frequency band associated with cognitive states.
(4) A mapping from frequency bands to RGB values.
(5) A live display influenced by RGB values.

Once again, we can view each item as part of a body query: (1) is the query tool, (2) is one bodily source, both (3) and (4) are query tool related interpretation criteria, and (5) may be seen as an instance of real-time documentation. In this case, however, the resulting documentation fulfills an annotation goal. While the previous example used the documentation as a transcription used by the performers, in this case the documentation is incorporated into the performance and serves to manifest both transitions between cognitive states and synchronization/desynchronization between the cognitive states of the participants.

The body query illustrated by this performance may be used to fulfill other goals. For example, in a project where the research inquiry is related to achieving certain cognitive states during practice, the resulting live documentation may fulfill an insight identification goal. In that case, the practitioner-researcher predetermines a target cognitive state (which then has a corresponding color or set of colors) and starts experimenting with the effect of certain actions on the projected color.

This example also shows that query tool related interpretations are not restricted to one discipline and may be built from several *know-that* pools. On one hand, frequency bands are selected according to known associations to cognitive states, an interpretation coming from neuroscience. On the other hand, frequency band mappings to colors were chosen according to "historically established in the western world cultural associations of specific colours with certain emotions". In this way, two different sets of previous knowledge are joined in a common interpretation for the body query in the context of this particular performance.

### 5.3  Schiavone et al. *Towards Real-Time Visualization of a Juggler's Brain*

The last project we review involves research on a particular artistic practice rather than research through artistic practice. The aim of the authors was to monitor the brain activity of a juggler while performing, with the long term goal of creating real-time visualizations of that activity [19]. Two subjects, one intermediate and one expert juggler, participated in the study. In the first part of the study, their EEG signals were recorded during five different conditions; in the second part of the study, the expert juggler was asked to perform three juggling patterns of increasing difficulty while their signal was recorded. All analysis was performed offline.

Following results from previous research, the authors conducted two types of analysis on the signal: power spectra across frequency bands, and spectral coherence between pairs of electrodes. Their results suggest that these measures may be used to differentiate between expert and non-expert jugglers, and between difficulty levels of different patterns.

This example shows an incomplete body query: it has a bodily source and a query tool but lacks interpretation criteria and documentation. We selected it because it illustrates how a body query may be designed from existing research. In this case, the results point the way towards query tool related interpretations regarding the experience of the performer and the difficulty of the juggling patterns. Further research along this line will provide a more robust foundation upon which the interpretation can be built. At that point, concrete documentation possibilities will appear.

We imagine, like the authors, the possibility of real-time visualization of the identified biomarkers. This kind of visualization may work as documentation to guide practice sessions during a PaR process, to annotate live performances to evidence the brain activity related to juggling, or as a training tool for non-expert jugglers. The body query suggested by this research stands in contrasts with those described in the previous examples: while they used BCI as part of the medium in the practice, this would use BCI as an introspection tool regarding the practice.

# 6   Discussion

We have presented a framework for using BCI tools in PaR, which is centered on the concept of body queries and how they generate documentation that fills a perceived gap in the types of descriptions available in artistic practice. The model combines PaR concepts with BCI-based body queries to provide information to be used in "thick descriptions" evidencing the research inquiry.

We believe the reviewed examples show the flexibility of the framework and how can it be applied in future PaR projects. Two of the examples use BCI as an integral part of the creative process and practice and illustrate how BCI-based body queries may be used as part of the practice or inquiry. In contrast, the last example illustrates another possible use of BCI in a PaR process, not as medium but as a means of documentation to reflect upon the practice in the context of the inquiry.

The framework is also useful because it moves the focus away from the technical details of implementing the BCI system towards the PaR process. This is important to avoid technoformalism [8, cited by 22], that is, to avoid focusing exclusively in the medium while abandoning the artistic concept that guides the research.

However, as we are focused on brain body queries, we must beware of reductionism, as each body query yields information of part of the body state. Practitioner-researchers must be careful when interpreting brain activity, it may be possible for a practitioner-researcher to build up a set of interpretations for a specific project but those interpretations may not be necessarily transferrable to another project. Also, agreed-upon interpretations based on neuroscience literature must be carefully weighed to avoid reductionism, and, ideally, interpretations should include multiple body queries.

We know future work should be done on body queries in general (expanding body-area networks to PaR, for example), nevertheless, we believe this framework represents a starting point in using BCI as a tool for PaR, possibly opening further lines of inquiry, both in each particular project and in PaR in general.

Finally, we want to emphasize that, the feedback and interlocked loops of doing-thinking, querying the body, and reflecting, illustrate the processes by which the metaphorical cogs of the practice are increasingly exposed as the tacit is made explicit.

# References

1. Aparicio, A.: Immobilis in mobili: performing arts, BCI, and locked-in syndrome. Brain-Comput. Interfaces **2**(2–3), 150–159 (2015). http://www.tandfonline.com/doi/abs/10.1080/2326263X.2015.1100366

2. Aparicio, A.: Brain affordances: an approach to design for performers with locked-in syndrome. In: Magnusson, T., Kiefer, C., Duffy, S. (eds.) Proceedings of the 2016 International Conference on Live Interfaces, pp. 224–227. REFRAME, Brighton (2016). http://reframe.sussex.ac.uk/reframebooks/archive2016/live-interfaces/
3. Cádiz, R., de la Cuadra, P.: Kara: a BCI approach to composition. In: Proceedings of the 2014 Internation Computer Music Conference, pp. 350–354. Michigan Publishing, University of Michigan Library, Ann Arbor (2014)
4. Chen, M., Gonzalez, S., Vasilakos, A., Cao, H., Leung, V.C.M.: Body area networks: a survey. Mob. Netw. Appl. 16(2), 171–193 (2011). http://link.springer.com/10.1007/s11036-010-0260-8
5. Cruz-Garza, J.G., Hernandez, Z.R., Tse, T., Caducoy, E., Abibullaev, B., Contreras-Vidal, J.L.: A novel experimental and analytical approach to the multimodal neural decoding of intent during social interaction in freely-behaving human infants. J. Vis. Exp. 104, e53406 (2015). http://www.jove.com/video/53406/a-novel-experimental-analytical-approach-to-multimodal-neural
6. Eaton, J., Williams, D., Miranda, E.: The space between us: evaluating a multi-user affective brain-computer music interface. Brain-Comput. Interfaces 2(2–3), 103–116 (2015)
7. Haseman, B.: A manifesto for performative research. Media Int. Aust. Inc. Culture Policy 118(1), 98–106 (2006). http://journals.sagepub.com/doi/abs/10.1177/1329878X0611800113
8. Heitlinger, S., Bryan-Kinns, N.: Understanding performative behaviour within content-rich digital live art. Digit. Creativity 24(2), 111–118 (2013). http://www.tandfonline.com/doi/abs/10.1080/14626268.2013.808962
9. Kübler, A., Holz, E.M., Riccio, A., Zickler, C., Kaufmann, T., Kleih, S.C., Staiger-Sälzer, P., Desideri, L., Hoogerwerf, E.J., Mattia, D.: The user-centered design as novel perspective for evaluating the usability of BCI-controlled applications. PLoS ONE 9(12), e112392 (2014)
10. Laureys, S., Pellas, F., Eeckhout, P.V., Ghorbel, S., Schnakers, C., Perrin, F., Berré, J., Faymonville, M.E., Pantke, K.H., Damas, F., Lamy, M., Moonen, G., Goldman, S.: The locked-in syndrome: what is it like to be conscious but paralyzed and voiceless? In: Laureys, S. (ed.) The Boundaries of Consciousness: Neurobiology and Neuropathology, Progress in Brain Research, vol. 150, pp. 495–611. Elsevier, Amsterdam (2005). http://www.sciencedirect.com/science/article/pii/S0079612305500347
11. Liberati, G., Pizzimenti, A., Simione, L., Riccio, A., Schettini, F., Inghilleri, M., Mattia, D., Cincotti, F.: Developing brain-computer interfaces from a user-centered perspective: assessing the needs of persons with amyotrophic lateral sclerosis, caregivers, and professionals. Appl. Ergon. 50, 139–146 (2015)
12. Lucier, A.: Statement on: music for solo performer. In: Biofeedback and the Arts, Results of Early Experiments, pp. 60–61. Aesthetic Research Center of Canada Publications, Vancouver (1976)
13. May, S.: Rethinking the cognitive turn. In: May, S. (ed.) Rethinking Practice as Research and the Cognitive Turn, pp. 11–38. Palgrave Macmillan, London (2015). http://link.springer.com/10.1057/9781137522733_2
14. Miranda, E.R.: Music neurotechnology: from music of the spheres to music of the hemispheres. Symmetry: Cult. Sci. 26(3), 353–378 (2015)
15. Nelson, R.: Conceptual frameworks for PaR and related pedagogy: from 'hard facts' to 'liquid knowing'. In: Nelson, R. (ed.) Practice as Research in the Arts, pp. 48–70. Palgrave Macmillan, London (2013). http://link.springer.com/10.1057/9781137282910_3

16. Nelson, R.: From practitioner to practitioner-researcher. In: Nelson, R. (ed.) Practice as Research in the Arts, pp. 23–47. Palgrave Macmillan, London (2013). http://link.springer.com/10.1057/9781137282910_2

17. Nelson, R.: Introduction: the what, where, when and why of 'practice as research'. In: Nelson, R. (ed.) Practice as Research in the Arts, pp. 3–22. Palgrave Macmillan, London (2013). http://link.springer.com/10.1057/9781137282910_1

18. Nelson, R.: Supervision, documentation and other aspects of praxis. In: Nelson, R. (ed.) Practice as Research in the Arts, pp. 71–92. Palgrave Macmillan, London (2013). http://link.springer.com/10.1057/9781137282910_4

19. Schiavone, G., Großekathöfer, U., à Campo, S., Mihajlović, V.: Towards real-time visualization of a juggler's brain. Brain-Comput. Interfaces **2**(2–3), 90–102 (2015). http://www.tandfonline.com/doi/full/10.1080/2326263X.2015.1101656

20. Wadeson, A., Nijholt, A., Nam, C.S.: Artistic brain-computer interfaces: state-of-the-art control mechanisms. Brain-Comput. Interfaces **2**(2–3), 70–75 (2015). http://www.tandfonline.com/doi/full/10.1080/2326263X.2015.1103155

21. Wolpaw, J.R., Birbaumer, N., McFarland, D.J., Pfurtscheller, G., Vaughan, T.M.: Brain-computer interfaces for communication and control. Clin. Neurophysiol.: Off. J. Int. Fed. Clin. Neurophysiol. **113**(6), 767–791 (2002). http://www.ncbi.nlm.nih.gov/pubmed/12048038

22. Zioga, P., Chapman, P., Ma, M., Pollick, F.: Enheduanna-a manifesto of falling: first demonstration of a live brain-computer cinema performance with multi-brain BCI interaction for one performer and two audience members. Digit. Creat. (2016). http://doi.org/10.1080/14626268.2016.1260593

# Using Brain Painting at Home for 5 Years: Stability of the P300 During Prolonged BCI Usage by Two End-Users with ALS

Loïc Botrel[✉], Elisa Mira Holz, and Andrea Kübler

Institute of Psychology, University of Würzburg, Würzburg, Germany
loic.botrel@uni-wuerzburg.de

**Abstract.** Brain painting (BP) is non-invasive electroencephalography (EEG) based Brain-Computer Interface (BCI) for creative expression based on a P300 matrix. The technology was transferred into a home setup for two patients with amyotrophic lateral sclerosis (ALS), who used the system for several years while being evaluated on performance and satisfaction. Holz and colleagues found that the use of BP increased quality of life. Additionally, they described that changes in the amplitude of the P300 ERPs could be observed between recalibrations of the BCI. In this paper, we quantified the evolution of the P300 peaks in the two BCI end-users (HP and JT). For HP, the P300 peak amplitude increased during 9 months, then progressively decreased for the following 51 months, but the BCI accuracy remained stable. JT's P300 peak amplitude did not significantly decrease during 32 months that separated the calibrations. Yet, JT's BCI accuracy declined which we may attribute to a decline in physical functioning due to ALS. Painters used online BCI for hundreds of hours (HP 755, JT 223) and both finished more than 50 named brain paintings. HP could use BP autonomously and regularly at home for 33 months without recalibration of the system, and JT for 10 months, suggesting the stability of P300 and SWLDA online classifiers in the long-term, and demonstrating the feasibility of having a P300 based system at home that requires few involvement of BCI experts.

## 1 Introduction

Brain painting (BP) is a brain-computer interface (BCI) controlled application that allows for creative expression. It is based on the well known P300 Speller paradigm [4], but with the particularity of presenting a matrix of icons that send commands to a virtual canvas. This non-invasive electroencephalography (EEG) based system was developed and successfully tested with healthy participants and patients [11]. To fulfill the translational purpose of the project, we adapted BP for independent home use, by simplifying the user interface, therefore allowing caregivers to operate the system without the direct assistance of BCI experts. BP was installed at the home of two end-users (HP, aged 78 and JT, aged 77). Both end-users, in the locked-in state due to amyotrophic lateral sclerosis (ALS), used the system assisted by their caregivers and family without

© Springer International Publishing AG 2017
D.D. Schmorrow and C.M. Fidopiastis (Eds.): AC 2017, Part II, LNAI 10285, pp. 282–292, 2017.
DOI: 10.1007/978-3-319-58625-0_20

requiring the presence of researchers on site. Further software and development cycles, following the user centered design (see [10] for guidelines) were implemented and led to a new BP version allowing users to draw lines, curves and select new forms. BP2 was tested with healthy participants, and installed at JT's home [1]. During several years and hundreds of sessions of painting, we regularly assessed HP's and JT's satisfaction, perceived control level and impact of BP on their quality of life [5,6]. Holz and colleagues previously found that the peak amplitude at Cz increased in 9 months of evaluation and decreased after 26 months, while Sellers and colleagues [12] showed that the ERPs remained stable across 18 months in a patients with ALS in the locked-in-state.

## 2    Objective

The amplitude of the P300 ERP is the physiological marker for BCI performance, which we acquired during recalibrations of the BCI over the extended period of 60 months for HP, and of 32 months for JT. We report in the present paper the evolution of the P300 ERP across the evaluated period and discuss its stability for the independent home use of BP.

## 3    Methods

### 3.1    BCI Feedback

To bring BP out of the lab to the end-users' home, we were strictly following the user-centered design [10]. We adapted the BP system (BP1 [11]) such that it could be used independently at home without requiring an expert to be present. Satisfaction, frustration, workload and quality of life were assessed and were reported in other studies [5,6]. As a first upgrade, we introduced a new feedback modality that replaced classical P300 intensification of the characters by overlays with the face of Einstein [7,8], which were proven to lead to better performance, also in patients. Additionally, a minor upgrade of the feedback was also implemented, allowing the end-users to immediately see their selections within the matrix, which they initially had to deduce from a status bar. JT received directly the upgraded BP1, with the face paradigm. After a while using BP1, participants expressed the wish to extend the functionalities of the interface, notably the ability to draw lines, obtain more shapes than only circles or squares, and then be able to fill the whole screen at once. Thus, BP2 was developed and integrated all those requests, with even more features such as writing text or inserting external images [1]. Those were evaluated in healthy participants [3], but the number of functionalities proposed in the matrices provided to the end-users was simplified to match their initial wishes, while avoiding overload with too many options.

Yet, BP2 contains line drawing functions, gradients and additional shapes. The line drawing feature relies on placing crosses at specific locations on the canvas, which are then linked. For more than 3 crosses, lines were automatically connected to each others forming a path. The path could be closed using the "open/close" path command. Instead of tracing a line, the closed path could be filled with color using the "fill/trace" path command allowed to switch between tracing a line for the path or filling its content. A smoothing function was also added to allow more natural paths to be drawn. (See Fig. 1 for a simulation of BP2 use for drawing shapes, lines and gradients)

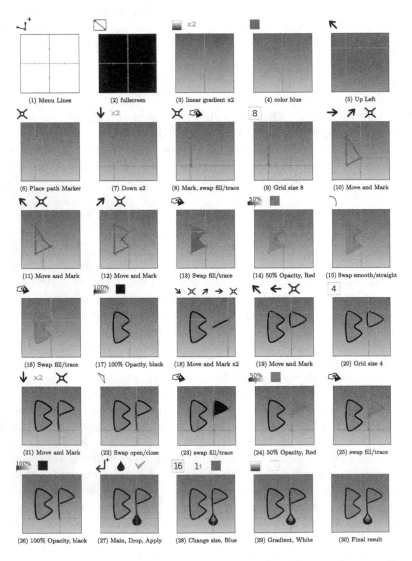

**Fig. 1.** Screenshots of BP2 simulating painting based on the new features (i.e. lines, curves, gradients, fullscreen) in 30 steps totalizing 53 selections. The thumbnails indicate the commands that were selected within the BP matrices during the simulation.

BP2 also facilitated caregiver's operation and allowed for short auto-calibration of the BCI, which provided a quick performance assessment, and a more robust adaptation to issues such as broken electrodes, wrong placement of the cap or lack of EEG gel. While those regular issues are easily spotted and solved in a laboratory environment, they represent a core challenge in home setups, especially during the first months of use.

## 3.2  Participants

Two patients with ALS in the locked-in state were provided with a BCI system at home. The study was approved by the Ethical Review Board of the Medical Faculty at the University of Tübingen.

**HP** is a female 77 years-old patient with ALS (spinal form). She was diagnosed in 2007, and is completely paralyzed except eye-movements, allowing her to use an eye-tracker for communicating, browsing Internet or sending emails. HP lives in her family house surrounded by her family and is permanently under caregiver supervision who oversee the operation of the artificial respirator and feeding. When she contacted the university of Würzburg, HP had an EEG amplifier (granted by g.tec[1]). As a former hobby painter, HP expressed interest in trying BP in her home environment, and received the first iteration of BP adaptation to home use in Jan. 2012. She then kept using the system within a period of 5 years and is by now still using it albeit we stopped data collection for evaluation.

**JT** is a male 76 years-old patient with ALS. He was diagnosed in 2006, was able to normally talk until 2014. Afterwards, he nevertheless retained the ability to move facial muscles enabling people to read his lips. JT was surrounded by close relatives and was under permanent supervision to oversee the function of the artificial respirator and feeding. JT was a retired architect and professional painter. After loosing grasp function due to ALS, JT was determined to keep painting; after contacting the university of Würzburg, he received BP at home in Sept. 2013. In the course of the year 2014, JT presented fasciculations in the neck that were both painful and created artifacts on the EEG. Retraining the classifier was sufficient to solve the issue[2]. JT kept actively painting until July 2015. But due to multiple health issues (e.g., neck pain) and practical reasons (assistant left his service), JT did not manage to regularly use BP after this period. JT deceased in Jan. 2017.

## 3.3  Calibrations

In the course of 5 years of use, HP had five calibration sessions of BP1. We visited HP four times to recalibrate the system, while the last session was remotely

---

[1]  g.tec medical engineering GmbH, www.gtec.at.

[2]  We initially planned to lower the low pass filter to 20 Hz, providing a cleaner averaged signal, but the classifier performed well. Filtering was therefore held as a backup plan in case the artifact would worsen.

supervized using shared desktop and voice communication. On the third session, we introduced the Einstein face paradigm. JT used BP1 for 10 months, after which we installed BP2 and recalibrated the system three times in the following 11 months of painting. The auto-calibration function was used once under researchers supervision on site, and JT continued using BP for 3.5 months until his assistant left his service. Four auto-calibration sessions, which were conducted in 2016 by untrained caregivers, did not provide a good signal quality, and were excluded from the analysis. Helped by his former assistant, JT performed a successful auto-calibration in June 2016 that is reported here. In total, we report 5 of the 9 calibrations that JT performed during a period of 32 months. Details about the timeline of calibration sessions is shown in Table 1.

**Table 1.** Offline calibration runs used for both online classifier training and statistical analysis

| User | Num | Date | Flash type | BP version | Calibration method |
|------|-----|------|-----------|-----------|--------------------|
| HP | 1 | 01.2012 | Intensification | BP1 | Researchers on site |
|  | 2 | 03.2012 | | | |
|  | 3 | 10.2012 | Einstein's face | | |
|  | 4 | 04.2014 | | | |
|  | 5 | 01.2017 | | | Remotely supervised |
| JT | 1 | 10.2013 | Einstein's face | BP1 | Researchers on site |
|  | 2 | 08.2014 | | BP2 | |
|  | 3 | 12.2014 | | | |
|  | 4 | 05.2015 | | BP2 autocalib | |
|  | 5–8 | n/a | | | Failed autocalibrations |
|  | 9 | 06.2016 | | | autocalibration |

*note: empty cells indicate no change*

### 3.4  Signal Processing and Classification

The feedback was provided by two LCD monitors directly in the field of view of the end-users, such that they could move their eyes between monitors. The P300 stimulation monitor was placed directly in front of them at a distance of about 60 cm, while the canvas monitor was placed on the right side.

The EEG was measured with a cap that allowed for easy set-up (g.GAMMAcap) holding eight active electrodes (Fz, Cz, P3, Pz, P4, PO3, PO4 and Oz, conform to the 10–20 system), and connected to a g.GAMMAbox and g.USBAmp amplifier (gtec.at, Austria). The EEG signal was recorded with a sampling rate of 256 Hz and was band-pass filtered between .1 and 40 Hz for both online and offline data analysis[3]. Both BP1 and BP2 relied on BCI2000 for signal acquisition and processing. For each calibration, a minimum of 5 target

---

[3] For P300 peak analysis and plots of JT, we band-pass filtered between .1 to 20 Hz.

selections with 15 repetitions was collected in a supervised fashion, resulting in a minimum of 150 targets repetitions and 900 non-targets repetitions. The EEG activity was extracted between 0 to 800 ms post stimulation. Averaged features and their $r^2$ determination coefficient were calculated using the P300-GUI (BCI2000 toolbox) based on Matlab (The MathWorks). The features were used to train a stepwise linear discriminant analysis (SWLDA) classifier [9]. The minimum number of sequence to reach 100% cross-fold validation accuracy provided by P300GUI, plus two was used for online painting. This number was selected when installing BP1 and BP2. Then the number was manually adjusted by the experimenters based on end-users' requests and cross-validation results.

### 3.5  P300 Peak Analysis

For the analysis of the P300 peaks, we selected the midline electrodes (Fz, Cz, Pz and Oz). To determine the temporal – time – position of target P300 peaks, we used the maximum $r^2$ between averaged target and non-targets amplitude, estimated for each calibration run and each electrode. No specific temporal constraint was applied for the identification of the peak (i.e. between 0 and 800 ms). Then, the peak amplitude at the corresponding time point was collected for every target stimulus.

To determine how the amplitude of the P300 ERP evolved during the years, and whether it was larger in different EEG channels, we conducted for each end-user a type III full-factorial ANOVA with target ERP peak as dependent variable. Calibration run and channel were used as between factors. For each combination of calibration run and channel, there was a minimum of 150 target peaks that entered the ANOVA. Post hoc tests were performed using Tukey's honest significant differences test (HSD).

## 4  Results

### 4.1  HP

The average target peak amplitude on midline electrodes was $M = 3.8\,\mu V$, $SEM = .17$. The ANOVA for HP yielded an interaction between channel and calibration ($F(12, 8980) = 6.5$, $p < .001$), a main effect of calibration $F(4, 8980) = 63.5$, $p < .001$), and a main effect of electrode ($F(3, 8980) = 90$, $p < .001$). Pairwise comparisons for the interaction between electrode and channel revealed that the target peak amplitude at Fz and Cz increased between the 1st and the 3rd calibration ($p_{adj} < .001$), then decreased between the 3rd and the 5th ($p_{adj} < .001$). For the parieto-occipital channels Pz and Oz, the target peak amplitude was significantly lower between the 1st calibration and calibrations 2, 3 and 5 ($p_{adj} < .001$), but did not significantly differ between each others for calibrations 2, 3, 4 and 5, excepted for calibrations 3 and 4 at Pz ($p_{adj} < .05$, see Fig. 2).

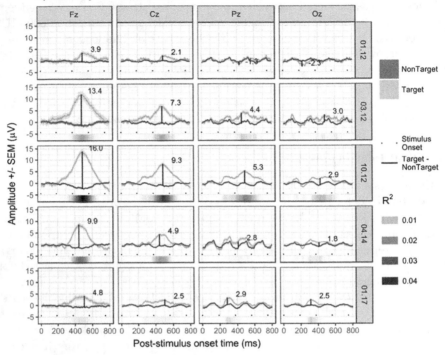

### Calibration runs HP

**a) ERPs by electrode and date**

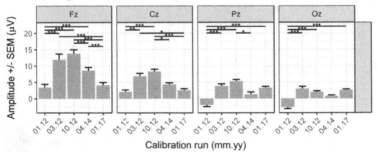

**b) Target Peak amplitude by electrode**

**Fig. 2.** Average plots using data acquired during online BCI calibration of HP, arranged by EEG electrode and calibration session. (a) The target and non-target ERPs, with a number indicating their amplitude difference. Points indicate the onset of the flash stimuli, and the black bars represent the determination coefficient of the corresponding features. (b) Average amplitude and standard error of the mean of the target peaks. Adjusted $\alpha$ levels: .001***, .01**, .05*.

Considering only brain painting sessions that lasted more than five minutes; in 5 years of using BP, HP had 484 painting sessions totalizing 755 h of painting via BCI ($M = 93.7$ min, $SD = 50.6$). Hp made more than 50 named paintings (see Fig. 3).

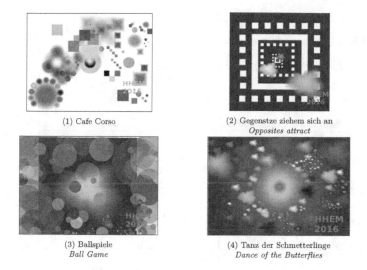

(1) Cafe Corso

(2) Gegenstze ziehem sich an
*Opposites attract*

(3) Ballspiele
*Ball Game*

(4) Tanz der Schmetterlinge
*Dance of the Butterflies*

**Fig. 3.** Four original brain paintings made by HP using BP1 during 2016.

## 4.2  JT

For JT, average target peak amplitude on midline electrodes was $M = 4.5\,\mu V$, $SEM = .16$. The ANOVA for JT yielded no significant main effects of calibration ($F(4, 5980) = 1.4, p = .21$), channel ($F(3, 5980) = .54$, $p = .66$) and no interaction between channel and calibration ($F(12, 5980) = 1.3$, $p = .24$, see Fig. 4). In a period of 2.5 years, JT had 225 painting sessions totalizing 223 h of painting via BCI ($M = 59.6\,min$, $SD = 33.1$). Using BP1, JT created 31 named paintings, and 19 with BP2, plus an additional serie of 10 paintings that are meant to be later integrated as models to follow in a tutorial for beginners (see Fig. 5).

## 5  Discussion

The current study with two end-users demonstrates that people in the locked-in state due to neurodegenerative disease can use a BCI at home for many years. Both HP and JT could paint for years based on a single calibration. Between calibration 4 and 5, HP painted during 33 months before we remotely performed another calibration. This observation demonstrates the stability of the P300 and the user friendliness of the BCI. Interrestingly, HP's P300 increased for 9 months which may indicate a better focus of attention due to training. The next calibrations revealed a reduced amplitude which may be attributed to disease progression but was not concomitant of changes made to the BCI paradigms (i.e. Einstein's faces). JT's P300 amplitude remained stable across the years despite physical decline from severe paralysis to the locked-in state, this decline was also reflected in his satisfaction and control levels [2]. Both artists continued to produce creative output through the years.

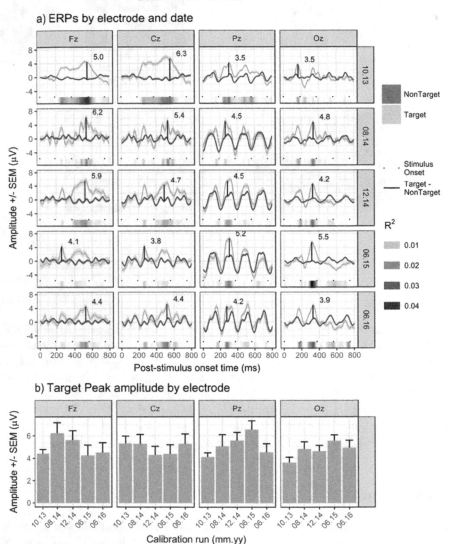

*Calibration runs JT*

**Fig. 4.** Average plots using data acquired during online BCI calibration of JT, arranged by EEG electrode and calibration session. (a) The target and non-target ERPs, with a number indicating their amplitude difference. Points indicate the onset of the flash stimuli, and the black bars represent the determination coefficient of the corresponding features. (b) Average amplitude and standard error of the mean of the target peaks.

Although the autocalibration feature worked well in preliminary tests in the lab, the conditions in which such calibrations took place by JT were not reliable (i.e. untrained caregiver, no regular practice), underlining the necessity of thorough training of significant others who support BCI use at home.

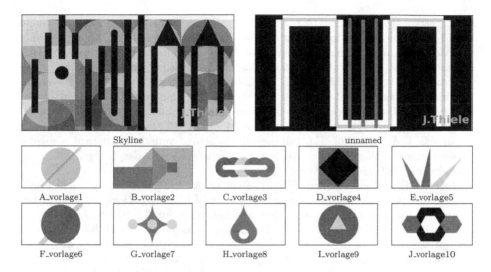

**Fig. 5.** Twelve original paintings by JT using BP2 during 2015. The serie of 10 smaller painting are intended to be translated into a BP2 beginners' tutorial.

The auto-calibration function should not be used at the very beginning of BCI home use. Instead, experts must set-up the system properly and ensure well function through remote supervision. Another option would be to record a few selections before starting a daily session, such that the newly acquired data can be compared with the actual classifier. Such a functionality would be convenient to evaluate more accurately the bias between self-reported accuracy and true accuracy. Yet, later when end-users – caregivers and patients alike – are familiar with BCI set-up and use, the autocalibration function can be introduced.

## 6   Conclusion

In the light of these results, and previous findings [5,6,12], we suggest that the P300 is a sufficiently stable EEG component that may be used in a BCI setup for years in patients with neurodegenerative disease. Furthermore, the SWLDA classifier used for target selection is sensitive even to smaller ERP amplitudes. Therefore, BP – or any P300 based BCI – is an option for (creative) expression and interaction usable at home without experts being present, even after years in the locked in state due to the neurodegenerative ALS.

## References

1. Botrel, L., Holz, E.M., Kübler, A.: Brain painting v2: evaluation of p300-based brain-computer interface for creative expression by an end-user following the user-centered design. Brain-Comput. Interfaces **2**(2–3), 135–149 (2015)

2. Botrel, L., Holz, E.M., Kübler, A.: Brain painting v2: long-term evaluation by an end-user at home - an update. In: Müller-Putz, G., Huggins, J.E., Steyrl, D. (eds.) Proceedings of the Sixth International Brain-Computer Interface Meeting: BCI Past, Present, and Future, p. 232. Verlag der Technischen Universität Graz (2016)
3. Botrel, L., Reuter, P., Holz, E.M., Kübler, A.: Brain painting version 2 - evaluation with healthy end-users. In: Müller-Putz, G., Bauernfeind, G., Brunner, C., Steyrl, D., Wriessnegger, S., Scherer, R. (eds.) Proceedings of the 6th International Brain-Computer Interface Conference 2014, pp. 32–35 (2014)
4. Farwell, L.A., Donchin, E.: Talking off the top of your head: toward a mental prosthesis utilizing event-related brain potentials. Electroencephalogr. Clin. Neurophysiol. **70**(6), 510–523 (1988)
5. Holz, E.M., Botrel, L., Kaufmann, T., Kübler, A.: Long-term independent brain-computer interface home use improves quality of life of a patient in the locked-in state: a case study. Arch. Phys. Med. Rehabil. **96**(3 Suppl.), S16–S26 (2015)
6. Holz, E.M., Botrel, L., Kübler, A.: Independent home use of brain painting improves quality of life of two artists in the locked-in state diagnosed with amyotrophic lateral sclerosis. Brain-Comput. Interfaces **2**(2–3), 117–134 (2015)
7. Kaufmann, T., Schulz, S.M., Grunzinger, C., Kübler, A.: Flashing characters with famous faces improves ERP-based brain-computer interface performance. J. Neural Eng. **8**(5), 056016 (2011)
8. Kaufmann, T., Schulz, S.M., Koblitz, A., Renner, G., Wessig, C., Kübler, A.: Face stimuli effectively prevent brain-computer interface inefficiency in patients with neurodegenerative disease. Clin. Neurophysiol.: Official J. Int. Fed. Clin. Neurophysiol. **124**(5), 893–900 (2013)
9. Krusienski, D.J., Sellers, E.W., Cabestaing, F., Bayoudh, S., McFarland, D.J., Vaughan, T.M., Wolpaw, J.R.: A comparison of classification techniques for the p300 speller. J. Neural Eng. **3**(4), 299–305 (2006)
10. Kübler, A., Holz, E.M., Riccio, A., Zickler, C., Kaufmann, T., Kleih, S.C., Staiger-Salzer, P., Desideri, L., Hoogerwerf, E.J., Mattia, D.: The user-centered design as novel perspective for evaluating the usability of BCI-controlled applications. PloS One **9**(12), e112392 (2014)
11. Munssinger, J.I., Halder, S., Kleih, S.C., Furdea, A., Raco, V., Hosle, A., Kübler, A.: Brain painting: first evaluation of a new brain-computer interface application with ALS-patients and healthy volunteers. Frontiers Neurosci. **4**, 182 (2010)
12. Sellers, E.W., Vaughan, T.M., Wolpaw, J.R.: A brain-computer interface for long-term independent home use. Amyotrophic Lateral Sclerosis: Official Publ. World Fed. Neurol. Res. Group Motor Neuron Dis. **11**(5), 449–455 (2010)

# Music Imagery for Brain-Computer Interface Control

Mei Lin Chen, Lin Yao, and Ning Jiang$^{(\boxtimes)}$

Department of Systems Design Engineering,
University of Waterloo, Waterloo, Canada
ning.jiang@uwaterloo.ca

**Abstract.** Brain-computer interface (BCI) provides an alternative way for lock in patients to interact with the environment solely based on neural activity. The drawback with independent BCIs is their lack in the number of commands – usually only two are available. This provides great challenges to the BCI's usefulness and applicability in real-life scenarios. A potential avenue to increasing the number of independent BCI commands is through modulating brain activity with music, in regions as the orbitofrontal cortex. By quantifying oscillatory signatures such as alpha rhythm at the frontal cortex, we can obtain a greater understanding of the effect of music at the cortical level. Similar to how desynchronization patterns during motor imagery is comparable to that in real movement, the imagination of music elicits response from the auditory cortex as if the sound is actually heard. We propose an experimental paradigm to train subjects to elicit discriminative brain activation pattern with respect to imagining high and low music scales. Each trial of listening to music (high or low scale) was followed by its respective music imagery. The result of this three subjects experiment achieved over 70% accuracy in independent BCI performance and showed similar distributions in Discriminative Brain Patterns (DBP) between high and low music listening and imagination, as shown in Fig. 1. This pilot study opens an avenue for increasing BCI commands, especially in independent BCI, which are currently very limited. It also provides a potential channel for music composition.

**Keywords:** Brain-computer interface (BCI) · Music imagination · Listening guided training

## 1 Introduction

Brain-computer interface (BCI) technologies provide an alternative mean of interacting with the environment independent of peripheral nerves and muscles, based solely on neural activities [1]. BCI technologies hold great potential to improve their autonomy and quality of life for those with severe and multiple motor disabilities such as lock-in syndrome. Generally, users can use the BCI system by consciously eliciting distinct, reproducible patterns of activity in particular brain regions through mental tasks. A decoding system detects these patterns of activity and translates them to the designated commands for external device control (e.g., computer cursor, robotic hands, rehabilitation devices) [2].

© Springer International Publishing AG 2017
D.D. Schmorrow and C.M. Fidopiastis (Eds.): AC 2017, Part II, LNAI 10285, pp. 293–300, 2017.
DOI: 10.1007/978-3-319-58625-0_21

**Fig. 1.** Sound stimuli of high and low scale composed with online NoteFlight software. *(1)* Shows the high music scale and *(2)* the low scale music scale.

Among the various BCI systems developed up to date [3], independent BCI without external stimulation has received vast amounts of interest [4–6]. Due to its independent nature, BCI systems based solely on cognitive tasks such as motor imagery [7], slow cortical potential [8], sensorimotor rhythms [9], and somatosensory attention orientation [10] have shown promising potential not only in communication and control but also in neurorehabilitation [11, 12]. However, there are still many drawbacks in these independent BCI systems, such that the degree of control commands is very limited – generally only two degrees of control available. Further, there is also the challenge of "BCI-Illiteracy", which is that BCI control does not work for a non-negligible portion of users (estimated 15 to 30%) [13]. Increasing the currently limited BCI commands by introducing novel BCI modalities would significantly improve the information transfer rate [14]. A larger range of diversified BCI systems would make BCI suitable for a greater number of users.

Brain responses to music stimulation opened a new window of opportunity for the study of music at the cognitive level. There's a potential for using music to modulate activities in brain structures such as the orbitofrontal cortex [15]. By quantifying oscillatory signatures such as alpha rhythm at the frontal cortex, we can obtain a greater understanding of the effect of music at the cortical level [16]. Similar to how desynchronization patterns during motor imagery models is comparable to that in real movement [17], the imagination of music elicits response from the auditory cortex as if the sound is actually heard [18]. Based on current works on EEG music studies [16, 19, 20], we will provide a novel paradigm to train the subjects to elicit distinguishable brain patterns with respect to imagination of low and high pitched piano music scales. The EEG activation patterns as a result of music imagery will be analyzed and translated into control for independent BCI system.

# 2   Methods

**Subjects**
Three healthy subjects, two male and one female, mean age 23, were recruited in the study. All three were naïve BCI subjects and all have normal hearing and normal or corrected to normal vision, none reported to be diagnosed with any neurological disorder or hearing impairment. This study was approved by the Ethics Committee of the University of Waterloo and all subjects signed a written informed consent before participation in the experiment.

**Sound Stimuli**
Two different ranges of sound stimuli (high and low scales) were administered to the subjects. The stimuli were composed with the online NoteFlight software, which can be found at www.noteflight.com. The high scale composes of a full 8-note ascending scale starting at C6 and ending at C7. The low scale composes of the same full 8-note ascending scale but starts at C2 and ends at C3. Both scales are electronically generated by the piano simulator on NoteFlight at 2/4 measure and tempo of 120 quarter notes per minute. See Fig. 1 for music sheet.

**EEG Recording**
EEG signals were recorded using the g.Nautilus system (g.tec, Austria). A 32-channel wireless g.Nautilus EEG cap was used to collect 32 channel EEG signals, and the active gel-based electrodes were placed according to the extended 10/20 system. The reference electrode was placed on the right earlobe and the ground electrode was placed on the forehead. A 60 Hz notch filter was applied during recording to the raw signals, which were sampled at a frequency of 250 Hz with 24-bit resolution.

**Experimental Procedure**
Subjects were seated in a comfortable chair at a distance of approximately 0.5 m away from a 23-inch Dell computer monitor. A built-in speaker beneath the monitor was facing the subject and was used to present the auditory stimuli. The subjects were asked to sit still, limiting their ocular and facial movements to a minimal. A total of 160 trails were performed by the subject in 4 runs. Subjects rested for 1–2 min between each run.

Each run consisted of 40 trials, and the trials were done in pairs of listening to either the high or the low music scale followed by the auditory imagination of the music scale that was just presented (high scale listening was followed by high scale imagination; low scale listening was followed by low scale imagination). 20 pairs of trails were performed in random order.

At the beginning of the first trial of the pair, a white cross ("+") appeared at the center of the black screen. After 3 s, either the high or the low music scale was auditorily presented to the subject. At 5.2 s, the screen turns black and the subject relaxed for 2 s, followed by an additional random rest period of 0 to 2 s to avoid adaptation. For the second trail of the pair, the same procedure is performed, except a faint 'pop' cue sound is played for 0.2 s to prompt the subject to begin imagining the music scale they just heard in the trial before. This procedure is shown visually in Fig. 2.

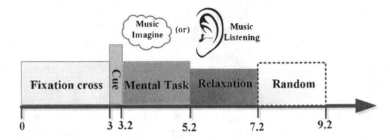

**Fig. 2.** Experiment protocol, subjects are instructed to perform music listening task or music imagination task during the mental task period. Each music listening task is followed by corresponding music imagination task, i.e. high scale listening is followed by high scale imagination after the next trial, and also to low scale music. After the music imagination trial, the next music listening trial will be presented randomly.

### EEG Data Processing

EEG signals were visually inspected and trails contaminated with muscle or eye movement activities were removed. A minimum of 35 out of 40 trials remained. The artifact-free EEG was re-referenced according to the average referencing method. Time-frequency decomposition of each trial along each EEG channel was undertaken to construct the spatio-spectral-temporal structure according to the predefined mental tasks. It was calculated every 200 ms with a hanning tapper, convoluted with a modified sinusoid basis in which the number of cycles linearly changed with frequency to achieve proper time and frequency resolution. The $R^2$ index was calculated based on the above spatio-spectral-temporal structures between different mental tasks, and used to locate the components of different EEG channels for the classification of the two corresponding mental tasks. The Discriminative Brain Pattern (DBP) was defined as a topographic plot of the $R^2$ index, which was averaged along the task-line time interval mentioned above, and along certain frequency bands, such as alpha of [8 13] Hz, beta of [13 26] Hz.

### Algorithm and Performance Evaluation

Spatial filtering technique was adopted for both reducing the number of channels and for enhancing the feature discrimination between different mental tasks. The spatial filters were determined with the Common Spatial Pattern (CSP) procedure, which has been extensively validated for BCI. The log variance of the first three and last three components of the spatially filtered signals were chosen as feature vectors, and linear discriminative analysis (LDA) was used for classification. During the online experiment, spatial filters and LDA parameters were retrained at every trial, i.e., the classification of the current trial was based on the 40 previous trials in the previous run and trials before the current trial in the same run.

As the most discriminative frequency bands are highly subject-dependent, the bands were selected as: lower alpha [8 10] Hz ($\alpha-$), upper alpha [10 13] Hz ($\alpha+$), lower beta [13 20] Hz ($\beta-$), upper beta [20 26] Hz ($\beta+$), alpha [8 13] Hz ($\alpha$), beta [13 26] Hz ($\beta$), alpha-beta [8 26] Hz ($\alpha\beta$), and [10 16] Hz ($\eta$, good for some subjects to our experience). A fourth- order Butterworth filter was applied to the raw EEG signals before the

CSP spatial filtering. A $10 \times 10$ fold cross-validation was utilized to evaluate the BCI performance among different frequency bands, and for selecting the sub-optimal frequency band.

## 3  Results

**Discriminative Brain Pattern Between Low and High Music in Listening and Imagination**

$R^2$ value distribution in spatial-spectral-temporal space with respect to music listening and imagination from subject s1 was presented as shown in Fig. 3. The discrimination information was mainly concentrated in the frontal cortex and laid between 20 to 35 Hz frequency range.

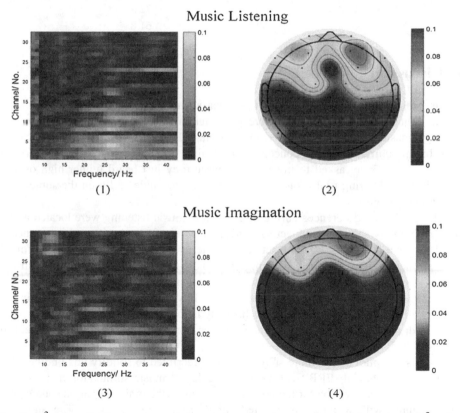

**Fig. 3.** $R^2$ value distribution in spatial-spectral-temporal space from subject s1. *(1)* $R^2$ value distribution across frequency and spatial domains in music listening task ($R^2$ was averaged along the temporal dimension corresponding to the third–fifth seconds from the beginning of the trial), the color bar indicates the $R^2$ values. *(2)* Topoplot of $R^2$ averaged between 25 and 30 Hz (Discriminative Brain Pattern) with respect to music perception task. *(3)* $R^2$ value distribution across frequency and spatial domains in music imagination task. *(4)* Topoplot of $R^2$ averaged between 25 and 30 Hz with respect to music imagination task. (Color figure online)

**Classification Performance of the Potential Music Imagination BCI System**

EEG signals during the mental task period were extracted for listening and imagination classes, and the first to third seconds from the beginning of the trial was extracted for idle state classes. The classification results between high and low pitch during the music listening are outlined in the second column of the Table 1; the classification results between high and low pitch during the music imagination are outlined in the third column; the results between Idle state and Imagination state are presented in the fourth column.

**Table 1.** Classification between low and high music

| Subject | Low vs. high music listening (%) | Low vs. high music imagination (%) | Music imagination vs. idle state (%) |
|---------|----------------------------------|------------------------------------|--------------------------------------|
| S1 | 77.0 | 82.8 | 73.7 |
| S2 | 70 | 62.3 | 72.8 |
| S3 | 53.1 | 75.5 | 61.8 |

## 4 Discussion

In this preliminary study, we have shown that an independent BCI based on music imagination is possible upon music perception training. The classification between low and high music imagination resulted in an average BCI performance of 73.5% accuracy. In this current proof-of-concept investigation, the subjects first listened to the music and then were asked to imagine the music they just heard (either high or low scale) in the following trial. This was done in order to guide and train the subjects in their music imagery.

The oscillation differences during high and low music listening were located at the frontal cortex as shown in subject s1, and the reactive frequency range was concentrated between 20 and 35 Hz. The activation patterns in music imagination were found to be similar to those in music listening. This indicates that it is possible to train the subject's music imagination through guided music listening followed by music imagination recall of the previously heard music. It was unexpected that the oscillation difference between high and low music listening is located at the frontal cortex instead of the auditory cortex [18], but a greater number of subjects in the future will help to explain this discrepancy.

As this is a pilot study, more subjects will be recruited to solidify this finding. The event related potential (ERP) with respect to different music stimulation and also the instructing void cue will be further analyzed to localize the brain activation source, and ERP features will also be investigated for discrimination analysis. The subject's musical experience and musical background may also play a significant role in the subject's ability to use music imagination BCI control. The subject's engagement in the music and personal preference may also come into play [16]. These will be taken into consideration in future data collection and analysis. The ultimate goal is to provide a way for subjects to use music imagery to control a BCI independent of the music listening cue prior to imagery.

There are a few limitations to this study, such that there is no control over the quality of the subjects' music imagery. Further, the subject's motivation level can also skew the results, such that if the subject was not motivated, the effect would be smaller [16].

In summary, the current work found a reactive frequency range concentrated between 20 and 35 Hz. The activation patterns in music imagination were found to be similar to those in music listening.

# 5  Conclusion

In this work, we have shown that imagination of low and high scale music can be discriminated on EEG signals and potentially be translated into a modality for independent BCI control, through providing music listening guided training. The music imagination based BCI system will expand the variety of BCI commands and hold the potential in music composition solely through brain activity.

**Acknowledgement.** We thank all volunteers for their participation in the study. This work is supported by the University Starter Grant of the University of Waterloo (No. 203859).

# References

1. Vallabhaneni, A., Wang, T., He, B.: Brain–computer interface. In: He, B. (ed.) Neural Engineering, pp. 85–121. Springer, Boston (2005)
2. He, B., Gao, S., Yuan, H., Wolpaw, J.R.: Brain–computer interfaces. In: He, B. (ed.) Neural Engineering, pp. 87–151. Springer, Boston (2013)
3. Hassanien, A.E., Azar, A.T. (eds.): Brain-Computer Interface: Current Trends and Applications, vol. 74. Springer International Publishing, Cham (2015)
4. Lesenfants, D., Habbal, D., Lugo, Z., Lebeau, M., Horki, P., Amico, E., Pokorny, C., Gómez, F., Soddu, A., Müller-Putz, G., Laureys, S., Noirhomme, Q.: An independent SSVEP-based brain-computer interface in locked-in syndrome. J. Neural Eng. **11**(3), 35002 (2014)
5. Kaufmann, T., Holz, E.M., Kübler, A.: Comparison of tactile, auditory, and visual modality for brain-computer interface use: a case study with a patient in the locked-in state. Front. Neurosci. **7**(7 July), 1–12 (2013)
6. Allison, B., McFarland, D., Schalk, G., Zheng, S., Jackson, M., Wolpaw, J.: Towards an independent brain - computer interface using steady state visual evoked potentials. Clin. Neurophysiol. **119**(2), 399–408 (2008)
7. Kevric, J., Subasi, A.: Comparison of signal decomposition methods in classification of EEG signals for motor-imagery BCI system. Biomed. Sig. Process. Control **31**, 398–406 (2017)
8. Mensh, B.D., Werfel, J., Seung, H.S.: BCI competition 2003—data set Ia: combining gamma-band power with slow cortical potentials to improve single-trial classification of electroencephalographic signals. IEEE Trans. Biomed. Eng. **51**(6), 1052–1056 (2004)
9. Kübler, A., Nijboer, F., Mellinger, J., Vaughan, T.M., Pawelzik, H., Schalk, G., McFarland, D.J., Birbaumer, N., Wolpaw, J.R.: Patients with ALS can use sensorimotor rhythms to operate a brain-computer interface. Neurology **64**(10), 1775–1777 (2005)

10. Yao, L., Sheng, X., Zhang, D., Jiang, N., Farina, D., Zhu, X.: A BCI system based on somatosensory attentional orientation. IEEE Trans. Neural Syst. Rehabil. Eng. **4320**(1), 1 (2016)
11. Ang, K.K., Guan, C., Chua, K.S.G., Ang, B.T., Kuah, C., Wang, C., Phua, K.S., Chin, Y.Z., Zhang, H.: Clinical study of neurorehabilitation in stroke using EEG-based motor imagery brain-computer interface with robotic feedback. In: 2010 Annual International Conference of the IEEE Engineering in Medicine and Biology Society, EMBC 2010 (2010)
12. Ramos-Murguialday, A., Broetz, D., Rea, M., Yilmaz, Ö., Brasil, F.L., Liberati, G., Marco, R., Garcia-cossio, E., Vyziotis, A., Cho, W., Cohen, L.G., Birbaumer, N.: Brain-machine-interface in chronic stroke rehabilitation: a controlled study. Ann. Neurol. **74**(1), 100–108 (2014)
13. Vidaurre, C., Blankertz, B.: Towards a cure for BCI illiteracy. Brain Topogr. **23**(2), 194–198 (2010)
14. Wolpaw, J.R., Birbaumer, N., McFarland, D.J., Pfurtscheller, G., Vaughan, T.M.: Brain–computer interfaces for communication and control. Clin. Neurophysiol. **113**, 767–791 (2002)
15. Koelsch, S.: Brain correlates of music-evoked emotions. Nat. Rev. Neurosci. **15**(3), 170–180 (2014)
16. Schaefer, R.S., Vlek, R.J., Desain, P.: Music perception and imagery in EEG: alpha band effects of task and stimulus. Int. J. Psychophysiol. **82**, 254–259 (2011)
17. Höller, Y., Bergmann, J., Kronbichler, M., Crone, J.S., Schmid, E.V., Thomschewski, A., Butz, K., Schütze, V., Höller, P., Trinka, E.: Real movement vs. motor imagery in healthy subjects. Int. J. Psychophysiol. **87**(1), 35–41 (2013)
18. Zatorre, R.J., Halpern, A.R.: Mental concerts: musical imagery and auditory cortex. Neuron **47**(1), 9–12 (2005)
19. Vlek, R.J., Schaefer, R.S., Gielen, C.C.A.M., Farquhar, J.D.R., Desain, P.: Shared mechanisms in perception and imagery of auditory accents. Clin. Neurophysiol. **122**(8), 1526–1532 (2011)
20. Reck Miranda, E., Sharman, K., Kilborn, K., Duncan, A.: On harnessing the electroencephalogram for the musical braincap. Sour. Comput. Music J. **27**(2), 80–102 (2003)

# An Experimental Study on Usability of Brain-Computer Interaction Technology in Human Spaceflight

Shanguang Chen[1,2(✉)], Jin Jiang[2], Jiabei Tang[3], Xuejun Jiao[2],
Hongzhi Qi[3], Yong Cao[2], Chunhui Wang[2], and Dong Ming[3]

[1] China Manned Space Agency, Beijing, China
shanguang_chen@126.com
[2] National Key Laboratory of Human Factors Engineering,
China Astronaut Research and Training Center, Beijing, China
[3] Tianjin University, Tianjin, China

**Abstract.** Over the past few decades, the extensive development of human-computer interaction has greatly improved the life of human beings. As a novel form of human-computer interaction (HCI), brain-computer interface (BCI) has shown its potential application values in some special areas such as mental typing, rehabilitation engineering, etc. It is known that the astronauts in space, especially in long duration spaceflight, are always occupied to deal with many complicated tasks. More effective HCI devices are required to aid astronauts to fulfill their tasks with lower mental workload. The rising of new HCI technologies including BCI may provide promising solutions for this problem. We took the advantages of China Tiangong-2 Space Lab in Nov. 2016 to carry out on-orbit experiments to examine the usability of BCI in space and factors influencing BCI performance. The experiment design adopted three typical paradigms of BCI including event-related potential (ERP) based BCI, motor imagery (MI) based BCI, and steady-state visual evoked potential (SSVEP) based BCI. Besides, three different experiment environments: normal experiment, simulated on-orbit experiment and real on-orbit experiment were conducted to compare the changing of physiological responses and BCI performance between ground and space. Thirty-five health participants took part in the normal experiment and simulated on-orbit experiment. Furthermore, the real on-orbit experiment was carried out in Tiangong-2 space lab in November 2016, and two crewmembers completed the tests as scheduled. The experimental results indicated that machine noise had significant effect on performance of P300 based BCI and MI based BCI between normal experiment and simulated on-orbit experiment. Additionally, negative emotion had significant effect on the performance of MI based BCI. Besides, the difference between average accuracy of normal experiment and on-orbit experiment was not significant. From the aspect of brain response, few differences were observed over the three BCI paradigms in the three experimental conditions. The results suggest that BCI technology is a very competitive ways of HCI which could be used in future space missions, however, further improvements are needed in both BCI hardware and adaptive algorithms for better performance.

© Springer International Publishing AG 2017
D.D. Schmorrow and C.M. Fidopiastis (Eds.): AC 2017, Part II, LNAI 10285, pp. 301–312, 2017.
DOI: 10.1007/978-3-319-58625-0_22

**Keywords:** Brain-computer interaction (BCI) · Human-computer interaction (HCI) · Human spaceflight · BCI usability

# 1    Introduction

Human-Computer Interface (HCI) focuses on developing the interfaces between users and computers. The first known use of the term HCI was in 1975, proposed by Carlisle [1]. Sometimes, HCI also refers to the same concept Human-Machine Interface (HMI). Specifically, the Association for Computer Machinery (ACM) defines human-computer interaction as "a discipline concerned with the design, evaluation and implementation of interactive computing systems for human use and with the study of major phenomena surrounding them" [2]. The keyboard-display is a traditional HCI system. Printers can input command by keyboard. After receiving the command, the operating system executes at once, and the executed result will display on the displayer. With the rapid development of computer science, the functions of HCI system are becoming more and more abundant, so are the interaction patterns between human and machine.

Over the past few decades of HCI development, human beings have entered into the world of intelligent HCI. HCI technology greatly improved the life of human beings, especially with the birth of brain-computer interface (BCI) technology. A major focus of BCI efforts is to allow a direct communication pathway between an enhanced or wired brain and an external device. In detail, a BCI system can translate signals generated by brain activities into control signals to allow commanding specific devices that could help patients communicate with the external environment without the participation of muscles [3]. Most widely-used BCI systems are established based on electroencephalogram (EEG), which is mainly divided into two patterns: spontaneous EEG or evoked EEG. From the perspective of experimental paradigm, there are mainly three typical BCI paradigms including motor imagery (MI) [4, 5], steady-state visually evoked potential (SSVEP) [6, 7] and event-related potential (ERP) [8, 9]. These different BCI paradigms have broad applications in many aspects, such as mental typewriting, rehabilitation engineering and augmented cognition. Nowadays, the technology of BCI is showing its enormous potential in the field of manned space.

With the steady progress of China's manned space project, the space flight time will continue to be extended, as well as the space mission will continue to be more complex in the future, which makes the cooperation pattern between astronauts and external equipment be constantly deepening. Therefore, breaking through the limitation of traditional human-computer information access and establishing new human-computer information interaction technology will be an inevitable trend of the future manned space development. Fortunately, the rising of brain-computer interface (BCI) as well as some other novel interaction technologies provide a promising solution for this problem.

However, the environment in space is so severe that the application of BCI in space environment will face great challenges. Specifically, weightlessness will cause bone loss and muscle atrophy; hypoxia will cause fatigue and even nausea and vomiting; and the change of space pressure makes the movement of astronauts become inconvenient. Different kinds of machine noise, as well as the negative emotion [10] of the astronauts themselves will also have interference on the task performance [11]. Thus, whether the BCI technology on ground still works in the space needs to be verified by experiments, while no related study has been reported so far. Aiming at this problem, this study implemented three typical BCI paradigms including ERP- BCI, MI-BCI and SSVEP-BCI, and explored the distinction of BCI between ground and space from the perspective of system performance and EEG responses.

# 2 Materials and Method

## 2.1 Participants

Thirty-five healthy participants (23 aged 25–33, and 12 aged 36–50) that owns the similar age and education level with astronauts of China took part in the normal experiment and simulated experiment. Additionally, two Chinese astronauts took part in the real on-orbit experiment. All of the participants and the two astronauts had normal hearing and normal or corrected-to-normal vision. All the participants and the two astronauts are novices of BCI.

## 2.2 Experimental Paradigm

In this study, three widely-used BCI paradigms described above were adopted. The three paradigms were implemented in the same software platform, as shown in Fig. 1.

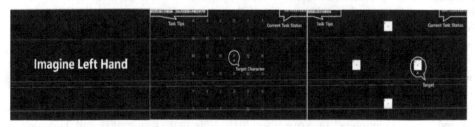

A. Interface of MI-BCI    B. Interface of ERP-BCI    C. Interface of SSVEP-BCI

**Fig. 1.** The interface of the Experimental software platform

Specifically, a P300-Speller proposed by Farwell and Donchin in 1988 [12] was taken as ERP-BCI. In this paradigm, a 6 * 6 character matrix was presented on the screen, with a random sequence of 12 flashes consisting of 6 rows and 6 columns that constitutes an Oddball-Paradigm [13]. The participants were required to sit in a comfortable state, and attending to the target character on the screen. Thus, when subjects caught the target stimuli, a P300 response emerged. In a word, this paradigm recognized the selected character of participants by distinguishing the difference between target and non-target stimuli.

SSVEP is a characteristic potential produced by modulation of the periodic visual stimuli. Specifically, when the subjects received a periodic flicker stimulation, the corresponding frequency modulated signal is generated in occipital region. Generally, visual stimuli frequency of 6–50 Hz could be used to induce SSVEP response. The first SSVEP-based BCI system was proposed by Gao et al. [18]. SSVEP-BCI technology aroused wide concern because of its high information transfer rate (ITR). Recently, SSVEP-BCI has been widely applied to the mental typewriting [19], intelligent wheelchair control [20] and computer games [21]. In this study, four squares flashing at 7 Hz, 9 Hz, 13 Hz, 15 Hz respectively were used as the SSVEP stimuli.

MI-BCI is based on sensorimotor rhythms (SMRs). SMRs was the fluctuation of the electromagnetic field recorded in the sensory motor cortex (posterior frontal and parietal lobe) [14–16]. The typical SMRs signal can be divided into three main bands: alpha/mu (8–12 Hz), beta (18–30 Hz), gamma (30–200 Hz or more). Previous researches had proved that SMRs changed with the change of motor behaviors. Specifically, the power of mu rhythm will weaken during the motor behaviors. This phenomenon was called event-related desynchronization (ERD) [17]. Besides, the ERD happened while participants are imagining the movements as well. MI-BCI was proposed based on this principle. In current study, left hand and right hand imaging were adopted as two MI commands.

### 2.3 Experimental Procedure

As mentioned above, three different experiments including normal experiment, simulated on-orbit experiment and real on-orbit experiment were implemented in this study in order to compare the difference of BCI system performance and EEG responses between ground and space. In detail, normal experiment means the general experiment on the ground; simulated on-orbit experiment is carried out on the ground space capsule, which introduced the interference of machine noise and negative emotions. In addition, the noise used in the simulated on-orbit experiment was acquired from Tiangong-1 in real space, and the intensity of the recorded noise was about 60 dB. The negative emotions were induced by negative videos. Real on-orbit experiment was carried out in Tiangong-2 in November 2016. Note that, Tiangong-1 and Tiangong-2 are the first target spacecraft and the first space laboratory of China respectively.

The experimental paradigm was developed by C# and MATLAB. Participants were instructed to sit in a comfortable position and keep their eyes staring at the center of the screen, with minimum eye movements or any other muscle artifacts throughout the whole experiment. The experiments are carried out in both offline and online, but only offline data was analyzed. The whole experiment procedure was indicated in Fig. 2. There were four groups of experiments in total, and each group mainly consisted of three parts: P300-BCI, SSVEP-BCI and MI-BCI in time order. In P300-BCI section, five characters were chosen, and each character should repeats 10 times. then the SSVEP-BCI was implemented. After one minute of relax, 16 motor imagery instructions (8 left and 8 right in random sequence) were carried out. Each group lasts about 10 min, with 1 min for relax between groups. The experiment lasts 46 min in total. In addition, the experiments repeat four times, with a control-experiment on ground

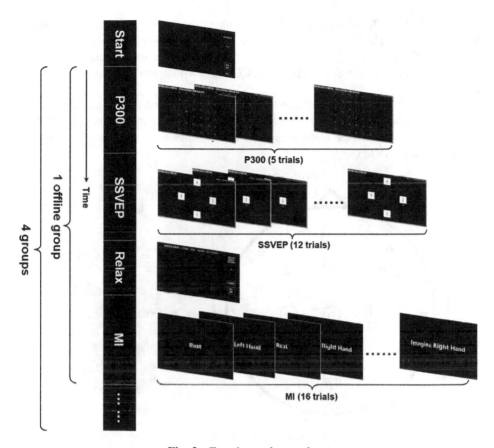

**Fig. 2.** Experimental procedure

before the astronauts step into the space, and three on-orbit experiments on the 3rd day, 13th day and 23rd day on orbit.

## 2.4  Data Acquisition and Processing

The EEG signals were recorded from 11 Ag/AgCl scalp electrodes placed according to Fig. 3, and amplified by a B-Alert X10 amplifier with a sampling rate of 256 Hz. During the data acquisition, all channels were referenced to the average of electrode REF1 and REF2. Electrode impedances were kept below 40 KΩ during data acquisition.

For ERP-BCI, the data were filtered with a 0.5–15 Hz band-pass filter. Following each flash, a time window of 700 ms of EEG data, was obtained from each of the 9 electrode channels and down sampled to a rate of 20 Hz. The down sampled features were concatenated across the channels to obtain a feature vector as the input of a linear discriminative analysis (LDA) classifier.

For SSVEP-BCI, the data were filtered with a filter bank of 10 band-pass filters (4–80 Hz, 11–80 Hz, 18–80 Hz, 25–80 Hz, 32–80 Hz, 39–80 Hz, 46–80 Hz, 53–80 Hz, 60–80 Hz, 67–80 Hz). Data of 5 s after the stimulus onset were taken as the features. A canonical correlation analysis (CCA) algorithm was used to recognize the target frequency.

For MI-BCI, the data were filtered with an 8–30 Hz band-pass filter. Data of 4 s after the cue onset were taken as the features. A common spatial pattern (CSP) filter was adopted to enhance the features and the new features were classified by a support vector machine (SVM).

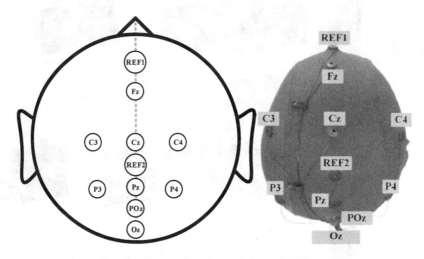

**Fig. 3.** Channel location and the real EEG cap

## 3    Results

### 3.1    Normal Experiment vs Simulated on-Orbit Experiment

The comparison results between normal experiment and simulated on-orbit experiment are summarized as follows:

For ERP-BCI, the classification accuracy is 0.75 in the normal experiment condition, 0.71 in the simulated on-orbit experiment with the machine noise, and 0.70 with the negative emotion. Furthermore, for comparison between normal experiment and simulated on-orbit experiment with machine noise, t-test result indicates that the difference of classification accuracy is significant: $p = 0.03 < 0.05$; for comparison between normal experiment and negative emotion introduced simulated on-orbit experiment, t-test result indicates that the difference of classification accuracy is not significant: $p = 0.85 > 0.05$. T-test results of P300 amplitude and latency in either comparison between normal and simulated on-orbit experiment with noise or comparison between normal and negative emotion introduced simulated on-orbit experiment were not significant.

For SSVEP-BCI, the classification accuracy is 0.70 in the normal experiment condition, 0.73 in the simulated experiment with noise, and 0.69 with negative emotion. Furthermore, for system performance, t-test results demonstrate that neither the effect of noise nor negative emotion was significant ($p > 0.05$). Moreover, for signal to noise ratio (SNR), t-test result indicates no significant difference as well ($p > 0.05$).

For MI-BCI, the classification accuracy is 0.87, 0.84 and 0.83 corresponding to the 3 experiments respectively. Furthermore, for comparison between normal experiment and simulated experiment with noise, t-test result indicates that the difference of classification accuracy is significant: $p = 0.02 < 0.05$; for comparison between normal experiment and negative emotion introduced simulated experiment, t-test result is significant as well: $p = 0.03 < 0.05$. However, no significant difference was observed from the aspect of brain response.

It can be inferred that the machine noise and negative motion have little effect on the selected three typical paradigms of BCI. The usability of BCI for on-orbit was preliminarily proved. However, whether the three paradigms are usable in zero-gravity environment or not still needs the verification of experimental data in Tiangong-2.

## 3.2   Normal Experiment vs Real Experiment on-Orbit P300-BCI

Figure 4 shows the change of average recognition rate with the number of repetitions. The left part of Fig. 4 represents the experimental result of astronaut 1, and the right represents astronaut 2. As depicted in Fig. 4, the recognition rate increased with the rising of the repetition number for both astronaut 1 and 2. In detail, for astronaut 1, the classification accuracy on ground was 1.00 when the repetition times was ten. The classification accuracy of the experiment on orbit was 0.90, 0.95 and 0.95 for the first, second and third experiment respectively. For astronaut 2, the classification accuracy of the experiment on ground was 0.90 when the repetition times was ten. The classification accuracy of the experiment on orbit was 1.00, 1.00 and 0.95 for the first, second and third experiment respectively. We can conclude that the average system performance for experiment on ground and orbit are 0.95 and 0.96 respectively. The system

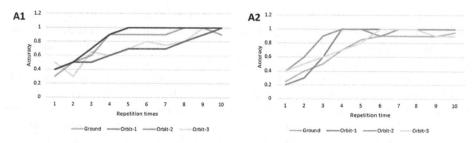

**Fig. 4.** Average recognition rates with changing repetition times. A1 and A2 are the experimental results of astronaut 1 and 2 respectively. Ground, Orbit-1, Orbit-2 and Orbit-3 represent the experiment on the ground, experiment on the 3rd day on-orbit, experiment on the 13th day on-orbit, experiment on the 23rd day on-orbit respectively.

performance of BCI between ground and orbit shows little difference. It demonstrates that P300 based BCI can be applied to on-orbit environment.

Figure 5 shows the amplitude and latency of P300 component in ERP. According to the figure, main conclusions can be summarized as follows: From the aspect of P300 amplitude, no obvious regularity was observed for astronaut 1 or 2. Besides, compared with that of astronaut 2, the P300 amplitude of astronaut 1 showed weak variety. From the aspect of latency, no obvious regularity was observed as well. Specifically, latency of astronaut 1 decreases at first, and then increases. While latency of astronaut 2 increases for a little bit and then decreases continuously.

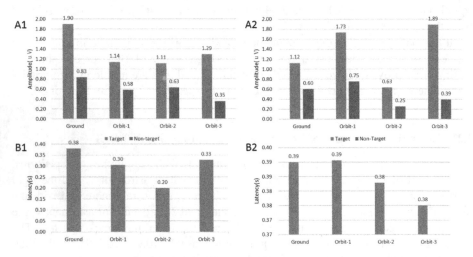

**Fig. 5.** The P300 amplitudes and latencies of the two astronauts. A1 and A2 represent the amplitude of astronaut 1 and 2 respectively. B1 and B2 represent the latencies of astronaut 1 and 2 respectively. Ground, Orbit-1, Orbit-2 and Orbit-3 represent the experiment on the ground, experiment on the 3$^{rd}$ day on-orbit, experiment on the 13$^{th}$ day on-orbit and experiment on the 20$^{th}$ day on-orbit respectively.

### 3.3   MI-BCI

Figure 6 displays the experiment result. The left part of Fig. 4 represents the experimental result of astronaut 1, and the right represents the experimental result of astronaut 2. For astronaut 1, MI accuracy on ground is 0.88, which is a little bit higher than that of the three on-orbit experiment: 0.74, 0.84 and 0.87 for the 3$^{rd}$ day on-orbit, 13$^{th}$ day on-orbit and 23$^{rd}$ day on-orbit respectively. Besides, the MI accuracy increases with the extension of on-orbit time. For astronaut 2, MI accuracy on ground is 0.79, which is lower than that of the three on-orbit experiment: 0.86, 0.84 and 0.85 for the 3$^{rd}$ day on-orbit, 13$^{th}$ day on-orbit and 23$^{rd}$ day on-orbit respectively. Whereas, MI accuracy on-orbit shows no obvious regularity compared with that of astronaut 1. In a word, MI accuracy of experiment on ground and on-orbit is very close. Thus, the effectiveness of MI-BCI applied to on-orbit environment was verified initiatively.

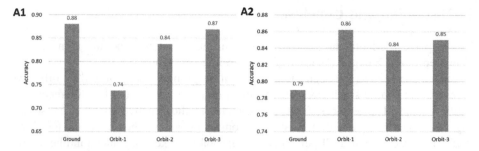

**Fig. 6.** Accuracies of the two astronauts of MI-BCI. A1 and A2 are the experimental results of astronaut 1 and 2 respectively. Ground, Orbit-1, Orbit-2 and Orbit-3 represent the experiment on the ground, experiment on the 3$^{rd}$ day on-orbit, experiment on the 13$^{th}$ day on-orbit and experiment on the 20$^{th}$ day on-orbit respectively.

### 3.4   SSVEP-BCI

Figure 7 shows the experiment result. The left part of Fig. 7 represents the experimental result of astronaut 1, and the right part represents the result of astronaut 2. For astronaut 1, the total accuracy of the experiment on ground is 0.81, which is much lower than that of the experiment on-orbit: 0.96, 1.00 and 0.96 for the 3$^{rd}$ day on-orbit, 13$^{th}$ day on-orbit and 23$^{rd}$ day on-orbit respectively. For astronaut 2, the total accuracy of the experiment on ground was 0.89, which is much lower than that of the experiment on-orbit: 1.00, 1.00, 0.96 for the 3$^{rd}$ day on-orbit, 13$^{th}$ day on-orbit and 23$^{th}$ day on-orbit respectively. Besides, the accuracy of the experiment on ground is much lower compared with that of experiment on-orbit for both astronaut 1 and 2. Therefore, we can conclude that SSVEP based BCI can be applied to on-orbit environment because of the better system performance.

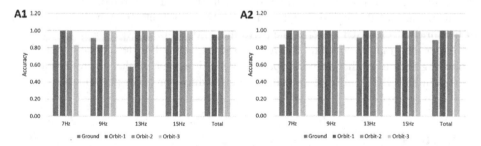

**Fig. 7.** Accuracies of the two astronauts for SSVEP-BCI. A1 and A2 are the experimental results of astronaut 1 and 2 respectively. Ground, Orbit-1, Orbit-2 and Orbit-3 represent the experiment on the ground, experiment on the 3$^{rd}$ day on-orbit, experiment on the 13$^{th}$ day on-orbit, and experiment on the 23$^{rd}$ day on-orbit respectively.

## 4   Discussion and Conclusion

This paper carried out three different experiment including experiment on ground, simulated on-orbit experiment and real on-orbit experiment.

In the comparison between the experiment on ground and simulated on-orbit, we have observed some significant differences in offline accuracy, but the differences are small. The small differences might be attributed to the negative effects of noise and negative emotions on attention processes. Some studies have shown that the top-down mechanism is crucial to BCI performance. The ability to keep the attention filter active during the selection of a target influences performance in BCI control [22].

Although the simulated experiment cannot simulate the effects of weightlessness, it excludes the effects of two major factors that may affect the performance of the BCI systems.

The results of experiment on-orbit suggests that the performance of the selected three paradigms on-orbit were close to that of experiment on ground. However, the experimental results were different between the two astronauts. For instance, astronaut 1 performed poorer on P300 and SSVEP based BCI than astronaut 2, but a better performance on MI-BCI.. This could be due to that astronaut 1 has a higher age compared with astronaut 2, which might have diminution of vision ability which is important in the P300 and SSVEP based BCI experiment.

Furthermore, we could find out that the two astronauts perform better on orbit than on ground in most cases. Two reasons may account to this phenomenon. First, the proficiency of astronauts becomes better as the number of times participating the experiment increases. Second, the zero-gravity might put some positive impact on the rhythm of EEG oscillation [23, 24]. As we have only two astronauts involved in the on-orbit experiments, the samples are apparently not enough. These hypotheses need to be further verified. In addition, it should be noted that according to the reports from the two crewmembers in Tiangong-2, some of the BCI parts were not so easy to use. Preparation time of on-orbit tests may be longer than that on ground.

In conclusion, although on-orbit environment had some effect on the brain response of the three selected BCI system. The performance of on-orbit experiment was close to or higher than that on ground. The results show that the BCI technology could be a promising HCI in further manned space mission, however, further improvements are needed in both BCI hardware and adaptive algorithms for better performance.

## References

1. Wolpaw, J.R., Birbaumer, N., Heetderks, W.J., et al.: Brain-computer interface technology: a review of the first international meeting. IEEE Trans. Rehabil. Eng. **8**(2), 164–173 (2000)
2. Carlisle, J.H.: Evaluating the impact of office automation on top management communication. In: Proceedings of the National Computer Conference and Exposition 7–10 June, pp. 611–616 (1976). doi:10.1145/1499799.1499885. Use of 'human-computer interaction' appears in references

3. Hewett, T.T., Baecker, R., Card, S., et al.: ACM SIGCHI Curricula for Human-Computer Interaction. ACM, New York (1992)

4. Wolpaw, J.R., McFarland, D.J.: Control of a two-dimensional movement signal by a noninvasive brain-computer interface in humans. Proc. Natl. Acad. Sci. U.S.A. **101**(51), 17849–17854 (2004)

5. Blankertz, B., Dornhege, G., Krauledat, M., et al.: The non-invasive Berlin brain–computer interface: fast acquisition of effective performance in untrained subjects. NeuroImage **37**(2), 539–550 (2007)

6. Cheng, M., Gao, X., Gao, S., et al.: Design and implementation of a brain-computer interface with high transfer rates. IEEE Trans. Biomed. Eng. **49**(10), 1181–1186 (2002)

7. Gao, X., Xu, D., Cheng, M., et al.: A BCI-based environmental controller for the motion-disabled. IEEE Trans. Neural Syst. Rehabil. Eng. **11**(2), 137–140 (2003)

8. Farwell, L.A., Donchin, E.: Talking off the top of your head: toward a mental prosthesis utilizing event-related brain potentials. Electroencephalogr. Clin. Neurophysiol. **70**(6), 510–523 (1988)

9. Treder, M.S., Schmidt, N.M., Blankertz, B.: Gaze-independent brain–computer interfaces based on covert attention and feature attention. J. Neural Eng. **8**(6), 066003 (2011)

10. Gumenyuk, V., Korzyukov, O., Alho, K., et al.: Effects of auditory distraction on electrophysiological brain activity and performance in children aged 8–13 years. Psychophysiology **41**(1), 30–36 (2004)

11. Zhu, Y., Tian, X., Wu, G., et al.: Emotional influence on SSVEP based BCI. In: 2013 Humaine Association Conference on Affective Computing and Intelligent Interaction (ACII), pp. 859–864. IEEE (2013)

12. Farwell, L.A., Donchin, E.: Talking off the top of your head. toward a mental prosthesis utilizing event-related brain potentials. Electroencephalogr. Clin. Neurophysiol. **70**(6), 510–523 (1988)

13. Fabiani, M., Gratton, G., Karis, D., et al.: Definition, identification, and reliability of measurement of the P300 component of the event-related brain potential. Adv. psychophysiol. **2**(S 1), 78 (1987)

14. Berger, H.: Ueber das Elektrenkephalogramm des Menschen. J. Psychol. Neurol. **94**(1), 16–60 (1931)

15. Jasper, H.H., Andrews, H.L.: Electro-encephalography: III. Normal differentiation of occipital and precentral regions in man. Arch. Neurol. Psychiatry **39**(1), 96–115 (1938)

16. Jasper, H., Penfield, W.: Electrocorticograms in man: effect of voluntary movement upon the electrical activity of the precentral gyrus. Archiv für Psychiatrie und Nervenkrankh. **183**(1–2), 163–174 (1949)

17. Rossi, G.F.: Brain stem facilitating influences on EEG synchronization experimental findings and observations in man. Acta Neurochir. **13**(2), 257–288 (1965)

18. Cheng, M., Gao, X., Gao, S., et al.: Design and implementation of a brain-computer interface with high transfer rates. IEEE Trans. Biomed. Eng. **49**(10), 1181–1186 (2002)

19. Allison, B., Luth, T., Valbuena, D., et al.: BCI demographics: how many (and what kinds of) people can use an SSVEP BCI? IEEE Trans. Neural Syst. Rehabil. Eng. **18**(2), 107–116 (2010)

20. Diez, P.F., Müller, S.M.T., Mut, V.A., et al.: Commanding a robotic wheelchair with a high-frequency steady-state visual evoked potential based brain–computer interface. Med. Eng. Phys. **35**(8), 1155–1164 (2013)

21. Chumerin, N., Manyakov, N.V., van Vliet, M., et al.: Steady-state visual evoked potential-based computer gaming on a consumer-grade EEG device. IEEE Trans. Comput. Intell. AI Games **5**(2), 100–110 (2013)

22. Riccio, A., Simione, L., Schettini, F., et al.: Attention and P300-based BCI performance in people with amyotrophic lateral sclerosis. Front. Hum. Neurosci. **7**(1), 732 (2013)
23. Schneider, S., Brümmer, V., Carnahan, H., et al.: What happens to the brain in weightlessness? A first approach by EEG tomography. Neuroimage **42**(4), 1316–1323 (2008)
24. Wollseiffen, P., Vogt, T., Abeln, V., et al.: Neuro-cognitive performance is enhanced during short periods of microgravity. Physiol. Behav. **155**, 9–16 (2016)

# A Brain-Computer Interface Based on Abstract Visual and Auditory Imagery: Evidence for an Effect of Artistic Training

Kiret Dhindsa[1]($\boxtimes$), Dean Carcone[2], and Suzanna Becker[2]

[1] School of Computational Science and Engineering,
McMaster University, Hamilton, ON, Canada
dhindsj@mcmaster.ca
[2] Department of Psychology, Neuroscience, and Behaviour,
McMaster University, Hamilton, ON, Canada
becker@mcmaster.ca

**Abstract.** Various kinds of mental imagery have been employed in controlling a brain-computer interface (BCI). BCIs based on mental imagery are typically designed for certain kinds of mental imagery, e.g., motor imagery, which have known neurophysiological correlates. This is a sensible approach because it is much simpler to extract relevant features for classifying brain signals if the expected neurophysiological correlates are known beforehand. However, there is significant variance across individuals in the ability to control different neurophysiological signals, and insufficient empirical data is available in order to determine whether different individuals have better BCI performance with different types of mental imagery. Moreover, there is growing interest in the use of new kinds of mental imagery which might be more suitable for different kinds of applications, including in the arts.

This study presents a BCI in which the participants determined their own specific mental commands based on motor imagery, abstract visual imagery, and abstract auditory imagery. We found that different participants performed best in different sensory modalities, despite there being no differences in the signal processing or machine learning methods used for any of the three tasks. Furthermore, there was a significant effect of background domain expertise on BCI performance, such that musicians had higher accuracy with auditory imagery, and visual artists had higher accuracy with visual imagery.

These results shed light on the individual factors which impact BCI performance. Taking into account domain expertise and allowing for a more personalized method of control in BCI design may have significant long-term implications for user training and BCI applications, particularly those with an artistic or musical focus.

**Keywords:** Brain-computer interface · Mental imagery · Individual differences · Performance predictors · Domain expertise · User-centred design · Auditory imagery · Visual imagery

© Springer International Publishing AG 2017
D.D. Schmorrow and C.M. Fidopiastis (Eds.): AC 2017, Part II, LNAI 10285, pp. 313–332, 2017.
DOI: 10.1007/978-3-319-58625-0_23

# 1  Introduction

Brain-computer interfaces (BCIs) allow a user to control a computerized device using their brain activity directly [53]. This is achieved by interpreting user intentions or reactions from brain recordings in real time. BCIs based on mental imagery are particularly flexible because they potentially allow for a high number of inputs, or mental commands, and because they can be implemented such that the user may issue his/her mental commands at will, rather than as a reaction to a stimulus (see for example [30,37]). Thus, mental imagery BCIs can be categorized as spontaneous BCIs (also called asynchronous BCIs) [7,13,24,31].

Further advances to mental imagery BCIs may bring a more conscious, creative, and free interactive BCI experience in the future. As signal processing and machine learning algorithms become more reliable and generalizable in translating mental commands recorded in electroencephalography (EEG) and other brain recording technologies into BCI outputs, BCI users will be able to interact with BCIs in more varied and personalized ways. However, current BCIs are much more restrictive than this. At present, BCIs are capable of recognizing only a few predetermined mental commands reliably, and users are asked to learn how to modulate specific neurophysiological signals using mental imagery which is narrowly defined by the design of the BCI itself.

Mental imagery BCIs are restricted to a few predefined mental commands because doing so simplifies the problem of translating brain activity into BCI outputs. If users are instructed to use mental images which have well-characterized neurological correlates, then the BCI will know what changes in brain activity to look for. By far the most common form of mental imagery used in BCI is motor imagery [37,49], in which the user imagines performing a specific action involving one or more parts of their body. Motor imagery is convenient in the BCI context because it is known to modulate the sensorimotor rhythm (SMR), an oscillation pattern typically in the 8–12 Hz frequency band over sensorimotor cortex (also known as the $\mu$ rhythm) [41], in a similar fashion as real motor actions [33,42]. Furthermore, different motor images can be localized spatially. For example, real and imagined left versus right hand movements result in a suppression of the SMR in a localized region on the opposite hemisphere of the brain [40]. Therefore, motor imagery lends itself to create a relatively simple mental imagery BCI.

Despite the advancement it has brought to the field, the current reliance on motor imagery to drive the development of mental imagery BCI methods and applications may be limited in the long term. Individuals vary significantly in their ability to voluntarily modulate their SMR [45,46], and the ability to modulate the sensorimotor rhythm is correlated with cognitive profile and past experience outside of the BCI context [1,9,18,19,47,52]. This may explain why an estimated 15%–25% of individuals are unable to control a BCI with motor imagery [4,22].

It has been suggested previously that making mental imagery BCIs more reliable for the general user may require more than merely training unsuccessful users to use different kinds of motor imagery or to modulate their SMR in different ways. Instead, the solution might be to allow different users to use different kinds of neurophysiological signals altogether [2]. In this study, we ask whether it is possible to use different kinds of mental imagery with a BCI designed for generalizability and to allow different users to use different specific mental imagery (we call this an Open-Ended BCI [14]). Furthermore, given that successful modulation of the SMR and successful use of BCIs based on motor imagery is at least partially dependent on individual factors, we ask whether it is also the case that success with different kinds of mental imagery depends on background experience relevant to the sensory modality used when controlling the BCI. In particular, we compare motor imagery to abstract visual imagery and abstract auditory imagery and ask whether success with any of these modalities is related to artistic or athletic background. The results of this study have potentially profound implications for BCI design and training, especially in the context of creative or artistic BCI applications.

## 2   Methods

Thirteen undergraduate and graduate participants practiced controlling an EEG-based BCI using three different kinds of mental imagery (data from three participants were excluded due to poor signal quality, so only data from ten participants are reported here). Visual imagery was used to change the size of a circle, auditory imagery was used to control the pitch of a tone, and motor imagery, used for comparison, was used to control the position of a circle on a computer display. Three 30-minute sessions were completed for one type of mental imagery over the course of one week (with some variation to accommodate the schedules of each participant) before moving to the next type of mental imagery. The order in which the three different types of mental imagery tasks were completed was counter-balanced across participants. The experiment was approved by the McMaster Research Ethics Board.

Participants were free to choose their own particular mental commands within each sensory modality. However, each participant was asked to make sure that their mental commands were very distinct and invoked rich and salient sensory imagery. Furthermore, since it was very difficult for participants to employ only one type of sensory imagery at the complete exclusion of others (e.g., as known from previous studies, it is difficult to engage in purely kinesthetic motor imagery without any accompanying visual imagery [36,48]), the requirement was only that the appropriate sensory modality was the most dominant and salient feature of each mental command. The mental commands chosen by each participant for each task are summarized in Table 2.

### 2.1   EEG Hardware

The Emotiv Epoc [16] was used to record EEG. The Epoc is a consumer-grade EEG headset previously shown to provide useful EEG but with poor signal quality compared to research-grade devices [3, 15, 25]. However, successful BCI studies have been conducted using this device in the past [10, 28].

The Emotiv Epoc is equipped with 14 saline-based electrodes with additional channels for Common Mode Sense (CMS) and Drven Right Leg (DLR) located at P3 and P4 according to the International 10–20 system (these are used for referencing and noise reduction). EEG is recorded with a sampling rate of 128 Hz and a 0.2–45 Hz bandpass filter along with 50 Hz and 60 Hz notch filters are implemented in the hardware. The electrode configuration is shown in Fig. 1.

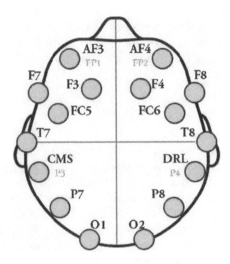

**Fig. 1.** Emotiv Epoc electrode layout. Symmetrically on each hemisphere is one electrode on visual cortex, one on parietal cortex, one on temporal cortex (with one near the border of temporal and frontal cortices), and three on frontal cortex.

## 2.2   Experimental Procedure

Before beginning the experiment, participants were asked to complete a brief questionnaire examining their background experience in the arts and in athletic activities. The questionnaire asked participants to indicate how many years of practice, how many hours per week they practice, and for their self-rated expertise in visual arts, music, and athletics/sports. The questions and responses are given in Table 3. The order of imagery tasks was then determined by counterbalancing with previous participants.

At the beginning of each session, an experimenter fit the EEG headset to the participant. Since the Emotiv Epoc does not allow for direct measurements of impedance, impedance was estimated using the proprietary toolbox that accompanies the device. In this toolbox, a colour-coded display indicates the signal quality at each electrode site. Electrodes were readjusted and saline solution was reapplied until all 14 sites showed "good" signal quality according to the proprietary software. In cases where good signal quality was especially difficult to achieve, at most two electrodes were allowed to show less than "good" signal quality.

Data collection was completed with Matlab 2013b [32], Simulink, and Psychtoolbox [8]. At the start of each session, on-screen text reiterated the description of the experiment and all necessary instructions, including instructions to avoid blinking, head/eye movements, jaw clenches, and any other muscular activity during the mental imagery period. Each session included 10 blocks of 20 trials, where each trial spanned approximately nine seconds (the structure of each trial is given in Fig. 2). The first block of every session was used for pretraining. Therefore, no classification was performed and no feedback was provided to the participant. These twenty trials were used to construct models with which to classify trials in the next block. The models were updated at the end of every block, and the newly updated models were used to classify trials in the next block.

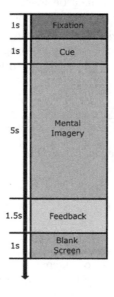

**Fig. 2.** The structure of each trial. A white fixation cross appeared for 1 s over a black background to indicate the start of a new trial. A textual cue (e.g., "low note", "shrink", "left", etc.) then appeared in white font in place of the fixation cross and persisted for 1 s. This cue was replaced by the fixation cross for 5 s, marking the mental imagery period. The feedback stimulus was then presented for 1.5 s corresponding to the classification confidence level. At the end of the trial, the screen was left blank for 1 s.

After each session, participants completed a questionnaire asking them to describe the specific mental commands used and to rate their level of interest in the task. The mental commands used by participants are summarized in Table 2. Correlational analyses comparing task interest and the accuracy of the BCI are given in Sect. 3.1.

## 2.3   EEG Processing Pipeline

Each BCI used the same processing pipeline so that performance across types of mental imagery could be fairly compared. Common spatial patterns (CSP) [34, 44] and power spectral density estimation (PSD) were used to extract features. Minimum-Redundancy Maximum-Relevance (MRMR) [39] was used for feature selection. Finally, a linear Support Vector Machine (SVM) [12] was used for binary classification.

**Feature Extraction: Common Spatial Patterns and Power Spectral Density Estimation.** CSP is a PCA-based supervised spatial filter typically used for motor imagery classification for EEG-based BCIs [34,44], but various extensions of CSP have also been used to classify other types of mental imagery in EEG (e.g., emotional imagery [21]). CSP is a supervised method that aims to construct a spatial filter which yields components (linear combinations of EEG channels) whose difference in variance between two classes is maximized.

The CSP filter $W$ is constructed with respect to two $N \times S_1$ and $N \times S_2$ EEG data matrices $X_1$ and $X_2$, where $N$ is the number of EEG channels and $S_1$ and $S_2$ are the total number of samples belonging to class one and class two respectively. The normalized spatial covariance matrices of $X_1$ and $X_2$ are then computed as follows:

$$R_1 = \frac{X_1 X_1^T}{trace(X_1 X_1^T)} \qquad R_2 = \frac{X_2 X_2^T}{trace(X_2 X_2^T)}, \tag{1}$$

where $T$ denotes the transpose operator. The composite covariance matrix is then taken using

$$R_c = R_1 + R_2. \tag{2}$$

The eigendecomposition of $R_c$

$$R_c = V \lambda V^T \tag{3}$$

can be taken to obtain the matrix of eigenvectors $V$ and the diagonal matrix of eigenvalues in descending order $\lambda$. The whitening transform

$$Q = V\sqrt{\lambda^{-1}} \tag{4}$$

is then computed so that $Q R_c Q^T$ has all variances (diagonal elements) equal to one. Because $Q$ is computed using the composite covariance matrix in Eq. 2,

$$R_1^* = QR_1Q^T \qquad and \qquad R_2^* = QR_2Q^T \tag{5}$$

have a common matrix of eigenvectors $V^*$ such that

$$R_1^* = V^*\lambda_1 V^{*T}, \qquad R_2^* = V^*\lambda_2 V^{*T}, \qquad and \qquad \lambda_1 + \lambda_2 = I, \tag{6}$$

where $I$ is the identity matrix. Hence, the largest eigenvalues for $R_1^*$ are the smallest eigenvalues for $R_2^*$ and vice versa. Since $R_1^*$ and $R_2^*$ are whitened spatial covariance matrices for $X_1$ and $X_2$, the first and last eigenvectors of $V^*$, which correspond to the largest and smallest eigenvalues in $\lambda_1$, define the coefficients for two linear combination of EEG channels which maximize the difference in variance between both classes. Given this result, the CSP filter $W$ is constructed with

$$W = (V^{*T}Q)^T \tag{7}$$

and is used to decompose EEG trials into CSP components like any other linear spatial filter:

$$C = WX_{EEG}. \tag{8}$$

For classification, $W$ can be constructed using only the top $M$ and bottom $M$ eigenvectors from $V^*$, where $M \in \{1, 2, \ldots \lfloor N/2 \rfloor\}$ is a parameter that must be chosen, or alternatively, only the top $M$ and bottom $M$ rows of $C$ can be used for feature extraction. Assuming the latter (i.e., that $W$ was constructed using all eigenvectors in $V^*$), then features $f_j$, $j = 1, \ldots 2M$, are extracted by taking the log of the normalized variance for each of the $2M$ components in $Z = \{1, \ldots M, N - M + 1, \ldots N\}$:

$$f_j = \log \left[ \frac{var(C_m)}{\sum_{i \in Z} var(C_i)} \right], \tag{9}$$

where $m \in Z$. These $2M$ features can then be used for classification.

Because CSP is a supervised spatial filter, it also allows for the estimation and visualization of the discriminative EEG spatial patterns corresponding to each class. In particular, the columns of $W^{-1}$ can be interpreted as time-invariant EEG source distributions, and are called the common spatial patterns [5,44].

This study involved three particular challenges with respect to the mental commands used by our participants: (1) a wide variety of mental commands were used between participants and between the three sensory modalities, (2) many of these mental commands were abstract and atypical for BCI use, and (3) the mental commands used by participants were not known a priori. Therefore, the EEG processing pipeline needed to cast a wide net in order to attempt to classify trials in the presence of these extra sources of variability. To do this, CSP models were computed from EEG after applying an 8–30 Hz 4th order Butterworth bandpass filter. We pre-selected $M = 2$, resulting in four CSP components and therefore four CSP features per trial. In addition to CSP features, the power of each CSP component was computed in non-overlapping 1 Hz bins, resulting in an additional 88 features per trial with which to attempt to find an optimally discriminative subset.

A total of 92 features per trial is too many for reliable classification given only a maximum of 180 trials for training, and only a small subset of these features were expected to have discriminative value. However, we could not know in advance which features would be useful because the choice of mental commands was left to the participants. In fact, it was expected that different features would be important for different types of mental imagery and for different participants, hence the need for feature selection.

**Feature Selection: Minimum-Redundancy Maximum-Relevance.** MRMR is a supervised feature selection method based on mutual information [39]. Its objective is to find a subset of features $Z$ which has maximum mutual information with the true class labels (maximum relevance) while at the same time minimizing the mutual information between the selected features themselves (minimum redundancy). MRMR was chosen for this study because its approach makes it particularly effective when the candidate features are highly correlated and where only a small subset contribute distinct discriminative information.

MRMR selects $K$ features, where $K$ is a chosen integer less than the total number of features. Features are selected from the list of candidate features sequentially. The first selected feature, $z_1$, is chosen by finding the candidate feature which has the highest mutual information with the class labels in a training set:

$$z_1 = \max_i I(F = \{f_i, i = 1, \ldots, N\}; Y), \tag{10}$$

where $f_i \in F$ are the individual candidate feature vectors in the candidate feature matrix of the training set $F$, $N$ is the total number of candidate features, $Y$ are the true class labels in the training set, and $I$ is the mutual information function. Each subsequent $k^{\text{th}}$ selected feature for $k = 2, \ldots K$ is chosen by maximizing the difference between relevance and redundancy, $D - R$, where

$$D = I(Z_k = \{z_i, i = 1, \ldots, k\}; Y), \tag{11}$$

which is estimated by

$$\bar{D} = \frac{1}{k} \sum_{z_i \in Z_k} I(z_i; Y) \tag{12}$$

in order to avoid computing potentially intractable joint probability densities, and

$$R = I(Z_k, Z_k), \tag{13}$$

which is estimated by

$$\bar{R} = \frac{1}{k^2} \sum_{z_i, z_j \in Z_k} I(z_i; z_j). \tag{14}$$

During model construction and model updates (i.e., after every block of 20 trials within each session), we test a classifier with $K = 5, 10, \ldots, 40$ and choose the model with the highest classification accuracy.

**Classification: Linear Support Vector Machine.** The linear SVM implementation from the libSVM Matlab toolbox was used [11]. In order to minimize the time between blocks, we did not optimize the SVM parameters $C$ and $G$ during model construction or model updates. The classifier, along with the CSP filter and list of selected features, was updated after every block of trials to incorporate all trials performed within that session (e.g., at the end of block 5, the models were recomputed using all of the 100 trials completed during that session). Each session was independent from previous sessions, even within the same sensory modality. New models were initialized and trained after the first block of every session without any reference to the models or trials obtained in previous sessions.

## 2.4   BCI Outputs and Feedback

Feedback was provided to participants after each trial according to the parameters given in Table 1. The feedback given was proportional to classifier confidence, where classifier confidence was the estimated probability of belonging to each class using a parametric model to fit posterior densities (see [11,26,27,43,54]). Using these probability estimates, weighted feedback could be presented between the two binary extremes for each type of mental imagery. For example, a classification decision in favour of a high tone in the auditory imagery case would result in a feedback tone with a frequency closer to the highest possible tone than the lowest possible tone. In contrast to using only binary feedback, participants were instructed to aim for maximally high tones or maximally low tones, thus training to improve classification confidence rather than just training to improve classification accuracy alone.

**Table 1.** The features of the BCI outputs for each type of mental imagery. The extreme outputs were shown during the pretraining block. In subsequent blocks, the feedback provided was somewhere in between the low and high extremes, based on classifier confidence, in the direction of the classifier's decision. Classifier confidence greater than 0.8 for either class also resulted in the extreme output.

| Imagery | Output type | Low extreme | Midpoint | High extreme |
|---------|-------------|-------------|----------|--------------|
| Motor | 100 pixel diameter white circle | −500 pixel shift | 0 pixel shift | 500 pixel shift |
| Visual | 150 pixel diameter white circle | 100 pixel diameter decrease | 0 pixel change | 100 pixel diameter increase |
| Auditory | Pure tones | 220 Hz (A3) | 440 Hz (A4) | 880 Hz (A5) |

## 2.5   Offline Analysis

Offline analysis using the Fieldtrip toolbox's [38] statistical thresholding-based artifact rejection was performed to remove trials contaminated by artifacts and reduce the risk that BCI performance could be explained by muscular activity. Visual inspection was performed after automatic artifact rejection in order to remove any trials which were not free of artifacts with high confidence. For each session, 15-fold cross-validation was performed where on each iteration all artifact-free trials belonging to that session were randomly partitioned into a training and test set (the test set contained 25% of the trials), feature extraction was performed using the same method as in online analysis (CSP filters were trained using only the training set), and a linear SVM was used.

## 3    Results

### 3.1    BCI Performance

BCI performance varied considerably across participants. Figure 3 shows the average classification accuracy of the last three blocks of each session (the last three blocks were used as an estimate of final model performance). Similarly, the results of offline analysis are shown in Fig. 4. There was no specific effect of

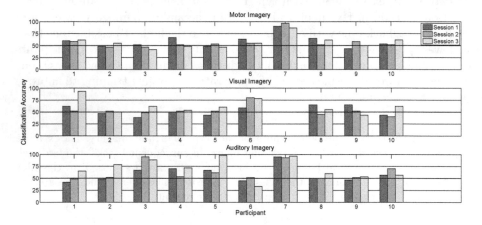

**Fig. 3.** Online classification accuracy over the final three blocks of each session. All participants and types of mental imagery are shown.

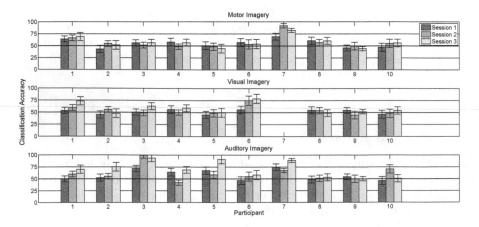

**Fig. 4.** Offline cross-validation accuracy for each session. Error bars show the standard deviation computed from all 15 cross-validation iterations.

task order ($F_{2,84} = 1.22$, $p = 0.30$) or sensory modality ($F_{2,84} = 2.39$, $p = 0.10$). However, there was weak but significant positive correlation between reported interest in the task and performance ($r = 0.28$, $p < 0.05$).

The specific mental commands performed by each participant are given in Table 2. The corresponding common spatial patterns are shown in Fig. 5.

**Table 2.** A summary of mental commands chosen by each participant for each training session. "Feedback stimulus" means the participant imagined the BCI outputs directly.

| Imagery | Motor | Visual | Auditory |
|---------|-------|--------|----------|
| P1 | Sweeping right arm/Sweeping left leg | Feedback stimulus | Piercing high note/Muffled low note |
| P2 | N/A | N/A | N/A |
| P3 | N/A | N/A | Opera singer/Chanting monks |
| P4 | Guitar chord with left hand/Slapping with right hand | Growing blue circle/Shrinking marble | Buzzy kazoo/Leonard Cohen singing |
| P5 | Boxing with right hand/Guarding with left hand | Self expanding/Shrinking a ball in hands | Jazz trumpet/Heavy metal vocals |
| P6 | Retracting hand from hot stove/Painting with brush | Moon getting closer/Car driving away | Opera singer/Chanting om |
| P7 | Punching with right hand/Stretching right arm to the left | *Withdrew from study* | Singing or playing high notes/Singing or playing low notes |
| P8 | Right hand and left hand actions (not described) | Feedback stimulus | Feedback stimulus |
| P9 | Lifting a dumbell/Dribbling a basketball | Car driving away/Balloon expanding | Bell ringing/Foghorn |
| P10 | Turning a car right/Turning a car left | Inflating a balloon/Deflating a balloon | Screeching chalkboard/Growling lion |

## 3.2  Effect of Background Experience

A significant effect of background expertise was found, as evaluated by our background experience questionnaire ($F_{2,80} = 14.0$, $p < 0.0001$, with variance explained $\omega^2 = 0.22$). Self-reported expertise in athletics, visual arts, or music was also significantly correlated with BCI performance ($r = 0.46$, $p < 0.0001$).

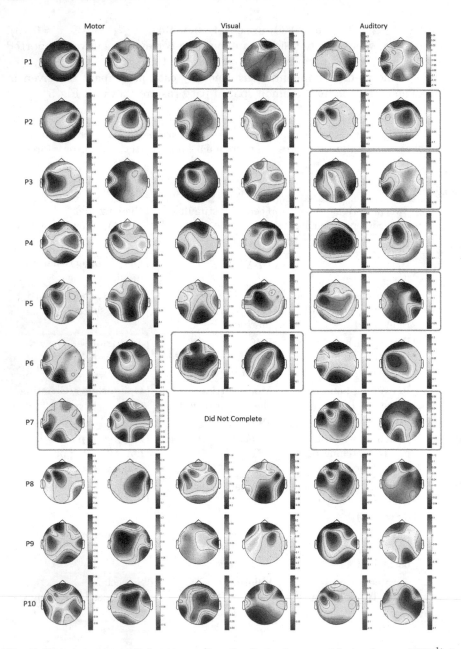

**Fig. 5.** The common spatial patterns (i.e., the first column and last column of $W^{-1}$) for the last session of each sensory modality for each participant. All trials within a session were used to construct the common spatial patterns shown here. The left pattern of each pair corresponds to the negative class (i.e., left shift, shrink, and low tone), and the right pattern corresponds to the positive class (i.e., right shift, grow, high tone). Sessions during which more than 70% classification accuracy was achieved are boxed in green. (Color figure online)

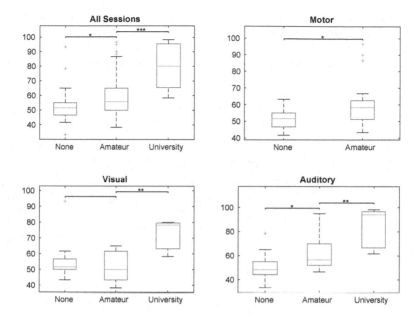

**Fig. 6.** BCI performance across sessions at varying levels of self-reported expertise in a relevant domain (athletics for motor imagery, visual art for visual imagery, and music for auditory imagery). $*p < 0.05$, $**p < 0.01$, $***p < 0.001$

BCI performance in all sessions organized by self-reported expertise in the corresponding domain is shown in Fig. 6.

## 4    Discussion and Conclusions

In this study we present two important findings which may impact how mental commands are chosen for BCI control. First, we found that by using a broad feature extraction approach, it was possible to enable user control over a BCI with abstract visual and auditory imagery, even when the specific mental commands were not known a priori. Second, it was found that participants were able to control a BCI using only one or two of the available types of mental imagery, and that this result may be related to the participant's artistic background.

### 4.1    Brain-Computer Interfacing with Abstract Mental Imagery

From Fig. 3, it can be seen that nine of out ten participants were able to achieve above chance level performance with at least one type of mental imagery on at least one session. Furthermore, eight out of ten participants achieved their best performance with 70% classification accuracy or above, where 70% is considered the minimum threshold for a communication device such as a BCI [23].

**Table 3.** Responses to the background experience questionnaire. The questionnaire asks participants to state the number of hours/week of practice, the number of years spent practicing, and a self-rating of their overall proficiency of performance level. Note that P1, P2, and P3 completed an earlier version of this questionnaire, so only their level of expertise is available.

| Imagery | Motor | | | Visual | | | Auditory | | |
|---|---|---|---|---|---|---|---|---|---|
| | Hrs/Wk | #Years | Level | Hrs/Wk | #Years | Level | Hrs/Wk | #Years | Level |
| P1 | N/A | N/A | 2 | N/A | N/A | 1 | N/A | N/A | 1 |
| P2 | N/A | N/A | 1 | N/A | N/A | 1 | N/A | N/A | 1 |
| P3 | N/A | N/A | 1 | N/A | N/A | 2 | N/A | N/A | 2 |
| P4 | 3 | 2 | 2 | 1 | 1 | 1 | 4 | 4 | 2 |
| P5 | 2 | 3 | 2 | 1 | 1 | 1 | 1 | 6 | 3 |
| P6 | 2 | 1 | 1 | 3 | 4 | 3 | 1 | 1 | 1 |
| P7 | 1 | 6 | 2 | 1 | 1 | 2 | 4 | 4 | 3 |
| P8 | 4 | 4 | 2 | 2 | 3 | 2 | 1 | 1 | 2 |
| P9 | 4 | 2 | 2 | 2 | 7 | 2 | 1 | 5 | 2 |
| P10 | 4 | 3 | 2 | 1 | 3 | 2 | 1 | 5 | 2 |

**Coding:**
- Hours/Week (*1 = less than 1 h, 2 = 1–2 h, 3 = 3–4 h, 4 = 5–10 h, 6 = 10+ h*).
- #Years (*1 = less than 1 year, 2 = 1–2 years, 3 = 3–4 years, 4 = 5–6 years, 5 = 7–8 years, 6 = 9–10 years, 6 = 10+ years*)
- Level (*1 = Do not practice/perform, 2 = Amateur, 3 = Varsity/University level, 4 = Professional*)

The results obtained through offline analysis validate the BCI performance levels achieved during the online training experiment. In several cases, classification accuracy was higher in offline analysis than in online analysis. The main differences between the two analyses were that in offline analysis trials contaminated by artifacts were removed. In addition, all trials were shuffled during offline analysis before partitioning training and test sets, resulting in the training data containing a mix of trials from different blocks of each session. These two differences together may have made offline analysis more robust than its online counterpart, but the offline analyses do suggest that BCI performance was not substantially driven by artifacts. However, it is important to note that it is possible that subvocal muscle activity, micro eye movements, or micro muscle activations impacted performance. This possibility is discussed in greater detail in Sect. 4.3.

## 4.2 Evidence for an Effect of Background Experience

It is interesting that most participants performed much better with one sensory modality compared to others. Participants most often performed best with auditory or visual imagery rather than motor imagery, even though motor imagery is usually considered simpler to classify. This might be explained by the electrode configuration of the Emotiv Epoc headset (this point is discussed further in Sect. 4.3). However, we also note that most of our participants reported having greater expertise in visual arts or music rather than in athletic performance or sports.

The differences in performance were not related to task order, perceived accuracy, or interest in each task (see Sect. 3.1). However, it was found that performance varied with background experience. Specifically, it was found that self-reported expertise or performance level in athletics/sports, visual arts, and music had an effect on BCI performance with different sensory modalities (see Sect. 3.2). While performance is also correlated with interest, which itself related to domain expertise, the effect of domain expertise specifically was stronger than the effect of interest in each task. Therefore, we conclude that domain expertise had a specific significant effect on BCI performance.

We suggest that results with a larger sample size and replication in other contexts is needed before these results should be incorporated into training humans to use a BCI. However, these results may have a profound impact on how BCI training is done. In particular, BCIs designed for artistic or creative applications, or BCIs designed to allow mental commands involving abstract visual or auditory imagery, may need to take into consideration the artistic background of its users during training. Likewise, BCIs intended as assistive or rehabilitative tools might benefit from designing for types of mental imagarey associated with any domain expertise acquired by the patient pre-injury. This observed effect of domain expertise may also have implications for BCI training more generally.

If it is indeed the case that artistic background or domain expertise more broadly has a significant impact on BCI performance, the suggestion to design BCIs which enable different users to employ different mental commands, even if different neurophysiological signals are used [14,17,35], must be examined more closely. Achieving this, however, requires the BCI community to meet the challenge of creating a truly generalizable BCI which does not need to know the kinds of mental imagery that will be used a priori.

There is also growing attention being brought to the need for improved BCI training and neurofeedback for humans [29]. While we do not explicitly present methods for this here, the results of this study may be relevant. In addition to improving methods for BCI training, the effect of background experience on BCI performance seen in the present study suggests that we should also consider which mental commands should be trained with which individuals in the first place.

The co-adaptive BCI approach is a good example of an advancement in the direction of individual-based mental command selection [50,51]. However, because it attempts to find an optimal subset of mental commands from a predefined set of choices, it cannot fully take advantage of individual factors influencing the best choice of mental commands. In order to do so with this approach would require an expontentially increasing number of combinations of mental commands to test. The BCI presented here takes a different approach to reach a similar goal. Rather than trying to find an optimal subset of mental commands from a list of mental commands, we left the choice of mental command open to the user and aimed to find an optimal set of features from a list of candidate features.

### 4.3 Limitations and Future Work

BCI performance and direct comparisons in performance between different sensory modalities or specific kinds of mental commands are limited in this study by the Emotiv Epoc hardware. The unchangeable electrode configuration of the headset is less optimal for some types of mental commands than others. In particular, no sensors are placed over locations C3 or C4, which are most commonly used to detect the sensorimotor rhythm which is modulated during motor imagery. Similarly, only two electrodes are available over the occipital cortices, which might have otherwise played a more central role in detecting visual imagery. Instead, the Emotiv Epoc relies most heavily on the frontal cortices, which may in part determine which specific mental commands were most successful. For example, perhaps mental commands with different emotional content or with differing degrees of cognitive load would be more successful with this electrode configuration, but it is not clear from descriptions of the mental commands used whether this was an explanatory factor in differences in BCI performance in this study.

The Emotiv Epoc is also known to have significantly lower a signal-to-noise ratio compared to research-grade devices [3,15,25] and to result in lower BCI performance (e.g.,[6,15], or comparing [28] and [20]). However, our aim here was not to achieve state of the art BCI performance, but rather to assess BCI performance in the context of abstract user-defined visual and auditory imagery and to compare this performance to relevant domain expertise.

It is possible that artifacts could have interfered with BCI performance in a significant way. We conducted an offline classification analysis using the same feature extraction methods and classifier as in the online experiment but included standard artifact rejection software included in the Fieldtrip toolbox [38]. We saw a slight improvement in classification accuracy, suggesting that at least common artifacts, such as eye blinks and jaw clenches, were not driving BCI performance. However, there remains the possibility that very subtle muscle activity, such as subvocal laryngeal contractions influenced BCI performance. These would require electromyography (EMG) electrodes to detect, and therefore we cannot confirm whether these significantly affected performance. We would not expect, however, that the tendency to perform subvocal laryngeal contractions or other types of muscle activity would be so highly related to domain expertise, especially given the variety of mental commands used in this study (many of which did not correspond to the actual skill participants had specific training in). Therefore, we do not expect that BCI performance was driven mainly by such subtle muscle contractions.

The exact reasons background expertise may impact BCI performance with abstract mental imagery remains unknown. It is possible that someone who is musically trained or merely innately musically talented is able to generate more salient, consistent, and rich auditory imagery than others. It is also possible that individuals who are able to produce such auditory imagery are also drawn to practising music. In addition to investigating the effect of background experience on BCI performance more broadly and with a larger sample of participants, it would be of great benefit to separate the effect of the quality (e.g., including saliency, consistency, and richness) of the mental commands themselves to see if these are highly correlated with background experience and if these factors are the primary drivers affecting the differences in BCI performance seen in this study.

**Acknowledgments.** This research was funded by a Discovery grant from the Natural Sciences and Engineering Research Council of Canada (NSERC) to SB and an NSERC PGS scholarship to KD.

# References

1. Allison, B., Luth, T., Valbuena, D., Teymourian, A., Volosyak, I., Graser, A.: BCI demographics: how many (and what kinds of) people can use an SSVEP BCI? IEEE Trans. Neural Syst. Rehabil. Eng. **18**(2), 107–116 (2010)
2. Allison, B.Z., Neuper, C.: Could anyone use a BCI? In: Tan, D.S., Nijholt, A. (eds.) Brain-Computer Interfaces, pp. 35–54. Springer, Heidelberg (2010)
3. Badcock, N.A., Mousikou, P., Mahajan, Y., de Lissa, P., Thie, J., McArthur, G.: Validation of the Emotiv EPOC EEG gaming system for measuring research quality auditory ERPs. PeerJ **1**, 2 (2013)
4. Blankertz, B., Sannelli, C., Halder, S., Hammer, E.M., Kübler, A., Müller, K.R., Curio, G., Dickhaus, T.: Neurophysiological predictor of SMR-based BCI performance. NeuroImage **51**(4), 1303–1309 (2010)
5. Blankertz, B., Tomioka, R., Lemm, S., Kawanabe, M., Muller, K.-R.: Optimizing spatial filters for robust EEG single-trial analysis. IEEE Signal Proc. Mag. **25**(1), 41–56 (2008)
6. Bobrov, P., Frolov, A., Cantor, C., Fedulova, I., Bakhnyan, M., Zhavoronkov, A.: Brain-computer interface based on generation of visual images. PLoS One **6**(6), e20674 (2011)
7. Borisoff, J.F., Mason, S.G., Bashashati, A., Birch, G.E.: Brain-computer interface design for asynchronous control applications: improvements to the LF-ASD asynchronous brain switch. IEEE Trans. Biomed. Eng. **51**(6), 985–992 (2004)
8. Brainard, D.H.: The psychophysics toolbox. Spat. Vis. **10**, 433–436 (1997)
9. Burde, W., Blankertz, B.: Is the locus of control of reinforcement a predictor of brain-computer interface performance? na (2006)
10. Carrino, F., Dumoulin, J., Mugellini, E., Khaled, O.A., Ingold, R.: A self-paced BCI system to control an electric wheelchair: evaluation of a commercial, low-cost EEG device. In: 2012 ISSNIP Biosignals and Biorobotics Conference (BRC), pp. 1–6, January 2012
11. Chang, C.C., Lin, C.J.: LIBSVM: a library for support vector machines. ACM Trans. Intell. Syst. Technol. **2**, 27:1–27:27 (2011). http://www.csie.ntu.edu.tw/cjlin/libsvm
12. Cortes, C., Vapnik, V.: Support-vector networks. Mach. Learn. **20**(3), 273–297 (1995)

13. del Millan, J.R., Mouriño, J.: Asynchronous BCI and local neural classifiers: an overview of the adaptive brain interface project. IEEE Trans. Neural Syst. Rehabil. Eng. **11**(2), 159–161 (2003)
14. Dhindsa, K., Carcone, D., Becker, S.: An open-ended approach to BCI: embracing individual differences by allowing for user-defined mental commands. In: Conference Abstract: German-Japanese Adaptive BCI Workshopp (2015). Front. Comput. Neurosci
15. Duvinage, M., Castermans, T., Petieau, M., Hoellinger, T., Cheron, G., Dutoit, T.: Performance of the Emotiv Epoc headset for P300-based applications. Biomed. Eng. Online **12**, 56 (2013)
16. Emotiv Systems. Emotiv - brain computer interface technology, May 2011. http://www.emotiv.com
17. Friedrich, E.V., Scherer, R., Neuper, C.: The effect of distinct mental strategies on classification performance for brain-computer interfaces. Int. J. Psychophysiol. **84**(1), 86–94 (2012)
18. Hammer, E.M., Halder, S., Blankertz, B., Sannelli, C., Dickhaus, T., Kleih, S., Müller, K.R., Kübler, A.: Psychological predictors of SMR-BCI performance. Biol. Psychol. **89**(1), 80–86 (2012)
19. Jeunet, C., NKaoua, B., Subramanian, S., Hachet, M., Lotte, F.: Predicting mental imagery-based BCI performance from personality, cognitive profile and neurophysiological patterns. PloS One **10**(12), e0143962 (2015)
20. Kindermans, P.-J., Verschore, H., Verstraeten, D., Schrauwen, B.: A p300 BCI for the masses: prior information enables instant unsupervised spelling. In: Advances in Neural Information Processing Systems, pp. 710–718 (2012)
21. Kothe, C.A., Makeig, S., Onton, J.A.: Emotion recognition from EEG during self-paced emotional imagery. In: Proceedings - 2013 Humaine Association Conference on Affective Computing and Intelligent Interaction, ACII, pp. 855–858 (2013)
22. Kübler, A., Müller, K.R.: An introduction to brain computer interfacing. In: Dornhege, G., del Millán, J.R., Hinterberger, T., McFarland, D., Müller, K.R. (eds.) Toward Brain-Computer Interfacing. MIT Press, Cambridge (2007)
23. Kübler, A., Neumann, N., Kaiser, J., Kotchoubey, B., Hinterberger, T., Birbaumer, N.P.: Brain-computer communication: self-regulation of slow cortical potentials for verbal communication. Arch. Phys. Med. Rehabil. **82**(11), 1533–1539 (2001)
24. Kus, R., Valbuena, D., Zygierewicz, J., Malechka, T., Graeser, A., Durka, P.: Asynchronous BCI based on motor imagery with automated calibration and neurofeedback training. IEEE Trans. Neural Syst. Rehabil. Eng.: Publ. IEEE Eng. Med. Biol. Soc. **20**(6), 823–835 (2012)
25. Lievesley, R., Wozencroft, M., Ewins, D., Lievesley, M., Wozencroft, R.: The Emotiv EPOC neuroheadset: an inexpensive method of controlling assistive technologies using facial expressions and thoughts? J. Assist. Technol. **5**(2), 67–82 (2011)
26. Lin, C.J., Weng, R.C., et al.: Simple Probabilistic Predictions for Support Vector Regression. National Taiwan University, Taipei (2004)
27. Lin, H.-T., Lin, C.-J., Weng, R.C.: A note on Platts probabilistic outputs for support vector machines. Mach. Learn. **68**(3), 267–276 (2007)
28. Liu, Y., Jiang, X., Cao, T., Wan, F., Mak, P.U., Mak, P.I., Vai, M.I.: Implementation of SSVEP based BCI with Emotiv EPOC. In: Proceedings of IEEE International Conference on Virtual Environments, Human-Computer Interfaces, and Measurement Systems, VECIMS, pp. 34–37 (2012)
29. Lotte, F., Larrue, F., Mühl, C.: Flaws in current human training protocols for spontaneous Brain-Computer Interfaces: lessons learned from instructional design. Front. Hum. Neurosci. **7**(September), 568 (2013)

30. Mak, J.N., Arbel, Y., Minett, J.W., McCane, L.M., Yuksel, B., Ryan, D., Thompson, D., Bianchi, L., Erdogmus, D.: Optimizing the P300-based brain-computer interface: current status, limitations and future directions. J. Neural Eng. **8**(2), 025003 (2011)
31. Mason, S.G., Birch, G.E.: A brain-controlled switch for asynchronous control applications. IEEE Trans. Biomed. Eng. **47**(10), 1297–1307 (2000)
32. MATLAB. Version 8.2.0 (R2013b). The MathWorks Inc., Natick, Massachusetts (2013)
33. McFarland, D.J., Miner, L.A., Vaughan, T.M., Wolpaw, J.R.: Mu and beta rhythm topographies during motor imagery and actual movements. Brain Topogr. **12**(3), 177–186 (2000)
34. Müller-Gerking, J., Pfurtscheller, G., Flyvbjerg, H.: Designing optimal spatial filters for single-trial EEG classification in a movement task. Clin. Neurophysiol. **110**(5), 787–798 (1999)
35. Neuper, C., Pfurtscheller, G.: Neurofeedback training for BCI control. In: Graimann, B., Pfurtscheller, G., Allison, B. (eds.) Brain-Computer Interfaces, pp. 65–78. Springer, Heidelberg (2010)
36. Neuper, C., Scherer, R., Reiner, M., Pfurtscheller, G.: Imagery of motor actions: differential effects of kinesthetic and visual-motor mode of imagery in single-trial EEG. Cogn. Brain. Res. **25**(3), 668–677 (2005)
37. Nicolas-Alonso, L.F., Gomez-Gil, J.: Brain computer interfaces, a review. Sensors **12**(2), 1211–1279 (2012)
38. Oostenveld, R., Fries, P., Maris, E., Schoffelen, J.M.: FieldTrip: open source software for advanced analysis of MEG, EEG, and invasive electrophysiological data. Comput. Intell. Neurosci. **2011**, 1–9 (2011)
39. Peng, H.C.: Feature selection based on mutual information criteria of max-dependency, max-relevance, and min-redundancy. IEEE Trans. Pattern Anal. Mach. Intell. **27**, 1226–1238 (2005)
40. Pfurtscheller, G., Neuper, C., Flotzinger, D., Pregenzer, M.: EEG-based discrimination between imagination of right and left hand movement. Electroencephalogr. Clin. Neurophysiol. **103**(6), 642–651 (1997)
41. Pfurtscheller, G., Lopes da Silva, F.H.: EEG event-related desynchronization (ERD), event-related synchronization (ERS). Electroencephalogr.: Basic Princ. Clin. Appl. Relat. Fields **4**, 958–967 (1999)
42. Pfurtscheller, G., Neuper, C.: Motor imagery activates primary sensorimotor area in humans. Neurosci. Lett. **239**(2), 65–68 (1997)
43. Platt, J., et al.: Probabilistic outputs for support vector machines and comparisons to regularized likelihood methods. Adv. Large Margin Classif. **10**(3), 61–74 (1999)
44. Ramoser, H., Müller-Gerking, J., Pfurtscheller, G.: Optimal spatial filtering of single trial EEG during imagined hand movement. IEEE Trans. Rehabil. Eng. **8**(4), 441–446 (2000)
45. Randolph, A.B.: Not all created equal: individual-technology fit of brain-computer interfaces. In: Proceedings of the Annual Hawaii International Conference on System Sciences, pp. 572–578 (2011)
46. Randolph, A.B., Jackson, M.M., Karmakar, S.: Individual characteristics and their effect on predicting mu rhythm modulation. Int. J. Hum.-Comput. Interact. **27**(1), 24–37 (2010)
47. Scherer, R., Faller, J., Friedrich, E.V., Opisso, E., Costa, U., Kübler, A., Müller-Putz, G.R.: Individually adapted imagery improves brain-computer interface performance in end-users with disability. PloS One **10**(5), e0123727 (2015)

48. Stinear, C.M., Byblow, W.D., Steyvers, M., Levin, O., Swinnen, S.P.: Kinesthetic, but not visual, motor imagery modulates corticomotor excitability. Exp. Brain Res. **168**(1–2), 157–164 (2006)

49. Thomas, E., Dyson, M., Clerc, M.: An analysis of performance evaluation for motor-imagery based BCI. J. Neural Eng. **10**(3), 031001 (2013)

50. Vidaurre, C., Sannelli, C., Müller, K.R., Blankertz, B.: Co-adaptive calibration to improve BCI efficiency. J. Neural Eng. **8**(2), 025009 (2011)

51. Vidaurre, C., Sannelli, C., Müller, K.-R., Blankertz, B.: Machine-learning-based coadaptive calibration for brain-computer interfaces. Neural Comput. **23**(3), 791–816 (2011)

52. Vuckovic, A., Osuagwu, B.A.: Using a motor imagery questionnaire to estimate the performance of a brain-computer interface based on object oriented motor imagery. Clin. Neurophysiol. **124**(8), 1586–1595 (2013)

53. Wolpaw, J.R., Birbaumer, N., McFarland, D.J., Pfurtscheller, G., Vaughan, T.M.: Brain-computer interfaces for communication and control. Clin. Neurophysiol. Official J. Int. Fed. Clin. Neurophysiol. **113**(6), 767–791 (2002)

54. Ting-Fan, W., Lin, C.-J., Weng, R.C.: Probability estimates for multi-class classification by pairwise coupling. J. Mach. Learn. Res. **5**(Aug), 975–1005 (2004)

# Brain-Computer Interfaces (BCI) Based 3D Computer-Aided Design (CAD): To Improve the Efficiency of 3D Modeling for New Users

Yu-Chun Huang[1(✉)] and Kuan-Lin Chen[2]

[1] Graduate Institute of Design Science, Tatung University,
No. 40, Sec. 3, Zhongshan N. Road, Taipei, Taiwan
ych@ttu.edu.tw
[2] Department of Electrical Engineering, National Taiwan University,
No. 1, Sec. 4, Roosevelt Road, Taipei, Taiwan
b00204005@ntu.edu.tw

**Abstract.** In current HCI interfaces (keyboard, mice, gesture and pen), users must learn a variety of different ways to achieve the same commend in 3D modeling in different softwares (such as Maya, 3D studio Max and Rihno). For instance, to achieve the frequently used commands, such as rotating and zoom in/zoom out, users have to memorize the multiple hotkey (keyboard + mice) or use the graphic icon to perform these actions. Moreover, it would be even more inconvenient if you cross different 3D modeling softwares (Maya and 3D studio Max). The rotation function hotkeys are totally different even if there are designed in the same company (Autodesk). To increase the efficiency of 3D modeling, the CAD users usually need to memorize complicated hotkey combinations for different softwares. Hence, the challenge of this research is to generate a universal, intuitive and natural way to perform the "rotate" and "zoom in/out" command in 3D CAD modeling. Also, this alternative "rotate" and "zoom in/out" input can be widely applied to other 3D CAD softwares. We create a "BCI embedded CAD" prototype that connects EPOC+ to maxscript (3D studio Max). Through the system, the user is able to enhance the ability in 3D modeling through "thinking the commends". In the future study, the BCI embedded CAD can be modified as a cross-platform 3D CAD manipulation that enables users to use imagination to control 3D modeling in different softwares (Maya, 3D studio Max, and Rihno) rather than traditional text-based commands or graphical icons.

**Keywords:** Human-computer interaction interface · Brain-computer interface · Computer-aided design

## 1 Introduction

Sculpturing a physical model in real world is easy and common for a designer. However, in the 20th century, with the development of "Computer-Aided Design/ Computer-Aided Manufactured (CAD/CAM)" (Lichten 1984), modeling has increased efficiently, but other problems came along to untrained users: the users need to learn

© Springer International Publishing AG 2017
D.D. Schmorrow and C.M. Fidopiastis (Eds.): AC 2017, Part II, LNAI 10285, pp. 333–344, 2017.
DOI: 10.1007/978-3-319-58625-0_24

how to use the 3D software via complicated and inconvenient interfaces, especially for the novices. Thus, researchers focus on the 3D input problem for many years (Aish 1979; Lim 2003; Dickinson et al. 2005; Jackie Lee et al. 2006). Aish (1979) aiming that 3D input systems should be able to create and modify 3D geometry intuitively in order to interpret and evaluate the spatial qualities of a design directly. However, in the 1980s, the CAD interface was limited to text-based commands; in the 1990s, it was limited to the windows, icons, menu and pointers-based (WIMP) and text hybrid dominated CAD system. We can see that in most 3D modeling systems, text-based command system and Graphic-User Interfaces (GUIs) are still the mainstream.

The keyboard and mice are essential for users to type in and select commands since the first CAD software—"Sketchpad" (Sutherland 1964), to recent CAD softwares —"Maya", "3D studio Max" and "Rihno". In order to create a more intuitive and friendly interface for users, Ishii and Ullmer (1997) suggested a new concept Tangible-User Interfaces (TUIs), which was able to create a seamless interaction across physical interfaces and digital information. Jackie Lee et al. (2006) proposed a TUI based "iSphere" to act as a hand sensor to manipulate 3D modeling in a realistic and spatial way. Lee and Ishii (2010) created a "Beyond and Collapsible pen" system, which was able to use gesture and pen tool to manipulate 3D model. Also, to increase the 3D modeling efficiency, Sharma et al. (2011) developed "MozArt" based on speaking, touching, and a toolbar/button-less interface for creating computer graphics models.

On the other side, Brain-computer interface (BCI) has been applied to the various fields: psychology recognition research from the original brainwaves (Paller and Kutas 1992), BCI embedded robot arm control through the imagination (Chapin et al. 1999; Lebedev and Nicolelis 2006), BCI game (Krepki et al. 2007), Virtual Reality (VR) navigation (forward and backward, left and right) through the imagination (Leeb et al. 2004) and BCI embedded smart space design (Huang 2006, 2011).

## 2   Problem and Objective

Different softwares usually have a variety of different ways to reach same commend functions. For instance, the ways of commending simple and frequently used functions, such as rotating and zoom in/zoom out object" are totally different in Maya, 3D studio Max and Rihno (Fig. 1). Moreover, it is even more challenging if crossing different 3D modeling softwares, such as between Maya and 3D studio Max, is required. Users are required to either memorize the multiple hotkey (keyboard + mice) or use the graphic icon to finish the action. This could sometimes be confusing and time-consuming. To increase the efficiency of 3D modeling, CAD users usually memorize complicated hotkey combinations for different softwares.

Hence, the goal of this research is to develop a more intuitive and natural way of commending frequently used functions in 3D CAD modeling across different softwares. We combine BCI into CAD system to generate a user-friendly interface in 3D CAD manipulation (see Fig. 2). By monitoring brainwaves emitted when intending to

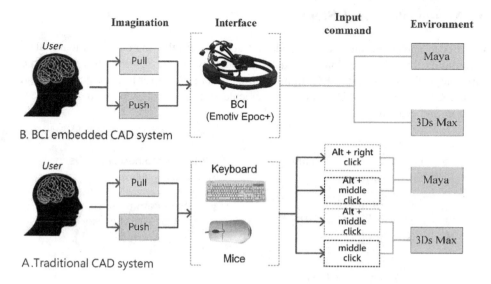

**Fig. 1.** Comparison between BCI CAD system and traditional CAD system

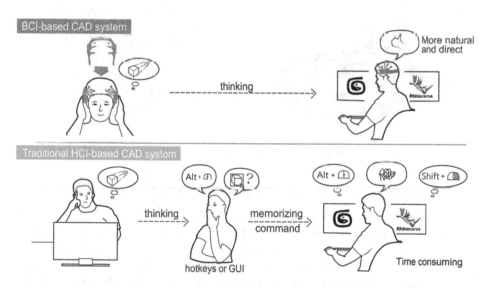

**Fig. 2.** Concept of BCI-CAD system

perform different commands, users are able to intuitively control 3D rotation, and room in/out command through imagination rather than relying on the traditional input commands (keyboard + mice or graphical icons).

# 3  Methodology and Steps

In order to implement the "BCI embedded CAD" system that the users can manipulate commands through "imagination", the methodology of the research is divided into three steps: the first step, the BCI training process via EPOC+ for new users; the second step, BCI embedded CAD system implementation; the third step, scenario demonstration and evaluations.

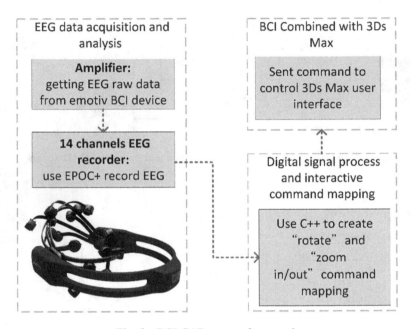

**Fig. 3.**  BCI-CAD system framework

## 3.1   The First Step: BCI Training Process via EPOC+ for New Users

For the past BCI devices, a long time training process is mandatory for users' brainwaves to be recognized at high accuracy. To ensure that the EPOC+ can be adapted quickly and widely for every users, the first step of this research is to find out how to create a short and effective training process for new users. After the training process, the users should achieve 90% accurate rate to control virtual objects in the 3D environment.

## 3.2   The Second Step: System Implementation

This step divided into three parts: EEG data acquisition and analysis, digital signal process and interactive command mapping and BCI combined with 3Ds Max by using C++ and maxscript (see Fig. 3).

### 3.3    The Third Step: Scenario Demonstration and Evaluations

In order to demonstrate the system prototype, the subjects are asked to build a box and try to use imagination command to zoom in/out the box in 3Ds Max. To evaluate the BCI-CAD efficiency, we created two different experiments to demonstrate the system.

## 4    BCI Training Process via EPOC+ for New Users

### 4.1    EPOC+ Installation

In the first part, in order to acquire accurate signal, the subjects follow the steps to install the EPOC+ system (see Fig. 4). First, the user has to wear the EPOC+ to his head. Second, the user opens the EPOC+ software to check the contact quality of each sensor (see Fig. 4-A). The sensor electrode figures correspond to the quality of the contact quality: from green, yellow, orange, red and black indicating high to low quality. Third, the user starts to train the neutral and command (push, pull, left or right) brainwaves (see Fig. 4-B). Forth, the user tries to use imagination command to move the virtual box (see Fig. 4-C).

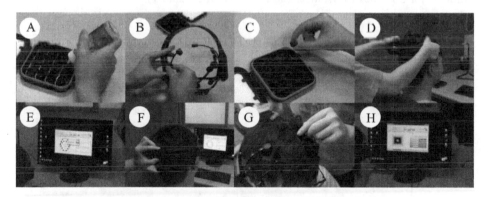

**Fig. 4.**   EPOC+ installation (Color figure online)

### 4.2    Experiments of BCI Training Methods

To enable the users to control the viewport in 3Ds Max through EPOC+, we need to design a training process that successfully zooms in/out of the virtual box via imagination. Therefore, the research first establishes an experiment procedure that enables achieving more than 80% of accuracy to control the imagination command—valid signal. "Valid signal" means, in 5 s, after the voice command (e.g. pull), the user can successfully complete a 3Ds Max command (zoom in the virtual box) via imagination through the EPOC device. Just like the fingerprints, different users exhibit different patterns of EEG brainwaves. To achieve high accuracy, each user has to finish the training process before using the BCI embedded CAD system (Fig. 5).

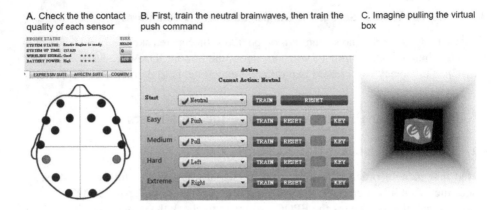

**Fig. 5.**  EEG data acquisition steps via EPOC+

Therefore in order to find out a short and effective training process for new users, we go through three different types of training procedure. In each training experiment, the user will test the "imagination command" by randomly testing "push" or "pull" command for 50 times to evaluate the accuracy (see Table 1).

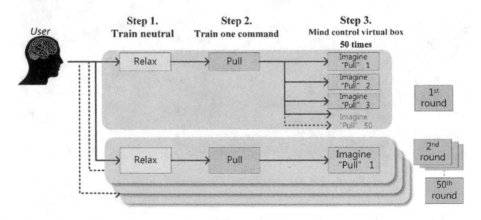

**Fig. 6.**  Steps of EPOC+ training process

## Training Experiment Type 1

The users first go through the neutral training 1 time and the push training 1 time and then try "imagination of push test" 10 time. The users would repeat the previous action for 10 times. Second the users go through the pull training 1 time and then tries the "imagination of pull test" 10 times and then repeat the previous action for 10 times. Finally, the users test the imaginations of push or pull for 50 times. The accuracy of imagination push or pull mix command is 76%.

**Training Experiment Type 2**
The users go through neutral training, push training and pull training for 10 times. Next, the users test the imaginations of push or pull for 50 times. The accuracy of imagination of push or pull mix command is 84%.

**Training Experiment Type 3**
The users go through each of neutral training, push training and pull training for 20 times. And then the users test the imaginations of push or pull for 50 times. The accuracy of imagination of push or pull mix commands is 84%.

**Table 1.** BCI training experiments

| Experiment type | Training procedure | Randomly test imagination of push or pull 50 times (Accuracy %) |
|---|---|---|
| Experiment type I | First step: Neutral training x1 time ⎫<br>Push training x1 time ⎬ Imagination of Push test x 10 times<br>Second step: Repeat first action 10 times<br>Third step: Pull training x1 time } Imagination of Pull test x 10 times<br>Firth step: Repeat third action 10 times<br>Fifth step: Randomly test imagination of push or pull 50 times | 76% |
| Experiment type II | First step: Neutral training x10 times<br>Push training x10 times<br>Pull training x10 times<br>Second step: Randomly test imagination of push or pull 50 times | 84% |
| Experiment type III | First step: Neutral training x20 times<br>Push training x20 times<br>Pull training x20 times<br>Second step: Randomly test imagination of push or pull 50 times | 84% |

As shown in Table 1, we found that longer training process in Experiment type III did not increase the accuracy rate as compared to Experiment type II. Our data suggests that new users can achieve the 80% accuracy after completing experiment type II, which takes approximately 20 min to finish.

## 5   System Implementation

In our proposed framework, there are two building blocks, namely, 3ds Max plug-in and Emotiv API, respectively. The main task here is to provide an interface between 3ds Max plug-in and Emotiv API to realize the communication in one direction from EPOC+ hardware to 3ds Max software. Therefore, the requirement is just a single plug-in file in 3ds Max by using the Emotive API (Fig. 6).

Customizing our own plug-in function in 3ds Max is simple since the software itself consists of many plugins. The most well-known part is the user interface around the 3ds Max, which allows users to set their own way via Maxscript or dynamic link library. All user-specified plug-ins can accomplish by using 3ds Max SDK. Hereby, to our proposed system, the plug-in is event-triggered by the zoom in/out signals from EmoEngine, provided by Emotiv API and response zoom in/out of the object in 3ds Max. By reading the state of the user's brainwaves through the EPOC+ and provide signal to judge whether the object should zoom in or out is the main program of our plug-in software.

When one completes the training step, he or she can simply download the plug-in and start to customize the zoom in/out feature by imagination (Figs. 7 and 8).

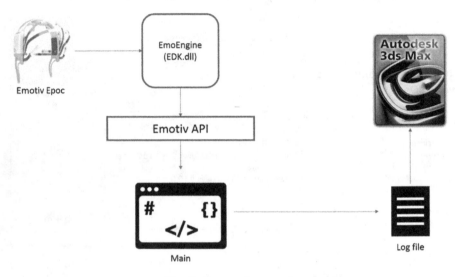

**Fig. 7.** System framework

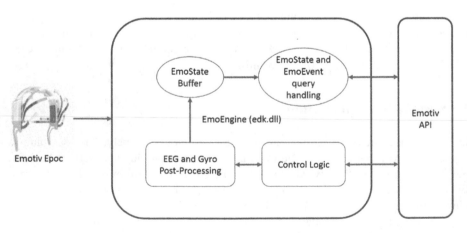

**Fig. 8.** The relationship between EmoEngine and Emotive

# 6  Scenario Demonstration and Evaluations

In order to evaluate the BCI-CAD system, we created two different experiments. And we found a 3Ds Max new user as our subject to get through the following experiment without telling him/her the hotkeys of the "zoom in" and "zoom out" in 3Ds Max. We asked him/her to find out commends either through the graphical icon or through imagination. The following experiments include: (1) traditional GUI-CAD experiments; (2) the BCI-CAD experiments.

## 6.1  Traditional GUI-CAD Experiments

We taught him/her to create a box in the viewport at 3Ds Max, and then we asked the subject to find out the commends of "zoom in" or "zoom out" to "push" or "pull" the virtual object in GUI. Then the subject was asked to speak loudly in every step before performing the GUI commands. We found that the new users could spend more than one minute looking for the "zoom in" icon. But once the user learned where to find the zoom in commend, they could easily find the "zoom out". The subjects generally spent approximately 2 min finishing the zoom in, zoom out tasks. The manipulate intention completely matches the intention.

## 6.2  BCI-CAD Experiments

Before starting the BCI-CAD experiment, the subject is asked to wear EPOC+ headset, and ensuring good electrode contact quality (electrode turn to green color). The subject was asked to create a box through mice and keyboard (just like in the previous experiment). Since we need to verify if the BCI-CAD system is more intuitive than GUI command based CAD, we asked the subject to use the mind command to control the virtual box in 3Ds Max instead of using the mice and keyboard (see Fig. 9-D, E, F). Meanwhile, the subject must speak loudly when imagining the commands.

As shown in Fig. 10, we could observe if the user's intention match the mind command. Sometime the real-time mind command was delayed due to the problem of maxscript and the huge 3Ds Max software. Sometimes, the BCI-CAD was triggered two times (see Fig. 10) with only one intention from the subject. However, almost every activity (zoom in or zoom out command) can be recognized through imagination. Without learning how to use keyboard or mice, the user could easily and naturally control the 3Ds Max viewport (Table 2). The manipulate intention also completely match the mind intention.

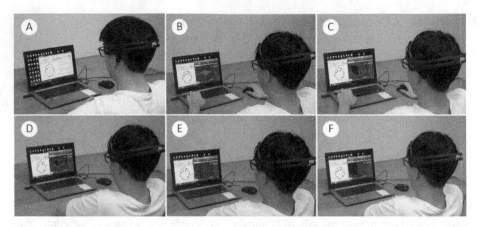

**Fig. 9.** Scenario demonstration: (A) user is wearing the EPOC+ headband, and check the electrode contact quality is good; (B, C) the user starts building a box in 3Ds MAX through mouse and keyboard; (D, E) the user starts to use imagination command to zoom out the box of the viewport; (F) the user smoothly zoom in the box of the viewport. (Color figure online)

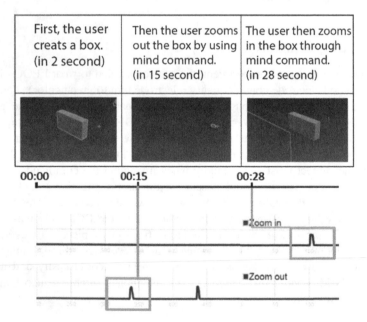

**Fig. 10.** Representation of real time mind-command activity

**Table 2.** Statistics of the intention and mind command

| 3Ds Max | Speak command | | Mind command | | Success rate | | |
|---|---|---|---|---|---|---|---|
| | Zoom in | Zoom out | Zoom in | Zoom out | Mix success rate | Zoom in | Zoom out |
| 00:10 | v | | v | | 100% | | |
| 00:46 | | v | | v | 100% | | |
| 01:29 | | v | | v | 100% | | |
| 01:45 | | v | | v | 100% | | |
| Command times | 1 | 3 | 1 | 3 | 100% | 100% | 100% |

## 7   Conclusion

The research creates a "BCI embedded CAD" system prototype, which build the connection between EPOC+ 3Ds Max via maxscript and C++. Through the system, the user is able to enhance the ability in 3D modeling through "thinking the commands". The training procedure is simple and efficient and users could finish the training process within 20 min. Furthermore, the users are able to achieve 80% accuracy by using the mind command to push or pull the viewport in 3Ds Max.

However, as in the scenario demonstration, sometimes the user used both "mind command" and "physical interface (keyboard or mice)" to control the virtual box. Therefore, the future study would focus on how to apply "BCI embedded CAD" system to cross 3D CAD platforms (3Ds Max, Rihno, and MAYA). The BCI embedded CAD users can perform more efficiently than traditional users.

As to the contribution, the research is significant not only in the architecture engineering but also the design fields. In our prototype, the system can only control on/off signal (pull or "invalid pull") to zoom in/out the viewport. The future study would be focused on how to partially adjust different viewports.

## References

Aish, R.: 3D input for CAAD systems. Comput. Aided Des. **11**(2), 66–70 (1979)

Chapin, J.K., Moxon, K.A., Markowitz, R.S., Nicolelis, M.A.: Real-time control of a robot arm using simultaneously recorded neurons in the motor cortex. Nat. Neurosci. **2**(7), 664–670 (1999)

Dickinson, J.K., Yu, Z., Zeng, Y., Antunes, H.: Pentablet as a {CAD} interface alternative. Robotics Comput.-Integr. Manuf. **21**(45), 465–474 (2005). 14th International Conference on Flexible Automation and Intelligent Manufacturings

Huang, Y.C.: A space make you lively: a brain-computer interface approach to smart space. In: 11th International Conference on Computer Aided Architectural Design Research in Asia (CAADRIA 2006), pp. 303–312 (2006)

Huang, Y.C.: How human-computer interface redefines original lifestyle in architecture? Adv. Mater. Res. **250**, 1088–1097 (2011)

Ishii, H., Ullmer, B.: Tangible bits: towards seamless interfaces between people, bits and atoms. In: Proceedings of the ACM SIGCHI Conference on Human Factors in Computing Systems, pp. 234–241. ACM (1997)

Jackie Lee, C.-H., Hu, Y., Selker, T.: iSphere: a free-hand 3D modeling interface. Int. J. Archit. Comput. **4**(1), 19–31 (2006)

Krepki, R., Blankertz, B., Curio, G., Müller, K.-R.: The Berlin Brain-Computer Interface (BBCI)– towards a new communication channel for online control in gaming applications. Multimedia Tools Appl. **33**(1), 73–90 (2007)

Lebedev, M.A., Nicolelis, M.A.: Brain-machine interfaces: past, present and future. Trends Neurosci. **29**(9), 536–546 (2006). Epub 2006 Jul 21

Lee, J., Ishii, H.: Beyond: collapsible tools and gestures for computational design. In: CHI 2010 Extended Abstracts on Human Factors in Computing Systems (CHI EA 2010), pp. 3931–3936. ACM, New York (2010)

Leeb, R., Gert, P.: Walking through a virtual city by thought. In: 26th Annual International Conference of the IEEE Engineering in Medicine and Biology Society, IEMBS 2004, vol. 2, pp. 4503–4506. IEEE (2004)

Lichten, L.: The emerging technology of CAD/CAM. In: Proceedings of the 1984 Annual Conference of the ACM on The Fifth Generation Challenge, pp. 236–241. ACM (1984)

Lim, C.: G pen: an intelligent designer's playmate. In: Association for Computer Aided Design in Architecture (2003)

Paller, K., Kutas, M.: Brain potentials during memory retrieval provide neurophysiological support for the distinction between conscious recollection and priming. J. Cogn. Neurosci. **4**(4), 375–392 (1992)

Sharma, A., Madhvanath, S., Shekhawat, A., Billinghurst, M.: Mozart: a multimodal interface for conceptual 3D modeling. In: Proceedings of the 13th International Conference on Multimodal Interfaces, pp. 307–310. ACM (2011)

Sutherland, I.E.: Sketch pad a man-machine graphical communication system. In: Proceedings of the SHARE Design Automation Workshop, pp. 6–329. ACM (1964)

# NeuroSnap: Expressing the User's Affective State with Facial Filters

Ryan Lieblein, Camille Hunter, Sarah Garcia, Marvin Andujar[✉],
Chris S. Crawford, and Juan E. Gilbert

Computer and Information Science and Engineering Department,
University of Florida, Gainesville, USA
{rlieblein, camilleh, sarahmgarcia, manduja,
chrisscrawford, juan}@ufl.edu

**Abstract.** The use of facial filters in social media have changed the way people communicate and share their emotions. Daily, users generate millions of videos content with visual filters, where they manually select and apply these filters on top of their video or images. This paper presents an artistic Brain-Computer Interface new method to express the user's affective state through facial filters. Therefore, this article presents NeuroSnap, an application modeled from Snapchat, where the user's affective state is expressed automatically with custom-designed facial filters. Each filter represents relaxation, alerted, or highly alerted based on the electroencephalography (EEG) waves. This paper also provides brief example scenarios with a focus on user experience on how users could interact with NeuroSnap. Lastly, this paper provides preliminary results on people's perception on this application and the accuracy of obtained values of both alpha and beta obtained from a mobile wireless BCI device.

**Keywords:** Artistic Brain-Computer Interfaces · Facial filters · Affective state · EEG · Visual artistic expression

## 1 Introduction

One concentration of Artistic Brain-Computer Interfaces (artistic BCI) is the visual artistic expression of the user's affective state [1–3]. One form of visual artistic representation is dynamic and interacting visualizations. These visualizations and illustrations can be used to provide new ways for users to express themselves in social media, video communication or just provide visual feedback to the user, which can personalize the user experience. In this paper, we introduce NeuroSnap, an artistic BCI application that displays visuals as facial filters to express the user's affective state. This application uses similar concepts from Snapchat [4] where it lets users apply a variety of graphics and filters to a live video using facial recognition. Snapchat is an image, text, and video messaging mobile application. The messages are only available for a short time, then disappear. Therefore, users cannot save or check an earlier message sent to them like other social media sites. Snapchat filters are the most adapted feature from users but are not based on the users' affective state gathered from the brain. Facebook (https://www.facebook.com) is also another social media that allows

© Springer International Publishing AG 2017
D.D. Schmorrow and C.M. Fidopiastis (Eds.): AC 2017, Part II, LNAI 10285, pp. 345–353, 2017.
DOI: 10.1007/978-3-319-58625-0_25

users to express how they feel about a particular content posted by other people. For ages, this social networking site used only on image for expression, the like button (Fig. 1a). However, this illustration was limiting the user from expressing other emotions (positive and negative). Recently, Facebook released five new images (Fig. 1b) that allow users express both positive and negative emotions. Also, it allows users express more than one positive expression. These initiatives from social media may show that users enjoy sharing their emotions through visual expressions. Social media studies show that receiving likes and views on pictures sent through social media causes excitement feelings for the user, resulting in the repeated use of these applications [2]. Nevertheless, user study research needs further investigation to determine the type of images that users prefer to use and to understand their perception from the existing ones.

**Fig. 1.** (a) Old like button (Image retrieved from: https://commons.wikimedia.org/wiki/File: Facebook_like_thumb.png). (b) New emotion reactions (Image retrieved from: http://www. webpronews.com/facebook-finally-makes-reactions-like-button-extension-available-globally-2016-02/).

In artistic BCI there are other forms of expressions that are not associated with emotion reactions or facial filters. Brain painting is a common method for ALS-patients and healthy users to express their affective state visually. Brain painting is a P300-brain painting application that allows users paint pictures using brain activity only [6]. Brain Painting lets users express themselves creatively and share their paintings with society. Users are also able to print their paintings to see their form of expression places at their home.

Unlike Brain Painting, NeuroSnap adapts the concept of expressing emotions through visual expression, but from the user's brainwaves to represent their affective state with a mobile BCI device. It is not a P300 application and automatically displays a visual filter over the user's face that conveys one of the three states: relaxed, focused, and complex thinking. Relaxed is when a user is not thinking about anything, focused is when a user is thinking of a particular thought while performing a task, but it is not performing a complex activity. Lastly, complex thinking is when a user is performing a difficult task that requires a lot of thinking and concentration.

The aim of this paper is to describe NeuroSnap and its implications to aid users automatically express their affective state with images known as facial filters positioned on top of the user's face represented on the computer. This application allows users to express their affective state through images in real-time without the need to express them verbally or through text. This paper also discusses different scenarios of how users can interact with the application from a user experience and human-computer interaction perspective. Lastly, it provides preliminary data of accuracy of obtained EEG values from the mobile BCI.

## 2  NeuroSnap

NeuroSnap is an application that allows users to express their affective state through facial filters. It measures electroencephalographic (EEG) signals from the user's scalp and decodes the EEG waves using proprietary algorithms from Emotiv and displays a particular filter representing the affective state based on the EEG waves: alpha and beta (frequency separated between low and high). The user can see the filters on the computer once the camera has detected the user's face using real-time facial detection and identified the highest averaged value of the EEG waves at a determined time (Fig. 2).

**Fig. 2.** The user wearing the Emotiv Insight as he waits for his affective state to be determined.

NeuroSnap is based on the popular mobile application Snapchat. Using the front and rear cameras of a mobile device, Snapchat users can take pictures and videos of themselves while manually choosing from a selection of filters to apply to their face. NeuroSnap, however, applies these facial filters automatically based on real-time brain data. Previous work has suggested that the elimination for control devices (i.e. a mouse or keyboard) is imperative to enhancing user experience [8]. A study conducted by Quinn and Fernstrom shows that hands-free applications are more user-friendly when working with digital interfaces. The following subsections describe more in detailed how NeuroSnap map the EEG waves with facial filters.

## 2.1  Facial Detection

NeuroSnap uses OpenCV computer vision library to access the computer's camera. It implements facial recognition via the Haar Cascades classifier for placement of the facial filter on top of the user's face. Haar Cascades is a machine learning technique to detect visual objects. It is capable of processing images rapidly with high detection rates [13]. This method uses pre-trained classifiers. NeuroSnap uses this technique's pre-trained classifiers, including face, eye, and smile classifiers to detect the position of the user's face on the screen. After receiving information on the location of the face inside the frame, a point is defined as the center of that area where we can then apply the facial filter. These classifiers continuously run while the application is in use and stop once the user terminates the program.

## 2.2  BCI Apparatus

The Emotiv Insight (Fig. 3) is a mobile, non-invasive, wireless electroencephalography (EEG) device. It consists of five channels (AF3, AF4, T7, T8, and Pz) with two left mastoid process references and its locations are based on the 10–20 international system (Fig. 4). Its signal resolution is 128–256 samples per second per channel

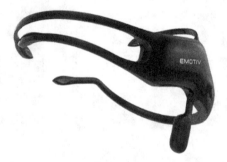

**Fig. 3.** The Emotiv Insight: a mobile 5 channels EEG device

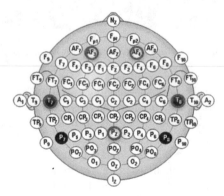

**Fig. 4.** Locations of Emotiv Insight channels on 10–20 international system. Channels are identified by a red circle. (Color figure online)

with 0.51 uV voltage resolution. In NeuroSnap, this BCI apparatus is used to measure EEG and obtain Alpha and Beta brainwaves to map the average values to the facial filters.

Currently, NeuroSnap supports Alpha (relaxed) and Beta (alerted) waves for facial filter expression. Channels AF3 and AF4 for obtaining data from Alpha and Beta, as they are located in the frontal lobe [9]. NeuroSnap measures and decodes EEG based on frequency using a predefined function from the Emotiv library. The obtained data was tested for accuracy and discussed in the results section Table 1 shows the specification of the EEG waves implemented in NeuroSnap and its affective meaning. According to Johnson et al., "Emotion recognition has emerged as a notable research topic in this field as it provides a window on the internal mental state of the user" [11]. Previous works in affective computing have shown that detecting alpha and beta brainwaves is an effective way of measuring attention levels in the brain. In a research study conducted by Oude Bos to recognize emotion from brain signals, alpha waves are described to be "typical for an alert, but a relaxed mental state," while beta waves are related to an active state of mind [7]. Beta waves are detected at 12 Hz, while alpha ranges from 8–12 Hz [12].

**Table 1.** EEG waves specification of their meaning and frequency ranges

| EEG waves | Affective representation | Frequency range |
|-----------|--------------------------|-----------------|
| Alpha     | Relaxed                  | 8–12 Hz         |
| Low Beta  | Lightly Focused          | 12–16 Hz        |
| High Beta | Highly Focused           | 16–25 Hz        |

NeuroSnap brings two essential functions together: the camera method and the EEG method. First, the non-invasive BCI apparatus obtains EEG signal from the user's brain in real-time. The Emotiv SDK has a post-processing method that returns Alpha, Low Beta, and High Beta waves. These values are then received by the camera function which continually detects if a face is present within the camera frame. If there is a face identified by the computer's camera, the function will check if any of the EEG waves are within the calibration thresholds. The facial filter applied is determined as follows:

- *Relaxation*: When the Alpha value is greater than the Low Beta and High Beta values, the mud mask filter is displayed to represent relaxation. (Figure 5).
- *Lightly Focused*: When the Low Beta value is greater than the Alpha and High Beta values, the light bulb is displayed to represent light focus (Fig. 6).
- *Highly Focused*: When the High Beta value is greater than the Alpha and Low Beta values, the thought bubble filter is displayed to represent high focus (Fig. 7).

**Fig. 5.** The relaxation filter applied to the user.

**Fig. 6.** The focused filter applied to the user.

**Fig. 7.** The complex thought filter applied to the user.

## 3   Preliminary Results

### 3.1   Survey

The purpose of the survey was to assess the interest of users wanting to use an application like NeuroSnap. This step is important because people's perception of the use of BCI devices could be negative and the success towards implementation of such devices in society is based on people's perception and implementation willingness. A total of 49 healthy participants (27 female & 22 males) between the ages of 18–26 completed the short survey. They answered two questions based on their usage of Snapchat and their interest in using a system that allows them to express their emotion or affective state using a BCI.

Figure 8 shows the results of the given survey. 34 participants have used Snapchat before, where 29 participants would be interested in using NeuroSnap, and five do not have an interest in using it. 15 people have not previously use Snapchat, but were introduced to NeuroSnap, 11 of them claimed they would be interested in using the application, whereas 4 participants would not use NeuroSnap. In summary, the results entail that 81.6% of the participants who have used Snapchat are interested in using a similar application using BCI.

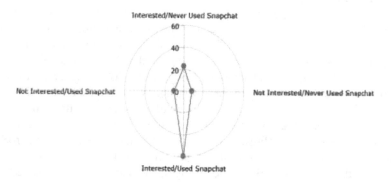

**Fig. 8.**   Survey responses results.

## 3.2   EEG Wave Accuracy Test

A test with four subjects was conducted to determine the accuracy of the EEG waves. The dataset for the fourth subject was discarded due to abnormality in the data. It consisted of two steps: the alpha step and beta step. During the alpha phase, the participants closed their eyes while listening to an alpha tone and raindrop through an earphone. The participants were instructed to perform no muscle movement and to not think about anything. The beta step consisted of watching a video of the FIFA 2015 video game (https://www.youtube.com/watch?v=Q21bznzy_HY). The video gets the participant in an alert state due to its intense used of sounds, colors, and picture frames. It is also a short video as recommended to use for elicitation [10]. This test is important to test the accuracy obtained data from mobile EEG devices. During the tests, it is expected to see higher alpha values during the alpha step and higher beta during the beta test. Table 2 shows that the participants demonstrated high levels of alpha during the alpha step and that the participants had noticeably high levels of beta during the beta step. During the alpha step, the alpha state of the participants was higher than the beta state, while in the beta step, the beta state was higher than alpha. This preliminary test shows that the acquired EEG wave from the mobile EEG device was accurate during the specific steps.

**Table 2.** Results of the participant's EEG wave accuracy test.

| Participants | EEG waves | Alpha step | Beta step |
|---|---|---|---|
| Participant one | Alpha | 0.34641 | 0.26556 |
| | Low Beta | 0.25922 | 0.41064 |
| | High Beta | 0.14000 | 0.41150 |
| Participant two | Alpha | 0.97470 | 0.08914 |
| | Low Beta | 0.20392 | 0.20651 |
| | High Beta | 0.09511 | 0.47331 |
| Participant three | Alpha | 0.28012 | 0.10384 |
| | Low Beta | 0.11410 | 0.11385 |
| | High Beta | 0.07750 | 0.24138 |

# 4    User Interaction

Upon launching the application, a window with the NeuroSnap title and instructions are displayed on the user's screen. The EEG device should then be mounted on the user's scalp. The user then presses any key on the keyboard to begin running the program. The welcome window closes, and a new window appears displaying the user from their front-facing camera or computer webcam (Fig. 2). When the user's face is detected, their current affective state is determined by NeuroSnap. Based on the Alpha and Beta values received from the EEG device, a facial filter is chosen and appears on the computer screen in real-time (Figs. 5, 6, and 7). After the steps above, NeuroSnap is hands-free. Therefore, there is no need for the user to make manual modifications or selections. As the user's affective state changes, the facial filters displayed on the camera screen will update accordingly. Also, each time the current facial filter is altered by the user's brain state, the application produces a screenshot of the user with the filter most recently applied, which is then added to a local folder. The user can then visit the local folder on their computer and browse through their screenshots. When the user is finished using NeuroSnap, the window can be closed from the top right-hand corner, shutting down the software.

# 5    Discussion/Summary

The purpose of this paper is to introduce a new method of visually expressing the user's affective state with a mobile BCI. NeuroSnap is a hands-free application that measures EEG and obtains the user's Alpha and Beta (low and high). The application uses an open-source computer vision software library, OpenCV, to manipulate the computer's camera to detect a user's face in real-time, using the Haar Cascades and apply an image filter over a particular region of the user's face. By receiving positive feedback from the participants in the survey, NeuroSnap can be useful for improving the public's perception on BCI-enabled technologies. Also, the preliminary results of alpha and beta test show that NeuroSnap accurately makes the decision on the facial filters based on brain data and not muscle or eye movements. The applicability of visually expressing the affective state can expand to scenarios such as sharing the current state in social media, improve the emotion expression via video chat, and explore the use of visual expression feedback for therapy. As BCI systems also have potential to serve as therapeutic tools [5].

Future work entails the following:

- Further, design various facial filters and perform user experience research studies to understand user's acceptability and usability. Also, classify the new designs in the arousal dimension.
- Improve the movement of the facial filters when users perform a head movement.
- Perform EEG classification with machine learning algorithms such as support vector machine (SVM).
- Implement theta wave for drowsiness detection.

# References

1. Andujar, M., Crawford, C.S., Nijholt, A., Jackson, F., Gilbert, J.E.: Artistic brain-computer interfaces: the expression and stimulation of the user's affective state. Brain-Comput. Interfaces 2(2–3), 60–69 (2015)
2. Donelly, E., Kuss, D.J.: Depression among users of social networking sites (SNSs): the role of SNS addiction and increased usage. J. Addict. Prev. Med. 1(2), 107 (2016)
3. Gürkök, H., Nijholt, A.: Affective brain-computer interfaces for arts. In: 2013 Humaine Association Conference on Affective Computing and Intelligent Interaction (ACII), pp. 827–831. IEEE, September 2013
4. Lichterman, J.: Snapchat reportedly has more daily users than Twitter. What does that mean for news? (2015). http://www.niemanlab.org/2016/06/snapchat-reportedly-has-more-daily-users-than-twitter-what-does-that-mean-for-news/
5. Mak, J.N., Wolpaw, J.R.: Clinical applications of brain-computer interfaces: current state and future prospects. IEEE Rev. Biomed. Eng. 2, 187–199 (2009)
6. Münßinger, J.I., Halder, S., Kleih, S.C., Furdea, A., Raco, V., Hösle, A., Kubler, A.: Brain painting: first evaluation of a new brain–computer interface application with ALS-patients and healthy volunteers. Front. Neurosci. 4, 182 (2010)
7. Oude Bos, D.: EEG-based emotion recognition-The Influence of Visual and Auditory Stimuli. Capita Selecta (MSc course) (2006)
8. Quinn, N., Fernstrom, M.: A multimodal artistic interface. In ACM SIGGRAPH 2005 Posters, p. 25. ACM, July 2005
9. Reuderink, B., Mühl, C., Poel, M.: Valence, arousal and dominance in the EEG during game play. Int. J. Auton. Adapt. Commun. Syst. 6(1), 45–62 (2013)
10. Rottenberg, J., Ray, R.D., Gross, J.J.: Emotion elicitation using films. In: Coan, J.A., Allen, J.J.B. (eds.) The Handbook of Emotion Elicitation and Assessment, pp. 9–28. Oxford University Press, London (2007)
11. Stikic, M., Johnson, R.R., Tan, V., Berka, C.: EEG-based classification of positive and negative affective states. Brain-Comput. Interfaces 1(2), 99–112 (2014)
12. Teplan, M.: Fundamentals of EEG measurement. Meas. Sci. Rev. 2(2), 1–11 (2002)
13. Viola, P., Jones, M.: Rapid object detection using a boosted cascade of simple features. In: Proceedings of the 2001 IEEE Computer Society Conference on Computer Vision and Pattern Recognition, CVPR 2001, vol. 1, pp. I-I. IEEE (2001)

# Tactile Stimulation Training to Enhance MRCP Detection in Chronic Stroke Patients

Natalie Mrachacz-Kersting[1](✉), Susan Aliakbaryhosseinabadi[1],
Martin Pedersen[1], Ning Jiang[2], and Dario Farina[3]

[1] Center for Sensory-Motor Interaction, The Faculty of Medicine,
Aalborg University, Aalborg, Denmark
nm@hst.aau.dk
[2] Department of Systems Design Engineering,
University of Waterloo, Waterloo, Canada
[3] Department of Bioengineering, Imperial College London, London, UK

**Abstract.** We have recently developed an associative Brain-Computer Interface (BCI) for neuromodulation in chronic and acute stroke patients that leads to functional improvements. The control signal is the movement related cortical potential (MRCP) that develops prior to movement execution. The MRCP increases in variability as a novel task is learned, which in turn significantly decreases the detection accuracy. In the current study we sought to investigate if tactile stimulation, often implemented in rehabilitation, may act as a primer to our associative BCI by decreasing MRCP variability. Six chronic stroke patients were exposed to one session of tactile stimulation, and the MRCP of an arm lifting task, repeated 30 times, extracted. Results reveal that for three patients the MRCP detection accuracy expressed as the rate of true and false positives was improved. In two patients however the detection accuracy declined while one patient was unable to complete the experiment. Since tactile stimulation is a common tool implemented by physiotherapists to train patients to perform dynamic movements with the appropriate muscle pattern to avoid compensatory actions by other muscles it will be important to decipher why it results in such differential effects across patients.

**Keywords:** Brain-computer-interface · Movement-related-cortical potential · Stroke · Tactile stimulation training · Detection accuracy

## 1 Introduction

A brain-computer-interface (BCI) designed for neuromodulation uses brain signals to control an external device without the conventional way of nerves and muscles [1, 2]. In previous studies we have shown significant improvements in the functionality of chronic and subacute stroke patients exposed to a novel associative BCI intervention [3, 4]. Patients were able to walk faster and increase their foot tapping frequency significantly following only three sessions of training [4]. We also reported significant plasticity induction at the level of the motor cortex using non-invasive transcranial magnetic stimulation [4, 5]. In this associative BCI, the reorganization of brain areas, necessary to re-learn motor tasks after brain damage, is enhanced by establishing a

© Springer International Publishing AG 2017
D.D. Schmorrow and C.M. Fidopiastis (Eds.): AC 2017, Part II, LNAI 10285, pp. 354–363, 2017.
DOI: 10.1007/978-3-319-58625-0_26

causal relationship between the patient's intention (interpreted with the BCI) and the artificial reproduction of the intended movement.

The rationale of this relies on the concept of associative brain plasticity, i.e., the reinforcement of cortical connections due to the coupling of efferent (brain command) and afferent signals (signals from the body generated during motion and sent to the brain along nerves) [5–7]. The associative BCI system interprets the patient's intention in terms of the movement to be executed and controls an electrical stimulation system, which artificially reproduces the intended movement in the target limb by delivering electrical current to the peripheral nerves. This approach, based on animal and human studies [8, 9] creates a strong causal connection between the intention to move expressed by the brain and the sensation of movement which arrives at the brain with afferent activity from the limb.

In these studies the control signal was the movement related cortical potential (MRCP). The MRCP is a slow negative potential that starts to develop approximately one to two seconds prior to movement onset, attains its largest amplitude just prior to movement onset, followed by a re-afferent phase [10]. The MRCP generated following a cue to the user comprises several well defined parts, which are known to be linked to specific neurophysiological mechanisms [11]. The first deflection, the early MRCP, commences immediately following the warning stimulus [12]. The late MRCP appears 1 to 0.5 s prior to the cue to perform the movement [12], is associated to the planning of voluntary movements and is altered in neurological disease [13]. During the movement execution and after the cue, a more complex waveform may be observed thought to be related to somatosensory feedback and the attention level during task execution [12].

Depending on the lesion site and the extend of the lesion, stroke patients generally exhibit a variable MRCP shape between trials and days although the time of peak negativity remains stable at least in chronic stroke patients [4] when referenced to a cue that indicates the patient to perform the movement. However, since the ultimate goal of our associative BCI is to provide high detection accuracy and thus a maximal number of precisely timed pairings of the MRCP and the artificially generated afferent signal, the trial to trial variability of the MRCP is problematic. Specifically as the algorithm is required to detect movement intent prior to the movement execution phase.

Clinicians attempt to restore normal functionality by using a variety of techniques to train the patient to react to external stimuli appropriately and as fast as possible. The main aim is to provide the patient with the correct way of executing the movement. One of these involves tactile stimulation that guides patients through initiation and completion of intended tasks. In the current study we investigated if such tactile stimulation may be used as a primer for our associative BCI intervention by training patients to execute the task in a similar manner. We hypothesized that the MRCP associated to the task becomes more stable following the tactile stimulation training, thus improving detection accuracy and consequently performance of our BCI algorithm.

## 2  Methods

### 2.1  Patients

Six patients at least one year post the injury (age of 18–35 mean 27.5 years) provided informed consent and agreed to participate in the study. Inclusion criteria were: 1. 18 years of age or above, 2. Ischemic stroke at least 12 month prior to the study, 3. Able to follow commands, 4. Ability to be active for at least one hour, 5. Able to voluntarily elevate the affected arm by a minimum of 5 cm (elbow) and 30 cm (hand). The patients were all affected on the left side of the brain due to an ischemic stroke. Table 1 provides patient demographics.

**Table 1.** Patient demographics

| Patient | Age | Gender | Months since stroke | Affected side |
| --- | --- | --- | --- | --- |
| 1 | 33 | Female | 18 | Left |
| 2 | 19 | Male | 17 | Left |
| 3 | 31 | Male | 12 | Left |
| 4 | 18 | Female | 48 | Left |
| 5 | 32 | Female | 36 | Both |
| 6 | 32 | Female | 12 | Left |

### 2.2  Movement Related Cortical Potential (MRCP)

Nine channels of monopolar EEG were recorded using an active EEG electrode system and g.USBamp amplifier (gTec, GmbH, Austria) from F3, FC5, FC1, T7, C3, Cz, Cp5, CP1 and P3 according to the standard international 10–20 system. The ground and reference electrodes were placed on Fz and the left earlobe, respectively. Impedance was maintained below 5 KΩ. Signals were filtered from 0 to 100 Hz and sampled at 256 Hz. A single channel of surface electromyography (EMG) was recorded from the right deltoid muscle to control for the subject's movement. The electrodes (Ambu Neuroline 720, Ag/AgC1) were placed parallel on the skin at the frontal aspect of the affected deltoid muscle.

Patients were asked to attempt to lift their arm contralateral to the lesion site 30 times. The patient set-up and position is depicted in Fig. 1A. A custom made Matlab script provided visual information via a screen positioned 2 m in front of the patient on when to mentally prepare, execute, and release the movement (Fig. 1B). The visual cue was comprised of five phases defined as focus, preparation, execution, hold and rest time. After a random duration to focus, a ramp appeared on the screen. A cursor moved along the ramp and when it reached the upward turn, the movement period commenced and patients had to perform and sustain a shoulder elevation while placing the lower arm and hand onto a pillow placed on their lap, followed by a rest period. A total of 30 trials were completed prior to and following the intervention. Patients were instructed to attempt to perform the movement as fast as possible when the cursor had reached the upwards turn and to maintain the new position for 2 s, following which they relaxed again 4–5 s prior to the next cue being provided.

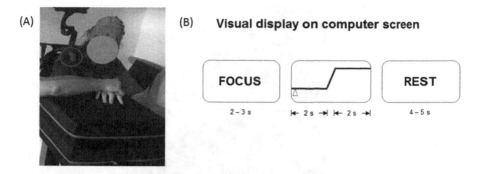

**Fig. 1.** Experimental set-up. (A) Patient set-up and position during the session. (B) The visual display shown to the patients during the single trials. FOCUS appeared on the screen initially followed by the schematic of a step-function. Subjects were required to start the movement once the moving cursor (triangle) reached the upward slope. The word REST appeared last on the screen.

### 2.3   Feature Extraction from the MRCP

EEG data were divided into epochs of 4 s (from 2 s before to 2 s after the visual cue) for each movement, band pass-filtered from 0.05 Hz to 10 Hz, and subsequently a Laplacian channel [14] was used, to enhance the MRCP in each epoch. A window of 500 ms on either side of task onset was chosen and if any epoch's peak negativity was outside the selected window it was discarded. This was to ensure that any mistrials where the patient commenced the movement too early or too late were not included in the final analysis. In addition, epochs containing eye-induced artifacts such as eye movements, eye blinks or extra-ocular muscle activity (Electrooculographic (EOG) activity) exceeding 125 µV were also discarded. Based on these remaining epochs, the mean peak negativity of the MRCP (PN) was defined as the time of occurrence of the minimum value of the averaged MRCP in relation to the visual cue. In addition the variability of the signal in the time of −1 to −0.5 ms prior to cue onset was extracted.

### 2.4   Tactile Stimulation Training

The tactile stimulation training commenced with a five minute massage and deep pressure application to the Flexor Retinaculum of the hand and the insertion point of the Biceps Brachii and Brachialis. These muscles were chosen as they were identified by the therapist of the patients as being the primary muscles limiting the task initiation and completion. This first phase of the training is intended to provide the patient with additional sensory input to the weak muscles so as to facilitate their activation in the next phase. In phase two, patients were asked to perform the task of elevating the shoulder and placing their affected arm onto a pillow located in front of them (Fig. 1A). The patients were instructed to initiate and start the movement, and if required, the therapist provided additional assistance to ensure the movement could be completed.

**Fig. 2.** The grip of the physiotherapist in the patients arm during the application of deep pressures to facilitate the movement of the patient. The start position for the right arm is also shown.

In case the patient did not commence the movement, the therapist held the grip on the patient's lower arm, providing periodic deep pressure as additional sensory input (Fig. 2). Patients completed on average five trials. The total duration of the training did not exceed 20 min.

### 2.5    MRCP Detection

Movement detection parameters were extracted from the EEG epochs using the Locality Preserving Projection (LPP) method followed by a linear discriminant analyses (LDA) classifier (LPP-LDA). The details of this technique are provided elsewhere [15]. The detection latency (DL) was defined as the difference between the movement detection time and the real movement onset as calculated from the EMG signals. The true positive rate (TPR) was defined as the number of true detections divided by the total true events. The false positive rate (FPR) was defined as the number of false detections divided by the number of total events. TPR and FPR were used as the detection features.

## 3    Results

An example of single trial MRCPs and the average MRCP across all electrode locations prior to the tactile stimulation training is depicted in Fig. 3. The single trials show greater variability compared to post tactile stimulation training (Fig. 4).

One patient was excluded from further analysis as this patient was unable to complete the entire experiment. For the remaining patients, an MRCP variability curve was calculated from individual pre and post training trials and the variability extracted

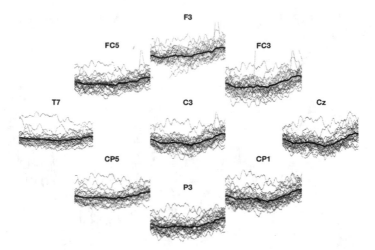

**Fig. 3.** Single trial MRCPs (dotted traces) and the average MRCP (thick traces) for all individual channels for one patient. No trials have been omitted thus data are for all 30 attempted movements. The MRCPs are produced during the motor task prior to the tactile stimulation intervention.

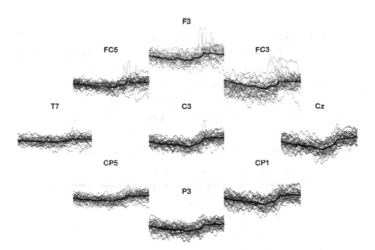

**Fig. 4.** Single trial MRCPs (dotted traces) and the average MRCP (thick traces) for all individual channels for one patient. No trials have been omitted thus data are for all 30 attempted movements. The MRCPs are produced during the motor task following the tactile stimulation intervention.

within $[-2\ 0]$ prior to movement onset. An example of the average MRCP and the associated variability curve for the single trials from one patient is shown in Fig. 5. The tactile stimulation training induced decreases in variability across patients (34–88%), however two patients exhibited large increases in variability (334 and 213%) thus the overall result was not significant.

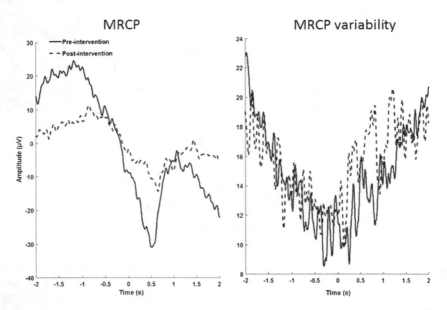

**Fig. 5.** The average MRCP and the associated variability for one patient. Data are the average of 26 trials.

Across all patients, the MRCP was detected at −254 ms (minus indicating prior to movement onset) and −262 ms before and following training respectively. The robustness of the detection algorithm was expressed as the rate of true positives (TPR) and false positives (FP) as a percentage. Prior to the training, these were: TPR: 51–85, FP: 16–45; and immediately following the training: TPR: 50–92, FP: 12–33. Due to the low patient numbers, no statistical comparisons were made (Table 2).

**Table 2.** Detection latency, TPR and FPR of movement detection

| Patient | Pre-intervention | | | Post-intervention | | |
|---|---|---|---|---|---|---|
| | Latency | TPR | FPR | Latency | TPR | FPR |
| 1 | −251.8 | .79 | .33 | −267.9 | .69 | .33 |
| 2 | −255.5 | .74 | .41 | −296.8 | .50 | .16 |
| 3 | −262.7 | .54 | .33 | −264.3 | .64 | .12 |
| 4 | −227.4 | .85 | .45 | −217 | .92 | .29 |
| 5 | −274.7 | .51 | .16 | −262.3 | .68 | .16 |

## 4   Discussion

In the current study we investigated the effects of adjuvant tactile stimulation tailored to guide patients through initiation and completion of the main task, on the variability of the MRCP. Three of the patients, had a decreased variability of the MRCP and concomitant improvements in detection accuracy, while in two patients the variability increased. The results in this small patient cohort indicate that for at least some patients, tactile stimulation training may be a primer to reduce MRCP variability and thus to enhance detection performance in an online associative BCI.

BCIs designed for neuromodulation attempt to restore motor function in individuals that have suffered from a central nervous system lesion such as a stroke [4, 16–24]. In these studies there are several control signals that are typically extracted from the ongoing EEG signals such as event related desynchronization/synchronization (ERDs and ERSs) [19, 20, 22–24], Mu rhythm [18] and the MRCP [4]. In all these BCI systems, it is necessary to train the detection algorithm prior to the actual BCI intervention. However, especially in ERD/ERS controlled BCIs the patients themselves also have to be trained to control the relevant brain signals where frequently 15 or more sessions are required [25, 26]. MRCP based BCIs on the other hand may be implemented from the first session as all patients are able to produce this signal modality.

The MRCP extracted from the EEG signal has several advantageous properties; 1. It can be recorded reliably from BCI naïve participants upon first time BCI use [3, 4]; 2. A relatively low number of channels is required for accurate detection [30]; 3. It can be detected prior to movement execution [31]. What is not known is how these signals change as the patient starts to recover. In studies on learning new skills in healthy subjects it is known that the area responsible for controlling specific muscles increases [27] and specific areas increase their response to artificial stimuli such as TMS [28]. As such it is expected that in stroke patients both in the chronic and the acute phase, similar changes may occur.

Recently we have shown that the MRCP is significantly affected by learning of a novel motor task as well as attention changes of the user [29]. Specifically the variability within the preparation phase is affected and it is this, which the detection algorithm is trained on. Since the associative BCI when implemented as part of the rehabilitation of stroke patients will lead to significant plasticity [3, 4], it is likely that the MRCP will increase in variability much like the learning of the novel task. This however may be viewed as a positive development and algorithms that can adapt to this new state of the user will have to be developed. However, an additional problem is posed when patients are unable to reliably repeat the specific task within the BCI. This may be related to the time of task execution (patients may vary in their response time to the cue provide from trial to trial) or the recruitment patterns of muscles (patients are unable to perform the movement appropriately due to variability in the pattern of muscle activation). Here, techniques that provide the patient with immediate feedback as to the task performance may aid in reducing task variability and as a consequence MRCP variability. Tactile sensory stimulation as applied in the current study, guides the patient by providing such feedback. Data from at least three patients suggest that it may be a useful technique in some patients to improve detection accuracy, though it remains to be investigated why some patients remain unresponsive.

# References

1. Wolpaw, J.R.: Brain-computer interfaces. Handb. Clin. Neurol. **110**, 67–74 (2013)
2. Wolpaw, J.R., Wolpaw, E.W.: Brain-Computer Interfaces - Principles and Practice. Oxford University Press, New York (2012)

3. Mrachacz-Kersting, N., Stevenson, A., Aliakbaryhosseinabadi, S., Lundgaard, A., Jørgensen, H., Severinsen, K., Farina, D.: An associative brain-computer-interface for acute stroke patients. In: International Conference on Neurorehabilitation, p. 248 (2016)

4. Mrachacz-Kersting, N., Jiang, N., Stevenson, A.J., Niazi, I.K., Kostic, V., Pavlovic, A., Radovanovic, S., Djuric-Jovicic, M., Agosta, F., Dremstrup, K., Farina, D.: Efficient neuroplasticity induction in chronic stroke patients by an associative brain-computer interface. J. Neurophysiol. **115**, 1410–1421 (2016)

5. Mrachacz-Kersting, N., Kristensen, S.R., Niazi, I.K., Farina, D.: Precise temporal association between cortical potentials evoked by motor imagination and afference induces cortical plasticity. J. Physiol. **590**, 1669–1682 (2012)

6. Cooke, S.F., Bliss, T.V.P.: Plasticity in the human central nervous system. Brain **129**, 1659–1673 (2006)

7. Stefan, K., Kunesch, E., Cohen, L.G., Benecke, R., Classen, J.: Induction of plasticity in the human motor cortex by paired associative stimulation. Brain **123**, 572–584 (2000)

8. Bliss, T.V.P., Lomo, T.: Long-lasting potentiation of synaptic transmission in the dentate area of the anaesthetized rabbit following stimulation of the perforant path. J. Physiol. (Lond.) **232**, 331–356 (1973)

9. Mrachacz-Kersting, N., Fong, M., Murphy, B.A., Sinkjaer, T.: Changes in excitability of the cortical projections to the human tibialis anterior after paired associative stimulation. J. Neurophysiol. **97**, 1951–1958 (2007)

10. Kornhuber, H.H., Deecke, L.: Changes in the brain potential in voluntary movements and passive movements in man: readiness potential and reafferent potential. Pflugers Arch. Gesamte Physiol. Menschen. Tiere. **284**, 1–17 (1965)

11. Walter, W.G., Cooper, R., Aldridge, V.J., McCallum, W.C., Winter, A.L.: Contingent negative variation: an electric sign of sensorimotor association and expectancy in the human brain. Nature **203**, 380–384 (1964)

12. Hamano, T., Luders, H.O., Ikeda, A., Collura, T.F., Comair, Y.G., Shibasaki, H.: The cortical generators of the contingent negative variation in humans: a study with subdural electrodes. Electroencephalogr. Clin. Neurophysiol./Evoked Potentials Sect. **104**, 257–268 (1997)

13. Ikeda, A., Shibasaki, H., Kaji, R., Terada, K., Nagamine, T., Honda, M., Kimura, J.: Dissociation between contingent negative variation (CNV) and Bereitschaftspotential (BP) in patients with parkinsonism. Electroencephalogr. Clin. Neurophysiol. **102**, 142–151 (1997)

14. McFarland, D.J., McCane, L.M., David, S.V., Wolpaw, J.R.: Spatial filter selection for EEG-based communication. Electroencephalogr. Clin. Neurophysiol. **103**, 386–394 (1997)

15. Xu, R., Jiang, N., Lin, C., Mrachacz-Kersting, N., Dremstrup, K., Farina, D.: Enhanced low-latency detection of motor intention from EEG for closed-loop brain-computer interface applications. IEEE Trans. Biomed. Eng. **61**, 288–296 (2014)

16. Daly, J.J., Cheng, R., Rogers, J., Litinas, K., Hrovat, K., Dohring, M.: Feasibility of a new application of noninvasive brain computer interface (BCI): a case study of training for recovery of volitional motor control after stroke. J. Neurol. Phys. Ther. **33**, 203–211 (2009)

17. Ang, K.K., Guan, C., Chua, K.S., Ang, B.T., Kuah, C., Wang, C., Phua, K.S., Chin, Z.Y., Zhang, H.: Clinical study of neurorehabilitation in stroke using EEG-based motor imagery brain-computer interface with robotic feedback. In: Conference Proceedings of IEEE Engineering in Medicine and Biology Society, vol. 2010, pp. 5549–5552 (2010)

18. Broetz, D., Braun, C., Weber, C., Soekadar, S.R., Caria, A., Birbaumer, N.: Combination of brain-computer interface training and goal-directed physical therapy in chronic stroke: a case report. Neurorehabil. Neural Repair **24**, 674–679 (2010)

19. Cincotti, F., Pichiorri, F., Arico, P., Aloise, F., Leotta, F., de Vico Fallani, F., Millan Jdel, R., Molinari, M., Mattia, D.: EEG-based brain-computer interface to support post-stroke motor rehabilitation of the upper limb. In: Conference Proceedings of IEEE Engineering in Medicine and Biology Society, vol. 2012, pp. 4112–4115 (2012)
20. Li, M., Liu, Y., Wu, Y., Liu, S., Jia, J., Zhang, L.: Neurophysiological substrates of stroke patients with motor imagery-based brain-computer interface training. Int. J. Neurosci. **124**, 403–415 (2014)
21. Young, B.M., Nigogosyan, Z., Nair, V.A., Walton, L.M., Song, J., Tyler, M.E., Edwards, D.F., Caldera, K., Sattin, J.A., Williams, J.C., Prabhakaran, V.: Case report: post-stroke interventional BCI rehabilitation in an individual with preexisting sensorineural disability. Front. Neuroeng. **7**, 18 (2014)
22. Mukaino, M., Ono, T., Shindo, K., Fujiwara, T., Ota, T., Kimura, A., Liu, M., Ushiba, J.: Efficacy of brain-computer interface-driven neuromuscular electrical stimulation for chronic paresis after stroke. J. Rehabil. Med. **46**, 378–382 (2014)
23. Ramos-Murguialday, A., Broetz, D., Rea, M., Laer, L., Yilmaz, O., Brasil, F.L., Liberati, G., Curado, M.R., Garcia-Cossio, E., Vyziotis, A., Cho, W., Agostini, M., Soares, E., Soekadar, S., Caria, A., Cohen, L.G., Birbaumer, N.: Brain-machine interface in chronic stroke rehabilitation: a controlled study. Ann. Neurol. **74**, 100–108 (2013)
24. Pichiorri, F., Morone, G., Petti, M., Toppi, J., Pisotta, I., Molinari, M., Paolucci, S., Inghilleri, M., Astolfi, L., Cincotti, F., Mattia, D.: Brain-computer interface boosts motor imagery practice during stroke recovery. Ann. Neurol. **77**, 851–865 (2015)
25. Buch, E., Weber, C., Cohen, L.G., Braun, C., Dimyan, M.A., Ard, T., Mellinger, J., Caria, A., Soekadar, S., Fourkas, A., Birbaumer, N.: Think to move: a neuromagnetic brain-computer interface (BCI) system for chronic stroke. Stroke **39**, 910–917 (2008)
26. Kai, K.A., Cuntai, G., Sui Geok Chua, K., Beng-Ti, A., Kuah, C., Chuanchu, W., Kok, S.P., Zheng, Y.C., Haihong, Z.: A clinical study of motor imagery-based brain-computer interface for upper limb robotic rehabilitation. In: Annual International Conference of IEEE, Engineering in Medicine and Biology Society, EMBC 2009, pp. 5981–5984 (2009)
27. Pascual-Leone, A., Nguyet, D., Cohen, L.G., Brasil-Neto, J.P., Cammarota, A., Hallett, M.: Modulation of muscle responses evoked by transcranial magnetic stimulation during the acquisition of new fine motor skills. J. Neurophysiol. **74**, 1037–1045 (1995)
28. Perez, M.A., Lungholt, B.K.S., Nyborg, K., Nielsen, J.B.: Motor skill training induces changes in the excitability of the leg cortical area in healthy humans. Exp. Brain Res. **159**, 197–205 (2004)
29. Mrachacz-Kersting, N., Jiang, N., Aliakbaryhosseinabadi, S., Xu, R., Petrini, L., Lontis, R., Dremstrup, K., Farina, D.: The changing brain: bidirectional learning between algorithm and user. In: Guger, C., Allison, B.Z., Edlinger, G. (eds.) Brain-Computer Interface Research: A State-of-the-Art Summary-4. Springer, Heidelberg (2015)
30. Jochumsen, M., Niazi, I.K., Rovsing, H., Rovsing, C., Nielsen, G.A.R., Andersen, T.K., Dong, N.P.T., Sørensen, M.E., Mrachacz-Kersting, N., Jiang, N., Farina, D., Dremstrup, K.: Detection of movement intentions through a single channel of electroencephalography. In: Jensen, W., Andersen, O., Akay, M. (eds.) Replace, Repair, Restore, Relieve – Bridging Clinical and Engineering Solutions in Neurorehabilitation, pp. 465–472. Springer, Cham (2014)
31. Niazi, I.K., Mrachacz-Kersting, N., Jiang, N., Dremstrup, K., Farina, D.: Peripheral electrical stimulation triggered by self-paced detection of motor intention enhances motor evoked potentials. IEEE Trans. Neural Syst. Rehabil. Eng **20**, 595–604 (2012)

# Digital Interface Brain Computer Interaction Method Based on Icon Control

Yafeng Niu[1,2(✉)], Chengqi Xue[1], Haiyan Wang[1], Wenzhe Tang[1],
Xinyu Zhang[1], Tao Jin[3], and Yingjie Victor Chen[4]

[1] School of Mechanical Engineering,
Southeast University, Nanjing 211189, China
nyf@seu.edu.cn
[2] Science and Technology on Electro-Optic Control Laboratory,
Luoyang 471023, China
[3] Mechanical and Electrical Engineering Institute,
China University of Petroleum, Qingdao 266580, China
[4] Department of Computer Graphics Technology,
Purdue University, West Lafayette, IN 47907, USA

**Abstract.** In order to explore the icon controlled digital interface for brain-computer interaction, we use Event-Related Potential technology, first of all, collect the icons from various digital interfaces, use the image processing software to process the icon images, the method comprises the following steps: communication between EEG and test computer, EEG experiment, off-line analysis of the original signal, time domain and frequency domain feature extraction of the group average EEG signal, microprocessor processing, and obtain the user computer function control command of the icon picture, then extract time domain and frequency domain characteristics of target icon picture EEG signal, and calculate the similarity between them, finally realize the triggering of control instruction of the target icon picture. This method can effectively realize icon brain-computer control of the digital interface, and provide the important reference for other elements to interact with the digital interface brain-computer interaction.

**Keywords:** Icon · Digital interface · Brain-computer interaction · Time domain · Frequency domain

## 1 Introduction

Human-computer interaction is the interaction between people and machine, in essence refers to the interaction between people and computer, or can be understood as people and machine that contains a computer. The ultimate aim of human-computer interaction research is to explore how to design a computer that can help people accomplish a mission more safely and more efficiently.

With the advent of the era of big data, advanced interactive technology shows the characteristics of "human-centered" and "natural interaction", and researches on human nature perception channels came into being such as voice, touch, somatosensory,

© Springer International Publishing AG 2017
D.D. Schmorrow and C.M. Fidopiastis (Eds.): AC 2017, Part II, LNAI 10285, pp. 364–377, 2017.
DOI: 10.1007/978-3-319-58625-0_27

augmented reality, eye control and brain control, in which brain control technology is one of the most cutting-edge interactive technology.

Brain control is based on brain-machine interface technology, speculate the brain's thinking activities by extracting EEG signal generated by human or animal brain, and translated into the corresponding command to control the external computer or other equipment. At present, brain control has infiltrated into military weapons and equipment, virtual reality, household equipment, games and medical fields.

The application of brain-computer interaction in digital interface gives the user an unprecedented experience. Researchers at home and abroad have carried out relevant research in the field of brain-computer interaction, mainly using brain waves to control computers and electromechanical devices. In 1991, Wolpaw et al. researched and published result that control the movement of the cursor by changing the amplitude of mu rhythm in the EEG signal, proposed the concept of brain drive control technology [1]. In 1999, Nature first published an article about the brain-computer interface which used slow potential to achieve spelling [2]. In 2003 Nature reported experiments made by Duke University which used monkey brain to control robot [3]. Professor Miller from Northwestern University achieved functional electrical stimulation control paralyzed muscles [4]. Pittsburgh University achieved human brain ECoG signal control robot [5]. Cheng M using the steady-state visual evoked potential experiment paradigm BCI system realized a four-degree-of-freedom artificial limb pouring process based on SSVEP control [6]. In 2010, Graz University of Technology achieved brain-computer interface paradigm which used event-related synchronization potential duration as the classification [7].

Research has found that the EEG signal will show a corresponding and regular pattern of change when people are in thinking activities or in the outside world induced by a stimulus [8]. At present, brain electrical signals used in brain-computer interface are: Slow cortical potential (SCP), P300, Motor imagery (MI) and Steady state visual evoked potential (SSVEP) [9]. In 2012, Zhang et al. proposed a way to improve the accuracy of brain-computer interaction recognition by using inverted face to induce vertex positive potential (VPP) and N170, combined with P300, experimental results showed that, compared to highlight icon and object stimulation, inverted face stimuli can induce stronger N170, VPP and P300, resulting in more discriminatory features [10].

The application of digital interface elements in brain-computer interaction, mainly using the experimental tasks to complete the visual movement, collecting tested brain waves at the same time, then match the EEG signal library in the computer microprocessors according to the processed EEG components, the command can be activated when the signal matches the data base, achieving the interaction without operation between digital interface elements EEG signal and computer.

In the field of digital interface BCI, Zhu et al. [11] proposed a smart typing method using multi-mode EEG control, which realized the remote control process of computer typing without body-typed motion. Guan et al. [12] proposed a virtual Chinese-English keyboard design using brain waves, which realized the direct input of Chinese and English information using brain waves; Liu et al. [13] proposed a extraction method of motor imagery EEG feature which can be used to control the cursor.

In the field of brain-computer interaction of ERP components, Wu et al. [14] proposed a novel BCI Chinese input virtual keyboard system based on the P300 potential;

Hong et al. [15] using N2 potential, proposed a brain-computer interaction method which used visual movement-related neural signals as the carrier. Li et al. [16] developed an experimental system for measuring brain stress by using EEG.

As stated above, in the field of digital interface brain-computer interaction, scholars mostly do text input research that based on brainwave, or realize the control of cursor through the movement imagination, practicality and application range are both very limited. In the brain-computer interaction field of ERP components, P300 and N200 potentials have already been used in brain-computer interaction. There are so many ERPs related to cognition but still lack of digital interface brain-computer interaction researches that using digital interface element cognition.

## 2    The Implement Method of Icon Brain-Computer Interaction

Icon is the most important element and component of the digital interface, and it will be one of the most important input ways of digital interface brain-computer interaction in the future. Integrated predecessors' research, this paper uses icon elements as cognitive objects, presents digital interface brain-computer interactive method based on icon control from the perspective of ERP application and then explores the interface elements on digital interface BCI control. The method in the paper mainly includes following steps: icon collecting and processing; acquiring user's computer function control commands of the icon pictures; time and frequency feature extraction of target icon image's EEG signals. Similarity calculation and activate control instruction of target icon pictures.

### 2.1    Icon Collection and Processing

Collect i function icon pictures from a variety of digital interface, which i = 1, 2...10, common function icon pictures are collected from the digital interface by using screenshot tool, function icon picture refer to close icon picture, save icon picture, undo icon picture, forward icon picture, enlarge icon picture, zoom icon picture, select icon picture, cut icon picture, maximize icon picture, minimize icon picture and other common icons. To avoid the interference of the difference of perspective and clarity, icons need to be processed, using Photoshop, Illustrator or Coreldraw etc. image processing softwares to process icons, get the png format icon picture, both area and pixels are 48px × 48px, then put the icon picture into the center of an area of 1024px × 768px white background image, generate the bmp format icon picture. As shown in Fig. 1, use the "magnifying glass" as an example, collect "magnifying glass" function icon picture from the Visio software, picture preview software, Photoshop CC and AutoCAD software etc. 10 digital interfaces, then generate images meet the test requirements by using graphics softwares.

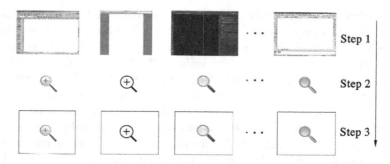

**Fig. 1.** Icon collection and processing schematic diagram

## 2.2 The User Computer Control Commands for Obtaining Icon Pictures

The user computer function control commands for obtaining icon pictures includes the following stages: communication between the EEG and the test computer, the testing process, the off-line analysis of the original signal, the extraction of the group average EEG signal in time and frequency features and the microprocessor processing.

**The Communications Between EEG Equipment and Test Computer.** Connect ERP device with the test computer loaded with the E-prime software to realize the communication between the ERP device and the computer. E-Prime is a set of computerized experimental design, generation and operation software for mental and behavioral experiments. ERP device is a Neuroscan event-related potential system. The communication between ERP device and test computer is by selecting the corresponding data transmission com interface in E-Prime, and inserting inline statement in E-Prime to achieve ERP device's triggering, recording, visual stimulation and EEG synchronization and marking.

**ERP Experimental Test Process.** 20 subjects were selected and each participant was tested 10 times for each icon image. Each icon image obtained 200 test samples, and 200 test samples formed a group. The testing process was as follows: A test image was presented to the subject, using the electrode cap worn on the head of the subject which is configured by ERP devices, the Scan software captured the primitive EEG signals of the subject during the stimulation period of the test image, sampling rate is 500 Hz and all the single test images were traversed to obtain subjects' original EEG signals of all the test images during the stimulus period. The presentation of the test image included the prompt stage, the visual stimulation presentation stage of icon images and the blank stage. At the prompt stage, there was a 32px × 32px black cross in the center of the screen, then disappeared after 1000 ms, at this stage, subjects need to concentrate. In the visual stimulus presentation stage of icon pictures, the center of the screen would present any single icon image in an area of 48px × 48px, subjects need to observe it carefully, the icon image would disappear after 1000 ms. In the blank stage, the screen showed a white blank screen, lasting for 1000 ms to eliminate the visual residue of subjects.

The number of subjects was 20, including 10 males and 10 females, all with university education background, aged between 20–30 years old, all right-handed, without history of mental illness or brain trauma, with normal vision or normal vision correction. The Neuroscan ERP system includes the Synamp2 signal amplifier, the Scan EEG recording analysis system and the 64-channels Ag/AgCl electrode cap, the electrodes are placed in accordance with the international 10–20 system. Before the EEG was recorded, Scan parameter settings include: the reference electrode was placed in bilateral mastoid connection. The ground electrode is placed in the connection midpoint between the FPZ electrode and the FZ electrode, both horizontal and vertical ocular electricity were recorded simultaneously, and the bandpass is 0.05–100 Hz, the sampling frequency is 500 Hz, electrode and scalp contact resistance are less than 5 kΩ. The visual stimulus program is running on the E-Prime, presented through the display, all the pictures' background is white in the test process, and all stimuli are located in the center of the screen, the test process diagram is shown in Fig. 2.

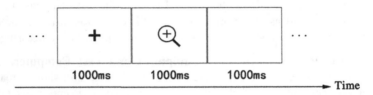

**Fig. 2.** Schematic diagram of ERP experiment testing process

**Raw Signals Offline Analysis.** This research use Scan software to offline analyze the raw EEG signals, which includes each EEG signal pre-processing and each group superposed average, aiming to obtain the group average EEG electrical signals $\overline{y_i(t)}$ of each icon. $\overline{y_i(t)}$ is the general expression of the group average EEG signals of each icon, denoting the group average EEG signals of the icon i.

Pre-processing is to respectively preview each raw EEG signal and to eliminate ocular artifacts, and then extract raw EEG signals segmentally, to obtain the icon i visual stimuli raw signal $y_i(t)$, t are the sampling time points and $t = 1000 + 2m$, null point of t is the time when visual guidance center appear, m are the sampling amounts of icon visual stimuli raw EEG signals and m is integer on [1, 500], finally, correct baseline of the icon visual stimuli raw signals $y_i(t)$ and eliminate artifacts. The icon visual stimuli raw signals $y_i(t)$ that the artifacts have been removed from 10 tests of 20 subjects respectively were processing by group superposition average, then get $\overline{y_i(t)}$.

Offline analysis is to re-analyze and re-process the recorded raw physiological signals. All processes of the offline analysis can be accomplished by Scan software. The process of offline analysis includes EEG preview, ocular artifacts elimination, raw EEG signals segmental extraction, baseline correction, artifacts elimination and group superposition average. EEG preview is to remove the obvious offset EEG data; Ocular artifacts elimination can be accomplished by the independent component analysis (ICA) refer to the plus or minus of EOG amplitude, the direction of EOG and the direction of EEG; Raw EEG segmental extraction is to segment the continuous recorded raw EEG data, according to the time point when each icon shows and the 1000 ms from start to end of the chosen icons that marker recorded. This time means a 1000 ms time period that we extract each icon from showing to disappearing; Baseline correction is to eliminate the offset that EEG relative to baseline, the baseline of this process is according to the signals when icons display; Artifacts elimination is to remove the higher amplitude artifacts of the EEG data which exist in the segmental period. The amplitude defaults of the artifacts elimination are between $\pm 50$–$\pm 100$ μv; Group superposition average obtains the relevant group average EEG signals by superpose and average all EEG data of all subjects. The group average EEG signals of each icon are the EEG signals after 200 times superposition average.

**The Time Domain and Frequency Domain Features Extraction of Group Average EEG Signals.** In this stage, we extract the time domain and frequency domain feature for group average EEG signals $\overline{y_i(t)}$ of each icon. The time domain feature $\overline{Y_i}$ contains average $\overline{Y_{i1}}$, absolute average amplitude $\overline{Y_{i2}}$, variance $\overline{Y_{i3}}$, average root value $\overline{Y_{i4}}$, peak-peak value $\overline{Y_{i5}}$, waveform factor, $\overline{Y_{i6}}$ kurtosis factor $\overline{Y_{i7}}$ and skewness factor.$\overline{Y_{i8}}$ The frequency domain feature $\overline{S_i}$ contains spectrum average amplitude $\overline{S_{i1}}$, spectrum variance $\overline{S_{i2}}$, the first spectrum feature frequency $\overline{S_{i3}}$ and the second spectrum feature frequency $\overline{S_{i4}}$.

(1)  The following method shows how to extract the time domain feature of the icon i group average EEG signal $\overline{y_i(t)}$:

The average $\overline{Y_{i1}}$ of the time domain feature $\overline{Y_i}$ in the icon i group average EEG signal $\overline{y_i(t)}$ is:

$$\overline{Y_{i1}} = \frac{1}{500} \sum_{1002}^{2000} \overline{y_i(t)} = \frac{1}{500} \sum_{m=1}^{500} \overline{y_i(1000+2m)} \tag{1}$$

Average amplitude $\overline{Y_{i2}}$:

$$\overline{Y_{i2}} = \frac{1}{500} \sum_{1002}^{2000} \left| \overline{y_i(t)} \right| = \frac{1}{500} \sum_{m=1}^{500} \left| \overline{y_i(1000+2m)} \right| \tag{2}$$

Variance $\overline{Y_{i3}}$:

$$\overline{Y_{i3}} = \frac{1}{499} \sum_{1002}^{2000} \left( \overline{y_i(t)} - \overline{Y_{i1}} \right)^2 = \frac{1}{499} \sum_{m=1}^{500} \left( \overline{y_i(1000+2m)} - \overline{Y_{i1}} \right)^2 \tag{3}$$

Average root value $\overline{Y_{i4}}$:

$$\overline{Y_{i4}} = \sqrt{\frac{1}{500} \sum_{1002}^{2000} \left( \overline{y_i(t)} \right)^2} = \sqrt{\frac{1}{500} \sum_{m=1}^{500} \left( \overline{y_i(1000+2m)} \right)^2} \tag{4}$$

Peak-peak value $\overline{Y_{i5}}$:

$$\overline{Y_{i5}} = \max\left(\overline{y_i(t)}\right) - \min\left(\overline{y_i(t)}\right) = \max\left(\overline{y_i(1000+2m)}\right) - \min\left(\overline{y_i(1000+2m)}\right) \tag{5}$$

Waveform factor $\overline{Y_{i6}}$:

$$\overline{Y_{i6}} = \frac{\sqrt{\frac{1}{500}\sum\limits_{1000}^{2000}\left(\overline{y_i(t)}\right)^2}}{\frac{1}{500}\sum\limits_{1000}^{2000}\left|\overline{y_i(t)}\right|} = \frac{\sqrt{\frac{1}{500}\sum\limits_{m=1}^{500}\left(\overline{y_i(1000+2m)}\right)^2}}{\frac{1}{500}\sum\limits_{m=1}^{500}\left|\overline{y_i(1000+2m)}\right|} = \frac{\overline{Y_{i4}}}{\overline{Y_{i2}}} \tag{6}$$

Kurtosis factor $\overline{Y_{i7}}$:

$$\overline{Y_{i7}} = \frac{\frac{1}{500}\sum\limits_{1002}^{2000}\left(\overline{y_i(t)}\right)^4}{\left(\frac{1}{500}\sum\limits_{1002}^{2000}\left(\overline{y_i(t)}\right)^2\right)^2} = \frac{\frac{1}{500}\sum\limits_{m=1}^{500}\left(\overline{y_i(1000+2m)}\right)^4}{\left(\frac{1}{500}\sum\limits_{m=1}^{500}\left(\overline{y_i(1000+2m)}\right)^2\right)^2} \tag{7}$$

Skewness factor $\overline{Y_{i8}}$:

$$\overline{Y_{i8}} = \frac{\frac{1}{500}\sum\limits_{1002}^{2000}\left(\overline{y_i(t)}\right)^3}{\left(\sqrt{\left(\frac{1}{500}\sum\limits_{1002}^{2000}\left(\overline{y_i(t)}\right)^3\right)}\right)^3} = \frac{\frac{1}{500}\sum\limits_{m=1}^{500}\left(\overline{y_i(1000+2m)}\right)^3}{\left(\sqrt{\left(\frac{1}{500}\sum\limits_{m=1}^{500}\left(\overline{y_i(1000+2m)}\right)^3\right)}\right)^3} \tag{8}$$

$y_i(t)$ are the icon i visual stimuli raw EEG signal and $\overline{y_i(t)}$ are the icon i group average EEG signal, t are the sampling time points and $t = 1000 + 2m$, m are the sampling amounts of icon visual stimuli raw EEG signals and m is integer on [1, 500].

(2)  The following method shows how to extract the frequency domain feature of the icon i group average EEG signals $\overline{y_i(t)}$:

First, group EEG signals $\overline{y_i(t)}$ of the icons are analyzed based on Fourier Transform respectively, then spectrum function $\overline{S_i(k)}$ of $\overline{y_i(t)}$ is obtained as follows:

$$\overline{S_i(k)} = \sum\limits_{1002}^{2000} e^{-i\frac{2\pi}{500}tk}\overline{y_i(t)} = \sum\limits_{m=1}^{500} e^{-i\frac{2\pi}{500}(1000+2m)k}\overline{y_i(1000+2m)} \tag{9}$$

$-i$ is the plural unit, t are sampling time points and $t = 1000 + 2m$, m are the sampling amounts of icon visual stimuli raw EEG signals and m is integer on [1, 500],k represent spectrum points and k is integer [1, 500].

Then, The following method shows how to extract the frequency domain feature $\overline{S_i}$ of the icon i group average EEG signal.

The spectrum average amplitude $\overline{S_{i1}}$ of the frequency domain feature $\overline{S_i}$ in the icon i group average EEG signal is:

$$\overline{S_{i1}} = \frac{\sum\limits_{k=1}^{500} \overline{S_i(k)}}{500} \tag{10}$$

Spectrum variance $\overline{S_{i2}}$:

$$\overline{S_{i2}} = \frac{\sum\limits_{k=1}^{500} \left(\overline{S_i(k)} - \overline{S_{i1}}\right)^2}{499} \tag{11}$$

The first spectrum feature frequency $\overline{S_{i3}}$:

$$\overline{S_{i3}} = \frac{\sum\limits_{k=1}^{500} \overline{S_i(k)} f_k}{\sum\limits_{k=1}^{500} \overline{S_i(k)}} \tag{12}$$

The second spectrum feature frequency $\overline{S_{i4}}$:

$$\overline{S_{i4}} = \sqrt{\frac{\sum\limits_{k=1}^{500} \overline{S_i(k)} \left(f_k - \overline{S_{i3}}\right)^2}{500}} \tag{13}$$

$\overline{S_i(k)}$ are obtained by Fourier Transform to the icon group average EEG signal $\overline{y_i(t)}$, and denote the spectrum of the icon i group average EEG signal $\overline{y_i(t)}$. $f_k$ are the frequency value of the $k_{th}$ spectrum points, and the calculation formula of $f_k$ is $f_k = \frac{k.Fs}{500}$. In this formula, Fs is the sampling frequency (500 Hz), k denote the spectrum points and k is integer on [1, 500].

**Microprocessor Processing.** In this process, the time domain feature and the frequency domain feature which extracted from the icon group average EEG signal are sent to the microprocessor, and have been translated into digital signals that users can recognize, they are used to the user computer function control command of the corresponding icons through the USB or other general input sent to the user computer, which are stored into the icon activation command module of the user computer. This process is aimed to activate the close icon, save icon, cancel icon, forward icon, zoom in icon, zoom out icon, select icon, cut icon, maximize icon or minimize icon in the user computer.

## 2.3 The Extraction of the Time Domain and Frequency Domain Features in EEG Signals of the Target Icons

This process connects the ERP devices to the user computer. Users should wear an electrode cap and observe certain target icons, then the certain target icon will have a 1000 ms stimuli to the users. We use Scan software in ERP devices, and collect the raw EEG signals when users are stimulated. The sampling frequency is 500 Hz. We do EEG preview, ocular artifacts elimination, baseline correction and artifacts elimination to the collected raw EEG signals, and then extract the time domain feature $Y_i$ and the frequency domain feature $S_i$ of the EEG signals $y_i'(t')$ that artifacts have been eliminated.

$y_i'(t')$ are the general expression of the EEG signals in the stimulation of certain target icon after artifacts elimination, representing the EEG signals of the target icon that correspond to the icon i. $t'$ are the sampling time points when observing the certain target icon, time null point is the time when certain target icon displays and $t' = 2n$, n are the sampling amounts and is integer on [1, 500].

The time domain feature $\overline{Y_i}$ contains average $\overline{Y_{i1}}$, absolute average amplitude $\overline{Y_{i2}}$, variance $\overline{Y_{i3}}$, average root value $\overline{Y_{i4}}$, peak-peak value $\overline{Y_{i5}}$, waveform factor $\overline{Y_{i6}}$, kurtosis factor $\overline{Y_{i7}}$ and skewness factor $\overline{Y_{i8}}$. The following method shows how to extract the time domain feature of the EEG signals $y_i'(t')$ in certain target icon which correspond to the icon i.

The average $Y_i$ of the time domain feature $Y_{i1}$ of the EEG signal $y_i'(t')$ in certain target icon which correspond to the icon i is:

$$Y_{i1} = \frac{1}{500} \sum_{2}^{1000} y_i'(t') = \frac{1}{500} \sum_{n=1}^{500} y_i'(2n) \tag{14}$$

Average amplitude $Y_{i2}$:

$$Y_{i2} = \frac{1}{500} \sum_{2}^{1000} |y_i'(t')| = \frac{1}{500} \sum_{n=1}^{500} |y_i'(2n)| \tag{15}$$

Variance $Y_{i3}$:

$$Y_{i3} = \frac{1}{499} \sum_{2}^{1000} (y_i'(t') - Y_{i1})^2 = \frac{1}{499} \sum_{n=1}^{500} (y_i'(2n) - Y_{i1})^2 \tag{16}$$

Average root value $Y_{i4}$:

$$Y_{i4} = \sqrt{\frac{1}{500} \sum_{2}^{1000} (y_i'(t'))^2} = \sqrt{\frac{1}{500} \sum_{n=1}^{500} (y_i'(2n))^2} \tag{17}$$

Peak-peak value $Y_{i5}$:

$$Y_{i5} = \max(y_i'(t')) - \min(y_i'(t')) = \max(y_i'(2n)) - \min(y_i'(2n)) \tag{18}$$

Waveform factor $Y_{i6}$:

$$Y_{i6} = \frac{\sqrt{\frac{1}{500}\sum\limits_{2}^{1000}(y_i'(t'))^2}}{\frac{1}{500}\sum\limits_{2}^{1000}|y_i'(t')|} = \frac{\sqrt{\frac{1}{500}\sum\limits_{n=1}^{500}(y_i'(2n))^2}}{\frac{1}{500}\sum\limits_{n=1}^{500}|y_i'(2n)|} = \frac{Y_{i4}}{Y_{i2}} \tag{19}$$

Kurtosis factor $Y_{i7}$:

$$Y_{i7} = \frac{\frac{1}{500}\sum\limits_{2}^{1000}(y_i'(t'))^4}{\left(\frac{1}{500}\sum\limits_{2}^{1000}(y_i'(t'))^2\right)^2} = \frac{\frac{1}{500}\sum\limits_{n=1}^{500}(y_i'(2n))^4}{\left(\frac{1}{500}\sum\limits_{n=1}^{500}(y_i'(2n))^2\right)^2} \tag{20}$$

Skewness factor $Y_{i8}$:

$$Y_{i8} = \frac{\frac{1}{500}\sum\limits_{2}^{1000}(y_i'(t'))^3}{\left(\sqrt{\left(\frac{1}{500}\sum\limits_{2}^{1000}(y_i'(t'))^3\right)}\right)^3} = \frac{\frac{1}{500}\sum\limits_{n=1}^{500}(y_i'(2n))^3}{\left(\sqrt{\left(\frac{1}{500}\sum\limits_{n=1}^{500}(y_i'(2n))^3\right)}\right)^3} \tag{21}$$

$y_i'(t')$ are the EEG signals of the certain target icon that corresponds to the icon i, $t'$ are the sampling time points and $t' = 2n$, n are the sampling amounts and n is integer on [1, 500].

The frequency domain feature $\overline{S}_i$ contains spectrum average amplitude $\overline{S}_{i1}$, spectrum variance $\overline{S}_{i2}$, the first spectrum feature frequency $\overline{S}_{i3}$ and the second spectrum feature frequency $\overline{S}_{i4}$. The following method shows how to extract the frequency domain feature of the EEG signals $y_i'(t')$ in certain target icon which correspond to the icon i:

First, EEG signals of certain target icon $y_i'(t')$ are analyzed based on Fourier Transform respectively, then spectrum function $S_i(k')$ of $y_i'(t')$ is obtained as follows:

$$S_i(k') = \sum\limits_{2}^{1000} e^{-i\frac{2\pi}{500}t'k'} y_i'(t') = \sum\limits_{n=1}^{500} e^{-i\frac{2\pi}{500}2nk'} y_i'(2n) \tag{22}$$

In which, $-i$ is the plural unit, $t'$ are EEG sampling time points and $t' = 2n$, n are the sampling amounts and n is integer on [1, 500], k' represent spectrum points and k is integer to [1, 500].

Then, extracting process of the frequency domain feature $S_i$ of the group average EEG signal are as follows:

The spectrum average amplitude $S_{i1}$ of the frequency domain feature $S_i$ in the certain target icon EEG signal $y_i'(t')$ that correspond to the icon i is:

$$S_{i1} = \frac{\sum\limits_{k'=1}^{500} S_i(k')}{500} \tag{23}$$

Spectrum variance $S_{i2}$:

$$S_{i2} = \frac{\sum\limits_{k'=1}^{500} (S_i(k') - S_{i1})^2}{499} \tag{24}$$

The first spectrum feature frequency $S_{i3}$:

$$S_{i3} = \frac{\sum\limits_{k'=1}^{500} S_i(k') f_{k'}'}{\sum\limits_{k'=1}^{500} S_i(k')} \tag{25}$$

The second spectrum feature frequency $S_{i4}$:

$$S_{i4} = \sqrt{\frac{\sum\limits_{k'=1}^{500} S_i(k')(f_{k'}' - S_{i3})^2}{500}} \tag{26}$$

$S_i(k')$ are obtained by Fourier Transform to the certain target icon EEG signal $y_i'(t')$ which correspond to the icon i, and denote the spectrum of the certain target icon EEG signal $y_i'(t')$. $f_{k'}'$ are the frequency value of the $k_{th}$ spectrum points, and $f_{k'}' = \frac{k' \cdot Fs}{500}$. In which, Fs is the sampling frequency (500 Hz), k' denote the spectrum points and k' is integer on [1, 500].

## 2.4    Similarity Calculation and Control Command of Activation Target Icons

This stage is aiming to calculate the time domain similarity A between the time domain feature $Y_i$ of certain target icon EEG signals after artifacts elimination and the time domain feature $\overline{Y}_i$ of the group average EEG signals which correspond to their icons. Then, calculate the frequency domain similarity B between target icon and the corresponding icon. If both of time domain similarity A and frequency domain similarity B > 90%, the control command of certain target icons will be triggered. As a result, EEG signals that are triggered by icons can control the interface.

Figure 3 depicts the process of activating control command of target icons in magnifying glass. In this figure, 1 denotes electrode cap, 2 denotes ERP devices, 3 denotes SCAN EEG signal processing module, 4 denotes microprocessor, 5 is the similarity of calculating on the EEG signal time domain and frequency domain features, 6 shows the circumstance that both of the time domain and frequency domain similarity is above 0.9, 7 trigger user computer "magnifying glass" command, 8 denotes the display device, 9 shows the target icon "magnifying glass" command has been activated, thus it can accomplish page zoom in.

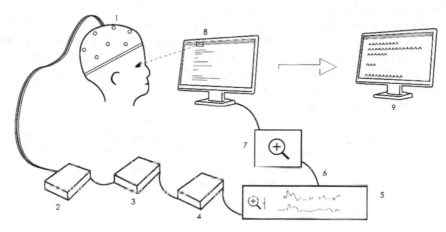

**Fig. 3.** The target icon control command activation process

The following calculation process shows the time domain similarity A between the certain target EEG signal of the icon i and the corresponding icon average EEG signal.

$$A = \sum_{j=1}^{8} \frac{1}{8} A_{ij}, \quad A_{ij} = \begin{cases} \frac{\overline{Y_{ij}}}{Y_{ij}}, & \overline{Y_{ij}} < Y_{ij} \\ \frac{Y_{ij}}{\overline{Y_{ij}}}, & \overline{Y_{ij}} \geq Y_{ij} \end{cases} \tag{27}$$

$A_{ij}$ is the $j_{th}$ time domain feature similarity of the icon i, $\overline{Y_{ij}}$ is the $j_{th}$ time domain feature value of the icon i group average EEG signal, $Y_{ij}$ is the $j_{th}$ time domain feature value of the icon i's certain target icon EEG signal. j is integer on [1, 8], and there are 8 indexes in time domain feature and each index weights $\frac{1}{8}$.

The calculation of frequency domain similarity B is as follows:

$$B = \sum_{l=1}^{4} \frac{1}{4} B_{il}, \quad B_{il} = \begin{cases} \frac{\overline{S_{il}}}{S_{il}}, & \overline{S_{il}} < S_{il} \\ \frac{S_{il}}{\overline{S_{il}}}, & \overline{S_{il}} \geq S_{il} \end{cases} \tag{28}$$

$B_{il}$ is the $l_{th}$ frequency domain feature similarity of the icon i, $\overline{S_{il}}$ is the $l_{th}$ frequency domain feature value of the icon i group average EEG signal, $S_{il}$ is the $l_{th}$ frequency domain feature value of the icon i's certain target icon EEG signal. l is integer on [1, 4], there are 4 indexes in frequency domain feature and each index weights $\frac{1}{4}$.

## 3   Discussion

This paper realizes the EEG control of the digital interface through using icons. In the future, we can try to use the selective attention mechanism of the navigation bar, the brain mechanism of color difference, in order to realize the brain-computer interaction of digital interface by using other elements.

In the early stage, brain-computer interaction needs to be carried out EEG experiment design according to EEG experimental standards and norms. In the using of navigation bar for brain-computer interaction, we can try to use the serial mismatch pattern to complete; in the using of color for brain-computer interaction, we can try to use Go-Nogo experimental paradigm. EEG features include time domain and frequency domain, wherein time domain and frequency domain extraction, classification and identification need to be achieved through the algorithm, and different mathematical algorithms will produce different effects. And other elements of brain-computer interaction, we can try to use wavelet algorithm and other mathematical methods. To achieve a high degree of matching between the EEG signal and the target command signal, various mathematical algorithms can be tried to reduce the error and improve the accuracy.

## 4   Conclusion

This paper first introduces the specific concept of brain-computer interaction, and analyzes the role of event-related potentials in brain-computer interaction. At the same time, the application of EEG assessment method in interface design, brain-computer interaction was proposed. Finally, integrating ERP experiments, signal feature extraction and classification technology, a digital interface BCI method of icon control was proposed, which is a new attempt and exploration in brain-computer interaction field. Finally, the realization of the brain-computer interaction method of other elements in the interface was discussed.

**Acknowledgements.** The paper is supported jointly by Science and Technology on Electro-optic Control Laboratory and National Aerospace Science Foundation of China (No. 20165169017), SAST Foundation of China (SAST No. 2016010) and National Natural Science Foundation of China (No. 71471037, 71271053, 51405514).

## References

1. Mason, S.G., Bashashati, A., Fatourechi, M., et al.: A comprehensive survey of brain interface technology designs. Ann. Biomed. Eng. **35**, 137–169 (2007)
2. Birbaumer, N., Ghanayim, N., Hinterberger, T., et al.: A spelling device for the paralysed. Nature **398**, 297–298 (1999)

3. Nicolelis, M.A.L.: Brain–machine interfaces to restore motor function and probe neural circuits. Nat. Rev. Neurosci. **4**, 417–422 (2003)
4. Ethier, C., Oby, E.R., Bauman, J.J., Miller, L.E.: Restoration of grasp following paralysis through brain-controlled stimulation of muscles. Nature **485**, 368–371 (2012)
5. Milekovic, T., Fischer, J., Pistohl, T., et al.: An online brain-machine interface using decoding of movement direction from the human electrocorticogram. J. Neural Eng. **9**, 046003 (2012)
6. Cheng, M., Ren, Y., Gao, X., et al.: Key technologies of rehabilitation robot control by EEG signal. Robot Tech. Appl. **4**, 45–48 (2003)
7. Allison, B.Z., Brunner, C., Kaiser, V., et al.: Toward a hybrid brain–computer interface based on imagined movement and visual attention. J. Neural Eng. **7**, 026007 (2010)
8. Gazzaniga, M.S., Ivry, R., Mangun, G.R.: Cognitive Neuro-Science. W. W. Norton and Company Inc., New York (2002)
9. Wang, X., Jin, J., Zhang, Y., et al.: Brain control: human-computer integration control based on brain-computer interface. Acta Automatica Sinica **39**, 208–221 (2013)
10. Zhang, Y., Zhao, Q., Jin, J., et al.: A novel BCI based on ERP components sensitive to configural processing of human faces. J. Neural Eng. **9**, 026018 (2012)
11. Zhu, Y., Ming, D., Qi, H., Cheng, L., Wan, B.: Patent application specification. CN200910069247 (2009). (in Chinese)
12. Guan, J., Li, M., Zhou, D., Chen, J., Liu, H., Chen, Y.: Patent application specification. CN201110269595 (2011). (in Chinese)
13. Liu, P., Hou, B., Zhou, G., He, J.: Patent application specification. CN201210085013 (2012). in Chinese
14. Wu, B., Su, Y., Zhang, J., Li, X., Zhang, J., Chen, W., Zheng, Y.: A virtual chinese keyboard BCI system based on P300 potentials. Acta Electronica Sinica **37**, 1733–1738 (2009)
15. Hong, B., Gao, Shang., Gao, X., Guo, F.: Patent application specification. CN200910076207 (2009). (in Chinese)
16. Li, X., Hong, J., Jiang, Y., Xu, F., Yao, L.: Patent application specification. CN201210006069 (2012). (in Chinese)

# Differences in Motor Imagery Activity Between the Paretic and Non-paretic Hands in Stroke Patients Using an EEG BCI

Zhaoyang Qiu[1], Shugeng Chen[2], Brendan Z. Allison[3], Jie Jia[2(✉)], Xingyu Wang[1], and Jing Jin[1(✉)]

[1] Key Laboratory of Advanced Control and Optimization for Chemical Processes, Ministry of Education, East China University of Science and Technology, Shanghai, People's Republic of China
jinjingat@gmail.com
[2] Department of Neurology, Huashan Hospital, Fudan University, Shanghai, People's Republic of China
shannonjj@126.com
[3] Department of Cognitive Science, University of California at San Diego, La Jolla, CA, USA

**Abstract.** Stroke is the leading cause of serious and long-term disability worldwide. Stroke survivors may recover some motor function after rehabilitation therapy. Many studies have shown that motor imagery (MI) based brain-computer Interface (BCI) can improve upper limb stroke rehabilitation. However, as stroke patients have suffered neurological damage, the brain regions associated with motor function might be compromised, thus impairing BCI performance. In this paper, we tried to explore whether stroke patients' imagination of hand movement differed between paretic versus non-paretic hands. Ten stroke patients (5 male, aged 21–69 years, mean $48.4 \pm 15.4$) participated in this study. They imagined moving either the left or the right hand according to cues. The common spatial patterns (CSP) approach was used to extract MI features, and a support vector machine (SVM) was used for classification. Results did not show that motor imagery accuracy for paretic hands was not substantially worse than with non-paretic hands. In tandem with other work assessing motor accuracy in healthy participants versus stroke patients, these results suggest that possible concerns about stroke patients' use of BCI-based motor imagery systems may not present serious obstacles to wider research and implementation.

**Keywords:** Motor imagery · Brain-computer interface · Stroke rehabilitation

## 1 Introduction

Stroke is one of the most common cerebrovascular diseases. It is the leading cause of serious and long-term disability worldwide [1–3]. A major consequence of stroke is impairment of motor function, often including hemiplegia of the upper limbs.

---

Z. Qiu and S. Chen—Equal Contribution

D.D. Schmorrow and C.M. Fidopiastis (Eds.): AC 2017, Part II, LNAI 10285, pp. 378–388, 2017.
DOI: 10.1007/978-3-319-58625-0_28

After rehabilitation therapy, some stroke survivors can partially regain their motor control, but most survivors are left with permanent motor disability, which may affect their ability to work, drive, type and conduct other daily activities [4].

At present, treatments to improve upper limb function may be divided into two categories: peripheral nerve intervention and of central nerve intervention. The methods of peripheral nerve intervention include specialized exercises, sensory integration training, and functional electrical stimulation (FES). The methods of central nerve intervention, which are much more experimental, include brain computer interfaces (BCIs), repetitive transcranial magnetic stimulation (rTMS), and transcranial direct current stimulation (tDCS).

Brain computer interface (BCI) systems have gained considerable attention in the research literature recently. BCI systems provide a new communication method for people with severe neuromuscular disabilities [5–7]. Various neurological phenomena can be used in BCI systems. Steady state visual evoked potentials (SSVEP) [8, 9], slow cortical potentials, P300 evoked potentials [10–15] and event-related desynchronization (ERD) [16]/event-related synchronization (ERS) [17] are the most prominent approaches in BCI systems.

Even if persons with stroke can no longer move an affected limb, they can still imagine moving it. Research has shown that motor imagery based BCIs can help induce brain plasticity in stroke survivors [1–3, 18]. It is well established that imagination of limb movement could result in event-related desynchronization (ERD) and event-related synchronization (ERS). Specifically, movement imagery (MI) affects the mu (8–12 Hz) and beta waves (13–30 Hz) in the EEG. Movement imagery produces significant ERD over the contralateral central area during imagination of right and left hand movement [19]. However, as stroke patients suffer neurological damage, the brain regions associated with motor function might be compromised [4]. This neurological damage could impair the ability to imagine movement. This study will explore any differences in BCI accuracy when classifying imagined movements of the paretic versus non-paretic hands.

## 2   Methods

### 2.1   Patients

Ten stroke patients (5 male, aged 21–69 years, mean 48.4 ± 15.4) participated in this study. Five of them, designated patients 1–5, have left hemiplegia, while patients 6–10 have right hemiplegia. All patients signed a written consent form prior to this experiment. The local ethics committee approved the consent form and experimental procedure before any patients participated. All patients were right handed according to self-reports. All subjects' native language was Mandarin Chinese.

### 2.2   Data Acquisition

In this study, EEG signals were sampled at 256 Hz through the g.USBamp (Guger Technologies, Graz, Austria). The band pass filter was set to 0.1 Hz–30 Hz.

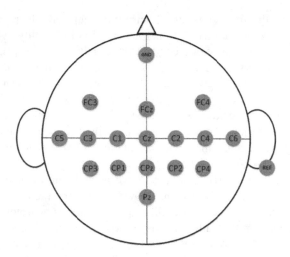

**Fig. 1.** The electrode distribution used in this study.

A 16-channel cap (FC3, FCZ, FC4, C5, C3, C1, CZ, C2, C4, C6, CP3, CP1, CPZ, CP2, CP4 and PZ) following the 10–20 international system was used for signal recording. Data were referenced to electrode REF located over the right mastoid with a forehead ground (GND), shown in Fig. 1.

## 2.3  Experimental Paradigms

After being prepared for EEG recording, the patients were seated in a comfortable chair in a shielded room. During data acquisition, patients were asked to relax and avoid unnecessary movement. The experimenter informed the patients that they would hear cues over a speaker that would instruct them to imagine moving either the left or the right hand. Figure 2 shows that each trial lasts eight seconds and starts with a warning "beep". Two seconds later, the cue (the command to imagine a left or right hand movement) is played. Patients were asked to imagine whatever type of hand movements that they felt was easiest for them. Six second later, a "relax" command is played, informing patients that the trial is over. Each patient participated in sixty trials within one recording session.

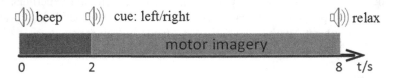

**Fig. 2.** Timing of a trial of the motor imagery paradigm. Each trial consisted of task and rest periods. Patients started to execute motor imagery tasks while the cue ("left" or "right") was played.

## 2.4    Feature Extraction

The EEG data were band-pass filtered using a third order Butterworth band pass filter from 8 to 30 Hz, since this frequency band included the range of frequencies that are most relevant in classifying motor imagery with EEG data.

The CSP algorithm is an effective feature extraction algorithm. It has been widely used in processing EEG data from motor imagery [20–25]. CSP is based on the simultaneous diagonalization of two covariance matrices. It finds a spatial filter to maximize variance for one class and minimize variance for another class at the same time to improve classification.

For the analysis, the original EEG signal data of a single trial is represented as a matrix $E_{N \times T}$, where $N$ is the number of channels, and $T$ is the number of sampling points for each channel. The CSP algorithm process is as follows:

Calculate spatial covariance of the EEG data:

$$C = (EE^T)/(tr(EE^T)) \tag{1}$$

$C_l$ and $C_r$ represent two spatial covariance matrixes (two classes of motor imagery). The composite spatial covariance matrix is $C_c$.

$C_c$ can be decomposed as:

$$C_c = U_c \lambda_c U_c^T \tag{2}$$

$U_c$ is the matrix of eigenvectors and $\lambda_c$ is the diagonal matrix of eigenvalues. In the process, the eigenvalues are arranged in descending order.

After whitening transformation:

$$P = \sqrt{\lambda_c^{-1}} U_c^T \tag{3}$$

Then $\overline{C_l}$ and $\overline{C_r}$ can be transformed into:

$$S_l = P\overline{C_l}P^T, S_r = P\overline{C_r}P^T \tag{4}$$

$S_l$ and $S_r$ share the same eigenvectors. If $S_l = B\lambda_r B^T$, then

$$S_r = B\lambda_r B^T, \ \lambda_l + \lambda_r = I \tag{5}$$

$I$ is the identity matrix. The projection matrix is achieved by the following equation:

$$W = (B^T P)^T \tag{6}$$

This is the expected spatial filter. Then the EEG signals can be projected on the first $m$ and last $m$ columns of $B$. So a single trial EEG data can be transformed into:

$$Z = WE \tag{7}$$

## 2.5   Classification Scheme

The support vector machine (SVM) is a machine learning method proposed in the 1990s [26]. It is mainly proposed for pattern recognition problems. Suppose the EEG data set $A \in R^d$ is from two classes, and could be divided by a hyperplane linearly. The resulting hyperplane could be expressed as: $WA + b = 0$. $W \in R^d$ is weight vector and $b$ is the intercept (scalar). The problem is transformed into finding the optimal hyperplane as follows:

$$\min J(W, \varepsilon) = \frac{1}{2}||W||^2 + c \sum_{i=1}^{n} \varepsilon_i, c \geq 0$$
$$s.t. \ y_i(W^T A^{(i)} + b) \geq 1 - \varepsilon_i, \varepsilon_i \geq 0, i = (1, \cdots n)$$

(8)

Where $A^{(i)}$ is a feature vector of a training sample, and $y_i$ is the category with labels, $\{-1, 1\}$, to which $A^{(i)}$ belongs. $W$ is the hyperplane coefficients vector. c is used to control the trade-off between the model complexity and empirical risk [27]. In this paper, the 10*10-fold cross validation accuracy approach were used to evaluate the performance of each patient.

## 3   Results

### 3.1   Feature Extraction

Figure 3 shows the ERD maps from patients 4 and 9 over channels C3 and C4. When patient 4 imagined right hand movement, ERD phenomena at channel C3 were stronger than at C4. When patient 9 performed the left-hand MI, ERD phenomenon at channel C4 were stronger than at C3.

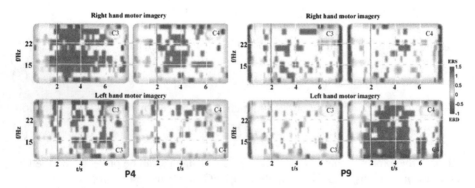

**Fig. 3.** The figure described two patients' ERD map during the right hand and left hand MI. "P" represents "patient".

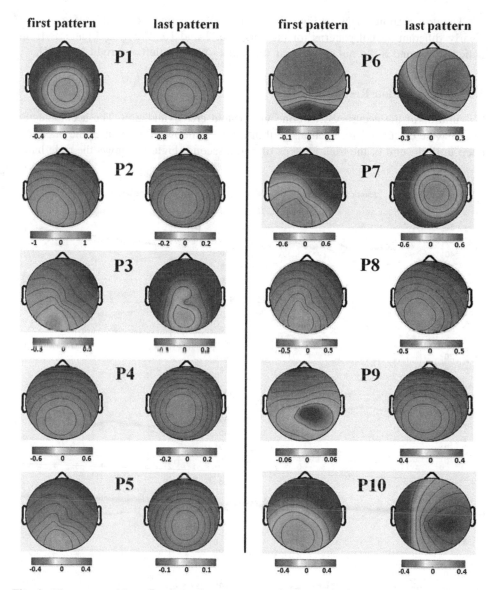

**Fig. 4.** The topographic maps of the first and last spatial patterns of ten patients. The patterns were extracted from averages of 60 trials. "P" represents "patient".

In the CSP algorithm, W is the projection matrix, and $W^{-1}$ is the inverse matrix of W. The columns of $W^{-1}$ are the time invariant vectors of EEG source distribution vectors called common spatial patterns [28]. Figure 4 shows the ten patients' first and last common spatial patterns. The first pattern was related to the ERD phenomena over left motor area of the cortex (obtained by maximizing the variance of the right hand MI EEG data). Accordingly, the ERD phenomenon over the right sensorimotor area of the cortex was related to the last pattern, corresponding to the left hand MI.

The topographic maps in Fig. 4 show that left vs. right left hand MI produced clearly different spatial patterns for patients 1, 6, 7 and 10. The spatial patterns from patients 2, 4 and 8 did not show clear differences between left and right hand MI.

## 3.2    Classification Results

Calculation of the accuracy was done via 10-fold cross validation. The accuracies in Fig. 5 were calculated for all trials within a time window of 1.5 s after the attention beep until the end of the trial, in steps of half a second. Figure 5 shows the right hand

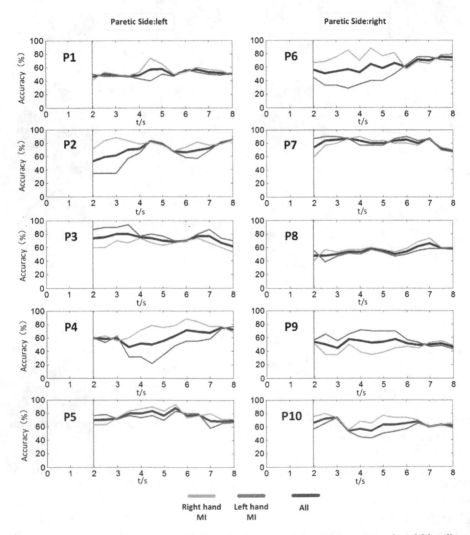

**Fig. 5.** The accuracy plots across all 60 trials for ten patients. The green, red and blue lines represent right hand motor imagery, left hand motor imagery and overall classification accuracies respectively. "P" represents "patient". (Color figure online)

MI, left hand MI, and overall classification results. Patients 1 to 5 have left hemiplegia, and patients 6 to 10 have right hemiplegia.

Results showed that patients 2, 4, 6 and 10 exhibited higher accuracies with the right hand MI than the left hand MI during most of the movement imagery period. For patients 3 and 9, the accuracies of left hand MI are higher than right hand MI. For the remaining patients, differences between the left and right hand MI are not obvious. Overall, these results do not support a relationship between which hand is paretic and classification of left vs. right MI. The higher accuracy during right hand MI (compared to left hand MI) may result from handedness or greater use of the right hand, but this suggestion requires further testing.

Figure 5 also shows that the accuracies varied across patients. The accuracies from patients 5 and 7 were above 80% during most of the MI period, while accuracies of patients 1, 8, and 9 were close to the chance level 50%. These performance results are generally consistent with work with healthy patients who have not trained to use a motor imagery BCI. There was no clear effect of paretic hand on accuracy.

## 4 Discussion

The primary goal of this study was to investigate whether there are differences between the motor imagery performance of the paretic and non-paretic hands for stroke patients. Ten stroke patients participated in our experiment. The results did not reveal a relationship between which hand was paretic (left vs. right) and either BCI performance or the separability of left vs. right hand MI.

Figure 3 displays the ERD maps from two patients. For patient 4, ERD phenomena at channel C3 were stronger than at C4 during right hand motor imagery. However, ERD phenomena at channel C4 were not stronger than at C3 during left hand motor imagery, but lower. This result is consistent with the classification accuracies in Fig. 5. Results in Fig. 5 showed that right hand MI yielded better performance than left hand MI for patient 4. For patient 9, ERD phenomena at channel C4 were significantly stronger than at C3 during left hand MI, while there were not obvious ERD changes over either channel during right hand MI. Again, the results in Fig. 5 are consistent, as patient p performed better with left hand MI than right hand MI.

Figure 5 shows that the MI accuracies do not show a strong relationship between the paretic vs. non-paretic hand. However, for many patients, regardless of paretic side, right hand MI yielded better classification accuracy than left hand MI. [29] reported that motor evoked potential amplitudes induced by MI of right (dominant hand) finger movement were significantly larger than those induced over the left (non-dominant hand). According to some relevant research, patients would perform better when they are familiar with (or skilled in) the action of complex MI. [30] reported that sports experts showed significant activation in the parahippocampus during imagery of professional skills relative to the novices. [31] found that the mean execution rate was significantly faster in a skilled MI condition relative to a novel condition. Hence, patients would perform better when they were familiar with the action of motor imagery. Since all patients were right handed, their right hands would be more skilled in some actions. This might lead to the better performance during right hand MI.

The overall accuracies from most patients were not high enough for reliable communication. In a motor imagery based BCI, users should learn how to modulate their brain activity proficiently. Future research could explore new ways to train stroke patients based partly on ongoing measures of EEG activity [1–3, 18], including paradigms in which users can choose their own mental activities relating to hand movement. Instead of learning to perform specific hand MI tasks such as imagining grasping or lifting, users could choose tasks such as writing, typing, or painting.

## 5  Conclusion

This study explored the differences between the MI of the paretic versus non-paretic hands for stroke patients. Results from ten patients did not show a strong relationship between BCI classification accuracy and which hand was paretic. The MI accuracies of the paretic hand might not be lower than the non-paretic hand. On the other hand, MI was more accurate for right than left hand MI, which may result from handedness and the subjects' freedom to choose their own MI task. Future work could explore training with self-selected imagery to improve performance, and explore the impact on rehabilitation of motor impairment resulting from stroke.

**Acknowledgments.** This work was supported in part by the Grant National Natural Science Foundation of China, under Grant Nos. 61573142, 61203127, 91420302 and 61305028. This work was also supported by the 13 Fundamental Research Funds for the Central Universities (WG1414005, WH1314023, and WH1516018) and Shanghai Chenguang Program under Grant 14CG31.

## References

1. Meng, F., Tong, K.Y., Chan, S.T., Wong, W.W., Lui, K.H., Tang, K.W., Gao, X.R.: BCI-FES training system design and implementation for rehabilitation of stroke patients. In: IEEE International Joint Conference on Neural Networks, pp. 4103–4106 (2008)
2. Soekadar, S.R., Birbaumer, N., Slutzky, M.W., Cohen, L.G.: Brain–machine interfaces in neurorehabilitation of stroke. Neurobiol. Dis. **83**, 172–179 (2014)
3. Pichiorri, F., Morone, G., Petti, M., Toppi, J., Pisotta, I., Molinari, M., Paolucci, S., Inghilleri, M., Astolfi, L., Cincotti, F., Mattia, D.: Brain-computer interface boosts motor imagery practice during stroke recovery. Ann. Neurol. **77**, 851–865 (2015)
4. Ang, K.K., Guan, C., Phua, K.S., Wang, C.C., Teh, I., Chen, C.W., Chew, E.: Transcranial direct current stimulation and EEG-based motor imagery BCI for upper limb stroke rehabilitation. In: Conference Proceedings of IEEE Engineering in Medicine and Biology Society, pp. 4128–4131 (2012)
5. Wolpaw, J.R., Birbaumer, N., McFarland, D.J., Pfurtscheller, G., Vaughan, T.M.: Brain–computer interfaces for communication and control. Clin. Neurophysiol. **113**, 767–791 (2002)
6. Jin, J., Allison, B.Z., Sellers, E.W., Brunner, C., Horki, P., Wang, X., Neuper, C.: An adaptive P300-based control system. J. Neural Eng. **8**, 036006 (2011)

7. Laar, B.V.D., Bos, D.P., Reuderink, B.B., Poel, M.: How much control is enough? Influence of unreliable input on user experience. IEEE Trans. Cybern. **43**, 1584–1592 (2013)

8. Cruz, J.N.D., Wan, F., Wong, C.M., Cao, T.: Adaptive time-window length based on online performance measurement in SSVEP-based BCIs. Neurocomputing **149**, 93–99 (2015)

9. Zhang, Y.S., Guo, D.Q., Cheng, K.W., Yao, D.Z., Xu, P.: The graph theoretical analysis of the SSVEP harmonic response networks. Cogn. Neurodyn. **9**, 305–315 (2015)

10. Jin, J., Daly, I., Zhang, Y., Wang, X.Y., Cichocki, A.: An optimized ERP brain–computer interface based on facial expression changes. J. Neural Eng. **11**, 1082–1088 (2014)

11. Chen, L., Jin, J., Zhang, Y., Wang, X.Y., Cichocki, A.: A survey of the dummy face and human face stimuli used in BCI paradigm. J. Neurosci. Methods **239**, 18–27 (2015)

12. Kaufmann, T., Schulz, S.M., Köblitz, A., Renner, G., Wessig, C., Kübler, A.: Face stimuli effectively prevent brain–computer interface inefficiency in patients with neurodegenerative disease. Clin. Neurophysiol. Off. J. Int. Fed. Clin. Neurophysiol. **124**, 893–900 (2013)

13. Jin, J., Sellers, E.W., Zhou, S., Zhang, Y., Wang, X., Cichocki, A.: A P300 brain computer interface based on a modification of the mismatch negative paradigm. Int. J. Neural Syst. **2**, 595–599 (2015)

14. Pan, J.H., Li, Y.Q., Gu, Z.H., Yu, Z.L.: A comparison study of two P300 speller paradigms for brain–computer interface. Cogn. Neurodyn. **7**, 523–529 (2013)

15. Yin, E., Zeyl, T., Saab, R., Hu, D., Zhou, Z., Chau, T.: An auditory/tactile visual saccade-independent P300 brain–computer interface. Int. J. Neural Syst. **26**, 1650001 (2015)

16. Pfurtscheller, G.: Graphical display and statistical evaluation of event-related desynchronization (ERD). Electroencephalogr. Clin. Neurophysiol. **43**, 757–760 (1977)

17. Pfurtscheller, G.: Event-related synchronization (ERS): an electrophysiological correlate of cortical areas at rest. Electroencephalogr. Clin. Neurophysiol. **83**, 62–69 (1992)

18. Jiang, S., Chen, L., Wang, Z., Xu, J.: Application of BCI-FES system on stroke rehabilitation. In: International IEEE/EMBS Conference on Neural Engineering, pp. 1112–1115. IEEE (2015)

19. Pfurtscheller, G., Neuper, C., Flotzinger, D., Pregenzerb, M.: EEG-based discrimination between imagination of right and left hand movement. Electroencephalogr. Clin. Neurophysiol. **103**, 642–651 (1997)

20. He, L., Gu, Z., Li, Y., Yu, Z.: Classifying motor imagery EEG signals by iterative channel elimination according to compound weight. In: Wang, F.L., Deng, H., Gao, Y., Lei, J. (eds.) AICI 2010. LNCS (LNAI), vol. 6320, pp. 71–78. Springer, Heidelberg (2010). doi:10.1007/978-3-642-16527-6_11

21. Nasihatkon, B., Boostani, R., Jahromi, M.Z.: An efficient hybrid linear and kernel CSP approach for EEG feature extraction. Neurocomputing **73**, 432–437 (2009)

22. Ang, K.K., Chin, Z.Y., Zhang, H.H., Guan, C.T.: Robust filter bank common spatial pattern (RFBCSP) in motor-imagery-based brain–computer interface. In: Conference Proceedings of the IEEE Engineering in Medicine and Biology Society, pp. 578–581 (2009)

23. Liu, C., Zhao, H.B., Li, C.S., Wang, H.: Classification of ECoG motor imagery tasks based on CSP and SVM. In: BMEI 3rd International Conference on IEEE, pp. 804–807 (2010)

24. Qiu, Z., Jin, J., Lam, H.K., Zhang, Y., Wang, X., Cichocki, A.: Improved SFFS method for channel selection in motor imagery based BCI. Neurocomputing **207**, 519–527 (2016)

25. Qiu, Z., Jin, J., Zhang, Yu., Wang, X.: Generic channels selection in motor imagery-based BCI. In: Wang, R., Pan, X. (eds.) Advances in Cognitive Neurodynamics (V). ACN, pp. 413–419. Springer, Singapore (2016). doi:10.1007/978-981-10-0207-6_57

26. Vapnik, V.N., Vapnik, V.: Statistical Learning Theory. Wiley, New York (1998)

27. Yang, Y., Wang, J., Yang, Y.Y.: Improving SVM classifier with prior knowledge in micro calcification detection. In: Conference Proceedings of the IEEE Image Processing, pp. 2837–2840 (2012)

28. Wang, L., Zhang, X., Zhong, X., Zhang, Y.: Analysis and classification of speech imagery EEG for BCI. Biomed. Sign. Proc. Contr. **8**, 901–908 (2013)

29. Yahagi, S., Kasai, T.: Motor evoked potentials induced by motor imagery reveal a functional asymmetry of cortical motor control in left- and right-handed human subjects. Neurosci. Lett. **276**, 185 (1999)

30. Wei, G., Luo, J.: Sport expert's motor imagery: functional imaging of professional motor skills and simple motor skills. Brain Res. **1341**, 52–62 (2010)

31. Lacourse, M.G., Orr, E.L., Cramer, S.C.: Brain activation during execution and motor imagery of novel and skilled sequential hand movements. Neuroimage **27**, 505–519 (2005)

# Multimodal Neural Interfaces for Augmenting Human Cognition

William J. Tyler[✉]

Arizona State University, Tempe, USA
wtyler@asu.edu

**Abstract.** Within the next decade multimodal neural interfaces (MNI's) could begin to transform society by expanding human cognitive abilities. Embodiments of such interfaces will include a combination of biometric and environmental sensors working in cooperation with noninvasive brain stimulation or neuromodulation devices to optimize human cognitive processes. These MNI's may, for example, monitor psychophysiological arousal using pupillometry and responsively stimulate noradrenergic activity in a manner to enhance sustained attention or vigilance. Other near-term applications may include MNI's that are designed to enable an individual to maintain a particular state of calm or flow state during stressful tasks by using algorithms to generate auricular vagal nerve stimulation waveforms based on real-time heart rate variability and electroencephalography data. Numerous other possibilities remain. The present paper provides a brief overview of several different types of biometric sensors and the neurophysiological systems they can monitor. This information is provided in context of their present limitations, as well as how neurophysiological sensors may be used in combination with noninvasive brain stimulation (NIBS) methods to augment human cognition and performance. Overall the paper attempts to provide a balanced and realistic examination of the issues remaining to be solved or addressed in order to reliably enhance human cognition. Efforts that combine high quality sensors for monitoring neurophysiological signatures of attention and psychophysiological markers of arousal with scientifically-grounded neurostimulation approaches in an integrated MNI solution will be necessary to achieve reliable and reproducible cognitive augmentation facilitated by future MNI's.

**Keywords:** Neuromodulation · Augmented cognition · Human intelligence · Brain machine interface · Human performance

## 1 Introduction

Over the past couple decades there have been numerous engineering and scientific advances, which have begun to open new possibilities for Human Computer Interactions (HCI's). Such advances include the recent and rapid emergence of wearable computing architectures and wireless biometric sensors. These advances have been driven in large part by innovations and technology development in the mobile health sector of the consumer electronics industry. In other words, consumer demands have driven the development of advanced biometric sensors like wearable electroencephalography

© Springer International Publishing AG 2017
D.D. Schmorrow and C.M. Fidopiastis (Eds.): AC 2017, Part II, LNAI 10285, pp. 389–407, 2017.
DOI: 10.1007/978-3-319-58625-0_29

(EEG) headbands and wearable health trackers like heart rate (HR) and activity monitors [1]. During this time other advances in neurotechnology have brought about a prolific expansion of noninvasive neuromodulation methods and devices. These neuromodulation and brain stimulation methods have been developed through decades of biomedical research and are used today in various embodiments to treat neurological and psychiatric disorders. Interestingly, over the past few years several embodiments of noninvasive neuromodulation devices have also emerged in the consumer electronics market.

Opening a new era in HCI's and human evolution, consumer electronics neuromodulation devices have begun to enter the marketplace intended as human performance enhancing machines (Fig. 1). It remains early in this new era of human-machine symbiosis and the technologies currently available remain rudimentary. However, billions of dollars of investments have recently been made into the neuromodulation and neural interface space over the past five years. These investments have been made in conjunction with major research and development efforts supported by federal research agencies, private investments including venture capital, as well as by large multinational consumer technology and communication corporations like Google, Qualcomm, Facebook, Samsung, and Apple [2, 3]. In addition to the usual suspect medical device companies like Medtronic and Boston Scientific, others including large pharma and biotech companies like the Bayer Corporation, Glaxo Smith Kline, Johnson & Johnson, and Pfizer have also become increasingly active in the space. Given these investments and the rapid proliferation of technologies being developed, by 2040 it can be expected that consumer neuromodulation devices will be routinely used to optimize and enhance human performance. A major point of this paper is to discusses how some of these future technologies may operate specifically to augment cognitive learning abilities while outlining some of challenges that will be associated with developing and validating them.

A new generation of multimodal neural interfaces (MNI's) that includes a combination of biometric and environmental sensors working in cooperation with noninvasive brain stimulation (NIBS) or neuromodulation devices will be best suited to enable robust HCI's capable of enhancing human cognition (Fig. 1). Research over the past couple decades has clearly shown that it is not essential to have information about brain activity or psychophysiological states in order to produce significant changes in cognitive abilities using NIBS techniques. The vast majority of the effects produced to date however have been fairly small. As we gain better abilities to acquire and process real-time insights into brain activity/behavior relationships, in parallel, the technologies for modulating brain activity will become more precise and effective. The convergence of these advances will lead to MNI's for augmenting cognition (Fig. 1). This paper surveys current state-of-the-art methods that are positioned to serve as a basis for MNI's capable of enhancing learning within the next decade. It is proposed that by first gaining a solid scientific grasp on how to enhance fundamental cognitive processes like associative learning or skill training, neuromodulation can begin to take aim towards optimizing higher cognitive functions, such as decision making or abstract reasoning.

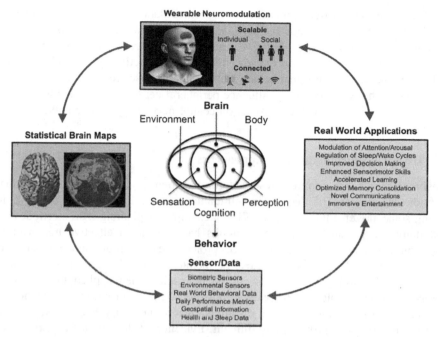

**Fig. 1.** Multimodal neural interfaces can integrate with existing and future information networks providing unique opportunities to understand and optimize human brain/behavior relationships. Wearable, connected neuromodulation systems (top) have recently been introduced to the consumer marketplace as devices intended to augment or optimize human experiences (right). These devices are safe and inexpensive however they remain in a rudimentary state with respect to biological efficacy. The introduction of noninvasive neural interfaces for modulating or sensing neural activity into mass markets will bring about rapid advances in their technological capabilities and biological efficacy. Already data from multiple sensors and devices can be captured by back-end or cloud services (bottom). These biometric, environmental, and behavioral data concomitant with neuromodulation data can help neuroscience understand how modulation of targeted brain circuits influences freely behaving humans in real world environments by creating statistical models and maps (left). The transposition of consumer information extracted from voluntarily and openly shared resources onto new insights gained from global human brain mapping efforts will certainly advance our understanding of how the human brain regulates behavior (center).

## 2 Neuromodulation Methods for Cognitive Modulation

Neuromodulation is a general term used to refer to a collection of approaches used to increase and/or decrease nervous system activity. There are pharmacological or chemical means of neuromodulation, psychological or behavioral means of neuro-modulation, as well as various forms of natural sensory stimulation or deprivation that can be used influence neuronal activity for desired outcomes. While these different forms of neuromodulation are of interest for their ability to enhance human cognitive performance, they are beyond the scope of the present paper. Rather the focus of this paper is on hardware-based approaches to neuromodulation and their embodiments as neural interfaces. The methods coarsely classified into one of two major categories, invasive or noninvasive [4, 5]. Invasive neuromodulation refers to the use of a surgically implanted electrode(s) to exert an effect on neural activity. Noninvasive neuromodulation methods do not require surgically implanted electrodes, but rather deliver energy across the skin to directly influence peripheral nerves and across bone, such as vertebrae or skull to exert direct actions on central nervous system activity.

## 2.1   Invasive Neuromodulation Approaches

Invasive methods are currently reserved for therapeutic or diagnostic applications. Methods and devices of deep-brain stimulation (DBS) have proven effective for treating some movement disorders [6, 7]. For example, implanting DBS electrodes into subthalamic nuclei and other motor circuits has proven an effective treatment for Parkinson's disease [7]. Interestingly, DBS protocols can exert an immediate effect on tremors and motor behaviors, which can be monitored in real time to guide treatment paradigms. DBS has produced less consistent results when applied to other brain circuits in a manner intended to generate positive cognitive or emotional outcomes.

Compared to treating movement disorders, treating neuropsychiatric disorders and cognitive diseases has proven more difficult. Evidence of this comes from the recent failure of two different placebo-controlled, randomized Phase II trials designed to evaluate the efficacy of DBS for treating major depressive disorder [8, 9]. Similarly, a separate Phase II trial assessing the efficacy of DBS of the fornix in treating mild Alzheimer's disease failed to demonstrate any significant cognitive benefits compared to controls [10]. Reinforced by the null outcomes of these DBS studies, it is speculated that deep-brain regions underlying cognitive or emotional processes need to be targeted in an individualized manner. It may also be the case however that there is significant variation in the representation of emotional or cognitive control regions at any given moment. Thus, the targeting of any one region within an individual using DBS electrodes may prove a difficult path forward for treating emotional or cognitive dysfunction. Further, the use of DBS for cognitive augmentation will always require a surgical procedure that obviously takes on a different risk (versus reward) profile compared to noninvasive options. Neural engineering efforts have however become increasingly focused on developing implantable neuromodulation technologies that are minimally invasive. Therefore it is expected that humans will eventually rely on implanted neuromodulation devices to enhance, augment or optimize their performance and experiences. Either way it is safe to presume that DBS methods will not be widely used to augment the cognition of healthy individuals within the next decade.

## 2.2   Noninvasive Neuromodulation

**Transcranial Magnetic/Electrical Stimulation.** Over the past several decades externally applied neuromodulation methods, such as transcranial magnetic stimulation (TMS) and transcranial electrical stimulation (tES) like transcranial direct current stimulation (tDCS) have been shown to be capable of safely modulating human brain function and behavior [4]. TMS modulates brain activity via electromagnetic induction [4]. On the other hand it is believed that more crude methods like tDCS diffusely affect brain activity by passing a weak electrical current the skin, skull, dura mater, cerebrospinal fluid and into cortex [11]. These top-down cortical modulation methods have also demonstrated therapeutic potential for treating a variety of neurological and psychiatric diseases. In particular, TMS can directly stimulate and robustly modulate cortical activity. The FDA has approved TMS devices for the treatment of major depressive disorder and migraine headaches. Additionally, TMS holds promise for treating a variety of other neurological diseases and psychiatric disorders. While TMS provides more diffuse modulation of brain activity than DBS, such sparse modulation may be an advantage when treating cognitive or emotional dysfunctions likely originating from aberrant activity patterns across spatially distributed, but interconnected circuits (Fig. 2).

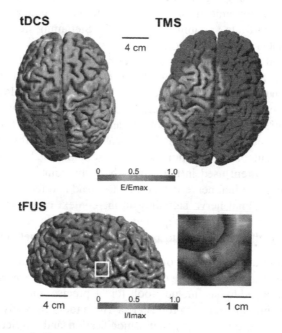

**Fig. 2.** Noninvasive methods of neuromodulation confer broad spatial resolutions. The spatial distributions of electric fields (EField) generated by transcranial direct current stimulation (tDCS) and transcranial magnetic stimulation (TMS) are illustrated as modeled using realistic, physiologically validated finite element modeling (top images; scale = 4 cm). The magnitudes of the EFields are illustrated as a ratio of the maximum for normalization and visualization purposes. The bottom panel of images illustrates the spatial distribution of the acoustic field generated by transcranial focused ultrasound (tFUS) at two different magnifications (scale = 4 cm and 1 cm) for comparison purposes. The magnitude of acoustic intensity is shown as a ratio to the maximum observed value for comparative visualization purposes. Note the superior spatial resolution conferred by tFUS compared to tDCS or TMS.

In numerous studies tDCS and transcranial alternating current stimulation (tACS) have been reported capable of enhancing and perturbing cognitive processes, such as working memory or creative problem solving when targeted to different brain regions [12, 13]. However, these findings have been inconsistent and/or produce marginal effects [14, 15]. Due largely to these variable outcomes, poor study designs, and lack of a cohesive mechanistic hypotheses, some neuroscientists have recently begun to challenge the idea that tDCS exerts its actions through direct effects on cortex. Further supporting these challenges, it has recently been shown that 1 mA tES produces a maximal electric field (Efield) strength of $\leq 0.5$ mV/mm in both non-human primates and humans [16]. While it seems tES does produce a nonzero Efield strength, it remains debatable whether or not such low Efield strengths can exert consistent and reliable effects on brain activity that are sufficient to alter human behavior, emotion, or cognition. Alternative bottom-up mechanisms, which have been shown to underlie non-invasive peripheral neuromodulation methods, may help explain some of the general outcomes observed in response to tDCS.

Interestingly tDCS targeting the PFC has been shown to modulate psychophsyiolgical arousal and autonomic nervous system activity as indicated by changes in cortisol levels and heart rate variability (HRV) [17]. Stemming from the conventional hypothesis that tDCS modulates cortical activity via top-down mechanisms, the explanation provided by Brunoni and colleagues was that tDCS acted on the prefrontal cortex to influence activity of the hypothalamic pituitary adrenal (HPA) axis and sympathoadrenal medullary (SAM) systems [17]. As discussed below in the context of peripheral nerve modulation however, alternate neural pathways involving the bottom-up modulation of brain circuit activity and autonomic function seem to better explain many of the observations made in response to tES including tDCS and tACS (including entrainment or perturbation of brain oscillations). For example, a major action of the direct current used in tDCS may be to modulate the activity of cranial nerves, such as the trigeminal nerve innervating the head and face. Any such effects as described below on cranial nerve signaling in the context of peripheral neuromodulation, such as modulating norepinephrine signaling could explain many of the short-term plasticity effects believed to be triggered by tDCS methods.

**Optical Neuromodulation.** In addition to electrical and magnetic methods of NIBS, there are also optical and acoustic methods. Some of the most powerful brain stimulation methods developed to date include tools for the precise stimulation and inhibition of neural circuits using optogenetic probes [18]. These tools currently offer the highest spatial resolution, but require both genetic modification and surgical procedures, so they are not presently a realistic option for broadly augmenting human cognition. Other less invasive, albeit less specific, forms of optical neuromodulation may be more readily useful however.

Photobiomodulation (PBM) implements certain wavelengths of light (typically near-infrared; NIR) to modulate a variety of intra- and extracellular signaling processes. Reflective of the source of photons and the relatively low energy levels used to influence target tissues with PBM, it can also be referred to as low-level laser therapy (LLLT). In this respect PBM is different from other forms of laser-mediated infrared (IR) stimulation, such as transient optical neural stimulation in which high-energy IR laser pulses are used to directly stimulate action potentials in peripheral nerves [19]. The focus here is rather on the use of low energy NIR photons that have been shown to modulate cortical activity following transcranial transmission.

Recent studies have shown NIR photons (>800 nm) can penetrate cortical depths up to a few centimeters [20, 21]. In fact a higher percentage of the energy transmitted by NIR photons across the skin and skull reach the cortex compared to electrical currents transmitted via DC tES fields. Several applications of transcranial PBM (tPBM) have shown that transmitting NIR photons from light emitting diodes (LEDs) to the cortex can enhance cognitive function in patents suffering from several neurological and psychiatric disorders [22, 23]. Interestingly, intranasal PBM has also been reported in a few cases to provide cognitive benefits to patients suffering from mild to moderate dementia [24]. Transcranial NIR laser therapy has also been shown to safely modulate emotional and cognitive function in healthy humans [25]. Further, intra-aural bright light therapy has been shown to enhance sensorimotor functions in athletes [26]. Despite the early promise of PBM, tPBM and LLLT, these viable options of modulating brain activity have been understudied to date. Further, studies into the potential of tPBM for cognitive enhancement are certainly warranted. This is true especially when considering the preliminary findings of safety and efficacy coupled with the fact that numerous off-the-shelf components can be used to engineer relatively simple tPBM optical neural interfaces that may be effective.

**Ultrasonic Neuromodulation.** About a decade ago it was shown that pulsed ultrasound (US) could directly and noninvasively stimulate action potentials and synaptic transmission by acting through nonthermal (mechanical) mechanisms on voltage-gated ion channel activity [27]. Since then the field of ultrasonic neuromodulation (UNMOD) has emerged through numerous demonstrations that US can be used to focally modulate the activity of brain circuits in different organisms including humans [28]. It has also been shown in numerous different experimental preparations that US can modulate peripheral neural circuits [28]. Since US can be transmitted and focused across bone including skull, it has a variety of potential applications as a noninvasive neural interface.

Transcranial focused US (tFUS) was recently shown to modulate cortical activity in humans in a manner that enhanced their somatosensory discrimination abilities [29]. Even more recently, tFUS was demonstrated to functionally stimulate brain circuit activity in the somatosensory and visual cortices of humans [30, 31]. Perhaps one of the greatest advantages of tFUS for neuromodulation is that it can confer spatial resolutions anywhere in the human brain equivalent to those of DBS electrodes and better than other noninvasive methods like TMS or tDCS (Fig. 2) [29]. Again as discussed elsewhere, this is true even in deep-brain circuits [28, 29]. Additionally, the use of holographic US makes it feasible to modulate multiple sites within a neural circuit simultaneously. This can be achieved in a manner such that the multifocal US neurostimulation patterns can be spatiotemporally modulated rapidly to convey complex sensory information embodied, for example, as an acoustic retinal prosthetic [32, 33]. Similarly US can be used to deliver haptic inputs (ultrahaptics), as well as for generating virtually interactive 3D objects in free space [34, 35]. Such contact-free or touchless neural interfaces implementing US and UNMOD pose a world of intriguing possibilities especially for entertainment purposes, which is likely why Disney Research and others are beginning development activities in the space [35]. Since optical holograms can be superimposed with ultrasonic holograms to create virtual multisensory environments that can be both seen and felt, the potential impact of this type of technology for augmenting cognition by creating virtually immersive multisensory learning environments on-demand in the future is staggering.

Although further research is needed and global efforts are ongoing, UNMOD has already shown that it may offer several advantages over electrical, chemical, magnetic, and optical neuromodulation methods [28, 29]. The increased application of US in NIBS studies and HCI's will prove to bring about many exciting advances in the near future. One of the more enticing prospects is a MNI embodiment, which incorporates the neuromodulation capabilities of US with its imaging abilities in an integrated, wearable form factor to both stimulate and image brain activity in freely behaving humans. Already in the art, the technological foundations and preliminary engineering specifications required to develop such a device exist.

**Peripheral Nerve Modulation.** Perhaps the most widely implemented form of electrical neuromodulation exists in the form of transcutaneous electrical nerve stimulation or TENS. This basic TENS method has been safely used for decades to modulate peripheral nerve activity and treat pain. Given the safety of TENS and similar transdermal neurostimulation devices there are already a large diversity of over-the-counter devices cleared by various regulatory agencies for a variety of medical, cosmetic (aesthetic), and recreational purposes. These basic methods also serve the foundation for modulation of a specific class of peripheral nerves, cranial nerves, which can provide powerful conduits to central regulators of brain activity. Depending on the stimulus parameters and protocols used, different outcomes can be achieved.

Since the head (skin, muscle, and sensory organs) is innervated by a dense matrix of peripheral nerve and cranial nerve (CN) fibers, it seems difficult that one could pass electrical currents across the skin on any part of the head without affecting the activity of general somatic or proprioceptive afferent fibers innervating that local vicinity. In fact, one of the only universal outcomes of all tES methods is that the methods induce skin sensations. These skin sensations are undoubtedly transmitted to the brain by CN fibers affected by electrical currents transmitted through cutaneous tissues. For example, tDCS electrodes placed over regions targeting PFC can modulate the activity of supraorbital and/or supratrochlear branches of trigeminal nerve (CN V) afferents, as well as temporal branches of the facial nerve (CN VII) and perhaps the vagal (CN X), accessory (CN XI) and/or hypoglossal (CN XII) nerves depending on the exact anode/cathode montage used. Collectively these the afferent fibers of these CN and other peripheral nerves innervating the head and neck feed directly into robust arousal systems like the ascending reticular activating system (RAS) located in the brain stem as discussed in greater detail below.

Afferent fibers of the trigeminal, facial, vagal, accessory, and hypoglossal CN's, as well as afferents of cervical nerves like cervical spinal nerves and the phrenic nerve project directly to sensory nuclei of the brain stem. The primary sensory information relayed by these fibers is transmitted to cortical areas via thalamocortical pathways. Prior to, during, and after signal propagation to cortex however, incoming peripheral signals carried by cranial and spinal nerve afferent pathways simultaneously undergo extensive local processing in a series of highly inter-connected structures including the reticular formation (RF) and RAS located in the brainstem (Fig. 3). This first station of information integration in the brain is where higher consciousness is thought to originate in brain stem circuits filtering, integrating, and processing incoming sensory information [36]. It is here that cranial and spinal nerves modulate the activity of the RAS nuclei the locus coeruleus (LC), raphe nuclei (RN), and pedunculopontine nuclei (PPN), as well as others responsible for the bottom-up regulation of cortical gain, psychophysiological arousal, and neurobiological responses to environmental stimuli and stressors [37–40].

Through bottom-up pathways the LC, RN, and PPN influence brain activity, human behavior, brain information processing, sleep/wake/arousal cycles, and higher cortical functions including attention and cognition by regulating levels of norepinephrine (NE), serotonin (5-HT), and acetylcholine (ACh) respectively [37–40] (Fig. 3). To those not skilled in the art of neuroscience it may not be obvious, but these signaling pathways and molecules are the classical targets of many potent classes of drugs, such as beta-blockers, SSRI's, MAOI's, and amphetamine derivatives used to treat diseases or to enhance human performance including cognition. Pharmacological methods swamp systems usually in an unspecific manner. Thus, peripheral neuromodulation may offer a more controlled way to achieve some of the same outcomes as many drugs. Further, since these pathways represent some of the most powerful endogenous neuromodulators known to exist in the brain, learning to harness their signaling abilities with pulsed transdermal electrical stimulation (pTES) of cranial nerves will be imperative to the success of future MNI's for augmenting human performance including cognition. This is true especially given the ease of access of CN's and the robust ability of pTES and similar transcutaneous electrical methods to modulate brain activity.

With respect to the safety, there exists a wealth of primary data and clinical endpoints demonstrating broad safety margins for electrical stimulation of peripheral nerves including the vagus [41, 42]. More specifically several implanted vagus nerve stimulator (VNS) electrodes intended for medical uses have been approved by the United States Food and Drug Administration (FDA) and the European Commission (CE Mark) for treatment of drug-resistant epilepsy, and also in the United States for treatment of drug-resistant depression. VNS is a safe and effective therapy that is widely believed to work by acting through bottom-up afferent effects on the neuromodulators NE and 5-HT, as well as glutamatergic and GABAergic neurotransmitter systems as discussed above [41, 43, 44]. Given repeated demonstrations that transdermal VNS has been shown to be effective in achieving similar clinical outcomes, there has become a shift towards favoring this non-invasive approach over surgically implanted cervical VNS devices.

Stimulation of the cervical and auricular branch of the vagus has been repeatedly demonstrated to induce short-term and long-term brain plasticity [41]. It has also been shown to modulate brain circuits and trigger signaling consequences supporting mechanisms of action for the observed plasticity [44–47]. Whether or not neurotechnology can be advanced to harness this plasticity in a useful manner for real world gains remains to be determined. However several recent studies have provided early

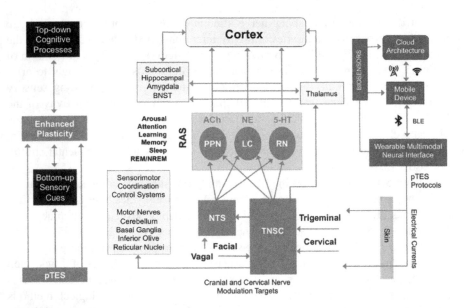

**Fig. 3.** Cranial nerve modulation enables bottom-up modulation of higher brain by influencing nuclei of the ascending reticular activating system. The schematic illustration shows brain circuits and general concepts involved in the bottom-up regulation of neural networks to enhance plasticity and performance using pulses transdermal electrical stimulation (pTES) methods. The delivery of pulsed electrical currents across the skin of the head, neck, or face using transdermal electrodes can modulate the activity of cranial and cervical nerves (blue pathways). The trigeminal, cervical, facial, and vagus nerves send afferent inputs to the trigeminal nucleus sensory complex (TNSC) and nucleus of the solitary tract (NTS) in the brain stem. These first nuclei then send projections to higher nuclei of the ascending reticular activating system (RAS). The RAS includes pedunculopontine nuclei (PPN), the locus coeruleus (LC), and raphe nuclei (RN), which transmit acetylcholine (ACh), norepinephrine (NE), and serotonin (5-HT) respectively to various parts of the brain. These regions and processes highlighted in red serve as the chief control centers in the brain for regulating arousal, attention, learning, memory, sleep onset, and stages of sleep. Either through automated or assisted algorithms that learn to control the timing and levels of RAS responses to pTES protocols, multimodal neural interfaces (MNI's) and their wireless data networks (represented in purple) will become powerful enhancers of endogenous brain plasticity. These MNI's may enable the switching on and off of sleep/wake states, optimized attention, increased sensory awareness, improved consolidation/retention of learned information, and other enhancements for tuning human performance. (Color figure online)

evidence that this may indeed be the case. In other potential applications high-frequency (kHz) pTES of trigeminal and cervical afferents via a small, wearable device attached to the side of the forehead and base of neck has been shown capable of significantly suppressing stress responses during fear conditioning by decreasing sympathetic tone and biochemical markers of noradrenergic activity in humans [48]. These effects are also thought to underlie the mechanisms of action responsible for the ability trigeminal and cervical pTES treatments delivered using a wearable device nightly before sleep onset to improve sleep quality and enhance mood as indicated by physiological, biochemical and behavioral measures [49]. These observations are also consistent with the sleep/wake and attention/arousal control functions of the neural circuitry being targeted by CN modulation (Fig. 3). Certainly being able to modulate sleep/wake cycles or trigger restorative micro-naps on-demand would have profound implications on human cognitive performance. Based on preliminary findings it appears the modulation of the cervical plexus and trigeminal-vagal circuits may provide a path to achieving such milestones [49]. We have ongoing studies devoted to determining if rapid, robust, and effective sleep control programs can indeed be delivered using high-frequency modulation of cervical plexus circuitry.

Superficial branches of the vagus, in particular the auricular branch of the vagus nerve, are located in anatomical regions such that achieving functional electrical coupling to them can be achieved using a number of industrial electrode designs including conventional transdermal neurostimulation approaches. These devices are similar to ear-bud style headphones lending themselves to realistic human interface designs of which we are already accustomed. At least one start-up company (Nervana, LLC) has recently begun to commercialize consumer-grade auricular vagal nerve stimulators integrated with headphones as a system intended to suppress sympathetic activity and promote relaxation. Stimulation of the left auricular vagus using transdermal vagal nerve stimulation (tVNS) has in fact been shown to be a safe and effective method of regulating ascending neuromodulatory brainstem circuits, as well as higher cortical regions. Data from several studies has shown that electrical modulation of vagal afferents, including tVNS of the auricular vagus nerve, in healthy humans can safely produce biochemical, behavioral, and neurophysiological effects that are consistent with an enhancement of skills training or learning [50–52]. Therefore it is expected that cranial nerve modulation and other NIBS methods can indeed be used to systematically enhance learning and/or skill training within the next ten years.

Some of the major hurdles that still remain in the field of CN modulation involve precise anatomical mapping of brain stem inputs and outputs, as well as to better characterize the pulse parameter space as a function of neurophysiological and biochemical outcomes. Basic scientific progress in these areas will surely enable cranial nerve modulation to become a powerful core of future MNI's. Also it is important to keep in mind that, as mentioned, the robust safety profile of NIBS methods including CN modulation has allowed these technologies to make recent entries into consumer markets. This transference into mass markets will also bring about the scaling of new insights, innovations, and discoveries, which has not yet been experienced in any neurotechnology sector to date. In other words, the mainstream adoption of neuromodulation devices for human performance enhancement will bring about dramatic changes to the HCI landscape and greatly influence the future potential of MNI's for augmenting human cognition.

# 3  Multimodal Neural Interfaces for Cognitive Applications

Over the past decade the technology industry sectors of wearable computing and mobile health (mHealth; digital health) have begun to introduce a bewildering number of connected biometric and environmental sensors to medical device and consumer health markets. By some estimates, the number of connected consumer devices may exceed 50 billion within the next couple years. New generations of smarter and more reliable medical-grade sensors are also expected to be continuously entering the consumer health marketplace over the coming few years [1]. Although While only a subset of sensors to date have been designed to operate as neural interfaces *per se*, as described below a variety of other sensor types can also provide quantitative and predictive information regarding brain/behavior relationships. Consolidated information collected from these sensors will train future MNI networks to bias or tune human brain circuit activity using neuromodulation functions for performance optimization (Fig. 1). Such closed-loop human-machine interfaces will transform the ways we interact with information, our environments, and each other.

## 3.1 Electrophysiological Sensors Integrated with Neuromodulation Devices

Common signatures of electrophysiological or neurophysiological activity used in modern neural interfaces include those acquired through electroencephalography (EEG) and electromyography (EMG) sensors. There are also numerous tethered and wireless sensors that report electrocardiographic (ECG) and neurophysiological activity. Many current generation heart rate (HR) monitors however implement pressure transducers or optical sensors, so HR signals are discussed in the context of psychophysiological sensors below. Conventional electrophysiological sensors detect micro-scale voltage fluctuations reflecting central and peripheral nervous system activity of the brain and neuromuscular systems respectively. As mentioned previously, increased consumer demands coupled with decreased component and manufacturing costs have led to the emergence of wearable EEG, EMG, and ECG systems over the past decade [1]. Since there are well-documented applications of these technologies in numerous clinical applications, the focus of these technologies here is on their future potential in supporting advanced HCI's.

Some consumer EEG and EMG devices are marketed and used as modern biofeedback systems connected to mobile applications that coach users through relaxation techniques including meditation. Other consumer-grade wearable EEG/EMG embodiments are useful for establishing local networks directly between a user's brain activity and a computer system, for example to control robotic actions [53]. Some of the most interesting uses of EEG to emerge recently however are applications designed to monitor and predict human cognitive function and performance.

It is relatively well established that EEG can be a useful tool for monitoring and predicting memory and cognitive performance under some conditions [54]. Other interesting EEG applications related to their potential for augmenting human cognition include the monitoring of cortical idling [55] and operator interruptibility [56]. Providing a demonstration that wearable sensors including EEG can predict susceptibility to worker (user) interruptions opens the possibility for MNI's to gate information flow to users at optimal times to ensure optimal cognitive performance [56]. Given that mobile EEG systems and psychophysiological sensors are readily available, one can imagine the rapid development of a total mobile learning solution that embodies a MNI enabling users to track, predict, and correct interruptibility using biometric signals as previously described [56]. Such an MNI would operate in a manner to predict a users susceptibility to disruption then in a closed-loop manner deliver cranial nerve (CN) modulation protocols to maintain attention as similarly illustrated in Fig. 3. Similar MNI embodiments utilizing EEG signals to monitor distractibility and attention while controlling CN modulation protocols to regulate arousal and attention can also be used to enhance vigilance during long periods of high cognitive demand or to optimize cognitive function when operating off natural circadian cycles.

Several issues need to be solved before EEG interfaces can reliably serve MNI's in closed-loop applications in the real world. First, given the growth of EEG sensors in consumer health markets it would be advantageous if certain industry standards were established. Such standards would be used to ensure data quality and sensor performance, as there remains considerable variability across devices [57]. The search for idealized dry electrodes has been on ongoing saga for the EEG industry especially as the demand for high quality mobile devices has grown the past few years. New generations of conductive polymers and micromechanical systems look to overcome these voids of quality dry electrode solutions soon.

Even with dry EEG electrodes, many mobile sensing headsets have poor quality industrial designs that are cumbersome and do not properly account for human factors in real world situations. One of the more interesting possible solutions however enables the recording of high quality EEG signals from within the ear canal (ear-EEG) [58, 59] or around the outer ear [60]. Again, headphones already exist in a friendly and familiar form factor that we are all already accustomed to. There is some resistance of individuals to use present day consumer neural interfaces because they make users feel awkward or unnatural. This is a problem, which can be solved by adopting industrial designs of familiar forms like ear bud headphones to in the development of future MNI systems. As elegantly demonstrated by Züger and Fritz (2015) the integration of EEG signals with psychophysiological signals can provide robust paths forward in the development of MNI's.

### 3.2   Psychophysiological Sensors for Closed-Loop Neuromodulation

While electrophysiological sensors directly detect changes in neural activity, psychophysiological sensors can record the activity of several different systems through various means to provide quantitative information about brain states. Microbolometer based near IR imaging of facial temperatures, which reflect capillary vasoconstriction dynamics controlled by the sympathetic nervous system and NE signaling, can remotely collect information about emotional arousal or whether an individual or individuals are in relaxed or stressed mental state [49]. Other optical sensors (photodiodes and CMOS detectors for example), pressure transducers (piezoelectric elements), ultrasonic sensors, gyroscopes and accelerometers have been used in a variety of ways to report information about brain states or make inferences about brain activity of particular circuits. As discussed below, many of these approaches to monitoring psychophysiological behaviors will be useful in the design of MNI's integrating neural sensing and modulation capabilities.

One of the most widely recorded mobile health signals that reports neurophysiological activity is HR. Examining HR and heart rate variability (HRV) can provide some unique insights into functional autonomic nervous system activity including vagal responses to sensory stimuli and environmental stressors [61, 62]. While HR and HRV certainly provide opportunities to better understand brain function; due to the complex variables and neural circuitry regulating the cardiac cycle, one might be cautioned in using it as a trigger in MNI applications intended to enhance cognitive function. Restated, HR/HRV signals alone are extremely difficult to interpret especially without extensive historical records from which accurate predictions can be made. In previous studies for example, we found facial temperature to be a better predictor of acute stress responses than HR or HRV [49]. There are obviously many contexts however when HR/HRV data can be useful in MNI applications and since these data can be captured from a variety of common devices, they should be captured anytime neuromodulation methods are implemented then integrated through cloud computing applications with other relevant streams of sensor data as similarly illustrated in Figs. 1 and 3. Other sensors capable of reporting psychophysiological and neurophysiological information will likely prove more useful in MNI's designed to augment cognitive processes.

Evidence in the literature indicates that pupillary responses and eye blink rates are two robust indicators of psychophysiological activity. Interestingly, standard CMOS or CCD detectors can be used to remotely sense pupil dynamics and eye blink rates, which makes them interesting candidates for reporting psychophysiological information to MNI's designed to work in a closed-loop manner with neuromodulation protocols. Pupil diameter (PD) has been shown to reflect states of attention [63] and to rapidly fluctuate with the levels of NE and ACh in the cortex [64]. Further supporting the tight relationship between PD and LC/NE activity, it was recently shown that PD significantly covaries with fMRI BOLD activity in the LC [65]. Similar to the ability of PD to report NE activity, spontaneous eye-blink rates (EBR) have been clincally validated to correlate with dopamine levels and function [66]. Eye blinks have also interestingly been shown to briefly activate the default mode network and may perhaps serve to transiently consolidate information from dorsal attention networks during sustained attention [67]. Combined with CN modulation by pTES for example (Fig. 3), PD and EBR can prove to be reliable neurophysiological variables used to inform or train MNI protocols.

Given that CN modulation by pTES and other methods has been to work, in part, by modulating LC/NE activity combined with the fact the PD is a reliable reporter of LC/NE activity, a next logical step in the development of MNI's for augmenting cognitive function would be to marry these two approaches in an integrated wearable design. Industrial designs like that of Google Glass or other head-mounted devices, such as wearable Tobii eye trackers lend themselves well to supporting the hardware required for monitoring PD and modulating trigeminal, vagal, or other CN's. In particular, PD has been shown to reflect cortical gain control mediated by LC activity [68], as well as to correlate with the stimulus dimensions of some forms of cued learning [69]. As such, one can envision a MNI that monitors PD in a manner to trigger specific pTES protocols that engage or disengage LC activity during learning. Further, PD could be used during training or learning as information that would act to alter the temporal rate(s) or stimulus characteristic of information being presented in sync with

CN modulation to optimize encoding and retention. The presentation of information could also be gated to a user as a function of PD to optimize creative problem solving or divergent thinking since PD has been shown to predict states of convergent and divergent thinking [70]. While many intriguing possibilities have been discussed throughout this paper, it seems most practical that the next stages of development focus on MNI applications that are grounded by strong scientific results. Therefore, future studies should consider the use of multiple sensors not only in an attempt to enhance brain function, but more importantly to better understand it while being able to safely modulate identified brain circuits and signaling systems in freely behaving humans. Modern neurotechnology has presented the computational sciences, neuroscience, bioengineering, medicine, social sciences, and us as humans (consumers) with a massive opportunity to gain better insights into one of the greatest mysteries of the universe – how brain activity produces dynamic and complex behaviors.

# 4   Conclusion

As described throughout this paper, many recent advances in neural interfaces and neurotechnologies have been driven by research, development, and innovation in the consumer electronics industry in wearable computing and mHealth (digital health) technology sectors. Given the increased demand and growing investments in this space, it is anticipated that wearable MNI's capable of both sensing and modulating brain activity or mental states will open new opportunities for HCI's. Major global impacts of closed-loop MNI's will likely first be experienced through neurotechnologies intended to augment human cognition – specifically to enhance learning or modulate attention. By first acquiring a solid scientific understanding of how various neuromodulation techniques affect plasticity and influence simple learning processes like associative learning or sensorimotor skill learning, future efforts can build upon this foundational knowledge to develop advanced MNI's capable of augmenting human cognition in transformative ways. It is expected that this will take some time, perhaps a couple decades, but the path has indeed been set in motion with industrial paced efforts occurring on a global scale. The future of MNI's for augmenting cognition looks to be bright and perhaps will bring about a world where performance enhancing technology becomes favored over, or used in conjunction with, today's standard pharmacological, chemical, and training methods. As a parting thought, one might imagine the impact of the learning tools of the year 2040 embodied as MNI's including ear-EEG sensors and intra-aural HR sensors integrated with transdermal auricular vagal nerve stimulating electrodes as an earbud style device that is designed to be worn connected to pair of glasses comprised of a CMOS to detect PD and EBR, a microbolometer to detect facial temperature, and a transparent OLED screen to present virtual information transposed onto the real world.

**Disclosure.** WJT is an inventor and co-inventor on numerous issued and pending patents describing the utility and design of neuromodulation methods, systems, and devices. WJT has no financial stakes or equity interests in companies or entities assigned rights to these patents.

# References

1. Piwek, L., Ellis, D.A., Andrews, S., Joinson, A.: The rise of consumer health wearables: promises and barriers. PLOS Med. **13**, e1001953 (2016)
2. Nelson, J.T., Tepe, V.: Neuromodulation research and application in the U.S. department of defense. Brain Stimul. Basic Trans. Clin. Res. Neuromodulation **8**, 247–252 (2014)
3. Waltz, E.: A spark at the periphery. Nat. Biotech. **34**, 904–908 (2016)
4. Wagner, T., Valero-Cabre, A., Pascual-Leone, A.: Noninvasive human brain stimulation. Annu. Rev. Biomed. Eng. **9**, 527–565 (2007)
5. Luan, S., Williams, I., Nikolic, K., Constandinou, T.G.: Neuromodulation: present and emerging methods. Front. Neuroeng. **7**, 27 (2014)
6. Hamani, C., Andrade, D., Hodaie, M., Wennberg, R., Lozano, A.: Deep brain stimulation for the treatment of epilepsy. Int. J. Neural Syst. **19**, 213–226 (2009)
7. Lozano, A.M., Snyder, B.J.: Deep brain stimulation for parkinsonian gait disorders. J. Neurol. **255**(Suppl. 4), 30–31 (2008)
8. Bergfeld, I.O., Mantione, M., Hoogendoorn, M.C., et al.: Deep brain stimulation of the ventral anterior limb of the internal capsule for treatment-resistant depression: a randomized clinical trial. JAMA Psychiatry **73**, 456–464 (2016)
9. Dougherty, D.D., Rezai, A.R., Carpenter, L.L., Howland, R.H., Bhati, M.T., O'Reardon, J.P., Eskandar, E.N., Baltuch, G.H., Machado, A.D., Kondziolka, D., Cusin, C., Evans, K.C., Price, L.H., Jacobs, K., Pandya, M., Denko, T., Tyrka, A.R., Brelje, T., Deckersbach, T., Kubu, C., Malone Jr., D.A.: A randomized sham-controlled trial of deep brain stimulation of the ventral capsule/ventral striatum for chronic treatment-resistant depression. Biol. Psychiatry **78**, 240–248 (2015)
10. Lozano, A.M., Fosdick, L., Chakravarty, M.M., Leoutsakos, J.M., Munro, C., Oh, E., Drake, K.E., Lyman, C.H., Rosenberg, P.B., Anderson, W.S., Tang-Wai, D.F., Pendergrass, J.C., Salloway, S., Asaad, W.F., Ponce, F.A., Burke, A., Sabbagh, M., Wolk, D.A., Baltuch, G., Okun, M.S., Foote, K.D., McAndrews, M.P., Giacobbe, P., Targum, S.D., Lyketsos, C.G., Smith, G.S.: A phase II study of fornix deep brain stimulation in mild Alzheimer's disease. J. Alzheimer's Dis. JAD **54**, 777–787 (2016)
11. Peterchev, A.V., Wagner, T.A., Miranda, P.C., Nitsche, M.A., Paulus, W., Lisanby, S.H., Pascual-Leone, A., Bikson, M.: Fundamentals of transcranial electric and magnetic stimulation dose: definition, selection, and reporting practices. Brain Stimul. **5**, 435–453 (2012)
12. Dubljevic, V., Saigle, V., Racine, E.: The rising tide of tDCS in the media and academic literature. Neuron **82**, 731–736 (2014)
13. Floel, A.: tDCS-enhanced motor and cognitive function in neurological diseases. Neuroimage **85**(Pt 3), 934–947 (2014)
14. Horvath, J.C., Forte, J.D., Carter, O.: Evidence that transcranial direct current stimulation (tDCS) generates little-to-no reliable neurophysiologic effect beyond MEP amplitude modulation in healthy human subjects: a systematic review. Neuropsychologia **66C**, 213–236 (2015)
15. Horvath, J.C., Forte, J.D., Carter, O.: Quantitative review finds no evidence of cognitive effects in healthy populations from single-session transcranial direct current stimulation (tDCS). Brain Stimul. Basic Transl. Clin. Res. Neuromodulation **8**(3), 535–550 (2015)
16. Opitz, A., Falchier, A., Yan, C.-G., Yeagle, E.M., Linn, G.S., Megevand, P., Thielscher, A., Deborah, A.R., Milham, M.P., Mehta, A.D., Schroeder, C.E.: Spatiotemporal structure of intracranial electric fields induced by transcranial electric stimulation in humans and nonhuman primates. Sci. Rep. **6**, 31236 (2016)

17. Brunoni, A.R., Vanderhasselt, M.A., Boggio, P.S., Fregni, F., Dantas, E.M., Mill, J.G., Lotufo, P.A., Bensenor, I.M.: Polarity- and valence-dependent effects of prefrontal transcranial direct current stimulation on heart rate variability and salivary cortisol. Psychoneuroendocrinology **38**, 58–66 (2013)
18. Fenno, L., Yizhar, O., Deisseroth, K.: The development and application of optogenetics. Annu. Rev. Neurosci. **34**, 389–412 (2011)
19. Wells, J., Konrad, P., Kao, C., Jansen, E.D., Mahadevan-Jansen, A.: Pulsed laser versus electrical energy for peripheral nerve stimulation. J. Neurosci. Methods **163**, 326–337 (2007)
20. Tedford, C.E., DeLapp, S., Jacques, S., Anders, J.: Quantitative analysis of transcranial and intraparenchymal light penetration in human cadaver brain tissue. Lasers Surg. Med. **47**, 312–322 (2015)
21. Henderson, T.A., Morries, L.D.: Near-infrared photonic energy penetration: can infrared phototherapy effectively reach the human brain? Neuropsychiatr. Dis. Treat. **11**, 2191–2208 (2015)
22. Naeser, M.A., Martin, P.I., Ho, M.D., Krengel, M.H., Bogdanova, Y., Knight, J.A., Yee, M. K., Zafonte, R., Frazier, J., Hamblin, M.R., Koo, B.B.: Transcranial, red/near-infrared light-emitting diode therapy to improve cognition in chronic traumatic brain injury. Photomed. Laser Surg. **34**, 610–626 (2016)
23. Hamblin, M.R.: Shining light on the head: photobiomodulation for brain disorders. BBA Clin. **6**, 113–124 (2016)
24. Saltmarche, A.E., Naeser, M.A., Ho, K.F., Hamblin, M.R., Lim, L.: Significant improvement in cognition in mild to moderately severe dementia cases treated with transcranial plus intranasal photobiomodulation: case series report. Photomed. Laser surg. (2017). http://online.liebertpub.com/doi/10.1089/pho.2016.4227
25. Barrett, D.W., Gonzalez-Lima, F.: Transcranial infrared laser stimulation produces beneficial cognitive and emotional effects in humans. Neuroscience **230**, 13–23 (2013)
26. Tulppo, M.P., Jurvelin, H., Roivainen, E., Nissila, J., Hautala, A.J., Kiviniemi, A.M., Kiviniemi, V.J., Takala, T.: Effects of bright light treatment on psychomotor speed in athletes. Front. Physiol. **5**, 184 (2014)
27. Tyler, W.J., Tufail, Y., Finsterwald, M., Tauchmann, M.L., Olson, E.J., Majestic, C.: Remote excitation of neuronal circuits using low-intensity, low-frequency ultrasound. PLoS ONE **3**, e3511 (2008)
28. Naor, O., Krupa, S., Shoham, S.: Ultrasonic neuromodulation. J. Neural Eng. **13**, 031003 (2016)
29. Legon, W., Sato, T.F., Opitz, A., Mueller, J., Barbour, A., Williams, A., Tyler, W.J.: Transcranial focused ultrasound modulates the activity of primary somatosensory cortex in humans. Nat. Neurosci. **17**, 322–329 (2014)
30. Lee, W., Kim, H.-C., Jung, Y., Chung, Y.A., Song, I.-U., Lee, J.-H., Yoo, S.-S.: Transcranial focused ultrasound stimulation of human primary visual cortex. Sci. Rep. **6**, 34026 (2016)
31. Lee, W., Kim, H., Jung, Y., Song, I.-U., Chung, Y.A., Yoo, S.-S.: Image-guided transcranial focused ultrasound stimulates human primary somatosensory cortex. Sci. Rep. **5**, 8743 (2015)
32. Hertzberg, Y., Naor, O., Volovick, A., Shoham, S.: Towards multifocal ultrasonic neural stimulation: pattern generation algorithms. J. Neural Eng. **7**, 056002 (2010)
33. Naor, O., Hertzberg, Y., Zemel, E., Kimmel, E., Shoham, S.: Towards multifocal ultrasonic neural stimulation II: design considerations for an acoustic retinal prosthesis. J. Neural Eng. **9**, 026006 (2012)
34. Carter, T., Seah, S.A., Long, B., Drinkwater, B., Subramanian, S.: UltraHaptics: multi-point mid-air haptic feedback for touch surfaces. In: Proceedings of the 26th Annual ACM Symposium on User Interface Software and Technology, pp. 505–514. ACM, St. Andrews (2013)

35. Sodhi, R., Poupyrev, I., Glisson, M., Israr, A.: AIREAL: interactive tactile experiences in free air. ACM Trans. Graph. **32**, 1–10 (2013)
36. Parvizi, J., Damasio, A.: Consciousness and the brainstem. Cognition **79**, 135–160 (2001)
37. Couto, L.B., Moroni, C.R., dos Reis Ferreira, C.M., Elias-Filho, D.H., Parada, C.A., Pela, I.R., Coimbra, N.C.: Descriptive and functional neuroanatomy of locus coeruleus-noradrenaline-containing neurons involvement in bradykinin-induced antinociception on principal sensory trigeminal nucleus. J. Chem. Neuroanat. **32**, 28–45 (2006)
38. Aston-Jones, G., Rajkowski, J., Cohen, J.: Role of locus coeruleus in attention and behavioral flexibility. Biol. Psychiatry **46**, 1309–1320 (1999)
39. Berridge, C.W., Waterhouse, B.D.: The locus coeruleus-noradrenergic system: modulation of behavioral state and state-dependent cognitive processes. Brain Res. Brain Res. Rev. **42**, 33–84 (2003)
40. Sara, S.J.: The locus coeruleus and noradrenergic modulation of cognition. Nat. Rev. Neurosci. **10**, 211–223 (2009)
41. Ben-Menachem, E., Revesz, D., Simon, B.J., Silberstein, S.: Surgically implanted and non-invasive vagus nerve stimulation: a review of efficacy, safety and tolerability. Eur. J. Neurol. **22**, 1260–1268 (2015)
42. McCreery, D.B., Agnew, W.F., Yuen, T.G.H., Bullara, L.: Charge density and charge per phase as cofactors in neural injury induced by electrical stimulation. IEEE Trans. Biomed. Eng. **37**, 996–1001 (1990)
43. George, M.S., Aston-Jones, G.: Noninvasive techniques for probing neurocircuitry and treating illness: vagus nerve stimulation (VNS), transcranial magnetic stimulation (TMS) and transcranial direct current stimulation (tDCS). Neuropsychopharmacology **35**, 301–316 (2010)
44. Krahl, S.E., Clark, K.B.: Vagus nerve stimulation for epilepsy: a review of central mechanisms. Surg. Neurol. Int. **3**, S255–S259 (2012)
45. Fang, J., Rong, P., Hong, Y., Fan, Y., Liu, J., Wang, H., Zhang, G., Chen, X., Shi, S., Wang, L., Liu, R., Hwang, J., Li, Z., Tao, J., Wang, Y., Zhu, B., Kong, J.: Transcutaneous vagus nerve stimulation modulates default mode network in major depressive disorder. Biol. Psychiatry **79**, 266–273 (2016)
46. Frangos, E., Ellrich, J., Komisaruk, B.R.: Non-invasive access to the vagus nerve central projections via electrical stimulation of the external ear: fMRI evidence in humans. Brain Stimul. Basic Transl. Clin. Res. Neuromodulation **8**, 624–636 (2015)
47. Kraus, T., Hösl, K., Kiess, O., Schanze, A., Kornhuber, J., Forster, C.: BOLD fMRI deactivation of limbic and temporal brain structures and mood enhancing effect by transcutaneous vagus nerve stimulation. J. Neural Transm. **114**, 1485–1493 (2007)
48. Tyler, W.J., Boasso, A.M., Mortimore, H.M., Silva, R.S., Charlesworth, J.D., Marlin, M.A., Aebersold, K., Aven, L., Wetmore, D.Z., Pal, S.K.: Transdermal neuromodulation of noradrenergic activity suppresses psychophysiological and biochemical stress responses in humans. Sci. Rep. **5**, 13865 (2015)
49. Boasso, A.M., Mortimore, H., Silva, R., Aven, L., Tyler, W.J.: Transdermal electrical neuromodulation of the trigeminal sensory nuclear complex improves sleep quality and mood. bioRxiv (2016)
50. Jacobs, H.I.L., Riphagen, J.M., Razat, C.M., Wiese, S., Sack, A.T.: Transcutaneous vagus nerve stimulation boosts associative memory in older individuals. Neurobiol. Aging **36**, 1860–1867 (2015)
51. Sellaro, R., van Leusden, J.W., Tona, K.D., Verkuil, B., Nieuwenhuis, S., Colzato, L.S.: Transcutaneous vagus nerve stimulation enhances post-error slowing. J. Cogn. Neurosci. **27**, 2126–2132 (2015)

52. Steenbergen, L., Sellaro, R., Stock, A.-K., Verkuil, B., Beste, C., Colzato, L.S.: Transcutaneous vagus nerve stimulation (tVNS) enhances response selection during action cascading processes. Eur. Neuropsychopharmacol. **25**, 773–778 (2015)
53. Minati, L., Yoshimura, N., Koike, Y.: Hybrid control of a vision-guided robot arm by EOG, EMG, EEG biosignals and head movement acquired via a consumer-grade wearable device. IEEE Access **4**, 9528–9541 (2016)
54. Klimesch, W.: EEG alpha and theta oscillations reflect cognitive and memory performance: a review and analysis. Brain Res. Rev. **29**, 169–195 (1999)
55. Pfurtscheller, G., Stancák Jr., A., Neuper, C.: Event-related synchronization (ERS) in the alpha band — an electrophysiological correlate of cortical idling: a review. Int. J. Psychophysiol. **24**, 39–46 (1996)
56. Züger, M., Fritz, T.: Interruptibility of software developers and its prediction using psycho-physiological sensors. In: Proceedings of the 33rd Annual ACM Conference on Human Factors in Computing Systems, pp. 2981–2990. ACM, Seoul (2015)
57. Nijboer, F., van de Laar, B., Gerritsen, S., Nijholt, A., Poel, M.: Usability of three electroencephalogram headsets for brain-computer interfaces: a within subject comparison. Interact. Comput. **27**, 500–511 (2015)
58. Mikkelsen, K.B., Kappel, S.L., Mandic, D.P., Kidmose, P.: EEG recorded from the ear: characterizing the ear-EEG method. Front. Neurosci. **9**, 438 (2015)
59. Schroeder, E.D., Walker, N., Danko, A.S.: Wearable ear EEG for brain interfacing, pp. 1005115–1005116 (2017)
60. Martin, G.B., Bojana, M., Stefan, D.: Identifying auditory attention with ear-EEG: cEEGrid versus high-density cap EEG comparison. J. Neural Eng. **13**, 066004 (2016)
61. Billman, G.E.: Heart rate variability - a historical perspective. Front. Physiol. **2**, 86 (2011)
62. Reyes del Paso, G.A., Langewitz, W., Mulder, L.J., van Roon, A., Duschek, S.: The utility of low frequency heart rate variability as an index of sympathetic cardiac tone: a review with emphasis on a reanalysis of previous studies. Psychophysiology **50**, 477–487 (2013)
63. Gabay, S., Pertzov, Y., Henik, A.: Orienting of attention, pupil size, and the norepinephrine system. Atten. Percept. Psychophys. **73**, 123–129 (2011)
64. Reimer, J., McGinley, M.J., Liu, Y., Rodenkirch, C., Wang, Q., McCormick, D.A., Tolias, A.S.: Pupil fluctuations track rapid changes in adrenergic and cholinergic activity in cortex. Nat. Commun. **7**, 13289 (2016)
65. Murphy, P.R., O'Connell, R.G., O'Sullivan, M., Robertson, I.H., Balsters, J.H.: Pupil diameter covaries with BOLD activity in human locus coeruleus. Hum. Brain Mapp. **35**, 4140–4154 (2014)
66. Karson, C.N.: Spontaneous eye-blink rates and dopaminergic systems. Brain **106**, 643–653 (1983)
67. Nakano, T., Kato, M., Morito, Y., Itoi, S., Kitazawa, S.: Blink-related momentary activation of the default mode network while viewing videos. Proc. Natl. Acad. Sci. U.S.A. **110**, 702–706 (2013)
68. Gilzenrat, M.S., Nieuwenhuis, S., Jepma, M., Cohen, J.D.: Pupil diameter tracks changes in control state predicted by the adaptive gain theory of locus coeruleus function. Cogn. Affect. Behav. Neurosci. **10**, 252–269 (2010)
69. Eldar, E., Cohen, J.D., Niv, Y.: The effects of neural gain on attention and learning. Nat. Neurosci. **16**, 1146–1153 (2013)
70. Chermahini, S.A., Hommel, B.: The (b)link between creativity and dopamine: Spontaneous eye blink rates predict and dissociate divergent and convergent thinking. Cognition **115**, 458–465 (2010)

# Human Cognition and Behavior in Complex Tasks and Environments

# Using Assessment to Provide Application in Human Factors Engineering to USMA Cadets

Michael W. Boyce[1(✉)], Charles P. Rowan[2], Devonte L. Baity[2],
and Michael K. Yoshino[2]

[1] Army Research Laboratory, Orlando, FL, USA
`michael.w.boycell.civ@mail.mil`
[2] United States Military Academy at West Point, West Point, NY, USA
`{charles.rowan,devonte.baity,michael.yoshino}@usma.edu`

**Abstract.** This paper discusses a collaboration between the Army Research Laboratory (ARL) and the United States Military Academy at West Point in teaching the fundamentals of human factors engineering through assessment and experimentation. To facilitate this, the cadets engage in a year-long capstone project where an ARL scientist serves as a mentor, often in conjunction with departmental faculty. This paper discusses a five-phase teaching process to assist in training the fundamentals of research. The five phases are: 1. Identification of research questions and background research. 2. The development of research protocols and their associated training, 3. The selection and understanding of appropriate assessment techniques, 4. The coordination and execution of data collection, and 5. Statistical analysis and reporting. This process uses an existing research experiment at ARL focusing on the impact of different types of display surfaces to support military tactical decision-making to serve as a case study. The research experiment used a hybrid of two research platforms: the Augmented REality Sandtable (ARES) and the Generalized Intelligent Framework for Tutoring (GIFT). An examination of the process as well as perspectives from the cadets assisting with the Perspectives from The ARL/USMA research and the cadets assisting with the research. These perspectives can help with the development of other similar programs aimed at combining research laboratories and academic institutions.

**Keywords:** Military tactics · Assessment · Capstone · Augmented reality sandtable · Generalized intelligent framework for tutoring · Cadets · USMA

## 1 Introduction

Bridging the gap between theoretical classroom learning and applied experimental research using technology is essential to the education of military cadets [1]. The department of Behavioral Sciences and Leadership (BS&L), engineering psychology program at the United States Military Academy at West Point (USMA) uses human factors engineering to make the classroom-applied connection. The relationship between organizations such as the USMA and the Army Research Laboratory (ARL) provide

D.D. Schmorrow and C.M. Fidopiastis (Eds.): AC 2017, Part II, LNAI 10285, pp. 411–422, 2017.
DOI: 10.1007/978-3-319-58625-0_30

opportunities for interdisciplinary teams that can contribute to the development of simulation and training systems and the teaching of human factors engineering to cadets supporting the research [2]. Human factors engineering has several different areas of military relevance such as:

- Human-agent teaming [3]
- User interface design for command and control [4]
- Cyber defense [5] and
- Situation awareness [6].

Human factors engineering, with its challenging and exciting problems, is diverse enough to meet any interest that a cadet may have. During the Fall of 2016, researchers at ARL and USMA decided to put together a capstone project with two cadets, a USMA faculty member, and an ARL researcher, who are the authors of this paper. This paper contributes to the existing literature by providing an Army-specific application to cadet training, guiding proper research techniques during capstone projects.

The capstone has specific requirements such as proposal development, oral presentations, and final reports. This research focuses on additional requirements that target the relationship between the researcher and the cadets while maintaining experimental rigor. These additional requirements sparked the development of a five-phase process that would provide different teaching moments throughout the capstone project. The five phases are: 1. Identification of research questions and background research. 2. The development of research protocols and their associated training, 3. The selection and understanding of appropriate assessment techniques, 4. The coordination and execution of data collection, and 5. Statistical analysis and reporting. Although these phases appear to be self-explanatory, it is the communication and interaction that provide and support positive outcomes.

Examples can assist in solidifying the understanding of a theoretical process. The example for this process is a research experiment involving the Augmented REality Sandtable [ARES, 7] and the Generalized Intelligent Framework for Tutoring [GIFT, 8] to provide an assessment of military tactics knowledge at the squad and platoon level. The experiment assesses the impact of surface projection on the accuracy, time on task, engagement, and physiological responses as cadets answer questions. This research is a follow-up to a pilot study [9] involving Reserve Officers' Training Corps (ROTC) cadets. There was also a replication study using USMA cadets, which was led by one of the co-authors as a part of another capstone [10].

The structure of this paper is organized as follows: Sect. 2 talks about the specific method used to support the capstone project in two different ways. The first is through the teaching process phases, and the second is the more traditional description of the method of the experiment. Section 3 will cover the effectiveness of the process by discussing the positives and negatives for each one of the phases. Section 4 is a discussion written by the cadet coauthors talking about their experience during the capstone project and working with ARL researchers. Section 5 provides a conclusion with potential recommendations for similar types of programs on the integration of the process and assessment into a military student population.

# 2   Method

## 2.1   Teaching Process Phases

### Identification of Research Questions and Background Research

The first step in helping the cadets formulate research questions to support the capstone project is to investigate into related literature and find the underlying principles which potentially guide the experimental design. The result of this investigation is a literature review on topics the cadets found interesting as well as the metrics or assessment tools that they can potentially use. The first obvious topic that they wanted to examine was the issue of time on task for decision making. Specifically, do different types of surface projection combinations lead to varying effects on time on task? Past research about different types of projected displays (i.e. 3-D perspective views versus 2-D views) has shown differential effects of task performance based on the specifics of the task and the display [11–14].

The cadets were also interested in examining areas of human factors engineering where standardized metrics for assessment exist. The two topics they chose were cognitive workload and system usability. The task was to research the various metrics associated with these topics so that they can make an educated decision on which metrics they thought were appropriate. The research question is: do the different display surfaces change the perceived usability of displays or workload of the participants? Existing research has performed comparisons across workload measures [15–17] and subjective usability metrics [18, 19]. It is from these three areas (time on task, workload, and usability) that the research protocol was created (Phase 2).

### The Development of Research Protocols and their Associated Training

Since the research has an ARL principle investigator (Boyce), the ARL Institutional Review Board (IRB) will serve as the IRB of record. In addition to the required Collaborative Institutional Training Initiative (CITI) Basic Course for Social & Behavioral Research Investigators, which ensures a foundational understanding of human subject protection, the cadets were also familiarized with the various sections of the ARL Protocol template such as background, equipment and apparatus, stimuli, and experimental design. It is from the experimental design that the selection of assessment techniques occurred (Phase 3).

### The Selection and Understanding of Appropriate Assessment Techniques

For the evaluation of time on task, the metric used was the amount of time it took a cadet to answer a question, a straightforward calculation. This was in contrast to workload and usability, where new metrics arise on a daily basis, with each one having its strengths and weaknesses.

As a part of their capstone project, the cadets had to submit a report explaining their study and the methods that they were planning to use. When assisting the cadets with the metric selection and reasoning for that selection, consistency and validation of the metrics were essential. The metrics chosen were:

*User Engagement Scale (UES)*
The UES is a 31-item survey which measures engagement across six dimensions: Perceived Usability, Aesthetics, Focused Attention, Felt Involvement, Novelty, and Endurability [20]. The UES is a modified version with questions reworded to meet the specifics of the military tactics domain.

*System Usability Scale (SUS)*
The SUS is a 10 item survey that provides participants five response options ranging from strongly disagree to strongly agree. Analysis across ten years of research indicated that the SUS demonstrated strong reliability, Cronbach's $\alpha$ = .91 [21]. A modified version of the SUS is a part of the experiment with questions reworded to specifically refers to the displays.

*Self-Assessmen Manikin (SAM)*
The SAM is a picture-oriented scale to assess the affect dimensions of valence, arousal, and dominance. SAM is composed of three sets of five figures (manikins), which stand for the three major affective dimensions [22].

*NASA-Task Load Index (NASA-TLX)*
NASA-TLX uses a six-dimension scale to assess subjective perception of workload. The six dimensions are: mental demand, physical demand, temporal demand, performance, effort, and frustration. After completing a task, participants are asked to rate each factor on a scale from low to high, which is followed by a series of pairwise comparisons to compare how individual dimensions relate to one another [23]. The scale could assist in accounting for variance in performance scores. It has over a 20 year period of research experiments and applications [24, 25].

**The Coordination and Execution of Data Collection**
Asignificant component of the relationship between ARL and USMA is the actual collection of the data. Data collection requires an identification of the appropriate subject population, the recruitment of that population, the setup of the experiment, and standardizing the execution of the experiment. Then, once the data collection is complete, it consists of backing up data to ensure safe storage.

A:  Identification of Appropriate Subject Population – To make sure that the questions that the experiment was asking the cadets were of appropriate difficulty, the second author of this paper (Rowan), performed informal pilot testing with cadets from various class years as well as from instructors who taught tactics content. Instructors that validated the content of the questions taught tactics to a range of military personnel from cadets at USMA to mid-career officers at the US Army Command and General Staff Officer Course. This ensured subject matter expertise validated each question and answer through iterative design. Once the correct population was established, the recruitment can begin through the USMA SONA System. The portion of the SONA system used was the population of cadets enrolled in a general psychology course at West Point.

B: Setup of the Experiment – USMA worked very closely with ARL personnel to ensure that the setup represented an identical setup to that which is in the protocol. It required setting up the appropriate structural supports and technology components as well as ensuring proper alignment of the ARES projection technology (Fig. 1).

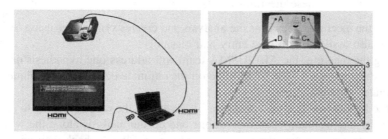

**Fig. 1.** Hardware setup and projection alignment

C: Standardizing the Execution of the Experiment – To keep consistency across the entire research team, the protocol included an experimental script. The script is important in training the cadets how to follow the experimental procedure.

Below is a small example of content from the script:

### *When the participant comes in:*

1. *Put up the signs*
2. *Read the following to the participant*

   *"Thank you for taking the time to participate in this study. Please have a seat so we can fill out the Informed Consent form. An informed consent explains the study and makes sure you understand what you're going to be doing. Please read through it carefully and let me know if you have any questions. You'll sign three consent forms: one for your records, one for the Army Research Laboratory (located in Orlando, Fl. and assisting with the research), and one for the department."*

3. *Make sure they sign in the appropriate places also make sure you sign as well. Make sure to give them a copy and put the participant number in the upper right.*
4. *Start the GIFT Control Panel (desktop shortcut)*

The script was also updated as needed to make it easier to follow the instructions (excluding actionable items).

D: Saving and Backing Up Data/Storage Procedures for Personally Identifiable Information (PII) – Since the experiment had hard copies of consent forms as well as the electronic data which was collected by GIFT, the data had to be stored in secure places at all times. With the assistance of the second author (Rowan), the cadets developed a process in which, after participants were finished, they would ensure that the data was in safe and locked storage.

**Statistical Analysis and Reporting.** At the time of this writing, statistical analysis is still underway. The method which allows ARL/USMA to work together on statistical analysis is regularly scheduled meetings to discuss research findings based on the hypotheses of the ARL experiment and the USMA capstone.

The structure of these meetings are as follows:

1. Before the meeting, ARL runs the analysis and creates syntax files using SPSS. The cadets also assisted with data entry and cleaning.
2. During the meeting, the ARL/USMA team will address one hypothesis or piece of data, which allows for the focus to be on the rationale behind the technique and the associated data assumptions.
3. For the hypotheses that the cadets are interested in, the role of ARL is to serve as a guide, by having them click the buttons and do the analysis along the way.
4. The cadets can then use the pre-generated syntax files to check their answers.

The hope with an approach like this is that at an undergraduate level, the cadets are receiving applied instruction on the techniques that they learned in their research methods and statistics classes.

## 2.2   Experimental Method

**Brief Summary.** This experiment assessed how displaying information onto different surfaces (flat vs. raised) can influence the performance (i.e. time on task and accuracy) and engagement (i.e. self-report surveys and electrodermal activity) of cadets in answering questions on military tactics.

**Experimental Conditions.** There are two experimental conditions: the flat condition consists of questions projected onto a flat white painted board, and the raised condition consists of one of four raised terrain boards which corresponds to the maps of the tactics questions (Fig. 2).

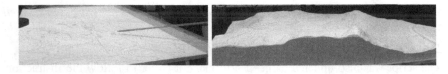

**Fig. 2.** Example of flat projection surface versus a raised projection surface

**Participants.** A total of 65 participants provided data for the experiment. The participants were cadets at USMA, West Point in their first or second year of studies at the academy. The reason for the selection of cadets is to support experiment goals of conducting research to support squad and platoon military instruction. The criteria for participation was that the participants were above 18 years of age.

## Apparatus and Materials

### ARES (Augmented REality Sandtable)

ARES proof-of-concept is a traditional sand table, filled with play sand, augmented with a commercial, off the shelf (COTS) projector, LCD monitor, laptop, and Microsoft Kinect and Xbox Controllers. For this experiment, the ARES projection technology combined with terrain boards was used rather than the actual sand table.

### GIFT (Generalized Intelligent Framework for Tutoring)

GIFT is an open source adaptive tutoring engine which can provide tailored learning experiences based on learner attributes. GIFT has recently moved online and is now completely accessible via the web at https://cloud.gifttutoring.org. For this research experiment, GIFT served as a content delivery and data aggregation tool (see Fig. 3 for the combination of ARES and GIFT).

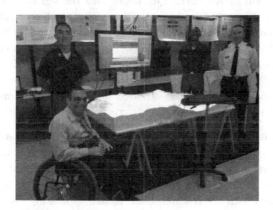

**Fig. 3.** Our team showing the ARES/GIFT combination (Left to Right: Dr. Boyce, CDT Yoshino, CDT Baity, MAJ Rowan)

### Microsoft Band 2 Physiological Sensor

The physiological variable of electrodermal activity (EDA) was monitored to analyze physiological response associated with arousal during the answering of the tactics questions. The EDA sensor used for the experiment was the Microsoft Band 2. The Microsoft Band 2 is a wearable, wireless biosensor that measures emotional arousal via skin conductance, a form of EDA that grows higher during states such as excitement, attention, or anxiety and lower during states of boredom or relaxation.

**Procedure.** Before their arrival, the participants were randomized and counterbalanced into one ordering of conditions, with either the flat condition presented first or the raised condition presented first, followed by the opposite condition. Upon arrival, participants received a brief overview of the study and were asked to fill out a paper informed consent form. Next, GIFT administered a demographics survey and the Self-Assessment Manikin survey. Following this, participants were asked to wear the Microsoft Band 2, which is an electrodermal sensor that is like a wrist watch.

Next, the participant was given a short introduction via GIFT explaining the scenario and the concepts to be covered in the lesson. This introduction leads into a series of training example slides. It is at this point that the participant was able to ask questions for clarification. They then were placed in the experimental scenario which consisted of military tactics questions followed by self-report surveys for each condition.

## 3  Effectiveness of the Process

With data analysis still underway, a way of looking at results is to examine the positives and negatives of each of the phases of the process. This provides insight into improvement and awareness of where things went wrong.

**Phase 1: Identification of Research Questions and Background Research**
Apositive output of this collaboration was the background research in the areas of display design, human performance, and system usability. The combination of sources from ARL, the USMA faculty members, as well as the literature review performed by the cadets, led to a solid understanding of the problem space. However, there were some negatives in Phase 1. ARL, who had already documented research in this area, primarily handled the creation of the research questions. Those predefined research questions narrowed the input that the cadets could have into this phase.

**Phase 2: The Development of Research Protocols and Their Associated Training**
Building a protocol is essential for performing human-subjects research, and the cadets appeared to do this very well for their class. They understood all the necessary sections to be built into their protocol. They went through the mandatory training, as well as additional discussions with the research team related to looking out for a participant's well-being. A challenge during this phase was that, since the ARL IRB was the IRB of record, most of the dealings with the protocol were handled by ARL, and, in the end, it was an ARL protocol that was used to run the study. It would have been an interesting experience for the cadets to be interacting with IRB board members/personnel.

**Phase 3: The Selection and Understanding of Appropriate Assessment Techniques**
The cadets research into the appropriate assessment techniques highlighted this phase. They examined the literature, expanding where they did not have enough sources, and began to understand the need to collect from multiple sources of data to understand the state of the participant. On the downside, this phase suffered from the fact that there were already specific measures in consideration and the cadets might not have wanted to go against the ARL design and bring in more innovative measures.

**Phase 4: The Coordination and Execution of Data Collection**
This phase was by orders of magnitude the most successful phase from all perspectives. Once the cadets gained familiarity with the experiment, the team could do up to six participants per day. Considering that the target number was 65, it goes to show how productive this relationship can be to gather scores of subject data (with the caveat that the classes have a limited enrollment, so it is a possibility to run out of available participants). On the downside, the number of participants in a brief period led to the

potential for errors by the experiment team. Generally speaking, when errors did occur, they were system related.

## Phase 5: Statistical Analysis and Reporting

This phase had some positives regarding making the conceptual connections between what the cadets were learning in class and its application to research. It also exposed them to different types of analyses that they may not have seen in class. However, the geographic separation between ARL and USMA forced all of these conversations to occur over the phone. It could have been done in smaller, more frequent sessions if the ARL researchers and the cadets were not so far apart.

Overall the process, while needing some adjustment, was successful at achieving its primary goals: to teach cadets and to produce quality research.

## 4  Discussion

### Cadet Experience – Cadets Michael Yoshino and Devonte Baity

In developing and executing the capstone project for the engineering psychology major at USMA, the opportunity was presented to collaborate with researchers from ARL on existing research efforts, supported by the first author of this paper from ARL. The capstone project for West Point seniors is integrated into our Human Factors Engineering (PL485) and Colloquium in Engineering Psychology (PL488E) capstone courses. The overarching goal is to apply the knowledge and skills learned throughout the major.

In PL485 (Human Factors Engineering) during the first semester of senior year, a literature review was created via a topic paper. This framed our project specifics—research questions, hypotheses, method, experimental design and project outlook—in a proposal paper, and ultimately presented progress both in an oral report and via a final paper. The most involved aspect of the project has been data collection, which required 60 h in the laboratory. ARL collaborated with us on-site at USMA for the bulk of this endeavor, during which there was an emphasis on sound, productive research. From the informed consent form to backing-up data, the proper handling of participants, and troubleshooting the study during a trial, this was a very informative experience. Additionally, the importance of following a script for consistency was stressed early on, and it was certainly a learning process to develop a proper, comprehensive script for the study. Overall, the team was able to make the most out of the time provided as well as participants' time with efficient, yet proper procedures that were well-rehearsed and executed.

Cadets are provided a substantial statistical background in our curriculum, with Probability and Statistics (MA206) and Applied Statistics (MA376) core courses, yet exposure to data on this scale is rather limited. ARL has been a valuable resource in helping to comprehend findings from data analysis in SPSS and making ties to the existing knowledge from statistics courses. From this, independent conclusions can be drawn from the data to present in the discussion and conclusion of the final capstone paper.

Regarding reservations, the only shortcoming we can identify about this process is the state in which we received it—largely refined and ready for data collection. Moving forward, we will seek further opportunities to play roles in the formative, developmental phases of a research experiment including the determination of theoretical and applied rationales derived from real-world problems as well as the generation of research questions and hypotheses.

## 5   Conclusion

This paper described a teaching process implemented through experimentation and collaboration with the United States Military Academy at West Point. The process assisted in discussing many of the relevant topic areas in human factors engineering such as proper statistical techniques, method selection, targeted research questions and human-subjects protection. In the end, the findings are producing promising results as well, which only makes the success of the capstone project even stronger.

A few recommendations that may help in the development of future collaborations:

- Find a way to spend as much time with the cadet as reasonably possible. One of the reasons that this team had such success is because there were many discussions in and out of the classroom related to metrics, human factors engineering, and performing an effective study.
- For areas like statistical analysis, build in extra time (co-located if possible) to allow for the cadets to understand the techniques and why they are doing them.
- Help them feel ownership of the project. Project ownership is very important, especially if the researcher has already created their experiment design. However, it is still possible to train cadets to speak confidently and knowledgeably about the research.

Following these recommendations can lead to successful collaboration, use of assessment, and teaching human factors engineering all at the same time!

**Acknowledgements.** The research described herein has been sponsored by the U.S. Army Research Laboratory. The statements and opinions expressed in this article do not necessarily reflect the position or the policy of the United States Government, and no official endorsement should be inferred.

## References

1. Alexander, A.L., Brunyé, T., Sidman, J., Weil, S.A.: From gaming to training: a review of studies on fidelity, immersion, presence, and buy-in and their effects on transfer in pc-based simulations and games. DARWARS Train. Impact Group **5**, 1–14 (2005)
2. Welch, R.W., Estes, A.C.: Project-based independent study capstone course. In: Structures Congress 2005: Metropolis and Beyond, pp. 1–12 (2005)
3. Chen, J.Y., Barnes, M.J.: Human–agent teaming for multirobot control: a review of human factors issues. IEEE Trans. Hum.-Mach. Syst. **44**, 13–29 (2014)

4. Hall, D.S., Shattuck, L.G., Bennett, K.B.: Evaluation of an ecological interface design for military command and control. J. Cogn. Eng. Dec. Making **6**(2), 165–193 (2012)
5. Vieane, A., Funke, G., Mancuso, V., Greenlee, E., Dye, G., Borghetti, B., Miller, B., Menke, L., Brown, R.: Coordinated displays to assist cyber defenders. Proc. Hum. Factors Ergon. Soc. Ann. Meet. **60**, 344–348 (2016)
6. Clasing, J.E., Casali, J.G.: Warfighter auditory situation awareness: effects of augmented hearing protection/enhancement devices and TCAPS for military ground combat applications. Int. J. Audiol. **53**, S43–S52 (2014)
7. Amburn, C.R., Vey, N.L., Boyce, M.W., Mize, J.R.: The augmented reality sandtable (ARES) (No. ARL-SR-0340). Army Research Laboratory (2015)
8. Sottilare, R.A., Brawner, K.W., Goldberg, B.S., Holden, H.K.: The Generalized Intelligent Framework for Tutoring (GIFT). Army Research Laboratory, Orlando, FL (2012)
9. Boyce, M.W., Reyes, R.J., Cruz, D.E., Amburn, C.R., Goldberg, B., Moss, J.D., Sottilare, R.A.: Effect of Topography on Learning Military Tactics - Integration of Generalized Intelligent Framework for Tutoring (GIFT) and Augmented REality Sandtable (ARES) (ARL-7792). Army Research Laboratory (2016)
10. Rowan, C., Dustin, M., Peasley, E.: ARES sandtable: the effects on topography on learning military tactics. In: 7th Annual Applied Human Factors and Ergonomics International Conference
11. Tory, M., Moller, T., Atkins, M.S., Kirkpatrick, A.E.: Combining 2D and 3D views for orientation and relative position tasks. In: Proceedings of the SIGCHI Conference on Human Factors in Computing Systems, pp. 73–80. ACM, Vienna (2004)
12. St. John, M., Smallman, H.S., Bank, T.E., Cowen, M.B.: Tactical routing using two-dimensional and three-dimensional views of terrain. In: Proceedings of the Human Factors and Ergonomics Society Annual Meeting, vol. 45, pp. 1409–1413 (2001)
13. St. John, M., Cowen, M.B., Smallman, H.S., Oonk, H.M.: The use of 2D and 3D displays for shape-understanding versus relative-position tasks. Hum. Factors: J. Hum. Factors Ergon. Soc. **43**, 79–98 (2001)
14. Dixon, S., Fitzhugh, E., Aleva, D.: Human factors guidelines for applications of 3D perspectives: a literature review. In: Display Technologies and Applications for Defense, Security, and Avionics III, pp. 73270K-73270K-73211. SPIE
15. Matthews, G., Reinerman-Jones, L.E., Barber, D.J., Abich, J.: The psychometrics of mental workload multiple measures are sensitive but divergent. Hum. Factors: J. Hum. Factors Ergon. Soc. **57**, 125–143 (2015)
16. Mracek, D.L., Arsenault, M.L., Day, E.A., Hardy, J.H., Terry, R.A.: A multilevel approach to relating subjective workload to performance after shifts in task demand. Hum. Factors: J. Hum. Factors Ergon. Soc. **56**, 1401–1413 (2014)
17. Hill, S.G., Iavecchia, H.P., Byers, J.C., Bittner, A.C., Zaklade, A.L., Christ, R.E.: Comparison of four subjective workload rating scales. Hum. Factors: J. Hum. Factors Ergon. Soc. **34**, 429–439 (1992)
18. O'Brien, H.L., Lebow, M.: Mixed-methods approach to measuring user experience in online news interactions. J. Am. Soc. Inf. Sci. Technol. **64**, 1543–1556 (2013)
19. Hornbæk, K., Law, E.L.-C.: Meta-analysis of correlations among usability measures. In: Proceedings of the SIGCHI Conference on Human Factors in Computing Systems, pp. 617–626. ACM
20. O'Brien, H.L., Toms, E.G.: The development and evaluation of a survey to measure user engagement. J. Am. Soc. Inf. Sci. Technol. **61**, 50–69 (2010)
21. Bangor, A., Kortum, P.T., Miller, J.T.: An empirical evaluation of the system usability scale. Int. J. Hum.-Comput. Interact. **24**, 574–594 (2008)

22. Bradley, M.M., Lang, P.J.: Measuring emotion: the self-assessment manikin and the semantic differential. J. Behav. Ther. Exp. Psychiatry **25**, 49–59 (1994)
23. Hart, S.G., Staveland, L.E.: Development of NASA-TLX (task load index): results of empirical and theoretical research. Adv. Psychol. **52**, 139–183 (1988)
24. Hart, S.G.: NASA-task load index (NASA-TLX); 20 years later. In: Proceedings of the Human Factors and Ergonomics Society Annual Meeting, pp. 904–908. Sage Publications
25. Grier, R.A.: How high is high? A meta-analysis of NASA-TLX global workload scores. Proc. Hum. Factors Ergon. Soc. Ann. Meet. **59**, 1727–1731 (2015)

# Towards Technologically Assisted Mindfulness Meditation Practice in Older Adults: An Analysis of Difficulties Faced and Design Suggestions for Neurofeedback

Simon Cook[1(✉)], Ronald M. Baecker[1], Cosmin Munteanu[1,2],
and Andrew Walker[1,2]

[1] Technologies for Ageing Gracefully Lab,
University of Toronto, Toronto, Canada
{Simon, Ron, Cosmin, Andrew}@taglab.ca
[2] Institute for Communication, Culture Information and Technology,
University of Toronto Mississauga, Mississauga, Canada

**Abstract.** Learning to meditate as an older adult can be difficult given the decreased ability to inhibit distractions in the elderly, and the important role of dealing with distractions in several types of meditation practice. Designing technologically assisted meditation practices in general is an area that is only beginning to be explored, and this is especially true for these kinds of technologies for older adults. In order to better design support for meditation practices for such a population we performed a qualitative study of 9 meditators aged 55+ in order to understand their specific needs, followed by a pilot study of a device which we designed in order to address these needs. Our analysis of these interviews yielded three themes. First was that there was an initial difficulty and discouraging experience when performing focused attention exercises which comprise a significant part of a beginner's meditation practice. Second was a difficulty understanding when you are "doing it right" and how to make sense of teachings. Third was an openness to making use of new technologies and ways of supporting their meditation practice as long as the new support does not interfere with what they considered the core parts of meditation to be. We then use these results to outline design considerations for a neurofeedback application to address these needs.

**Keywords:** Mindfulness · Older adults · Neurofeedback · Meditation · Attention

## 1 Introduction

An aging population and increased life expectancy brings with it significant difficulties, but also affords new opportunities. One difficulty to be addressed is how to allow for those with age-related cognitive decline due to neurodegenerative diseases to live fulfilling and meaningful lives. Pharmacological interventions to treat the underlying biochemical causes of these diseases will be an essential part of treatment, but

© Springer International Publishing AG 2017
D.D. Schmorrow and C.M. Fidopiastis (Eds.): AC 2017, Part II, LNAI 10285, pp. 423–442, 2017.
DOI: 10.1007/978-3-319-58625-0_31

non-pharmacological interventions have an important role to play as well in the absence of a complete pharmacological solution. One possible avenue of research is the design of interventions that would increase cognitive reserve. There is increasing evidence for mindfulness meditation practice as such a non-pharmacological intervention that would increase cognitive reserve [1–5].

However, learning mindfulness meditation can be difficult. Since there are no outward signs of performance when meditating, a teacher's feedback cannot be easily based on the performance of the student. For older adults with reduced mobility, learning from an experienced teacher may also pose a significant challenge. Additionally, learning to meditate is an effortful activity, and it can be unclear based on instructions for meditating what the state is that the learner is trying to reach, especially if it is unfamiliar. Finally, while periods of mind wandering can be an instructive and important part of meditation, especially long periods of mind wandering can be discouraging and not instructive for learning how to stay focused in the desired way. While these issues are mentioned in the literature, little work has been done to understand the needs of older adults in particular with respect to learning meditation. In order to aid older adults in learning to meditate we need to understand the difficulties they face and how these difficulties can be addressed by new technologies.

Engineering good interventions for technologically assisted meditation practice is an area that is only beginning to be explored, and is currently often situated in the context of neurofeedback. Neurofeedback, that is, the use of real-time feedback based on signals from a user's brain, is designed to allow the user to change their brain activity towards or away from some target brain activity using the aforementioned feedback. Its application with respect to meditation is an attempt to ameliorate both the effort and teacher feedback issues of learning meditation. By providing feedback based on meditation relevant brain activity, it is claimed that a user utilizing such a neurofeedback device would more easily be able to reach and stay in the desired kinds of meditative state.

The goal of this paper is therefore to understand in a general sense the difficulties that older adults face in meditation, and whether they are open to the use of technology to support meditation. We then use this data to argue that for neurofeedback as a plausible approach to addressing these difficulties.

## 2    Background

**Mindfulness Meditation**

The clinical application of meditation practices has been gaining increasing prominence in the last 30 years in the form of the Mindfulness Based Stress Reduction (MBSR) program for treating a number of issues [6]. MBSR and variants of it have been found to be an effective at helping to treat depression [7], anxiety [8, 9], addiction [10], eating disorders [11], and chronic pain [12], among others. Though the meditation practices that are used in these programs are based on Vipassana meditation, a traditional Vajrayana Buddhist practice, they have taken on a decidedly western secular flavour in MBSR.

Jon Kabat-Zinn offers a commonly used definition of mindfulness as "the awareness that emerges through paying attention on purpose, in the present moment, and non-judgmentally to the unfolding of experience moment by moment" [13]. Mindfulness meditation in this context is composed of two kinds of practices that are conducive to cultivating mindfulness [14] and are typically practiced seated and with eyes closed for beginners.

First is focused attention, which is the practice of directing one's attention to some object of meditation, either endogenous or exogenous, and attending to the character of that object in focus. When one notices that their attention has drifted from the original object, attention is brought back in an accepting and non-judgmental way and for beginners the object of meditation is typically the sensations of breath.

Open-monitoring meditation is similar to focused attention meditation but the focus of attention is loosened from the original object to the process of attending itself. Open-monitoring is typically taught after one has some experience with focused attention meditation. Similar kinds of vigilance towards distraction are practiced, along with the practice of bring attention back to the process of attending when it wanders. Often, open-monitoring is preceded in a practice session by focused attention meditation in order to calm the mind and reduce distractions.

Though strong inferences can be made from the wealth of neuroscientific, psychological, and cognitive scientific evidence on some relevant cognitive functions involved in meditation and classical Buddhist texts on meditation describe difficulties faced by beginner and experienced meditators [15], this should be supplemented with qualitative research to investigate this particular context. Unfortunately, there is a dearth of first-person accounts of individuals learning meditation in general [16], with an even sparser base of evidence for older adults. Addressing this gap in the literature is the purpose of this study. Additionally, much of the qualitative research focuses on the improvements that practitioners experience, backgrounding the difficulties that might be faced [17].

### Related Work in Understanding the Needs of Older Adults When Learning Meditation

Of the few studies of older adults learning to meditate that have been performed, only one stands out as being closely related to the question of concern in this paper. Morone et al. [16] investigated the effects of mindfulness meditation on older adults (mean age 74.3), specifically those with chronic pain. Though they found themes of barriers to meditation and the processes of meditation in their interviews, they did not expand on these themes in their analysis and instead focused on themes of outcomes for pain, sleep, attention, and well-being. From their example quotes for the theme of barriers to meditation they included the following:

"I always fall asleep after 15 to 30 min (of meditation)." [16]
"It seems like there is never a good time to meditate." [16]

Additionally, in their processes of meditation they mention that becoming familiar with meditation and attending in the desired way was difficult.

All other qualitative research on this topic so far has either been of a different population, or focused on different questions, or both. Most of the research that does gather data about difficulties faced when learning meditation does not make these issues the focus of their study and do not report in detail their results. McCollum and Gehart [18] studied a class of therapists with an unreported mean age who were learning mindfulness meditation and analyzed their journal entries in which they were prompted to write about what impeded their goal of practicing daily among other things. Despite mentioning that they explicitly prompted the subjects to write about what impeded their goal of daily meditation practice and that "often included ways in which they struggled with meditating and the frustrations they encountered with the practice", they did not describe in any detail what these difficulties were. They do note that "Although most students reported having 1 or 2 weeks during which it was difficult to keep up with their daily practice of mindfulness, most reported meeting or exceeding this goal most weeks of the semester".

Shonin et al. [19] similarly background the difficulties faced by their subjects in learning their meditation training program in lieu of focusing on the perceived benefits of the practice. They found that all participants reported similar 'challenges of being aware', which was that it was difficult to maintain a regular practice, and that learning to deal with their 'racing mind' was a challenge.

Lomas et al. [20] addresses some of these gaps by focusing their qualitative study of meditators explicitly on the challenges they faced. Specifically, they looked at issues faced by male meditators. All of their subjects reported meditation being difficult at least some of the time, with many reporting difficulties with maintaining attention, mind wandering, self-doubt, and physical discomfort. Significantly, participants described mindfulness meditation as a difficult skill to learn which required practice. Meditation could also be at times boring or mundane, making it uninteresting to engage in, and that it was sometimes difficult to find the nuance and the challenge in the experience to make it worthwhile. In contrast, the practice of meditation also brought up difficult and powerful emotions and thoughts, though participants generally understood this as the point of the practice, and overall participants thought that meditation contributed to well-being and psychological development. Difficulty focusing and dealing with negative thoughts also showed up in the diaries of those taking an MBSR course [21] in one of the few other qualitative studies of the difficulties of meditation of note.

## Neurofeedback for Assisting Meditation

Giving users feedback about their own brain activity with the goal of changing that brain activity, that is, neurofeedback, has recently seen interest as a way of helping beginners learn meditation [22]. While the focus of our study is on problems that older adults face when meditating, in the context of this work in neurofeedback and meditation we discuss below the implications of our results for designing neurofeedback technologies for older adults in particular. Given our argument that such a technology shows possible promise for seniors, four recent papers are significant for placing this work in that context.

Bhayee et al. [23] offered the first study comparing a neurofeedback assisted mindfulness meditation practice using consumer grade EEG hardware to an active control group on measures of attention and working memory and found an increase in these relevant measures compared to the control group. Their design used auditory feedback using wind and storm sounds which would increase in intensity based on greater estimated distraction, and decrease with greater estimated stability of attention.

While this is a promising start and points to the viability of neurofeedback assisted mindfulness meditation in general, several limitations make future work built on this more difficult. First, their use of proprietary and unstated combination of frequency bands for determining the feedback makes replication without using their particular device and setup difficult. The use of an unstated machine learning algorithm trained on calibration conditions specific to each user poses similar difficulties. Additionally, while they state that the feedback is based on estimated distraction and attention stability, these terms are left undefined in the paper, and it is unclear both the neuro-physiological mechanisms they think underlie them, as well as whether they are the same as the sense in which they are used in their evaluation measures.

Slightly different from earlier discussed neurofeedback designs but still relevantly similar is the work of Sas and Chopra [24]. Using a consumer grade EEG headset, they provided auditory binaural beat neurofeedback of frontal low alpha (relaxation, 6 Hz–10 Hz) and theta activity (high working memory requirements, 4–6 Hz), and found that subjects reported increased subjective ratings of deepness of meditative state compared to monaural feedback and controls.

Similar to Sas and Chopra [24], Kosunen et al. [25] used a virtual reality environment paired with neurofeedback provided by a non-consumer grade EEG device based on frontal low alpha and theta activity similar to Sas and Chopra [24] from F3, F4, C3, C4, P3, and P4. They found an increase in self-reported measures of relaxation, feeling of presence, and deepness of meditation compared to their no feedback control group.

Different from these three studies is Lutterveld et al. [26], on our which our design detailed below is primarily based, which instead of using non-localized EEG data of frontal lobe activity, they used a high-density EEG device to provide visual feedback based on PCC gamma band (40–57 Hz) activity. They found that subjects were able to volitionally control the feedback signal in the direction of increased effortless awareness, and that the feedback signal corresponded to the subject's experience of effortless awareness.

## Moving Forward: Connecting Neurofeedback Technology to Meditation for Older Adults

While older adults have been shown to be able to use neurofeedback systems in some contexts [27] none of the neurofeedback assisted meditation research has been performed with older adults. Given this, it is still unclear that neurofeedback assisted meditation practice actually meets any need that older adults might have when learning meditation. While they might be able to use such technologies broadly speaking, and may even be able to use them to help improve their meditation practice, it could be the case that the significant difficulties faced by older adults may be poorly addressed by these developing methods. Our study is designed start directly addressing these questions by understanding first the difficulties that older adults face in learning meditation.

# 3  Methods

## Participants

The sample consisted of 9 adults aged 55 and older (average 71 years, from 56–85 years old, 5 females, 4 males). Participants (see Table 1) were recruited through local meditation classes, religious institutions, hospitals, and medical services that offered meditation classes. Inclusion criteria were that participants had either completed a meditation course, participated in a meditation retreat, or had been practicing meditation for over 1 year. It was also required that their meditation include vipassana, zen, transcendental, or mindfulness. There was no pre-interview screening.

**Table 1.** Participant details

| Participant # | Age | Meditation experience |
|---|---|---|
| 1 | 67 | 3 years vipassana (intermittent, maximum 6 weeks daily). 40 Years Yoga. 10 years various traditions (very infrequently) |
| 2 | 76 | 28 years vipassana (consistent, daily) |
| 3 | 70 | 3 years vipassana (consistent, daily) |
| 4 | 56 | 15 years informally in various traditions (infrequently, intermittent). 3 years zen (often daily, but not consistently. No regular or scheduled practice) |
| 5 | 82 | 26 years vipassana (consistent, daily). 8 weeks various traditions (infrequently) |
| 6 | 65 | 30 years various traditions (frequently), mostly guided meditations |
| 7 | 85 | 8 years transcendental meditation (intermittent, infrequently). 24 years vipassana (consistent, frequently) |
| 8 | 74 | 16 years vipassana (consistent, frequently) |
| 9 | 65 | 42 years vipassana (consistent, frequently) |

## Procedure

A single semi-structured interview was administered to participants at either their place of residence or a private room in our research laboratory. Audio from the interviews was recorded and coded by the author and a research assistant using a coding scheme developed by those doing the coding. A copy of the interview guide is included as Appendix A. The interview asked open-ended questions designed to explore the difficulties that the participants faced in learning and maintaining a meditation practice and how they addressed those difficulties along with their comfort with technology and its use in meditation. The interview guide was pilot tested on two participants whose data was not included and refined before gathering the data of the participants included in this study. Compensation was provided in the form of travel expenses for participants and a non-alcoholic beverage of the participant's choice. Following the interview participants were encouraged to ask any additional questions they had about the study and larger research project.

**Data Analysis**

Each interview was transcribed by the author or a research assistant, and then analyzed for coding. A modified grounded theory [28] approach was taken to understanding the data, with the coding performed iteratively. Initial open coding was performed by the author and a research assistant independently on each transcript. The author and the research assistant discussed some of the experiences of the author in interviewing the participants and his thoughts on the interviews and research questions prior to this initial coding. This was followed by meetings to discuss the data and find agreement on a set of codes. From this discussion, we reviewed our coding results, performed selective coding, and identified several overarching themes that are presented below.

Prior to conducting the interviews and coding data the author possessed general knowledge in the fields of psychology, human-computer interaction, and neuroscience. Additionally he had specific theoretical knowledge of age-related cognitive decline and various meditation practices. The author had also intermittently practiced Vipassana meditation for 5 years. This experience informed the research questions, the interview process, and the coding of the data in a way that is compatible with current qualitative research practices. The second coder had never meditated in any tradition and did not have a background in psychology. These differences in background help to cross-validate the coding and theme generation process. Neither coder had interacted with any of the meditation communities which the participants were a part of prior to this study, with the exception of participant 1, which the author had attended at a time not concurrent with participant 1's involvement in that community.

Throughout the periods of conducting interviews and coding of the resulting data the author further consulted literature on age-related cognitive decline, the meditation practices of the participants, and current technologies for assisting meditation. This informed the interviews as well as the coding to clarify the emerging analysis. While this is not entirely consistent with classic Straussian/Glaserian grounded theory [29, 30], it is consistent with the sort of modified grounded theory described by Cutcliffe [28].

## 4 Results

While several themes emerged from the data, we focus our analysis on those most relevant to difficulties faced by beginner the design of technologies to assist meditation (summarized in Table 2). The four of most concern to us here are a difficulty dealing with distractions and learning to train attention, a difficulty understanding when they are "doing it right", physical difficulties due to age, and an openness to the use of technology to help learn meditation. In the following sections, we explore each of these themes in depth with some analysis of implications that they suggest.

**Theme: Difficulty Dealing with Distractions and Learning to Train Attention**

Across all participants that practiced some kind of Vipassana or Zen meditation (Participants 1, 2, 3, 4, 5, 7, 8, and 9) there was an acknowledgment of the difficulty of maintaining the right kind of attention and dealing with an active mind. All of these participants highlighted this as a particular challenge for beginners, one that leads to significant discomfort.

**Table 2.** Themes and design implications from the results.

| Theme | Participants | Implications |
|---|---|---|
| Dealing with distractions | 1, 2, 3, 4, 5, 7, 8, 9 | ($1_a$) Dealing with distractions and mind wandering may be essential part of meditation experience<br>($1_b$) Design should help beginners get to more expert kinds of focused attention<br>($1_c$) Cannot distract from the process of meditating |
| Understanding how to "do it right" | 1, 2, 3, 5, 7 | ($2_a$) Experiencing the unfamiliar mental states cultivated by meditation is essential<br>($2_b$) "Doing it right" doesn't necessarily mean having no distractions<br>($2_c$) "Doing it right" necessitates the design encouraging exploration, not having a narrow training regimen<br>($2_d$) Should be a tool for exploration |
| Physical difficulties | 2, 3, 4, 7 | ($3_a$) Existing tools and solutions available adequately meet needs<br>($3_b$) Encouraging low arousal mental states is necessarily desirable |
| Openness to technology | All | ($4_a$) What the mind is doing should not differ significantly from traditional meditation practices<br>(4b) Technology should not encourage attitudes that run counter to mindfulness<br>($4_c$) Should leave room for effort and difficulty |

Participant 1 described how, as a beginner, it was difficult *"to be able to actually think about my breath for more than you know, two or three consecutive breaths before I would be going off in a direction"*. For them, it was discouraging to realize how little control over their mind they had, and how this did not match up with what they were told they should be doing. This led them to finding it more difficult to decide to practice meditation regularly, since *"sitting meditation is just so difficult for me that it... When something is difficult for you, I don't necessarily seek it out"* (Participant 1). Despite considering a greater control over their mind and emotions as one of their goals of meditating and an explicit desire to maintain a regular meditation practice they found that this contributed to them ceasing a regular meditation practice for a time. However, this did not stop Participant 1 from returning to try to learn again:

> *"I actually did the whole six weeks, meditating almost every day, and never really got into it. [Later] I started it all over again, just kind of seeing. Maybe I will learn to sit still and meditate"*

This identifies a source of difficulty, an initial motivation to pursue meditation, connects that difficulty decreases in their practice of meditation, and finally a recognition that they would like to overcome that difficulty and continue meditating.

This theme of difficulty in attending and dealing with mind wandering was present in participants who went on to become experienced meditators as well. Participants 2, 4, 5, 7, 8, and 9, each with 15 years of Vipassana meditation or more all described how encountering how busy their mind was and how difficult it was to maintain attention were difficulties when they were beginners. Additionally, Participant 5 and Participant 7, who are both meditation teachers, described how this is a difficulty they see in all participants including older adults. This leads to our first design implication, which is:

(a) **Dealing with distractions and mind wandering is an essential part of learning to meditate**

As Participant 5 said,

*"[T]he hardest part, the way is that people, students come up and ask questions, and it's 'my mind won't do it immediately when I wanted it to do it' and you have to say that, yeah, it's very difficult. Sometimes your mind will be distracted, and to embrace that, and to learn it as an opportunity to learn how to bring a distracted mind back. It's an opportunity to learn not to resist, or to see it is an unwanted thing, and to understand that everything's on a continuum, and that you won't be in a deep concentrated state all the time, sometimes you're in a very distracted state"*

This is consistent with the kinds of difficulties described by the qualitative studies of meditation detailed earlier [16, 20], and with traditional Buddhist texts describing these kinds of meditation practices [31]. This consistency of results lends credence to this being a legitimate difficulty for beginners in general, and its presence in older adults suggest that it does not stop becoming a problem as one ages.

Interestingly, the experienced meditators described how this is a difficulty that in some ways does not ever go away. As Participant 5 described it:

*"You will sometimes have a deeper meditation, and sometimes you'll be really distracted. Everything's on the continuum."*

The experienced meditators saw this as a part of meditation that could not be eliminated, that it is unavoidable for anybody practicing meditation to find themselves easily distracted sometimes. With practice, it is easier to deal with distractions and stay regularly focused. Participant 7 described it as

*"When you first start to meditate, to try to get into it, it's like getting that car started. Like pushing this car. [...] Then now, it's like, I just give it a little nudge and I jump in, and away I go"*

The persistence but changing nature of this difficulty and its perceived essential role in even experienced meditation practice leads us the consideration that:

(b) **Helping novices have the kind of attention that experts do would make meditation easier**

While this might seem obvious in retrospect, it could have been the case that the relevant difference was not one of attention, and establishing this helps narrow our focus later. Given this, it is essential to be clear on what is meant by "dealing with distractions and mind wandering" in order to evaluate the effectiveness of any possible design, and in order to elucidate possible points at which a technology could intervene.

Another major design implication is that

(c) **It should not distract the user from focused attention meditation**

This is implied by the way that distraction from the target of one's meditation practice is seen as a difficulty. Any design that pulls the user's attention away from meditation while they are in focused attention or open monitoring states in order to interact with it or make sense of its outputs is necessarily a distraction.

### Theme: Difficulty Understanding When You Are "Doing It Right" and How to Make Sense of Teachings

Participants also reported that learning meditation requires more than just hearing some instructions; it needs practice until one can experience what the instruction is trying to teach. That is, having these experiences repeatedly over time makes it clearer what the instruction is about and develops relevant skills.

This manifests in a difficulty in understanding whether a beginner meditator is "doing it right". Participant 1 described how

*"The difficulty would be to measure up to the expectation of what we are being told"*

This difficulty is echoed by Participant 3:

*'Am I doing it right? What do I look like? Everyone else knows what they are doing but me"*

For Participant 2, it was the non-judging attitude advocated by mindfulness meditation in particular that was difficult to grasp:

*"Could I trust that what I am doing is the right thing? Even when I knew that there was no right thing."*

Participants 5 and 7 described this difficulty as they saw it in their students. They described the importance of practice and of exploring and experiencing for oneself the things that are being told to you by a teacher. To them, the teaching is a way of helping to guide and assist a person to get them to a place where they could explore more on their own. In the words of Participant 5:

*"[J]ust learn, practice the technique, just practice. The experiential wisdom is all about the moment it comes. [...] I could talk at her until the cows come home, but until she actually understood through her own experience that she needed to calm her distracted mind, [...] then she understood what I was trying to say to her*

From this, we take that

(a) **Experiencing novel mental states cultivated by meditation is essential to learning**

For Participant 7 and others, they mention that it is the non-judging and exploratory attitude that can be especially hard to understand, and that this difficulty is part of the reason for the concerns that one is not "doing it right":

*"[I] don't care how you do it, I just want you to observe all the sensations in your body, don't miss them, and notice the changing nature. That's all there is to it. So you have to get them to stop doing it wrong, and they can get into a lot of difficulty, because sometimes you're looking for something; you want something to happen. That's the way we're brought up, you know - am I doing it right?"*

We draw three key considerations that may inform future design work from these regularities, which are that:

(b) **"Doing it right" doesn't necessarily mean having no distractions**
(c) **"Doing it right" does mean having the right attitude towards learning**
(d) **Helping users have the right attitude means helping encourage exploration and avoiding tightly constrained training programs**

An expectation of being guided along a tightly constrained training regimen that would have clear intermediate goals is to miss how taking an exploratory stance entails accepting the possibility of uncertainty. Therefore any design needs to communicate how it affords exploration and if possible prime the user into mental states that are more exploratory. One possible avenue for fleshing out what this means for design is an application of work on fixed and growth mindsets in psychology. In particular, how an exploratory growth mindset could be instilled in users [32] may have implications for pushing users away from the kind of attitude that would be unhelpful.

### Theme: Physical Difficulties

The theme that contained the most older adult specific concerns was that there were specific physical difficulties that participants attributed to age which made meditation difficult. Participants 2, 3, 4, and 7 all described how as they got older that sitting upright in the typical posture taught to meditators caused them significant discomfort. For newer meditators this made it difficult to continue practicing, but each one persisted to find a way to comfortably meditate. Participant 4 remarked that

*"Considering it is a very passive physical activity, I remember physically it was demanding, just to hold that posture. As you get older different joints get stiff. Even now if I meditate I use a chair, not sitting on the floor. Although I like the idea, it doesn't work"*

Participant 2 saw the traditional methods that they saw as easier for younger adults as preferable when learning, but that alternative methods were acceptable as well as long as they didn't interfere with what they saw as the core parts of the practice. For them:

*"I use a chair now. Sitting on the ground I just can't do it anymore. [...] Part of it is ego that I had to adjust to. Sorry guys I am 76 it is just the way it is! But you are 24 and you have to do it!"*

From this we draw the conclusion that while they exist

(a) **Aging related physical difficulties are not a significant barrier to learning meditation**

It is not clear that making a more comfortable seat would even be helpful, since it is desirable to be alert and awake during meditation. Participant 3 remarked how they found being sleepy and concerns about being sleepy an impediment to learning meditation, which is reflected in traditional meditation texts which describe meditation as being a state of alert wakefulness [31].

(b) **Encouraging low-arousal mental states is not necessarily desirable**

The design of appropriate seats for meditation is already filled with traditional and modern designs that we will not explore further here. Most significantly for our concerns here and for neurofeedback designs in particular is that the design should not encourage a low arousal and sleepy mental states.

**Theme: Technology to Help**

A fourth theme of using technology to help emerged naturally from participants explaining their experience of meditation and their difficulties, as well as from explicit questions about the role of technology in their practice. Technology played a role in each participant's meditation practice, with recorded guided meditation (Participants 2, 3, 4, 5, 6, 7, 8, and 9), seating (Participants 2, 3, 4, 5, 7, and 9), timer apps (Participant 1, 3, 5, 7, and 8), and internet communities (Participants 6 and 9) as the most prominent uses of technology. Each one of these technologies assisted with different difficulties in the participant's practice. For some, guided meditations helped with learning the skill of meditating, and provided helpful reminders during practice of generally what one should be doing. For others, the role that guided meditations played was more about using the sounds of chanting, bells, and the voice of a teacher to calm themselves. For this second group, guided meditations played a significant role in helping to relax (participants 4 and 6). Timers were universally used during practices that committed to meditating for a set length of time in order to mark the end of a practice so that the user did not have to interrupt their meditation to see how long they had been meditating for.

Several participants (Participants 2, 3, 4, 5), in describing their use of technology to help their practice made note of how they saw the potential for technology to be both a help and a hindrance to learning meditation, and that the relationship between a technology being a long term benefit and a short term crutch was complicated. Participant 2 thought that

*"bells and whistles reduce people's strength within themselves"*

However, they still left room open for using technology to help meditation, that

*"you can actually have training programs that [are] for those people who are struggling with like, oh my god, focusing on my breath, this is crazy hard. Something they can use for a few minutes, when they can't get through their body. To help them understand that subtlety that they have deep inside"*

This skeptical optimism articulated by Participant 5 was focused on design considerations outlined above, that

*"There's a bit of a craving and aversion that comes up [with how people approach technology], that kind of goes in the opposite direction of what we want to do"*

They were concerned that what would be lost in the pursuit of using technology is how

*"[P]art of this technique is acceptance and being alert and aware and accepting reality as it is and not as you want it to be. [...] If we were getting caught up in the mechanics of meditation we forget [...] that you will sometimes have a deeper meditation, and sometimes you'll be really distracted"*

This, together with some of the design implications this we draw the design implication that

Despite these concerns, they saw the technology that they did use as in no way a hindrance to their meditation practice. All participants were open in some way to the possibility of using new technologies, which could improve meditation practice either for themselves or for beginner meditators.

Several things can be learned from the technology that they currently do use. While guided meditations were seen to be helpful at times, all participants who used them except for Participant 9 saw them as a tool that should not be relied on regularly, and that the value of meditation lies in pursuing the practice on one's own without a guiding voice. This and the importance of taking the right attitude towards practice and the necessity of dealing with distractions even for experienced meditators leads to our final design implications.

(a) **What the mind is doing should not differ significantly from traditional meditation practices**
(b) **Technology should not encourage attitudes that run counter to mindfulness**
(c) **Should leave room for difficulty**

While beginner meditators might at first want to ease all difficulties they encounter, all experienced and beginner meditators with the exception of Participant 9 saw this as undesirable in the long-term. For Participant 2, 5, and 7, what they would learn if there were no difficulties would not be meditation.

## 5  Discussion

An important aspect to note about these results is that in terms of the difficulties faced by the participants in learning meditation, it does not appear at first that they differ significantly from those of younger adults, such as the subjects of Lomas et al. [20] and Shonin et al. [19]. Participants who were themselves meditation teachers reported that beginner meditators of any age experienced these same kinds of difficulties. While some subjects reported age specific physical difficulties, they either embraced those difficulties as part of being aware of one's experience in a non-judging mindful way, or had simple low-tech solutions with which they were comfortable. This is not to say that the design for any solution should be the same for both older and younger adults, but only that their difficulties are roughly the same from the perspective of this kind of qualitative data analysis.

Given this, it may appear at first that the mental difficulties associated with learning meditation are both the same in kind and in extent for older adults and younger adults. However, we think that there is reason to believe that while the difficulties are of the same kind, that older adults would find learning to meditate more difficult than younger adults would.

Additionally, five of the subjects mentioned that these difficulties resulted in them or others that they knew either ceasing to meditate for some extended periods or to give up entirely. Understood in the context of helping older adults learn to meditate as a way of improving cognitive reserve, then helping people get past these hurdles as a beginner takes on additional importance, and goes some way towards justifying solving these difficulties as important design goals.

A final high-level consideration is that whatever a design to assist learning mindfulness meditation should be subject to three constraints. First, it should not be intrusive into the experience of the user when they are successfully meditating. Second, in order to be compatible with existing practices it should not require the user to do anything significantly different from a standard practice in terms of actions during meditation. For example, controlling the device should not require the user's eyes to be open (since they are closed in early mindfulness meditation practices), or for the user to need to move to manipulate any input devices (since beginner mindfulness meditation practices are done seated and completely still). An extension of this leads to our third constraint, which is that since there are no outward signs of the user's attention any solution must be sensitive to the internal mental states of the user.

Together, the need to determine if any differences in reported difficulties exists between older and younger beginner meditators along with the constraint that the design must be sensitive to the internal mental states of the user necessitate turning to the cognitive neuroscience, psychology, and cognitive science of attention, meditation, and mind-wandering.

## Decomposing Mindfulness into Cognitive Processes

Given our earlier definition of mindfulness meditation, we can begin to decompose it into its constituent cognitive processes. Using the Liverpool Mindfulness Model, regular mindfulness practice develops attentional processes that are engaged in regulatory processes of emotion and cognition [33]. When meditating, one is engaged in a cycle of mind wandering, noticing that one's mind has wandered, disengaging from the object of attention in the mind wandering, orienting attention back to the original object of meditation, and finally sustaining attention on the desired object of meditation to broken up eventually by a distraction and return to mind wandering. These attentional processes can be broken down into five brain networks that are roughly responsible for them.

Important for present purposes is the identification of mind wandering with activity in the default mode network. As detailed further below, our neurofeedback design is intended to increase the salience of the feedback during extended periods of mind wandering, thus engaging the salience network and bringing the user out of their mind wandering to the task of disengaging from both the provided feedback and the content of their mind wandering.

Recent work on the dynamics of mind wandering is helpful for clarifying both what our proposed neurofeedback design is for and what the associated mental processes are. As Christoff et al. [34] argue, prior to the mid-1990's the dominant support that the task-centric view enjoyed in cognitive psychology and cognitive neuroscience led to resting state activity being viewed as noise and not comprised of any meaningful or related brain or mental activity. Even with the discovery of the default mode network, a series of interconnected brain areas involved in memory and reasoning (primarily consisting of the medial prefrontal cortex, posterior cingulate cortex, and angular gyrus), the dominant view became that default mode network activity was related to task-unrelated thought. Instead, mind wandering, and by some extension particular kinds of default mode network activity, should be thought of as describing the character of thought as being fleeting and moving from topic to topic with relatively few constraints including contents which can be task related, instead of committed to an overly narrow content and task based view [34].

This view gives a sharper focus to mind wandering in the context of potential neurofeedback designs and in meditation. First, it becomes clear that detecting mind wandering is not a matter of detecting the content of what the mind has wandered to, but instead the brain activity relevant for the kind of way in which thought changes generally in mind wandering. With respect to meditation, this makes sense of and permits the way that one's mind can be wandering where the contents are composed of things that are roughly the desired content of one's meditation. That is, it illuminates the difference (phenomenologically, pychological, and neurophysiologically) between mind wandering composed of the content of one's breath, and mindful focused attention of one's breath.

Second, it makes clear that mind wandering is not a simple binary with a clear distinction between mind wandering and focus. If mind wandering describes a range of loosely (automatically and deliberately) constrained thought with regulatory contributions from several brain networks [34], then it is possible at least in principle for some hypothetical neurofeedback design to be sensitive to the degree to which a user is experiencing mind wandering. Recent results by Lutterveld et al. [26] substantiate this claim, who found that subjects were able to volitionally control a visual feedback signal based on source localized posterior cingulate cortex gamma band (40–57 Hz) activity in the direction of increased effortless awareness, and that the feedback signal corresponded to the subjects experience of effortless awareness. Additionally, decreases in gamma band activity in that region corresponded to increases in mind wandering.

### Refining Analysis of Interview Results

This decomposition of the cognitive processes that are constitutive of mindfulness meditation can be used to shed new light on the results of our interviews with subjects. When subjects say that they encounter difficulties when dealing with distractions and mind wandering, it can be described as an overly active default mode network and regulatory issues that would appropriately decrease activation in the DMN and switch to salience network activity and disengagement with the distraction from the executive control network. With this connection established and the requisite theoretical machinery in place, we can now make a connection to another body of research that was before not possible: age-related differences in working memory, attention, and the influence of distractions on both.

Older adults show decreased performance on tasks of working memory and attention when presented with distractions, compared to younger adults, a difference which is partly attributed to neuroanatomical changes in the frontoparietal executive control network [35]. This decreased ability to inhibit distracting stimuli makes them less able to bring to bear the necessary cognitive resources for attention demanding tasks more difficult when distracted, leading to decreased activation in the frontoparietal regions during the tasks compared to younger adults [36].

While there is currently no research directly showing that older adults spend less time in effortless awareness associated brain states when confronted with exogenous or endogenous distractions, we believe that these results provide some preliminary support for the following claims. Older adults, when distracted during meditation and engaged in mind wandering will show on average increased default mode network activity, and the activity of their default mode network would be negatively correlated with subsequent frontoparietal executive control network activity when they attempt to disengage from the distraction. What this means phenomenologically is that we expect that they would experience disengaging from their distractions and mind wandering as more effortful than younger adults and be successful at it less often. Then, given the importance of being able to recognize and disengage with distractions during meditation, we would also expect that they would spend less time in a state of effortless awareness or focused on their object of meditation since those steps follow engagement of the executive control network. In other words, older adults might more often find themselves pulled back into their mind wandering before they could break out of it and resume meditation, compared to younger adults.

The second theme of difficulty understanding when they are "doing it right" makes more sense in this context as well. If these earlier claims are the case, and given the importance of actually experiencing and spending time in a meditative state for resolving issues found in this theme, then it becomes clear that this can be a very significant hurdle for older adults learning to meditate. With decreased time spent in focused awareness, and increased time spent in mind wandering and the difficult activity of bringing oneself out of it, then it is hard to see what the kind of focus described in meditation is like.

### Recommendations for Neurofeedback Design

The themes from our interviews, the high level constraints which our analysis yielded, and our specific breakdown of the constitutive cognitive processes underlying meditation, our analysis of these processes in the context of older adults provide a strong foundation for outlining our recommendations for the design of a neurofeedback technology to assist learning meditation.

Our first recommendation is that some sort of neurofeedback, or at least some passive BCI seems necessary. This follows from our earlier design implication from our interviews that it should be sensitive to difficulties of a user dealing with distractions and when they are "doing it right", combined with the need for the user to not actively control the system through any intentional input of their own. If the user to were to alert the system that their mind has been wandering by traditional input methods then it is already too late, since the user has already noticed their mind wandering. Additionally, if that method of signaling to the system required additional attention, then it necessarily also affects the process of meditation in a way that differs from traditional practices. This is because it is at that moment that the user should be returning their attention back to the object of meditation and disengaging from their distraction, rather than engaging in giving some input to the system. Therefore, the only possible design is one that is controlled passively by changes in the user's attention.

Second is that the output of the system cannot be visual. This is because the eyes of the user should be closed in traditional beginner meditation practices, and differing from this would be a violation of the constraint that the process of meditation should not significantly differ from traditional practices.

Third is that the system should not give any feedback to the user when they are in attentional states that are not mind wandering that could distract them. This also follows from several design implications discussed earlier and is in accordance with assertions in traditional Vipassana meditation literature and contemporary mindfulness meditation practices [13]. If it were to give feedback while the user is being mindful about something that is not the output of the system then it runs the risk of distracting them from their meditation with the feedback, defeating the purpose of helping them spend less time distracted. Additionally, several participants in articulating the way in which any technology to assist learning meditation should not differ from traditional meditation practice mentioned how they would not like any additional content added to their experience when they are not distracted. While systems which provide feedback that become transparently incorporated into one's attention are possible [37, 38] and are an exciting avenue for future work in this area, in the absence of something like this, it should only give feedback during mind wandering.

Given that the system is giving feedback about mind wandering, then a fourth recommendation is that it should not give any feedback immediately after determining that the user's mind is wandering. Assuming some perfect system that is able to determine that a user's mind is wandering immediately following the start of mind wandering, then giving feedback at that time would run counter to two of our design implications. From the recognition that effort of meditation is seen by meditators as a benefit, and that noticing that one's mind is wandering is an essential part of the practice, it follows that removing the possibility of a user ever noticing when their mind has been wandering would be unacceptable. This is not to say that giving any feedback at all about mind wandering would necessarily run counter to these requirements. If recognizing that one's mind has wandered is an important part of learning meditation, then very long periods of mind wandering in some ways represent lost opportunities for noticing that one's mind has been wandering. The requirement then becomes that it should help cue the user into their mind wandering some amount of time after their mind has started wandering, but before the end of their meditation practice. This tension was recognized well by Participant 1, who offered the solution that if something were to tell them that their mind was wandering then:

> "I would like it to, with some sort of settable delay, tell me when I am distracted. But with a programmable delay right? And then poke me or something, let me know when my mind is wandering. [...] I would want it to be adjustable. So as I got better and better at it I could put more delay on it"

While this differs from many traditional neurofeedback designs that give a much tighter feedback loop, it is a necessary requirement for meditation in particular.

Finally, evidence from our earlier decomposition of the cognitive processes involved in meditation make it clear that PCC gamma activity is a good marker for mind wandering, and thus a good target for controlling the feedback of a system which is sensitive to mind wandering in its user.

## 6 Evaluation and Future Work

We plan to conduct a series of three studies to evaluate a design that follows these recommendations. Our first experiment is designed to assess whether such a system can improve performance on standard measures of sustained visual attention compared to a sham feedback control. Given that vigilance of attention on the target of meditation is a central component of early parts of learning mindfulness meditation, then improvements on sustained attention measures when using the device should increase the plausibility that it would improve some of these relevant parts of beginner meditation practice.

Our second experiment is designed to show that users can associate feelings of attentional focus and effortless awareness with real-time auditory, rather than visual, representations of their PCC activity and volitionally control the direction of feedback in the direction of increased effortless awareness compared to a sham feedback control, based on the experimental design of Lutterveld et al. [26].

Finally, we plan to run a study of older adults using our planned system to learn meditation, compared to a standard audiobook alternative method of learning meditation without a teacher present. By assessing user acceptance using Davis' [39] Technology Acceptance Model (TAM), we plan to assess the user's perceived ease of use, perceived usefulness, and attitude towards using the system.

# 7    Conclusions

Meditation is difficult to learn in general, and our results indicate that this is a difficulty for older adults as well. From our results, they face difficulties dealing with distractions and mind wandering along with difficulties understanding whether they are "doing it right". Further consideration of the cognitive processes of meditation and age-related differences in distractibility and attention point to learning meditation being perhaps more difficult for older adults than younger adults, although our study's limitations suggest that further research is needed to verify this hypothesis. In any case, our results are also encouraging for the prospect of using technology to assist older adults learn meditation, as our participants were generally open to its use in these contexts. However, this openness was conditional on it being "not too complicated to use" (Participant 1), that it also did not differ significantly from existing meditation practices, and that the use of the technology did not distract them from meditation. While the development of technologies to assist meditation are still in their infancy, we argued for several recommendations for such a technology based on our results. Designs should be sensitive to the internal mental states of the user without requiring their attention, they should not use visual feedback, they should not give feedback to the user unless they are distracted from mind wandering, and that any feedback should be delayed in order to keep a desirable amount of challenge in meditation. Finally, we see neurofeedback systems as necessary to meet these recommendations. Together this provides a starting point for further investigating technologies to assist meditation for older adults.

# References

1. Marciniak, R., Sheardova, K., Čermáková, P., Hudeček, D., Šumec, R., Hort, J.: Effect of meditation on cognitive functions in context of aging and neurodegenerative diseases. Front. Behav. Neurosci. **8**, 17 (2014)
2. Newberg, A.B., Serruya, M., Wintering, N., Moss, A.S., Reibel, D., Monti, D.A.: Meditation and neurodegenerative diseases. Ann. N.Y. Acad. Sci. **1307**(1), 112–123 (2014)
3. Luders, E.: Exploring age-related brain degeneration in meditation practitioners. Ann. N.Y. Acad. Sci. **1307**(1), 82–88 (2014)

4. Gard, T., Hölzel, B.K., Lazar, S.W.: The potential effects of meditation on age-related cognitive decline: a systematic review. Ann. N.Y. Acad. Sci. **1307**(1), 89–103 (2014)
5. Larouche, E., Hudon, C., Goulet, S.: Potential benefits of mindfulness-based interventions in mild cognitive impairment and Alzheimer's disease: an interdisciplinary perspective. Behav. Brain Res. **276**, 199–212 (2015)
6. Cullen, M.: Mindfulness-based interventions: an emerging phenomenon. Mindfulness **2**(3), 186–193 (2011)
7. Jain, S., et al.: A randomized controlled trial of mindfulness meditation versus relaxation training: effects on distress, positive states of mind, rumination, and distraction. Ann. Behav. Med. **33**(1), 11–21 (2007)
8. Baer, R.A.: Mindfulness training as a clinical intervention: a conceptual and empirical review. Clin. Psychol. Sci. Pract. **10**(2), 125–143 (2003)
9. Toneatto, T., Nguyen, L.: Does mindfulness meditation improve anxiety and mood symptoms? A review of the controlled research. Can. J. Psychiatry **52**(4), 260–266 (2007)
10. Bowen, S., Marlatt, A.: Surfing the urge: brief mindfulness-based intervention for college student smokers. Psychol. Addict. Behav. **23**(4), 666–671 (2009)
11. Baer, R.A.: Mindfulness-Based Treatment Approaches: Clinician's Guide to Evidence Base and Applications. Academic Press, Cambridge (2015)
12. Kabat-Zinn, J.: An outpatient program in behavioral medicine for chronic pain patients based on the practice of mindfulness meditation: theoretical considerations and preliminary results. Gen. Hosp. Psychiatry **4**(1), 33–47 (1982)
13. Kabat-Zinn, J.: Mindfulness-based interventions in context: past, present, and future. Clin. Psychol. Sci. Pract. **10**(2), 144–156 (2003)
14. Lutz, A., Slagter, H.A., Dunne, J.D., Davidson, R.J.: Attention regulation and monitoring in meditation. Trends Cogn. Sci. **12**(4), 163–169 (2008)
15. Engler, J.: Being somebody and being nobody: a reexamination of the understanding of self in psychoanalysis and Buddhism. In: Psychoanalysis and Buddhism: An Unfolding Dialog, pp. 35–79 (2003)
16. Morone, N.E., Lynch, C.S., Greco, C.M., Tindle, H.A., Weiner, D.K.: I felt like a new person. The effects of mindfulness meditation on older adults with chronic pain: qualitative narrative analysis of diary entries. J. Pain **9**(9), 841–848 (2008)
17. Irving, J.A., Dobkin, P.L., Park, J.: Cultivating mindfulness in health care professionals: a review of empirical studies of mindfulness-based stress reduction (MBSR). Complement. Ther. Clin. Pract. **15**(2), 61–66 (2009)
18. McCollum, E.E., Gehart, D.R.: Using mindfulness meditation to teach beginning therapists therapeutic presence: a qualitative study. J. Marital Fam. Ther. **36**(3), 347–360 (2010)
19. Gordon, W.V., Shonin, E., Sumich, A., Sundin, E.C., Griffiths, M.D.: Meditation awareness training (MAT) for psychological well-being in a sub-clinical sample of university students: a controlled pilot study. Mindfulness **5**(4), 381–391 (2014)
20. Lomas, T., Edginton, T., Cartwright, T., Ridge, D.: Cultivating equanimity through mindfulness meditation: a mixed methods enquiry into the development of decentring capabilities in men. Int. J. Wellbeing **5**(3) (2015)
21. Kerr, C.E., Josyula, K., Littenberg, R.: Developing an observing attitude: an analysis of meditation diaries in an MBSR clinical trial. Clin. Psychol. Psychother. **18**(1), 80–93 (2011)
22. Brandmeyer, T., Delorme, A.: Meditation and neurofeedback. Front. Psychol. **4**, 688 (2013)
23. Bhayee, S., et al.: Attentional and affective consequences of technology supported mindfulness training: a randomised, active control, efficacy trial. BMC Psychol. **4**, 60 (2016)
24. Sas, C., Chopra, R.: MeditAid: a wearable adaptive neurofeedback-based system for training mindfulness state. Pers. Ubiquit. Comput. **19**(7), 1169–1182 (2015)

25. Kosunen, I., Salminen, M., Järvelä, S., Ruonala, A., Ravaja, N., Jacucci, G.: RelaWorld: neuroadaptive and immersive virtual reality meditation system. In: Proceedings of the 21st International Conference on Intelligent User Interfaces, New York, NY, USA, pp. 208–217 (2016)
26. van Lutterveld, R., et al.: Source-space EEG neurofeedback links subjective experience with brain activity during effortless awareness meditation. NeuroImage
27. Wang, J.-R., Hsieh, S.: Neurofeedback training improves attention and working memory performance. Clin. Neurophysiol. **124**(12), 2406–2420 (2013)
28. Cutcliffe, J.R.: Methodological issues in grounded theory. J. Adv. Nurs. **31**(6), 1476–1484 (2000)
29. Glaser, B.G.: Doing Grounded Theory: Issues and Discussions. Sociology Press, Mill Valley (1998)
30. Strauss, A., Corbin, J.M.: Basics of Qualitative Research: Grounded Theory Procedures and Techniques. Sage Publications Inc, Thousand Oaks (1990)
31. Bodhi, B.: In the Buddha's Words: An Anthology of Discourses from the Pali Canon. Simon and Schuster, New York (2005)
32. Yeager, D., Paunesku, D., Walton, G., Dweck, C.: How can we instill productive mindsets at scale? A review of the evidence and an initial R&D agenda. In: White paper prepared for the White House meeting on "Excellence in Education: The Importance of Academic Mindsets
33. Malinowski, P.: Neural mechanisms of attentional control in mindfulness meditation. Front. Neurosci. **7**, 8 (2013)
34. Christoff, K., Irving, Z.C., Fox, K.C.R., Spreng, R.N., Andrews-Hanna, J.R.: Mind-wandering as spontaneous thought: a dynamic framework. Nat. Rev. Neurosci. **17**(11), 718–731 (2016)
35. Campbell, K.L., Grady, C.L., Ng, C., Hasher, L.: Age differences in the frontoparietal cognitive control network: implications for distractibility. Neuropsychologia **50**(9), 2212–2223 (2012)
36. Reuter-Lorenz, P.A., Cappell, K.A.: Neurocognitive aging and the compensation hypothesis. Curr. Dir. Psychol. Sci. **17**(3), 177–182 (2008)
37. Bach-y-Rita, P., Kercel, S.W.: Sensory substitution and the human–machine interface. Trends Cogn. Sci. **7**(12), 541–546 (2003)
38. Hartcher-O'Brien, J., Auvray, M.: The process of distal attribution illuminated through studies of sensory substitution. Multisens. Res. **27**(5–6), 421–441 (2014)
39. Davis, F.D.: A technology acceptance model for empirically testing new end-user information systems : theory and results. Thesis, Massachusetts Institute of Technology (1985)

# Dynamic Task Sharing Within Human-UxS Teams: Computational Situation Awareness

Scott Grigsby[✉], Jacob Crossman, Ben Purman, Rich Frederiksen, and Dylan Schmorrow

Soar Technologies, Inc., Ann Arbor, MI, USA
scott.grigsby@soartech.com

**Abstract.** In current military operations, a team of human operators, often distributed across multiple locations, is required to manage even a single Unmanned Vehicle (UxV). For future multi-UxV control, effective dynamic task sharing strategies – the ability to quickly re-assign tasks and responsibilities between operators or between operators and autonomous systems - will vastly improve team coordination. However, for task hand-off to be executed effectively, the task assignee needs to be quickly brought up to speed with sufficient situation awareness to effectively handle their new tasking. We have implemented a system, called Computational Situation Awareness (CSA), that encodes the awareness maintenance process into the control station itself. CSA generates a computational "mental" model of an expert's SA and maintains multi-level awareness of the mission and state of the unmanned systems. This allows the system to predict information requirements and drive cueing and other mitigations for individuals and across the team. By tracking user tasks and system state related to those tasks, CSA builds an understanding of the task's progress thus enabling it to better determine what information the user needs to maintain task relevant SA without bogging them down. By encoding workload assessment and situation awareness into the operator control station itself, the control station becomes a partner with the operator (or team of operators) in making sense of the data. This enables it to manage task sharing and offloading and share information in terms that aids rather than distracts, thus improving each operator's mission effectiveness.

**Keywords:** Situation awareness · Workload · Human-Machine teaming · Decision support

## 1 Introduction

Supervisory control of multiple UxVs is a challenge, due to the cognitive burdens it places on the operator. These burdens include:

1. Staying aware of all important mission activities and events
2. Predicting outcomes and activities so as to proactively address them
3. Making decisions about how to best deploy aircraft
4. Shifting and regaining awareness when multiple activities occur simultaneously
5. Triaging and offloading tasks when overloaded
6. Recognizing faults or failures

© Springer International Publishing AG 2017
D.D. Schmorrow and C.M. Fidopiastis (Eds.): AC 2017, Part II, LNAI 10285, pp. 443–460, 2017.
DOI: 10.1007/978-3-319-58625-0_32

Prior work suggests that, under the right conditions, supervisory control should provide an operator with the ability to control 4–8 UAVs simultaneously given the right conditions (i.e. that the level of automation is correct, and required situation awareness is maintained) [1]. Current systems fall far short of this level – most requiring multiple people to manage one aircraft.

The Multi Autonomous Ground-robotic International Challenge 2010 (MAGIC 2010) [2] provided an opportunity to test the limits of human supervisory control in a reasonably complex ground domain. In this competition, multiple robots executed ISR and dangerous object interaction tasks under the supervision of one or two operators. For this environment, Soar Technology, Inc. (SoarTech) developed the SAGE user interface designed to keep operators (and competition judges) aware of the overall mission as well as important events that were critical to the mission. Though only one of several factors that influenced the results, SAGE (along with a significant amount of robot autonomy [3]) helped a team of two operators efficiently control 14 ground robots. This results suggested an opportunity to apply new technologies to the problem of multi-vehicle control – specifically, technology that can enhance and expand operator situation awareness.

This prior work has led to the further research, development, and evaluation of what we call **Computational Situation Awareness (CSA)**. CSA is stand-alone software that maintains multi-level awareness of the mission and state of the unmanned systems. CSA Ingests (via networking protocols) data regarding the mission, UAV state, and some user-entered data. CSA then maintains an internal operating picture, detects task, failure, and mission-relevant events, and estimates user workload. The purpose of this technology is to help the operator continuously orient him/herself to the situation with the goal of making faster and better decisions.

## 2 Approach

Multi-UAV missions require a combination of global situation awareness (e.g., the state of the whole mission) and awareness of specific details such as the activity of a specific track, or the cause of a failure. Alternating between these types of macro and micro views of a mission is known to cause loss of situation awareness and thus can lead to poor decisions or change blindness.

To aid the user, CSA maintains situation awareness within the system itself and, unlike the human, CSA does not get distracted, attending equally effectively to all aspects of the mission. Unlike other systems, CSA maintains this awareness at multiple levels as defined by Endsley [3]:

1. **Perception:** Like most command and control systems, CSA maintains an internal operating picture (IOP) with the locations and states of each entity.
2. **Comprehension:** Unlike most other systems, CSA monitors this perception data for important relationships that matter in the mission. When discovered, these relationships trigger *events*. Events are a key output of CSA – they represent situations that require user attention. Events are maintained in a queue and are color coded to indicate priority. Events are CSA's means of orienting the user to critical situations.

Without CSA, the operator would need to use scan-and-assess techniques to maintain the same awareness making it difficult to maintain both macro- and micro-awareness.

3. **Projection:** CSA also projects some information into the future – for example, computing estimated task completion time. This projection data is integrated back into CSA's internal operating picture allowing events to be proactively triggered on predicted situations.

This multi-level IOP can be used for purposes beyond event detection. Our existing Lucid system uses this data to estimate the workload required of the user to execute the mission. This estimate associates a multi-dimensional workload model with each event and task in the IOP, and from the collection of these models, it computes an overall workload. This estimate is used within the system to automatically offload tasks to other users when overloaded.

CSA's ability to maintain its own internal operating picture can form the basis for situation awareness for both human users and autonomous entities. Within a decision support application, CSA would output its events using a smart interaction module to display alerts or events, allocate tasks, or otherwise inform missions, allowing the human user to take intelligent actions. Within an autonomous control system, CSA would be used to track and inform the entities decision processes directly.

## 2.1 CSA Architecture and System Integration

Computational Situation Awareness is implemented as a software module that ingests a broad range of state data and outputs filtered state data, events, and workload estimates. Figure 1 illustrates the CSA data flow.

The central component of CSA is the internal operating picture (IOP), which stores state data. This store is implemented as an in-memory store with separate indexed data structures for assets, tasks, tracks, and other relevant state items.

The IOP is maintained by a set of processes that are continuously processing incoming state messages from simulation (though the source is unimportant) and either (L1) simply storing them, (L2) making additional computational inferences on them, or (L3) making projections based on them. The Ln labels indicate the level of processing provided by these functions in Endsley's levels of SA terminology [4].

The basic SA processes set the stage for event detection. Event detection finds patterns in the IOP that match to mission, task, and failure situations that are of interest to the user. Some of these events are hard coded (e.g., the task start/completion tasks and the failure tasks). Others are informed by user requests (e.g., the force protection zone and restricted areas). These events are prioritized and output to the network where any component can subscribe to them. Each event is associated with a specific client (based on the task offloading work we will discuss in the next sub-section) and, thus, clients that do not "own" an event, display the event differently (grayed out, low on the event queue).

Events can be added to the CSA module relatively easily by simply implementing an event class and logic. There is support in the infrastructure for various spatio-temporal computations that can be reused to support new events. New event classes can easily be added within a day or two.

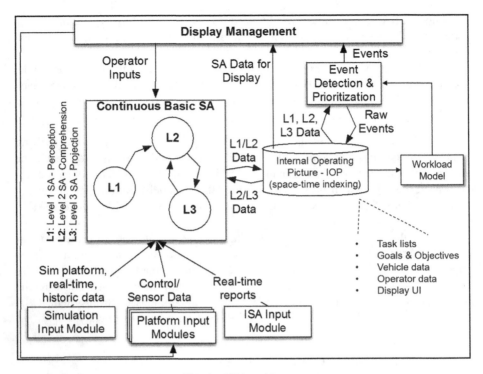

**Fig. 1.** CSA architecture

As an example, Table 1 summarizes the classes of events that were supported as of the end of our Lucid effort. The shaded rows highlight the events that the user can request explicitly. The "zone" based events are created in two cases: (1) when mission plan data is received force protection and restricted operating zones are created around objectives and dangerous areas, and (2) when the user creates a zone of interest using the polygon drawing tools in the UI. The track-based events are created when users select to "watch" a track. In these cases the user is alerted when new information about that track becomes available, when the track is lost, and when the track changes course significantly. These user-driven events are a critical component to CSA's utility as they let the user specify how the CSA system should help him/her. In our evaluation, these user-driven events were most valuable in helping the operators execute the mission.

## 2.2   Real-Time Workload Assessment and Offloading

The IOP is also used to infer the workload on the user in any given situation. When the workload is estimated to be above a single operator's capacity to execute effectively, events and tasks are offloaded to another operator. The basic workload assessment capability uses a 3-dimensional model to estimate workload in the cognitive, visual, and manual dimensions (these three dimensions are taken from Wickens [5], but here the auditory mode is not incorporated to simplify the model for initial implementation).

**Table 1.** Classes of events that CSA can detect (Lucid implementation)

| Event name | Type | Description |
|---|---|---|
| Orbit point start | Task | Detect when orbit starts |
| Search route start/end | Task | Detects when route search starts and when end of route is reached |
| Search area start/end | Task | Detects when areas search starts and ends |
| Follow vessel | Task | Detects when tracking starts (failure event detects when it is lost |
| Asset task hasn't changed | Task | Detects when an asset has not been tasked recently (default: 5 min) |
| Force protection (user) | Mission | Detects when red/yellow tracks are discovered within a specified region |
| Restricted operating zone (user) | Mission | Detect blue forces in an unsafe area |
| Area of operation breach (user) | Mission | Detect that an asset has left an expected area of operation |
| New info available (user) | Mission | Detects when new data is available to track – Automatically created for any track being followed |
| Track change (user) | Mission | Detects when a track changes course (45 deg) or is lost – Automatically created for any track being followed |
| Fuel warning | Fault | Detects when a vehicle is at risk of not making back to carrier group with fuel levels |
| High/low altitude | Fault | UAV breaks an altitude boundary |
| Lost comms | Fault | UAV has lost communications |
| Near max comms range | Fault | Reaching limit of direct line-of-sight communication (Fire Scout-B) |
| Not making expected progress | Fault | Asset appears to be moving incorrectly (not following expected path) |

The basic architecture for workload estimation is illustrated in Fig. 2. Events and state data (most importantly, tasks) are pulled from the IOP. For each event and task, the system looks up the workload model for that event and reads the expected

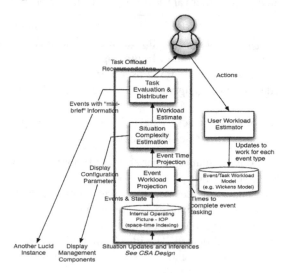

**Fig. 2.** Workload estimation architecture.

instantaneous workload value for that event at the given time. The expected instantaneous workload values are aggregated, using Eq. 1, to form an overall estimated workload. This value is fed into the task evaluation and distribution function where decisions are task distribution are made.

The equation used to compute the overall workload is as follows:

$$W(t) = \sum_{i=1}^{N} max_{k=1,2,3}\{w_k(t - t_i)\} + g(t) \tag{1}$$

$$g(t) = 0.1 \times 1.25^N \tag{2}$$

Here $W(t)$ is the estimated workload computed as the maximum of the accumulated component (e.g., cognitive, visual, manual) workloads. Component workloads are computed as functions of time, where each $t_i$ is the start time for the $i$th event or task. The $g(t)$ component approximates the non-linear effects caused by multiple simultaneous active events (attention switching). Its constant values were tuned during laboratory tests such that workload values approximated to 1.0 when a user appeared to be overloaded. g(t) presents some problems as it scales exponentially over the whole range of N, which is not realistic and can overestimate the workload for high Ns. It works reasonably well for N < 15, but provides excessive estimates. A future version will likely replace the exponential with a sigmoid function to model a diminishing effect as N increases to large numbers.

This model is similar in concept to the Wickens' model [5], but differs in that it scales to an arbitrary number of tasks and events and accounts for change in workload over time such as temporal delays, workload ramp up, and workload ramp down. Our model also designed to be more precise in that it seeks to derive a number that can be compared to the user's full load level (e.g., 1.0 = fully loaded).

The decision when to offload is not straightforward. We found in our discussions with users during the evaluation that there are several ways tasks can be divided within a team.

1. They can be broken up purely based on their **timing** (e.g., round robin distribution, or secondary user gets all tasks after the main user becomes overloaded).
2. They can be broken up based on **load balancing** (e.g., the choice of which user gets which tasks is made so as to minimize user workload differences).
3. They can be made based on **geography** (e.g., each user takes care of a geographic segment)
4. They can be made based on **asset ownership** (e.g., each user gets events and tasks associated with the assets that he/she owns).

In practice, during our evaluation, operators used more than one of these approaches when they were given a choice.

We only had time and resources to select one offloading method for our initial implementation. We selected a variant of (2) for its simplicity. The variation was that the algorithm tries to load users one at a time – meaning it will not balance the load until at least one user is fully allocated. The idea behind this strategy is that it allows the secondary operator(s) to focus on other tasks while the primary operator is able to do the task alone. The algorithm is as follows:

1. Assign all unassigned events to the user with the highest workload (this is the primary user).
2. If this user's workload estimate is < 1.2 (combined) then stop, otherwise –
3. Find the maximum workload event assigned to the high workload user that has occurred in the last 30 s. (i.e. offload the event that is the biggest component of the workload.
4. Assign this event to the lower workload user if (event.workload < 0.9 (high_user.workload - low_user.workload))

We note a couple of key points regarding this algorithm. First, events/tasks are not offloaded until the workload level reaches 1.2. This allows for the lack of precision in the workload model numbers. They are not intended to be correct to a single decimal place. Second, it moves tasks to other users from largest to smallest. The idea is to take the major focus tasks away from the primary user, so the primary user can continue to maintain global SA.

A crucial aspect of task offloading is maintaining situation awareness of the task parameters during handoff. Here CSA provides the appropriate mission parameters for the secondary operator. When the task is assigned or re-assigned, it is accompanied by a clickable "mini-brief" and recommendation with information drawn from the CSA IOP (Fig. 3) to enable the operator to quickly come up to speed on the task.

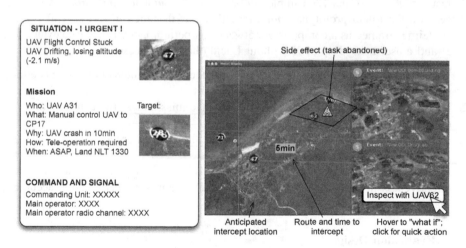

**Fig. 3.** Sample mini-brief (left) and recommendation panel (right) for task offloading

## 2.3 Architecture and Sample System Integration

The first implementation of CSA was within a system, called Lucid, to enhance operator situation awareness when executing control over multiple unmanned aerial vehicles (UAVs) to fulfill an ISR mission.

The Lucid system forms an innovative operator control unit (OCU) with a goal of decreasing operator: UAV ratios. Our specific research goals were:

1. Achieve operator:UAV ratios of 1:4 or better
2. Minimize operator interaction time
3. Maximize allowable neglect time (time the operator can neglect the system without degrading mission performance)
4. Maximize operator situation awareness
5. Lessen primary operator workload by automatically distributing tasking

Lucid was implemented in two pieces. First, CSA and workload estimation were combined into a single software component that was executed within a Java virtual machine. These technologies were then integrated with a supervisory control interface (RaptorX). Display and control capabilities were encapsulated within a plugin that resided in a RaptorX front end. These two components talk with each other using the Lightweight Communication Protocol (LCM). A proxy at the RaptorX end converts LCM traffic into native RaptorX TCP CommPath traffic so that the user interface plugins can send and receive data. The system as a whole is integrated with our own simulation environment, called SimJr, which provides simulated real-world data feeds and allows us to test and evaluate the system. The interface to SimJr is also a network interface using LCM.

## 3    Evaluation and Results

To test the efficacy of our CSA implementation, we implemented a rigorous evaluation process on the Lucid prototype. Our evaluation was designed to test several claims. Each claim is framed as a comparison between an operator using Lucid (the evaluation case) and a user using Raptor X without Lucid (the control case).

1. Using Lucid, operators will interact less with the system. Interaction here is defined to include control tasks and manipulation tasks.
2. Using Lucid, operators will be able to attend the mission less frequently in order to do other tasks.
3. Using Lucid, operators will have increased situation awareness of the mission, operating area, and asset state.
4. Using Lucid, operators will complete missions more effectively. We will measure effectiveness in terms of high value individuals identified, classification accuracy, reaction time, and task failures.

### 3.1    Evaluation Design

The Lucid evaluation was executed as a comparative study using a single control (or base) case and a single evaluation case. Both cases used the same scenario design and simulation and RaptorX as the core user interface. Communication between operators occurred only via a chat window. The independent variable for the study and the difference between the two cases is presence or absence of the Lucid capabilities, which are presented to the user as extensions of the Raptor X capability. Table 2 compares the features available in each configuration.

Operators were provided with a laptop computer with Raptor X and the Lucid plugin installed. Separate machines were used to run the simulation. Manual data was

**Table 2.** Evaluation configurations

|  | Control case | Evaluation case |
|---|---|---|
| Users | • Primary operator<br>• Supporting operator | SAME |
| Human communication | • Text chat | SAME |
| Simulation | • SimJr running battlegroup/harbor scenario | SAME |
| Secondary task | • Elementary math using tablet | SAME |
| Front end | • Raptor X<br>• Assets Commands<br>• Polygon overlay drawing | • Raptor X<br>• Assets Commands<br>• Polygon overlay drawing<br>• Event detection/queue<br>• Situation mini-briefs<br>• Decision overlay (if possible) |
| Task sharing | • Ad hoc using chat | • Auto event passing<br>• Manual event passing (via chat) |

collected (1) by the operators using predefined web forms/spreadsheets and (2) by the experiment director when required. At the end of each day, the team met in a hot wash to summarize what happened that day including collecting subjective feedback on performance.

Each test run (mission) has three main phases: planning/preparation (5 min), execution, and wrap up. The planning phase is short because the operators executed the same basic mission over and over (including training runs) and thus did not need much time to plan out activities. The mission execution phase was interrupted twice to measure situation awareness – once at 15 min and once at 30 min. During intermediate situation awareness testing the simulation was paused and the RaptorX screen blanked. For final situation awareness testing the simulation was paused, but the RaptorX screen remained visible. The wrap-up phase consists of structured questions and gathering of data from that mission. Each session typically ran 75–80 min.

Two operators executed each mission: a primary operator and a support operator:

**Primary Operator:** The primary operator is responsible for the overall mission including situation awareness, classification of tracks, and control of UAVs. The primary operator can offload tasks to the support operator when desired.

**Support Operator:** The support operator is responsible for any tasks the primary operator request for the secondary operator to execute.

The only exceptions to this structure were three runs made near the end of the evaluation when a second operator was not available. In these cases, a primary operator executed the mission alone.

**Metrics**

We collected a wide range of data associated with each of our experimental claims. A substantial volume of data was collected in the form of automatically generated logs from the RaptorX platform, including user actions with timing, and from the simulation (to capture ground truth of entity locations and timing of simulated events). For subjective workload measurement, we used an HTML version of the NASA Task Load IndeX (TLX) [6, 7], a widely employed multi-dimensional rating procedure that derives an overall workload score based on a weighted average of ratings on six subscales: Mental Demands, Physical Demands, Temporal Demands, Own Performance, Effort and Frustration. To assess situation awareness, we developed an adaptation of the Situation Awareness Global Assessment Technique (SAGAT) [4]. We supplemented the standard SAGAT procedure where subjects place entities on a map to demonstrate their awareness of the geographic situation with scenario-specific questions about mission-relevant conditions such as threats to own force and status of adversary activities.

**User's Mission and Tasks**

Overall, the operators were responsible for monitoring activity at a port. They were given initially 4, and as the mission progressed as many as 6 UAVs to execute the mission. These assets could be used to obtain tracks of vessels and ground vehicle in and around the port. Each track was associated with a set of property data (e.g., location, size, cargo, type), the completeness of which is dependent on the quality of the sensor reading on the vehicle. All operators were given the following mission brief:

> "You are responsible for monitoring activity in a port city. You have some UAVs at your disposal and can use them to obtain tracks of surface vessels and ground vehicle in and around the port. Each track has some associated data, the completeness of which is dependent on the quality of the sensor reading on the vehicle. Intelligence reports suggest that adversary forces intend to move explosives and other equipment out of the city by sea. Past experience suggests that operations like this begin by moving explosives from a bomb-making factory to a training site, then moving to a dock where they are transferred onto a ship. Ships used for such transfers usually arrive only shortly before the contraband coming from the training site is to be loaded. The locations of the training site and two or three bomb factories are known, as are the locations of all the docks. It is not known which bomb factory will supply the training site, or which dock will be used for the transfer. An informant reports that the ship to be used is the Trojan Steed, which can be distinguished by its white color, cargo of large crates, and like new condition."

Figure 4 provides an overview of the mission geography including the overall mission area view with the carrier group to the southeast.

Figure 5 is a close-up view of the land region where ground vehicles moved. These figures are taken from the RaptorX display.

Within the general activity of the harbor, the user is to detect three events:

1. A vehicle arriving at a known training site from one of two known bomb labs. The operator was required to identify the source location for this vehicle.
2. A vehicle leaving the training site at some point and moving to a dock to meet up with the Trojan Steed (sea vessel). The operator was required to identify whether or not the ground vehicle did meet up with the Trojan Steed.
3. Any vessel approaching the carrier group. The scenario supported carrier threats from either an opponent force destroyer or a fishing vessel. The operator had to correctly identify which vehicle threatened the battle group (as soon as possible).

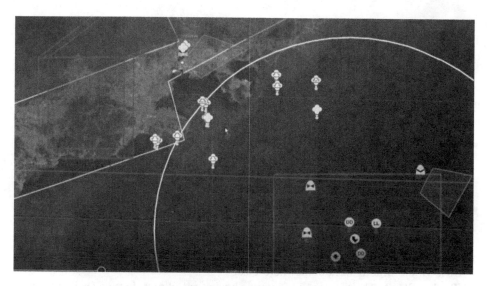

**Fig. 4.** Overall mission region

**Fig. 5.** Close-up of harbor area.

In support of detecting these mission-level events, the operator also attempted to complete these supporting actions:

1. Identifying the track of the vehicle that moved from a bomb site to the training area.
2. Identifying the track of the vehicle that moved from the training site to the dock or some other location.
3. Identifying the ship named "Trojan Steed" and its track.

We developed two different movement models – one for the sea and one for land. The sea vessels were spawned at both fixed and random locations in the sea (most at the beginning of the mission) and within the port. They each selected random destination and moved toward those destinations at rates dependent on the vessel type. The land vessels were spawned randomly along a road network and were given random destinations. Movement speeds were constant. The high value individuals (HVIs) were also randomized, but in a constrained manner:

- **Bomb Vehicle:** The vehicle moving from the bomb lab to the training camp. This vehicle spawned at a random time early in the mission. It source was randomly selected between two different bomb lab locations (one on the east, the other on the west).
- **Dock Vehicle:** The vehicle moving out of the training camp, possibly to a dock. This vehicle spawned a random (but constrained) number of seconds after the bomb vehicle arrived at the training camp. Its destination was randomized such that 50% of the time it went to the dock where the Trojan Steed was headed, while the other 50% of the time it went somewhere else.
- **Trojan Steed:** The sea vessel of interest begins out of port, but moves into the port to a dock during the mission. The Trojan Steed was randomly selected to be one of two sea vessels, one to the east and one to the west of the port mouth. Other clutter sea vessels with similar attributes were placed near each location. The Trojan Steed's dock destination was assigned randomly at startup (dependent in part on whether it would meet the dock vehicle that run).
- **Military Destroyers and Threatening Fishing Vessels:** Two destroyers patrolled the mouth of the port. At the beginning of the mission a threat was randomly selected among these vessels and a fishing fleet out of the port. The threat vehicle (either the military destroyer or a fishing vessel) would approach the carrier group over time.

To achieve the mission objectives the user can do two primary things: command UAVs and inspect/update information about tracks. The user can also execute supporting actions that help make decisions and commands easier. Table 3 lists the actions that a user can execute. Some of these activities can only happen when the user is using the Lucid plugin to RaptorX.

In addition to the main tasks, various situations can arise that require operator attention. Table 4 lists the situations that may occur during a mission and the expected operator response (or type of response). In many cases the operator has freedom in the details of the action taken.

Finally, the operators were asked to execute a secondary task whenever their primary task was not urgent or all consuming. The secondary task was the game "Tetris" executed on a tablet computer. The purpose of this secondary task is twofold:

1. To ensure that the user minimizes work on the main task (i.e., doesn't do "filler" tasks).
2. To estimate the allowable neglect time.

At the beginning of each scenario, the operator was asked to execute the secondary task as much as possible, running up as high a score as possible. At the start of the

**Table 3.** Available user actions in the Lucid and non-Lucid configurations.

| Action | Description | Lucid only |
|---|---|---|
| *UAV commands (speed and altitude can be set for each)* | | |
| Go to point | Go to a point in space and orbit or hover. Active sensor remains forward looking | |
| Observe point | Go to point or circular route where it is possible to keep sensor coverage on the point | |
| Search area | Fly in a circular pattern through an area such that every point in the area will be observed by the sensor at least once | |
| Search route | Fly along a route with the sensors oriented forward along the route | |
| Follow surface vessel | Position asset to keep vessel in view of its sensors. Move in order to keep vessel in view | |
| *Track annotation* | | |
| View track information | The user can select a track and view the known information for that track (e.g., location, type, etc.). Some fields may be unknown | |
| Mark track ID | The user can set the ID to one of the known HVIs | |
| Mark track force | For unknown entities, the user can mark the force of the track (i.e., Hostile, Suspected, or Unknown). Tracks marked as Hostile and Suspected have different colors so that they appear visually clear | |
| Mark track intent | For the foreign military surface vessel, the user can select the track and set the intent either "Patrol Harbor" or "Approach Battlegroup" | |
| *Map markup* | | |
| Create waypoints | The user can drop a waypoint on the map and assign a type to it: "Control" for use in tasking UAVs and "Location of Interest" to mark the main mission tasks | |
| Create routes and areas | The user can define routes as a series of waypoints and give them names. These can be used for route-based tasks | |
| *Other* | | |
| Chat | The user can chat in a standard chat window with the other operator | |
| *Event management* | | |
| Create watchbox | The user can create a box or radius and configure it to be watched by the system | X |
| Create watch on track | The user can mark a track to be watched for certain behaviors | X |
| Move event and asset control to other station | The user can select and offload an event (with an asset, if desired) to the other operator | X |

**Table 4.** Failure events that could occur during a mission.

| Situation | Symptom | Timing | Expected response |
|---|---|---|---|
| UAV runs low on fuel | Observe the fuel level in the asset details display | Fuel loss is permanent | Return the vehicle to the carrier group. If desired, launch reserve aircraft |
| UAV loses communication | Vehicle will appear to "freeze" for a period of time. The vehicle will continue its last action | Random. Comms loss may occur for 30 s to 2 min | Monitor for comms reacquisition. Possibly task another entity to complete that vehicle's mission |
| UAV navigation failure | Vehicle will drift away from planned route s and altitudes | Random. Navigation failures will repeat occurring periodically for up to 30 s each time | Possibly task another entity to complete that vehicle's mission |
| UAV breaches area of operations | Vehicle will be present in an area designated as "no fly" in the mission. Vehicle is removed from mission ("shot down") | This is not a random event, it only occurs when the operator loses track of the vehicle | Launch another vehicle or continue mission with one less vehicle |
| Track lost while attempting to auto-track | Aircraft will stop following sea vessel and just orbit the last known location | Permanent until re-acquired | User must direct asset to location where it can see the vessel to track and tell it to begin tracking again |

mission the operators press the "start" button on the secondary task application, and pause when not executing this task. When the mission is complete, the operators end the secondary task and report their score and time. In practice, some operators did not correctly report their score/time so some data was lost.

## 3.2 Evaluation Results

The overall finding of our evaluation is that Lucid had a moderate, positive effect on primary **operator efficiency and effectiveness**. Further findings include:

1. Mission Effectiveness
    (a) With Lucid, users had a higher effectiveness on the ground tracking task. Ground tracking was by far the most difficult aspect of the mission.
    (b) With Lucid, users more effectively kept HVIs in sensor view.
2. Interaction
    (a) With Lucid, the primary operator issued fewer commands
    (b) With Lucid, the primary operator executed fewer track views
    (c) With Lucid, the primary operator sent less chat to the secondary operator
3. Situation Awareness
    (a) With Lucid, subjective situation awareness was higher
    (b) With Lucid, there were significantly more correct SAGAT answers

4. Neglect Time
   (a) With Lucid, the primary user spent more time on the secondary task (result not significant)
   (b) One user was able to execute secondary tasks while operating alone

Here we highlight four of the more interesting findings from the evaluation relevant to CSA, workload monitoring, and task offloading.

Primary operators using Lucid selected and viewed tracks data much less frequently (Fig. 6 left). This effect is statistically significant with a 35% reduction in track inspection (p < 0.05 for the 3-tailed T-test). We hypothesize that this is mainly due to Lucid's CSA providing some of the scanning/check tasks that the user would have to do in the baseline system. Because of Lucid's alerts for tasking, failures, and especially mission issues (like track changes), the operator could focus on one area for a period of time without missing as much.

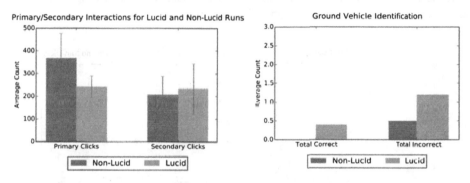

**Fig. 6.** Task counts for track-views (left) and ground vehicle identification (right).

Another interesting finding was that, overall, users attempted to identify ground tracks much more frequently when using Lucid than without (Fig. 6 right). In each mission, there are two ground vehicles to identify, and using Lucid the operator almost always made an attempt to identify both. Without Lucid, the operator only attempted to identify a single ground vehicle every 2 runs. Our conclusion is that Lucid aided the user in executing the ground-tracking mission, mainly through its alerts on tracks near the areas of interest, but also through its general reduction in required interaction time, providing more time to analyze tracks. The error rate was high using Lucid - on average, the user misclassified roughly one ground vehicle on every Lucid run, while correctly classifying roughly one ground vehicle every 2 runs. However, classification of ground vehicles was very difficult given the dozens of clutter vehicles and the many possible variations on the sources and destinations of the HVI vehicles. Thus, this error rate is not a surprise.

A surprising result is that the operators (especially the primary operator) issue far fewer chat lines when using Lucid than without (Fig. 7 left). For the primary user, the reduction is 44% with p < 0.05 using the usual 2-tailed T-test. We did not hypothesize that Lucid would reduce chat. We are uncertain as to why we see this effect. We believe that there are at least three possibilities: (1) a combination of the events and offloading reduced the need to communicate basic information about what was happening and where it was occurring, (2) the primary operator took more control during the Lucid runs and had the secondary operator do less, and (3) the primary operator, due to the stream of events felt more overwhelmed or engrossed in the details that he/she chatted less frequently. We cannot make any final conclusions as to which of these is true given our data, but we believe alternative (1) is most likely by elimination. Alternative (3) is not supported by the subjective evaluations (especially the TLX scores which show no difference in subjective workload between Lucid and non-Lucid runs). For alternative (2), we broke out the tasking activities by primary and secondary operator (Fig. 7 right). If alternative (2) were true we'd expect that for Lucid runs the secondary operator would issue many fewer UAV tasks than in the non-Lucid runs. This is not the case, in fact, the opposite is true (though not significantly so). This leaves us with alternative (1) as being most likely, and it is supported by the subjective and objective increase in SA shown above. This suggests that Lucid may be helping with shared situation awareness as well as individual awareness.

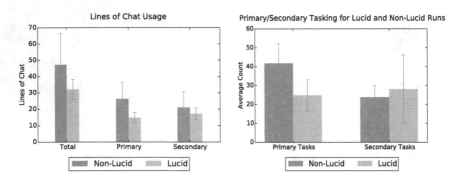

**Fig. 7.** Lines of chat (left) and workload estimate distributions (right)

Finally, as previously stated, Lucid did not have an effect on subjective workload based on the TLX measure – users felt workload with or without Lucid was comparable. This is not surprising in and of itself as the goal of Lucid was not to reduce workload per se, but to use workload measures to help balance task loading and allow the primary user to do more and be more effective.

## 4    Conclusions

The Lucid effort made significant strides toward developing a computational situation awareness capability that can aid a user in maintaining mission awareness and that can reduce some of the tedious work associated with executing ISR missions.

Our most important finding is that Lucid's CSA functionality appears to significantly reduce the manual interaction and intra-team interaction required for ISR missions using multiple UAVs. We hypothesize this effect is caused by (1) a reduction in the scan/check process required to maintain situation awareness and (2) better targeted tasking (few tasks issued, better sensor coverage). However, users did not report lower workload. This suggests that users were trading one type of work for another. In this case, we believe that Lucid reduced the user's manual workload allowing the primary user to focus more attention on cognitive and visual aspects of the problem. Our hypotheses is supported by the fact that operators using Lucid were able to execute the most challenging parts of the mission, ground target tracking, more often and more effectively when using Lucid.

This insight leads us to conclude that CSA's event detection and queuing capability, can be an effective complement to many standard common operating picture displays. CSA adds a layer of situation awareness and appears to improve the user's orientation to important mission items. It also enables a user to manage the mission better by reducing interaction (especially for SA tasks) and increases user focus on the critical tasks.

## 5 Future Directions

To achieve greater performance improvements (e.g., 2–3x), it would be most beneficial to combine CSA's capabilities with other improvements such as adding visualizations to the user interface that are specifically designed to take advantage of both event detection and workload estimation. Furthermore, while CSA's event detection appears to be a useful capability as implemented, further work to expand and refine this capability would allow it to be applied to more situations and have a larger impact. Potential areas for improvement include:

- Making events role specific and adding offloading strategies based on role, geography, and assets.
- Enhancement of the user-specified mission events. The users most liked these events and it is likely that these events were the biggest factor in the CSA's positive effects.
- Expand events to include compound events (combinations of situations that warrant attention).
- Further integrate event detection with UI elements. We spent relatively little time configuring the user interface to highlight event elements. Other related work suggest that such visualization improvements could increase the impact of the event detection system.

Finally, while we were able to implement a rudimentary workload estimation capability, Lucid's workload model would benefit from additional refinement. In particular, improvements to the workload model could be accomplished by using the evaluation data as a basis for model tuning/learning. For example, each workload function could be modeled as a probability distribution and the system could learn the parameters of these distributions using user activity. This would be most effective if combined with physiological sensors such as eye trackers, heart rate monitors, and EEG/MRI to input real-time objective of workload in addition to the task estimates.. Additionally, the following activities could improve the utility of the model

- Integration of user activity into the online model (e.g., the clicks)
- Implementation of UI configuration changes based on workload
- Use of workload to decide when to use autonomy rather than human control

**Acknowledgements.** This research was sponsored by a Small Business Innovation Research (SBIR) award through NAVAIR PMA (contract #N68335-14-C-0015). The views and conclusions contained in this document are those of the authors and should not be interpreted as representing the official policies, either expressed or implied of the U.S. Navy or U.S. Government. The U.S. Government is authorized to reproduce and distribute reprints for Government purposes notwithstanding any copyright notation herein.

# References

1. Cummings, M.L., Bruni, S., Mercier, S., Mitchell, P.J.: Automation architecture for single operator, multiple UAV command and control. Int. C2 J. **1**(2), 1–24 (2007)
2. Crossman, J., Marinier, R., Olson, E.: A hands-off, multi-robot display for communication situation awareness to operators. In: International Conference on Collaboration Technologies and Systems, Denver, pp. 109–116 (2012)
3. Ranganathan, P., Morton, R., Richardson, P., Strom, J., Goeddel, R., Bulic, M., Olson, E.: Coordinating a team of robots for urban reconnaissance. In: Proceedings of the Land Warfare Conference, LWC 2010, Brisbane (2010)
4. Endsley, M.R.: Toward a theory of situation awareness in dynamic systems. Hum. Factors **37**(1), 32–64 (1995)
5. Wickens, C.D.: Multiple resources and mental workload. Hum. Factors **50**(3), 449–455 (2008)
6. Hart, S.G., Staveland, L.E.: Development of NASA-TLX (task load index): results of empirical and theoretical research. In: Hancock, P.A., Meshkati, N. (eds.) Human Mental Workload. North Holland Press, Amsterdam (1988)
7. Hart, S.G.: NASA-task load index (NASA-TLX): 20 years later. In: Proceedings of the Human Factors and Ergonomics Society 50th Annual Meeting, pp. 904–908. HFES, Santa Monica (2006)

# Developing a High-Speed Craft Route Monitor Window

Odd Sveinung Hareide[1]([✉]), Frode Voll Mjelde[1],
Oeystein Glomsvoll[1], and Runar Ostnes[2]

[1] Navigation Competence Center,
Royal Norwegian Naval Academy, Bergen, Norway
oddsveinung.hareide@sksk.mil.no
[2] Institute of Ocean Operations and Civil Engineering,
Norwegian University of Science and Technology, Aalesund, Norway

**Abstract.** High-speed navigation in littoral waters is an advanced maritime operation. Reliable, timely and consistent data provided by the integrated navigation systems increases safe navigation. The workload of the navigator is high, together with the interaction between the navigator and the navigation system. Information from the graphical user interface in bridge displays must facilitate the demands for the high-speed navigator, and this article presents how eye tracking data was used to identify user requirements which in combination with a human centred design process led to the development of an improved software application on essential navigation equipment.

**Keywords:** Navigation · High-speed · Eye tracking · GUI · HCD

## 1 Introduction

Conducting a safe high-speed passage in littoral waters is a demanding task. With increasing demands for efficiency, and increasing use of technology and Human Machine Interaction (HMI), the daily job for the navigator has changed. Good Situational Awareness (SA) for the navigator has been emphasized as a critical component to avoid navigation accidents [1], and thus there are several technological initiatives aimed to enhance the SA of the navigator.

The extensive use of technology on ship bridges has caused concern about poor system usability for human interaction. One concern relates to how new technology aiming to increase the safety of operation, actually ends up doing the opposite [2]. Involving the human element in the design of systems is therefore imperative to minimize the potential human error in the operation and to increase safe navigation.

Eye tracking technology is a tool that can inform the designer about operator behaviour. It can monitor the eye's movement, and the collected data can be analysed to identify what kind of equipment that is used and how much time the navigator addresses that specific equipment. Analysing the data further can identify equipment and interfaces that steal time from the navigator's main task, and consequently lowers the navigator's SA. This study gives an example of how collecting and analysing Eye tracking data in combination with a Human-Centred Design (HCD) process resulted in

© Springer International Publishing AG 2017
D.D. Schmorrow and C.M. Fidopiastis (Eds.): AC 2017, Part II, LNAI 10285, pp. 461–473, 2017.
DOI: 10.1007/978-3-319-58625-0_33

a new and more user friendly design of the High-Speed Craft (HSC) route monitor window.

## 2    Background

High speed navigation has evolved since the first Hydrofoils in the early 20th century, and in the 1990s with catamaran hulls. A HSC is defined as a craft capable of maximum speed, in knots (kn), equal to or exceeding [3]:

$$7.192 \, x \, \nabla^{0,1667}$$

$\nabla$ = volume of displacement corresponding to the design waterline ($m^3$).
  For the Skjold-class in Fig. 2, this implies:

$$7.192 \, x \, 641^{0,1667} = 21,1 \, kn$$

Which concludes that the Skjold-class is a HSC, since the top speed is more than 21,1 kn.

The Norwegian coastline has been used to transport people for centuries, where the last decade has shown an increased need for even more efficient (faster) journeys. Norwegian yards and ship owners have a long tradition of building, utilizing and optimizing HSCs, most recently shown by the first hybrid HSC "Vision of the Fjords" [4]. Similarly, The Royal Norwegian Navy (RNoN) has a long tradition of operating HSCs, such as Fast Patrol Boats, to deter an enemy from attacking from the sea towards the coast. The challenging task of navigating a HSC in littoral waters has been emphasized, especially when it comes to the workload for the navigator [5]. The main difference between civilian and military maritime high-speed navigation, is that the civilian navigator usually sails established routes. The military navigator must be prepared to navigate in unknown and confined waters, often with poor or restricted data quality [6]. Littoral high speed navigation relies on a consistent methodology to achieve safe and efficient navigation [7], and the design of bridge equipment, layout and Graphical User Interfaces (GUI) must be in compliance with this methodology for successful interaction between the system and the navigator [8]. This underlines the importance of facilitating for systems that support the navigator in managing such demanding tasks.

### 2.1    e-Navigation

Todays' ship bridges are equipped with a well of displays and electronic aids, such as the Electronic Chart Display and Information System (ECDIS). The International Maritime Organization (IMO) has defined the modern and future collection, integration, exchange, presentation and analysis of marine information on board as e-Navigation [9], where the ultimate goal of e-Navigation is to enhance safety and security at sea.

Several studies indicate the close and important relationship between the bridge equipment, the navigators' attention span and the bridge crews' use of available resources [10–13]. To improve harmonization and user friendly bridge design, one solution is the Integrated Navigation System (INS). The purpose of the INS is to "enhance the safety of navigation by providing integrated and augmented functions to avoid geographic, traffic and environmental hazards". Route monitoring is one such task performed by the INS, defined as "continuous surveillance of own ships position in relation to the pre-planned route and the waters" [14]. As such, modern HSCs utilize INS to provide more, and real time, information for the navigator when conducting the passage. Figure 1 shows an example of an INS.

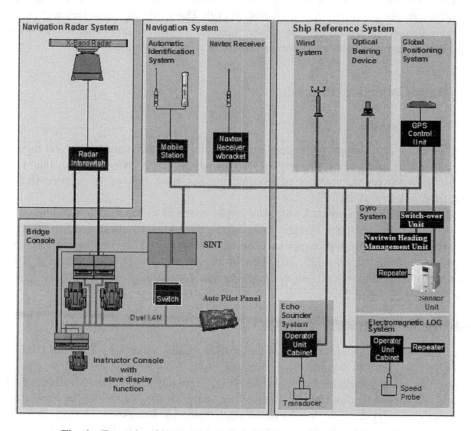

**Fig. 1.** Example of integrated navigation system (Courtesy of RNoN)

The INS layout in Fig. 1 outlines the complex structure of connecting multiple sensors to facilitate an integrated presentation of navigation information. The data collected is presented for the navigator on Multi-Function Displays (MFDs) in order to conduct navigational tasks.

There is an increased awareness of the need for efficient bridge design in high-speed operations [15]. The e-Navigation initiative has led to guidelines for HCD emphasizing the importance of including context and purpose in the design process [16]. The International Standardization Organization (ISO) has developed and released a standard for HCD for interactive systems. The standard identifies the importance of an iterative process that must include the end user to evaluate the ergonomics of human-system interaction [17]. This corresponds to other recommendations for designing HSCs based on a user perspective [18]. Reports from the maritime community identifies that several navigators find bridge systems difficult to access, and that they add noise and end up decreasing SA [10]. IMO will rectify some of these problems through its work on e-Navigation, expected to be finalized in 2019. Other initiatives are represented in the ongoing work with the Standard mode (S-mode) in ECDIS. S-mode is expected to contribute to standardisation and to provide detailed requirements for HMI and data presentation [19]. The work and initiatives within the e-Navigation scope underlines the present need for guidelines and standardisation for equipment placement and information presentation on a maritime bridge.

## 3   Data Collection Process

### 3.1   Eye Tracking

Eye Tracking is a method for collecting data of the eye's movement [20], and its use has expanded rapidly since the early 1970s. The original drive for eye tracking data was within research on the process of reading, but has later evolved to be used in the maritime industry as well [21, 22].

To improve design, eye tracking data can be analysed to better understand how the operator interacts with the systems [23, 24]. Eye tracking has been used to identify differences in the levels of experience between navigators [22], and to evaluate and improve maritime training [25, 26]. This article presents the development of a HSC route monitor window based on eye tracking data collected in the RNoN [27].

### 3.2   RNoN Eye Tracking Data Set

The data set is collected in field- and simulator studies using Eye Tracking Glasses (ETGs) [26], during daytime operations on board RNoN Corvettes and in similar conditions in the simulator. The Corvettes (Fig. 2) are capable of speeds exceeding 60 knots, and the navigation team consists of the Officer of the Watch and the Navigator. The navigation system on the Corvettes is delivered by Kongsberg Defence Agency (KDA), and the eye tracking data set was collected from the ECDIS and radar application from Kongsberg Maritime (KM). The ETGs were mounted on the navigator, who is the person responsible for conducting the passage.

The field study was conducted when navigating in littoral waters in the northern parts of Norway. The simulator study was conducted in the Skjold-class bridge simulator at RNoN Navigation Competence Centres' (NCC) Navigation Simulator (Nav-Sim), in a similar area as the field study. Eight navigators from the RNoN attended the trials, with an navigation experience spanning from two to six years, with both male and female participants [26]. The data was collected with the SensoMotoric

**Fig. 2.** Royal Norwegian Navy Corvette, Skjold-class (Courtesy of RNoN)

Instruments second generation ETGs and the Tobii Pro Glasses 2 [27], and analysed in the supplied and recommended software (BeGaze and the Tobi Pro Glasses Analyzer). 2 h and 57 min of eye tracking data has been processed and analysed in this study.

Eye tracking data in this type of study is unique, but it has still got its' weaknesses. The field data set and the simulator data set are not identical, but the area of operation is similar. There are also differences in the environment when collecting data in a field study versus a simulator study. The light and weather conditions are a challenge, both with regards to the data collection, and also concerning differences in the field study- and the simulator data set. The total amount of participants is eight, of both sexes, and they have a span in experience. The amount of military HSC navigators are limited, and it is difficult to introduce more participants to the data set. The difference between the conduct of the passage concerning sexes is not elaborated. Two different types of ETGs were used in order to collect more experience on different types of ETGs. However, this also hampers the resemblance of the data set. The analysing process of the data is semi-automatic, and is a time consuming task. As a rule of thumb 10 min of data takes 60 min to analyse. There is an uncertainty introduced in the manual task of the analysis due to the ambiguity of the data, and a 10% loss of data is also expected due to weaknesses in the ETG design. Collecting eye tracking data is the easy part and analysing is the challenging part [20].

When analysing eye tracking data, there are several eye tracking metrics and visualization techniques that can be used and applied to better understand the data [28]. One should note that some of the eye tracking data can be notorious ambiguous events. One example is backtracks, which is the specific relationship between two subsequent saccades where the second goes in the opposite direction of the first [20]. In order to conduct a more thorough analysis of the eye tracking data, it is recommended to use Subject Matter Experts (SMEs), to better understand the meaning of the data.

## 4  Route Monitor Window

The route monitor window is an important tool for the navigator, and results from the eye tracking data showed a high frequency of use during operation. Figure 3 shows the GUI as it is presented in Kongsberg ECDIS version 3.4.

**Fig. 3.**  GUI route monitor window

The route monitor dialog is used to display information about the selected route and to monitor the ships progress along it. The window consists of information about the route and its validation status, together with the current position of the ship and the upcoming information regarding the planned route. It also provides a button to enter the Autopilot (AP) mode, and information about Estimated Time of Arrival (ETA) to the final destination.

Information vital for high-speed navigation is highlighted by red boxes in Fig. 3, consisting of:

1. Information about turning object and next heading mark.
2. Time to Wheel Over Point (when the turn of the ship is to be conducted).
3. The course on the next leg.
4. The distance of the next leg.
5. Cross Track Deviation (XTD) which provides information about the ships actual position compared to the planned route.

The route monitor window is found in the lower right corner of the ECDIS application, and is presented as a KM standard size dialog window as shown in Fig. 4.

**Fig. 4.** Route monitor window seen from the perspective of the navigator

The distance from the navigator to the route monitor window is approximately 2 metres, and the size of the route monitor window is small, dependent on the size of the MFD. The navigators expressed concern about the accessibility of the information in the route monitor window. To investigate this concern, the scan pattern of the navigator was visualized through analysis of the collected eye tracking data (Fig. 5).

The circles in Fig. 5 represent fixation and the lines represent saccades. Fixation is defined as the state when the eye is remaining still over a defined period on a specific point, and fixation time is defined as how long the eye lingers on a specific fixation. The size of the circle indicates the time period of fixation; the bigger the circle, the longer the fixation. A saccade is defined as the rapid eye motion between two fixations, understood as movement from one fixation to another [20]. When analysing the eye

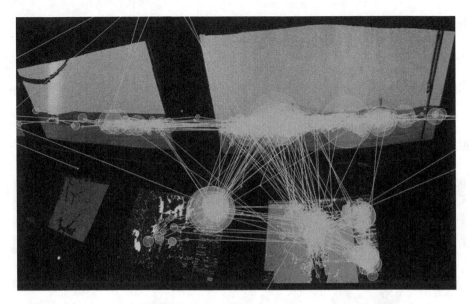

**Fig. 5.** Scan pattern of the navigator

tracking data together with the visualization techniques, it is identified that the route monitor window GUI is taking too much of the navigators' attention, and thus a HCD process of optimizing this GUI is initiated. This process is laid down in earlier work [28]. The results from the study was combined with RNoN standard operating procedures (SOPs) to manufacture a new HSC route monitor window that is better aligned to the HSC navigator's need.

### 4.1 Developing a High-Speed Craft Route Monitor Window

In close cooperation with SMEs and the supplier, an iterative process in accordance with IMO's guidelines for software quality assurance and HCD for e-Navigation [16] was started (Fig. 6).

The process is as follows:

1. Identification of challenge in design and HMI [27].
2. Create workgroup with SMEs and supplier to start the iterative HCD process of changing the GUI [16].
   i. Activity 1: Understand and specify the context of use.
   ii. Activity 2: Identify the user requirements.
   iii. Activity 3: Produce and/or develop design solutions to meet user requirements.
   iv. Activity 4: Evaluate the design against usability criteria;
      i. Test the new software in a 1:1 simulator [26].
   v. Activity 5: Maintain operational usability.

This method is illustrated in Fig. 6.

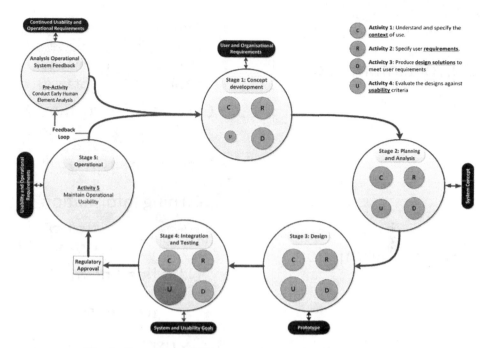

**Fig. 6.** Overview of HCD process for e-navigation systems (16)

The use of SMEs in a workgroup were essential for all activities leading up to the proposed design, and will be vital for trials and evaluations of the final design.

Activity 1 and 2 resulted in several design suggestions for activity 3, leading up to the conceptual content design of the route monitor window shown in Fig. 7. The supplier followed up the conceptual design with proposing a solution that fits the layout of the existing MFD (Fig. 8). The final proposal from the supplier will be tested later against usability criteria in activity 4.

**Activity 1.** When identifying the user requirements, it is important to start with the context of use. The context of use is to perform navigation on board a HSC in littoral waters, with the use of modern electronic navigational equipment such as the INS. It involves operations in narrow and open waters and in all types of weather and sea states, and ship movements and vibrations is expected to be high. The ship must also operate in demanding arctic waters, with no daylight during wintertime, which also drives the need for suitable night palettes in the GUI. In addition to this, the navigators' night vision is essential when conducting the advanced operation of maritime warfighting. Thus, the need for minimum light pollution from the MFDs is crucial.

This context suggests a need for frequent use of the route monitor window, a suggestion identified in a recent maritime usability study [23].

**Activity 2.** Level of accessibility of information provided in the route monitor window becomes a crucial design parameter. The GUI design must focus on user suitability while at the same time be coherent with RNoN SOPs. The SOPs in this context are the

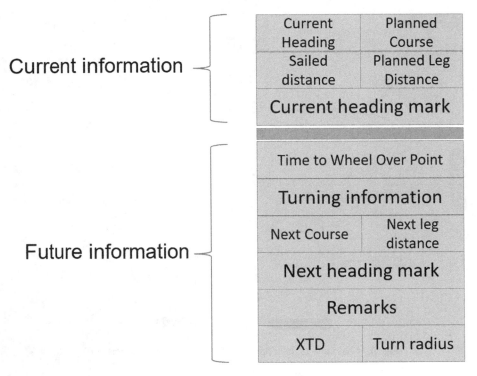

**Fig. 7.** Conceptual content of HSC route monitor window

rules and regulations for conducting a safe passage, which in the RNoN are known as the phases of navigation, with coinciding voice procedures [7].

The phases of navigation are in place to ensure that the navigator is aware and appreciative of the current and future environment to maximize the capabilities of the HSC. Figure 7 shows the results of Activity 2; a conceptual design of the new route monitor window for presenting the navigator with need-to-know information of the current and future route.

**Activity 3.** Human engineering design criteria are essential for successful design and solutions for high speed navigation [15, 18]. The conceptual content (Fig. 7) aims to ensure maritime SA for the navigator, and the goal for activity three is to balance user requirements with supplier and bridge equipment capabilities and constraints.

One such constraint is the size of the window, which limits the amount of information available for stacking. The window size is regulated by the design of the Kongsberg K-Bridge INS [29] and must be taken into consideration when designing a new GUI. Optimization of the new HSC route monitor window was made through suitable trade-offs between the supplier design criteria and the end user requirements.

Guidelines and requirements for HCD of display information systems were used to optimize system performance with consideration of inherent human capabilities and limitations as part of the total design trade-off space [30]. Specific considerations were given to the information architecture, including; the amount of information, density and presentation, text format and pattern coding, information grouping and label orientation.

Current information is presented on top (i.e. "what am I doing now"?) followed by future information (i.e. "what should I do next"?) on the bottom. Related information is grouped in sequences, limited by what kind of information that is necessary and sufficient to maintain maritime SA. This allows the navigators' scan pattern to flow from top-to-bottom and left-to-right with data presented in a readily usable form [30], avoiding critical data from being obscured by pagination or scrolling.

The coding used in turning - and heading mark information is in accordance with the RNoN SOPs [31].

Based on inputs from RNoN working groups, Activity 3 resulted in a preliminary suggestion for the new GUI from the supplier (KDA), shown in Fig. 8.

**Activity 4.** The final design suggestion from the supplier will be tested at RNoN NCC NavSim (expected early April 2017). The testing will be performed by RNoN HSC navigators and human factors specialists to ensure that operator interaction requirements are met. Once the design is proven to maintain operational usability for achieving required performance for HSC navigation, the new HSC route monitor window will be implemented in the fleet to foster design standardization.

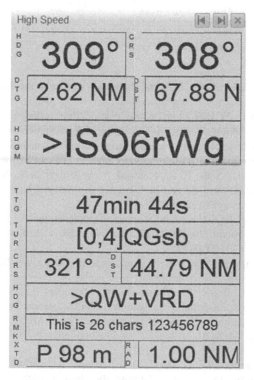

**Fig. 8.** HSC route monitor window suggestion from supplier

# 5   Conclusion

Today and in the future, there will be comprehensive interaction between humans and systems. This article has explained the process of refining and operationalizing a specific HSC route monitor window. Eye tracking data is an efficient Method to identify the level of user interaction with bridge systems, and can be utilized to aid the development of an improved software application. The guidelines for HCD activity 1–5 worked as an iterative process with a particular focus on combining operator requirements with system and human capabilities and limitations. The process resulted in an optimized design of a route monitor window specifically tailored to HSC navigation that will be thoroughly tested for user suitability. The final implementation of the product on-board RNoN ships is expected to minimize the potential human error in the operation and to increase safe navigation.

## 5.1   Future Work

Test and collect eye tracking data set of the new SW GUI in RNoN NCC NavSim. Implement the improved GUI in the RNoN (activity 5 in the HCD process).

**Acknowledgement.** The Royal Norwegian Navy has sponsored this work. A special thanks to the crew of the Royal Norwegian Navy Corvettes and the navigators in the Royal Norwegian Navy for passionate involvement in this work.

# References

1. McCafferty, D.B., Baker, C.C.: Trending the causes of marine incidents. American Bureau of Shipping (2006)
2. Wingrove, M.: Does ECDIS increase the risk of ship collisions? (2016). http://www.marinemec.com/news/view,does-ecdis-increase-the-risk-of-ship-collisions_42825.htm
3. IMO: International code of safety for high-speed craft. Resolut. MSC **36**, 63 (2000)
4. Aa B: Vision of the fjords (2016). http://www.braa.no/visionofthefjords/
5. Gould, K., Røed, B.K., Saus, E.-R., Koefoed, V.F., Bridger, R.S., Moen, B.E.: Effects of navigation method on workload and performance in simulated high-speed ship navigation. Appl. Ergon. **40**(1), 103–114 (2008)
6. Glomsvoll, O., Bonenberg, L.K.: GNSS jamming resilience for close to shore navigation in the northern sea. J. Navig. **70**, 33–48 (2017). © The Royal Institute of Navigation 2016, doi:10.1017/S0373463316000473
7. Hareide, O.S., Ostnes, R.: Scan pattern for the maritime navigator. TransNav – Int. J. Mar. Navig. Saf. Sea Transp. (2017, in press)
8. Dobbins, T., Hill, J., Brand, T., Thompson, T., McCartan, S.: Standardised information architecture to suuport the dynamic navigation (DYNAV) standard operating procedure. In: Human Factors Conference, The Royal Institution of Naval Architects, p. 7 (2016)
9. IMO: E-navigation IMO (2017). http://www.imo.org/en/OurWork/safety/navigation/pages/enavigation.aspx
10. Fagerholt, R.A., Kongsvik, T., Moe, H.K., Solem, A.: Broutforming på hurtigbåter. Kartlegging av problemer med utforming og funksjonalitet på teknisk utstyr på hurtigbåt-bro. Rapport. NTNU Samfunnsforskning AS (2014)

11. Hareide, O.S.: Control of Position Sensor Input to ECDIS on High Speed Craft. University of Nottingham, Nottingham (2013)
12. Hareide, O.S., Ostnes, R.: Comprehension of the eye of the navigator. Coord. Mag. **XII**(8), 13–20 (2016)
13. Norris, A.: Integrated Bridge Systems. ECDIS and Positioning, vol. 2. Nautical Institute, London (2010). 215 p.
14. IMO: Resolution MSC.252(83): Adoption of the Revised Performance Standard for Integrated Navigation Systems, p. 49, London (2007)
15. Røed, B.K.: Designing for High-Speed Ships. Norwegian University of Science and Technology, Trondheim (2007)
16. IMO: Guideline on Software Quality Assurance and Human-Centred Design for e-Navigation. In: NCSR (ed.) IMO, London, p. 26 (2016)
17. ISO: 9241-210:2010. Ergonomics of human system interaction-Part 210: Human-centred design for interactive systems (2010)
18. Dobbins, T.: High speed craft design from a human centred perspective. RINA (ed.) RINA, London (2004)
19. NCSR: Development of guidance on the Standardised (or S) Mode of operation of navigation equipment (including plans for a testbed by the Republic of Korea in 2017). In: IMO (cd.) (2016)
20. Holmqvist, K., Nyström, M., Andersson, R., Dewhurst, R., Jarodzka, H., Van de Weijer, J.: Eye tracking: a comprehensive guide to methods and measures. OUP Oxford (2011)
21. Bjørneseth, F.B., Renganayagalu, S.K., Dunlop, M.D., Homecker, E., Komandur, S. (eds.): Towards an experimental design framework for evaluation of dynamic workload and situational awareness in safety critical maritime settings. In: Proceedings of the 26th Annual BCS Interaction Specialist Group Conference on People and Computers. British Computer Society (2012)
22. Forsman, F., Sjors, A., Dahlman, J., Falkmer, T., Lee, H.C.: Eye tracking during high speed navigation at sea. J. Transp. Technol. **02**(03), 8 (2012)
23. Bergstrom, J.R., Schall, A.: Eye Tracking in User Experience Design. Elsevier, Amsterdam (2014)
24. Bjørneseth, F.B., Clarke, L., Dunlop, M., Komandur, S. (eds.): Towards an understanding of operator focus using eye-tracking in safety-critical maritime settings. In: International Conference on Human Factors in Ship Design and Operation (2014)
25. Renganayagalu, S.K., Komandur, S., Rylander, R.: Maritime simulator training: eye-trackers to improve training experience. In: Advances in Human Aspects of Transportation Part III: AHFE Conference, pp. 66–72 (2014)
26. Hareide, O.S., Ostnes, R.: Comparative study of the Skjold-class bridge- and simulator navigation training. Eur. J. Navig. **14**(4), 57 (2016)
27. Hareide, O.S., Ostnes, R.: Maritime usability study by analysing eye tracking data. In: Internation Navigation Conference Proceedings, p. 17 (2016)
28. Hareide, O.S., Ostnes, R., Mjelde, F.V. (eds.): Understanding the Eye of the Navigator. In: European Navigation Conference. Confedent International, Helsinki (2016)
29. Kongsberg: K-Bridge Integrated Navigation System: Kongsberg (2016). https://www.km.kongsberg.com/ks/web/nokbg0397.nsf/AllWeb/62F2BB1A93881801C1257CB7003A7687/$file/KM_K_Bridge.pdf?OpenElement
30. DOD US: Design Criteria Standard, Human Engineering, MIL-STD-1472G. In: Defence Do (ed.) (2012)
31. RNoN: SNP 500. In: Centre, N.C. (ed.) Royal Norwegian Naval Academy, Bergen (2012)

# A Review of Personnel Selection Approaches for the Skill of Decision Making

Irwin Hudson[1(✉)], Lauren Reinerman-Jones[2], and Grace Teo[2]

[1] U.S. Army Research Laboratory – Human Research and Engineering
Directorate Advanced Training and Simulation Division, Orlando, FL, USA
irwin.l.hudson.civ@mail.mil
[2] Institute for Simulation and Training, University of Central Florida,
Orlando, FL, USA
{lreinerm,gteo}@ist.ucf.edu

**Abstract.** Personnel Selection has been a long standing focus in the fields of Organizational Psychology, Human Factors Psychology, Business Management, Human Resources, and Industrial Engineering. Assessment methods in personnel selection can be categorized into subjective and objective methods. Selection assessments are often broad in attempting to capture the essence of person for success in a role or organization. However, this type of approach often yields inconclusive and biased subjective results. Therefore, focusing on key skills seems to be more beneficial. The skill of focus for this effort is decision making. Since those who make more good decisions are often influential and rise to leadership positions, it is imperative that better ways to uncover, assess, predict, or enhance DM skills, be developed. To do so, a review and firm understanding of personnel selection and decision making is necessary.

**Keywords:** Personnel selection · Decision making · Assessment · Physiological response · Subjective measures

## 1 Introduction

Selection has been a long standing focus in the fields of Organizational Psychology, Human Factors Psychology, Business Management, Human Resources, and Industrial Engineering. Each of these fields approach the challenge of selecting the right person for the job from a slightly different angle. For example, Human Factors Psychologists focus on task performance, whereas Industrial Engineers think in terms of manpower necessary to accomplish tasks. However, assessments for personnel selection have centered around a few traditional approaches. Those will be discussed first before examining a new method for assessing skills and utilizing ever-expanding technologies available for repeatable and objective assessment, which include simulations to present stimuli and physiological measures. That alternative approach is the basis for the present experiment. Specifically, the goal for this work is to is to determine if physiological responses assessed during a battery of tasks would improve prediction of decision making performance in a real-world task that incorporates the components of the battery, beyond the prediction associated with traditional assessment methods.

© Springer International Publishing AG 2017
D.D. Schmorrow and C.M. Fidopiastis (Eds.): AC 2017, Part II, LNAI 10285, pp. 474–485, 2017.
DOI: 10.1007/978-3-319-58625-0_34

# 2  Traditional Approaches to Personnel Selection

Assessment methods in personnel selection can be broadly categorized into subjective and objective methods. Subjective methods include personality measures, stress and coping style inventories [1], interviews, and supervisor ratings [2]. Objective measures include work samples [3], biographical data such as gender and age [4], situational judgment tests [5], and aptitude tests [6]. This section introduces several traditional approaches used in personnel selection in various organizations, clubs, teams, and businesses.

## 2.1  Personality Measures and Stress Coping Inventories

The American Psychological Association (APA) defines personality as the variations in characteristic patterns of thinking, feeling, and behavior [7], across individuals, and personality traits of an individual typically describe the individual's inclinations towards certain patterns of thinking, feeling, and behaving.

A widely used framework in personality research is the 5-factor (i.e., "Big Five") model. The Big Five personality inventory taps five traits: Neuroticism, Openness, Conscientiousness, Agreeableness, and Extraversion [8]. A study which relates personality to DM examined the career decisions made by various groups. While investigating career DM difficulties [9], researchers combined emotional levels and personality measures in three sample groups: (a) 691 deliberating individuals who entered a career self-help website, (b) 197 students in a university preparatory program, and (c) 286 young adults from the general population. As hypothesized, increased levels of personality-related and emotional DM difficulties were associated with greater levels of neuroticism, agreeableness, perfectionism and the need for cognitive closure, but were not strongly associated with high levels of extraversion, openness to experience, and career decision self-efficacy.

However, such studies that link personality traits to DM are relatively rare. Rather than relate any particular personality trait to DM, studies are more likely to show evidence that personality traits relate to job performance [10]. For instance, Conscientiousness has been shown to be predictive of performance [11]. Since superior job performance is unlikely without good DM, this may suggest a potential indirect link between personality and DM. While personality measures such as that which assesses the "Big Five" personality traits have demonstrated some utility in personnel assessment, evidence suggests that room exists for improving assessments of DM for selection, and that other measures be used.

Besides personality measures, stress coping inventories have also been utilized in personnel selection. For instance, selection of personnel for jobs such as law enforcement often includes an assessment of stress coping style and ability. This is because the job of law enforcement officers typically involves making high-stakes decisions under time pressure, Selection for such positions may include administering stress coping inventories to obtain information about stress tolerance and coping styles [3].

## 2.2 Interviews

Another common assessment method used in personnel selection is the interview. Interviews are favored by both supervisors [12] and human resources (HR) practitioners [13]. Although structured, competency-based interviews have been used to assess specific competencies such as decision-making, there are few studies that validate the use of the selection interview for assessing decision-making skill. Besides, more often than not, interviews are unstructured and results subject to a variety of interviewer bias including the "halo" effects, stereotyping, contrast effects among others [14].

## 2.3 Supervisor Ratings

Another common personnel selection method is the use of supervisory ratings of various competencies that can include decision-making ability [2]. However, measures of job performance with such ratings have been heavily criticized by researchers for having poor reliability and insufficient validity [15, 16]. Furthermore, supervisory ratings can be misinterpreted, misread, affected by extraneous influences, or lose accuracy due to its susceptibility to effects such as the "halo" or recency effects [17]. These issues have led researchers to conclude that subjective measures in personnel selection may not be sufficient.

## 2.4 Aptitude Measures

In the effort to address the aforementioned issues of subjective measures, as well as other problems such as social desirability [18] and "faking good" [19] in the personnel selection context, researchers have turned to assessment methods that are more objective. For example, United States Military Entrance Processing Command administers the Armed Service Vocational Aptitude Battery (ASVAB) to determine qualification for enlistment in to the US Armed Forces [20]. The ASVAB assesses knowledge and ability on various subjects (i.e., math, science, and electronics) to inform selection and deployment decisions. The premise is that decisions made in different military vocations would require specific abilities. This is also the notion underpinning assessment instruments such as the Adult Decision Making Competence [21], which assesses vulnerability to certain cognitive biases associated with DM (e.g., resistance to framing and the ability to apply decision rules). Other ability tests utilized in assessing DM potential include critical thinking and logical reasoning tests. For example, the Watson-Glaser Critical Thinking Appraisal [22] has been widely used in managerial selection to assess the ability to reflect and evaluate arguments and uncover assumptions and inferences in the process of logical thinking [23]. The challenge with aptitude tests is that they offer broad assessments and do not match-up directly with the skill of making decisions.

## 2.5 Situational Judgment Tests

On the other hand, situational judgment tests (SJT) can be developed to assess DM in a specific context (e.g., cross-cultural work scenarios, customer service). An item in an

SJT typically consists of a real-world situation accompanied by possible courses of action or responses to that situation. Respondents rate the effectiveness of each behavior or select what they think is the most effective course of action from the response options [5]. Since actual situations and response options are used in their development, SJTs incorporate features that correspond to events encountered during operations and, in so doing, are able to better portray the multidimensional nature of real-world decision making. However, like many personnel assessment methods, they can often be context- or task-specific, and may not be useful in assessing potential for skill development.

## 2.6  Biographical Data and Bio Data Measures

Another assessment method in selection utilizes biographical data and bio data of candidates that tend to relate to the desired qualities or job competencies. Studies supporting the use of bio data in assessment of DM include that by Manley et al. [24], which report that assessments of conscientiousness and locus of control using biographical data fared better in predicting ethical decision making compared to the self-report assessments of the same constructs. Despite the ability of bio data to tap specific constructs, the most common biographical data used in personnel selection are still the applicants' gender, age, and experience.

### 2.6.1  Gender

Appropriately, researchers have investigated the possibility of gender as a huge contributor in good or bad DM [4]. There is a specific area of research that examines if the gender effect in strategy and risk propensity in financial DM is more robust than certain contextual factors [25]. For example, the research investigates if level of task familiarity and framing of the task would account for more differences in DM strategies and risk preferences than would gender. The results provided by Powell & Ansic claimed that females are less risk seeking than males, irrespective of familiarity and framing, costs, or ambiguity. The results also revealed that each gender adopts different strategies in financial DM environments. 0.

However, these strategies have no significant impact on performance of the individual [25]. Since it is easier to observe strategies than either risk propensity or the results of daily DM, differences in DM strategies serve to reinforce the stereotype that proposes that females perform less favorably in the financial arena than that of their male counterparts. This view, suggesting that women are more risk-averse than men, has been around for a long time and is becoming increasingly widespread [26]. Consequently, this type of stereotypical thinking perpetuates throughout the financial community and is the basis for the so-called *glass ceiling* for women in corporate promotion ladders [4]. To this end, men are more likely to be trusted than women to make the risky decisions that may be vital for an organization's success. Similar stereotyping in the investment broker arena suggests that these perceptions disadvantage female clients, as well [27]. Wang suggested that women are typically, more conservative in their investing, and therefore, are usually offered investments with lower risks, which generates lower expected returns.

Research investigating male and female DM performance in correlation to leadership aimed to understand whether the proposed performance differences in gender existed [28]. Results of a meta-analytic review of 17 studies examining gender differences and leadership showed that male and female leaders exhibited equal amounts of initiating structure and consideration. Both male and female leaders attained an equal amount of satisfied subordinates. However, according to Dobbins and Platz [28], male leaders rated higher on the effective chart than female leaders in a laboratory setting. The findings in their meta-analytic review recommended imposing a moratorium on research correlating leadership performance between genders. The foundation for this selection approach is subjective in nature, due to the use of heuristics and biases. Therefore, a more objective approach to assessing and determining DM potential should provide results that are more descriptive.

### 2.6.2   Age and Experience

Another traditional approach to assessing and characterizing the skill of DM is via age and experience. In addition, like other traditional methods, researchers have explored the prospect of using age and experience to identify potential DM skills. An investigation where age and DM experience influences managerial DM performance, discovered that age was the more prevalent factor supporting this assertion [29]. There was little evidence supporting the notion that older managers were less adept at processing information and making decisions.

However, according to modern neuropsychological models, there are some age-related cognitive changes associated with deterioration in the frontal lobe, which has been associated with DM processes [30]. However, on the contrary, these models did not consider the potential parceling of the frontal lobes into dorsolateral and ventromedial regions. Three tasks of executive function and working memory (i.e., tasks dependent on dorsolateral prefrontal dysfunction), along with three tasks of emotion and social DM (i.e., tasks dependent on ventromedial prefrontal dysfunction) were assessed for age effects [30]. Although age-related variations in performance were discovered on dorsolateral prefrontal dysfunction tasks, there were no age-related variations observed during the majority of the ventromedial prefrontal dysfunction tasks and therefore, the results support the theory that instead of an overall degradation in executive function with age, there is a specific dorsolateral prefrontal cognitive relates to aging [30].

A main drawback in using biographical and biodata is that it rests heavily on the notion that past behavior predicts future behavior and assumes that individuals would not exceed their existing level of skill. This assumption is also true for other traditional assessment methods as well. Hence, their use can be limited in assessing DM skill or potential. Given all this, it may be necessary to explore measures beyond self-report, behavioral, or even tests of judgment and ability. A possible alternative approach may be to use physiological measures.

## 3   An Alternative Approach to Selection

Neuroscience research has implicated certain physiological structures and responses, such as the ventromedial prefrontal cortex, parietal lobe, amygdala, that are indicative of various DM processes [31] and skill development [32]. Findings of physiological changes related to DM have inspired the use of physiological measures for personnel assessment. The rationale for the use of physiological measures is that cognitive processes can be reflected in physiological responses. For instance, lie detector tests based on galvanic skin response (GSR) are linked to cognitive processes underlying integrity [33]. The experience of high workload has been associated with heart rate variability (HRV) changes and fixation durations [34], and the cognitive processes related to cerebral blood flow velocity (CBFV) are involved in certain vigilance tasks [35].

A new assessment using a multidimensional approach, whereby a Transcranial Doppler (TCD) measured cerebral blood flow velocity to the brain, and the Dundee Stress State Questionnaire (DSSQ) assessed stress, during a short battery of tasks predicted subsequent vigilance task performance [36, 37]. Specifically, the results of three short high information-processing tasks captured the core components and attributes that comprise vigilance tasks, which are primarily two categories: 1. Simultaneous or successive vigilance tasks and 2. Sensory or cognitive. The TCD recorded CBFV during the presentation of the three short tasks and a pre to post-DSSQ. Basic scientific principle of using different complex real world vigilance tasks validated the approach: 1. Simultaneous, sensory air traffic control, 2. Successive, cognitive verbal math problems, and 3. Long distance driving where vigilance was only one element. In other words, the integration of the short battery, CBFV, and stress response as an instrument for selecting personnel with optimal vigilance skill should predict task agnostic vigilance.

Different university student samples substantiated the effectiveness of the battery for predicting final period vigilance performance, which is the time where task performance suffers and errors are more likely to occur. In other words, the battery should be predictive even with a different sample. Results showed that utilizing this multidimensional approach accounted for up to 24% of vigilance performance variance [36].

# 4 Advancing the Multidimensional Approach

The present effort sought to extend the seminal work by Reinerman-Jones and colleagues [34, 36, 38] in two key ways. The first way was to apply the method to a different skill – that of decision-making. This would entail identification of a different task battery. Second, the inclusion of additional physiological measures would be used to account for more variance than did just the TCD. However, an extensive literature review of decision making and decision making assessment was first needed.

## 4.1 The Reason for the Skill of Decision Making

Like the skill of vigilance, the skill of DM is quantifiable and some people are better at making decisions than others [39]. Since those who make more good decisions are often influential and rise to leadership positions [40], it is imperative that better ways to uncover, assess, predict, or enhance DM skills, be developed. This realization is evident in the amount of resources that organizations and companies invest to ensure that they select the right leader who will make reasoned, timely, and intelligent decisions that are crucial to the success of an organization [41]. Identifying an individual's DM skill level for proper job selection and placement will enable a greater return on investment, lower attrition, and greater productivity [42]. Therefore, the purpose for this research is to establish an effective assessment tool that supports talent management – in particular, personnel selection, by focusing on the assessment of the skill of decision-making.

## 4.2    Current Theories and Models of Decision Making

There are several theories on how humans make decisions. In general, there are (i) theories that prescribe the best ways to make decisions (i.e. normative theories), and, (ii) theories that describe how decisions are actually made (i.e., descriptive theories).

### 4.2.1    Normative Theories

Normative theories outline the ideal standard or model of DM, and are based on what is considered to be the normal or correct way of making decisions. Normative theories are based on empirical assumptions for interpreting how or what the world should be. Along with empirical assumptions, normative theories also comprehensively include the social value systems or moral judgments of a mass on which to base their normative questions. The underlying theme of normative theories is that decision-makers are rational and will seek to select options that maximize utility by systematically consider all options thoroughly before making the decision [43]. However, the usefulness of normative theories has been challenged by observations by descriptive DM theorists who posit that human decision making often involve the use of heuristics and the presence of bias.

### 4.2.2    Descriptive Theories

Descriptive theories of decision making include the Prospect theory, and the Naturalistic decision making theory [44]. The pivotal contribution of the Prospect Theory is the notion that human decision making often involves the use of heuristics and bias. Heuristic methods are used to speed up the problem solving process for finding a satisfactory solution and ease the cognitive load of the decision making process [45]. On the other hand, a bias is defined as any particular tendency, trend, inclination, feeling or opinion that is preconceived or unreasoned [46]. Given Hick's Law [47] which states that the time taken for a decision is a function of the number of options, heuristics and bias serve as cognitive shortcuts that enable a decision to be reached in a timely manner. Nevertheless, although heuristics are helpful in making decisions, they can also lead decision makers down the wrong path, if not utilized properly.

Naturalistic decision-making theories emerged as a means of studying how people make decisions and perform cognitively complex functions in demanding real-world situations [44]. Essential characteristics of Naturalistic decision making theories include proficient decision makers, context-bound informal modeling, empirical based prescription, situation-action decision rules, and process orientation [48]. The study of Naturalistic DM highlights important decision theories neglected previously by the other models such as the use of expertise and the ability to generate options. Naturalistic DM also introduces important concepts including recognition primed decision-making (RPDM), coping with uncertainty, team DM, and decision errors [44].

## 4.3 Physiological Measures Associated with DM

Apart from selecting a new skill, the other aspect of the alternative approach is the use of various physiological measures. Some of the physiological sensors available for this application are shown in Table 1.

**Table 1.** Physiological sensors

| Sensor | Definition |
|---|---|
| Electroencephalogram (EEG) | Sensor that detects electrical activity in your brain using small, flat metal discs (electrodes) attached to your scalp [49]. Your brain cells communicate via electrical impulses and are active all the time, even when you're asleep. This activity shows up as wavy lines on an EEG recording. The types of waveforms have been indicative of various types of cognitive processing |
| Electrocardiogram (ECG or EKG) | Sensor that checks measures the electrical activity of your heart. Fluctuations in heart rate and other associated metrics (HRV and IBI) have been tied to responses to stress, workload, and other cognitive demands [50] |
| Function near-infrared (fNIR) | Sensor of functional neuroimaging that measures brain activity through hemodynamic responses associated with oxygen used to process information [51] |
| Transcranial doppler (TCD) | Sensor that measures the velocity of blood flow through the brain's blood vessels by means of ultrasound [52]. Changes in task load have been shown to have a paralleled effect in CBFV [37] |
| Eye tracker | Sensor that tracks where your eyes are focused. It determines your presence, attention, focus, drowsiness, consciousness, or other mental states [53]. This information can be used to gain deep insights into consumer behavior or to design revolutionary new user interfaces across various devices |

Studies have found that brain regions that are activated in moral DM relate to areas involved in cognitive processing in the right dorsolateral prefrontal cortex and bilateral inferior parietal lobe, emotional processing in the medial prefrontal cortex, parietal lobe, and amygdala, and finally, conflict processing in the anterior cingulate cortex [31]. Further results from patients with brain lesions implicate the ventromedial prefrontal cortext in moral DM [54]. General activation of these frontal lobe regions may be accessed by physiological measures from the electroencephalogram (EEG) and prefrontal cortex fNIR. Moreover, as proposed in the "somatic marker hypothesis" [55], the emotions that may be evoked during moral DM may be reflected in the autonomic nervous system. Autonomic nervous system activity can be accessed via the measures of cardiac activity (i.e., via electrocardiogram (ECG)).

Another experiment revealed a reduction in the high frequency component of heart rate variability (HRV) and an increase in the low-to-high frequency ratio during time pressure stress situations compared to the control settings, while no changes were shown in the low frequency component of HRV [56]. The results of their experiment imply that HRV is a more impressible and discriminatory measure of mental stress, which suggests that variables derived from heart rate physiology reflect a central command for managing stress and making decision under pressure.

In regards to critical thinking and brain activity, researchers claim that the consciousness and precision of certain tests to measure frontal lobe functions proves to have substantial influence on research findings [57] and they concluded that frontal lobe lesions prevail to be the attributing cause of the "bewildering array" of deficits. Metabolic responses such as those indexed by $rSO_2$ and CBFV have also been linked to DM. For instance, a metabolic experiment by Masicampo and Baumeister [58] related the availability of metabolic substrates (e.g., glucose) to resources that are required for certain DM processes. The hypothesis was based on the assertion that serious complex processing and self-restraint in DM requires large amounts of glucose, which in turn means, that heuristic strategies are more prevalent when this fuel is depleted [58]. This suggests a link between metabolic responses that tap blood flow activity to the brain to processes required for complex judgment. Other research utilizes an EEG measure called $N_2$ to reflect executive inhibition ability, which suggests better performance on "No-Go" DM tasks [59].

## 5  Future Direction

Based upon the above review, it is clear that personnel selection and decision making are complex constructs and assessments for each are varied. However, it is also necessary to develop an effective assessment for the skill of decision making given that it takes many good decisions to be successful and only one bad decision to set back a career, an entire organization, or an entire country. A battery of tasks can be developed and physiological measures selected for instantiation like the Reinerman et al. work [36].

## References

1. Heslegrave, R.J., Colvin, C.: An Exploration of Psychological and Psychophisiological Measures as Predictors of Successful Performance Under Stress. Battelle Memorial Institute, Columbus, OH (1996)
2. Piedmont, R.L., Weinstein, H.P.: Predicting supervisor ratings of job performance using the NEO personality inventory. J. Psychol. **128**(3), 255–265 (1994)
3. Ones, D.S., Viswesvaran, C.: Integrity tests and other criterion-focused occupational personality scales (COPS) used in personnel selection. Int. J. Sel. Assess. **9**(1–2), 31–39 (2001)
4. Johnson, J.E., Powell, P.L.: Decision making, risk and gender: Are managers different? Br. J. Manag. **5**(2), 123–138 (1994)
5. Weekley, J.A., Ployhart, R.E.: An Introduction to Situational Judgment Testing. Lawrence Eribaum Associates, Mahwah (2006)
6. Ghiselli, E.E.: The validity of aptitude tests in personnel selection. Pers. Psychol. **26**(4), 461–477 (1973)

7. American Psychological Association: Glossary of Psychological Terms (2002). American Psychological Association. www.apa.org/research/action/golossary.aspx?tab=5

8. Costa, P.T., McCrae, R.R.: Normal personality assessment in clinical practice: the NEO personality inventory. Psychol. Assess. **4**(1), 5–13 (1992)

9. Gati, I., Gadassi, R., Saka, N., Hadadi, Y., Ansenberg, N., Friedmann, R., Asulin-Peretz, L.: Emotional and personality-related aspects of career decision-making difficulties: facets of career indecisiveness. J. Career Assess. **19**(1), 3–20 (2010)

10. Highhouse, S., Lake, C.J.: Assessing decision-making competence in managers. In: Judgment and Decision Making at Work, p. 326 (2013)

11. Hurtz, G.M., Donovan, J.J.: Personality and job performance: the big five revisited. J. Appl. Psychol. **85**, 869–879 (2000)

12. Lievens, F., Highhouse, S., De Corte, W.: The importance of traits and abilities in superfisors' hireability decisions as a funcrions as a method of assessment. J. Occup. Organ. Psychol. **78**, 453–470 (2005)

13. Topor, D.J., Colarelli, S.M., Han, L.: Influence of traits and assessment methods on human resource practitioners' evaluations of job applicants. J. Bus. Psychol. **21**, 361–376 (2007)

14. Aamodt, M.: Industrial/Organizational Psychology: An Applied Approach. Nelson Education, Toronto (2012)

15. Mills, R., Sinclair, M.: Aspects of inspection in a knitwear company. Appl. Ergon. **7**(2), 97–107 (1976)

16. Wickens, C.D., Mavor, A.S., McGee, J.P.: Flight to the Future: Human Factors in Air Traffic Control. National Academies Press, Washington (1997)

17. Borman, W.C.: Job behavior, performance, and effectiveness. In: Dunnette, M.D., Hough, L. M. (eds.) Handbook of Industrial Organizational Psychology, vol. 2, 2nd edn, pp. 271–326. Consulting Psychologists Press, Palo Alto (1991)

18. Reynolds, W.M.: Development of reliable and valid short forms of the Marlowe-Crowne Social Desirability Scale. J. Clin. Psychol. **38**(1), 119–125 (1982)

19. Viswesvaran, C., Ones, D.S.: The effects of social desirability and faking on personality and integrity assissment for personnel selection. Hum. Perform. **11**(2–3), 245–269 (1998)

20. Moreno, K.E., Wetzel, C.D., McBride, J.R., Weiss, D.J.: Relationship between corresponding armed services vocational aptitude battery (ASVAB) and computerized adaptive testing (CAT) subtests. Appl. Psychol. Meas. **8**(2), 155–163 (1984)

21. Bruin, W., Parker, A.M., Fischhoff, B.: Individual differences in adult decision-making competence. J. Pers. Soc. Psychol. **92**(5), 938–956 (2007)

22. Ku, K.Y.: Assessing students' critical thinking performance: urging for measurements using multi-response format. Think. Skills Creativity **4**(1), 70–76 (2009)

23. Lake, C.J., Highhouse, S.: Assessing decision-making competence in managers. In: Judgment and Decision Making and Work, p. 326 (2013)

24. Manley, G.G., Benavidez, J., Dunn, K.: Development of a personality biodata measure to predict ethical decision making. J. Manag. Psychol. **22**(7), 664–682 (2007)

25. Powell, M., Ansic, D.: Gender differences in risk behaviour in financial decision-making: an experimental analysis. J. Econ. Psychol. **18**(6), 605–628 (1997)

26. Schubert, R., Brown, M., Gysler, M., Brachinger, H.W.: Finacial decision-making: are women really more risk-averse? Am. Econ. Rev. **89**(2), 381–385 (1999)

27. Wang, P.: Brokers still treat men better than women. Money **23**(6), 108–110 (1994)

28. Dobbins, G.H., Platz, S.J.: Sex differences in leadership: how real are they? Acad. Mang. Rev. **11**(1), 118–127 (1986)

29. Taylor, R.N.: Agen and experience as deterrminants of managerial information processing and decision making performance. Acad. Manag. J. **18**(1), 74–81 (1975)

30. MacPherson, S.E., Phillips, L.H., Della Sala, S.: Age, executive function and social decision making: adorsolateral prefrontal theory of cognitive aging. Psychol. Aging **17**(4), 598–609 (2002)

31. Greene, J.D., Nystrom, L.E., Engell, A.D., Darley, J.M., Cohen, J.D.: The neural bases of cognitive conflickt and control in moral judgment. Neuron **44**(2), 389–400 (2004)

32. Menon, V., Room, H.S.: Cognitive neuroscience of mathematical skill development. In: Conference of Neurocognitive Development, vol. 9 (2009)

33. Sackett, P.R., Burris, L.R., Callahan, C.: Integrity testing for personnel selection: an update. Pers. Psychol. **38**(1), 119–125 (1982)

34. Reinerman-Jones, L., Matthews, G., Barber, D., Abich, J.: Psychophysiological metrics for workload are demand-sensitive but multifactorial. In: Proceedings of the Human Factors and Ergonomics Society Annual Meeting, vol. 58. Sage Publications (2014)

35. Warm, J.S., Parasuraman, R.: Cerebral hemodynamics and vigilance. In: Neuroergonomics: The Brain at Work, pp. 146–158 (2007)

36. Reinerman, L.: Cerebral blood flow velocity and stress as predictors of vigilance. Doctoral dissertation. Universiy of Cinncinnati, OH (2006)

37. Matthews, G., Warm, J.S., Reinerman-Jones, L.E., Langheim, L.K., Washburn, D.A., Tripp, L.: Task engagement, cerebral blood flow velocity, and diagnostic monitoring for sustained attention. J. Exp. Psychol. Appl. **16**, 187 (2010)

38. Reinerman-Jones, L.: Assessing multidimensional complex decision making with situational judgment tests. In: International Multi-Disciplinary Conference on Cognitive Methods in Situation Awareness and Decision Support (CogSIMA), pp. 49–55. IEEE (2016)

39. Becker, S.W., Brownson, F.O.: What price ambiguity? Or the role of ambiguity in decision-making. J. Polit. Econ. **72**, 62–73 (1964)

40. Myatt, M.: Self-Made Man - No Such Thing. Forbes Magazine, New York (2011)

41. Handbook, US Army: Military Leadership. US Government Printing Office (1973)

42. Higgins, E.T.: Making a good decision: value from fit. Am. Psychol. **55**(11), 1217 (2000)

43. Einhorn, H.J., Hogarth, R.M.: Behavioral decision theory: processes of judgment and choice. Ann. Rev. Psychol. **19**(1), 1–31 (1981)

44. Klein, G.: Naturalistic decision making. Hum. Factors: J. Hum. Factors Ergon. Soc. **50**, 456–460 (2008)

45. Grunig, R., Kuhn, R.: Successful Decision-Making: A Systematic Approach to Complex Problems. Springer Science & Business Media, Heidelberg (2013)

46. Plous, S.: The Psychology of Judgment and Decision Making. McGraw-Hill Book Company, New York (1993)

47. Hick, W.E.: On the rate of gain of information. Q. J. Exp. Psychol. **4**(1), 11–26 (1952)

48. Lipshitz, R., Klein, G., Orasanu, J., Salas, E.: Taking stock of naturalistic decision making. J. Behav. Dec. Making **14**(5), 331–352 (2001)

49. Berka, C.L.: Real-time analysis of EEG indexes of alertness, cognition, and memory acquired with a wireless EEG headset. Int. J. Hum.-Comput. Interact. **17**(2), 151–170 (2004)

50. Henelius, A., Hirvonen, K., Holm, A., Korpela, J., Muller, K.: Mental workload classification using heart rate metrics. In: Annual International Conference of the IEEE Engineering in Medicine and Biology Society, pp. 1836–1839. IEEE (2009)

51. Ayaz, H., Shewokis, P.A., Brunce, S., Izzetoglu, K., Willems, B., Onaral, B.: Optical brain monitoring for operator training and mental workload. Neuroimage **59**(1), 36–47 (2012)

52. Aaslid, R.: Transcranial Doppler Sonography. Springer Science & Business Media, Heidelberg (2012)

53. Batista, J.: A drowsiness and point of attention monitoring system for driver vigilance. In: IEEE Intelligent Transportation Systems Conference, pp. 702–708 (2007)

54. Mendez, M.F., Anderson, E., Shapira, J.S.: An investigation of moral judgment in frontotemporal dementia. Cogn. Behav. Neurol. **18**(4), 193–197 (2005)
55. Damasio, A.R., Everitt, B.J., Bishop, D.: The somatic marker hypothesis and the possible functions of the prefrontal cortex [and discussion]. Philos. Trans. R. Soc. London B: Biol. Sci. **351**(1346), 1413–1420 (1996)
56. Hjortskov, N., Rissen, D., Blangsted, A.K., Fallentin, N., Lundberg, U., Sogaard, K.: The effect of mental stress on heart rate variability and blood pressure during computer work. Eur. J. Appl. Physiol. **92**(1–2), 84–89 (2004)
57. Reitan, R.M., Wolfson, D.: A selective and critical review of neuropsychological deficits and the frontal lobes. Neuropsychol. Rev. **4**(3), 161–198 (1994)
58. Masicampo, E.J., Baumeister, R.F.: Toward a physiology of dual-process reasoning and judgment: lemonade, willpower, and expensive rule-based analysis. Psychol. Sci. **19**(3), 255–260 (2008)
59. De Neys, W., Novitsky, N., Ramautar, J., Wagemans, J.: What makes a good reasoner? Brain potentials and heuristic bias susceptibility. Proc. Ann. Conf. Cogn. Sci. Soc. **32**, 1020–1025 (2010)

# Macrocognition Applied to the Hybrid Space: Team Environment, Functions and Processes in Cyber Operations

Øyvind Jøsok[1,4(✉)], Benjamin J. Knox[1], Kirsi Helkala[1],
Kyle Wilson[3], Stefan Sütterlin[2,5], Ricardo G. Lugo[2],
and Terje Ødegaard[2]

[1] Norwegian Defence Cyber Academy, Lillehammer, Norway
{ojosok, bknox}@cyfor.mil.no, khelkala@mil.no
[2] Department of Psychology, Inland Norway University of Applied Sciences,
Lillehammer, Norway
{Stefan.Sutterlin, Ricardo.Lugo, Terje.Odegaard}@inn.no
[3] The Applied Cognition and Cognitive Engineering (AC2E) Research Group,
University of Huddersfield, Manchester, UK
K.Wilson@hud.ac.uk
[4] Child and Youth Participation and Development Research Program,
Inland Norway University of Applied Sciences, Lillehammer, Norway
[5] Center for Clinical Neuroscience, Oslo University Hospital, Oslo, Norway

**Abstract.** As cyber is increasingly integrated into military operations, conducting military cyber operations requires the effective coordination of teams. This interdisciplinary contribution discusses teams working in, and in relation to the cyber domain as a part of a larger socio-technical system, and the need for a better understanding of the human factors that contribute to individual and team performance in such settings. To extend an existing macrocognitive model [19] describing functions and processes into a conceptual framework that maps cognitive processes along cyber-physical and tactical-strategic dimensions (the Hybrid Space; [4]) to gain a better understanding of environmental complexity, and how to operate effectively in a cyber team context. Current experience from conducting cyber network defence exercises at the Norwegian Defence Cyber Academy and implications for future education and training are discussed.

**Keywords:** Macrocognition · Cyber domain · Team · Cognitive engineering · Hybrid space · Human factors · Socio technical system · Cyber · Military · Operations

## 1  Introduction

Across multiple domains teams are being increasingly called upon to perform complex problem identification and problem-solving tasks in novel contexts and situations [1, 71]. This is revealed in the military context, where formal recognition of the cyber domain as a domain of operations [2], presents significant team challenges due to its

© Springer International Publishing AG 2017
D.D. Schmorrow and C.M. Fidopiastis (Eds.): AC 2017, Part II, LNAI 10285, pp. 486–500, 2017.
DOI: 10.1007/978-3-319-58625-0_35

emergent nature and novelty in the conflict arena [4–6, 65]. Cyber is the enabler of networked operations[1], allowing enhanced information flow to support humans in planning, command and control activities [7]. But it also escalates nonlinearity, complexity and unpredictability [8, 10], creating an environment too rapid and complex for human cognitive abilities to handle [12].

While the focus of research and development within the area of military cyber operations has been technology centered [13, 14], a growing amount of researchers have identified that the introduction of cyber as an operational domain places enhanced demands on teams [4, 10, 15, 16] and effective team coordination appears to be necessary for good cyber defence [17]. Combined with the integration of cyber operations into lower levels of military hierarchical structures [20, 21], this could lead to a significant shift in team dynamics, as roles, task demands and command functions are subsequently affected. [4, 10, 22]. The result is: *"Personnel operating in the cyber domain represent a group of actors facing work that is characterized by a unique pattern of human-technological interaction bearing cognitive and physical challenges across the digital, physical, and the social domain."* [22, p. 3]. How these demands manifest across team performance remains unexplored, which presents a challenge for education and training of individuals and teams within the area of cyber operations, as no common best practices or guidelines currently exist [3, 23].

While research on cyber operations has tended to investigate the possibility of enhancing performance by means of augmented cognition (e.g. aiding humans through the means of technology), there remains a case that the human element might be one of the greatest untapped sources of cyber defence effectiveness [14, 16, 17]. Currently, there is no consensus on how to assess the performance of teams in a cyber operation context [17]. This may be due to limited understanding of team processes in the complex problem solving environment of the cyber domain, when they are assessed against existing 'team' research that is generally considered to have flaws and limitations [1, 18]. For this reason, this paper assumes that good team performance cannot be assessed simply based upon the team who captured the flag first. Instead we argue that there is a need to investigate team processes in cyber defence training exercises as a path to assessing team and judging performance.

This paper first introduces the macrocognitive model by Schraagen et al. [19] and the Hybrid Space framework ([4]; Fig. 1) as conceptual tools for improving team performance in cyber operations. The paper will then look at team macrocognition in a cyber operations environment before finally describing contextual viewpoints from the perspective of cyber defence exercises conducted at the Norwegian Defence Cyber Academy (NDCA). Functions and processes that can be fostered in education and training will be discussed.

---

[1] Network enabled operations, definitions and maturity specifications see e.g.; [7, 9, 11].

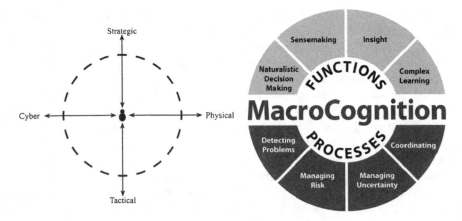

**Fig. 1.** The Hybrid Space conceptual framework [4] and macrocognition - functions and processes [19, 63].

## 2   Macrocognition and the Hybrid Space Framework Applied to Cyber Defence Teams

Located within the field of cognitive engineering [25] and empirically grounded in naturalistic decision making studies [24, 26, 27], the term macrocognition emerged from a need to address the broad variety of cognitive processes in a natural setting [1, 28, 70]. Macrocognition is subject to a variety of definitions that resemble each other by the commonality of explaining cognition in natural environments and later as 'the adaptation to complexity' [26, 28–32].

Macrocognition provides a framework (see Fig. 1) to study cognitive processes as they affect real-world task performance, and is addressed as a complement rather than a competitor to microcognition[2] [33, 70]. These processes include a range of internal and external cognitive activities [30] that are interoperable across team members for developing a set of alternative solutions [34]. The strength of this approach is that it encompasses both individual and team processes: *"Macrocognition is defined as the internalized and externalized high level mental processes employed by teams to create new knowledge during complex, one of a kind, collaborative problem solving."* [25, p. 7].

The Hybrid Space framework (see Fig. 1) can be used to map cognitive processes and to present a multidomain environment where cyber - as the key enabler - reduces distance between established hierarchical structures and formal rank and knowledge power relations [4, 22]. This occurs as decision makers and teams have to acknowledge and understand how to prioritize multiple assets based on known and unknown vulnerabilities and risks [4]. Mastering an environment where cognitive and physical challenges occur simultaneously across many situational dynamics and between several

---

[2] Klein et al. [30] coins the term microcognition for the purposes of explaining macrocognition. Microcognition refers to the study of cognition in controlled environments aiming at investigating the building blocks of cognition [30].

domains of interest [22, 35, 36] will rely on unprecedented levels of understanding [37, 69]. These higher levels of cognitive development are yet to be fully understood and require research to support agile manoeuvres in the information age [8].

The Hybrid Space conceptual framework primarily focuses on describing a cognitive landscape and the individual's perspective and perception of this [4]. However its applicability is not limited to individual actions; *"At all operational levels agents[3] can affect and are affected by abstraction levels of team and individual performance"* [4, p. 7]. Knox et al. [22] utilise the versatility of the Hybrid Space framework when addressing the issue of communication in socio-technical systems. They demonstrate the importance of the human factor by inferring from research in other safety-critical socio-technical systems such as acute medical care and aviation. A logical expansion of this contribution is to consider team processes in military socio-technical systems from the perspective of cyber defence units, where multiple operators are expected to act simultaneously as well as communicate and share knowledge.

The Hybrid Space adds a new dimension to observe and understand macrocognition functions and processes as they interact in a cyber-physical system. The macrocognition model, when applied to the cyber context does not account for vertical plane considerations as presented by the Hybrid Space. For example; the power dynamics in a team between tactical and strategic have direct impacts on team communication and coordination for functions and processes contributing to better performance.

## 3  Macrocognition in the Hybrid Space

In addressing cyber defence team issues, three possible factors that contribute to the breakdown of performance have been identified; team structure, team communication and information overload [38]. The conjunctions and reciprocal influence of these factors are not discussed in detail, but observed repeatedly in training as; *"...a group of individuals working independently with little to no communication or collaborative effort with team members."* [38, p. 221]. Even if research in this area is not mature enough to infer conclusively, this behaviour can be partly attributed to high cognitive load and partly to organizational policies [38]. However, analysts often spend a lot of time and effort searching the web for information that is often held by other members of the team, and simple communication efforts could fulfil the information need [16]. This indicates that the analysts' actions may actually be contributing to increased cognitive load. This leads to a decrease in communication and collaboration effort and as a result levels of overall understanding (individual and team) might suffer. This insight suggests that the individual and team dynamics are reciprocal cognitive processes, and understanding team dynamics in cyber defence teams can be approached from a naturalistic decision making research perspective through macrocognitive frameworks [26, 32, 69].

---

[3] In this context an agent can be both human and non-human [4].

## 3.1 Environment

Even though teamwork is a well researched construct, focus has been primarily on behavioural coordination in known tasks, and less on collaborative performance in novel situations [1, 38]. The macrocognitive functions that support teamwork in the Hybrid Space have to be viewed as processes that occur all of the time, often simultaneously, and some functions may serve as strategies to support the execution of additional novel functions [30]. Despite the interconnectivity of the functions, they can serve to support cognitive task analysis in naturalistic environments [31].

In discussing the macrocognitive environment, Klein et al. [30] identify a series of distinguishing features that form the context in which naturalistic decision making normally takes place [31]. These features are amongst others: ill-defined goals and ill-structured tasks; uncertainty, ambiguity, and missing data; shifting and competing goals; dynamic and continually changing conditions; action-feedback loops (real-time reactions to changed conditions); time stress; high stakes; multiple players; organizational goals and norms; experienced decision makers [31]. This list of features resembles the prerequisites for the Hybrid Space conceptual framework, where multiple agents in multiple domains interact and bring their own goals and assets into play. In the same way that Jøsok et al. [4] identify metacognitive skills as vital for performance in the Hybrid Space; research on macrocognitive constructs could bridge gaps between cyber team-members working in a hybrid environment that is defined by high stakes, ill-defined goals and tasks, information load, uncertainty and dynamic conditions [13, 14, 17, 38].

## 3.2 Structure

The role of cyber security teams is to protect assets that can be harmed via the cyber domain or in the cyber domain [39]. Within the area of team research it is generally accepted that a team needs to have a purpose and a goal, defined roles and a level of interdependence, as well as the fact that efficiency relies on team members' task- and team relevant knowledge and their understanding of these factors [40]. The current environmental issues in cyber defence teams make it difficult to meet these needs. Empowerment of lower ranks and cognitive readiness[4] to adapt to change is currently emerging as a requirement to perform successfully in the modern battlespace [4, 10, 22].

The tension between team goals and procedures, compared to organizational norms is a problem in this space [4]. At both inter and intra team level, one of the main contributing factors is that today's network and communications systems enable information to be shared and gathered in real-time, speeding up and blurring the interaction of agents, increasing the number of interactions between components dramatically, resulting in an inability to predict with confidence the consequences, (especially long term consequences) when parts of the system are altered by human actions [10].

---

[4] *"Cognitive readiness is the mental preparation (including skills, knowledge, abilities, motivations, and personal dispositions) an individual needs to establish and sustain competent performance in the complex and unpredictable environment of modern military operations"* [43, p. I-3].

Figure 2 encompasses a team with individually distributed responsibility and workload across the Hybrid Space. The leader will try to establish lines of communications to keep up to speed with the evolving situation, interacting with both the environment and team-members, engaging in a form of knowledge building process connecting pieces of information and aggregate these into higher levels of understanding [10]. In a military structure, the leader will also be expected to brief on the current situation to ranking officers or other stakeholders based on the current situational awareness of the total team knowledge and understanding. A logical action will be to position himself in an overarching role, with low levels of 'hands-on' and more context-related sensemaking. While this team concept model should work in relatively stable contexts in the physical world, the attributes of cyber make this difficult (e.g. ill-defined borders, concepts of time and space, absence of ground truth, the lack of law and policies, ambiguous ethical dilemmas etc.). However, hierarchical structuring of teams may have a negative impact on communication [41]. As several research contributions show, putting a team of experts together does not equal effective team performance. Factors ranging from a lack of organizational need or support, managemental errors or interindividual issues [42, 44–46] can all affect performance. This is somewhat addressed in the cyber defence team context when team coordination is identified as one of the main obstacles to performance. For example; internal team division of responsibility and established lines of communication during an incident were often brought into question [38]. In our view, this can also be described as a 'growing pain' [7] for military operations in the context of cyber operations. In a military context the contrarian asymmetries resulting from 'authority gradient' (leader: high; operator: low) and technical competence (leader: low; operator: high) distorts the common conception of a team. The leader's source of input is filtered by a complete information processing cycle on lower ranking expert levels; they rephrase, summarize and simplify before the collection of several complementary acting team members - at operator level - provide the informational input for the leader. This situation of contrarian asymmetrics probably needs entirely new ways of team development efforts, because of the special coordination and communication requirements needed in such a context [22]. Figure 3 provides a more accurate representation of the division of labor, coordination and communication demands that manifests itself in an operational context where any person can be the leader any given time.

## 3.3  Communication

The way team members are located across the space to cover the entire operational context has been acknowledged in the Orienting, Locating, Bridging (OLB) model [22]. This model is based on the assumption that one domain alone is not sufficient to make sense of the actions taken and the transferability of meaning to another domain. Using the OLB model, the interaction between members will be emergent and based on the current individual need to advance in the problem solving effort. The team would also be empowered to self-organize during problem solving if the traditional conceptions applied does not work, or had to be revised as the goals are reconceptualized

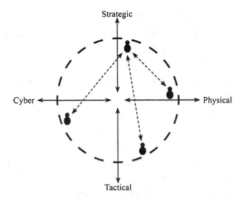

**Fig. 2.** Hierarchical structure, complicated relations

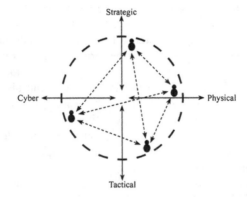

**Fig. 3.** Hierarchical structure, complex relations

based on improved understanding, or changing conditions in the environment. Klein [47] argues that complex settings require a more adaptive philosophy that breaks with fixed goals and fixed roles and task paradigms. Not just adapting to the goal, and changing the course of action, but changing the goals because of discoveries made during execution [47, 67]. Klein [47, 48] calls for a flexible execution that appreciates the process of setting goals, learning and discovery through planning and eventually redefining goals based on new insight into newly discovered, earlier invisible, relationships and dependencies. This will often lead to deeper understanding of the problem rather than to a solution [48]. Without a formal hierarchy, team members are free to share information as they wish [18]. Hence communication and coordination can be categorized as positively-complex between all team members. An example of this can be found among engineers working who demonstrated great team-work and cognitive flexibility to support their understanding of the STUXNET malware [53]. They analysed the code, and attempted to make sense of it individually and as a collaborative effort. They shared ideas across domains (i.e., not only looking at the code). In the end, for the code to make sense, they needed greater insight and had to start paying attention to the world around them and the geopolitical situation [49]. This multi-domain, coordinating and detecting process was achieved through complex learning functions and demonstrates macrocognition in action, in a Hybrid Space environment.

While sensemaking is considered a process in macrocognition [30], in the cyber context it relies on a state of cyber situational awareness. Obtaining and presenting an agreed recognized cyber picture is a contested area in the military, and a number of scientific papers are concerned with *aspects* related to situational awareness that are in fact only sub components (i.e. sensors, recognized cyber picture, strategic picture, physical operations etc.) leaving the overall situational awareness unmentioned [23]. Consequently some argue the cyber situational awareness is just a part of the overall situational awareness, and that cyber information needs to be combined with other information from other domains in order to make sense [23]. In practical terms this suggests that team members as well as operator and commander, need mutual appreciation towards each other's perspective in order to communicate efficiently to support each other's sensemaking [22].

Terms like the 'strategic corporal' [50–52] try to address the symptoms of this change, the solution however is disputed. To enhance team communication and coordination efforts, team members must be empowered to share knowledge and make decisions based on the current shared team knowledge, reducing the perception of the leader as a command and control mechanism. This means that the attitude of each team member is important; as each team member is required to maintain effort towards building individual knowledge, whilst also engaging in uninterrupted sharing based on own and team insight relating to the current context and problem space. In researching naturalistic decision making, Klein [26] observed that experts were not necessarily searching for the optimal choice, but looking to find an action that was workable, timely and cost effective [31]. While this is probably workable in a tactical situation in the physical domain, this approach may not be good enough in an operational cyber setting. These 'experts' heavily relied on the recognition of patterns in their environment for decision making. However, the often complex and intangible relationships in cyber, confront teams with previously unknown factors that influence the decision making process. Therefore they would probably have to engage in what Klein describes as "complex recognition primed decision making strategy" [31], where the precondition is that the situation does not match the experts' prior experiences. Hence the expert cannot apply recognition primed decision making directly, meaning they are required to engage in learning and discovering new knowledge and exploring new and adaptable ways to tackle the current issue. This shifts the goalposts for team research; from performance and efficiency, to, adaptability and appreciation of learning and sharing. In this situation, the 'all capturing' Hybrid Space framework is appropriate to gain insight into cyber-physical understanding, consideration for multiple domains, and interpretation of information emerging from different channels; all leading to greater appreciation for different domain perspectives within a learning team. Klein et al. [54] claim that any human sensemaking of events will start with some kind of framework, even if the framework is minimal. However some events in cyber operations may be counter-intuitive, and hence require more effort to make sense of, as seemingly logical reasoning may lead to faulty conclusions [55]. In conditions such as these, the adaptive characteristics of the Hybrid Space demonstrate how 'fit for purpose' it is for framing macrocognitive functions and processes in a new and complex field.

## 3.4    Information Load

Often in cyber operations the context complexifies the decision making process as the communication flow can be distorted by high cognitive load and information saturation [4, 12, 22, 38]. While the general, domain independent, assumption has been that more information available equals better decisions, there is still little known about how information sharing actually contributes to cyber situational awareness [23]. As long as humans are required to perceive and process information, there will be a point at which information overload becomes a reality. This leads to diminishing positive effects of information sharing due to reduced situational awareness [7].

In expert teams, individuals with specialized competence must actively acquire knowledge from the environment and each other to agree upon a full understanding of a problem space [18]. This dynamic form of problem-solving in a team can essentially be that of a 'moving-target' as processes are parallel, interdependent and continuous [1]. As for the Hybrid Space context, one could imagine the space itself sliding or moving along its axis, shifting the focus of the team to a more distant part of the space. This is a common problem recognized by several macrocognitive researchers in trying to understand complex socio-technical systems, and presents the researcher with 'moving target complications' in measurements [27, 64]. As experienced by military commanders [10], changes in both real-world scenarios and technology requires resilience and adaptability in work [27]. As the complexity of relations are augmented by technology *"...work cannot be adequately understood in terms of simplistic causal chain decomposition"* [56, p. 15].

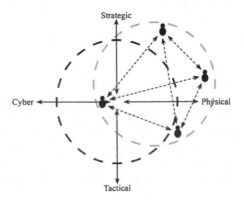

**Fig. 4.** Sliding space

As complexity increases [12] at an individual level, strategies of oversimplification are often applied [57]. At a team level, an often used strategy is distribution of workload and division of responsibility across an hierarchical team of domain experts [41, 46].

Both oversimplification (meaning also filtering out a lot of information before communicating it, limiting the recipient's information base for his/her decisions) and workload distribution are also an additional burden for communication capabilities. The process of gaining information is never ending, and in the Hybrid Space the attribution of attacks is difficult and making sense of intent and impact between domains can be confusing. The relationship between uncertainty and risk is also somewhat intangible, but still interconnected as i.e. acknowledgment of uncertainty would be to taking risk into account or to prepare to avoid or confront risks [58]. This is recognized in the Hybrid Space [4] when stating that: *"Assets and their vulnerabilities are interconnected. If an asset is lost, this loss has an effect on other assets and their vulnerabilities"* [4, p. 178].

It is well documented that inability to detect problems is the cause of many accidents [59], and in the Hybrid Space context the question of problem detection is particularly interesting (e.g. problem detection in the cyber domain relies on a unique human computer interaction and understanding; problems can emerge in one or several domains at different times, but still be interconnected; the effect of attacks might not be kinetic, but only have a cognitive impact i.e. lead to unthoughtful decisions that reduce operational freedom of own forces). While previous attempts to understand problem detection has been more incremental towards a threshold of detection, more complex domains seem to take advantage of higher level cognitive skills like re-conceptualization [59, 61].

Where the Hybrid Space conceptual framework [4] describes the environment in which cyber teams operate, the macrocognitive framework [19] adds understanding to the functions and processes that individuals and teams engage in within this space. Knowledge gained from observing and studying cognition in naturalistic settings in a cyber operation context [65], shed light on the current problems that have to be tackled to ensure that individuals and teams receive proper education and training [60] to operate in this complex multi-domain environment.

## 4  Research Based Cyber Defence Education - NDCA Context

The Norwegian Defence Cyber Academy (NDCA) conducts cyber defence exercises as part of a three year education cycle for officer cadets training to lead and operate in the cyber domain. Learning to operate in an environment where macrocognition shapes critical decision making supports exercising troops develop increased appreciation for team structures, grounded communication and the hazards of information overload.

The exercises are designed to ensure a positive learning environment for motivating, developing and nurturing the necessary and evolving individual and team skill-sets required to lead adaptively [68], and function as effective members in cyber teams. Fundamentally this requires creating an adaptable operative learning environment, that replicates multiple levels of complexity and cross domain dynamics [66]. In these conditions it becomes straightforward to expose trainees to novelty, as well as to the emerging nature of macrocognition in a cyber domain team context. Founded upon real world conflicts, exercise scenarios are holistic and capture the dynamics of the Hybrid Space by encompassing both cyber-physical problems as well strategic-tactical tension [4], ensuring naturalistic complexity. Context sensitive real world scenarios allow novices and practitioners to engage in authentic sensemaking based on available newsfeeds, online information and own mental frameworks. The complexity of the scenarios requires the teams engage in learning activities to gain understanding of detected problems, to coordinate in order to decide on the best course of action as well as communicate risk, limitations and uncertainties to the designated operational commander. The objective is to create an environment where standard operation procedures cannot be applied and teams have to continually adapt to complexity and novelty. No frameworks are imposed upon exercising personnel regarding team configuration. They are encouraged to self-synchronize and are supported rather than assessed by their appointed expert mentor. As they learn to manage the broad spectrum of team demands required to operate effectively, they themselves discover and develop a deeper appreciation for the functions and processes of macrocognition (see Fig. 1) in a cyber critical team context. As they iterate through increasingly complex cyber attacks - that arrive in their network as part of larger geo-political scenario - their individual and team dynamics are trained, tuned and tested.

The cyber defence exercises apply the Hybrid Space framework as a means of grounding communication partners within a cognitive space that is influenced by tactical/strategical and cyber-physical/socio-technical dimensions. Participants' ability to consciously apply macrocognitive functions is built upon the three-phase OLB model [22]. For example; to create a learning environment that exposes these competencies, students attending a cyber defence exercise in 2016 were tasked to design and create their own 'recognized cyber picture'. This demanded they present information relevant for building cyber situation awareness as part of the wider operational and strategic scenario. The product needed to be versatile enough that data could be verbally and visually presented to a non-technical strategic level commander. The purpose was to ensure the teams were able to increase the commander's understanding of how the cyber situation affects the physical context, and needs to be integrated into decision making.

Critically and possibly uniquely, the research team is an integrated part of the exercise planning team. This allows observing for decision making and team processes in a naturalistic way as the 'exercise becomes the lab', meaning research methods can be applied, triangulated formatively and summatively and cognitive load can be managed in order to ensure information overload leads to positive learning outcomes among participants. All the while, researchers and experts mentor and encourage metacognitive process as well as observe for macrocognitive functions. Applying the Hybrid Space framework as both a tool to encourage metacognition in cadets, as well as a tool for researchers to gather data on, for example; team workload [62], establishing training, education and performance metrics for individuals and teams working in the cyber domain becomes less intangible.

## 5 Conclusion and Future Work

In this paper we gave a brief introduction of macrocognitive concepts and the Hybrid Space framework, and discussed their applicability for improving team performance in cyber operations. As an educational example, we discussed how the NDCA uses macrocognitive processes and the Hybrid Space framework in research-based cyber defence education.

Despite attempts by teams to self-evaluate improvements in their performance, or judgements based upon 'capture the flag type' competitions, there does not exist a well-defined definition for good performance in cyber defence. The development of objective and valid criteria of success in cyber defence, the operationalization of individual and team performance, and finally the isolation of predictors for performance are challenges for future research. The placement of macrocognitive processes within the Hybrid Space acknowledges the cognitive dimensions of tactical versus strategic considerations and the hybridity of environmental events encompassing cyber events and physical correspondents and thus provides an adaptation of the macrocognitive model in a cyber defense context. Current conceptions of team organisation, team leadership and team interaction might have to be re-conceptualized due to the impact of the cyber domain.

**Acknowledgements.** The authors would like to thank the Ving 69 at the NDCA for the contributions to this article.

# References

1. Fiore, S.M., Rosen, M.A., Smith-Jentsch, K., Salas, E., Letsky, M., Warner, N.: Toward an understanding of macrocognition in teams: predicting processes in complex collaborative contexts. Hum. Fact.: J. Hum. Fact. Ergon. Soc. **52**, 203–224 (2010)
2. NATO: Warsaw Summit Communiqué (2016, press release). http://www.nato.int/cps/en/natohq/official_texts_133169.htm?selectedLocale=en
3. NATO: Cyber Defence Pledge (2016, press release). http://www.nato.int/cps/en/natohq/official_texts_133177.htm?selectedLocale=en
4. Jøsok, Ø., Knox, Benjamin J., Helkala, K., Lugo, Ricardo G., Sütterlin, S., Ward, P.: Exploring the hybrid space - theoretical framework applying cognitive science in military cyberspace operations. In: Schmorrow, Dylan D.D., Fidopiastis, Cali M.M. (eds.) AC 2016. LNCS (LNAI), vol. 9744, pp. 178–188. Springer, Cham (2016). doi:10.1007/978-3-319-39952-2_18
5. Tikk-Ringas, E., Kerttunen, M., Christopher, S.: Cyber security as a field of military education and study. Joint Force Q. **75**, 57–60 (2014)
6. Williams, B.T.: The joint force commander's guide to cyberspace operations. Joint Force Q. **73**(2nd quarter), 12–19 (2014)
7. Buchler, N., Fitzhugh, S.M., Marusich, L.R., Ungvarsky, D.M., Lebiere, C., Gonzalez, C.: Mission command in the age of network-enabled operations: social network analysis of information sharing and situation awareness. Front. Psychol. **7**(937) (2016). doi:10.3389/fpsyg.2016.00937
8. Alberts, D.S., Haynes, R.E.: Power to the Edge. Command and Control in the Information Age. DoD Command and Control Research Program: Department of Defence (2003). (ISBN 1-893723-13-5)
9. Alberts, D.S., Huber, R.K., Moffat, J.: NATO NEC C2 maturity model. DTIC Document (2010)
10. McChrystal, S., Collins, T., Silverman, D., Fussell, C.: Teams of Teams: New Rules of Engagement for a Complex World. Penguin, New York (2016)
11. Wilson, C.: Network centric operations: background and oversight issues for congress (2007)

12. Zachary, W., Rosoff, A., Miller, L.C., Read, S.J.: Context as a cognitive process: an integrative framework for supporting decision making. Paper presented at STIDS (2013)

13. Knott, B.A., Mancuso, V.F., Bennett, K., Finomore, V., McNeese, M., McKneely, J.A., Beecher, M.: Human factors in cyber warfare: alternative perspectives. Paper presented at Proceedings of Human Factors and Ergonomics Society Annual Meeting (2013)

14. Mancuso, V.F., Christensen, J.C., Cowley, J., Finomore, V., Gonzalez, C., Knott, B.: Human factors in cyber warfare II emerging perspectives. Paper presented at Proceedings of Human Factors and Ergonomics Society Annual Meeting (2014)

15. Gutzwiller, R.S., Fugate, S., Sawyer, B.D., Hancock, P.: The human factors of cyber network defence. Paper presented at Proceedings of Human Factors and Ergonomics Society Annual Meeting (2015)

16. Rajivan, P., Janssen, M.A., Cooke, N.J.: Agent-based model of a cyber security defence analyst team. Paper presented at Proceedings of Human Factors and Ergonomics Society Annual Meeting (2013)

17. Forsythe, C., Silva, A., Stevens-Adams, S., Bradshaw, J.: Human Dimension in Cyber Operations Research and Development Priorities. Paper presented at International Conference on Augmented Cognition (2013)

18. Grand, J.A., Braun, M.T., Kuljanin, G., Kozlowski, S.W.J., Chao, G.T.: The dynamics of team cognition: a process-oriented theory of knowledge emergence in teams. J. Appl. Psychol. **101**(10), 1353–1385 (2016). doi:10.1037/apl0000136

19. Schraagen, J.M., Klein, G., Hoffman, R.R.: The Macrocognition Framework of Naturalistic Decision Making. Ashgate Publishing Limited, Aldershot (2008)

20. Army, U.: Integration of cyberspace capabilities into tactical units. US Army Cyber Command (2016)

21. Tan, M.: The multi-domain battle. Def. News Weekl. (2016). http://www.defencenews.com/articles/the-multi-domain-battle

22. Knox, B.J., Jøsok, Ø., Helkala, K., Khooshabeh, P., Ødegaard, T., Sütterlin, S.: Socio-technical communication: the hybrid space and the OLB-Model for science-based cyber education. J. Mil. Psychol. (2017, submitted)

23. Franke, U., Brynielsson, J.: Cyber situational awareness–a systematic review of the literature. Comput. Secur. **46**, 18–31 (2014)

24. Letsky, M.P.: Macrocognition in teams: macrocognition in collaboration and knowledge interoperability. Paper presented at Panel Presentation at 51st Annual Meeting of the Human Factors and Ergonomics Society, Baltimore MD (2007)

25. Letsky, M., Warner, N., Fiore, S.M., Rosen, M., Salas, E.: Macrocognition in complex team problem solving. DTIC Document (2007). http://oai.dtic.mil/oai/oai?verb=getRecord&metadataPrefix=html&identifier=ADA481422

26. Klein, G.: Naturalistic decision making. Hum. Fact.: J. Hum. Fact. Ergon. Soc. **50**(3), 456–460 (2008)

27. Hoffman, R., Klein, G., Miller, J.: Naturalistic investigations and models of reasoning about complex indeterminate causation. Inf. Knowl. Syst. Manag. **10**(1–4), 397–425 (2011)

28. Hoffman, R.R., McNeese, M.D.: A history for macrocognition. J. Cogn. Eng. Decis. Mak. **3**(2), 97–110 (2009)

29. Kahneman, D., Klein, G.: Conditions for intuitive expertise: a failure to disagree. Am. Psychol. **64**(6), 515 (2009)

30. Klein, G., Ross, K.G., Moon, B.M., Klein, D.E., Hoffman, R.R., Hollnagel, E.: Macrocognition. IEEE Intell. Syst. **18**(3), 81–85 (2003)

31. Klein, G., Klinger, D.: Naturalistic decision making. Hum. Syst. IAC Gatew. **2**(1), 16–19 (1991)

32. Klein, G., Wright, C.: Macrocognition: from theory to toolbox. Front. Psychol. **7**(54) (2016). doi:10.3389/fpsyg.2016.00054

33. Klein, D.E., Klein, H.A., Klein, G.: Macrocognition: linking cognitive psychology and cognitive ergonomics. Paper presented at Proceedings of 5th International Conference on Human Interactions with Complex Systems, University of Illinois at Urbana-Champaign, Urbana-Champaign (2000)

34. Deshmukh, A.V., McComb, S.A., Wernz, C.: Agents as collaborating team members. In: Letsky, M.P., Warner, N.W., Fiore, S.M.F., Smith, C.A.P. (eds.) Macrocognition in Teams: Theories and Methodologies. Ashgate Publishing Ltd., Aldershot (2008)

35. Kegan, R., Lahey, L.L.: Immunity to Change: How to Overcome It and Unlock Potential in Yourself and Your Organization. Harvard Business Press, Boston (2009)

36. Joiner, W.B., Josephs, S.A.: Leadership Agility: Five Levels of Mastery for Anticipating and Initiating Change, vol. 307. Wiley, New York (2006)

37. Defence, M.O.: Future Trends Programme - Future Operating Environment 2035, United Kingdom (2015). https://www.gov.uk/government/publications/future-operating-environment-2035

38. Champion, M.A., Rajivan, P., Cooke, N.J., Jariwala, S.: Team-based cyber defence analysis. Paper presented at 2012 IEEE International Multi-disciplinary Conference on Cognitive Methods in Situation Awareness and Decision Support (2012)

39. von Solms, R., van Niekerk, J.: From information security to cyber security. Comput. Secur. **38**, 97–102 (2013)

40. Fiore, S.M., Ross, K.G., Jentsch, F.: A team cognitive readiness framework for small-unit training. J. Cogn. Eng. Decis. Mak. **6**(3), 325–349 (2012)

41. Brun, W., Ekornås, B., Kobbeltvedt, T., Pallesen, S., Hansen, A., Laberg, J.C., Johnsen, B. H.: Betydningen av felles mentale modeller for beslutningstaging i operative team. Nor. Mil. J. **11**(11–03), 22–27 (2003)

42. Dyer, W.G., Dyer, J.H., Dyer, D.: Team Building: Proven Strategies for Improving Team Performance. Wiley, New York (2013)

43. Morrison, J.E., Fletcher, J.D.: Cognitive readiness (2002)

44. Hackman, J.R.: Why teams don't work. In: Scott Tindale, R., Heath, L., Edwards, J., Posavac, E.J., Bryant, F.B., Suarez-Balcazar, Y., Henderson-King, E., Myers, J. (eds.) Theory and research on small groups, pp. 245–267. Springer, Heidelberg (2002)

45. Hackman, J.R.: Groups That Work and Those That Don't. Jossey-Bass, San Francisco (1990)

46. Urban, J.M., Bowers, C.A., Monday, S.D., Morgan Jr., B.B.: Workload, team structure, and communication in team performance. Mil. Psychol. **7**(2), 123–139 (1995). doi:10.1207/s15327876mp0702_6

47. Klein, G.: Flexecution as a paradigm for replanning, part 1. IEEE Intell. Syst. **22**(5), 79–83 (2007)

48. Klein, G.: Flexecution, part 2: understanding and supporting flexible execution. IEEE Intell. Syst. **22**(6), 108–112 (2007)

49. Gibney, A.: Zero Days. World War 3.0. Magnolia Pictures (2016)

50. Krulak, C.C.: The strategic corporal: leadership in the three block war. Mar. Mag (1999). http://oai.dtic.mil/oai/oai?verb=getRecord&metadataPrefix=html&identifier=ADA399413

51. Liddy, L.: The strategic corporal: some requirements in training and education. Education, training and doctrine. Aust. Army J. **2**, 139 (2004)

52. Lemay, A., Leblanc, S.P., De Jesus, T.: Lessons from the strategic corporal: implications of cyber incident response. Paper presented at Proceedings of 2015 ACM SIGMIS Conference on Computers and People Research (2015)

53. Lindsay, J.R.: Stuxnet and the limits of cyber warfare. Secur. Stud. **22**(3), 365–404 (2013)

54. Klein, G., Moon, B., Hoffman, R.R.: Making sense of sensemaking 2: a macrocognitive model. IEEE Intell. Syst. **21**(5), 88–92 (2006)
55. Lugo, R.G., Sütterlin, S., Knox, B.J., Jøsok, Ø., Helkala, K., Lande, N.M.: The moderating influence of self-efficacy on interoceptive ability and counterintuitive decision making in officer cadets. J. Mil. Stud. (2016)
56. Hoffman, R.R., Patterson, E., Miller, J.: Some challenges for macrocognitive measurement. In: Macrocognition Metrics and Scenarios: Design and Evaluation for Real-World Teams, pp. 11–28 (2009)
57. Fiore, S.M.F., Rosen, M., Salas, E., Burke, S., Jentsch, F.: Agents as collaborating team members. In: Letsky, M.P., Warner, N.W., Fiore, S.M.F., Smith, C.A.P. (eds.) Macrocognition in Teams: Theories and Methodologies. Ashgate Publishing Ltd., Aldershot (2008)
58. Lipshitz, R., Strauss, O.: Coping with uncertainty: a naturalistic decision-making analysis. Org. Behav. Hum. Decis. Process. **69**(2), 149–163 (1997)
59. Klein, G., Pliske, R.M., Crandall, B., Woods, D.: Features of problem detection. Paper presented at Proceedings of Human Factors and Ergonomics Society Annual Meeting (1999)
60. Arnold, T., Harrison, R., Conti, G.: Towards a career path in cyberspace operations for army officers. Small Wars J. 18 August 2014. http://smallwarsjournal.com/jrnl/art/towards-a-career-path-in-cyberspace-operations-for-army-officers. Accessed 4 Jan 2017
61. Hoffman, R.R., Shattuck, L.G.: Should we rethink how we do OPORDs? Mil. Rev. **86**(2), 100 (2006)
62. Lugo, R.G., Jøsok, Ø., Knox, B.J., Helkala, K., Sütterlin, S.: Team workload demands influence on cyber detection performance. Paper submitted for review at 13th International Conference on Naturalistic Decision Making 2017, Bath, UK (2017)
63. MacroCognition LLC. http://www.macrocognition.com
64. Rosen, M.A., Fiore, S.M., Salas, E., Letsky, M., Warner, N.: Tightly coupling cognition: understanding how communication and awareness drive coordination in teams (2008)
65. D'Amico, A., Whitley, K., Tesone, D., O'Brien, B., Roth, E.: Achieving cyber defence situational awareness: a cognitive task analysis of information assurance analysts. Paper presented at Proceedings of Human Factors and Ergonomics Society Annual Meeting (2005). http://journals.sagepub.com/doi/abs/10.1177/154193120504900304
66. Jones, R.M., O'Grady, R., Nicholson, D., Hoffman, R., Bunch, L., Bradshaw, J., Bolton, A.: Modeling and integrating cognitive agents within the emerging cyber domain. Paper presented at Proceedings of Interservice/Industry Training, Simulation, and Education Conference (I/ITSEC) (2015)
67. LePine, J.A.: Adaptation of teams in response to unforeseen change: effects of goal difficulty and team composition in terms of cognitive ability and goal orientation. J. Appl. Psychol. **90**(6), 1153–1167 (2005). doi:10.1037/0021-9010.90.6.1153
68. London, M., Sessa, V.I.: The development of group interaction patterns: How groups become adaptive, generative, and transformative learners. Hum. Resour. Dev. Rev. **6**(4), 353–376 (2007)
69. Sawyer, B.D., Finomore, V.S., Funke, G.J., Mancuso, V.F., Funke, M.E., Matthews, G., Warm, J.S.: Cyber vigilance effects of signal probability and event rate. Paper presented at Proceedings of Human Factors and Ergonomics Society Annual Meeting (2014)
70. Wilson, K.M., Helton, W.S., Wiggins, M.W.: Cognitive engineering. Wiley Interdiscipl. Rev.: Cogn. Sci. **4**(1), 17–31 (2013)
71. Salas, E., Cooke, N.J., Rosen, M.A.: On teams, teamwork, and team performance: discoveries and developments. Hum. Fact.: J. Hum. Fact. Ergon. Soc. **50**(3), 540–547 (2008)

# Nuclear Reactor Crew Evaluation of a Computerized Operator Support System HMI for Chemical and Volume Control System

Roger Lew[1($\boxtimes$)], Thomas A. Ulrich[1,2], and Ronald L. Boring[2]

[1] University of Idaho, Moscow, ID, USA
rogerlew@uidaho.edu
[2] Idaho National Laboratory, Idaho Falls, ID, USA
{thomas.ulrich,ronald.boring}@inl.gov

**Abstract.** A Computerized Operator Support System (COSS) functional prototype was developed as an assistive technology for operators. The COSS was implemented as a hybrid control board for the Chemical Volume Control System (CVCS) of a three loop Combustion Engineering pressurized water reactor and implemented full-scope, full-scale, glass top control room simulator. The hybrid control board simulated a modernized control room with both analog and digital instrumentation and control. The digital portions consisted of large digital overview and smaller touch displays, while the analog portion consisted primarily of safety indicators and controls. The glass top nature of the simulator allowed the COSS configuration to be compared to the existing fully analog configuration. A cooperative research and development agreement with a major US utility allowed for two separate licensed three-person crews of commercial reactor operators to evaluate the COSS. The evaluation revealed stylistic issues, operation insights, and design considerations that will guide control room modernization efforts and influence next generation control systems and Human Machine Interfaces.

**Keywords:** Nuclear power · Nuclear human factors · Control room · Computerized Operator Support Systems (COSS) · Process control

## 1 Introduction – Lab Paradigms to the Real World

The U.S. nuclear power plant (NPP) industry is interested in extending their current 40-year licensing periods by 20 or even 40 years to safely, reliably and securely meet U.S. energy demands. The Department of Energy (DOE) Light Water Reactor Sustainability (LWRS) program provides pathways for national labs to collaborate with academic and industry partners on R&D efforts to accomplish this objective [1]. Idaho National Laboratory (INL) and major US utility have arranged Cooperative Research and Development Agreement (CRADA) that is affiliated with the LWRS Program to support Main Control Room (MCR) modernization activities [2]. Fully modernizing a

© Springer International Publishing AG 2017
D.D. Schmorrow and C.M. Fidopiastis (Eds.): AC 2017, Part II, LNAI 10285, pp. 501–513, 2017.
DOI: 10.1007/978-3-319-58625-0_36

MCR in a single outage cycle is unfeasible. Utilities are therefore upgrading systems in a piecemeal fashion. INL's role is to help formulate an end-state vision for the MCR, as well as conduct a series of operator studies to validate design concepts and operator performance using new systems. The utilities benefit from this arrangement by obtaining plant and system specific knowledge and guidance. DOE and other utilities benefit because DOE shares generalizable findings. Furthermore, conducting control room studies with licensed operators is an expensive and time-consuming endeavor. With the CRADA arrangement, the utilities contribute operator time and support to carry out running full-scale, full-scope scenarios.

DOE's Office of Nuclear Energy (DOE-NE) has a Nuclear Energy Enabling Technologies (NEET) Program that aims to develop "crosscutting technologies that directly support and complement the Department of Energy, Office of Nuclear Energy's (DOE-NE) advanced reactor and fuel cycle concepts, focusing on innovative research that offers the promise of dramatically improved performance [3]." LWRS focuses efforts on near-future challenges and objectives for existing NPPs. In contrast, NEET focuses more on future technologies that could have long-lasting benefits beyond our current fleet of light water reactors. The complementary nature of a LWRS-CRADA and an ongoing NEET funded project provided a unique opportunity to conduct an evaluation of a Computerized Operator Support System (COSS) with licensed operators in the summer of 2016. As part of a CRADA workshop to evaluate an end-state control room concept, we could conduct scenarios with operators using COSS prototype with advanced control schemes and fault diagnosis system. This iteration of COSS was implemented for the Chemical Volume Control System (CVCS) of a three-loop Combustion Engineering pressurized water reactor.

Our COSS prototype has gone through several design-evaluation iterations [4]. Previous iterations have examined how to integrate a fault diagnosis system (PRO-AID) and utilize the fault diagnosis information to benefit the operators by incorporating Computer Based Procedures with soft controls. Our previous concepts have functioned as digital only interfaces. Next-generation plants will feature mostly digital controls, but modernized control rooms are unlikely to have the same level of control automation or digital control.

U.S. utilities are modernizing their control systems to increase reliability and reduce operating costs, but are proceeding by keeping existing analog safety systems in place [5]. Re-working these systems is time-consuming and expensive. Modification of safety critical systems would also require extensive review from the Nuclear Regulatory Commission. With proper maintenance, these systems can remain in place and function for the extended lifetime of the plants. As a result, modernized control rooms will likely contain a mix of digital and analog controls (hybrid control boards). In our COSS evaluation, the Human Machine Interface (HMI) simulated hybrid control boards with both analog and digital instrumentation and control. The digital portions consisted of large digital overview and smaller touch displays, while the analog portion consisted primarily of the remaining safety indicators and controls.

To understand the context of COSS in the future of nuclear power we must understand that utilities are actively developing modernization roadmaps 20+ years into the future. Specifications that are being written today might take seven to ten years to come to fruition. The U.S. nuclear industry has a commendable safety track-record partially because the nuclear industry as a whole is conservative at adopting control technology. COSS concepts and their underlying engineering technologies are plausible but not yet commercially viable. Our goal with formative evaluations is to ensure COSS evolves into a product that would be of real-world value to operators and nuclear control operations. COSS demonstrations have a secondary effect in shaping how operations culture evolves to incorporate advanced control schemes and fault diagnosis systems.

## 2 Computerized Operator Support System Prototype

A COSS or Computerized Operator Support System is defined here as a conglomeration of traditional and advanced control system technologies and human factors interaction concepts that are designed to function as a whole to assist operators in monitoring, controlling, and managing control processes in normal and abnormal operating conditions.

The term *designed* is of critical importance to understanding the definition. A control system and human machine interface could incorporate the technologies in a haphazard fashion. The resulting product could, on paper, have the same functionality, but be suboptimal to plant operations and operator interactions. The COSS concept is philosophically distinguished by incorporating design thinking into the creation of the product. Design thinking is a synthetic inductive process (solution-focused) in contrast to traditional scientifically rooted human factors that tends to be analytic and deductive (problem-focused) [6]. The COSS concepts were conceived by thinking about what would be most ideal to the operators should a problem arise, and then fitting technology to the solution. In this manner it is a user-centered design process rather than an engineering driven design process.

This iteration of COSS was implemented for the Chemical Volume Control System (CVCS) of a three-loop Combustion Engineering (CE) pressurized water reactor (PWR). The CVCS is housed within containment and is part of the primary reactor coolant system. It serves a number of important functions necessary for running the plant for long-periods of time. It is responsible for maintaining the chemistry of the primary coolant by filtering out contaminants as well as controlling born concentration through addition and dilution. The CVCS also provides a high-pressure water supply for the reactor coolant pump seals, and is used to manage the inventory of primary coolant. The Human Machine Interface (HMI) simulated a hybrid control board with both analog and digital instrumentation and control such as those anticipated to be found in modernized Generation II NPPs. The digital portion of the hybrid CVCS consisted of two large digital overviews with two smaller touch displays, while the analog portion consisted primarily of safety indicators and controls. The prototype was deployed in the INL Human System Simulation Laboratory (HSSL) full-scale, full-scope, reconfigurable glass top nuclear control room simulator [7]. The HSSL

**Fig. 1.** The human systems simulation laboratory nuclear control room simulator. The hybrid COSS-CVCS is represented on the group of 3 bays depicted on the far left.

simulator allowed the hybrid COSS control board configuration to be compared to a more traditional digital HMI as well as the existing analog configuration (see Fig. 1).

The COSS prototype emulates several advanced technologies to help operators monitor and control the CVCS while also enhancing their ability to detect and mitigate faults. A control room can have over 2,000 analog indicators and controls in addition to indications from the plant computer and other sources. Operators must constantly monitor and integrate information across sources to assess the current state of the plant. As plants are modernized, digital infrastructure supplants existing analog systems. Digital infrastructure can be advantageous because it allows additional information to be provided to operators, but this extra information may also compete for the operator's attention. One approach to organizing and prioritizing the available information is to use large overview displays to provide operators "at a glance" system status information. More detailed system and component level information is available by "digging" down through hierarchically organized displays.

Most NPP control rooms predate the existence of modern digital alarm list displays. With existing control rooms the alarms are grouped into windows at the top of each control board. This arrangement can be beneficial to operators because they can quickly assess the state of the plant on scanning the alarm tiles. The arrangement of the alarms is static and the operators can rely on their ability to recognize familiar or unfamiliar patterns. The CVCS prototype incorporated a like-for-like digital annunciator window replacement with an alarm list. The digital replacements offer lower maintenance and replacement costs compared to their analog counterparts. The like-for-like replacement maintains the operator's ability to scan the alarm boards and to respond to incoming alarms with existing procedures. The annunciator windows also provide a means of grouping alarms and prioritizing their importance. Less critical alarms can be sent to the alarm list. While the alarm list may not facilitate rapid scanning it does have some unique advantages over the annunciator windows. The alarms in the list are time stamped and can be interactively filtered to identify critical information.

One of the core innovative components of our COSS system is an advanced online sensor validation and fault diagnosis system (PRO-AID) developed at Argonne National Laboratory. The PRO-AID system actively monitors plant sensors and components. When a fault occurs it can detect and inform operators to abnormal conditions before plant variables exceed alarm thresholds. Once a fault is recognized by PRO-AID, the HMI highlights what component(s) that may be at fault. Computer Based Procedures (CBP) integrated with an expert knowledge system provide operators actions to mitigate undesirable plant events and return the plant to a safe operating condition with the least amount of upset possible. This additional information could be sufficient to avoid the costly endeavor of taking the plant offline.

Here we conducted an interface evaluation workshop with licensed operators. The workshop was intended to accomplish several goals. The first was to assess whether the COSS concept could aid operators during abnormal events. Secondly, we sought to capture operator impressions regarding the acceptance of COSS-like technology in the control room. The COSS prototype provided higher levels of automation compared to existing control systems. Operators may feel uncomfortable relinquishing control to technological systems. Lastly, we the operators were used to identify potential shortcomings of the COSS concept and to ideate potential remediations and improvements.

## 3   Method

In August of 2016 two crews of licensed reactor operators visited INL to participate in a LWRS-CRADA workshop. Each crew consisted of three individuals, and the crews participated on consecutive weeks. This allowed us to capture unbiased first impressions from each operating crew. The HSSL nuclear control room simulator was configured to represent the control room of the visiting crews. Prior to the data collection the crews conducted a small loss of coolant scenario to familiarize themselves with the glass-top controls and to validate the indicators and controls functioned as expected in the virtual control room.

### 3.1   Study Design

Each crew conducted a fault scenario with three variations of a CVCS control board. As a control condition the conventional analog control board was represented. In this condition the board was represented as it currently exists in the operator's plant. A second condition represented a hybrid analog/digital control board with large overview displays and a digital HMI. The second condition represented currently available technology would be commercial available for control room upgrades. The final condition incorporated advanced COSS concepts that are not yet commercially available. The following subsections describe these conditions in more detail.

**Description of Conventional Boards.** In the conventional layout the controls are arranged as a process. The mimic depicts the major components of the CVCS and their arrangement and function in the system thus providing the organizational structure on the board. The piping of the mimic is color coded to segregate the CVCS into sub-systems (e.g., letdown path is orange, charging and seal injection is red). The benefit of a mimic format allows operators to identify the function and status of the component from its placement in the mimic diagram without having to rely on memory and the component's labeling or looking back and forth between the board and documentation. The tradeoff to the mimic layout is that the spatial arrangement of the indicators and controls is not intuitive if operators are not familiar with the mimic's layout. During normal operations, most of the activity is concentrated on the right half of the board. The left half represents I&C for boric acid recovery, boration, and dilution. The indicators and controls on the board with green and red labels are safety related.

**Description of Digital HMI.** The digital HMI implementation consists of two large overview displays placed throughout on the vertical sections of the control boards to provide at a glance monitoring of plant subsystems and overall plant status. The large displays are intended be visible from across the control room. Below the large overview displays are four touch panel displays for reactor operators to interact with the CVCS. The remaining instrumentation was envisioned as a hybrid of analog and digital indicators and controls. The safety-related I&C along with a few additional non-safety-related I&C were relocated to the apron section of the panel. The layout of the controls was organized in the form of process mimic to maintain the positive aspects of the mimic organization while capitalizing on training carry-over from operator experience with the conventional board.

The left overview is for monitoring CVCS. The overview is organized as a piping and instrumentation diagram (P&ID) and is intended for monitoring during normal and abnormal operating conditions. The right overview is for monitoring Reactor Coolant System (RCS) coolant inventory. The RCS coolant inventory overview allows operators to monitor the reactor status, steam generator levels, RCS loop temperatures, and the pressurizer. The RCS and CVCS are tightly coupled. Pressurizer level is controlled through CVCS letdown, and the CVCS provides make-up for small RCS coolant losses. The RCS board resides to the right of.

Below the large overview displays are four touch panel displays. No other input such as keyboard, trackpad or mouse was provided. Therefore, all control functionality was implemented such that it could be performed using a touch interface. Buttons on the display were made substantially taller compared to an interface designed for cursor input. For numeric entry an onscreen numeric keypad was presented. The touch displays allowed operators to monitor and control sub-systems and components of the

CVCS such as seal-injection, boration, dilution, and automatic makeup. For the study, digital HMI screens and controls needed for the test scenario were developed. These included screens for monitoring seal injection and makeup and screens for controlling letdown flow, temperature, and back pressure as well as charging pressure.

The physical size of the displays was taken into consideration when laying out the content for the screens. Because the overview displays are roughly twice the height and width of the smaller displays, it is possible to have four times the amount of legible content on the overview screens.

All the HMI screens were implemented in a style known as dullscreen. With the dullscreen concept the screens appear monochromatic when the annunciators and instruments are within normal operating ranges, allowing high-contrast and salient color indications to grab the operators attention should something unexpected or noteworthy happen. The conventional approach to designing HMI screens identifies the minimum allowable size for text and other graphical elements and then "consistently" uses these minimum allowable sizes throughout the entire interface to maintain legibility. The downside is that everything is equally illegible. By employing graphic design and visual perception principles to the design, information can be hierarchically prioritized, and more pertinent information can be made more salient and legible to distant observers. Graphic design has long known that slight variations of font size, font weight, white-space, and typeface, and kerning can produce drastic differences in how information is perceived [8]. Graphic design is the art of manipulating these variations to produce a design that conveys the intended message. The science of visual perception excels at understanding the basic principles of contrast perception, text legibility, saliency, but is lacking when it comes to understanding how multiple nuanced elements to produce the gestalt, the whole perception of the features.

**Description of COSS.** Among the numerous goals of the workshop, we sought to evaluate how operators used the conventional boards, compared to the hybrid boards with the digital HMI described above, to an advanced concept digital HMI known as a The COSS builds on the digital HMI by conceiving additional control technologies and user interactions. The COSS implemented Type 2 computer based procedure (CBP) system that provided real-time variable status embedded in the procedure and guidance for selection the appropriate path (see Fig. 2).

The COSS also behaved as if it had an underlying prognostic diagnosis system known as PRO-AID developed by Argonne National Laboratory. PRO-AID is capable of determining system faults such as leaks and blockages from available sensor data. The spatial sensitivity of the diagnosis is dependent on the richness of the available instruments. One of the unique features of PRO-AID is that it only requires defining the system at the P&ID level. The PRO-AID system then trains from steady-state data to be able to recognize faults. This is significantly more feasible than having to develop a first principles model representation of the system.

Fault detections from PRO-AID are conveyed to operators through the HMI screens using a highly salient and distinct yellow-green color. The CVCS overview is organized as a P&ID to support conveying fault diagnostics from PRO-AID. The fault diagnostics require highlighting sections of piping and components to show operators

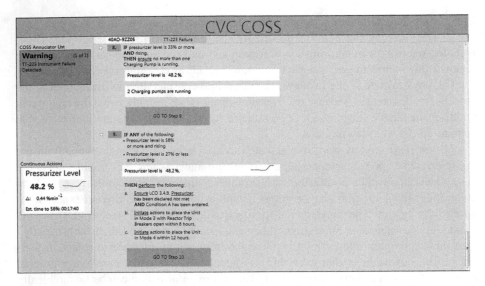

**Fig. 2.** The COSS features a type 2 computer based procedure, a fault diagnosis system and continuous monitoring of important plant variables. The purple lines are auto-scaling trends. (Color figure online)

the location of a detected fault. The COSS would then diagnose and alert operators to the problem. The CBP was used to guide operators down the appropriate course of action.

**Fault Description.** During normal operation some of the high-pressure RCS coolant is diverted the CVCS. The flow that is diverted and reduced in pressure through the letdown path. Then the flow passes through demineralization tanks and into a volume control tank (VCT). The VCT supplies coolant to charging pumps that increase the pressure so that coolant can be pushed back into the RCS. The fault scenarios caused letdown flow to become isolated or stop. In all scenarios, the letdown isolation event was produced by an instrumentation and control malfunction but the exact cause varied slightly to keep the operators from becoming complacent with the scenarios.

With the conventional boards, the letdown isolation resulted from a setpoint failure of a temperature controller that varies shell side component cooling water (CCW) flow to maintain the temperature of the letdown flow. The setpoint fails high with a ramp of 100 s which causes the CCW flow to increase briefly before closing to its minimum value of 20%. The reduced cooling flow through the letdown heat exchanger results in the letdown flow temperature increasing. A temperature interlock linked to a temperature controller downstream of the letdown heat exchanger was then triggered to close to prevent melting the resin in the demineralizers.

With the digital HMI and COSS conditions the letdown isolation is caused by a failure a temperature sensor failing high, then jumping around for a few seconds, then failing low. The COSS implementation also conveyed the fault diagnosis on the CVCS Overview (see Fig. 3). The cascade of events is the same as previously described.

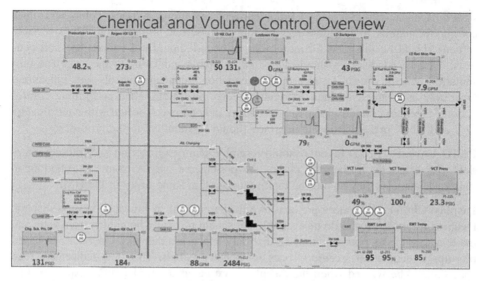

**Fig. 3.** CVCS large overview display post fault condition resulting in letdown flow becoming isolated. The large overview was implemented with a dullscreen concept that increases the saliency of the alarms. (Color figure online)

## 4   Results

Licensed reactor operators are a rare and expensive commodity when it comes to conducting human factors studies. As a consequence traditional quantitative performance measures are of limited validity due to sample size constraints. Here we relied on qualitative methods to elicit and capture operator feedback. Following each scenario an independent human factors consultant with 30+ years of experience in nuclear human factors engineering led a semi-structured discussion. The format presented the operators with the same set of questions for each condition. The semi-structured format allowed for additional follow-up questions and discussion. During discussion several human factors practitioners took notes. After the workshop these notes were compiled and several themes emerged with content relating to: layout, controls, automation, and COSS functionality. The high-level points pertaining to the CVCS COSS are summarized below.

### 4.1   HMI Layout and Style

**Hierarchical Organization.** Operators expressed preference for hierarchical organization with task based displays. The displays should normally be dedicated to a single screen or set of screens belonging to a single subsystem even if it is possible to bring up a screen from any subsystem. It was recommended that the overview displays be as large as possible to permit the information on the display(s) to be readable from a distance. The overview screens should provide a holistic and rapid depiction of the system. Operators prefer use of graphical representations, mimics, colors and other coding techniques to facilitate recognition of important information. The overview screens should be intended for monitoring only and should not contain any soft controls. Task based displays should tailor the available indicators to the task. The presentation scheme needs to clearly differentiation between controls and indicators. Operators are trained to look for confirmatory indications after performing control actions. Operators would like to have feedback indicators co-located with controls. The *tags* and labels presented in the interface should be identical to the procedures.

**P&ID Layouts.** P&ID layouts should resemble plant engineering and training materials. For example, if charging pumps are presented C, B, A from top-to-bottom in training materials, they should be represented in that same order in the HMI.

**Display Clutter.** Operators are sensitive to the amount of information on a display. Detailed information should be available but should normally be hidden from view and made accessible as pop-up windows that only appear on demand. Operators preferred pop-ups to dedicating *faceplate* space for detailed panels. They felt dedicated screen space would be wasted when the faceplates are being used. Operators expressed that the use of trends should be carefully considered. In the correct context the trend indicators provide valuable information permitting operators to better to predict future states. But, too many trends can be overwhelming and could lead to what the operators called "death by information." Operators had mixed feelings regarding auto-scaling Tufte styled very small line charts (sparklines [9]). Some operators expressed that they wish they could set the axis limits.

**Use of Color.** The study found operators strongly disliked the dullscreen implementation of the HMI in which the use of color is reserved exclusively to convey only important information. Operators strongly preferred the traditional red and green valve status indicators, even when compared to high contrast monochromatic indicators within the dullscreen implementation. The interface incorporated black and purple trend lines to distinguish multiple axes. The operators thought that more contrast was needed between the two colors.

### 4.2   Controls

**Maintaining Hard Controls.** Operators thought it was important to keep hard controls (analog buttons, dials, switches, etc.) for critical and time sensitive actions such as tripping a turbine or scramming the reactor.

**Soft Control Accidental Activation.** Operators expressed anxiety about soft control buttons being accidently being clicked because of user error or spurious touch panel input. Operators suggested that certain control actions need to have confirmation dialogs to prevent control actions from taking place from accidental input. Operators even suggested that buttons should remove focus to avoid being accidentally triggered and that the cursor should automatically move away from clickable button if it is left on top of a button for a set period of time.

**Touchscreen Reliability/Secondary Input Device.** Operators were concerned that a touchscreen failure could interfere with operations and suggested that a backup input device such as trackpad should be provided. In the event of a screen failure it should be possible to quickly and easily reconfigure what is shown on the displays. Operators also noted that they can use the mouse pointer to indicate what they are looking at on the screen to support peer checking.

Some operators are shorter, making it difficult for them to operate touchscreens. A trackpad on the apron would provide an ergonomic solution for these operators.

**Ergonomic Considerations.** Standing workstations present ergonomic considerations to maintain touchpanels in the reach envelope of 5th percentile females to 95th percentile males by stature. In accordance with NUREG-0700 the font on the displays need to maintain at least 16 min of arc across individuals [10].

## 4.3 COSS Functionality

**Computer Based Procedure.** They liked the capability to show plant data linked to a procedure step (decision aiding automation), which is defined as a Type 2 CBP system. They did not want the CBP system to take actions automatically to control the process (defined as a Type 3 CBP system) without their permission. They commented that the CBP system decision aiding automation was very useful, but suggested that problem diagnosis decision aiding also would be very helpful. They said that this capability should permit early identification of a developing problem and permit them to take earlier actions to mitigate the developing problem.

The CBP guided operators through procedures by highlighting the current step, as well as providing plant variable values within the procedure step itself. The COSS also provides contextual information within the procedure steps. Specifically, the COSS displays trend information within the procedure step to provide historical information about the relevant variable so that operators can assess abnormal fluctuations. Both crews noted the significant improvement with this integrated information.

Operators wanted the ability to be able to look ahead in the procedure. They also wanted the current step to be more apparent by being stylized differently.

An ad-hoc scenario variation where the reactor operators were using CBPs at the control boards versus at the senior reactor operator (SRO) workstation revealed operators might respond more quickly when CBPs are available at the board, but operators reported concern with a keyhole effect where they are inclined to focus too much on the CBP. A suggestion was that the SRO should have the ability to monitor their progression through the procedure from their workstation so that the SRO can maintain broad situational awareness of the plant and the information that the ROs are actively viewing.

**PRO-AID Fault Detection.** The plants current instrumentation may not be sufficient for increased levels of automation or for diagnostic systems like PRO-AID. Plants may need to consider upgrading instrumentation to realize automation benefits.

Operators emphasized the importance of the interface to provide a transparent view of PRO-AID systems functioning so operators can validate the diagnostics and build trust in the system. The PRO-AID fault diagnosis system monitors sensors to detect faults and determines faults using logic that operators might use.

## 5    Conclusions and Discussion

The operators who participated in this study lacked familiarity with modern DCS capabilities and digital HMI concepts and functionality. We must remember most nuclear control rooms were originally designed and implemented several decades ago. The nuclear industry has an aging workforce. Control system upgrades are being implemented with more recent technology. In comparison to decades past, there are many cases were control automation can handle tasks at least as reliably as human operators. When control automation is adopted the role of operators shifts from continuously manipulating controls to monitoring and anticipating the automated system. In some circumstances this may be a philosophical departure from current operations. In particular, the COSS implemented higher levels of automation than operators were accustomed to, but operators expressed a desire for this automation after sufficient familiarity was attained and if sufficient reliability could be established. The information obtain from the evaluations will be incorporated into the CVCS-COSS and evaluated with licensed crews. The roadmap from prototype to actual control technology is long and arduous but we hope our operator centric design approach influence control room modernization in the short-term and lead to next-generation advanced control systems in the long-term. The PRO-AID fault diagnostic system plays an important role in making COSS technologically feasible, though there is still work to be done in regard to the underlying technology that would drive an actual COSS implementation. Our work here lays the design concept groundwork for how to integrate these technological systems once they mature.

## 6    Disclaimer

This work of authorship was prepared as an account of work sponsored by an agency of the United States Government. Neither the United States Government, nor any agency thereof, nor any of their employees makes any warranty, express or implied, or assumes any legal liability or responsibility for the accuracy, completeness, or usefulness of any information, apparatus, product, or process disclosed, or represents that its use would not infringe privately-owned rights. Idaho National Laboratory is a multi-program laboratory operated by Battelle Energy Alliance LLC, for the United States Department of Energy.

## References

1. Kovesdi, C.R., Joe, J.C., Boring, R.L.: Migration of Older to New Digital Controls Systems in Nuclear Power Plant Main Control Rooms, INL/EXT-16-38576. Idaho National Laboratory, Idaho Falls (2016)

2. Thomas, K.D.: First-of-a-Kind Control Room Modernization Project Plan. INL/EXT-16-38026. Idaho National Laboratory, Idaho Falls (2016)
3. DOE-NE: Nuclear Energy Enabling Technology (2017). https://energy.gov/ne/nuclear-reactor-technologies/nuclear-energy-enabling-technologies
4. Boring, R.L., Thomas, K.D., Ulrich, T.A., Lew, R.T.: Computerized operator support systems to aid decision making in nuclear power plants. Procedia Manuf. **3**, 5261–5268 (2015)
5. Thomas, K.D.: Crossing the digital divide. Power **155**(11), 81–84 (2011)
6. Brown, T.: Change by Design: How Design Thinking Transforms Organizations and Inspires Innovation. Harper Collins, New York (2009)
7. Boring, R., Agarwal, V., Fitzgerald, K., Hugo, J., Hallbert, B.: Digital Full-Scope Simulation of a Conventional Nuclear Power Plant Control Room, Phase 2: Installation of a Reconfigurable Simulator to Support Nuclear Plant Sustainability, INL/EXT-13-28432. Idaho National Laboratory, Idaho Falls (2013)
8. Saltz, I.: Typography Essentials: 100 Design Principles for Working with Type (Design Essentials). Rockport Publishers, Beverly (2011)
9. Tufte, E.: The Visual Display of Quantitative Information. Quoted in "ET Work on Sparklines" (1983). http://www.edwardtufte.com/bboard/q-and-a-fetch-msg?msg_id=000AI
10. U.S. Nuclear Regulatory Commission: Human-System Interface Design Review Guidelines, NUREG-0700, Revision 2 (2002)

# Understanding the Success of Pokémon Go: Impact of Immersion on Players' Continuance Intention

Lili Liu[1,2(✉)], Christian Wagner[2], and Ayoung Suh[2]

[1] College of Economics and Management, Nanjing University of Aeronautics
and Astronautics, Nanjing, China
[2] School of Creative Media and Department of Information Systems,
City University of Hong Kong, Hong Kong, Hong Kong SAR
{llili2, c.wagner, ahysuh}@cityu.edu.hk

**Abstract.** Pokémon Go (PG) is one of the most successful mobile games in recent history. The uniqueness of PG appears to be its combination of augmented reality (AR) and location-based gaming. In the game, players use a mobile device's positioning capability to locate, capture, and battle the in-game creatures (called Pokémon), which are blended into the real environment and visible there through the mobile screen. The game accrued over 550 million installs in its first 80 days since launch, but player interest faded fast. PG had lost at least a third of its daily users by the middle of August 2016. So far, little is known why players continue or discontinue play. Understanding this will be vital to the future success of PG. Extant explanations of player participation in games focus predominantly on the impact of immersion. It appears that PG offers possibilities for creating various immersive experiences, which sustain players' continuance intention. However, the construct of immersion has yet to be well established and the role of immersion in the AR context remains unclear. To fill these gaps in research, this study seeks to investigate different immersive experiences and their impacts on a player's continuance intention. The paper reports on the result of a qualitative survey with 92 Pokémon players, and affirms that sensory immersion, spatial immersion, tactical immersion, strategic immersion, narrative immersion, and social immersion are key determinants of players' continuance intention. Theoretical and practical implications are discussed.

**Keywords:** Pokémon Go · Sensory immersion · Spatial immersion · Tactical immersion · Strategic immersion · Narrative immersion · Social immersion · Continuance intention

## 1 Introduction

Pokémon Go (PG), a location-based augmented reality (AR) mobile game, has become one of the most successful games in recent history. The user appeal of PG became visible immediately after launch. For example, it gained over 20 million active daily users (who use it for longer periods than Facebook, Twitter, and Snapchat combined) within two weeks [9]. Besides, PG accrued more than 550 million installs in its first 80 days [13]. Interestingly enough, many components of PG are not new. Foursquares and

© Springer International Publishing AG 2017
D.D. Schmorrow and C.M. Fidopiastis (Eds.): AC 2017, Part II, LNAI 10285, pp. 514–523, 2017.
DOI: 10.1007/978-3-319-58625-0_37

Geocaching, for instance, introduced the element of location-based gaming, while AR games have been around for more than a decade [12]. The uniqueness of PG appears to be its combination of Augmented Reality (AR) with location-based gaming. In the game, players use a mobile device's positioning capability to locate, capture, and battle the in-game creatures (called Pokémon), which are blended into the real environment and visible there through the mobile screen.

PG requires players to be physically active in order to play the game, by navigating in real world settings [4]. Prior studies indicate that sustained and regular play of PG positively affects human well-being. More specifically, regular players of PG may make significant adjustments to their daily routines and to the amount of time spent outside, which improves their physical and cognitive well-being [2], mental health [11], and social interactions with other players [17]. However, players' interest in PG fades fast. PG had lost at least a third of its daily users by the middle of August 2016 [9]. Nevertheless, millions were still playing the game and making in-app purchases four months after the game was released [5]. In order to maintain the long-term success of PG, it is crucial to understand why players continue playing PG. Yet little is known about the determinants of players' continuance intention after early experiences.

Extant explanations of player participation in games focus predominantly on the impact of immersion. Combing AR and location-based gaming, PG appears to define a new genre in games, which offers possibilities for creating various immersive experiences that retain players' continuance intention. However, the construct of immersion has yet to be well established and the role of immersion in the AR context remains unclear. The purpose of this research is, therefore, to investigate different immersive experiences players have perceived, and their impacts on players' continuance intention. In light of prior studies on game immersion, we first elaborated on the construct of immersion by identifying its six sub-dimensions: sensory immersion, spatial immersion, tactical immersion, strategic immersion, narrative immersion, and social immersion [1, 3, 7, 10]. Next, we conducted a qualitative study to verify the existence of the above-mentioned six immersive experiences and their impact on players' continuance intention. This study contributes to the theoretical understanding on the immersive experiences occurring in AR games. The findings may also aid developers in their efforts to sustain AR games or other AR applications through enhanced immersive experiences.

This paper consists of six sections. In next section, we explore PG as a game, describing its features. We then discuss the theoretical background, the categorization and definitions of immersive experiences, followed by methods, results, theoretical and practical implications, and finally limitations and future research are discussed.

## 2   Background

### 2.1   Pokémon Go

Pokémon Go is a free-to-pay, location-based AR mobile game that encourages players to play and travel simultaneously between real world and virtual environments [15]. It uses real-world locations for users to navigate and explore in order to play the game. PG is a casual game, with low barriers to entry and the ability to play meaningfully within minutes. In the game, players search for virtual characters called 'Pokémon', typically in outside public places. PG is collaborative. Players can help each other to become more successful, both in identifying Pokémon and in luring them to be caught. PG has a complete set of gamification elements, including points, levels, badges, a market for resources, and the ability to purchase resources with real or virtual currency. In order to level up, the players need to visit as many places as possible to capture more virtual monsters and earn more game points.

While virtual collecting and battling games have existed for around 30 years, PG is the first mobile game that largely involves players' physical movement. The player's gameplay in the real world is as important as virtual game activity. Players need to use real-world locations displayed by the game to search information about the locations of Pokémon. Players also need to navigate throughout their physical environment (i.e., their hometown), explore new areas, and visit specific sites to play successfully. This differentiates PG from traditional video and online games, which were typically screen-bound. PG is the first mobile game that represents a new integrative genre, where the virtual, the spatial, the social, and the physical are fully transcended [8]. However, the novelty effect of PG has not sustained player attention, leading to a significant drop in participation levels over time. This phenomenon raises interesting and challenging questions for how to maintain players' continuance participation in PG.

## 2.2 Immersive Experiences

The use of AR in games has repeatedly been proven to increase users' immersive experiences [e.g., 14, 19]. Although immersion is commonly described as the overall cognitive experience that players have while playing a digital game (Brown and Cairns), there have been attempts to define immersion as a multi-dimensional construct. Given that distinct designs of games generate different types of immersion, researchers have recognized the need to elaborate on the construct of immersion by characterizing its dimensional attributes. Through the extensive literature review, we identify six different immersion dimensions: sensory, spatial, tactical, strategic, narrative, and social [1, 3, 7, 10]. PG offers the opportunities for all of these types of immersive experiences to occur. For example, players of PG have a first-person perspective on the displayed virtual world and real world. Therefore, PG offers the opportunity for sensory immersion, and arguably also a high degree of spatial immersion. PG, as a massively multi-player online game, promotes face-to-face interaction among players thus providing a considerable level of social immersion. Players appear to experience these different types of immersion while playing PG. However, little research has systematically examined how different types of immersion influence players' continuance intention. Therefore, more nuanced understanding on immersive experiences in game playing becomes vital. The categorization and definitions of immersive are discussed as follows.

**Sensory immersion** relates to the audio/visual execution of games [10]. This dimension of immersion is easily recognizable as it can be intensified through intensifying its components, such as creating more compelling graphics or interacting on a larger screen or with a directional sound system. For example, large screens close to users' faces combined with strong, directional sounds easily overpower the sensory information from the real world, leading the user to focus entirely on the augmented reality supported environment and its stimuli.

**Spatial immersion** occurs when a user feels the synthetic world is perceptually convincing, that he or she is really"there (in the game world)", and that the game world looks and feels "real" (Arsenault).

**Tactical immersion** is the moment-by-moment immersion in the act of playing the game [1, 10]. It corresponds in part to the challenge factor and wholly to the control factor of the game system. Tactical immersion is experienced for instance when performing tactile operations that involve skill. When players want to continue the experience to become more skilled in using input devices to achieve better results, they are tactically immersed.

**Strategic immersion** is experienced in the encounter of mental challenges, or the need to think carefully and act intelligently [1, 10]. The strategic immersion can be caused by intellectual engagement in mental skills such as strategic thinking or logical problem solving. Tactical immersion and strategic immersion are highly correlated and can be summarized as challenge-based immersion. This is the feeling of immersion that is at its most powerful when a player is able to achieve a satisfying balance of challenges and abilities. Challenges can be related to motor skills or mental skills, but usually involve both to some degree.

**Narrative immersion** occurs when players become invested in the story of the game world [1]. It is similar to what is experienced while reading a book or watching a movie. The desire to know how the story will unfold may create curiosity, suspense and excitement, and thus makes the player want to continue the activity, which thus results in narrative immersion. Using a range of narrative tools such as cues, exciting characters, interesting events, or developing story-arc, can make a player want to continue and thus cause this form of immersion.

**Social immersion** causes are correlated with interaction with others, both in the virtual world and the real world. Social immersion occurs as an outcome when a player desires to keep playing the game with others and returns to the game world in order to feel connected with them. Examples of PG attributes that induce social immersion can include collaborative quests, challenges and puzzles, which may only be solvable together with others.

Best practices of designing a successful and sustainable game may not depend on producing a single immersion but rather a blending of different immersions. Alternatively, the lack of one immersive dimension may lead to an overall inferior experience that undermines enjoyment and thus hampers continuance participation. The research will therefore aim to provide empirical evidence to inform theory plus a set of instructional patterns and design principles for game designers.

# 3 Methodology

This study followed a qualitative approach. The data was collect on Feb 23, 2017 by using an online survey on Amazon Mechanical Turk. The survey was in English language and meant for international audience. Before the survey was launched, it was pre-tested with five long-terms players (who have played PG for at least one month), based on which few modifications were made. This study intended to investigate the impact of immersion on players' continuance intention to participate in PG over time, thus only those players who had played PG for relatively long time were selected as valid respondents. After making basic inquiries as to demographics, the survey contained a series of open-ended questions targeted at affirming the existence of different immersive experiences and their impacts on players' continuance intention to participate in PG. More specifically, we asked six open-ended questions regarding the sensory, spatial, tactical, strategic, narrative, and social immersions respectively.

1. Sensory immersion: Please tell us whether you kept playing PG because you like the visual/audio design. (Yes/No, please add explanations for your answer)
2. Spatial immersion: Please tell us whether you kept playing PG because the world in the game looks and feels "real", and you could feel that you are really part of the game world. (Yes/No, please add explanations for your answer)
3. Tactical immersion: Please tell us whether you kept playing PG because you like to develop your gaming skills. (Yes/No, please add explanations for your answer)
4. Strategic immersion: Please tell us whether you kept playing PG because you like the mental challenges you encountered, challenges that require you to think carefully and act intelligently. (Yes/No, please add explanations for your answer)
5. Narrative immersion: Please tell us whether you kept playing PG because you like the storyline (e.g., the story of training/evolving Pokémon) within the game. (Yes/No, please add explanations for your answer)
6. Social immersion: Please tell us whether you kept playing PG because you like the interaction with other players. (Yes/No, please add explanations for your answer)

The qualitative method is helpful to obtain in-depth information concerning the formulation of immersive experiences and their perceived relatedness, hence suitable to be adopted at the preliminary stage of a research topic [18]. All participants had self-reported long-term experiences in playing PG. In total, the survey received 92 valid responses. The detailed demographic information is presented in Table 1.

**Table 1.** Participants' demographic information

| Category | | Number | Percentage |
|---|---|---|---|
| Gender | Male | 57 | 61.96% |
| | Female | 35 | 38.04% |
| Age | 18–20 years old | 3 | 3.26% |
| | 21–25 years old | 35 | 38.04% |
| | 26–30 years old | 30 | 32.61% |
| | 31–35 years old | 13 | 14.13% |
| | 36–40 years old | 4 | 4.35% |
| | 41–50 years old | 5 | 5.43% |
| | Over 50 years old | 2 | 2.17% |
| Education | High school or below | 15 | 16.30% |
| | College | 37 | 40.22% |
| | University | 24 | 26.09% |
| | Graduate school or above | 16 | 17.39% |

# 4   Results

We summarized the nomination frequencies and explanations (quotations from respondents) for each immersive experience in Table 2. Respondents reported immersive experiences at differing frequencies. Taking sensory immersion as an example, 81 out of 92 respondents (88%) reported that they had perceived sensory immersion, which was the reason that kept them continue playing PG. Reasons for their confirmation on sensory immersion included: "The splash screen and map are attractively put together and the sounds are decent"; "The Pokémon were adorable"; and "Everything was well designed and visually pleasing". On the contrary, 11 players (12%) reported that they had not perceived sensory immersion. Explanations for their disconfirmation on sensory immersion contained: "I didn't care about those; I just wanted to catch Pokémon"; "I always turned off the AR"; and "I had it mute".

**Table 2.** Summary of confirmations and explanations for each immersive experience

| Immersive experiences | Number of yes | Percentage of yes | Reasons for confirmations | Number of no | Percentage of no | Reasons for confirmations |
|---|---|---|---|---|---|---|
| Sensory immersion | 81 | 88.04% | "The splash screen and map are attractively put together and the sounds are decent." "The Pokémon were adorable!" "Everything was well designed and visually pleasing" | 11 | 11.96% | "I didn't care about those; I just wanted to catch Pokémon." "I always turned off the AR " "I had it mute" |
| Spatial immersion | 66 | 71.74% | "It felt real and like the Pokémon were in front of me." "I found it hard to discern items in the game from the real world. For instance upon finding a pikachu he appeared to be on a chair, almost perfectly aligned." "The location based aspect really brought it to life" | 26 | 28.26% | "You were still looking through your phone." "It does not feel real to me" |
| Tactical immersion | 39 | 42.39% | "It made me better at throwing curve balls." "I enjoyed fighting in the local gyms and trying to hold onto the top spot" | 53 | 57.61% | "I don't see how that would develop gaming skills. It is not hard to play, a few swipes and that's that." "Does not take skill to play it at all." "I didn't care much about development of skills; I just enjoyed catching them all" |

(*continued*)

**Table 2.** (*continued*)

| Immersive experiences | Number of yes | Percentage of yes | Reasons for confirmations | Number of no | Percentage of no | Reasons for confirmations |
|---|---|---|---|---|---|---|
| Strategic immersion | 34 | 36.96% | "Planning how to catch and where gets me thinking and wondering." "There's a lot of thought to type advantages and the balance of types to put in your primary fighting team." "In Gyms you need to use type advantages in order to ensure victory." "Hunting for different Pokémon with different strategies" | 58 | 63.04% | "The game was too easy." "It didn't really trigger any mental challenges." "It's not challenging" |
| Narrative immersion | 47 | 51.09% | "Catching and leveling them up was the best part." "The story is quite interesting." "That's what's drawn me to the series in general." "I liked the storyline; it improves the fun part" | 45 | 48.91% | "There wasn't really a story line in the game. "There is no storyline. Just repetitive capture and challenging gyms." "What storyline? I would not count catching and evolving Pokémon a storyline. More like a mechanic" |
| Social immersion | 64 | 69.57% | "I could play with friends." "I enjoyed going to new places and talking to people I normally would have ignored." "I liked the interaction with many players because it made me feel part of a community." "Group playing is interestin" | 28 | 30.43% | "I barely interacted. Play alone mostly." "I was in a sparsely populated area and there were not that many other players to interact with." "There was not much interaction with others. The only thing you could do is battle a gym" |

Figure 1 displayed the nomination frequencies for various combinations of immersive experiences. For example, 15 out of 92 players (16.30%) confirmed that they had perceived two immersive experiences, while 13 out of 92 players (14.13%) had perceived five immersive experiences. Besides, 14 participants reported that they had experienced all the six immersions (sensory, spatial, tactical, strategic, narrative, and social), while surprisingly one player suggested that he/she had not perceived any immersive experience at all.

The non-zero responses for all immersion types provide justification for the six immersive experiences we identified from literature. They also suggest that different types of immersion were operating at different levels. Overall we observed one type of

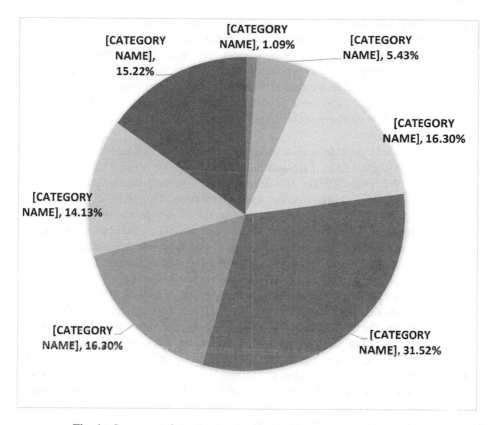

**Fig. 1.** Summary of nomination frequencies for various combinations

very strong immersion (sensory), two types of strong immersion (spatial, social), and three types of weak immersion (tactical, strategic, narrative). Sensory immersion was strongest, whereas narrative, tactical, and strategic immersion were weakest. The differences between the different levels of immersion were statistically significant based on Chi-square tests (x = 7.61, p = .01; x = 6.56, p = .01). Our findings further indicate that majority of respondents (93.48%) have experienced multiple immersions rather than a single immersion, which supported our statement that different immersions are not isolated from each other. Therefore, in order to design a successful game, practitioners should make effort to produce a blending of different immersions.

## 5  Discussion

The purpose of this study was to provide insights into the sustainability of PG, with special focus on the impact of immersion on players' continuance intention. In doing so, we firstly elaborate on the construct of immersion by identifying its sub-dimensions, and then verify the categorization and impact of different type of immersion on players' continuance intention to play PG based on a qualitative study. Our preliminary results suggest that PG users are affected by immersive experiences during game play, but not at equal levels. Sensory immersion dominated the immersive experiences, whereas the game story and the tasks were considered less immersive. The different immersion levels, put in relation to PG's popularity development raise the question whether sensory immersion is the factor that arouses user interest to initiate game play, with game realism and social experience sustaining game play for a while. However that a lack of meaningful story elements with challenging tasks will relatively soon lead to a decline in user interest.

The present study provides valuable first insights into the immersive experiences in location-based AR game (e.g., PG), and thus, extends our knowledge on immersion in game studies. We introduce six sub-dimensions of immersion, including sensory, spatial, tactical, strategic, narrative, and social immersion. This study also adds useful knowledge that assist the developers and managers of AR games in their efforts to provide the players with meaningful and positive immersions, which facilitates players' continuance participation. The recent changes to PG, with the introduction of more character movements, and more elaborate scoring mechanisms, seem to suggest that PG developers try to extend the tactical and strategic immersion experience within PG, thus trying to sustain player interest longer than before.

This study has few notable limitations. For example, although providing important insights regarding the sustainability of PG, the study did not investigate the actual effects of sensory, spatial, tactical, strategic, narrative, and social immersion on players' continuance intention. A more detailed empirical study will be useful to reveal the nuanced impact of above-mentioned six immersive experiences on players' continuance intention. Furthermore, this study has only scratched the surface of investigating immersion as a multi-dimensional construct, yet laid the groundwork for the possibility to design for immersion. Future study may generate better understanding of immersive experiences by manipulating them in an experiment.

# References

1. Adams, E.: Postmodernism and the three types of immersion. Gamasutra: Art Bus. Making Games 9 (2004)
2. Armanet, J.: Could Pokémon Go improve people's health? (2016). https://www.theguardian.com/healthcare-network/2016/jul/27/pokemon-go-improvehealth-walking. Accessed 28 Feb 2017
3. Arsenault, D.: Dark waters: spotlight on immersion. In: Proceedings Of the Game-On North America, pp. 50–52 (2005)
4. Baranowski, T.: Pokémon Go, go, go, gone? Games Health J. 5(5), 293–294 (2016)
5. BBC. Pokémon Go update seeks to revive interest (2016). http://www.bbc.com/news/technology-38291993. Accessed 28 Feb 2017
6. Brown, E., Cairns, P.: A grounded investigation of game immersion. In: Proceedings of CHI Extended Abstracts on Human Factors in Computing Systems, pp. 1297–1300. ACM (2004)
7. Cairns, P., Cox, A., Nordin, A.I.: Immersion in digital games: review of gaming experience research. In: Handbook of Digital Games, pp. 339–361 (2014)

8. Clark, A.M., Clark, M.T.: Pokémon Go and research qualitative, mixed methods research, and the supercomplexity of interventions. Int. J. Qual. Methods **15**(1), 1–3 (2016)
9. Digital Stat. Hot game: Amazing Pokémon Go statistics (2016). http://expandedramblings. com/index.php/pokemon-go-statistics/. Accessed 28 Feb 2017
10. Ermi, L., Mäyrä, F.: Fundamental components of the gameplay experience: analysing immersion. Worlds in Play: International Perspectives on Digital Games Research **37**(2), 37–53 (2005)
11. Fernando, G.: How Pokémon Go is helping people with social anxiety and depression (2016). http://www.news.com.au/technology/homeentertainment/gaming/how-pokemon-go-is-helpingpeople-with-social-anxiety-and-depression/newstory/bdf546cd7979d0c11480fcb-596e61538. Accessed 28 Feb 2017
12. Hoang, T., Baker, S.: Why Pokémon Go has been a viral success. Business Insider (2016). http://www.businessinsider.com.au/why-pokemon-gohas-been-a-viral-success-2016-7. Accessed 28 Feb 2017
13. Kari, T.: Pokémon GO 2016: exploring situational contexts of critical incidents in augmented reality. J. Virtual Worlds Res. **9**(3), 1–12 (2016)
14. Liu, L.L., Ip, R., Shum, A., Wagner, C.: Learning effects of virtual game worlds: an empirical investigation of immersion, enjoyment and performance. In: Proceedings of the Twentieth Americas Conference on Information Systems, Savannah, pp. 1–11 (2014)
15. Pokémon Go: Explore (2016). http://www.pokemongo.com/en-au/explore/. Accessed 28 Feb 2017
16. Sánchez, G., Vela, G., Simarro, F.M., Padilla-Zea, N.: Playability: analysing user experience in video games. Behav. Inf. Technol. **31**(10), 1033–1054 (2012)
17. Serino, M., Cordrey, K., McLaughlin, L., Milanaik, R.L.: Pokémon Go and augmented virtual reality games: a cautionary commentary for parents and pediatricians. Curr. Opin. Pediatr. **28**(5), 673–677 (2016)
18. Strauss, A., Corbin, J.: Basics of Qualitative, 2nd edn. SAGE Publications, Thousand Oaks (1998)
19. Wagner, C., Dibia, V.: Exploring the effectiveness of online role-play gaming in the acquisition of complex and tacit knowledge. Issues Inf. Syst. **14**(2), 367–374 (2013)

# Extempore Emergency Response Technique with Virtual Reality Gaming

Trinh Nguyen$^{(\boxtimes)}$ and Godwin Nyong$^{(\boxtimes)}$

University of Hawaii at Manoa, Honolulu, HI, USA
{trinhpp, godwinn}@hawaii.edu

**Abstract.** This paper provides an overview of Vietnam's technology penetration and the games industry, together with the social and cultural factors and issues, to propose the idea of integrating the gaming logic and attraction with Virtual Reality technology to improve Extempore Emergency Response Technique (EERT). The key research methodology is secondary research through journals, reports, statistics, as well as local news and updates. From the social perspective, Vietnam struggles to reduce the fatal consequences of increasing disasters and accidents in both rural and urban areas year by year. However, people's awareness of safety and appropriate emergency response remains minimal. From the technical perspective, this country is the global highlight with wide internet penetration, quick adoption of new technology, and being one of the biggest and fastest-growing markets for the games industry. The future development of smartphone games, especially VR games is expected to be tremendous in Vietnam, which facilitate various game design to combine with EERT training. Hence, implementing entertaining training solution would not only provide users with entertainment moments, but also uphold society's awareness of self-protection skills.

**Keywords:** Virtual reality · Augmented Reality · Vietnam · Games · Emergency response · Training

## 1 Introduction

This paper discusses the potential of integrating the gaming appeal into Virtual Reality training for Extempore Emergency Response Technique (EERT), a method that employs and utilize minimal investment of resource and equipment for maximal outcome on emergency response training.

VR application in emergency training is not a new concept. However, it limits the interest in formal and expensive trainings for limited audiences such as the military or firefighters. While the vast majority of civilians, typically in developing countries, are exposed to several disasters and accident as fire, earthquakes, flood, and stampede, there are limited training opportunities to this group. In particular, by November 2015, Vietnam had recorded 2694 cases of fire and explosion, 86 deaths with 283 people injured. It is also a country of widely available and low-cost internet, plus the significant growth of the gaming industry. Hence, applying advanced VR technology and gaming attraction to disaster response training is commercially potential in Vietnam as well as other countries.

© Springer International Publishing AG 2017
D.D. Schmorrow and C.M. Fidopiastis (Eds.): AC 2017, Part II, LNAI 10285, pp. 524–536, 2017.
DOI: 10.1007/978-3-319-58625-0_38

## 2  Key Findings

### 2.1  History of Virtual Reality in SBT (Simulation-Based Training)

The idea of virtual reality was seeded in the 1930s in a science fiction story by writer Stanley G. Weinbaum, which described a user experienced a fictional world through holographic, smell, taste, and touch by wearing goggles. The real beginning of VR started from 1965 with Ivan Sutherland's doctoral thesis which presented a concept that a computer hardware would be used to create a virtual world which user can realistically interact with that environment. The first VR/AR head mounted display that was connected to the computer was invented by Ivan and his student. However, the name "Virtual Reality" was only created in 1987 by Jaron Lanier, founder of the visual programming lab (VPL) [9] (Fig. 1).

 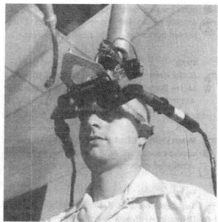

**Fig. 1.** VR head mounted display invented by Ivan Sutherland

The 21st century remarks with tremendous development of the VR technology, including investment of the leading technology names as Samsung Gear VR, Sony's PlayStation VR, HTC Vive, Google's Cardboard, Facebook Oculus Rift, and the Japanese's Fove [10] (Fig. 2).

### 2.2  Virtual Reality (VR) vs. Augmented Reality (AR)

Two most confused terms in the rising technology discussion topic are Virtual Reality (VR) and Augmented Reality (AR) both use the same coding language and similar technicality. However, VR creates a complete virtual world that users can interact with while AR blends the virtual contents and objects into the real world, which users can identify the differences. AR has achieved more commercial success than VR so far [3].

Two typical characteristics of VR is the ability to create presence and immersion. As creating a virtual world, it aims to make the user feel that he is actually present in

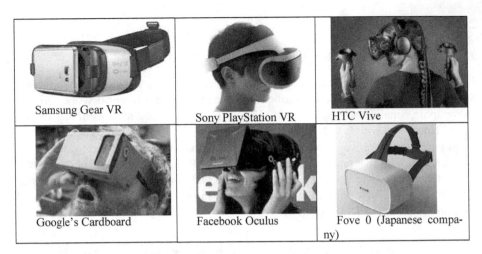

**Fig. 2.** Present popular VR headsets

the virtual environment though the level of immersion depends on the computer hardware, equipment, and the user's acceptance [12].

### 2.3   Application in Simulation Based Training (SBT)

VR application in simulation-based training is not a new idea since it has been adopted by the military for dangerous situations combat and aircraft training [21]. The eye-tracking technology is believed to evolve user interaction in the virtual environment [13], which facilitates trainings for individual or group response in disasters.

VR training systems can be monitored by human instructors or a computer-based simulator. Without the present of an experienced instructor, the simulator can correct the trainee to appropriate response to a situation [12]. In particular, a research to examine firefighters training results has demonstrated that the firefighters group trained with VR or blueprints before outperformed the control group (no training) in both time and accuracy [4]. If proper setting and implementation of virtual reality is applied broadly to simulation-based training, more lives can be saved from emergency situations.

## 3   Extempore Emergency Response Technique (EERT)

EERT advocates the use of regular readily available day to day household or body items as emergency supply to mitigate or resolve emergency situations; examples include cutting bed sheets to use as strips for bandages, using trash bag to collect water and socks as water filter can be the only option in certain emergency situations, or using ropes and water pipe to escape from a high floor fire. EERT can be a determining factor between life and death when there is a lack of availability of the necessary tools or resource in the case of an emergency or disaster. It encourages the minimalist approach to problem solving in the case of an emergency or disaster.

In Vietnam, the concept of EERT has only been noticed in the last few years when the number of death and injured people in preventable accidents considerably increases. The popular mean is via instructing articles, video clip or human training like in the picture below. However, the fundamental of emergency response technique is not only the knowledge that a person has, but also the calmness of that person in the situation. According to a local newspaper, both response knowledge and emotional reaction of Vietnamese in the emergency remains zero due to the lack of proper society attention on the matter and effective training approach [17] (Fig. 3).

**Fig. 3.** A police officer provides EERT in an apartment building [11].

The authors see an opportunity to replicate quick and efficient EERT in Vietnam to address the lack of sufficient emergency personnel both in the urban and rural areas. The cheap and wide coverage of internet and smartphone and the commercial success of gaming in Vietnam facilitate a new form of training EERT via the combination of VR technology and gaming logic.

## 3.1 Vietnam Review

There are various reasons why a developing country such as Vietnam would benefit from Virtual Reality as a training platform for Extempore Emergency Response

Technique (EERT). The first and obvious being cost saving since it advocates the use of the most basic equipment for life saving emergency situation.

## 3.2  Cultural Factor

Rebuilding the country after long period of war, Vietnam has chosen to sacrifice quality and healthy development to achieve huge capital investment which embraces the capitalists' exploitation of both urban and rural workers. According to the Ministry of Labor estimates, every year Vietnam lost around 2,500 people killed in workplace accidents. The whole country only has 496 labor inspectors in 2008 [16]. Accepting passive exposure to accident risks has become a common attitude of both Vietnam's regulators and people.

The high collectivism culture also hinders people to easily accept new thinking and behavior. One of the authors used to be laughed by her own friends for wearing the helmet while riding motorbike because people are not enforced by law to do that a few years ago. Similarly, there has been a social media debate when a girl escaping from a fire karaoke bar in Hanoi with her bra covering her nose in Sep 2016. Despite several praises that she was smart to properly respond in emergency, the majority criticized her for her "funny reaction" [6].

The close-minded perspective in self-protection requires an innovative approach to improving people's knowledge and attitude toward EERT, which technology development can provide (Fig. 4).

**Fig. 4.** Hanoi fire incident in a Karaoke bar

### 3.3   Social and Environmental Factor

Delay in emergency response and first aid care after an accident; coupled with the lack of readily available paramedic training is a growing concern in Vietnam.

By November 2015, Vietnam had recorded 2694 cases of fire and explosion, 86 deaths with 283 people injured. The total value of damage is estimated VND876 billion (US$38.6 Million) according to the general statistics office of Vietnam. One of the most recent fatal fire happened in Ho Chi Minh City killing three entire family members, as the family could not escape from three layers well-locked doors in their home [24]. This incident and the fatal outcome of the fire in Hanoi indicates the limitation of emergency response in Vietnam and the need to adequately address the situation void of cultural and social constraints.

Nevertheless, Vietnam is easily a buffet receipt for preventable accident and disaster. Per Viet Nam Emergency Response Plan, "at least one-third of Vietnam's 63 provinces are affected by El Niño-induced drought, with 18 provinces in the South Central, Central Highlands, and Mekong Delta regions severely affected", (Viet Nam: "Emergency Response Plan 2016/17", 2016). The continuous drought has threatened safe water supply for millions of people in these regions. However, drought is only one of several emergencies affecting Vietnam on a frequent basis, often leaving the local population without knowledge on how to respond and thus leading to medical emergencies.

Formal training in emergency response is relatively uncommon with most useful resources available only in foreign languages such as English and as such is difficult to understand by the local population. The issue with the inadequate distribution of resource and dissemination of information is also an impending factor. Website articles and television programs have been used; however, it has shown not to be attractive enough to generate enough interest amongst the population.

### 3.4   Vietnam – Wide, Cheap Yet Low-Quality Internet

Vietnam's internet quality is ranked below more than 100 other countries; however, it is the paradise for free and cheap Wi-Fi. The widely available internet is not only popular among cities, the rural areas also experience the strong growth of the internet and computing practices. In relatively low-income rural regions, locals who cannot afford their own computers can visit Internet Cafes with considerable numbers of computers [18] (Fig. 5).

In parallel with the internet, smartphone penetration is a tremendous trend in Vietnam. Among 48% population using the internet, half of them access the internet via their mobile devices [2]. Vietnam is also a quick adopter of technology. The availability of low-cost VR solutions such as Cardboard VR or Sky VR which costs VND200,000 (US$9) [21]. provide cost-effective tool for young people to experience VR. Affordable smartphone is now allowing VR-based training to reach everyone, whether with or without access to Internet Cafes or personal computer (Fig. 6).

**Fig. 5.** An internet-shift café in Vietnam

**Fig. 6.** Two university students design the "made in Vietnam" VR glasses

### 3.5    Vietnam – Ava Promising Game Market

Vietnam is one of the largest online game markets of value in Southeast Asia with sales of approximately $200 million in 2012 [19]. Particularly popular in Vietnam are virtual online games, which allow computer users to solve challenges in a virtual reality. With the recent increase in broadband adoption across Vietnam with 412% increase, Vietnam is clearly a fit for online knowledge dissemination [1].

Gaming also belongs to the top 3 interests among online activities according to Appota report 2015 and 2016. Casual games dominate gamers' taste, while various game types occupy their market share too (Fig. 7).

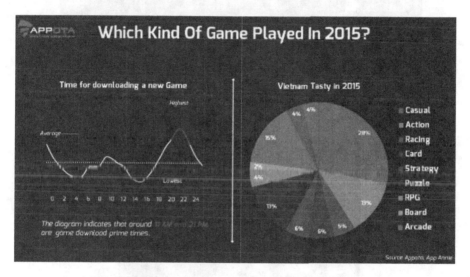

**Fig. 7.**  APPOTA report: games market share in Vietnam

Vietnamese youth are willing to experience new technology and gaming experience. Several types of services are available as special equipment in shopping malls and even a "hybrid" VR game which has a staff stand behind and help the consumer "experience" movement and effects while wearing the VR headset. This funny approach attracts many customers to their stores [15] (Figs. 8 and 9).

VR games do not always need to provide dramatic effects to be popular. The "Summer Lesson", one of the best-selling VR games in Japan is a typical example. The gamer will play the role of a tutor for a high school student during her summer break for one week. Yet this simple design effectively increases the immersive and memorable experience of the users. Bandai Namco, the game developer has initiated penetration of this game to Southeast Asia by providing English subtitles [22] (Fig. 10).

Bandai Namco's target in Southeast Asia indicates the importance of this region in the games industry. SEA is forecasted to lead the global industry growth by 13.1%. The Big6, which includes Vietnam accounts for 99% of the region's revenue. Vietnam, in

**Fig. 8.** A VR game area in a shopping mall

**Fig. 9.** The "hybrid" model which a person will create "physical effects" while the user experience VR headset.

**Fig. 10.** A scene from "The Summer Lesson" game

particular, is expected to witness the highest growth for smartphone games (Casual Games Association, 2017). It is indicative that any future activity will need to either compete or corporate with the time customers spend on game activities.

## 4    Can Gaming Logic Be Integrated to SBT to Make It More Interesting

Extempore Emergency Response Technique (EERT) advocates the use of the resources in the immediate environment and improvising accordingly for protection and safer outcome, much as the girl in the fire incident in Hanoi who used her bra against the fume of the fire.

Combining current technology infrastructure and the potential growth of Vietnam market, Virtual Reality can utilize virtual gaming for Extempore Emergency Response Technique (EERT) training. Such training could easily be duplicated implemented across internet cafes in Vietnam (Fig. 11).

The popularity and increasing awareness of The Summer Lesson VR game provides different ideas regarding a gaming approach to enhance people's awareness of EERT, either by immersing the user into a virtual disaster or simply coaching and saving a virtual character out of emergency. Although the lack of physical practice, frequent exposure to a situation will enhance outcome like the research on firefighters (Fig. 12).

**Fig. 11.** Tsunami response training with virtual reality

**Fig. 12.** Be a friend with the high-school girl and save her in dangerous situations?

# 5   Conclusion

As a developing country with low awareness of safety standard and emergency response technique, Vietnam suffers thousands of deaths and injuries caused by fire, work accidents, and other types of disaster every year. Limited solutions are available, including instructing radio and TV program, news and articles on the internet. However, these media contain several shortcomings, being uninteresting, theoretical, and lack of experience and practice just to name a few.

Given the development and penetration of the internet, smartphones, and other technology, the use of virtual reality gaming for Extempore Emergency Response Technique training presents an opportunity for training across various sectors of the economy. It would lead to the reduction of dependency and resource stretching at regular educational training institutions in the country. Implementing entertaining training solution would not only provide users with entertainment moments, but also uphold society's awareness of self-protection skills.

# References

1. Belson, D.: Akamai state of the Internet report. Q1, Technical report, Akamai, August 2011, p. 14 (2011)
2. Appota Corp.: Vietnam Mobile Market Report 2015, p. 5 (2011). http://www.slideshare.net/appota/vietnam-mobile-market-report-2015
3. Vamien, M.: Tech Times, Augmented Reality vs. Virtual Reality: What are the Differences and Similarities? (2014). http://www.techtimes.com/articles/5078/20140406/augmented-reality-vs-virtual-reality-what-are-the-differences-and-similarities.htm. Accessed 8 Feb 2017
4. Bliss, J., Tidwell, P., Guest, M.: The effectiveness of virtual reality for administering spatial navigation training to firefighters. Presence: Teleop. Virtual Environ. **6**(1), 73–86 (1997). doi:10.1162/pres.1997.6.1.73
5. Casual Games Association: Southeast Asia Games Market, New Zoo Games Market Report, pp. 2–12 (2017). https://cdn2.hubspot.net/hubfs/700740/Reports/Newzoo_Casual_Connect_South_East_Asia_Games_Market_Report.pdf
6. Trần, H.: Cô Gái Dung Áo Ngực Thoát Khỏi Đám Cháy Quán Karaoke 8 Tầng, VnExpress (2016). http://vnexpress.net/tin-tuc/cong-dong/anh/co-gai-dung-ao-nguc-thoat-khoi-dam-chay-quan-karaoke-8-tang-3470006.html. Accessed 30 Nov 2016
7. UN Vietnam: Details for Viet Nam: Emergency Response Plan 2016/17 (2016). http://www.un.org.vn/en/publications/publications-by-agency/doc_details/501-viet-nam-emergency-response-plan-201617.html?tmpl=component. Accessed 30 Nov 2016
8. General Statistics Office of Vietnam: Social and economic situation in eleven months of 2015 (2015). https://www.gso.gov.vn/default_en.aspx?tabid=622&ItemID=15482. Accessed 29 Nov 2016
9. Virtual Reality Society: History of Virtual Reality (2017). http://www.vrs.org.uk/virtual-reality/history.html. Accessed 6 Feb 2017
10. Lamkin, P.: The Best VR headsets: The Top Virtual Reality Devices To Go and Buy Now, Wareable (2017). https://www.wareable.com/headgear/the-best-ar-and-vr-headsets. Accessed 7 Feb 2017

11. Laptopaz.vn: Facebook (2015). https://www.facebook.com/laptopaz.vn/videos/491415374 353980. Accessed 10 Feb 2017

12. Louka, M.N., Balducelli, C.: Virtual reality tools for emergency operation support and training. In: Proceedings of TIEMS (The International Emergency Management Society), Oslo (2001)

13. Metz, R.: Startups are Building New Ways to Interact with Virtual Reality, MIT Technology Review (2017). https://www.technologyreview.com/s/543316/the-step-needed-to-make-virtual-reality-more-real/. Accessed 8 Feb 2017

14. Người Việt Dung Internet Nhiều Nhất Từ 20 - 24h. Ictnews.vn (2016). http://ictnews.vn/internet/nguoi-viet-dung-internet-nhieu-nhat-tu-20-24h-123850.ict. Accessed 30 Nov 2016

15. Online Games: Thiết Bị Chơi Game Thực Tế Ảo 'Chạy Bằng Cơm' Đinh Của Đinh. Gamek.vn (2017). http://gamek.vn/thiet-bi-choi-game-thuc-te-ao-chay-bang-com-dinh-cua-dinh-20170127015345461.chn. Accessed 10 Feb 2017

16. Rupasingha, W.: Rising work-related deaths and diseases in Vietnam, World Socialist Web Site. Wsws.org (2017). https://www.wsws.org/en/articles/2011/01/viet-j21.html. Accessed 10 Feb 2017

17. Nguyễn, D.: Sự Thật Kỹ Năng Thoát Hiểm Của Người Việt (2014). http://baodautu.vn/su-that-ky-nang-thoat-hiem-cua-nguoi-viet-d13848.html

18. Buu Dien: Vietnam Free Wi-Fi Paradise, VietNamNet (2015). http://english.vietnamnet.vn/fms/science-it/148843/vietnam—free-wi-fi-paradise.html

19. Victor, V.: Video Game Culture in Vietnam (2015). https://www.linkedin.com/pulse/video-game-culture-vietnam-victor-vautrin?trk=hp-feed-article-titleMinh. Accessed 30 Nov 2016

20. Trang: Virtual Reality Glasses: Now for the Masses, News VietNamNet (2016). http://english.vietnamnet.vn/fms/science-it/152262/virtual-reality-glasses–now-for-the-masses.html. Accessed 30 Nov 2016

21. Virtual Reality Society: Virtual Reality in the Military (2017). http://www.vrs.org.uk/virtual-reality-military/. Accessed 8 Feb 2017

22. Michael, L.: VR Game Summer Lesson Gets English Sub for SEA Release. GMA News (2016). http://www.gmanetwork.com/news/story/585494/scitech/technology/vr-game-summer-lesson-gets-english-sub-for-sea-release. Accessed 10 Feb 2017

23. Selena, L.: Why Virtual Reality is (Still) the Next Big Thing (2017). http://kernelmag.dailydot.com/issue-sections/features-issue-sections/15399/state-of-tech-2016-virtual-reality/

24. Nguyên, T.T.: Xác Định Nguyên Nhân Cháy Tiệm Cưới Hỏi (2016). http://www.tintaynguyen.com/xac-dinh-nguyen-nhan-chay-tiem-cuoi-hoi-3-nguoi-tu-vong/226227/. Accessed 30 Nov 2016

# Author Index

Printed in the United States
By Bookmasters